Professional ADO.NET

Paul Dickinson

Fabio Claudio Ferracchiati

Kevin Hoffman

Bipin Joshi

Donny Mack

John McTainsh

Matthew Milner

Jan Narkiewicz

Doug Seven

D1314252

Wrox Press Ltd. ®

Professional ADO.NET

Published by Wrox Press Ltd,
Arden House, 1102 Warwick Road, Acocks Green,
Birmingham, B27 6BH, UK
Printed in the United States
ISBN 1-861005-27-X

Trademark Acknowledgements

Wrox has endeavored to provide trademark information about all the companies and products mentioned in this book by the appropriate use of capitals. However, Wrox cannot guarantee the accuracy of this information.

Credits

Authors
Paul Dickinson
Fabio Claudio Ferracchiati
Kevin Hoffman
Bipin Joshi
Donny Mack
John McTainsh
Matthew Milner
Jan Narkiewicz
Doug Seven

Technical Reviewers
Kapil Apshankar
Martin Beaulieu
Paul Churchill
Michael Cohen
Chris Crane
Dan Green
Jeffrey Hasan
Lauren Hightower
Christian Holm
Mark Horner
Jody Kerr
Don Lee
Alex Lowe
Rob MacDonald
Craig McQueen
Arun Nair
J Boyd Nolan PE
Phil Powers-De George
Trevor Scott

Category Manager
Sonia Mullineux

Technical Architect
Alastair Ewins

Technical Editors
David Barnes
Claire Brittle

Author Agents
Avril Corbin

Project Administrators
Chandima Nethisinghe

Index
Martin Brooks

Production Project Coordinator
Emma Eato

Layout
Emma Eato
Natalie O'Donnell

Figures
Natalie O'Donnell

Cover
Chris Morris

Proof Reading
Chris Smith

About the Authors

Paul Dickinson

Paul was born very early on in life and has continued to age at a reasonable pace. He first discovered his computing prowess with the advent of the Atari ST and Kick Off 2. People came from far and wide only to be humiliated with his crushing one-twos and deadly banana shots. In order to better himself he went off to UMIST to study Computation. Proving that academia wasn't for Paul he graduated unspectacularly and spent several years cutting his software development teeth writing software to control mass spectrometers. His most recent resting place involves developing information management systems for laboratories. On the frequent occasions that Paul isn't in front of a computer he can be found hurtling round country roads in hired sports cars or searching for the perfect donner kebab. He'd like to thank his beautiful wife Sue for giving him the will to sit in darkened rooms working all hours ;-) Paul can be reached at www.pauldickinson.com.

Fabio Claudio Ferracchiati

Fabio Claudio Ferracchiati is a software developer and technical writer. In the early years of his ten-year career he worked with classical languages and old Microsoft tools like Visual Basic and Visual C++. After five years he decided to dedicate his attention to the Internet and all the related technologies. In 1998 he started a parallel career writing technical articles for Italian and international magazines. Actually he works in Rome for CPI Progetti Spa (http://www.cpiprogetti.it) where he develops Internet/intranet solutions using Microsoft technologies. Fabio would like to thank Wrox people and every one of his CPI colleagues. In particular he would like to thank Angelo for his kindness.

Let him spend particular words for his love, Danila. She helps him morally in his job and she renounces to stay with him during the working days and the week-ends. Also, she helps him with his diet. Yes, it is very hard preparing carrots, salads, vegetables every day (a little voice inside him says: "it's harder eating them..."). He is sure; he could never find a girl like her and he doesn't want to. Thanks for all.

Kevin Hoffman

Kevin Hoffman is a software technology junkie who is currently eating and breathing anything and everything that has to do with the .NET Framework. He started programming in BASIC on a Commodore VIC-20 that his grandfather had repaired after being found in the trash, and has been a tech addict ever since, working at everything from nationwide UNIX mainframe support to as a Software Engineer for one of the most popular e-commerce web sites on the Internet. Recently he has found that he loves to write and teach about programming as much as he loves doing it himself.

I would like to dedicate my work for this book to my mother Marie, who has always been a treasured source of infinite love and support. Also I would like to dedicate my work to my brother Kurt and sister-in-law Nina who have both always been encouraging and supportive.

Bipin Joshi

Bipin Joshi is a software developer from Mumbai having skills in Microsoft technologies. Currently he works on .NET technologies with Mastek Ltd – a global applications outsourcing company having offshore software development centers in India. He runs his personal web site at www.bipinjoshi.com, which provides articles, tutorials, and sourcecode on variety of .NET topics. He also contributes regularly to other popular web sites. When away from computers he spends time in deep meditation exploring the Divine. He can be reached via his web site – www.bipinjoshi.com.

This work is dedicated to my Baba, Aai, and Bhau (father, mother, and brother). Without their wonderful support and encouragement this would not have been possible.

Donny Mack

Donny Mack, MCP, MCSD, Microsoft .NET MVP, is a native of Washington State, and is one of the co-founders of DotNetJunkies.com – an education company solely dedicated to ASP.NET and other web related .NET technologies. DotNetJunkies.com is a free online centralized resource web site used by .NET developers to feed their .NET passion. Prior to founding DotNetJunkies.com with Doug Seven, Mack worked at Microsoft Corporation as a Visual InterDev/ASP Support Professional assisting developers from all over the world in troubleshooting and utilizing new advances in technology to improve application performance and functionality. Mack's need for bleeding edge technology is such that he spends his waking hours, (and some of his non-waking hours), writing code and developing content for DotNetJunkies.com. Mack is an MCP, MCSD, and one of the few Microsoft .NET MVP's in the world and has worked closely with Doug Seven and the ASP.NET development team throughout the development of the technology.

John McTainsh

I started coding at high school on the Apple II and ZX81 in 1982. In the early days I worked mostly with the Motorola chipset in assembly making simple but fast games and programming microcontrollers. I completed my engineering degree in 1988 and moved to Asia to work in the offshore oil and gas exploration industry. Starting as a commercial diver I soon got back into coding, developing control systems for underwater robots in C and C++. Since then I have written many control systems and various other application and drivers, mostly for PC hardware. I currently live in Australia and work as a team leader developing public safety software for computer aided dispatch systems used by Police, Fire, and Ambulance vehicles.

I would like to thank my parents for a great upbringing and wife and daughter for putting up with my tap tap coding late into the night. Thanks Claudia, Rebecca, Dorothy, and Albert.

Matthew Milner

Matt Milner works as a Technical Architect for BORN in Minneapolis where he designs and builds Microsoft solutions for clients in a variety of industries. Matt's primary focus has been using Windows DNA architecture and he is excited about the move to .NET and all the powerful new features. When Matt is not working at the computer, he spends his time in his woodshop, reading, or enjoying the many great natural resources of Minnesota.

Jan Narkiewicz

Jan D. Narkiewicz is Chief Technical Officer at Software Pronto, Inc (jann@softwarepronto.com). Jan began his career as a Microsoft developer thanks to basketball star, Michael Jordan. In the early 90's Jan noticed that no matter what happened during a game, Michael Jordan's team won. Similarly, no matter what happened in technology Microsoft always won (then again this strategy is ten years old and may need some revamping). Clearly there was a bandwagon to be jumped upon. Over the years Jan managed to work on an email system that resided on 17 million desktops, helped automate factories that make blue jeans you have in your closet (trust me you own this brand) and kept the skies over the Emirate of Abu Dhabi safe from enemy aircraft. All this was achieved using technology such as COM/DCOM, COM+, C++, VB, C#, ADO, SQL Server, Oracle, DB2, ASP.NET, ADO.NET, Java, Linux, and XML. In his spare time Jan is Academic Coordinator for the Windows curriculum at U.C. Berkeley Extension, teaches at U.C. Santa Cruz Extension, writes for *ASP Today* and occasionally plays some football (a.k.a. soccer).

Doug Seven

Doug Seven is the co-creator of DotNetJunkies.com, a free online centralized resource Web site used by developers to learn more about the .NET Framework – specifically ASP.NET. Seven comes to DotNetJunkies.com by way of technical roles at Nordstrom, Microsoft and GiftCertificates.com, and as a Training Specialist at Seattle Coffee Company. At Microsoft Seven was a Technical Lead in the Developer Support group where he taught classes in Visual Basic and ADO to Technical Routers, the first-tier support group. After leaving Microsoft, Seven worked as a Web Developer for GiftCertificates.com before leaving to pursue life as a DotNetJunkie.

Seven has authored several resource materials covering the .NET Framework, including "*Programming Data-Driven Web Applications with ASP.NET*" and contributing to "*ASP.NET: Tips, Tutorials and Code*" as well as countless magazine and Web site articles.

In his spare time, Seven, a self-proclaimed workaholic, enjoys writing code and answering technical questions. On the rare occasions when he can squeeze in a social life, he likes to learn about fine wines and sit by the pool, in the sun.

My work on this book is a direct credit to the great support I have received from my family and friends. Specifically I would like to thank Dawniel Giebel for all of her understanding, support, and most of all, for sharing her love, life, and wine; Donny Mack for continuing to fight the good fight with me; Mark Anders, Rob Howard, Scott Guthrie, and Susan Warren for answering all my questions so quickly; Dene "Madam D." Holdsworth, Jason Pace, and Tres Henry for being the number one fans of DotNetJunkies.com – someday we'll be as cool as GotDotNet.com; Alex Lowe, Trevor Scott, David Barnes, Claire Brittle, Craig McQueen, and Jeffery Hasan for all the great review work to make this book excellent; Avril Corbin, Alastair Ewins, Chandy Nethisinghe, Charlotte Smith, and Helen Cuthill at Wrox for everything; Ed Hickey for the best professional advice I ever received, "Write code everyday…even if its just one line"; Jon Serious for letting me play around with SeriousDotNet.com; Lance Hayes for being the greatest country music aficionado in the world; Corinne "Jimi" Gurkey and Willy G. for being so cool all the time; Dave Sceppa for being a great ADO resource while I was at Microsoft, for being generally sarcastic all the time, and for writing great books.

Table of Contents

Table of Contents

Table of Contents

Table of Contents

Table of Contents

Table of Contents

Table of Contents

Introduction

What is ADO.NET?

ADO.NET is a large set of .NET classes that enable us to retrieve and manipulate data, and update data sources, in very many different ways. As an integral part of the .NET framework, it shares many of its features: features such as multi-language support, garbage collection, just-in-time compilation, object-oriented design, and dynamic caching, and is far more than an upgrade of previous versions of ADO.

ADO.NET is set to become a core component of any data-driven .NET application or Web Service, and understanding its power will be essential to anyone wishing to utilize .NET data support to maximum effect.

What Does This Book Cover?

This book provides a thorough investigation of the ADO.NET classes (those included in the `System.Data`, `System.Data.Common`, `System.Data.OleDb`, `System.Data.SqlClient`, and `System.Data.Odbc` namespaces). We adopt a practical, solutions-oriented approach, looking at how to effectively utilize the various components of ADO.NET within data-centric application development.

We begin our journey in **Chapter 1** by looking at a brief history of data access in general, then looking more closely at ADO.NET itself. This includes looking at some of the features and comparing it to ADO 2.6. This theme continues into **Chapter 2**, which looks at the .NET data providers, which provide connectivity to a variety of data stores.

Chapter 3 moves on to delving into Visual Studio .NET and how this graphical user interface makes using ADO.NET intuitive and easy to handle. The chapter includes a number of examples to demonstrate the principles learned.

Now that we are a little more comfortable with ADO.NET, we can begin to delve deeper into the specifics of the technology. **Chapter 4** looks at the `DataReader`: what it is, why you would use it and also how you would use it in a number of situations. This in-depth look continues in **Chapter 5**, where we learn about the `DataSet`, while **Chapter 6** introduces and explores the `DataAdapter`.

Chapter 7 takes a closer look at the `DataSet`, which enables us to work with data while disconnected from the data source; this includes an introduction to how the XML Schema Definition (XSD) language is useful when manipulating `DataSets`. This leads us nicely into **Chapter 8**, where we explore the use of XML with the `DataSet`, covering various issues such as data marshalling and data filtering, amongst others.

Chapter 9 continues the look at the `DataSet` by examining constraints, relations and views, all of which influence the way that data is presented and manipulated. The chapter introduces the DataView and includes some examples.

Chapter 10 moves on to look at the topic of transactions, an important item in the business world where either all the operations must succeed, or all of them must fail. The chapter examines, amongst other things, isolation levels and their impact, performance, and advanced techniques.

The concept of mapping is explored in **Chapter 11**: this is where we can give our own names to unintuitive column headings in order to understand the material better.

Chapter 12 looks at creating our own Data Services component: the benefits, the creation and deployment, and using it once it exists. The chapter also looks at tips for better performance of data service components. This leads well into **Chapter 13**, where we look at ADO.NET and Web Services, in particular exchanging data, using XML, and security.

Chapter 14 looks again at the issue of XML, this time showing how SQL Server 2000 has native support for this cross-platform standard of data retrieval. The chapter is example-based, showing all the native XML options at every step.

Chapter 15 moves off into the more theoretical realm of performance and security. Both are important considerations if we will be dealing with thousands of data access demands every minute. The chapter covers many ways to increase performance and tighten security.

Chapter 16 discusses integration and migration, particularly accessing ADO from .NET and how to handle the migration from ADO to ADO.NET.

Chapter 17 allows us to create our own custom .NET data provider. It goes through the whole process: why we need our own provider, the architecture and design, and the actual implementation. The chapter also shows a number of ways that we can utilize our custom provider. The same method is employed by **Chapter 18**, which finishes the book by building a case study that uses ADO.NET in the middle layer of a multi-tier system that tracks packages for a fictional inner city bicycle courier company.

Who is This Book For?

This book is aimed at experienced developers, who already have some experience of developing or experimenting within the .NET framework, with either C# or Visual Basic .NET. We do not cover the basics of C# or Visual Basic .NET, and assume some prior experience of Microsoft data access technologies.

What You Need to Use This Book

To run the samples in this book you need to have the following:

❑   Windows 2000 or Windows XP

❑   The .NET Framework SDK. The code in this book will not work with .NET Beta 1.

The complete source code for the samples is available for download from our web site at http://www.wrox.com/Books/Book_Details.asp?isbn=186100527X.

Conventions

We've used a number of different styles of text and layout in this book to help differentiate between the different kinds of information. Here are examples of the styles we used and an explanation of what they mean.

Code has several fonts. If it's a word that we're talking about in the text – for example, when discussing a For...Next loop, it's in this font. If it's a block of code that can be typed as a program and run, then it's also in a gray box:

```
<?xml version 1.0?>
```

Sometimes we'll see code in a mixture of styles, like this:

```
<?xml version 1.0?>
<Invoice>
    <part>
        <name>Widget</name>
        <price>$10.00</price>
    </part>
</invoice>
```

In cases like this, the code with a white background is code we are already familiar with; the line highlighted in gray is a new addition to the code since we last looked at it.

Advice, hints, and background information comes in this type of font.

> **Important pieces of information come in boxes like this.**

Bullets appear indented, with each new bullet marked as follows:

❑ **Important Words** are in a bold type font

❑ Words that appear on the screen, or in menus like the File or Window menu, are in a similar font to the one you would see on a Windows desktop

❑ Keys that you press on the keyboard, like *Ctrl* and *Enter*, are in italics

Customer Support

We always value hearing from our readers, and we want to know what you think about this book: what you liked, what you didn't like, and what you think we can do better next time. You can send us your comments, either by returning the reply card in the back of the book, or by e-mail to feedback@wrox.com. Please be sure to mention the book title in your message.

How to Download the Sample Code for the Book

When you visit the Wrox site, http://www.wrox.com/, simply locate the title through our Search facility or by using one of the title lists. Click on Download in the Code column, or on Download Code on the book's detail page.

The files that are available for download from our site have been archived using WinZip. When you have saved the attachments to a folder on your hard-drive, you need to extract the files using a de-compression program such as WinZip or PKUnzip. When you extract the files, the code is usually extracted into chapter folders. When you start the extraction process, ensure your software (WinZip, PKUnzip, etc.) is set to use folder names.

Errata

We've made every effort to make sure that there are no errors in the text or in the code. However, no one is perfect and mistakes do occur. If you find an error in one of our books, like a spelling mistake or a faulty piece of code, we would be very grateful for feedback. By sending in errata you may save another reader hours of frustration, and of course, you will be helping us provide even higher quality information. Simply e-mail the information to support@wrox.com; your information will be checked and if correct, posted to the errata page for that title, or used in subsequent editions of the book.

To find errata on the web site, go to http://www.wrox.com/, and simply locate the title through our Advanced Search or title list. Click on the Book Errata link, which is below the cover graphic on the book's detail page.

E-Mail Support

If you wish to directly query a problem in the book with an expert who knows the book in detail then e-mail support@wrox.com, with the title of the book and the last four numbers of the ISBN in the subject field of the e-mail. A typical e-mail should include the following things:

- ❑ The **title of the book**, **last four digits of the ISBN**, and **page number** of the problem in the Subject field

- ❑ Your **name**, **contact information**, and the **problem** in the body of the message

We *won't* send you junk mail. We need the details to save your time and ours. When you send an e-mail message, it will go through the following chain of support:

- ❑ Customer Support – Your message is delivered to our customer support staff, who are the first people to read it. They have files on most frequently asked questions and will answer anything general about the book or the web site immediately.

- ❑ Editorial – Deeper queries are forwarded to the technical editor responsible for that book. They have experience with the programming language or particular product, and are able to answer detailed technical questions on the subject.

- ❑ The Authors – Finally, in the unlikely event that the editor cannot answer your problem, he or will forward the request to the author. We do try to protect the author from any distractions to their writing; however, we are quite happy to forward specific requests to them. All Wrox authors help with the support on their books. They will e-mail the customer and the editor with their response, and again all readers should benefit.

The Wrox Support process can only offer support to issues that are directly pertinent to the content of our published title. Support for questions that fall outside the scope of normal book support is provided via the community lists of our http://p2p.wrox.com/ forum.

p2p.wrox.com

For author and peer discussion join the P2P mailing lists. Our unique system provides **programmer to programmer**™ contact on mailing lists, forums, and newsgroups, all in addition to our one-to-one e-mail support system. If you post a query to P2P, you can be confident that it is being examined by the many Wrox authors and other industry experts who are present on our mailing lists. At p2p.wrox.com you will find a number of different lists that will help you, not only while you read this book, but also as you develop your own applications. Particularly appropriate to this book is the ADO.NET list.

To subscribe to a mailing list just follow these steps:

1. Go to http://p2p.wrox.com/

2. Choose the appropriate category from the left menu bar

3. Click on the mailing list you wish to join

4. Follow the instructions to subscribe and fill in your e-mail address and password

5. Reply to the confirmation e-mail you receive

6. Use the subscription manager to join more lists and set your e-mail preferences

Why this System Offers the Best Support

You can choose to join the mailing lists or you can receive them as a weekly digest. If you don't have the time, or facility, to receive the mailing list, then you can search our online archives. Junk and spam mails are deleted, and your own e-mail address is protected by the unique Lyris system. Queries about joining or leaving lists, and any other general queries about lists, should be sent to `listsupport@p2p.wrox.com`.

1

Data Access and .NET

In this chapter, we're just going to take a fairly quick overview of ADO.NET. This will be fast-paced, and we won't shy away from showing snippets of code, as this really is the best way to get to grips with the concepts. Hopefully this chapter will give you a solid understanding of the basic workings of ADO.NET, and give you a taste of some of its best features. By the end of the chapter, we hope that you'll be convinced of the advantages of ADO.NET, and eager to go further into the book!

ADO.NET is the latest in a long line of data access technologies released by Microsoft. ADO.NET differs somewhat from the previous technologies, however, in that it comes as part of a whole new platform called the .NET Framework. This platform is set to revolutionize every area of development, and ADO.NET is just one aspect of that. We'll therefore start by looking quickly at the main features of .NET.

The .NET Framework

It's no exaggeration to say that Microsoft's release of its new development and run-time environment, the .NET Framework, will revolutionize all aspects of programming in the Microsoft world. The benefits of this new platform will be felt in all areas of our code and in all types of application we develop. The .NET Framework is in itself a huge topic, and we can't cover every aspect in detail here, but since it's important to understand the basic principles behind .NET before attempting any ADO.NET programming, we'll quickly review the basics here.

For more information about programming in the .NET environment, check out Professional .NET Framework, *ISBN 1-861005-56-3.*

The Common Language Runtime

The foundation on which the .NET Framework is built is the **Common Language Runtime** (CLR). The CLR is the execution environment that manages .NET code at run time. In some ways, it is comparable to the Java Virtual Machine (JVM), or to the Visual Basic 6 runtime (`msvbvm60.dll`). Like these, the .NET Framework needs to be installed on any machine where .NET programs will be run. Unlike these, however, the CLR was designed specifically to support code written in many different languages. It's true that many different languages have been written that target the JVM (at present more than there are for .NET), but multiple-language support wasn't one of the primary design considerations of the JVM. In the case of the CLR, this really was one of the most important considerations.

In order to achieve cross-language support, all .NET programs are compiled prior to deployment into a low-level language called **Intermediate Language** (IL). Microsoft's implementation of this language is called **Microsoft Intermediate Language**, or MSIL. This IL code is then just-in-time compiled into native code at run time. This means that, whatever the original language of the source code, .NET executables and DLLs are always deployed in IL, so there are no differences between components originally written in C# and those written in VB .NET. This aids cross-language interoperability (such as the ability to derive a class written in one language from one written in any of the other .NET languages). However, it also allows applications to be deployed without modifications onto any supported platform (currently Windows 9x/ME, Windows NT4, Windows 2000, or Windows XP) – the JIT compiler handles optimizations for the processor/OS of the deployment machine.

Microsoft provides compilers for four .NET languages:

- ❑ C# – a new C-based language designed specifically for the .NET Framework. Most of the code in this book will be in C#.

- ❑ Visual Basic.NET – a version of the Visual Basic language updated for .NET (for example, with full object-oriented features, structured exception handling, and many of the other things VB developers have been demanding for years!).

- ❑ JScript.NET – Microsoft's implementation of the JavaScript scripting language, updated for .NET.

- ❑ Managed C++ – C++ with "managed extensions" to support .NET features that couldn't be implemented using the existing features of the language. Unlike the first three languages, the C++ compiler doesn't come free with the .NET Framework SDK, but is shipped with Visual Studio.NET.

- ❑ J# – essentially Visual J++ (including Microsoft extensions to Java such as COM support) for the .NET Framework. Beta 1 of J# was released during the writing of this book, and can be downloaded from http://msdn.microsoft.com/visualj/jsharp/beta.asp.

As well as these Microsoft languages, many more languages (such as COBOL, Perl, and Eiffel) will be supplied by third-party companies (more information for these three languages can be found at http://www.adtools.com/dotnet/index.html for COBOL, http://aspn.activestate.com/ASPN/Downloads/PerlASPX/More for PERL, and http://msdn.microsoft.com/library/techart/pdc_eiffel.htm for Eiffel).

Garbage Collection

One of the most important services provided by the CLR is **garbage collection**. In C and C++, if an object is instantiated, the memory it uses needs to be released before it can be reused. Failure to do this results in a "memory leak" – unused memory that can't be reclaimed by the system. As the amount of leaked memory increases, the performance of the application obviously deteriorates. However, because the error isn't obvious and only takes effect over time, these errors are notoriously difficult to trace. The CLR solves this problem by implementing a garbage collector. At periodic intervals (when there is no more room on the heap), the garbage collector will check all object references, and release the memory held by objects that have run out of scope and can no longer be accessed by the application. This exempts the programmer from having to destroy the objects explicitly, and solves the problem of memory leaks. There are a couple of points to remember here: firstly, we can't predict exactly when the garbage collector will run (although we can force a collection), so objects can remain in memory for some time after we've finished with them; secondly, the CLR won't clear up unmanaged resources – we need to do that ourselves. The usual way of doing this is to expose a method named Dispose, which will release all external resources and which can be called when we've finished with the object.

The Common Language Infrastructure

Although the .NET Framework is currently only available for Windows platforms, Microsoft has submitted a subset of .NET (the **Common Language Infrastructure**, or CLI) to the European Computer Manufacturers' Association (ECMA) for acceptance as an open standard. Versions of the CLI are in development for the FreeBSD and Linux operating systems. Similarly, specifications for C# and IL (the latter termed **Common Intermediate Language**, or CIL) have also been submitted to ECMA, and non-Microsoft implementations of the CLI will also implement these.

Assemblies

.NET code is deployed as an **assembly**. Assemblies consist of compiled IL code, and must contain one primary file (except in the case of dynamic assemblies, which are stored entirely in memory). This can be an executable (.exe) file, a DLL, or a compiled ASP.NET web application or Web Service. As well as the primary file, an assembly can contain resource files (such as images or icons) and other code modules. Most importantly, however, assemblies contain **metadata**. This metadata consists of two parts: the **type metadata** includes information about all the exported types and their methods defined in the assembly. As well as IL code, .NET assemblies contain a section known as the **manifest**. This section contains the **assembly metadata**, or information about the assembly itself, such as the version and build numbers.

This metadata allows assemblies to be completely self-describing: the assembly itself contains all the information necessary to install and run the application. There's no longer any need for type libraries or registry entries. Installation can be as simple as copying the assembly onto the target machine. Better still, because the assembly contains version information, multiple versions of the same component can be installed side-by-side on the same machine. This ends the problem known as "DLL Hell", where an application installing a new version of an existing component would break programs that used the old version.

The Common Type System

The foundation on which the CLR's cross-language features are built is the **Common Type System** (CTS). In order for classes defined in different languages to be able to communicate with each other, they need a common way to represent data – a common set of data types. All the predefined types that are available in IL are defined in the CTS. This means that all data in .NET code is ultimately stored in the same data types, because all .NET code compiles to IL.

The CTS distinguishes between two fundamental categories of data types – **value types** and **reference types**. Value types (including most of the built-in types, as well as structs and enumerations) contain their data directly. For example, a variable of an integer type stores the integer directly on the program's stack. Reference types (including String and Object, as well as arrays and most user-defined types such as classes and interfaces) store only a reference to their data on the stack – the data itself is stored in a different area of memory known as the heap. The difference between these types is particularly evident when passing parameters to methods. All method parameters are by default passed by value, not by reference. However, in the case of reference types, the value is nothing more than a reference to the location on the heap where the data is stored. As a result, reference-type parameters behave very much as we would expect arguments passed by reference to behave – changing the value of the variable within the body of the method will affect the original variable, too. This is an important point to remember if you pass ADO.NET objects into a method.

The Common Language Specification

One important point to note about the CTS is that not all features are exposed by all languages. For example, C# has a signed byte data type (sbyte), which isn't available in Visual Basic.NET. This could cause problems with language interoperability, so the **Common Language Specification** (CLS) defines a subset of the CTS, which *all* compilers must support. It's perfectly possible to expose features that aren't included in the CLS (for example, a C# class with a public property of type sbyte). However, it's important to remember that such features can't be guaranteed to be accessible from other languages – in this example, we wouldn't be able to access the class from VB.NET.

.NET Class Libraries

Finally, we come to perhaps the most important feature of all – a vast set of class libraries to accomplish just about any programming task conceivable. Classes and other types within the .NET Framework are organized into **namespaces**, similar to Java packages. These namespaces can be nested within other namespaces, and allow us to identify our classes and distinguish them from third-party classes with the same name.

Together with the .NET Framework, Microsoft provides a huge set of classes and other types, mostly within the System namespace, or one of the many nested namespaces. This includes the primitive types such as integers – the C# int and VB.NET Integer types are just aliases for the System.Int32 type. However, it also includes classes used for Windows applications, web applications, directory services, file access, and many others – including, of course, data access. These data access classes are collectively known as ADO.NET. In fact, .NET programming is effectively programming with the .NET class libraries – it's impossible to write any program in C# or VB NET that doesn't use these libraries.

Not Another Data Access Technology?

Given the revolutionary nature of .NET, and the fact that new class libraries have been introduced for almost every programming task, it's hardly surprising that developers are now faced with learning yet another data access technology. After all, it seems that a new data access strategy comes along every year or so. However, it's not quite time to throw away all your existing knowledge – ODBC and OLE DB can both be used from ADO.NET, and it's going to be quite some time before ADO.NET can access any data source directly. And even ADO, for which ADO.NET is a more-or-less direct replacement, can have its uses in certain scenarios. It's therefore worth spending a moment reviewing the development of data access over the last few years.

Brief History of Data Access

At first, programmatic access to databases was performed by native libraries, such as DBLib for SQL Server, and the Oracle Call Interface (OCI) for Oracle. This allowed for fast database access because no extra layer was involved – we simply wrote code that accessed the database directly. However, it also meant that developers had to learn a different set of APIs for every database system they ever needed to access, and if the application had to be updated to run against a different database system, all the data access code would have to be changed.

ODBC

As a solution to this, in the early 1990s Microsoft and other companies developed **Open Database Connectivity**, or ODBC. This provided a common data access layer, which could be used to access almost any relational database management system (RDBMS). ODBC uses an RDBMS-specific driver to communicate with the data source. The drivers (sometimes no more than a wrapper around native API calls) are loaded and managed by the ODBC Driver Manager. This also provides features such as connection pooling – the ability to reuse connections, rather than destroying connections when they are closed and creating a new connection every time the database is accessed. The application communicates with the Driver Manager through a standard API, so (in theory) if we wanted to update the application to connect to a different RDBMS, we only needed to change the connection details (in practice, there were often differences in the SQL dialect supported). Perhaps the most important feature of ODBC, however, was the fact that it was an open standard, widely adopted even by the Open Source community. As a result, ODBC drivers have been developed for many database systems that can't be accessed directly by later data access technologies. As we'll see shortly, this means ODBC still has a role to play in conjunction with ADO.NET.

DAO

One of the problems with ODBC is that it was designed to be used from low-level languages such as C++. As the importance of Visual Basic grew, there was a need for a data access technology that could be used more naturally from VB. This need was met in VB 3 with **Data Access Objects** (DAO). DAO provided a simple object model for talking to Jet, the database engine behind Microsoft's Access desktop database. As DAO was optimized for Access (although it can also be used to connect to ODBC data sources), it is very fast – in fact, still the fastest way of talking to Access from VB 6.

RDO

Due to its optimization for Access, DAO was very slow when used with ODBC data sources. To get round this, Microsoft introduced **Remote Data Objects** (RDO) with the Enterprise Edition of VB 4 (32-bit version only). RDO provides a simple object model, similar to that of DAO, designed specifically for access to ODBC data sources. RDO is essentially a thin wrapper over the ODBC API.

OLE DB

The next big shake-up in the world of data access technologies came with the release of **OLE DB**. Architecturally, OLE DB bears some resemblance to ODBC: communication with the data source takes place through **OLE DB providers** (similar in concept to ODBC drivers), which are designed for each supported type of data source. OLE DB providers implement a set of COM interfaces, which allow access to the data in a standard row/column format. An application that makes use of this data is known as an **OLE DB consumer**. As well as these standard data providers, which extract data from a data source and make it available through the OLE DB interfaces, OLE DB also has a number of service providers. These form a "middle tier" of the OLE DB architecture, providing services that are used with the data provider. These services include connection pooling, transaction enlistment (the ability to register MTS/COM+ components automatically within an MTS/COM+ transaction), data persistence, client-side data manipulation (the Client Cursor Engine, or CCE), hierarchical recordsets (data shaping), and data remoting (the ability to instantiate an OLE DB data provider on a remote machine).

The real innovation behind OLE DB was Microsoft's strategy for Universal Data Access (UDA). The thinking behind UDA is that data is stored in many places – e-mails, Excel spreadsheets, web pages, and so on, as well as traditional databases – and that we should be able to access all this data programmatically, through a single unified data access technology. OLE DB is the base for Microsoft's implementation of this strategy. The number of OLE DB providers has been gradually rising to cover both relational database systems (even the opensource MySQL database now has an OLE DB provider), and non-relational data sources such as the Exchange 2000 Web Store, Project 2000 files, and IIS virtual directories. However, even before these providers became available, Microsoft ensured wide-ranging support for OLE DB by supplying an OLE DB provider for ODBC drivers, This meant that right from the start OLE DB could be used to access any data source that had an ODBC driver. As we shall see, this successful tactic has been adopted again for ADO.NET.

ADO

ActiveX Data Objects (ADO) is the technology that gave its name to ADO.NET (although in reality the differences are far greater than the similarities). ADO is merely an OLE DB consumer – a thin layer allowing users of high-level languages such as VB and script languages to access OLE DB data sources through a simple object model; ADO is to OLE DB more or less what RDO was to ODBC. Its popularity lay in the fact it gave the vast number of Visual Basic, ASP, and Visual J++ developers easy access to data in many different locations. If OLE DB was the foundation on which UDA was built, ADO was the guise in which it appeared to the majority of developers. And, in certain scenarios, ADO still represents a valid choice for developers on the .NET Framework. Moreover, because many of the classes and concepts are similar, knowledge of ADO is a big advantage when learning ADO.NET. We will look at the relationship between ADO and ADO.NET in more detail later on in the chapter.

First, though, let's take an overview of ADO.NET itself.

Introduction to ADO.NET

Although we've presented it as something of an inevitability that .NET would bring a new data access API, we haven't yet really said why. After all, it's perfectly possible to carry on using ADO in .NET applications through COM interoperability. However, there are some very good reasons why ADO wasn't really suited to the new programming environment. We'll look quickly at some of the ways in which ADO.NET improves upon ADO called from .NET, before looking at the ADO.NET architecture in more detail.

Advantages of Using Managed Classes

Firstly, and most obviously, if we're using .NET then COM interoperability adds overhead to our application. .NET communicates with COM components via proxies called Runtime Callable Wrappers, and method calls need to be marshaled from the proxy to the COM object. In addition, COM components can't take advantage of the benefits of the CLR such as JIT compilation and the managed execution environment – they need to be compiled to native code prior to installation. This makes it essential to have a genuine .NET class library for data access.

Cross-Language Support

Another factor is the fact that ADO wasn't really designed for cross-language use; it was aimed primarily at VB programmers. As a result, ADO makes much use of optional method parameters, which are supported by VB and VB.NET, but not by C-based languages such as C#. This means that if you use ADO from C#, you will need to specify *all* parameters in method calls; for example, if you call the Connection.Open method and don't want to specify any options, you will need to include the adConnectUnspecified parameter! This makes ADO programming under .NET considerably more time-consuming.

Cleaner Architecture

As we noted above, ADO is no more than a thin layer over OLE DB. This makes the ADO architecture slightly cumbersome, as extra layers are introduced between the application and the data source. While much ADO.NET code will still use OLE DB for the immediate future, this will decrease as more native .NET data providers become available. Where a native provider exists, ADO.NET can be much faster than ADO, as the providers communicate directly with the data source. We will look in more detail at the ADO.NET architecture in the next section.

XML Support

One of the key features of the .NET Framework is its support for XML. XML is the standard transport and persistence format throughout the .NET Framework. While ADO had some support for XML from version 2.1 onwards, this was very limited, and required XML documents to be in exactly the right format. We will take a quick look at ADO.NET's XML support later in this chapter, and examine it in detail in Chapter 8.

Optimized Object Model

Finally, it's important to remember that the .NET Framework is aimed squarely at developing distributed applications, and particularly Internet-enabled applications. In this context, it's clear that certain types of connection are better than others. In an Internet application, we don't want to hold a connection open for a long time, as this could create a bottleneck as the number of open connections to the data source increase, and hence destroy scalability. ADO didn't encourage disconnected recordsets, whereas ADO.NET has different classes for connected and disconnected access, and doesn't permit updateable connected recordsets. We'll look at this issue in more detail later in the chapter.

Architectural Overview of ADO.NET

Now that you're hopefully convinced of why you should use ADO.NET, we can look at how ADO.NET works in more detail. The ADO.NET object model consists of two fundamental components: the **DataSet**, which is disconnected from the data source and doesn't need to know where the data it holds came from; and the **.NET data provider**. The .NET data providers allow us to connect to the data source, and to execute SQL commands against it.

.NET Data Providers

At the time of writing, there are three .NET data providers available: for SQL Server, for OLE DB data sources, and for ODBC-compliant data sources. Each provider exists in a namespace within the `System.Data` namespace, and consists of a number of classes. We'll look at each of these providers shortly.

Data Provider Components

Each .NET data provider consists of four main components:

❑ **Connection** – used to connect to the data source

❑ **Command** – used to execute a command against the data source and retrieve a `DataReader` or `DataSet`, or to execute an `INSERT`, `UPDATE`, or `DELETE` command against the data source

❑ **DataReader** – a forward-only, read-only connected resultset

❑ **DataAdapter** – used to populate a `DataSet` with data from the data source, and to update the data source

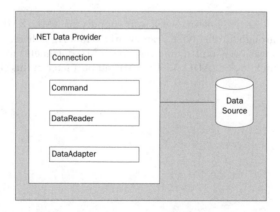

Note that these components are implemented separately by the .NET providers; there isn't a single `Connection` class, for example. Instead, the SQL Server and OLE DB providers implement `SqlConnection` and `OleDbConnection` classes respectively. These classes derive directly from `System.ComponentModel.Component` – there isn't an abstract `Connection` class – but they implement the same `IDbConnection` interface (in the `System.Data` namespace). We'll have a look at how this works in more detail later on in the chapter.

The Connection Classes

The connection classes are very similar to the ADO `Connection` object, and like that, they are used to represent a connection to a specific data source. The connection classes store the information that ADO.NET needs to connect to a data source in the form of a familiar connection string (just as in ADO). The `IDbConnection` interface's `ConnectionString` property holds information such as the username and password of the user, the name and location of the data source to connect to, and so on. In addition, the connection classes also have methods for opening and closing connections, and for beginning a transaction, and properties for setting the timeout period of the connection and for returning the current state (open or closed) of the connection. We'll see how to open connections to specific data sources in the section on the existing .NET providers.

The Command Classes

The command classes expose the `IDbCommand` interface and are similar to the ADO `Command` object – they are used to execute SQL statements or stored procedures in the data source. Also, like the ADO `Command` object, the command classes have a `CommandText` property, which contains the text of the command to be executed against the data source, and a `CommandType` property, which indicates whether the command is a SQL statement, the name of a stored procedure, or the name of a table. There are three distinct execute methods – `ExecuteReader`, which returns a `DataReader`; `ExecuteScalar`, which returns a single value; and `ExecuteNonQuery`, for use when no data will be returned from the query (for example, for a SQL `UPDATE` statement).

Again like their ADO equivalent, the command classes have a `Parameters` collection – a collection of objects to represent the parameters to be passed into a stored procedure. These objects expose the `IDataParameter` interface, and form part of the .NET provider. That is, each provider has a separate implementation of the `IDataParameter` (and `IDataParameterCollection`) interfaces:

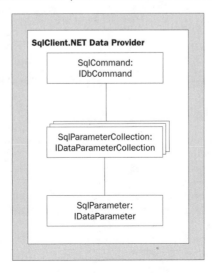

The DataReader

The DataReader is ADO.NET's answer to the connected recordset in ADO. However, the DataReader is forward-only and read-only – we can't navigate through it at random, and we can't use it to update the data source. It therefore allows extremely fast access to data that we just want to iterate through once, and it is recommended to use the DataReader (rather than the DataSet) wherever possible. A DataReader can only be returned from a call to the ExecuteReader method of a command object; we can't instantiate it directly. This forces us to instantiate a command object explicitly, unlike in ADO, where we could retrieve a Recordset object without ever explicitly creating a Command object. This makes the ADO.NET object model more transparent than the "flat" hierarchy of ADO.

The DataAdapter

The last main component of the .NET data provider is the DataAdapter. The DataAdapter acts as a bridge between the disconnected DataSet and the data source. It exposes two interfaces; the first of these, IDataAdapter, defines methods for populating a DataSet with data from the data source, and for updating the data source with changes made to the DataSet on the client. The second interface, IDbDataAdapter, defines four properties, each of type IDbCommand. These properties each set or return a command object specifying the command to be executed when the data source is to be queried or updated:

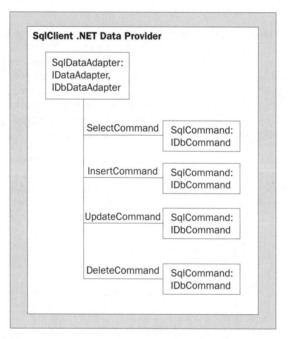

Note that an error will be generated if we attempt to update a data source and the correct command hasn't been specified. For example, if we try to call Update for a DataSet where a new row has been added, and don't specify an InsertCommand for the DataAdapter, we will get this error message:

```
Unhandled Exception: System.InvalidOperationException: Update requires a valid
InsertCommand when passed DataRow collection with new rows.
```

We'll look briefly at how we avoid this error when we discuss the DataSet.

Existing Data Providers

Three .NET data providers are currently available; these allow us to access any type of data source that we could access using ADO 2.1. The reason we've said ADO 2.1 rather than 2.5 (or later) is that the OLE DB 2.5 interfaces – IRow, IStream, etc. (exposed by the ADO Record and Stream objects) – are not supported by the OleDb provider. This means that we'll still need to use "classic" ADO with data sources such as web directories and the Exchange 2000 Web Store, until such time as ADO.NET equivalents for the Internet Publishing (MSDAIPP) and Exchange 2000 (ExOLEDB) OLE DB providers become available.

The SqlClient Provider

The SqlClient provider ships with ADO.NET and resides in the System.Data.SqlClient namespace. It can (and should) be used to access SQL Server 7.0 or later databases, or MSDE databases. The SqlClient provider can't be used with SQL Server 6.5 or earlier databases, so you will need to use the OleDb .NET provider with the OLE DB provider for SQL Server (SQLOLEDB) if you want to access an earlier version of SQL Server. However, if you can use the SqlClient provider, it is strongly recommended that you do so – using the OleDb provider adds an extra layer to your data access code, and uses COM interoperability behind the scenes (OLE DB is COM-based).

The classes within the SqlClient provider all begin with "Sql", so the connection class is SqlConnection, the command class is SqlCommand, and so on. Let's take a quick look at the ADO.NET code to open a connection to the pubs database on SQL Server. As with most of the code in this chapter (and in fact in the book), we'll use C#:

```
using System.Data.SqlClient;    // The SqlClient provider namespace

// Instantiate the connection, passing the
// connection string into the constructor
SqlConnection cn = new SqlConnection(
    "Data Source=(local);Initial Catalog=pubs;User ID=sa;Password=");
cn.Open();                      // Open the connection
```

The using directive in the first line isn't compulsory, but it saves a lot of typing – otherwise, we'd need to write System.Data.SqlClient.SqlConnection, rather than just SqlConnection. Notice that if you're coding in C#, you don't need to add a reference to System.Data.dll (where the SqlClient and OleDb providers live), even if you're using the command-line compiler. With the other languages, you will need to add the reference unless you're using Visual Studio.NET (which adds the reference for you).

Next, we instantiate the SqlConnection object – the SqlClient implementation of the IDbConnection interface. We pass the connection information into the constructor for this object, although we could instantiate it using the default (parameter-less) constructor, and then set its ConnectionString property. The connection string itself is almost identical to an ADO connection string – the one difference being that we don't, of course, need to specify the provider we're using. We've already done that by instantiating a SqlConnection object (rather than an OleDbConnection object). Finally, we call the Open method to open the connection. Unlike the ADO Connection object's Open method, we can't pass a connection string into this method as a parameter, so we *must* specify the connection information before opening the connection.

The OleDb Provider

If you're not using SQL Server 7.0 or later, it's almost certain that your best bet will be to use the OleDb provider, at least until more .NET providers are released. There are a couple of exceptions to this rule – if your data source has an ODBC driver, but not an OLE DB provider, then you will need to use the Odbc .NET provider. Support for MSDASQL (the OLE DB provider for ODBC drivers) was withdrawn from the OleDb provider somewhere between Beta 1 and Beta 2 of the .NET Framework, so there really is no alternative to this. This was probably done to prevent the use of ODBC Data Source Names (DSNs) with ADO.NET, except where ODBC really is required. Even in ADO, using DSNs involved a substantial performance penalty (particularly when an OLE DB provider was available), but the extra layers would be intolerable under .NET. Think of the architecture involved: ADO.NET – COM interop – (optional) OLE DB services – OLE DB provider – ODBC driver – data source!

The second situation where the OleDb provider doesn't help us has already been mentioned. If you need to access a data source using the Exchange 2000 or Internet Publishing Provider (IPP), then I'm afraid that for the moment there's no alternative to COM interop and old-fashioned ADO; the OleDb provider doesn't currently support the IRecord and IStream interfaces used by these providers.

The OleDb provider acts much like traditional ADO – it is essentially just a .NET wrapper around OLE DB (except that the OLE DB service providers are now largely obsolete, as this functionality – and more – is provided by ADO.NET). So as well as specifying that we're going to use the OleDb .NET provider (by instantiating the OleDbConnection etc. objects), we need to specify the *OLE DB* data provider that we want to use to connect from OLE DB to the data source. We do this in the same way as in ADO – by including the Provider property in the connection string, or by setting the Provider property of the OleDbConnection object.

Like the SqlClient provider, the OleDb provider resides in System.Data.dll, and ships with the .NET Framework. The classes that compose the provider are in the System.Data.OleDb namespace, and all have the prefix "OleDb" (OleDbConnection, OleDbCommand, and so on). Let's have a look at this in action by opening a connection to the Access Northwind database (in this case NWind.mdb):

```
using System.Data.OleDb;     // The OleDb provider namespace

// Instantiate the OleDbConnection object
OleDbConnection cn = new OleDbConnection(
    @"Provider=Microsoft.Jet.OLEDB.4.0;Data Source=C:\NWind.mdb");
cn.Open();                   // Open the connection
```

The @ character before the connection string is used in C# to indicate a "verbatim" string; that is, any escape characters are ignored. It's particularly useful with file paths (to avoid having to escape the backslash character).

There's nothing very different here to the previous example, except that we need to include the Provider property in the connection string, as we mentioned above. So, although we're using different objects, we've only changed three things:

❑   The using directive at the start of the code

❑   The connection string

❑   The prefix "OleDb" whenever we instantiate the provider-specific objects

This is also the natural-choice provider to use to connect to an Oracle database:

```
using System.Data.OleDb;

OleDbConnection cn = new OleDbConnection("Provider=MSDAORA;" +
    "Data Source=orcl.julian_new.wrox.com;User ID=scott;" +
    "Password=tiger");
cn.Open();
```

As with ADO, we pass in the name of the Oracle OLE DB provider (MSDAORA), the service name (here orcl.julian_new.wrox.com) as the Data Source, and the schema in the Oracle database as the User ID (scott in this case).

The Odbc Provider

Unlike the other two .NET providers, the Odbc provider isn't shipped with the .NET Framework. The current beta version can be downloaded as a single .exe file of 503KB from the MSDN site (http://www.microsoft.com/downloads/release.asp?ReleaseID=31125). Simply run this executable to install the classes – this program will install the assembly into the Global Assembly Cache, so the classes will automatically be globally available on the local machine. However, you will need to add a reference to the assembly (System.Data.Odbc.dll) to your projects to use the provider.

The Odbc provider should be used whenever you need to access a data source with no OLE DB provider (such as PostgreSQL or older databases such as Paradox or dBase), or if you need to use an ODBC driver for functionality that isn't available with the OLE DB provider. Architecturally, the Odbc provider is similar to the OleDb provider – it acts as a .NET wrapper around the ODBC API, and allows ADO.NET to access a data source through an ODBC driver.

The Odbc provider classes reside in the System.Data.Odbc namespace, and begin with the prefix "Odbc". For example, we can connect to a MySQL database like this (here we're connecting to a copy of the Access Northwind database that I've imported to MySQL):

```
using System.Data.Odbc;    // The Odbc provider namespace

// Instantiate the OdbcConnection object
OdbcConnection cn = new OdbcConnection(
    "DRIVER={MySQL};SERVER=JULIAN;DATABASE=Northwind;UID=root;PWD=");
cn.Open();                  // Open the connection
```

The only difference here is that we use an ODBC rather than an OLE DB connection string (exactly as we would connecting to an ODBC data source from ADO). This could be a pre-configured connection in the form of a Data Source Name (DSN), or it could be a full connection string (as above) specifying the ODBC driver to use, the name of the database server and the database on the server, and the user ID (UID) and password (PWD) to use.

The DataSet

The other major component of ADO.NET is the DataSet; this corresponds very roughly to the ADO recordset. It differs, however, in two important respects. The first of these is that the DataSet is *always* disconnected, and as a consequence doesn't care where the data comes from – the DataSet can be used in exactly the same way to manipulate data from a traditional data source or from an XML document. In order to connect a DataSet to a data source, we need to use the DataAdapter as an intermediary between the DataSet and the .NET data provider:

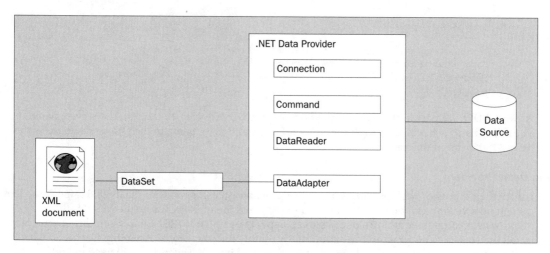

For example, to populate a `DataSet` with data from the `Employees` table in the `Northwind` database:

```
// Open the connection
OleDbConnection cn = new OleDbConnection(
    @"Provider=Microsoft.Jet.OLEDB.4.0;Data Source=C:\NWind.mdb");
cn.Open();

// Create a new DataAdapter object, passing in the SELECT command
OleDbDataAdapter da = new OleDbDataAdapter(
    "SELECT EmployeeID, FirstName, LastName FROM Employees", cn);

// Create a new DataSet
DataSet ds = new DataSet();

// Fill the DataSet
da.Fill(ds, "Employees");

// Close the connection now we've got the data
cn.Close();
```

After opening the connection just as we did before, there are three steps involved to populating the `DataSet`:

❑ Instantiate a new `DataAdapter` object. Before we fill the `DataSet`, we'll obviously need to specify the connection information and the data we want to fill it with. There are a number of ways of doing that, but probably the easiest is to pass the command text for the SQL query and either a connection string or an open connection into the `DataAdapter`'s constructor, as we do above.

❑ Create the new `DataSet`.

❑ Call the `DataAdapter`'s `Fill` method. We pass the `DataSet` we want to populate as a parameter to this method, and also the name of the table within the `DataSet` we want to fill. If we call the `Fill` method against a closed connection, the connection will automatically be opened, and then re-closed when the `DataSet` has been filled.

The DataTable Class

This last parameter gives a clue to the second important difference between a DataSet and an ADO recordset – the DataSet can contain more than one table of data. True, something similar was available in ADO with data shaping, but the tables in a DataSet can even be taken from different data sources. And, better still, we don't have the horrible SHAPE syntax to deal with. To achieve this, ADO.NET also has a DataTable class, which represents a single table within a DataSet. The DataSet has a Tables property, which returns a collection of these objects (a DataTableCollection). The DataTable represents data in the usual tabular format, and has collections of DataColumn and DataRow objects representing each column and row in the table:

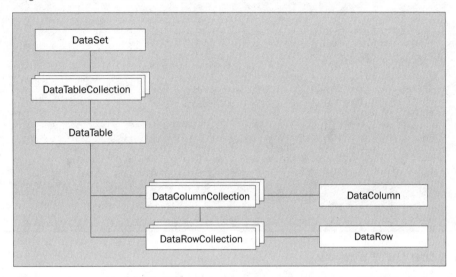

The DataColumn class corresponds to the Field object in ADO, but ADO didn't have any object representing a single row of data, so the DataRow class represents a big advance!

If we want to access the data in our DataTable, we have to access the appropriate DataRow object, and index into that to get the data for a particular column. The index can be either the numerical index of the column (0 for the first column, and so on), or the name of the column. The following example first iterates through the DataColumnCollection to retrieve the names of the column in the first table of the DataSet. We then iterate through each row and each column for the current row, and display the data in a crude command-line table:

```
// Display the column names
foreach (DataColumn dc in ds.Tables[0].Columns)
    Console.Write("{0,15}", dc.ColumnName);

// Add a newline after the column headings
Console.Write("\n");

// Display the data for each row
// Loop through the rows first
foreach (DataRow dr in ds.Tables[0].Rows)
{
    // Then loop through the columns for the current row
```

```
      for (int i=0; i<ds.Tables[0].Columns.Count; i++)
         Console.Write("{0,15}", dr[i]);

      // Add a line break after every row
      Console.Write("\n");
   }
```

If you execute this code snippet using the `DataSet` we populated earlier, you should see something like this:

Updating the Data Source

Actually, if we're just going to iterate through the data like that, we'd be much better off just using a `DataReader`. The `DataSet` should only really be used when we need to manipulate the data on the client. Unfortunately, however, this is where things get tricky. As we mentioned above, if we just try to make changes to the `DataSet` and then call the associated `DataAdapter`'s `Update` method, we'll get an error message telling us that the appropriate command object hasn't been set.

The easiest way to build the command object is to use the provider's CommandBuilder object. To see this in action, let's change the `FirstName` of the last record from "Anne" to "Anna":

```
// Change the value in the DataSet
ds.Tables[0].Rows[8]["FirstName"] = "Anna";

// Re-connect to the data source
cn.Open();

// Create an OleDbCommandBuilder object, passing the DataAdapter
// into the constructor
OleDbCommandBuilder cmdBuilder = new OleDbCommandBuilder(da);

// Display the UpdateCommand
Console.WriteLine(cmdBuilder.GetUpdateCommand().CommandText);

// Update the data source
```

```
da.Update(ds.Tables[0]);

// Close the connection again
cn.Close();
```

This is fairly straightforward. We pass our DataAdapter into the OleDbCommandBuilder's constructor, so it is automatically connected to our data source. We avoid the InvalidOperationException error just by instantiating the CommandBuilder for this DataAdapter – this will automatically build the commands for us. We can retrieve the text of the generated commands by calling the CommandBuilder's GetUpdateCommand, GetInsertCommand, etc., methods. As we're only updating a record (not deleting or inserting any records), we'll just show the UPDATE command. To do this, we call the GetUpdateCommand method, which returns a command object (in our case, an OleDbCommand, because we're using the OleDb provider). The CommandText in this case is:

```
UPDATE 'Employees' SET 'FirstName' = ? , 'LastName' = ? WHERE ( 'EmployeeID' = ?
AND 'FirstName' = ? AND 'LastName' = ? )
```

Now we can call the DataAdapter's Update method. This has several overloads, and can take as a parameter the DataSet (with or without the name of a table within the DataSet), or a DataTable, or an array of DataRow objects. Here we just pass in the DataTable we want to update. Finally, we re-close the connection.

ADO.NET and XML

Perhaps the single most impressive new feature of ADO.NET is its built-in support for XML. In fact, XML is now the standard persistence format for ADO.NET DataSets. While we've been able to save recordsets in XML format since ADO 2.1, the default format remained the proprietary Advanced Data TableGram (ADTG) format, and XML support was always limited. We couldn't, for example, load an arbitrary XML document into an ADO recordset – the document had to be in exactly the right format.

XML support in ADO.NET is far more complete – XML is absolutely integral to ADO.NET, and not just an add-on. XML is the format used to serialize and transport DataSets. Serializing a DataSet as an XML document (to a file, a stream, or a TextWriter object) is a trivial matter:

```
// Save the DataSet as an XML file
ds.WriteXml(@"C:\CSharp\Employees.xml");
```

The format of the generated XML document is far more readable than the ADO equivalent – the columns are represented by elements, not attributes, and there aren't a lot of unnecessary XML namespaces:

```
<?xml version="1.0" standalone="yes"?>
<NewDataSet>
  <Employees>
    <EmployeeID>1</EmployeeID>
    <FirstName>Nancy</FirstName>
    <LastName>Davolio</LastName>
  </Employees>
  <Employees>
```

```
         <EmployeeID>2</EmployeeID>
         <FirstName>Andrew</FirstName>
         <LastName>Fuller</LastName>
      </Employees>
      <!-- and so on... -->
   </NewDataSet>
```

In addition, we can load any well-formed XML document into a DataSet, without having to use a predefined structure (although we might lose content if the structure of the document is not basically tabular). For example (you will need to add a using System.IO; directive to the start of your code for this sample to work):

```
// Store the XML document in a string
string xmlDoc = @"<?xml version='1.0'?>
                    <books>
                        <book>
                            <title>Pro ADO.NET</title>
                            <publisher>Wrox Press</publisher>
                        </book>
                    </books>";

// Load this into a StringReader
StringReader sr = new StringReader(xmlDoc);

// Create a new DataSet and read in the XML
DataSet ds = new DataSet();
ds.ReadXml(sr);

// Display the column names and row data as a table
foreach (DataColumn dc in ds.Tables[0].Columns)
{
    Console.Write("{0,-15}", dc.ColumnName);
}
Console.Write("\n");

foreach (DataRow dr in ds.Tables[0].Rows)
{
    Console.WriteLine("{0,-15}{1,-15}", dr[0], dr[1]);
}
```

Here we just create a very simple XML document and store it in a string. We'll use the DataSet's ReadXml method to load the XML document into the DataSet. This doesn't accept an XML document as a string as a parameter, but it does accept a StringReader (this class resides in the System.IO namespace), so we create a new StringReader from our string, and pass that into the ReadXml method. Finally, we display the DataSet in tabular format much as we did before.

When we execute this, we should see the following:

```
Command Prompt                                                    _ □ ×
C:\527X Pro ADO.NET\Chapter 1>csc DataSetXml.cs
Microsoft (R) Visual C# Compiler Version 7.00.9254 [CLR version v1.0.2914]
Copyright (C) Microsoft Corp 2000-2001. All rights reserved.


C:\527X Pro ADO.NET\Chapter 1>DataSetXml
title           publisher
Pro ADO.NET     Wrox Press

C:\527X Pro ADO.NET\Chapter 1>_
```

Typed DataSets

As XML is everywhere behind the scenes in .NET, there is a whole range of tools available for working with XML documents and schemas. One of the most impressive of these is xsd.exe, which can (among some other neat tricks) take an XML Schema Definition (XSD) schema as input and generate from it a strongly typed DataSet. And it goes without saying that we can use the DataSet to generate the XSD schema automatically.

For example, we can generate an XSD schema for the Employees table in Northwind using the code:

```
OleDbConnection cn = new OleDbConnection(
    @"Provider=Microsoft.Jet.OLEDB.4.0;Data Source=C:\NWind.mdb");
cn.Open();
OleDbDataAdapter da = new OleDbDataAdapter("SELECT * FROM Employees", cn);
DataSet ds = new DataSet();
da.Fill(ds, "Employees");
cn.Close();
ds.WriteXmlSchema("Employees.xsd");
```

We can then run xsd.exe against this schema, using the option /d to indicate that we want to generate the source code for the strongly typed DataSet. To use xsd.exe from the command prompt, switch to the directory that contains the XSD schema and type this command (this assumes that the C:\Program Files\Microsoft.NET\FrameworkSDK\Bin directory has been added to the PATH environment variable):

```
xsd Employees.xsd /d
```

This generates a C# file named Employees.cs, which defines a class named NewDataSet, derived from DataSet, together with strongly typed DataTable and DataRow classes. As the NewDataSet class derives from DataSet, it has all the functionality of a normal DataSet. However, the typed DataRow class exposes each column in the row as a property of the appropriate data type (for example, a varchar column will be exposed as a string).

To see the typed DataSet in action, compile this C# file into a DLL:

```
csc /t:library Employees.cs
```

We can now use this assembly (Employees.dll) to create a strongly typed DataSet. The NewDataSet class has a nested EmployeesRow class (derived from DataRow). This class has a public property to return the value for each column in the table. This means that, instead of typing dr["FirstName"], we can now just type dr.FirstName:

```
// Open and populate the typed DataSet as normal...
OleDbConnection cn = new OleDbConnection(
    @"Provider=Microsoft.Jet.OLEDB.4.0;Data Source=C:\NWind.mdb");
cn.Open();
OleDbDataAdapter da = new OleDbDataAdapter("SELECT * FROM Employees", cn);

// The only difference is that we use a NewDataSet instead of a DataSet
NewDataSet ds = new NewDataSet();
da.Fill(ds, "Employees");
cn.Close();

// Display the data for each row
foreach (NewDataSet.EmployeesRow dr in ds.Employees.Rows)
{
    Console.WriteLine("{0,15}{1,15}", dr.FirstName, dr.LastName);
}
```

A small difference, you might think, and not worth the trouble of generating the class. And, if you're using Notepad, that's probably true. But if you're using a powerful IDE with IntelliSense and auto-completion, such as Visual Studio.NET, what this means is that the column names will be displayed as properties of the row:

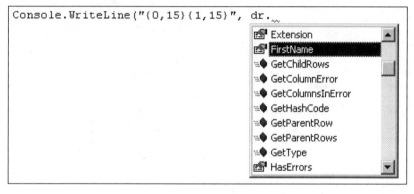

In other words, no more errors because you've mistyped or misremembered the name of a database column! In addition, it improves the readability of the code, and helps to minimize errors by enforcing strong typing at compile time – there's less danger of attempting to insert a value of the wrong type into a column.

ADO.NET and ADO 2.6

As ADO.NET is more or less a direct replacement for ADO 2.6 within the .NET world, and because most developers using it will be familiar to some degree with traditional ADO, it's worth taking a moment to consider some of the differences between the two technologies.

There are two chief differences between ADO.NET and ADO 2.6. Firstly, ADO.NET is specifically geared towards two distinct environments: disconnected resultsets, and read-only, forward-only connected access to the data source. Secondly, ADO.NET doesn't present a single, unified object model to the developer regardless of the data source – it uses provider-specific classes implemented by the .NET provider itself.

Disconnected Data Access

The first of these scenarios for which ADO.NET is optimized is the disconnected resultset. As we've seen, this is implemented by the `DataSet`, which is fully malleable and updateable, but which doesn't retain a persistent connection to the data source itself. The `DataSet` is similar in some ways to the disconnected recordset in ADO, but with the `DataSet` the disconnection is automatic, whereas previously developers explicitly had to disconnect the recordset from the data source and close the connection (a source of much confusion and many errors). For example, a typical method to return a disconnected recordset might contain ADO 2.6 code like this (in VB 6):

```
Dim cn As ADODB.Connection
Dim rs As ADODB.Recordset

Set cn = CreateObject("ADODB.Connection")
cn.Open "Provider=SQLOLEDB;Data Source=JULIAN;Initial Catalog=pubs;" & _
        "User ID=sa;Password="
Set rs = CreateObject("ADODB.Recordset")
rs.LockType = adLockBatchOptimistic        ' Specify the lock type
rs.CursorLocation = adUseClient            ' Specify that we're using
                                           ' OLE DB's Client Cursor Engine
rs.CursorType = adOpenStatic               ' Specify the cursor type
rs.Open "SELECT * FROM authors", cn        ' Open the recordset
Set rs.ActiveConnection = Nothing          ' Disconnect the recordset
cn .Close                                  ' Close the connection
Set cn = Nothing
```

Now, in ADO.NET, whenever we create a `DataSet`, it is automatically disconnected – in fact, as we've seen, we have to use the `DataAdapter` as an intermediary between the `DataSet` and the data provider. For example:

```
OleDbConnection cn = new OleDbConnection(@"Provider=Microsoft.Jet.OLEDB.4.0;
                                         Data Source=C:\NWind.mdb");
cn.Open();
OleDbDataAdapter da = new OleDbDataAdapter("SELECT * FROM Employees", cn);
DataSet ds = new DataSet();
da.Fill(ds, "Employees");
cn.Close();
```

This approach is far more transparent, and less prone to error, as well as being a good deal shorter! We don't need to specify additional information such as the `CursorType`, because the disconnected `DataSet` is by definition static. (Actually, we get a static cursor in ADO too, whatever type we specify, because the Client Cursor Engine (CCE) only supports static cursors; however, we *can't* specify the cursor type for a `DataSet`, so it's one less thing for us to worry about.)

Read-Only, Forward-Only Access

The second situation for which ADO.NET is optimized is where we want to iterate through each row in a resultset, one row at a time. In this scenario, we're not going to be making any changes to the data, and we're only going to be moving forward through the resultset, so we don't want to wait for the entire resultset to load before we start iterating through it. For this type of access, it makes sense to keep the connection to the data source open until we've finished iterating through the data. It's for precisely these situations that the DataReader was designed. Again, because we have a class designed specifically for the task, we can write much cleaner code. For example, to iterate through an ADO recordset we might use the following VB 6 code:

```
Dim cn As ADODB.Connection
Dim rs As ADODB.Recordset

Set cn = New ADODB.Connection
cn.Open "Provider=Microsoft.Jet.OLEDB.4.0;Data Source=C:\NWind.mdb"

Set rs = New ADODB.Recordset
rs.Open "SELECT * FROM Employees", cn, adOpenForwardOnly, adLockReadOnly

While Not rs.EOF
    MsgBox rs!FirstName & " " & rs!LastName
    rs.MoveNext
Wend

rs.Close
cn.Close
```

The ADO.NET equivalent would be:

```
OleDbConnection cn = new OleDbConnection(@"Provider=Microsoft.Jet.OLEDB.4.0;
                                          Data Source=C:\NWind.mdb");
cn.Open();
OleDbCommand cmd = new OleDbCommand("SELECT * FROM Employees", cn);
OleDbDataReader dr = cmd.ExecuteReader(CommandBehavior.CloseConnection);
while (dr.Read())
{
    Console.WriteLine (dr["FirstName"] + " " + dr["LastName"]);
}
dr.Close();
```

Notice how we no longer have to specify the cursor or lock types – we already know we want a forward-only, read-only cursor, so we don't have to remember half a dozen parameters when we open the DataReader.

The next nice touch is that the Read method automatically moves us to the next row. With ADO, it was easy to write code that went into an infinite loop because we forgot to add a MoveNext call. Not any more – DataReader.Read moves the DataReader's internal row pointer forward one row, and makes the data in that row available. The method itself returns a Boolean value of true while there's still data to be read, and false when EOF is reached. So, instead of needing separate calls to MoveNext and EOF, we can do the two in one go. Result – no more infinite loops!

The only point to watch here is that the DataReader starts on BOF, so we have to call Read at least once before we can access the data.

The gist of these changes is that where we had a single object (the `Recordset`) doing all the work in ADO 2.6, we now have specialized classes for the two most common scenarios. This means that a lot of the obscure (and often misunderstood) parameters we used to have when opening a recordset or executing a command can be abolished, and we can be sure that we're getting exactly the type of object we want. The disadvantage, of course, is if we want a non-standard way of accessing our data, for example a connected resultset that we can navigate through and update. ADO.NET just doesn't provide this.

It's worth remembering, though, that the whole of the .NET Framework was designed with one eye on distributed computing over the Internet, and particularly on exposing functionality through Web Services. Leaving database connections open in this way could seriously impact on the scalability of an application, and it's in keeping with the aims of .NET to prevent this (even if it does seem a bit nannyish). If you really do need this functionality, then for the time being at least, you're probably better off using "classic" ADO.

> *It's still possible to update the data source by executing commands using the command classes, of course. Combining these with the `DataReader` can be the most efficient technique if you need connected access, but you will need a fair bit of custom code to simulate a true updateable connected recordset.*

Provider-Specific Classes

The second major difference between ADO.NET and ADO is that there are specific sets of classes for each of the providers. In ADO, we simply used `Connection`, `Command`, and `Recordset` objects, regardless of the data source we were accessing; if we changed the database system used (say, upgraded from Access to SQL Server), then in theory at least all we needed to change was the connection string. Now we need to create a specific `SqlConnection`, `OleDbConnection`, etc. object, depending on the data provider.

In some ways, this is more analogous to the situation in OLE DB, where our first task was usually to instantiate the OLE DB provider using `CoCreateInstance`:

```
CoInitialize(NULL);
CoCreateInstance(CLSID_MSDASQL, NULL, CLSCTX_INPROC_SERVER, IID_IDBInitialize,
    (void **) &pIDBInitialize);
```

However, once we'd done this, we used standard interfaces to execute commands against the database. In ADO.NET the differences between the provider-specific classes are greater, as we have separate classes for the `Command`, `DataReader`, and `DataAdapter` (and so on), too. If we want to change the RDBMS used by our code, we need to change the namespaces imported into the project, and the code to declare and instantiate all provider-specific classes used, as well as the connection string.

This on its own may be a trivial search-and-replace task, but there's an even greater difference here. As we've seen, the common methods and properties for the .NET provider classes are defined in interfaces in the `System.Data` namespace. For example, the `ExecuteReader` method is defined in the `IDbCommand` interface. So far, that is much like OLE DB, where (for example) the `Execute` method is defined in the `ICommand` interface. However, with OLE DB we're dealing with the interfaces directly; with ADO.NET, we deal instead with objects, which implement these interfaces. The ADO.NET programmer doesn't need to know whether the methods and properties called are defined in the interface, or are specific to the provider.

To clarify this, let's look at the interface definition for `IDbConnection`. Just four properties and five methods are defined:

```
public interface System.Data.IDbConnection
{
    // Properties
    string ConnectionString { get; set; }
    int ConnectionTimeout { get; }
    string Database { get; }
    ConnectionState State { get; }

    // Methods
    System.Data.IDbTransaction BeginTransaction();
    System.Data.IDbTransaction BeginTransaction(
        System.Data.IsolationLevel il);
    void ChangeDatabase(string databaseName);
    void Close();
    System.Data.IDbCommand CreateCommand();
    void Open();
} // end of System.Data.IDbConnection
```

Now let's see how that's implemented by the OleDbConnection object. To save space, some members have been omitted from the definition below. All of the members defined by IDbConnection are implemented; the highlighted members are those that aren't implementations of the IDbConnection members:

```
public sealed class System.Data.OleDb.OleDbConnection :
    System.ComponentModel.Component,
    System.ComponentModel.IComponent,
    IDisposable,
    ICloneable,
    System.Data.IDbConnection
{
    // Properties
    public string ConnectionString { virtual get; virtual set; }
    public int ConnectionTimeout { virtual get; }
    public string Database { virtual get; }
    public string DataSource { get; }
    public string Provider { get; }
    public string ServerVersion { get; }
    public ConnectionState State { virtual get; }

    // Events
    public event OleDbInfoMessageEventHandler InfoMessage;
    public event StateChangeEventHandler StateChange;

    // Methods
    public System.Data.OleDb.OleDbTransaction BeginTransaction();
    public System.Data.OleDb.OleDbTransaction
        BeginTransaction(System.Data.IsolationLevel isolationLevel);
    public virtual void ChangeDatabase(string value);
    public virtual void Close();
    public System.Data.OleDb.OleDbCommand CreateCommand();
    public virtual System.Runtime.Remoting.ObjRef CreateObjRef(Type
        requestedType);
    public System.Data.DataTable GetOleDbSchemaTable(Guid schema, object[]
```

```
                    restrictions);
        public virtual void Open();
        public static void ReleaseObjectPool();
    } // end of System.Data.OleDb.OleDbConnection
```

Notice that OleDbConnection (and the other connection classes) derive from the Component class, and implement a number of other interfaces beside IDbConnection. The implementations of the members of these interfaces have been omitted. What we see is that, even ignoring these members (which aren't directly related to the class's functionality), there are an extra three properties, two events, and three methods. Some of these are implemented by the other providers (such as the StateChange event), others aren't (for example, the GetOleDbSchemaTable method has no equivalent in the SqlClient or Odbc providers). Short of checking the documentation, there's no way of knowing for sure whether a method or property is common to all providers.

This extensibility is potentially both a big advantage and a big disadvantage. On the one hand, it allows developers of .NET data providers an enormous amount of flexibility. Not only can extra members be added, but individual providers can even add extra classes and other types (for example, the SqlClient provider has a SqlDebugging class with no equivalent in the other providers). This gives provider developers the ability to allow data from a particular data source to be accessed in a more appropriate way, and gives scope for providers to be developed for data sources that don't fit so comfortably into the existing model, in much the same way as the OLE DB 2.5 interfaces allowed the development of the MSDAIPP and ExOLEDB OLE DB providers.

The downside, of course, is that if provider developers all go their own way and develop numerous extensions to their providers, developers using ADO.NET will need to be familiar with each provider that they have to use. This could be seen as a setback for the goal of Universal Data Access, and a partial return to datasource-specific APIs. Hopefully, however, the fixing of the core functionality in the ADO.NET interfaces will ensure that differences between the providers remain relatively minor.

As a side note, it's worth pointing out that if you really do want to write provider-independent code, you can code against the interfaces directly:

```
// Instantiate the Connection as normal
OleDbConnection oleDbConn = new OleDbConnection(
    @"Provider=Microsoft.Jet.OLEDB.4.0;Data Source=C:\NWind.mdb");

// Cast it to the IDbConnection interface
IDbConnection cn = (IDbConnection)oleDbConn;

// Now code against this interface
cn.Open();
IDbCommand cmd = cn.CreateCommand();
cmd.CommandText = "SELECT * FROM Employees";
IDataReader dr = cmd.ExecuteReader();
while (dr.Read())
{
    Console.WriteLine("{0} {1}", dr["FirstName"], dr["LastName"]);
}
```

We instantiate a connection object as normal (after all, the actual connection is always going to be provider-specific), and then cast it to the IDbConnection interface. We can then call the connection's methods as defined in the interface. For example, the CreateCommand method returns an instance of the IDbCommand interface, rather than an instance of the OleDbCommand class. As all providers have to support these interfaces, this technique allows us to write code that's completely provider-independent (except for the initial connection). However, interfaces don't provide any implementations of their members, so the provider-specific implementations will be used. For example, when we call IDbCommand.ExecuteReader, it is still the ExecuteReader method of the OleDbCommand class that will be executed.

Using ADO 2.x in .NET

Although we've stressed that you should use ADO.NET rather than ADO whenever possible, there are still a couple of scenarios where there's really no alternative but to use traditional ADO. We've mentioned these already, but it's worth reiterating them in one place:

❑   If you absolutely *have* to use a connected recordset, and need to be able to update the data source. One reason for this might be the more flexible lock and cursor types available in ADO. If your application has a small enough number of users to permit simultaneous connections and you need to be able to see changes to the data source as they are made, then ADO may be a better choice.

❑   If you need to use the ADO Record and Stream objects, for example if you're using the OLE DB provider for Exchange 2000 (ExOLEDB) or Internet Publishing (MSDAIPP). Until the OleDb provider is updated to support the OLE DB 2.5 interfaces or .NET providers for these data sources become available, you'll need to use ADO.

To use ADO 2.x from .NET, we need to create a **Runtime Callable Wrapper** (RCW) for the COM component. We can do this in Visual Studio.NET by selecting the ADODB library from the COM tab of the Add Reference dialog box:

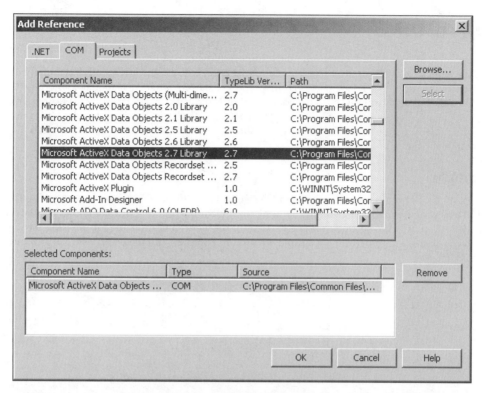

Alternatively, we can use the command-line tool `TlbImp.exe` to import the type library into .NET:

Note that this doesn't install the assembly into the Global Assembly Cache, so you'll need to make sure that the DLL is in the same directory as the code that calls it.

Once we've got our RCW for the ADODB library, using it is similar to using it from VB 6. The one major point to be aware of if you're writing C# code is that C# doesn't support optional parameters to method calls, so *all* parameters will need to be included. This complicates method calls significantly, so make sure you've got a reference to the ADO object model handy!

Using ADO.NET

As we've already mentioned, one of the most important features of the .NET Framework is its cross-language support. Although most of the code in this book will use C#, ADO.NET is equally easy to use from any of the other .NET languages. To help you get started, whatever language you're using, we'll have a quick look at writing ADO.NET code in all of Microsoft's .NET languages. For these examples, we'll just open up a connection to the pubs database in SQL Server, retrieve the data from the authors table into a DataReader, and iterate through this, displaying the au_fname and au_lname fields for each row.

C# Example

As most of the examples in the book are in C#, we'll start with that language. In fact, we've already seen most of this code before – the code for opening up the connection to a SQL Server is identical to the code we looked at in the section on the SqlClient provider, and the code for iterating through the provider is almost the same as the example we used to compare connected access in ADO and ADO.NET:

```
using System;
using System.Data.SqlClient;

class CSharpAdoExample
{
  static void Main(string[] args)
  {
    // Create the SqlConnection object and open the connection
    SqlConnection cn = new SqlConnection(
      "Data Source=JULIANS2;Initial Catalog=pubs;User ID=sa;Password=");
    cn.Open();

    // Create and execute the SqlCommand
    SqlCommand cmd = new SqlCommand(
      "SELECT au_fname, au_lname FROM authors", cn);
    SqlDataReader dr = cmd.ExecuteReader();

    // Iterate through the DataReader and display the au_fname and au_lname
    while (dr.Read())
    {
      Console.WriteLine(dr["au_fname"] + " " + dr["au_lname"]);
    }
  }
}
```

If this C# source file is called CSharpAdoExample.cs, we can compile it from the command line simply by typing csc CSharpAdoExample.cs. There's no need to add any references.

Visual Basic.NET Example

The equivalent VB.NET code really only differs from the C# in its syntax. While there are some more fundamental differences between the two languages (such as C#'s support for pointers and unsafe code), these generally don't affect ADO.NET programming directly. This is because the ADO.NET classes are CLS-compliant, and therefore don't expose features which aren't supported by all .NET compilers.

```
Imports System
Imports System.Data.SqlClient

Module VBAdoExample

  Sub Main()

    ' Declare our variables
    Dim cn As SqlConnection
    Dim cmd As SqlCommand
    Dim dr As SqlDataReader

    ' Create the SqlConnection object and open the connection
    cn = New SqlConnection("Data Source=JULIANS2;" & _
      "Initial Catalog=pubs;User ID=sa;Password=")
    cn.Open()

    ' Create and execute the SqlCommand
    cmd = New SqlCommand("SELECT au_fname, au_lname FROM authors", cn)
    dr = cmd.ExecuteReader()

    ' Iterate through the DataReader and display the au_fname and au_lname
    While dr.Read()
      Console.WriteLine(dr("au_fname") & " " & dr("au_lname"))
    End While
  End Sub

End Module
```

Remember that if you compile VB.NET files containing ADO.NET code from the command line, you need to add references to the assemblies System.dll and System.Data.dll. For example:

```
vbc VbAdoExample.vb /r:System.dll /r:System.Data.dll
```

JScript.NET Example

JScript.NET is much the simplest of the five languages. The actual syntax is almost identical to the C# version, except that by default JScript.NET is weakly typed (so we declare all our ADO.NET objects as vars). Also, with JScript.NET we don't need to include our application-level code within a class or any type of Main function (this is generated by the JScript compiler):

```
import System;
import System.Data.SqlClient;

// Create the SqlConnection object and open the connection
var cn = new SqlConnection(
  "Data Source=JULIANS2;Initial Catalog=pubs;User ID=sa;Password=");
cn.Open();

// Create and execute the SqlCommand
var cmd = new SqlCommand("SELECT au_fname, au_lname FROM authors", cn);
var dr = cmd.ExecuteReader();
```

```
// Iterate through the DataReader and display the au_fname and au_lname
while (dr.Read())
{
    Console.WriteLine(dr["au_fname"] + " " + dr["au_lname"]);
}
```

As with C#, we don't need to reference the `System.dll` or `System.Data.dll` assemblies, so we can compile the source code just using `jsc JsAdoExample.js`.

Managed C++ Example

C# and C++ are syntactically related, but the differences between C# and managed C++ are far greater than those between C# and VB.NET:

```
// Standard header include
#include "stdafx.h"

// Reference external assemblies
#using <mscorlib.dll>
#using <System.dll>
#using <System.Data.dll>

// Import namespaces
using namespace System;
using namespace System::Data::SqlClient;

// This is the entry point for this application
#ifdef _UNICODE
int wmain(void)
#else
int main(void)
#endif
{
    // Create the SqlConnection object and open the connection
    String* connectString =
        "Data Source=JULIANS2;Initial Catalog=pubs;User ID=sa;Password=";
    SqlConnection* cn = new SqlConnection(connectString);
    cn->Open();

    // Create and execute the SqlCommand
    String* cmdString = "SELECT au_fname, au_lname FROM authors";
    SqlCommand* cmd = new SqlCommand(cmdString, cn);
    SqlDataReader* dr = cmd->ExecuteReader();

    // Iterate through the DataReader and display the au_fname and au_lname
    while(dr->Read())
    {
        String* firstName = dr->get_Item("au_fname")->ToString();
        String* lastName = dr->get_Item("au_lname")->ToString();
        String* authorName = firstName->Concat(firstName, " ", lastName);
        Console::WriteLine(authorName);
    }
    return 0;
}
```

Notice that we need to reference any external assemblies (such as `System.Data.dll`) using the `#using` directive, as well as adding a `using` directive (no '#' this time) from import a namespace (as in C#). If you've not seen Managed C++ before, the most striking difference to C# is that reference types are implemented using pointer syntax (for example, C++ `String*` corresponds to C# `string`). The ADO.NET classes are, of course, reference types, so we need to use the indirect member access operator (`->`), rather than the direct member selection operator (`.`) with them.

The most important difference in the ADO.NET code here is that we can't use the column name to index into the `DataReader` to extract the data for that column, but instead have to call the `get_Item` method. Finally, we can't concatenate strings using the + operator, but need to use the `Concat` method. This method takes up to four single strings, or an array of strings, and joins them into a single string. Note that it's not a static method, so it must be called on an instance of `String*`, even though it doesn't necessarily affect that instance.

J# Example

Java syntax is very similar to C# syntax, so this looks very similar to the C# example:

```
import System.*;
import System.Data.*;
import System.Data.SqlClient.*;

// Summary description for Class1.
public class Class1
{
  public static void main(String[] args)
  {
    SqlConnection cn = new SqlConnection("Data Source=JULIANS2;" +
      "Initial Catalog=pubs;User ID=sa;Password=");
    cn.Open();
    SqlCommand cmd = new SqlCommand(
      "SELECT au_fname, au_lname FROM authors", cn);
    SqlDataReader dr = cmd.ExecuteReader();
    while (dr.Read())
    {
      System.out.println(dr.get_Item("au_fname") + " " +
        dr.get_Item("au_lname"));
    }
  }
}
```

The interesting thing to note about J# is that we can use both traditional Java packages, and .NET namespaces (both imported using the `import` keyword). For example, in the above code, we use the traditional Java `System.out.println` method to print to the console, but we could just as easily have used the .NET `System.Console.WriteLine` method. ADO.NET code is, of course, always .NET-specific.

ADO.NET Events

There's just one last feature of ADO.NET that we'll introduce before we leave this chapter – ADO.NET events. In concept, ADO.NET events are very similar to ADO events – events are generated when something significant happens, such as a connection is opened or closed. As in ADO, events are exposed as members of the ADO.NET objects, and our code can inform an object that we want to be notified when a particular event occurs. When that happens, a specially designated method known as an event handler is executed.

If events in ADO.NET are conceptually similar to events in ADO, unfortunately the way we implement event handlers is somewhat different. And worse, the way it's done is quite different depending on the language you use. However, the general procedure is the same. Firstly, we need to get a reference to the object that will generate the events. Next, we need to inform the object that we want to be notified when particular events are raised. Finally, we have to write the event handler that will be invoked whenever the event is raised for that object.

Let's have a quick look at how this works in C# and VB.NET. We'll use as an example the OleDbConnection's StateChange event, which is generated whenever the connection is opened or closed. Events in .NET make use of a special category of data type known as a **delegate**. A delegate is essentially a reference to a method – in this case a reference to our event handler method. To ask to be notified of an event, we need to add this delegate to the StateChange event.

In C# we do this simply by using the += operator. We get a reference to the delegate by creating a new object of the appropriate event handler type (in this case StateChangeEventHandler), and passing our function into the constructor:

```
// C# code
cn.StateChange += new StateChangeEventHandler(cn_StateChange);
```

In VB.NET, we get a reference to the delegate using the AddressOf function, and use the AddHandler function to add this to the OleDbConnection's StateChange event:

```
' VB .NET code
AddHandler cn.StateChange, AddressOf cn_StateChange
```

Next, we need to write the event handler method itself. In this case, we'll just write the new state to the console. Event handlers have predetermined signatures, and our method must conform to this. There are always two parameters – the object that raised the event, and an object containing additional arguments. The type of this object varies according to the type of the event handler. For the StateChange event, it is of type StateChangeEventArgs.

Here's the C# code for the event handler:

```
public static void cn_StateChange(object sender,
        System.Data.StateChangeEventArgs e)
{
    Console.WriteLine("Connection state changed: {0}",
        ((OleDbConnection)sender).State);
}
```

Notice that the sender is passed into the method as type object, so we need to cast it to the actual type of the sender (in this case, OleDbConnection) before we can access its methods and properties.

If we don't turn on `Option Strict`, VB.NET doesn't require this casting, so the code is slightly simpler:

```
Private Sub cn_StateChange(sender As Object, _
    e As System.Data.StateChangeEventArgs)
   Console.WriteLine("Connection state changed: {0}", sender.State)
End Sub
```

Otherwise, we will need to declare the `OleDbConnection` object at the class or module level, and access its `State` property directly:

```
Console.WriteLine("Connection state changed: {0}", cn.State)
```

To see how these fit together, here's the full listing of the C# code. The VB.NET code is available for download at the Wrox web site.

```csharp
using System;
using System.Data;
using System.Data.OleDb;

class AdoEventsExample
{
   public static void Main()
   {
      // Instantiate the OleDbConnection
      OleDbConnection cn = new OleDbConnection(
          @"Provider=Microsoft.Jet.OLEDB.4.0;Data Source=C:\NWind.mdb");

      // Hook our event handler into the event
      cn.StateChange += new StateChangeEventHandler(cn_StateChange);

      // Open and close the connection to test the event handler
      cn.Open();
      cn.Close();
   }

   // The definition for the event handler
   public static void cn_StateChange(object sender,
       System.Data.StateChangeEventArgs e)
   {
      Console.WriteLine("Connection state changed: {0}",
          ((OleDbConnection)sender).State);
   }
}
```

The output when we run this program is:

```
Command Prompt                                                    _ □ ×
C:\527X Pro ADO.NET\Chapter 1>csc AdoEventsExample.cs
Microsoft (R) Visual C# Compiler Version 7.00.9254 [CLR version v1.0.2914]
Copyright (C) Microsoft Corp 2000-2001. All rights reserved.


C:\527X Pro ADO.NET\Chapter 1>AdoEventsExample
Connection state changed: Open
Connection state changed: Closed

C:\527X Pro ADO.NET\Chapter 1>
```

Summary

This hasn't been too long a chapter, but we have covered a lot of ground. However, we've only really just begun to scratch the surface of what ADO.NET can do, and hopefully we've shown you just enough of its capabilities to encourage you to delve further and deeper into this vast library. As a quick recap, here are some of the things we covered:

❑ An overview of the main features of the .NET Framework

❑ The main developments in data access technologies over the last few years and how ADO.NET fits into the picture

❑ The three .NET data providers, their main components, and the `DataSet`

❑ The XML support built into ADO.NET

❑ How ADO.NET differs from ADO 2.6

❑ ADO.NET events

2

The .NET Data Providers

In most of today's applications we have two key components: the application and the data store. An application in today's Internet-driven, information-abundant world almost always requires access to some sort of data, and in many cases that data is in a database, such as Microsoft SQL Server, Oracle, or one of the many other databases available. Regardless of the database, there must be a mechanism in place to connect to the data and execute commands against that data. In the .NET Framework, that mechanism is the **data provider**.

A .NET data provider is used to connect to a database, execute commands, and retrieve results. The data providers are designed to be lightweight and efficient, creating a minimal layer between the application and the database. The data providers are designed for fast, efficient access to data for manipulation, or forward only, read-only access to data. A data provider is composed of four objects:

- ❑ Connection
- ❑ Command
- ❑ DataReader
- ❑ DataAdapter

A connection object provides connectivity to the database; a command object enables database commands, such as T-SQL commands or stored procedures, to be executed against the database; a datareader provides a forward only, read-only, memory efficient stream of data from the database to the application; and a DataAdapter provides a bridge between a DataSet and the database. The DataAdapter uses command objects to execute SELECT, INSERT, UPDATE, and DELETE commands against the database and return any requested data into, or reconcile data from, a DataSet.

In Chapter 5 we will discuss the DataSet at great length, but for now, all we need to know is that the DataSet is a disconnected representation of the database. A DataSet contains DataTables, Relations, and Constraints, allowing it to replicate the entire database, or select parts of the database, in a disconnected fashion, using XML as its underlying persistence format.

In the following figure we see an overview of the .NET data providers in an ADO.NET application.

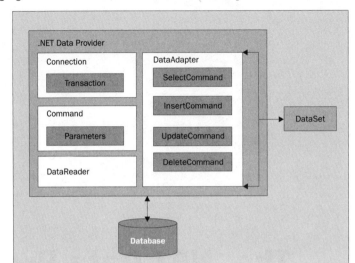

A data provider can be written for any data source, but the .NET Framework ships with two data providers:

❑ **SQL Server Data Provider**
A data provider designed explicitly for use with SQL Server 7.0 or greater. This data provider uses a proprietary protocol to connect directly to SQL Server 7.0 or greater without the OLE DB layer.

❑ **OLE DB Data Provider**
The data provider designed for use with all OLE DB-compliant data sources. While this data provider can be used with SQL Server 7.0 or greater, it is recommended that the SQL Server Data Provider be used.

> **A third data provider, the ODBC Data Provider, is available as a separate download from Microsoft (as of the .NET Framework SDK Beta 2), at http://www.microsoft.com/downloads/release.asp?ReleaseID=31125.**

Each data provider has its purpose, its benefits, and its drawbacks. In this chapter we will discuss and demonstrate the SQL Server Data Provider and the OLE DB Data Provider.

The SQL Server Data Provider

The SQL Server Data Provider was specifically designed by Microsoft for use with SQL Server 7.0 or later. It uses a proprietary protocol to communicate directly with SQL Server without the added weight of using an OLE DB or ODBC layer. Since this data provider is streamlined for use with SQL Server it results in very fast and efficient transfer of data. In applications that use Microsoft's SQL Server 7.0 or later, the SQL Server Data Provider is recommended. For applications that use SQL Server 6.5 or earlier, we must use the OLE DB Data Provider.

The classes for the SQL Server Data Provider are found in the `System.Data.SqlClient` namespace.

The OLE DB Data Provider

The OLE DB Data Provider is for use with databases that support OLE DB interfaces. This data provider uses native OLE DB through COM interoperability to access the database and execute commands. To use the OLE DB Data Provider we must also have a compatible OLE DB provider. The following OLE DB providers are, at the time of writing, compatible with ADO.NET :

- **SQLOLEDB** – Microsoft OLE DB Provider for SQL Server

- **MSDAORA** – Microsoft OLE DB Provider for Oracle

- **Microsoft.Jet.OLEDB.4.0** – OLE DB Provider for Microsoft Jet

The OLED DB Data Provider does not support OLE DB 2.5 interfaces, such as those required for Microsoft OLE DB Provider for Exchange and Microsoft OLE DB Provider for Internet Publishing. The OLE DB Data Provider also does not support the MSDASQL Provider (Microsoft OLE DB Provider for ODBC). The OLE DB Data Provider is the recommended data provider for applications that use SQL Server 6.5 or earlier, Oracle, or Microsoft Access.

The classes for the OLE DB Data Provider are found in the `System.Data.OleDb` namespace.

> To use either of the data provider we must include the `System.Data` namespace as well as the data provider appropriate namespace.

Meet the Players

In both the SQL Server Data Provider and the OLE DB Data Provider there are four key classes that are derived from the following ADO.NET interfaces, found in the `System.Data` namespace:

- `IDbConnection` – `SqlConnection` and `OleDbConnection`

- `IDbCommand` – `SqlCommand` and `OleDbCommand`

- `IDataReader` – `SqlDataReader` and `OleDbDataReader`

- `IDbDataAdapter` – `SqlDataAdapter` and `OleDbDataAdapter`

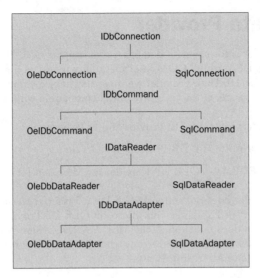

ADO.NET exposes a common model for the .NET data providers. This allows us to write code once that can be used for either data provider. This is achieved through the use of the ADO.NET data provider interfaces. By defining object instances against the interfaces, the appropriate class will be instantiated and used.

For example, the following code will work against either the SQL Server or OLE DB Data Provider:

```
public IdataReader getData(con As IDbConnection)
{
    IDbCommand cmd = con.CreateCommand();
    cmd.CommandText = "SELECT * FROM Customers";
    IDataReader reader = cmd.ExecuteReader();

    return reader;
}
```

In the preceding code, we have a procedure that takes a connection object as an input argument. The connection object is referenced as the `IDbConnection` interface. The application will not create an instance of the `IDbConnection` interface, but rather it will create an instance of the class that inherits from the interface. If we are using the `System.Data.SqlClient` namespace in our application, then the object will be an instance of the `SqlConnection` class; if we are using the `System.Data.OleDb` namespace, then the object will be an instance of the `OleDbConnection` class.

The same technique is used for the command and data reader instances. As a result, this method will work for either data provider without any code changes.

Let's take a look at each of the key classes in the ADO.NET Data Providers.

Connection

The connection classes inherit, as we just saw, from the `IDbConnection` interface. They are manifested in each data provider as either the `SqlConnection` (for the SQL Server Data Provider) or the `OleDbConnection` (for the OLE DB Data Provider). The connection class is used to open a connection to the database on which commands will be executed.

Unlike previous versions of ADO, connections must be explicitly closed to release the actual database connection. The database connection *will not* be implicitly released when the connection object falls out of scope or is reclaimed by garbage collection; the connection must be explicitly closed using the `Connection.Close()` method.

> **Managing connection state (whether the connection is open or closed) is very important in ADO.NET. Leaving a connection open can use unnecessary resources, causing you application's memory footprint to grow. ADO.NET does help manage this by automatically pooling connections, as we will discuss later, but explicitly closing a connection is required to release the actual database connection.**

Command

The command classes inherit from the `IDbCommand` interface. As with the connection class, the command classes are manifested as either the `SqlCommand` or the `OleDbCommand`. The command class is used to execute T-SQL commands or stored procedures against a database. Commands require an instance of a connection object in order to connect to the database and execute a command. In turn, the command class exposes several execute methods, depending on what expectations you have.

❑ **ExecuteReader** – returns a stream of data in the form of an object that inherits from the `IDataReader` interface (`SqlDataReader` or `OleDbDataReader`).

```
SqlDataReader myReader = myCommand.ExecuteReader();
```

❑ **ExecuteScalar** – returns a singleton value, such as an aggregate value like those returned from `COUNT()` or `SUM()` aggregate functions.

```
MyCommand.CaommandText = "SELCT COUNT(*) FROM Customers";
int numberOfCustomers = (int)myCommand.ExecuteScalar();
```

❑ **ExecuteNonQuery** – does not return records, but does return an integer indicating how many rows were affected by the command execution.

```
int rowsAffected = MyCommand.ExecuteNonQuery();
```

DataReader

The datareader classes inherit from the `IDataReader` interface. Continuing the trend, the data reader are manifested as either a `SqlDataReader` or an `OleDbDataReader`. The datareader is a forward-only, read-only stream of data from the database. This makes the datareader a very efficient means for retrieving data, as only one record is brought into memory at a time. Calling `Command.ExecuteReader()` will return a datareader object. We can use the `DataReader.Read()` method to iterate through the rows in the returned stream of data. The `Read()` method will advance to the next record in the stream.

```
while(reader.Read())
{
    //Do something with the value
}
```

Each datareader (`OleDbDataReader` and `SqlDataReader`) exposes several methods for retrieving the values of the record fields, each of which takes the zero-based column ordinal as its input argument. Each datareader object exposes a different set of methods, but the following list are methods exposed by both the `OleDbDataReader` and the `SqlDataReader`:

❑ `GetBoolean()`
Gets the value of a specified column as a Boolean

❑ `GetByte()`
Gets the value of a specified column as a byte

❑ `GetBytes()`
Reads a stream of bytes from the offset specified column offset into the buffer as an array starting at the given buffer offset

❑ `GetChar()`
Gets the value of a specified column as a character

❑ `GetChars()`
Reads a stream of characters from the specified column offset into the buffer as an array starting at the given buffer offset

❑ `GetDataTypeName()`
Gets the name of the source data type

❑ `GetDateTime()`
Gets the value of the specified column as a `DateTime` object

❑ `GetDecimal()`
Gets the value of the specified column as a `Decimal` object

❑ `GetDouble()`
Gets the value of the specified column as a double-precision floating-point number

❑ `GetFieldType()`
Gets the data type of the specified column

❑ `GetFloat()`
Gets the value of the specified column as a single-precision floating point number

❑ `GetGuid()`
Gets the value of the specified column as a globally-unique identifier (GUID)

❑ `GetInt16()`
Gets the value of the specified column as a 16-bit signed integer

❑ `GetInt32()`
Gets the value of the specified column as a 32-bit signed integer

❑ `GetInt64()`
Gets the value of the specified column as a 64-bit signed integer

❑ `GetName()`
Gets the name of the specified column

❑ `GetOrdinal()`
Gets the column ordinal, given the name of the column

❑ `GetSchemaTable()`
Returns a `DataTable` that describes the column metadata of the `DataReader`

- ❏ GetString()
  Gets the value of the specified column as a string

- ❏ GetTimeSpan()
  Gets the value of the specified column as a TimeSpan object

- ❏ GetValue()
  Gets the value of the column at the specified ordinal in its native format

- ❏ GetValues()
  Gets all the attribute columns in the current row

When the data type of the column is not known, we can use the ToString() method of the System.Object class to get the value as a string.

```
while(reader.Read())
{
   myString = reader.Item(0).ToString();
   myInt = reader.GetInt32(1);
}
```

A connection object can only contain one datareader at a time, so we must explicitly close the datareader when we are done with it. This will free the connection for other uses.

> **If the command that is being executed returns a datareader and one or more output parameters, those parameters are not accessible until the datareader has been closed.**

When a command returns multiple result sets in a single datareader, the NextResult() method is used to step to the next result set.

```
public void getData(con As IDbConnection)
{
    IDbCommand cmd = con.CreateCommand();
    cmd.CommandText = "SELECT * FROM Customers; SELECT * From Employees";
    IDataReader reader = cmd.ExecuteReader();

    do
    {

       while(reader.Read())
       {
          Response.Write(reader.Item(0).ToString());
          Response.Write(reader.Item(1).ToString());
       }
    }

    while(reader.NextResult() == false);
}
```

DataAdapter

The `DataAdapter` classes inherit from the `IDbDataAdapter` interface and are manifested as `SqlDataAdapter` and `OleDbDataAdapter`. The `DataAdapter` is intended for use with a `DataSet` and can retrieve data from the data source, populate `DataTables` and constraints, and maintain the `DataTable` relationships. The `DataSet` can contain multiple `DataTables`, disconnected from the database. The data in the `DataSet` can be manipulated – changed, deleted, or added to – without an active connection to the database. This is a big jump forward in design and functionality from previous versions of ADO. In Chapter 5 we will discuss the `DataSet` in depth.

The `DataAdapter` can be used to reconcile the data changes between the `DataSet` and the database. The `DataAdapter` consolidates a connection and four command objects: `SelectCommand`, `InsertCommand`, `UpdateCommand`, and `DeleteCommand`. The `SelectCommand` is used for retrieving data from the database, while the other three methods are used for reconciling data changes in the `DataSet`.

The `DataAdapter` exposes a `Fill()` method, which is used to fill a `DataTable` in a `DataSet`. The `Fill` method takes in a `DataSet` instance as a required argument and a table name as an optional argument. If a table name is not specified, the `DataTable` will be given a default name (`Table`, `Table1`, `Table2`, etc.). The following code shows how to use the SQL Server Data Provider to connect to the `Northwind` database and populate a `DataSet` with a representation of the `Customers` table.

```
using System;
using System.Data;
using System.Data.SqlClient;

public class UsingTheDataAdapter
{

    public static void Main()
    {

        DataSet ds = new DataSet();
        SqlDataAdapter sda = new SqlDataAdapter(
            "SELECT * FROM Customers",
            "server=localhost;database=Northwind;uid=sa;pwd=;");

        sda.Fill(ds, "Customers");

        for(int i=0; i < ds.Tables["Customers"].Rows.Count-1; i++)
        {
            Console.WriteLine("{0} - {1}",
                ds.Tables["Customers"].Rows[i][0].ToString(),
                ds.Tables["Customers"].Rows[i][1].ToString());
        }

    }

}
```

In the preceding code we create an instance of a `DataSet` (ds) and a `SqlDataAdapter` (sda). In the `SqlDataAdapter` constructor we pass in the T-SQL command and the connection string to use. When we invoke the `sda.Fill()` method, the connection is opened, the command is executed, a `DataTable` named "Customers" is created in the `DataSet`, and the connection is closed.

> The data adapter objects will manage opening and closing a connection for the
> command to execute, unless we explicitly open the connection. If the connection object
> that the data adapter is using is explicitly opened, using `Connection.Open()`, before
> the `Fill()` method is invoked, the data adapter will not close the connection. We
> must explicitly close the connection in this scenario.

Establishing Connections

The ADO.NET connection classes are used to make a connection between your application and a data
source. The connection class is instantiated, a connection string is set, and the connection is opened.
Once the connection is opened, commands may be executed over the connection to retrieve or
manipulate data in the database. Once we are done with the connection, it must be closed to release the
resource. As previously stated, it is critical that we explicitly close the connection, using the
`Connection.Close()` method, to release the actual database connection – the actual connection will
not be released even if the connection object falls out of scope and is garbage-collected.

The SqlConnection and OleDbConnection Classes

Each of the .NET Data Providers provides a connection class that derives from the `IDbConnection`
interface. With the exception of the format of the connection string used to connect to a database, the two
data provider connection classes work in the same way. The `SqlConnection` class is used to connect to a
Microsoft SQL Server 7.0 or greater database. For any other database that supports OLE DB, such as
Microsoft Access, Oracle, or previous versions of SQL Server, use the `OleDbConnection` class.

Constructing a Connection

The `SqlConnection` and `OleDbConnection` classes each expose two constructors for creating
instances of these classes in our applications. The first constructor creates a new instance of the
connection class, while the second constructor creates an instance of the connection class using the
connection string provided.

The following code demonstrates the two constructors:

```
SqlConnection con = new SqlConnection();
```

Or:

```
SqlConnection con = new
   SqlConnection("server=localhost;database=Northwind;uid=sa;pwd=;");
```

Notice in the preceding example that there was no "`provider`" value in the connection string. In classic
ADO we would define the OLE DB provider that should be used when opening the connection; we
would specify that the Microsoft OLE DB Provider for SQL (`SQLOLEDB`) should be used. In the
preceding example, we create a new instance of the `SqlConnection` class, which we know will be
connecting to a SQL Server database, because we are using the SQL Server Data Provider. As
mentioned previously, the SQL Server Data Provider does not use OLE DB, but rather connects to SQL
Server directly. The `SqlConnection` class does not expose a `Provider` property, and a provider
definition is not allowed in the connection string. The connection string should simply point to the
server and database to be connected to (and contain any security information of course).

When using the `OleDbConnection` class, however, an OLE DB Provider is required. The following OLE DB providers are compatible with ADO.NET:

❑ **SQLOLEDB** – Microsoft OLE DB Provider for SQL Server

```
OleDbConnection con = new
    OleDbConnection("Provider=SQLOLEDB;Data Source=localhost;" +
    "Initial Catalog=Northwind; Integrated Security=SSPI;");
```

❑ **MSDAORA** – Microsoft OLE DB Provider for Oracle

```
OleDbConnection con = new
    OleDbConnection("Provider=MSDAORA;Data Source=localhost;" +
    "Initial Catalog=Southwind; Integrated Security=SSPI;");
```

❑ **Microsoft.Jet.OLEDB.4.0** – OLE DB Provider for Microsoft Jet

```
OleDbConnection con = new
    OleDbConnection("Provider=Microsoft.Jet.OLEDB.4.0;" +
    "Data Source=C:\Program Files\Microsoft " +
    "Office\Office\Samples\Northwind.mdb; ");
```

> We cannot use the **MSDASQL** provider because the OleDb Data Provider does not support the OLE DB Provider for ODBC. The ODBC Data Provider is required for use with ODBC data sources. This is a separate download available on the Microsoft Web site, **http://www.microsoft.com/net/**, and is not shipped with the .NET Framework SDK.

When constructing an instance of the `OleDbConnection` class, you can pass the connection string to the constructor. An `OleDbConnection` object will be constructed with the connection string set to the value passed in. The connection string must include a `Provider=` clause that identifies which OLE DB provider to use.

Storing Connection Strings in the Configuration File

The .NET Framework uses XML-formatted text files for maintaining configuration information. The configuration files may contain everything from assembly references, versioning information, authentication information, and key-value pairs of application-specific data. Applications may have one or more configuration file. In Web applications, this file must be named `web.config`. In Console applications, the configuration file also ends in `.config`, but is prefixed with the application name, such as `MyApp.exe.config`. Windows Forms applications do not use configuration files.

The XML structure of the configuration files is similar whether the application is a Web application or a Console application. In either case, the configuration file may include an element named `<appSettings>`. It is in this element that key-value pairs may be stored.

Storing connection strings in the configuration file allows us to maintain them in only one place, which makes for easy modification if the connection strings change. Additionally, since the configuration file is an XML-formatted text file, the connection string can be changed, but the application does not need to be recompiled. This enables easy deployment of the application in scenarios where the connection string will change for each user. For scenarios where we do not want the user to have access to the connection string, we can store the value in a class (as a property), or in the system registry.

Unlike using an include file in a web application, and creating a constant value for the connection string, the configuration file doesn't need to be included in each Web Form that needs to access the connection string. Rather, values in the **<appSettings>** element of the configuration file are available to any class in the application, whether the class is a Web Form class, or a business logic or data access layer class.

For each connection string in the application, add a new <add> element to the <appSettings> element in the configuration file, as follows:

```
<?xml version="1.0" encoding="utf-8" ?>
<configuration>
    <appSettings>
        <add key="constring"
             value="server=localhost;database=Northwind;uid=sa;pwd=;"/>
    </appSettings>
</configuration>
```

The key attribute is the name by which we will refer to this connection string and the value attribute is the actual connection string.

The classes for accessing the configuration file are found in the System.Configuration namespace.

To create a connection using a connection string stored in the configuration file, we add a reference to the System.Configuration namespace and use the ConfigurationSettings class, as seen in the code below.

```
using System;
using System.Data;
using System.Data.SqlClient;
using System.Configuration;

public class UsingConfigSettings
{
    public static void Main()
    {
        SqlConnection con = new SqlConnection(
            ConfigurationSettings.AppSettings["constring"]);

        SqlCommand cmd = new SqlCommand();
        cmd.CommandText = "SELECT * FROM Customers";
        cmd.Connection = con;

        con.Open();
        SqlDataReader reader = cmd.ExecuteReader();

        while(reader.Read())
        {
            Console.WriteLine("{0} - {1}",
                reader.GetString(0),
                reader.GetString(1));
        }

        con.Close();
    }
}
```

In the preceding code example we import the `System.Configuration` namespace, which provides us with access to the configuration classes without having to use fully qualified names. We construct the con object as an instance of the `SqlConnection` class, and use the `ConfigurationSettings` class to access the `<appSettings>` element of the configuration file, and return the constring value.

Connection Events

The connection classes expose three events: `Disposed`, `StateChange`, and `InfoMessage`. These events fire under certain circumstances. The `Dispose` event is inherited from the `System.Component` class, and is fired when the object is destroyed, so we won't discuss it here.

StateChange

The `StateChange` event works similarly to the `InfoMessage` event, in that creating a method and using the `Handles` keyword will handle the event. The `StateChange` event fires whenever the state of the connection changes from open to closed, or the other way around. We can code an event handler for the `StateChange` event to perform some function whenever the state of the connection changes.

In the following code we create an event handler for the `StateChange` event and simply write the current state to the screen.

```
using System;
using System.Data;
using System.Data.SqlClient;
using System.Configuration;

public class RaisingStateChange
{
    public static SqlConnection con;

    public static void Main()
    {
        con = new SqlConnection(
            ConfigurationSettings.AppSettings["constring"]);

        con.StateChange +=
            new StateChangeEventHandler(StateChange);

        SqlCommand cmd = new SqlCommand();
        cmd.CommandText = "SELECT TOP 5 * FROM Customers";

        cmd.Connection = con;

        con.Open();
        SqlDataReader reader = cmd.ExecuteReader();

        while(reader.Read())
        {
            Console.WriteLine("{0} - {1}",
                reader.GetString(0),
                reader.GetString(1));
        }

        con.Close();

    }
```

```
    public static void StateChange(object sender, StateChangeEventArgs e)
    {
        Console.WriteLine("{0} - {1}",
            "ConnectionState",
            e.CurrentState.ToString());
    }
}
```

In the preceding code we created SqlConnection and SqlCommand objects. We created a method, StateChange(), to handle the StateChange event of the SqlConnection object. This is done by defining the con.StateChange event as an instance of the StateChangeEventHandler class, and passing in the StateChange() method. When the connection is opened, the StateChange event is raised, and the con_StateChange() method is fired. The same occurs when the connection is closed.

InfoMessage

This event fires whenever the provider sends a warning or informational message to the client. The event handler for the InfoMessage event takes the sender and either a SqlInfoMessageEventArgs or an OleDbInfoMessageEventArgs object as it arguments. The event arguments supply data for the InfoMessage event to the handler.

In the following code we raise the InfoMessage event by using a T-SQL PRINT command. The PRINT argument gets sent to the event handler as an error, and is accessible in the SqlInfoMessageEventArgs.Errors collection.

```
using System;
using System.Data;
using System.Data.SqlClient;
using System.Configuration;

public class RaisingInfoMessage
{
    public static SqlConnection con;

    public static void Main()
    {
        con = new SqlConnection(
            ConfigurationSettings.AppSettings["constring"]);

        con.InfoMessage +=
            new SqlInfoMessageEventHandler(InfoMessage);

        SqlCommand cmd = new SqlCommand("PRINT 'This is a test'", con);

        con.Open();
        SqlDataReader reader = cmd.ExecuteReader();

        while(reader.Read())
        {
            Console.WriteLine("{0} - {1}",
                reader.GetString(0),
                reader.GetString(1));
        }

        con.Close();
```

```
    }

    public static void InfoMessage(object sender,
        SqlInfoMessageEventArgs e)
    {
        for(int i=0; i < e.Errors.Count; i++)
        {
            Console.WriteLine("{0} - {1}",
                "InfoMessage",
                e.Errors[0].ToString());
        }
    }
}
```

In the preceding code we use a T-SQL PRINT command to raise the InfoMessage event. To handle the event we create a method, InfoMessage(), and define the con.InfoMessage event as an instance of the SqlInfoMessageEventHandler class, passing in the InfoMessage() method as the argument. When the SqlCommand (cmd) executes the T-SQL command, the InfoMessage event is raised, and the InfoMessage() method is fired.

Connection Pooling in the Data Providers

The .NET Data Providers manage connection pooling automatically, so the developer does not have to manage them. Through connection string modifiers, we can explicitly control the pooling behavior.

The OLE DB Data Provider pools connections using OLE DB session pooling. Connection pooling in OLE DB can be disabled using a connection string argument. The following connection string disables pooling and automatic transaction enlistment:

```
Provider=SQLOLEDB;OLE DB Services=-4;Data Source=localhost;Integrated
Security=SSPI;
```

> *For a full list of OLE DB Service values, see "Overriding Provider Service Defaults" in the MSDN Library* (http://msdn.microsoft.com/library/default.asp?url=/library/en-us/oledb/htm/oledboverriding_provider_service_defaults.asp).

The SQL Server Data Provider relies on Windows 2000 Component Services to manage connection pooling. Each connection pool is associated to one connection string. When a connection is being created, the SQL Server Data Provider looks for a pool that uses the exact connection string for the connection. If one is not found, then a new pool is created; if a pool is found, a connection within that pool is used. The connection pools live throughout the active process.

When a connection pool is created, multiple connection objects are created within that pool so that the minimum pool size requirement is satisfied. If needed, new connections are added to the pool, up to the maximum pool size. A new connection is needed when all of the connections in the pool are currently being used and a new connection is requested. If the maximum pool size has been reached, and a new connection is needed, the request is queued until a connection becomes available. An error is raised if the Connection.Timeout value elapses before a connection becomes available. To make a connection available in the pool, it must be explicitly closed by calling either the Close() or Dispose() method. When the connection is closed, it is returned to the pool.

Previously we saw that we must explicitly close a connection to release the actual connection to the database. Invoking the Dispose() method will close the connection and destroy the object. When an object is destroyed or falls out of scope it becomes available for garbage collection. If we do not explicitly close the connection to the database, the connection object may be garbage-collected, but the actual connection will remain open, and it will not be returned to the connection pool.

Using Commands

The command classes (OleDbCommand and SqlCommand) are used to execute commands on a data source across a connection. Once a connection is established, a command can be used to execute a T-SQL statement or a stored procedure, based on the value assigned to the CommandType property. The command class constructors take a SQL statement or stored procedure name and a connection object as their arguments.

The SqlCommand and OleDbCommand Classes

The two command classes are virtually identical, with the only real difference being that the SqlCommand class exposes an execute method for returning an XML stream that the OleDbCommand class does not. This is a capability given to the SqlCommand class based on the XML capabilities of SQL Server 7.0 and greater.

Using a Command with a T-SQL Statement

The command classes expose a CommandType property. By default, this property is set to "CommandType.Text", indicating that a T-SQL statement will be used as the CommandText property. Possible values for the CommandType property are:

- ❑ CommandType.Text – a SQL statement
- ❑ CommandType.TableDirect – a table name whose columns are returned
- ❑ CommandType.StoredProcedure – the name of a stored procedure

To create a command that executes a T-SQL statement, construct the command with the statement and a connection object, as seen below:

```
SqlConnection con = new
    SqlConnection(
    ConfigurationSettings.AppSettings["constring"]
);

SqlCommand cmd = new
    SqlCommand("SELECT * FROM Customers", con);
```

The preceding code creates a SqlConnection object using a connection string stored in the application's configuration file, then creates a SqlCommand using the T-SQL statement SELECT * FROM Customers. The SqlCommand uses the SqlConnection that was created just above it.

The syntax to create an OleDbCommand is identical, using the OLE DB Data Provider classes.

```
OleDbConnection con = new
    OleDbConnection(
    ConfigurationSettings.AppSettings["constring"]
);
```

```
OleDbCommand cmd = new
    OleDbCommand("SELECT * FROM Customers", con);
```

The command classes expose four possible constructors (the same constructors are available for both the OleDbCommand and the SqlCommand):

❑   SqlCommand cmd = new SqlCommand();

Creates a new SqlCommand with no properties set and no associated connection

❑   SqlCommand cmd = new SqlCommand(string CommandText);

Creates a SqlCommand with the CommandText property set, but no associated connection

❑   SqlCommand cmd = new SqlCommand(string CommandText,
        SqlConnection con);

Creates a SqlCommand with the CommandText property set, and the specified SqlConnection as the Connection property.

❑   SqlCommand cmd = new SqlCommand(string CommandText,
        SqlConnection con,
        SqlTransaction trans);

Creates a SqlCommand with the CommandText property set, the specified SqlConnection as the Connection property, and a SqlTransaction for the command to execute in

The CommandText and Connection properties can be set explicitly as seen in the following code:

```
SqlConnection con = new
    SqlConnection(
    ConfigurationSettings.AppSettings["constring"]
);
```

```
SqlCommand cmd = new SqlCommand();
cmd.CommandText = "SELECT * FROM Customers";
cmd.Connection = con;
```

Executing the Command

To execute a command and return any results we invoke one of the exposed execute methods:

❑   ExecuteNonQuery()

❑   ExecuteReader()

❑   ExecuteScalar()

❑   ExecuteXmlReader() (SqlCommand only)

ExecuteNonQuery

ExecuteNonQuery() is used for executing commands that do not return a result set, such as update, insert, or delete commands. The ExecuteNonQuery() method returns an integer value indicating the number of rows affected by the command. For all other types of commands –1 is returned. In the following code, ExecuteNonQuery() returns the number of rows affected by the DELETE command.

```
SqlConnection con = new SqlConnection(
    ConfigurationSettings.AppSettings["constring"]);

SqlCommand cmd = new SqlCommand();
cmd.CommandText = "DELETE FROM Customers WHERE CustomerID = 'SEVEN'";
cmd.Connection = con;

con.Open();

Console.WriteLine("{0} - {1}",
    "cmd.ExecuteNonQuery()",
    cmd.ExecuteNonQuery().ToString());

con.Close()
```

ExecuteReader

ExecuteReader() returns an object that implements the IDataReader interface, such as an OleDbReader or a SqlDataReader. The ExecuteReader() method can take an optional argument, a member of the CommandBehavior enumeration. The CommandBehavior enumeration specifies a description of the results and the effect on the database of the query command; its members are:

❑   CloseConnection – the connection is closed when the associated datareader is closed.

❑   KeyInfo – the query returns column and primary key information. The query is executed without any locking on the selected rows. When using KeyInfo, the SQL Server Data Provider appends a FOR BROWSE clause to the statement being executed.

❑   SchemaOnly – the command returns column information only and does not affect the database.

❑   SequentialAccess – the results of the query are read sequentially to the column level. This allows for reading of large binary data using the GetChars or GetBytes methods.

❑   SingleResult – returns a single result.

❑   SingleRow – returns a single row of data.

The following code demonstrates how to implement the ExecuteReader() method using the CommandBehavior.SingleRow parameter to return the first record in the result set.

```
SqlConnection con = new SqlConnection(
    ConfigurationSettings.AppSettings["constring"]);

SqlCommand cmd = new SqlCommand();
cmd.CommandText = "SELECT * FROM Customers";
cmd.Connection = con;

con.Open();
```

```
SqlDataReader reader = cmd.ExecuteReader(CommandBehavior.SingleRow);

while(reader.Read())
{
    Console.WriteLine("{0} - {1}",
        reader.GetString(0),
        reader.GetString(1));
}
```

```
con.Close()
```

In the preceding code example we create an instance of the `SqlDataReader` (reader). The `ExecuteReader()` method populates the datareader with the first row in the result set.

ExecuteScalar

The `ExecuteScalar()` method returns the first column of the first row in the result set; all other columns and rows are ignored. This method is particularly useful for returning aggregate values, such as the result of a `SELECT COUNT(*)` SQL statement. Using `ExecuteScalar()` is less code intensive, and requires fewer system resources than using `ExecuteReader()` and then invoking the `DataReader.Read()` method to get the returned value. The `ExecuteReader()` method creates a datareader stream on the connection, preventing anything from using the connection until the datareader is closed; `ExecuteScalar()` does not do this.

The following code demonstrates how to implement the `ExecuteScalar()` method.

```
SqlConnection con = new SqlConnection(
    ConfigurationSettings.AppSettings["constring"]);
```

```
SqlCommand cmd = new SqlCommand();
cmd.CommandText = "SELECT COUNT(*) FROM Customers";
cmd.Connection = con;

con.Open();

Console.WriteLine("{0} - {1}",
    "cmd.ExecuteScalar()",
    cmd.ExecuteScalar().ToString());
```

```
con.Close();
```

In the preceding code example, `ExecuteScalar()` is used to return the value of the aggregate `SELECT COUNT(*)` command.

ExecuteXmlReader

The `ExecuteXmlReader()` method is only available for the `SqlCommand` object. The `CommandText` property for a `SqlCommand` class that is invoking the `ExecuteXmlReader()` method should contain a SQL command with a valid `FOR XML` clause, or a command that returns `ntext` data in valid XML format.

You can find more information about using the SQL FOR XML clause at the Microsoft web site – Extreme XML: A Survey of Microsoft SQL Server 2000 XML Features (http://msdn.microsoft.com/library/default.asp?url=/library/en-us/dnexxml/html/xml07162001.asp)

The following code demonstrates how to invoke the `ExecuteXmlReader()` method using a `SELECT FOR XML` command against SQL Server 7.0 with XML support or SQL Server 2000.

```
SqlConnection con = new SqlConnection(
    ConfigurationSettings.AppSettings["constring"]);

SqlCommand cmd = new SqlCommand();
cmd.CommandText = "SELECT * FROM Customers FOR XML AUTO, XMLDATA";
cmd.Connection = con;

con.Open();

XmlReader reader = cmd.ExecuteXmlReader();
while(reader.Read())
{
    Console.WriteLine(reader.ReadOuterXml());
}

con.Close();
```

In the preceding code we select all of the records from the `Customers` table in the `Northwind` database and return them as an XML stream, in the form of an `XmlReader` object, using the `ExecuteXmlReader()` method.

The `XmlReader` class exposes a `Read()` method, which reads the next node of the XML stream. As we read through the XML stream, we use the `ReadOuterXml()` method to read the content, including the mark-up of each node and all of its children.

Using a Command with a Stored Procedure

In the same way as we use a command object to execute T-SQL statements against a database, we can use the command objects to execute stored procedures on the database. As discussed previously, the command classes have a `CommandType` property that takes one of three possible `CommandType` enumeration values, `Text`, `StoredProcedure`, or `TableDirect`. By default, the `CommandType` is set to `CommandType.Text`.

By constructing the command object with a stored procedure name, or setting the `CommandText` to a stored procedure name, we can execute that stored procedure on the database. The only other step necessary is to set the `CommandType` to `CommandType.StoredProcedure`. This is demonstrated in the following code, where we execute the `Northwind` database's "Ten Most Expensive Products" stored procedure.

```
SqlConnection con = new SqlConnection(
    ConfigurationSettings.AppSettings["constring"]);

SqlCommand cmd = new SqlCommand("Ten Most Expensive Products", con);
cmd.CommandType = CommandType.StoredProcedure;

con.Open();

SqlDataReader reader = cmd.ExecuteReader();

while(reader.Read())
{
Console.WriteLine("{0} - {1:C}",
    reader.GetString(0),
    reader.GetDecimal(1));
}

con.Close();
```

In the preceding code we construct a new SqlCommand object (cmd), passing in the name of a stored procedure ("Ten Most Expensive Products") and a SqlConnection object (con) as its arguments. Next, we set the CommandType property of the cmd object to the CommandType.StoredProcedure enumerator. We invoke the ExecuteReader() to return a SqlDataReader. Using the Read() method, we iterate through the result stream and use the GetString() and GetDecimal() methods of the datareader to write the results to the command window:

```
C:\WINNT\System32\cmd.exe                                        _ |□| ×|
Microsoft Windows 2000 [Version 5.00.2195]
(C) Copyright 1985-2000 Microsoft Corp.

C:\>E:\Wrox\ProADONet\C02\CSharp\myApp.exe
Côte de Blaye - $263.50
Thüringer Rostbratwurst - $123.79
Mishi Kobe Niku - $97.00
Sir Rodney's Marmalade - $81.00
Carnarvon Tigers - $62.50
Raclette Courdavault - $55.00
Manjimup Dried Apples - $53.00
Tarte au sucre - $49.30
Ipoh Coffee - $46.00
Rössle Sauerkraut - $45.60

C:\>_
```

Using the SqlParameter and OleDbParameter Classes

The .NET Data Providers include classes for creating parameter objects that can be added to a command's ParametersCollection. The parameters are created with a name, data type, input or output specification, and a value if applicable. Both the SqlParameter and OleDbParameter classes function in the same way: however, the SqlParameters are passed to the SQL Server as named parameters and must map to parameter names in the stored procedures.

Creating Parameterized T-SQL Queries

We can create parameterized T-SQL queries by adding one or more parameters to the T-SQL statement, and adding the same parameters to the command's Parameters collection. This is demonstrated in the following code.

```
SqlConnection con = new SqlConnection(
    ConfigurationSettings.AppSettings["constring"]);

SqlCommand cmd = new
    SqlCommand("SELECT * FROM Customers WHERE Country = @country", con);
cmd.Parameters.Add(
    new SqlParameter("@country", SqlDbType.VarChar, 50)).Value = "USA";

con.Open();

SqlDataReader reader = cmd.ExecuteReader();

while(reader.Read())
{
```

```
        Console.WriteLine("{0} - {1}",
            reader.GetString(0),
            reader.GetString(1));
    }

    con.Close();
```

In the preceding code example, we create a new `SqlCommand` object and pass in a T-SQL statement that uses a parameter in the `WHERE` clause. Next, we add a new `SqlParameter` to the `SqlCommand.Parameters` collection. For the `SqlParameter` constructor we pass in the parameter name and the data type of the parameter. The data types are defined using an values of `SqlDbType` or `OleDbType`, depending on the .NET Data Provider being used.

By default, the `Parameter` objects are created as input parameters, but setting the `Direction` property of the `Parameter` object can also set them as output parameters. The two possible enumerators for the `Direction` property are `ParameterDirection.Output` or `ParameterDirection.Input`.

The following example adds an output parameter to the preceding code:

```
SqlConnection con = new SqlConnection(
    ConfigurationSettings.AppSettings["constring"]);

SqlCommand cmd = new
    SqlCommand("SELECT * FROM Customers WHERE Country = @country; " +
    "SELECT @count = COUNT(*)  FROM Customers WHERE Country = @country",
    con);
cmd.Parameters.Add(new
    SqlParameter("@country", SqlDbType.VarChar, 50)).Value = "USA";
cmd.Parameters.Add(new SqlParameter("@count", SqlDbType.Int));
cmd.Parameters["@count"].Direction = ParameterDirection.Output;

con.Open();

SqlDataReader reader = cmd.ExecuteReader();

while(reader.Read())
{
    Console.WriteLine("{0} - {1}",
        reader.GetString(0),
        reader.GetString(1));
}

reader.Close();

Console.WriteLine("{0} - {1}",
    "Count",
    cmd.Parameters["@count"].Value.ToString());

con.Close();
```

In the preceding example we add a new `SqlParameter`, `@count`, to the parameters collection and set its `Direction` property to `ParameterDirection.Output`. Notice that we close the `SqlDataReader` prior to accessing the output parameter value; output parameters are not accessible until the datareader has been closed.

Executing Parameterized Stored Procedures

The same steps are used to execute a parameterized stored procedure. In the following code we execute a command that calls a stored procedure that returns a result set and one output parameter.

Add the following stored procedure to the Northwind database:

```
CREATE PROCEDURE [GetTenCustAndOutputParam]
@country varchar (50),
@count int output
AS
SELECT * FROM Customers WHERE Country = @country
SELECT @count=COUNT(*) FROM Customers WHERE Country = @country
GO
```

The preceding stored procedure returns the total count of records in the Customers table as an output parameter named @count, as well as a result set of records in the Customers table where the Country field has the value of the @country input parameter. The code to execute is nearly identical to the previous code example, except that we define the SqlCommand as a stored procedure.

```
SqlConnection con = new SqlConnection(
    ConfigurationSettings.AppSettings["constring"]);

SqlCommand cmd = new SqlCommand("GetTenCustAndOutputParam", con);
cmd.CommandType = CommandType.StoredProcedure;
cmd.Parameters.Add(new
    SqlParameter("@country", SqlDbType.VarChar, 50)).Value = "USA";
cmd.Parameters.Add(new SqlParameter("@count", SqlDbType.Int));
cmd.Parameters["@count"].Direction = ParameterDirection.Output;

con.Open();

SqlDataReader reader = cmd.ExecuteReader();

while(reader.Read())
{
    Console.WriteLine("{0} - {1}",
        reader.GetString(0),
        reader.GetString(1));
}

reader.Close();

Console.WriteLine("{0} - {1}",
    "Count",
    cmd.Parameters["@count"].Value.ToString());

con.Close();
```

In the preceding code we create a SqlCommand to execute the previously listed stored procedure. We add two SqlParameters to the SqlCommand's ParametersCollection, named @country and @count. Next we define the @count parameter as an output parameter by setting the Direction property to ParameterDirection.Output.

Summary

In this chapter we began digging into the .NET Data Providers. As we discussed, the .NET Data Providers are the mechanism used to connect an application to a database, such as SQL Server, Access, or Oracle. The data providers expose four primary classes: connection, command, datareader and `DataAdapter`. In this chapter we covered the connection and command classes. The datareader will be covered in-depth in Chapter 4, and the data adapter will be covered in Chapter 6.

In this chapter we looked at how the connection classes work, how to open and close connections, how to use the application configuration file to store connection strings, and how to handle the connection class events. From there, we saw how to execute a `Command` on a connection using either a T-SQL statement or a stored procedure. We investigated how to implement the various execute methods: `ExecuteNonQuery()`, `ExecuteReader()`, `ExecuteScalar()`, and `ExecuteXmlReader()` (`SqlCommand` only). Additionally, we looked at how to use the `Parameter` classes to execute parameterized queries or stored procedures. In the following chapters, we will be working with these classes and methods extensively.

3

Visual Studio .NET and ADO.NET

Throughout the book you may use Visual Studio .NET to write code, to compile, and to debug. Visual Studio .NET offers more features to manage ADO.NET classes. Thanks to the data components, we can write ADO.NET applications without writing any code by using the various wizards. By the end of this chapter you will be able to use every Data component offered by Visual Studio .NET to create applications that use ADO.NET classes.

This chapter focuses on using Visual Studio .NET to work with ADO.NET classes. For general information about the classes, see the relevant chapters later in the book.

In this chapter we will look at:

- ❑ Using `SqlConnection` and `OleDbConnection` to specify connection parameters
- ❑ Using `SqlCommand` and `OleDbCommand` to specify SQL commands
- ❑ Using `SqlDataAdapter` and `OleDbDataAdapter` to retrieve records from the database and to fill `DataSet` and `DataTable` objects
- ❑ Using the `DataSet` to manage in-memory database structures and data
- ❑ Using the `DataView` component to filter and sort data in a dataset
- ❑ Using the `DataGrid` to display and edit data on a web page or Windows form

To create complex applications, some coding is unavoidable. We will look at the code that Visual Studio .NET generates automatically, so that we can customize it to our specific needs.

Connection Classes

As we have seen, the .NET framework includes two data providers – one for OLE data sources, and one especially for SQL Server 7.0 and above. We use both of these providers in a very similar way, but the components have different names to differentiate them. OleDbConnection provides connections to OLE data sources, and SqlConnection provides connections to SQL Server 7.0 and above.

Microsoft has also released an ODBC .NET provider, although at the time of writing it had only been tested using three ODBC drivers:

❑   Microsoft SQL ODBC driver

❑   Microsoft Jet ODBC driver

❑   Microsoft ODBC driver for ORACLE

The ODBC driver is not included in the .NET framework, but can be obtained from the Microsoft web site.

SqlConnection and OleDbConnection Data Components

ADO.NET connection objects establish a connection to a specified database. Visual Studio .NET offers two data components to help you to manage connection objects:

❑   The OleDbConnection data component to connect to a database using the OLE DB .NET data provider

❑   The SqlConnection data component to connect to a Microsoft SQL Server database using the SQL .NET data provider

The following figure shows the Visual Studio .NET Toolbox, where these components are located (if the toolbar is not showing in Visual Studio .NET, press *Ctrl+Alt+X* to show the toolbox):

To use them, just drag one either *onto* the web or Windows form and observe the new object inserted automatically *below* the form, in an area called the **tray**:

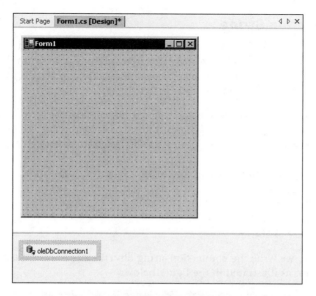

This drag operation generates code automatically. The first snippet declares the object:

```
private System.Data.OleDb.OleDbConnection oleDbConnection1;
```

The second is generated inside the `InitializeComponent` method, which the Visual Studio .NET designer generates to initialize every object contained in the form (if you can't see this snippet of code in your application's script, you have to click the '+' next to **Windows Form Designer generated code** to expand the code):

```
#region Windows Form Designer generated code
/// <summary>
/// Required method for Designer support - do not modify
/// the contents of this method with the code editor.
/// </summary>
private void InitializeComponent()
{
  this.oleDbConnection1 = new System.Data.OleDb.OleDbConnection();
  //
  // Form1
  //
    . . .
}
#endregion
```

The snippet of code above shows the connection object creation inside a `#region`, `#endregion` code zone generated by the Designer, which delimits private code.

> **Visual Studio .NET does allow you to change the code inside the private region code, but it would be better to think of this code as 'untouchable', because these directives are used to make the code more maintainable, so changing anything here could cause untold damage elsewhere.**

Adding the Connection String

The connection string contains the information used by the object to connect to the database. Usually, a connection string contains the database server name, the database name, and the username and password to use. Sometimes a connection string also contains specific data-provider information, such as the security model or data encryption method.

You can add a connection string to the data component in two ways:

1. Using the ConnectionString property from the Properties window

2. Using the Data Link Properties dialog box

A connection string looks something like the following:

```
Provider=Microsoft.Jet.OLEDB.4.0;Data Source=C:\PRO.ADO.NET\example1\example1.mdb
```

Using the first method, we write the connection string directly into the ConnectionString property in the Properties window, as illustrated in the figure below:

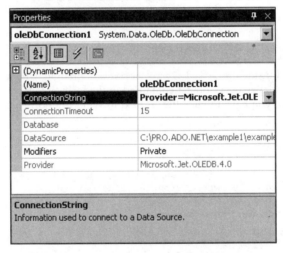

Setting the ConnectionString property in the Properties window will add the following line of code within the Designer region:

```
//
// oleDbConnection1
//
this.oleDbConnection1.ConnectionString = "Provider=Microsoft.Jet.OLEDB.4.0;Data
Source=C:\\PRO.ADO.NET\\example1\\example1.mdb";
```

To use the second method, we create a new data connection item by selecting <New Connection...> from the drop-down list for the ConnectionString property in the Properties window. This will generate a connection string by letting us select settings in a dialog box. If the connection is successful, the generated connection string will be assigned to the Connection object, and added to the Data Connections listed in the Server Explorer window (which we can display by selecting Server Explorer from the View menu).

We can also add a connection to the Server Explorer by right-clicking on the Data Connections item and selecting **Add Connection**. It will then appear as an option in the drop-down list in the **ConnectionString** property of `Connection` components. If you can't see the Server Explorer window, you can use the *Ctrl+Shift+S* keys combination in order to display it, as well as the **View** menu.

We will now take a look at the dialog box that this method of generating a connection string uses. Although the same dialogue box appears for both OLE DB and SQL connections, we use it in a slightly different way for the different connections.

For an OLE DB connection, the first step is to choose an OLE DB data provider from the **Provider** tab in the **Data Link Properties** dialog box:

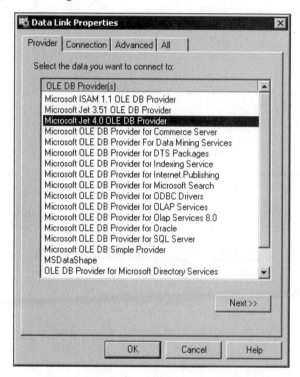

For `SqlConnection` objects, we do not specify a provider. The default choice of provider, Microsoft OLE DB Provider for SQL Server, will provide us with the choice of connection settings that we need.

After selecting the correct provider, click **Next** to move to the **Connection** tab. There are various parameters that need to be set – the exact parameters are dictated by the choice of provider. The following illustration shows the connection settings for the Microsoft Jet 4.0 OLE DB Provider:

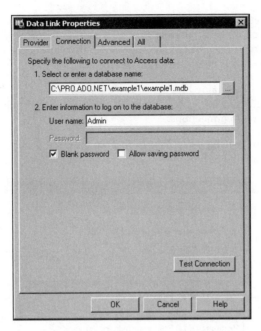

For this particular provider we need to specify the database filename, and optionally a username and password. We can check the settings using the Test Connection button.

Just for completeness, the figure below shows the parameters for SqlConnection, or an OLE DB Connection to SQL Server:

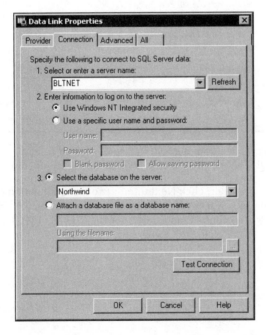

As you can see, there are more parameters for this type of connection. Here is a summary of how to use them:

❑ **Server name** – the server that contains the database. If the database will run on the same machine as the application, use Localhost.

❑ **Log on information** – we need to choose the security model to use to connect to the database. The Use Windows NT integrated security option allows users who are logged into NT to connect to the database without SQL Server-specific accounts. To implement this kind of security model, you have to set the Microsoft SQL Server database specifying the Windows NT Authentication Mode or the Mixed Mode. Using the second option, Use a specific user name and password, you need to specify a valid SQL Server account that gives appropriate permission for accessing the database. For the Northwind database we can use sa.

❑ **Database** – select the database that you wish to access, in one of two ways – the logon credentials must be valid for that database.

Going back to our Microsoft.Jet connection, clicking OK will create a new data connection item and display it in the Data Connections tree within the Server Explorer window:

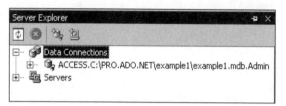

If you used the <New Connection...> option in the ConnectionString pull-down, the new connection string will be assigned automatically. If you used Add Connection in the Server Explorer, you can assign the connection string to the Connection component by selecting it from the ConnectionString pull-down on the Connection's property window. Of course this means that the same connection string can be used for several Connection objects, by selecting an existing string from the pull-down.

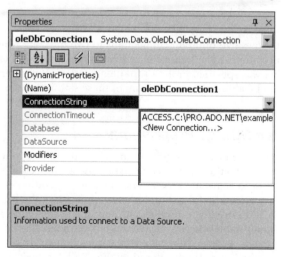

Choosing a connection string will add some new code in the region used by the Designer:

```
#region Windows Form Designer generated code
/// <summary>
/// Required method for Designer support - do not modify
/// the contents of this method with the code editor.
/// </summary>
private void InitializeComponent()
{
  this.oleDbConnection1 = new System.Data.OleDb.OleDbConnection();
  //
  // oleDbConnection1
  //
  this.oleDbConnection1.ConnectionString =
@"Provider=Microsoft.Jet.OLEDB.4.0;Password="";User ID=Admin;Data
Source=C:\PRO.ADO.NET\Example1\example1.mdb;Mode=Share Deny None;Extended
Properties="";Jet OLEDB:System database="";Jet OLEDB:Registry Path="";Jet
OLEDB:Database Password="";Jet OLEDB:Engine Type=5;Jet OLEDB:Database Locking
Mode=1;Jet OLEDB:Global Partial Bulk Ops=2;Jet OLEDB:Global Bulk
Transactions=1;Jet OLEDB:New Database Password="";Jet OLEDB:Create System
Database=False;Jet OLEDB:Encrypt Database=False;Jet OLEDB:Don't Copy Locale on
Compact=False;Jet OLEDB:Compact Without Replica Repair=False;Jet OLEDB:SFP=False";

  //
  // dbConn
  //
  dbConn.ConnectionString =
@"Provider=Microsoft.Jet.OLEDB.4.0;Password="""";User ID=Admin;Data
Source=C:\PRO.ADO.NET\Example7\bltairlines.mdb;Mode=Share Deny None;Extended
Properties="""";Jet OLEDB:System database="""";Jet OLEDB:Registry Path="""";Jet
OLEDB:Database Password="""";Jet OLEDB:Engine Type=5;Jet OLEDB:Database Locking
Mode=1;Jet OLEDB:Global Partial Bulk Ops=2;Jet OLEDB:Global Bulk
Transactions=1;Jet OLEDB:New Database Password="""";Jet OLEDB:Create System
Database=False;Jet OLEDB:Encrypt Database=False;Jet OLEDB:Don't Copy Locale on
Compact=False;Jet OLEDB:Compact Without Replica Repair=False;Jet OLEDB:SFP=False";
}
#endregion
```

The above code snippet shows two different connections to two different Microsoft Access databases using the Microsoft Jet provider. A giant connection string has been added to the code automatically after the connection string was specified in the Properties window. If we were coding the connection string manually, we would be able to leave out many of these settings so the string would be much shorter.

Retrieving Connection Strings Programmatically

If you are creating a desktop application, or you are moving your web application from the development server to the production server, you can't define a connection string directly in your code pointing to a specific path or to a specific server. The Windows operating system offers a centralized way to store and to retrieve general information on your application: the Registry. You can use the Registry during the application installation process to store the correct path and filename of your database or the correct server name where your database is running. The examples in this chapter, before connecting to the database, have to retrieve the connection string from the Windows Registry, which they do simply by using the methods offered by the .NET framework.

The `Microsoft.Win32` namespace contains every method and property needed to manage registry entries effectively. Let's imagine that our installation program has added the following entry to the Windows Registry:

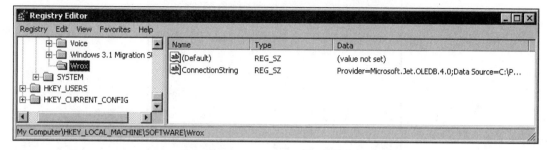

During the constructor function execution, we can retrieve the connection string using two simple lines of code:

```
public Form1()
{
  //
  // Required for Windows Form Designer support
  //
  InitializeComponent();

  //
  // TODO: Add any constructor code after InitializeComponent call
  //
  RegistryKey key = Registry.LocalMachine.OpenSubKey("SOFTWARE\\WROX");
  oleDbConnection1.ConnectionString =
      key.GetValue("ConnectionString").ToString();
}
```

The `RegistryKey` object represents a registry key pointer containing every value within the key itself. The `OpenSubKey` method from the `LocalMachine` object opens a sub-key returning a registry key pointing to the path specified as a parameter. In the example above, we need to open the `HKEY_LOCAL_MACHINE\SOFTWARE\Wrox` sub-key. After retrieving the pointer to the sub-key, we can retrieve the `ConnectionString` value simply using the `GetValue` method exposed by the `RegistryKey` class.

Adding an Event

Managing an event from the Visual Studio .NET application is a piece of cake. Selecting the Events button in the Properties window will show every event that the object exposes, and we can then assign that event to a particular event handling method:

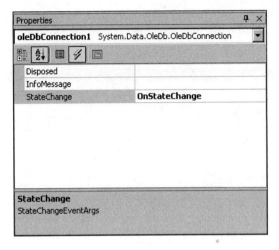

This will automatically create event handler management code within the Designer region:

```
#region Windows Form Designer generated code
/// <summary>
/// Required method for Designer support - do not modify
/// the contents of this method with the code editor.
/// </summary>
private void InitializeComponent()
{
   this.oleDbConnection1 = new System.Data.OleDb.OleDbConnection();
   //
   // oleDbConnection1
   //
   this.oleDbConnection1.StateChange += new
       System.Data.StateChangeEventHandler(this.OnStateChange);

   . . .

}
#endregion
```

And a new empty event handler managing method will be inserted at the end of the code:

```
private void OnStateChange(object sender,
             System.Data.StateChangeEventArgs e)
{

}
```

The StateChange event is fired each time the connection state changes. For example, we can use this event to inform the user of the database connection state by displaying a message in the status bar of the application (you can find this example in the Example1 folder of the download code):

The code behind the "big" button retrieves the data using an `OleDbDataAdapter` together with a `DataSet` object, while the `StateChange` event handler writes every connection change inside the status bar:

```
private void button1_Click(object sender, System.EventArgs e)
{
  // Create an OleDbDataAdapter to retrieve data from the database
  OleDbDataAdapter da = new OleDbDataAdapter("SELECT ID FROM " +
          "tabUsers",oleDbConnection1);
  // Fill the DataSet object
  DataSet ds = new DataSet("ds");
  da.Fill(ds);
}

private void OnStateChange(object sender, System.Data.StateChangeEventArgs e)
{
  // Build the string message
  string strMessage;
  strMessage = "Connection state changed from " + e.OriginalState + " to "
      + e.CurrentState;
  // Write the message into the status bar
  sb.Text = strMessage;
}
```

Command Data Components

The `Connection` object alone is not sufficient to retrieve data or to modify a record from the database, because it indicates only which are the parameters to use to connect to the database, and establishes a connection based on these parameters. ADO.NET offers two classes that use the connection object: either a `DataAdapter` object to fill a `DataTable` or a `DataSet`, or the `Execute` method series provided by the `Command` class itself. You can use an object created from one of these classes – `DataAdapter` or `Command` – to retrieve data, to update some records, to add a new record, and to delete records.

We use the `Command` object that corresponds to the connection we are using – `OleDbCommand` for an `OleDbConnection`, and `SqlCommand` for a `SqlConnection`.

SqlCommand and OledbCommand Data Components

Visual Studio .NET offers two data components to execute commands against a database connection:

❑ The `SqlCommand` data component manages SQL commands specific for a Microsoft SQL Server database, accessed using a `SqlConnection` object

❑ The `OleDbCommand` data component manages SQL commands for data sources accessed through an OLE data provider

These can be accessed from the Toolbox, as before. To use the command components, we first need a corresponding connection component. After that, simply drag the command data component onto the form in Visual Studio .NET:

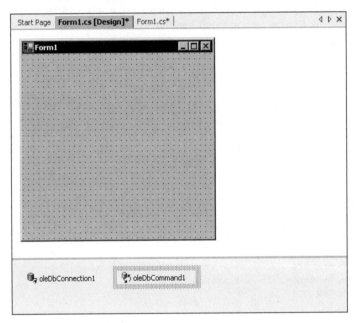

The drag operation inserts two new lines of code automatically in your source code. The first is added within the main class, in order to declare a `OleDbCommand` variable:

```
private System.Data.OleDb.OleDbCommand oleDbCommand1;
```

> The **private** data-hiding descriptor can be modified either manually or better from the **Modifiers** property inside the **Properties** window.

The second line is added within the Designer `private` region and creates a new object from the `OleDbCommand` class, assigning it to the `oleDbCommand1` variable:

```
#region Windows Form Designer generated code
/// <summary>
/// Required method for Designer support - do not modify
```

```
/// the contents of this method with the code editor.
/// </summary>
private void InitializeComponent()
{
   this.oleDbConnection1 = new System.Data.OleDb.OleDbConnection();
   this.oleDbCommand1 = new System.Data.OleDb.OleDbCommand();


   . . .

}
#endregion
```

> If you want to change the default auto-assigned object name you can write a new name within the **(Name)** property inside the **Properties** window. Visual Studio .NET will change every command reference with the new name, automatically.

Before executing the SQL command, we need to specify the database connection that the command data component will use. From the Properties window, selecting the Connection property means that you can select from the combo box the name of the connection object previously inserted in the project. The Visual Studio .NET IDE gives you the opportunity to create a new connection object directly from the combo box selecting the New item:

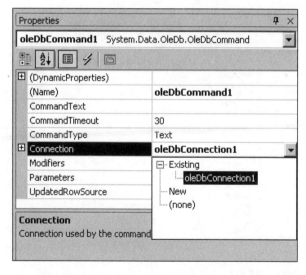

In the figure above we have selected the connection component that we had already added to the form.

Defining a Query Command

Visual Studio .NET allows developers to create a SQL query using a powerful visual tool called Query Builder, which is similar to the Query Analyzer in SQL Server and the query wizard in Access. To use it, click on the '...' button next to the CommandText property in the Properties window.

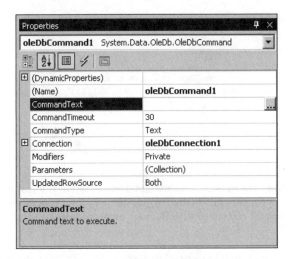

The following dialog box will appear:

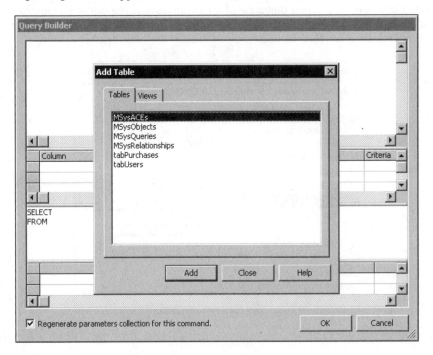

In the Add Table dialog box, select the tables that will be used in the query and click the Add button. All the tables from the database provided in the connection object will be visible here. After adding the relevant tables, we can define relations between the tables (if you have added more than one). Simply drag the column identifier onto the related column within the parent table and a SQL JOIN instruction will be added to the query, automatically:

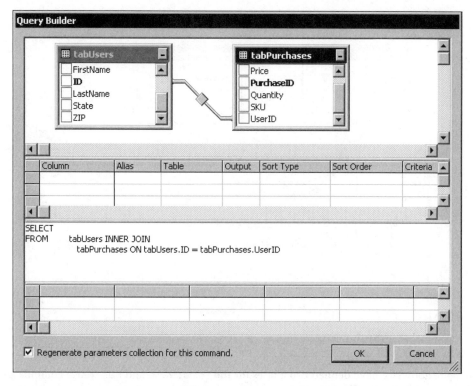

For example, in the figure above two tables have been related using the user identification column and an INNER JOIN SQL instruction has been added to the query.

Now we can choose which columns will appear in the query by selecting the checkbox next to the column name. Every related column name will be automatically added to the SELECT instruction. We can also define an alias for a column name by adding a new column name in the Alias cell. Finally we can add a WHERE condition by adding a Criteria expression for the related column. We can use a column as criteria but not have it appear in the query result, simply by un-checking the Output column:

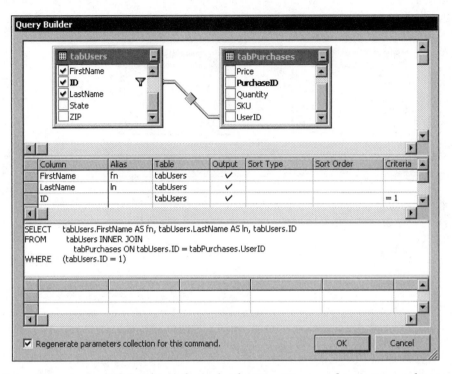

In the figure above we have defined two aliases for the FirstName and LastName columns and a criteria expression for the ID column.

> If you check the **Regenerate parameters collection for this command** check-box, every column you add, remove, or modify from the query will regenerate parameters in the collection.

After confirming the query expression with the OK button, new row code will be added automatically:

```
#region Windows Form Designer generated code
/// <summary>
/// Required method for Designer support - do not modify
/// the contents of this method with the code editor.
/// </summary>
private void InitializeComponent()
{
  . . .

  //
  // oleDbCommand1
  //
  this.oleDbCommand1.CommandText = "SELECT tabUsers.FirstName AS fn, " +
        "tabUsers.LastName AS ln, tabUsers.ID FROM tabUse" +
        "rs INNER JOIN tabPurchases ON tabUsers.ID = " +
        "tabPurchases.UserID WHERE (tabUsers." +
```

```
            "ID = 1)";

    this.oleDbCommand1.Connection = this.oleDbConnection1;

    . . .
}
#endregion
```

In the above example, we have hard-coded the criteria. Often we will want to run the same query with different criteria. We could concatenate strings to produce the command SQL. This can be a pain though – particularly where the user has the option to enter search criteria that might contain single quote characters, which the SQL interpreter will think signifies the end or beginning of a string, and usually generate an error.

Visual Studio .NET offers a better way to provide parameter queries. For each parameter, insert a placeholder in the command text, and use the data command object to specify the value.

> **For OLE DB data provider queries you have to use the "?" placeholder.**
> **For Microsoft SQL Server queries you have to use the "@" placeholder.**

In the following example (Example3), a simple user interface allows users to look for employees inside the Employee table contained in the Northwind database:

The first operation is defining the SELECT statement that retrieves the employees' first names and last names based on the query criteria. You can build the query as we have seen before or simply write it within the **CommandText** property in the SqlCommand data component property.

```
SELECT FirstName, LastName FROM Employees WHERE (LastName LIKE @Find)
```

After that we have to add the parameter in the SqlCommand collection. It can be done by simply selecting the ellipsis (...) button in the **Parameters** property within the **Properties** window. The following dialog box appears, allowing you to add, modify, and delete command parameters.

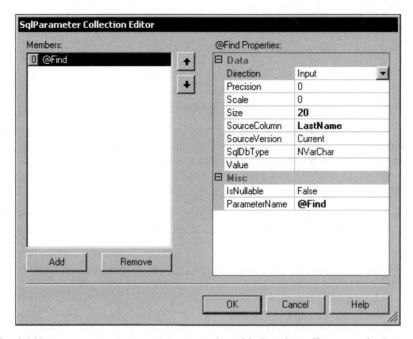

Pressing the Add button causes a new parameter to be added to the collection, which is ready to be shaped according to your preferences. You will find more explanation about the dialog box above in the next section of this chapter.

Behind the Find button there is the code that executes the query and fills the listbox with the records retrieved:

```
private void btnFind_Click(object sender, System.EventArgs e)
{
  // The SqlDataReader class provides a way to read a forward-only
  // stream of rows from a Sql Server database
  SqlDataReader drEmployee = null;

  try
  {
    // Open connection to the database
    sqlConnection1.Open();

    // Fill the parameter with the value retrieved from the text field
    sqlCommand1.Parameters["@Find"].Value = txtFind.Text;

    // Execute the query
    drEmployee = sqlCommand1.ExecuteReader();

    // Fill the list box with the values retrieved
    lbFound.Items.Clear();
    while(drEmployee.Read())
    {
      lbFound.Items.Add(drEmployee["FirstName"].ToString() + " " +
```

```
              drEmployee["LastName"].ToString());
     }
  }
  catch(Exception ex)
  {
     // Print error message
     MessageBox.Show(ex.Message);
  }
  finally
  {
     // Close data reader object and database connection
     if (drEmployee != null)
       drEmployee.Close();

     if (sqlConnection1.State != ConnectionState.Closed)
       sqlConnection1.Close();
  }
}
```

The code above does not need to check for string variable content such as single quotes, because it is done automatically. Any special characters that the user entered are automatically 'escaped' so that they do not get misinterpreted by the SQL interpreter.

Executing a Stored Procedure

A stored procedure is a SQL function that is compiled and stored in the Microsoft SQL Server database. We can call it from our .NET applications, and these procedures can take parameters and return values – like procedures in other programming languages. As it is compiled into the database, it will be a lot faster than writing complex SQL commands into your .NET application, where they will need to be re-interpreted by the database every time the query is run. Let's look at a simple stored procedure, called InsertNewAuthor, that inserts a new record into the tabAuthors table in the WroxDB database (scripts for the creation of which are available for download):

```
CREATE PROCEDURE InsertNewAuthor
@FirstName varchar(50),
@LastName varchar(50)
AS
INSERT INTO tabAuthors (Author_FirstName, Author_LastName)
VALUES (@FirstName, @LastName)
return @@IDENTITY
```

The table we are looking at requires three columns:

❑   An identity column identifier called AuthorID as primary key, which is auto-numbered

❑   A varchar data type column called Author_FirstName

❑   A varchar data type column called Author_LastName

This procedure creates a new row, assigning the Author_FirstName and Author_LastName values. Finally, @@IDENTITY is a parameter that will contain the AuthorID column value just created (as @@IDENTITY is a special way of returning the primary key of a table).

To use the stored procedure above we provide two parameters, the FirstName and the LastName, which you can see defined as input parameters in the code above (@FirstName and @LastName). For example, the next snippet of code adds a new record using the EXEC SQL command within the database to execute the stored procedure:

```
EXEC InsertNewAuthor 'Fabio Claudio','Ferracchiati'
```

Executing a stored procedure in a .NET application is really simple using Visual Studio .NET. These are the required steps (you can see this in Example2):

1. Set the CommandType property to StoredProcedure using the drop-down in the Properties window

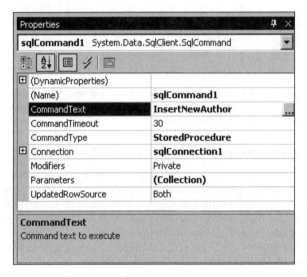

2. Specify the name of the stored procedure to use in the CommandText property of the Properties window

3. Select Yes on the Regenerate parameters message box that appears after the second step

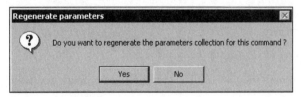

After these steps, Visual Studio .NET will insert several lines of code to prepare the command object to execute the correct stored procedure:

```
//
// sqlCommand1
//
this.sqlCommand1.CommandText = "InsertNewAuthor";
```

```
this.sqlCommand1.CommandType = System.Data.CommandType.StoredProcedure;
this.sqlCommand1.Connection = this.sqlConnection1;
this.sqlCommand1.Parameters.Add(new
    System.Data.SqlClient.SqlParameter("@RETURN_VALUE",
    System.Data.SqlDbType.Int, 4,
    System.Data.ParameterDirection.ReturnValue, true, ((System.Byte)(10)),
    ((System.Byte)(0)), "", System.Data.DataRowVersion.Current, null));

this.sqlCommand1.Parameters.Add(new
System.Data.SqlClient.SqlParameter("@FirstName", System.Data.SqlDbType.Char,
    50, System.Data.ParameterDirection.Input, true, ((System.Byte)(0)),
    ((System.Byte)(0)), "", System.Data.DataRowVersion.Current, null));

this.sqlCommand1.Parameters.Add(new
System.Data.SqlClient.SqlParameter("@LastName", System.Data.SqlDbType.Char,
    50, System.Data.ParameterDirection.Input, true, ((System.Byte)(0)),
    ((System.Byte)(0)), "", System.Data.DataRowVersion.Current, null));
```

Visual Studio .NET has retrieved the stored procedure's parameters automatically, and it has also obtained properties like the parameter data type, size, parameter name, and so on.

We can change the parameters collection by calling the **SqlParameter Collection Editor**, which we do by selecting the '...' button for the **Parameters** property in the **Properties** window.

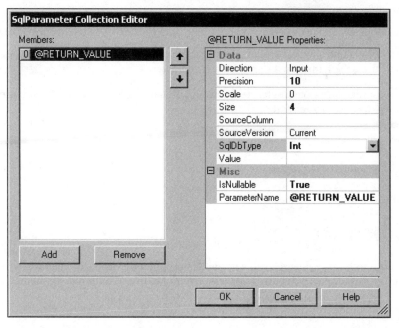

The left panel of the dialog box, **Members**, lists all the parameters that the stored procedure exposes. In the right panel , you can define the parameter's characteristics, such as its own parameter name or the data type. Let's see every option in detail:

- ❑ **Direction** – indicates whether the member is just an input parameter, just an output parameter, or both. You have to use an input parameter when you want to provide a value to the stored procedure. You have to specify an output parameter when you expect a return value from the stored procedure. Finally, you can select the input/output parameter type when you first want to provide a value to the stored procedure and then you expect a return value filled from the stored procedure within the same parameter.

- ❑ **Precision** – this property is valid just for the number data types and indicates the number of digits in a number.

- ❑ **Scale** – this property is valid just for the number data types and indicates the number of digits after the decimal point.

- ❑ **Size** – this property is valid just for the alphanumeric data types and indicates the parameter size. It has to be exactly the same size as was declared for the stored procedure parameter.

- ❑ **SourceColumn** – use this field to associate the parameter to the source column in the database. It is very useful in update processes, but not useful for a stored procedure retrieving records.

- ❑ **SourceVersion** – use this field to specify the version of the data within the data source. Really useful for update operations; not useful in a stored procedure that retrieves records.

- ❑ **SqlDbType** – indicates the parameter data type.

- ❑ **Value** – in this property you can set a value for the parameter. Not really useful in stored procedure case.

- ❑ **IsNullable** – indicates whether the parameter can be a `null` value (`true`) or not (`false`).

- ❑ **ParameterName** – indicates the name of the parameter. For Microsoft SQL Server stored procedures, the name must start with a @ character.

After the stored procedure's parameter declaration, you have to follow these steps in order to execute the stored procedure from your code:

1. Open the database connection

2. Set each value to supply to the stored procedure

3. Call the `ExecuteNonQuery` method

4. Close the database connection

Imagine we want to insert a new record, with details supplied by the user. The form would have textboxes to supply the record details. The code behind an 'insert' button could be like this:

```
private void button1_Click(object sender, System.EventArgs e)
{
  try
  {
    if ((txtFirstName.TextLength > 0)&&(txtLastName.TextLength > 0 ))
    {
      // Open the connection to the database
      sqlConnection1.Open();
```

```
        // Fill the stored procedure parameters with text fields
        // values
        sqlCommand1.Parameters[1].Value = txtFirstName.Text;
        sqlCommand1.Parameters[2].Value = txtLastName.Text;

        // Execute the stored procedure
        sqlCommand1.ExecuteNonQuery();

        // Print to video the final result
        MessageBox.Show("The new author has been added with the " +
        "following identifier: " + sqlCommand1.Parameters[0].Value);

        // Clear text fields
        txtFirstName.Clear();
        txtLastName.Clear();
    }
}
catch (Exception excpt)
{

    // Show error message
    MessageBox.Show(excpt.Message);
}
finally
{
    // If the connection has been opened, close it
    if (sqlConnection1.State != ConnectionState.Closed)
        sqlConnection1.Close();
}
}
```

Data Adapter Components

The DataAdapter transfers data from a data source to a dataset, and back again – a key ability of ADO.NET. Datasets allow us to work with data without remaining connected to the data source. Also, the same DataSet class can handle data retrieved from many different sources – SQL Server connections, OLE DB connections, XML, or the user interface. The DataAdapter enables the DataSet to update a database using SQL commands stored within the InsertCommand, UpdateCommand, and DeleteCommand properties.

Once again, we have separate classes for OLE DB connections, and direct connections to SQL Server 7 or above databases: OleDbDataAdapter and SqlDataAdapter. DataAdapters will probably start to appear for all kinds of data sources, and it is possible to write our own – see Chapter 17 on creating .NET data providers.

Visual Studio .NET offers a wizard for developers to create a working data adapter object for their data source by selecting a few options.

The wizard offers similar features for SQL and OLE DB connections. However, some OLE databases do not support stored procedures, Microsoft Access for example. In these cases, the wizard will disable these options.

Dragging a data adapter component onto the form will display the wizard. After the welcome step, which summarizes all the operations available using the tool, the wizard gives us a choice between available database connections, and the option to create a new one:

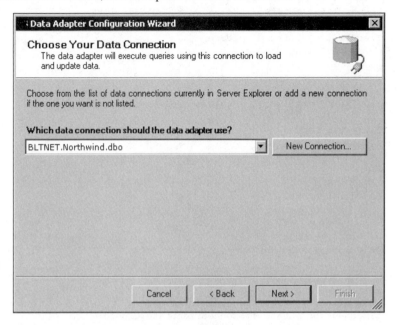

Choosing a New Connection will display Data Link Properties, and we can create a connection in the way we saw earlier in the chapter. Once the connection has been chosen, we move on to select the method that the data adapter will use to access the database:

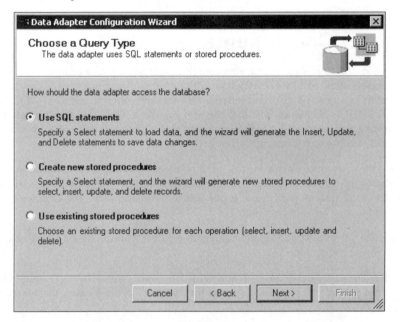

Each of these is worth considering. Here's an overview of each one:

- ❑ Use SQL statements – allows developers either to specify a SQL statement to retrieve data from database or to build a new query using the Query Builder visual tool. The wizard will automatically generate update, delete, and insert commands based on the select statement.

- ❑ Create a new stored procedure – creates stored procedures instead of SQL statements in the application's code. The wizard will automatically generate update, delete, and insert commands based on the select statement. **This option is disabled for databases that do not implement stored procedures.**

- ❑ Use existing stored procedures – allows developers to choose existing stored procedures to select, update, insert, and delete records.

> **The wizard allows a developer to generate SQL statements automatically only when the query does not contain more than one table. So, you will have to manually add your insert, update, and delete statements if you have tables joined together in your query.**

The Use SQL Statements Option

In this case the wizard will ask us to specify a new SELECT statement, which it will use to fill the dataset and to generate the three update commands:

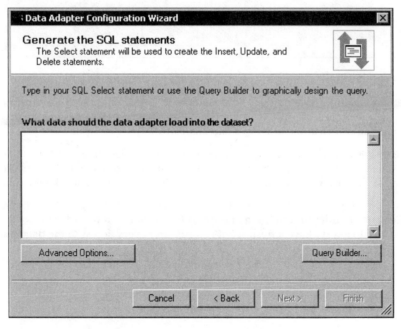

In the step illustrated above you have two possibilities:

- ❑ Insert the SQL query instruction manually in the text field
- ❑ Use the Query Builder visual tool

If you fancy writing the SQL straight out, just write it into the box. Otherwise use the **Query Builder** button, which builds a SELECT statement using the **Query Builder** visual tool. We have looked at this tool earlier in the chapter.

At this stage, we can click Advanced Options and set some additional details:

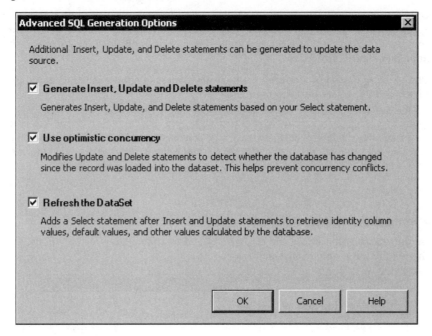

Let's see each option in detail:

❑ **Generate Insert, Update and Delete statements** – generates three statements based on the SELECT query instruction. The other two options are related to this one, so if you clear the option you will clear the other two automatically.

❑ **Use optimistic concurrency** – adds a WHERE condition to the INSERT, UPDATE, and DELETE statements generated automatically by the wizard in order to guarantee to users that they are not going to change records that have been modified by other users, otherwise the command will fail.

❑ The **Refresh the DataSet** – appends a SELECT statement after the INSERT and UPDATE statements in order to retrieve the newly added or modified record. This is necessary when you want to always have a fresh set of records after every access to the database.

Clicking the **Next** button moves on to a final summary, and then clicking **Finish** will close the wizard and add the Data Adapter and its associated code.

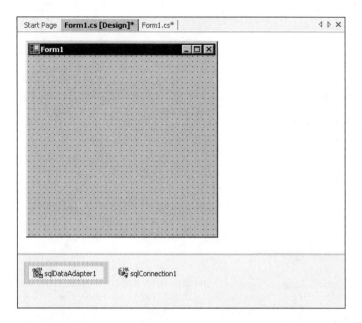

> The wizard can be re-run at any time by right-clicking the `DataAdapter` component in the form's tray and selecting **Configure Data Adapter...**

It's worth taking a look at the code that the wizard generates. Let's take a look at how different code is generated depending on the **Advanced Options** that we select.

If you clear all the **Advanced Options**, so that the wizard does not generate any update commands, we get the following code. Three variables are declared:

```
private System.Data.SqlClient.SqlDataAdapter sqlDataAdapter1;
private System.Data.SqlClient.SqlConnection sqlConnection1;
private System.Data.SqlClient.SqlCommand sqlSelectCommand1;
```

In the body of the `InitializeComponent` function, they are constructed and initialized:

```
this.sqlDataAdapter1 = new System.Data.SqlClient.SqlDataAdapter();
this.sqlConnection1 = new System.Data.SqlClient.SqlConnection();
this.sqlSelectCommand1 = new System.Data.SqlClient.SqlCommand();

...

//
// sqlSelectCommand1
//
this.sqlSelectCommand1.CommandText = "SELECT Title, FirstName, LastName, " +
                "HomePhone, EmployeeID FROM Employees";

//
```

```
// sqlDataAdapter1
//
this.sqlDataAdapter1.SelectCommand = this.sqlSelectCommand1;
```

The command object, sqlSelectCommand1, contains the SELECT statement specified in the related wizard step, and the Command property of the DataAdapter object is set to the sqlSelectCommand1 object.

With only the Generate Insert, Update and Delete statements option selected, the wizard will analyze your query to create the following three statements:

```
//
// sqlDataAdapter1
//
sqlDataAdapter1.DeleteCommand = this.sqlDeleteCommand1;
sqlDataAdapter1.InsertCommand = this.sqlInsertCommand1;
sqlDataAdapter1.SelectCommand = this.sqlSelectCommand1;
//
// sqlInsertCommand1
//
sqlInsertCommand1.CommandText = "INSERT INTO Employees(Title, FirstName, " +
            "LastName, HomePhone) VALUES (@Title, @Fir" +
            "stName, @LastName, @HomePhone)";

sqlInsertCommand1.Connection = this.sqlConnection1;
sqlInsertCommand1.Parameters.Add(new SqlParameter("@Title", SqlDbType.NVarChar,
30, ParameterDirection.Input, true, ((System.Byte)(0)),
    ((System.Byte)(0)), "Title", DataRowVersion.Current, null));

sqlInsertCommand1.Parameters.Add(new SqlClient.SqlParameter("@FirstName",
    SqlDbType.NVarChar, 10, ParameterDirection.Input, false,
        ((System.Byte)(0)), ((System.Byte)(0)), "FirstName",
        DataRowVersion.Current, null));

. . .

    . . .

//
// sqlUpdateCommand1
//
sqlUpdateCommand1.CommandText = "UPDATE Employees SET Title = @Title, " +
            "FirstName = @FirstName, LastName = @LastName" +
            ", HomePhone = @HomePhone WHERE (EmployeeID = "
            + @Original_EmployeeID)";

sqlUpdateCommand1.Connection = this.sqlConnection1;
sqlUpdateCommand1.Parameters.Add(new SqlClient.SqlParameter("@Title",
    SqlDbType.NVarChar, 30, ParameterDirection.Input, true,
        ((System.Byte)(0)), ((System.Byte)(0)), "Title",
        DataRowVersion.Current, null));

sqlUpdateCommand1.Parameters.Add(new SqlClient.SqlParameter("@FirstName",
    SqlDbType.NVarChar, 10, ParameterDirection.Input, false,
```

```
          ((System.Byte)(0)), ((System.Byte)(0)), "FirstName",
       DataRowVersion.Current, null));

. . .


. . .

//
// sqlDeleteCommand1
//
sqlDeleteCommand1.CommandText = "DELETE FROM Employees
   WHERE (EmployeeID = @EmployeeID)";
sqlDeleteCommand1.Connection = this.sqlConnection1;
sqlDeleteCommand1.Parameters.Add(new SqlClient.SqlParameter("@EmployeeID",
   SqlDbType.Int, 4, ParameterDirection.Input, false, ((System.Byte)(0)),
       ((System.Byte)(0)), "EmployeeID", DataRowVersion.Original, null));
```

As you can see from the code above, the INSERT, UPDATE, and DELETE commands have been created automatically. The wizard has recognized the primary key column, even if it was not present in the query, adding a WHERE condition inside both the UPDATE and DELETE statements.

In an application it could happen that you are attempting to update a record that has been removed by another user; using the code above, an exception would be raised and the program would fail the operation. To obtain major control over these kinds of exceptions you can select the **Use optimistic concurrency** option, which will create extra code:

```
//
// sqlUpdateCommand1
//
sqlUpdateCommand1.CommandText = @"UPDATE Employees SET Title = @Title, " +
        "FirstName = @FirstName, LastName = @LastName,
        " + "HomePhone = @HomePhone WHERE" +
        " (EmployeeID = @Original_EmployeeID) AND " +
        "(FirstName = @Original_FirstName) AND " +
        "(HomePhone = @Original_HomePhone OR " +
        "@Original_HomePhone1 IS NULL AND HomePhone IS" +
        " NULL) AND (LastName = @Original_LastName) AND" +
        + " (Title = @Original_Title OR @Original_Title1" +
        + " IS NULL AND Title IS NULL)";
```

In the snippet above, the UPDATE statement has changed and the record will be updated only if the original column values have not been changed. The DELETE statement also changes, so that a row will only be deleted if it has not been modified in the data source since the dataset was filled.

Finally, to ensure that you always have a set of fresh records inside your DataSet object, you can select the **Refresh the DataSet** advanced option in order to retrieve the records each time a new database operation is performed:

```
//
// sqlInsertCommand1
//
sqlInsertCommand1.CommandText = "INSERT INTO Employees(Title, FirstName, " +
        "LastName, HomePhone) VALUES (@Title, @Fir" +
```

```
"stName, @LastName, @HomePhone); SELECT Title,
" + " FirstName, LastName, HomePhone, Em" +
"ployeeID FROM Employees WHERE (EmployeeID = "
+ "@@IDENTITY)";
```

In the statement above, a `SELECT` instruction has been appended to the `INSERT` command in order to retrieve the last record inserted. However, if you have many records to insert or to update, it is better not to use this option but to refresh the `DataSet` at the end of your database operations. Using the **Refresh the DataSet** option will execute two commands for each database operation, slowing down general performance.

The "Create new stored procedures" Option

This option allows developers to create four stored procedures to select, update, insert, and delete records, instead of using SQL statements in our application. The first two wizard steps are identical to those if we were using SQL statements – we choose the database connection parameters and the `SELECT` string. The third step is different because it asks us to choose four stored procedure names that will be created in the database automatically (based on the `SELECT` string we have provided):

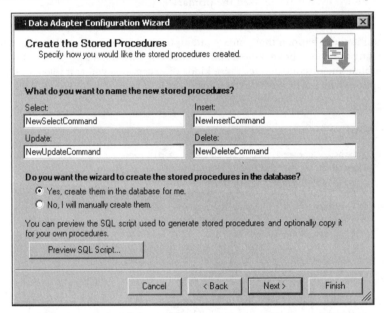

We can change the default names for the stored procedures and choose whether to let the wizard create the stored procedures in the database automatically. The **Preview SQL Script** button shows the script that the wizard will run against the database, but does not provide the ability to modify the instructions:

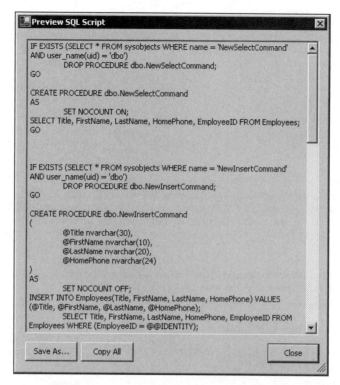

After this step, the wizard will display a summary of every operation it is going to do. Clicking the Finish button will create the stored procedures, and add the following code to the project:

```
//
// sqlSelectCommand1
//
sqlSelectCommand1.CommandText = "NewSelectCommand";
sqlSelectCommand1.CommandType = CommandType.StoredProcedure;
sqlSelectCommand1.Connection = sqlConnection1;

sqlSelectCommand1.Parameters.Add(new SqlParameter("@RETURN_VALUE",
  SqlDbType.Int, 4, ParameterDirection.ReturnValue, false,
    ((System.Byte)(0)), ((System.Byte)(0)), "", DataRowVersion.Current,
    null));

//
// sqlInsertCommand1
//
sqlInsertCommand1.CommandText = "NewInsertCommand";
sqlInsertCommand1.CommandType = CommandType.StoredProcedure;
sqlInsertCommand1.Connection = sqlConnection1;

sqlInsertCommand1.Parameters.Add(new SqlClient.SqlParameter("@RETURN_VALUE",
  SqlDbType.Int, 4, ParameterDirection.ReturnValue, false,
    ((System.Byte)(0)), ((System.Byte)(0)), "", DataRowVersion.Current,
    null));
```

```
sqlInsertCommand1.Parameters.Add(new SqlClient.SqlParameter("@Title",
   SqlDbType.NVarChar, 30, ParameterDirection.Input, true,
      ((System.Byte)(0)), ((System.Byte)(0)), "Title", DataRowVersion.Current,
      null));

. . .


//
// sqlUpdateCommand1
//
sqlUpdateCommand1.CommandText = "NewUpdateCommand";
sqlUpdateCommand1.CommandType = CommandType.StoredProcedure;
sqlUpdateCommand1.Connection = sqlConnection1;
sqlUpdateCommand1.Parameters.Add(new SqlClient.SqlParameter("@RETURN_VALUE",
   SqlDbType.Int, 4, ParameterDirection.ReturnValue, false,
      ((System.Byte)(0)), ((System.Byte)(0)), "", DataRowVersion.Current,
      null));

sqlUpdateCommand1.Parameters.Add(new
   System.Data.SqlClient.SqlParameter("@Title",
      System.Data.SqlDbType.NVarChar, 30,
      System.Data.ParameterDirection.Input, true, ((System.Byte)(0)),
      ((System.Byte)(0)), "Title", System.Data.DataRowVersion.Current, null));

sqlUpdateCommand1.Parameters.Add(new SqlClient.SqlParameter("@FirstName",
   SqlDbType.NVarChar, 10, ParameterDirection.Input, false,
      ((System.Byte)(0)), ((System.Byte)(0)), "FirstName",
      DataRowVersion.Current, null));

. . .


//
// sqlDeleteCommand1
//
sqlDeleteCommand1.CommandText = "NewDeleteCommand";
sqlDeleteCommand1.CommandType = CommandType.StoredProcedure;
sqlDeleteCommand1.Connection = sqlConnection1;

sqlDeleteCommand1.Parameters.Add(new SqlClient.SqlParameter("@RETURN_VALUE",
   SqlDbType.Int, 4, ParameterDirection.ReturnValue, false,
      ((System.Byte)(0)), ((System.Byte)(0)), "", DataRowVersion.Current,
      null));

sqlDeleteCommand1.Parameters.Add(new SqlClient.SqlParameter("@EmployeeID",
   SqlDbType.Int, 4, ParameterDirection.Input, false, ((System.Byte)(0)),
      ((System.Byte)(0)), "EmployeeID", DataRowVersion.Original, null));

. . .
```

In the fragment of code above you can see how the wizard has inserted the stored procedures in the code.

The "Use existing stored procedures" Option

You can use the last wizard option when you want to use existing stored procedures to select, insert, update, and delete records in the database. The wizard will analyze every parameter that you have provided to the stored procedures, creating all the code necessary to execute them.

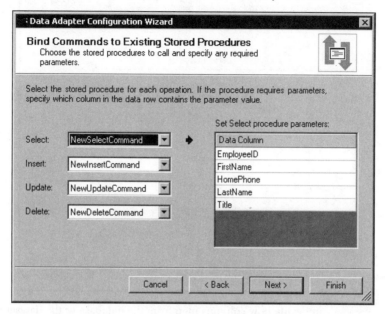

The wizard's step above shows four combo boxes where you can select every stored procedure that you want to use in your code. The **Select** stored procedure is mandatory, while you can omit the other three.

> **If you remove a parameter from a stored procedure and then use the wizard to update your code, you will continue to see the same stored procedure's parameters, even the deleted one. The same behavior is encountered when you add a new parameter to the stored procedure or when you change its name, dimension, data type, and so on. Actually, the only thing you can do in order to retrieve the correct stored procedure structure is close Visual Studio .NET and then restart it.**

The code generated by the wizard will contain calls to the stored procedures specified during the steps.

Table Mappings

The ADO.NET class library offers a way to map column names from the database to the `DataSet` using the `DataTableMapping` and `DataColumnMapping` objects. Usually, mapping classes are really useful when you have to manage tables that have unclear or short column names. In fact, you can define new names for the columns used by the `DataSet` object in order to improve the code readability. For more information on mapping, see Chapter 11. Visual Studio .NET offers a visual tool that allows developers to map the column names generating the code automatically. You can display the Table Mappings visual tool by clicking on the '...' button in the `DataAdapter` object's TableMappings property contained in the Properties window:

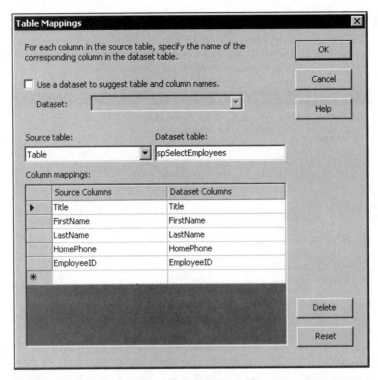

In the figure above you can decide how columns map from the database to the dataset by relating names from the **Source Columns** and the **Dataset Columns** in the grid. You can check **Use a dataset to suggest table and column names** if your project contains one or more dataset files whose schema will be used to suggest the table and column names to map to.

A typical scenario where you can use the **Table Mappings** dialog box would be receiving a `DataSet` object from a Web Service and wanting to insert its data into a database. The database table and column names will often be different from the names in the dataset, so we must map the database names to the dataset names.

Finally, we can remove a mapping row by selecting it and pressing the **Delete** button, or we can roll back all the changes we have made by the **Reset** button.

Let's see the code generated by the wizard:

```
sqlDataAdapter1.TableMappings.AddRange(new Common.DataTableMapping[] {
  new Common.DataTableMapping("Table", "spSelectEmployees", new
  Common.DataColumnMapping[] {new Common.DataColumnMapping("Title",
  "Title"),
new Common.DataColumnMapping("FirstName", "FirstName"), new
  Common.DataColumnMapping("LastName", "LastName"), new
  Common.DataColumnMapping("HomePhone", "HomePhone"), new
  Common.DataColumnMapping("EmployeeID", "EmployeeID")})});
```

The code creates a new `DataTableMapping` object, with related `DataColumnMapping` objects.

> Even if you don't want to create a mapping mechanism, because the source column names are the same as in the dataset, Visual Studio .NET will create them anyway. You cannot delete the respective rows of code because they have been written in the private code region, and changing its content it would render the tool useless.

DataSet Data Component

The `DataSet` implements a disconnected mechanism to improve database connection performance, and to manage data exchange using XML. Visual Studio .NET offers many visual tools to help developers manipulate datasets.

The `DataSet` object is independent from the data provider, so we use the same `DataSet` component for connections using `OleDbConnection`, `SqlConnection`, and any other `Connection` component that might be developed in the future.

Dragging the data component onto the form will raise the following dialog box, where we select whether we want to create a typed or an untyped dataset:

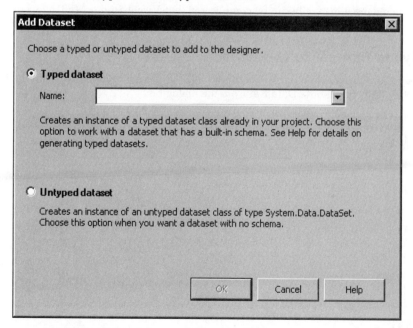

This dialog box allows developers to choose between two options:

- ❑ Typed DataSet – create an object based on an existing subclass of the `DataSet` class that incorporates schema information into the class definition.

- ❑ Untyped dataset – create an instance of the `DataSet` class, which incorporates no schema information. This option allows us to create an empty dataset with no initial schema.

Visual Studio .NET offers a complete set of tools to manage typed datasets, so in the following section of the chapter we will focus our attention on this aspect. Adding an untyped dataset is more or less the same as declaring a dataset object with coding instructions – we have the ability to set a few properties at design-time, such as the namespace and the prefix. The really interesting Visual Studio .NET features are offered by typed datasets.

The Typed Dataset

A typed dataset is a subclass of the `DataSet` class that implements properties and methods specific to the data structure that it will be used to manipulate; it also includes column type information. These properties and methods provide easy ways to access tables, columns, relations, and so on. They also ensure that the dataset is only used to store data of the appropriate type for its columns, helping to avoid errors when the dataset is written back to the data source.

Imagine you want to manage a `myTable` table that has a `myID` column: with the typed dataset it will be as simple as calling the following instruction:

```
myDataSet.myTable.myID;
```

Creating a typed dataset manually can be complicated, but Visual Studio .NET offers the tools to accomplish this easily.

Adding a Typed Dataset to the Project

Adding a `DataSet` object inside the Visual Studio .NET project is really easy. From the Project menu, select Add New Item and choose Data Set from the dialog box:

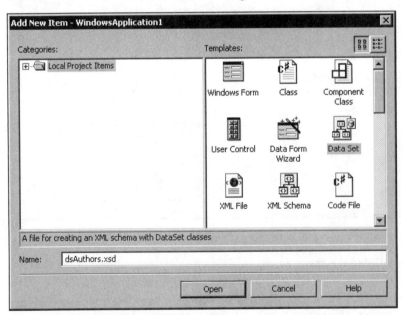

After choosing a valid filename and pressing the Open button, a new `DataSet` class will be generated automatically (this can be seen in Example5):

```
public class dsAuthors : System.Data.DataSet {

    public dsAuthors() {
        this.InitClass();
    }

    private dsAuthors(SerializationInfo info, StreamingContext context) {
        this.InitClass();
        this.GetSerializationData(info, context);
    }

    protected override bool ShouldSerializeTables() {
        return false;
    }

    protected override bool ShouldSerializeRelations() {
        return false;
    }

    protected override void ReadXmlSerializable(XmlReader reader) {
        this.ReadXml(reader, XmlReadMode.IgnoreSchema);
    }

    protected override System.Xml.Schema.XmlSchema GetSchemaSerializable() {
        System.IO.MemoryStream stream = new System.IO.MemoryStream();
        this.WriteXmlSchema(new XmlTextWriter(stream, null));
        stream.Position = 0;
        return Xml.Schema.XmlSchema.Read(new XmlTextReader(stream), null);
    }

    private void InitClass() {
        this.DataSetName = "dsAuthors";
        this.Namespace = "http://tempuri.org/dsAuthors.xsd";
    }
}
```

As shown above, the class does not contain database information, but it has overridden all the necessary methods to serialize the data and the constructor to initialize internal variables to the default values.

> In order to display the code generated by the Visual Studio .NET tool, you have to select the **Show All Files** button within the Solution Explorer window, as shown in the following screenshot.

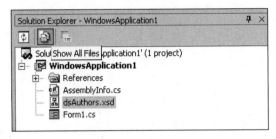

There are two ways to create the dataset schema: we can drag tables from a database connection in the **Server Explorer** onto the dataset, or we can drag the XML Schema components in the **Toolbox** window onto the dataset designer (this option allows for creating the dataset manually). Usually the first method is used to retrieve information from a database, and the second when the data will be retrieved from an XML document. However, we can use whichever one we like, even if retrieving a schema automatically is faster than if we had made it manually.

The following image shows the complete list of XML Schema components that you can use for your dataset schema definition (the best way to get more information on these components is to use the Help files that come with Visual Studio .NET):

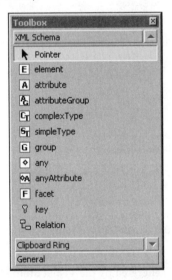

Although you need a sound understanding of XML to manually create an XML schema, you can, if you do not have such a solid basis, always choose either to infer the XML schema using the `DataSet`'s `InferXmlSchema` method, or load an existing one using an untyped dataset object.

When you work with database information, you can drag the desired tables directly onto the dataset designer from the **Server Explorer** – Visual Studio .NET will create the related schema automatically. It will analyze every column contained in the selected tables and create element keys and other elements with the correct data types. Moreover, if the tables are joined by relationships then Visual Studio .NET will automatically create relations inside the XML schema.

The following figure shows what the dataset designer will look like if we drag the authors table, from the pubs database that ships with Microsoft SQL Server, onto the dataset designer:

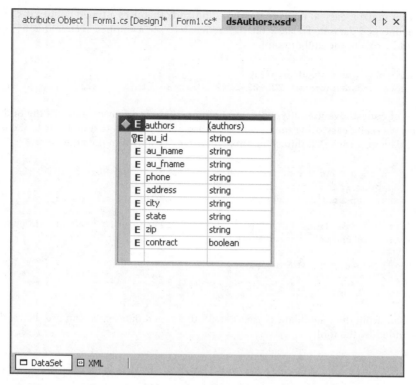

We can see the XML tags that define the typed dataset by clicking on the **XML** tab underneath the Dataset Designer. We can remove XML elements (whole tables or individual columns) graphically by right-clicking them and choosing **Delete** from the context menu, or by selecting them and pressing the *Delete* key.

As we define the dataset's schema, Visual Studio .NET will generate a class that inherits from the `DataSet` and implements the schema.

Let's see what has been added:

- ❑ The main class derived from the `DataSet` parent class will contain a new `DataTable` derived class wrapped around the table specified in the designer. Naturally, for each table inserted in the `DataSet`, the tool will create a related `DataTable` derived class.

- ❑ A new `DataRow` derived class will be added to the main class, which wraps the table's row information.

- ❑ A new `EventArgs` derived class will be added in the main class to implement the row change event.

- ❑ The `DataSet` derived class will offer a new property for each table inserted into the dataset; the properties will be named after the table that they point to.

- ❑ Every new class will contain an ad hoc method to add a row to the data table contained in the dataset, a read-only property for each column present in the table, a method to find a row by providing the primary key, and, four event handlers specific for the rows contained in the table.

These features make it easy to manage the data, and code that uses a typed dataset is clearer than code that uses an untyped dataset. To show the difference, let's see a snippet of code that uses our generated dataset to add a row to the authors table:

```
dsAuthors ds = new dsAuthors();
ds.authors.AddauthorsRow("222-22-2222","Ferracchiati","Fabio Claudio",true);
```

The snippet of code above uses a typed dataset wrapped around four columns of the authors table. As you can see, it's really easy using the new AddauthorsRow method to add a row to the dataset. Using an untyped dataset means that things became contorted, as shown in the code here:

```
SqlConnection dbConn = new SqlConnection("data source=BLTNET;initial
   catalog=pubs;integrated security=SSPI;persist security" + "
   info=True;workstation id=BLTNET;packet size=4096");

SqlClient.SqlDataAdapter daAuthors = new SqlClient.SqlDataAdapter("SELECT
   au_lname, au_fname, contract, au_id FROM authors", dbConn);

DataSet ds = new DataSet("dsAuthors");

daAuthors.Fill(ds);
```

Retrieving data from the typed dataset is easier. With a typed dataset we can use the read-only properties added by the tool:

```
ds.authors.au_lname;
```

However, when using an untyped dataset we must use the following:

```
ds.Tables["authors"].Rows[0][" au_lname"];
```

Relating Two or More Tables

Relating two or more tables in the dataset object is as important as relating them in the database. We can assign constraints between tables that cascade updates and deletes, or check for integrity rules.

The dataset designer makes it easy to create relationships between tables. You have to drag the tables onto the designer and drag the column that composes the relation over to the other column in the other table. If two or more columns compose the relation, you can select all of them and drag them directly onto the other table.

> **Visual Studio .NET offers a different dragging mechanism to Microsoft Access and Microsoft SQL Server: when you have two tables side by side in the diagram and you want to relate the column from the left table to one in the right table, you must drag the source column from the left-hand side of the parent table. Also, it doesn't matter what column you drag *to* – the DataSet Designer will select one for you, and give you the option to change it if you wish.**

After dragging a column onto a related table, the Dataset Designer prompts us to define the relationship's details:

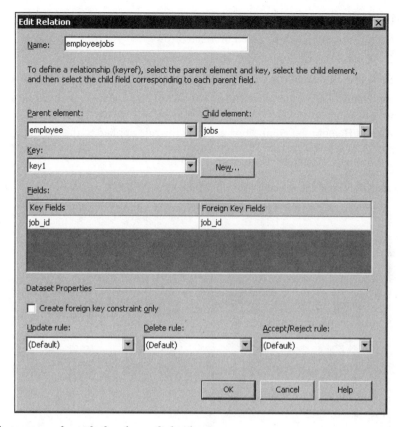

Let's see what we can do with the above dialog box:

- In the **Name** text field we specify the name that will be assigned to this relationship in the dataset object.

- The **Parent element** combo box enables us to select a different parent table for the relationship.

- The **Child element** combo box enables us to select a different child table for the relationship.

- The **Key** combo box enables us to select a parent key. This could be a single column or a set of columns. If we have created the relationship by dragging, we don't need to change this. The **New** button enables us to specify a column or set of columns to act as the key in the parent table.

- The **Fields** listview allows us to set columns in the child table that correspond with the key columns we have selected for the parent table. Visual Studio .NET will attempt to choose these automatically, but sometimes it is necessary to change them.

- The **Create foreign key constraint only** checkbox specifies that a dataset should only enforce constraints between the tables, and not retrieve data from both the tables. The resulting dataset will be more efficient, but contain fewer methods.

- **Update rule** and **Delete rule** enable us to choose how the dataset should behave when a row in the parent table is updated or deleted. If the constraint only checkbox has been checked, the constraint rule will be applied to these operations, guaranteeing the data's referential integrity. They can assume one of the following values:

- ❑ (Default) – set to whatever the default is set to

- ❑ None – no action will be taken on related rows

- ❑ Cascade – cascades the update/delete across to all related rows

- ❑ SetNull – all related rows will be set to DBNull as a result of the update action

- ❑ SetDefault – all of the related rows affected by the update action will be set to their default values as indicated by their DefaultValue property

- ❑ The Accept/Reject rule: combo box contains the rule applied to the dataset when the AcceptChanges and RejectChanges methods are called. It can assume one of the following values: (Default), None, and Cascade.

After clicking the OK button, the relationship will be added to the XSD, and shown in the Dataset Designer:

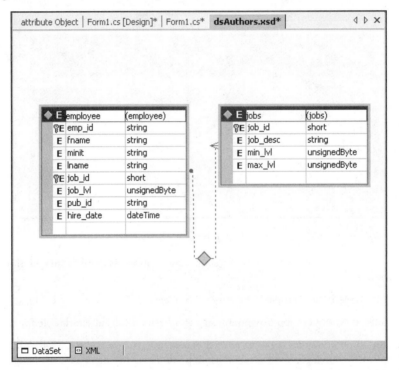

Generating and Filling a Typed DataSet Object

Visual Studio .NET allows developers to generate a strongly typed DataSet class by right-clicking a data adapter component in the tray and selecting Generate Dataset. Visual Studio .NET will study the SELECT statement provided when creating the data adapter and will generate a new XSD schema file and a new source file containing the complete typed dataset class.

The following screenshot shows the schema for a typed DataSet class created using the data adapter menu command:

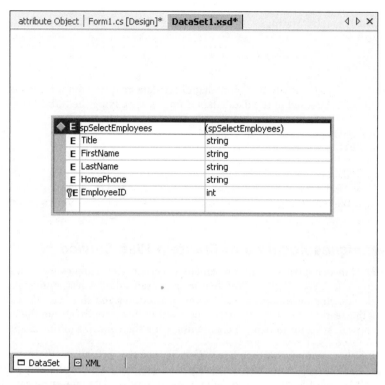

Below you can see the XML representation of the DataSet:

```xml
<xsd:schema id="dsEmployee"
targetNamespace="http://www.tempuri.org/dsEmployee.xsd"
xmlns="http://www.tempuri.org/dsEmployee.xsd"
xmlns:xsd="http://www.w3.org/2001/XMLSchema" xmlns:msdata="urn:schemas-microsoft-
com:xml-msdata" attributeFormDefault="qualified" elementFormDefault="qualified">
  <xsd:element name="dsEmployee" msdata:IsDataSet="true">
   <xsd:complexType>
    <xsd:choice maxOccurs="unbounded">
     <xsd:element name="Employees">
      <xsd:complexType>
       <xsd:sequence>
        <xsd:element name="Title" type="xsd:string" minOccurs="0" />
        <xsd:element name="FirstName" type="xsd:string" />
        <xsd:element name="LastName" type="xsd:string" />
        <xsd:element name="HomePhone" type="xsd:string" minOccurs="0" />
        <xsd:element name="EmployeeID" msdata:ReadOnly="true"
             msdata:AutoIncrement="true" type="xsd:int" />
       </xsd:sequence>
      </xsd:complexType>
     </xsd:element>
    </xsd:choice>
   </xsd:complexType>
   <xsd:unique name="Constraint1" msdata:PrimaryKey="true">
    <xsd:selector xpath=".//Employees" />
```

```
      <xsd:field xpath="EmployeeID" />
    </xsd:unique>
  </xsd:element>
</xsd:schema>
```

Filling the `dataset` object is really easy now that every data adapter component is declared in the code. Just call the `Fill` method of the data adapter object, specifying the `DataSet` object to fill:

```
// Fill the employee dataset
daEmployee.Fill(dsEmployee);
```

We can display the data contained in the dataset in various ways, such as using a data grid component, filling text fields, and saving the data using the XML language and then using an XML template to display the record. We will now go on to explore different ways of displaying a dataset using Visual Studio .NET.

Using the Techniques Acquired to Create a Web Service

For the purposes of this chapter, we will now create a Web Service using every data aspect that we have seen until this moment. Very briefly, a Web Service represents the biggest innovation introduced by the .NET framework: allowing developers to call remote procedures and show results within their own applications. As this feature is so important, it is covered in more depth later in the book – all we need to know now is how to set it up so that we can demonstrate the concepts of this chapter.

The fictional BltAirlines company airline has a Web Service that lists all the flights that its organizes for the present day. The Wrox Intranet Portal has a special section, useful for the employees, which displays all the BltAirlines flights retrieved using its Web Service. The employee can choose a flight then inform the related office, which will go on to book the selected flight. Naturally, the scenario could be extended to allow particular employees to book a flight directly, maybe by calling another remote procedure, but this is beyond the scope of this simple example, which just shows how to join together the data components we have studied.

Creating the Web Service

Let's start creating the Web Service. From the **New Project** menu in Visual Studio .NET choose **ASP.NET Web Service** and call it **BltAirlinesWebService**. The project will contain a service that we will use to add a remote procedure that will return a dataset containing the flights list. Now we can create the database and the table that will contain every flight. You can choose the database you prefer – I chose Microsoft SQL Server – and use that to build the **BltAirlinesDB** database, specifying the following columns in the **tabFlights** table (scripts for creation of this database are available in the download):

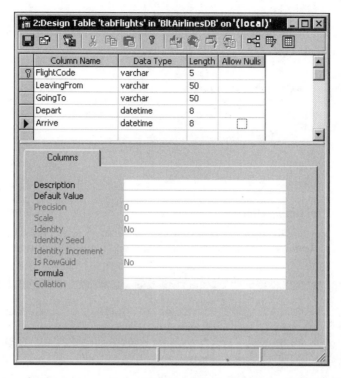

Now we can create a database connection within the **Server Explorer** window and drag the table onto an empty typed dataset, called **WebService**, that you have to add to the project:

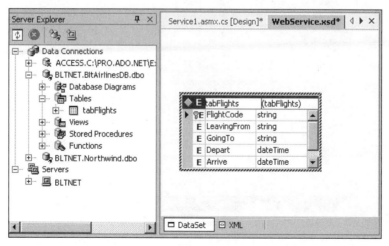

So, now we need to create a `DataAdapter` to fill the dataset with the data retrieved from the table. Drag the `SqlDataAdapter` data component from the **Toolbox** window onto the web service design page and use the wizard steps to create an object that only retrieves the records without inserting, updating, and deleting them. This is accomplished by clearing the **Generate Insert, Update and Delete statements** checkbox from the **Advanced** dialog box. I chose to create a stored procedure to retrieve the data, but you may need to choose another option if you have used another database.

The last operation we have to do consists of inserting a typed data set data component pointing to the dataset we have added in the project. Now that the Visual Studio .NET tool has added all the code, we have just to define the web method that returns the dataset:

```
[WebMethod]
public dsWebService RetrieveFlights()
{
    // Fill the dataset
    da.Fill(ds);

    // Return it
    return ds;
}
```

Creating the Wrox Portal Application

The Wrox Intranet portal will allow employees to book a flight by retrieving the flights list directly from the BltAirlines site. (Of course, you remember that actually booking a flight online is beyond the scope of this chapter!)

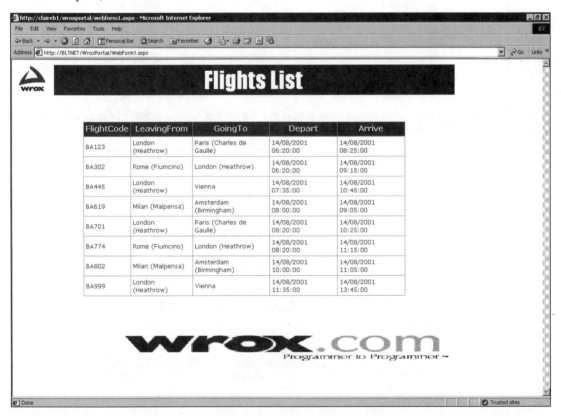

The first operation is adding a web reference to the Web Service. You can select the **Add Web Reference...** menu from the **Project** menu and add the URL where the Web Service is located:

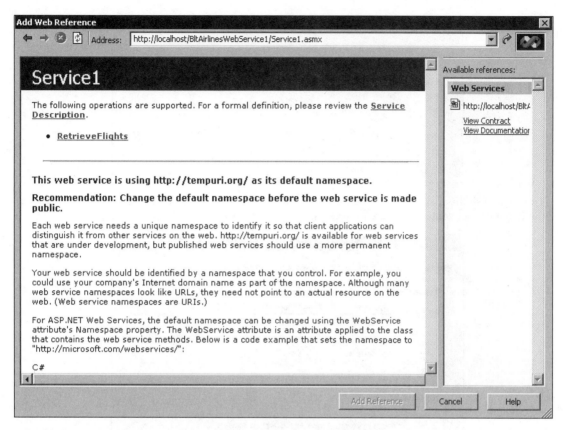

In the figure above you can see the list of methods exposed by the **Service1** Web Service. In this case just one method is available: the `RetrieveFlights` procedure. This method returns a dataset containing the list of flights retrieved by the Web Service. We need to call this method within our code:

```
private void Page_Init(object sender, EventArgs e)
{
  //
  // CODEGEN: This call is required by the ASP.NET Web Form Designer.
  //
  InitializeComponent();

  WebApplication1.localhost.Service1 flights = new
          WebApplication1.localhost.Service1();

  ds = flights.RetrieveFlights();

  . . .

}
```

The method is exposed by the `Service1` Web Service, so we need to create an instance of this object and then call it. The `ds DataSet` data component has been added from the **Toolbox** window, specifying that it is to create a typed dataset based on the object created during the web reference linking.

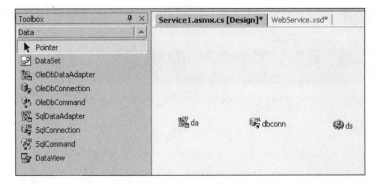

To accomplish this task, just drag the `DataSet` data component on the Design service page and select the typed dataset contained in the project, as illustrated below:

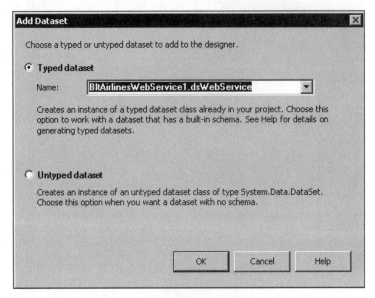

Now that the dataset is retrieved we can choose a way to display its records. I chose the **DataGrid** web server control that you'll learn to use at the end of the chapter.

The DataView Data Component

The final data component that we will look at is the `DataView`. The `DataView` enables developers to filter and sort data in a dataset.

In Visual Studio .NET we can create a `DataView` object by dragging the icon from the Toolbox to a form or other container, in the same way as we have done previously. In this section we will see how to create and use a `DataView` data component using the features of Visual Studio .NET.

Using the DataView to View Selected Rows

Usually, a `DataView` data component is added to the project to display a sub-set of the records in a `DataSet` or `DataTable`. Using a `DataView` data component, we can accomplish two kinds of filtering operation:

1. Filter the dataset records using a filter expression – for example, all rows where `lastname` begins with B

2. Filter the dataset records using their own row state – for example, all rows that have been changed, or all rows that have been marked for deletion

> A typed dataset contains a **DataView** object accessible from the **DefaultView** property in the code. So, we do not need to add a data view data component when we have a typed dataset in our code. However, we might choose to add one if we want to set the data view properties at design-time using Visual Studio .NET tools.

Let's list the main properties offered by the data component that are necessary for the correct execution of the application:

❑ **Name** – the object's name

❑ **AllowDelete, AllowEdit, AllowNew** – specify whether the data view data component allows update operations

❑ **Table** – specifies the underlying `DataTable`

Filtering Rows Using a Filter Expression

The `DataView` offers a `RowFilter` property, which we can use to provide a filter expression. We can set the filter expression in the property field. Its syntax is similar to an SQL WHERE clause. The following figure illustrates a filter that retrieves a specific row in the `tabFlights` table of the typed `DataSet` called ds:

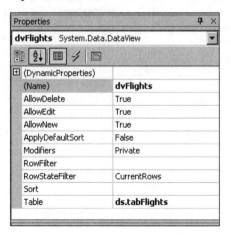

Visual Studio .NET will generate the code that will filter the content of the dataset retrieving just the row having the value specified.

```
//
// dvFlights
//
this.dvFlights.RowFilter = "FLIGHTCODE=\'BA101\'";
```

Filtering Rows on Row State

When a `DataSet` is filled from a data source, each record will be marked as Unchanged. When we use a data adapter to write changes back to a data source, it will only make database calls for rows that have changed in some way. So, when we delete a record from a dataset, we are really marking the row as deleted – the data remains in memory until we call the dataset's `AcceptChanges` method.

The `DataView` data component offers the RowStateFilter property just to filter the dataset records having a particular row state. By default it will be set to CurrentRows, which displays Unchanged rows, New rows, and Current Modified rows. However, for our purposes, we will need to check only Deleted:

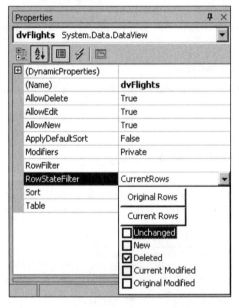

You can modify the state filter by changing the state of the checkboxes in the property pull-down. The tool will generate the related code to allow the data view to retrieve filtered records:

```
//
// dvFlights
//
dvFlights.RowStateFilter = System.Data.DataViewRowState.Deleted;
```

The example above will only display rows that are marked as deleted – useful if we want to tell the user what rows they are about to delete when they choose to update the data source.

In the following example, a windows form shows two data grids: the first contains the current rows retrieved and stored in a typed dataset, while the second shows just the records removed from the typed dataset:

Producing an application like this is simple. Firstly, we need two dataview data components pointing to the same typed data set. The first dataview shows the current records, while the second object is filtered to display only the removed records. At the beginning, the Removed data grid will not display any records, but it will be filled automatically as we select and remove records from the first data grid. This could be a good way to inform the user about every change made to the records before updating the data source.

Using the DataView to Sort Rows

Another useful feature offered by the DataView is sorting the dataset content for display. If we want to sort records by the date and time values contained in the Depart column, we can specify the column name in the Sort property, as illustrated in the figure below:

The syntax for the Sort property is similar to the SQL ORDER BY clause. We can specify a descending sort simply by putting the DESC instruction after the column name. We can also can sort data using more than one column, separating each column name with a comma.

The DataGrid Component

Visual Studio .NET provides an enhanced version of the DataGrid component already available in Visual Basic 6. The new features added to this new version are extremely useful. The first thing to note is that a new version of the component is provided, even for web applications. The web version is really powerful: it creates an HTML representation of the data contained in the data source to which it is bound. We can choose to create pages based on simple HTML that display in any browser, or to generate the code specifically for Internet Explorer so that some DHTML code is generated.

The DataGrid class is located in the System.Web.UI.WebControls namespace.

In this final part of the chapter we will look at the DataGrid web and Windows form components. First, the web forms DataGrid.

DataGrid Web Component

The web DataGrid component is a web server control that generates an HTML table. The control can bind to a dataset, a datatable, a dataview, or an array. The DataGrid is read-only by default, but can be easily customized to accomplish updates, insertions, and deletions. Moreover, the DataGrid component enables the user to select a sort-column, and adds particular events to manage the records.

To use the DataGrid component, simply drag it from the Web Forms tab within the Toolbox onto the aspx page.

Binding the DataGrid Component to a Data Source

To use the DataGrid component correctly we need to bind it to a data source. This data source could be a dataset, a datatable, or a data view object – we use the DataSource and DataMember properties to make the selection:

In the figure above, the datagrid is bound to a typed dataset called ds, and we are looking at the tabFlights table within that dataset. Also, we can set the DataKeyField property, which specifies the column that uniquely identifies a given row in this table. This value does not need to be displayed, but it is necessary to specify a DataKeyField if you wish to use the datagrid to edit data.

After defining the data source, we need to add a few code instructions to populate the dataset and refresh the content of the datagrid. Each time the datagrid changes we must call the DataBind method, in order to display data source changes. So, in the Page_Init event handler, after the component initialize phase, add the following instructions:

```
// Fill the data set using the data adapter component
daFlights.Fill(dsFlights);

// Populate the data grid
dgFlights.DataBind();
```

The result looks unrefined, but is fully working:

FLIGHTCODE	LeaveFrom	GoingTo	Depart	Arrive	FirstName	LastName	ID_PILOT
BA101	Rome	London	8/16/2001 9:55:00 AM	8/16/2001 11:55:00 AM	Tom	Cruise	2
BA157	Milan	London	8/15/2001 11:25:00 AM	8/15/2001 1:25:00 PM	John	Smith	1
BA201	Paris	London	8/17/2001 1:55:00 PM	8/17/2001 3:55:00 PM	Tom	Cruise	2

121

Formatting the DataGrid

As you can see from the figure above, the datagrid's default properties make the table look rather sparse. However, Visual Studio .NET provides two ways to improve the component's appearance:

❑ The Auto Format wizard

❑ The Property Builder wizard

You can select these wizards by right-clicking on the datagrid component and choosing the respective menu item.

The Auto Format wizard shows a list of templates to choose from:

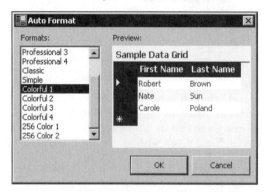

After clicking the OK button, the layout and the schema will be applied to the datagrid immediately:

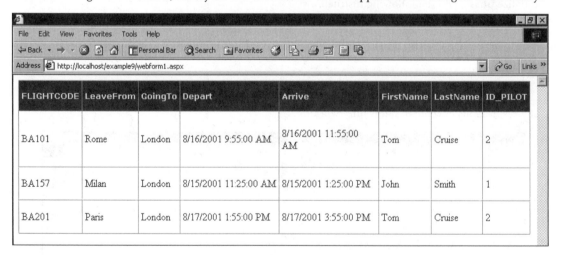

The Property Builder wizard allows developers to choose a style for each datagrid section, such as Header and Footer. In this way we have more options than with the Auto Format wizard:

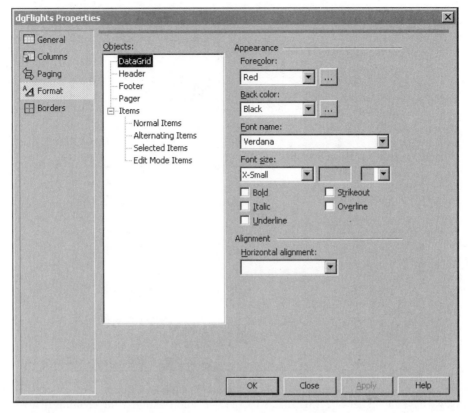

We can associate a style with each element contained in the **Objects** tree view, and preview the results using the **Apply** button. We can change the appearance of each of the following objects:

- ❑ The **DataGrid** object represents the appearance of the whole datagrid

- ❑ The **Header** object represents the header of the datagrid

- ❑ The **Footer** object represents the footer of the datagrid

- ❑ The **Pager** object represents the buttons that enable the user to move between different pages, when the datagrid is divided into pages

- ❑ The **Normal Items** object represents the appearance of normal rows

- ❑ The **Alternating Items** object allows us to have a different style for alternate rows, which can help users to scan across a row because not all rows look identical

- ❑ The **Selected Items** object represents the style of currently selected row

- ❑ The **Edit Mode Items** object represents the appearance of rows as they are being edited

We can also configure the columns that will displayed in the data grid component. By default the columns are displayed automatically, retrieving their names from the data source. We can modify this and specify which columns to display, what to call them, and how to display them. To do this, select the **Columns** tab in the left pane of the **Property Builder**, which will display the following:

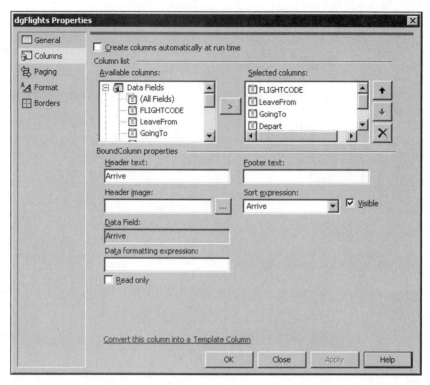

By default, the **Create columns automatically at run time** is checked. Before setting up the columns manually, we have to uncheck it. After that, we can select and customize the columns that will be displayed in the datagrid. Let's look at our options:

- ❏ The **Available columns** tree view lists for items: **Data Fields** contains all the fields within the data source bounded to the datagrid component; **Button Column** allows us to add a button to each row of the datagrid to accomplish particular tasks (there are five buttons already defined to select a datagrid's row, to edit, update, cancel an update, and delete a row); **HyperLink Column** allows us to define a URL link for the data grid's column value; **Template Column** allows us to add controls other than buttons to the data grid's rows.

- ❏ The **Selected columns** listbox enables us to change the order of the columns and remove those that we don't want to display.

- ❏ **Header text** specifies the text that will appear as the title of the column.

- ❏ **Footer text** specifies the text that will appear on the datagrid column footer.

- ❏ **Header image** specifies a path and a filename for an image file that you want use in the datagrid column header. The image will replace the header text.

- ❏ **Sort expression** contains the column that will be used to sort the grid.

- ❏ **Visible** allows us to hide and to show a column. Making the column invisible, instead of removing it, will allow you to hide and display the column programmatically.

- ❏ **Data formatting expression** allows us to define a formatting expression applied to the column before it is shown.

❑ Read only specifies that a column should be read-only even when in edit mode.

These properties give us great control over the appearance of the web form's datagrid component.

Sorting DataGrid Records

The DataGrid component offers an easy way to sort column elements displayed in the page. There are three easy steps:

1. Set the AllowSorting property to true from the Properties window, or from the General tab in the Property Builder.

2. Add an event handler to the SortCommand datagrid event, which is raised each time the user sorts the records. We can easily add it from the Property window by selecting the events list and double-clicking on the SortCommand event.

3. Add just a few code instructions to sort and to display the sorted column records.

The code to accomplish the sort operation is shown below:

```
private void dgFlights_SortCommand(object source,
System.Web.UI.WebControls.DataGridSortCommandEventArgs e)
{
  dvFlights.Sort = e.SortExpression;
  dgFlights.DataBind();
}
```

The DataGridSortCommandEventArgs object contains the element to which the sort has to be applied. The code applies the sort to a DataView object associated with the data source.

Selecting, Editing, Updating, and Deleting DataGrid Records

The DataGrid component offers some properties to allow users to edit data. Using these properties we can:

❑ Select a row, consequently changing the datagrid's SelectIndex property

❑ Edit a datagrid record, showing text fields where the data has changed

❑ Update the edited record

❑ Delete a datagrid row

Selecting a DataGrid Row

Often, a datagrid acts as a menu, allowing the user to select a particular row. For example, an e-commerce site might show a grid listing available items, and allow users to select what they want to buy. To create a datagrid that does this, open the Property Builder and add a Select Button column. We can specify the column's header, the caption that should appear in each cell, and the command name.

We can also choose a different style to be shown when the row is selected. From the Property Builder, change the selected tab to Format and specify a new style for the Selected Items object.

The last and most important operation is to retrieve the content of the selected row. To do this, add an event handler to the SelectedIndexChanged event and insert some instructions. The following code snippet shows how to add a confirmation message when a specific row is selected:

```
private void dgFlights_SelectedIndexChanged(object sender,
                                         System.EventArgs e)
{
    DataGridItem dgi = ((DataGrid)sender).SelectedItem;

    outputText.InnerHtml =
        "The flight " + dgi.Cells[1].Text + " has been booked";
}
```

The sender object is the DataGrid component that raised the event. We retrieve the selected DataGridItem using the SelectedItem property. Then we can retrieve the datagrid's cells using the Cells collection exposed by the object. The final result is shown below:

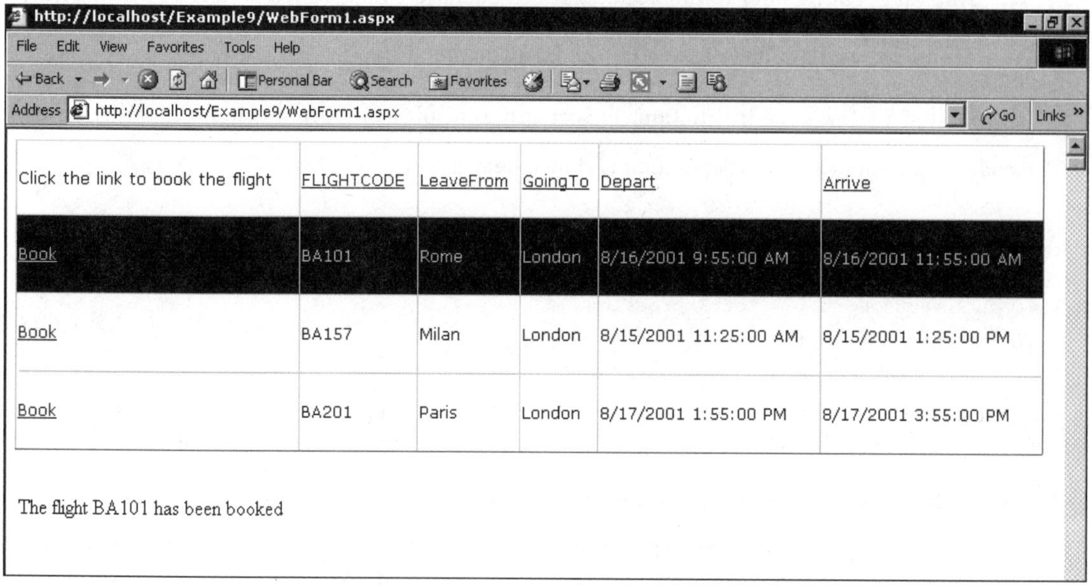

Putting a DataGrid Row into Edit Mode

The DataGrid component offers an easy way for users to edit and modify its content. We can add an edit button to each row that will put that row into edit mode. In order to add the editing functionality, we need to add the Edit, Update, Cancel button column object. We can optionally specify the text that will be shown on the buttons within the datagrid. Then we have to add the EditCommand event handler, inserting the necessary code to put the chosen row into edit mode. The code below manages the EditCommand event:

```
private void dgFlights_EditCommand(object source,
System.Web.UI.WebControls.DataGridCommandEventArgs e)
{
    dgFlights.EditItemIndex = e.Item.ItemIndex;
    dgFlights.DataBind();
}
```

The DataGridCommandEventArg object passed to the event handler contains the item index of the edited row, which we use to specify which row should be made editable.

Updating a Data Grid Row

After the editing operations, the user can select the Update button (which doesn't always look like a button, but you can see it to the left of the screenshot) in order to reflect the changes back to the database. In the following example the user can change the quantity of goods ordered in a basket:

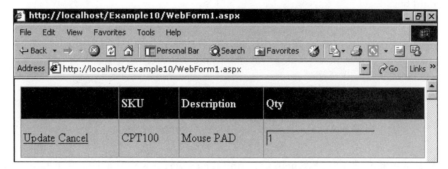

The Update button link will raise the `UpdateCommand` event, which we catch in order to update the data source with the new value:

```
private void dgBasket_UpdateCommand(object source,
System.Web.UI.WebControls.DataGridCommandEventArgs e)
{
  string strQTY = ((TextBox)e.Item.Cells[3].Controls[0]).Text;
  ds.Basket[0].Qty = System.Int16.Parse(strQTY);

  dgBasket.EditItemIndex = -1;
  dgBasket.DataBind();
}
```

Using the `Cells` collection exposed by the `DataGrid` component, we retrieve the text contained in the cell. If we didn't use a template for the column, the cell will always contain a single text field – so we only retrieve the first item in the controls collection. If the cell contains multiple components, we can retrieve them one at a time using their index in the `Controls` collection.

The Cancel button cancels the update operation and returns to the normal view. We use the `CancelCommand` event to implement this behavior:

```
private void dgBasket_CancelCommand(object source,
System.Web.UI.WebControls.DataGridCommandEventArgs e)
{
  dgBasket.EditItemIndex = -1;
  dgBasket.DataBind();
}
```

The first instruction puts all of the rows into normal mode without updating the data source, the second rebinds the data to the datagrid.

Deleting a DataGrid Row

The `DataGrid` operation that we will look at is row deletion. To add this feature, we must:

❑   Insert a Delete button object into the data grid, using the Property Builder dialog box

❑   Add an event handler for the `DeleteCommand` event

❑   Add the code to update the data source

The first two steps are very similar to operations we have already seen. The code required in the event handler could be:

```
private void dgBasket_DeleteCommand(object source,
System.Web.UI.WebControls.DataGridCommandEventArgs e)
{
  dsBasket.BasketRow row =
    ds.Basket.FindBySKU(e.Item.Cells[1].Text);
  ds.Basket.RemoveBasketRow(row);

  dgBasket.DataBind();
}
```

This handler, used the `FindBySKU` method to find the correct row in the dataset, is based on the primary key of the row that is being deleted. The `e.Item.Cells[1].Text` instruction retrieves the SKU value present on the selected item that is the primary key column for the template. It then removes that row from the dataset, and finally rebinds the datagrid to the data.

Breaking a DataGrid into Pages

If a datagrid contains a lot of records, it can be a good idea to display a limited number of rows per page, and allow users to move between pages. Usually, just ten rows are displayed for each page, but we can change this by setting the Page size in the Paging sheet of the Properties Builder:

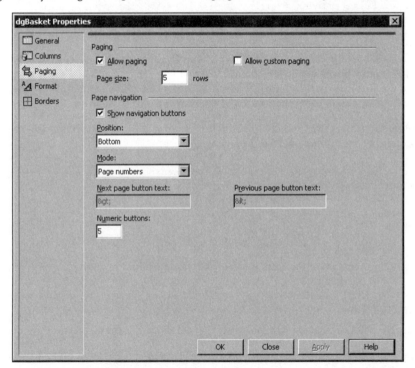

We also choose where to display the navigation buttons and whether to display navigation buttons as numbers or as Next/Previous buttons. To enable these settings, make sure Allow Paging is checked. This will cause the datagrid to display a new navigation bar, as shown in the next figure:

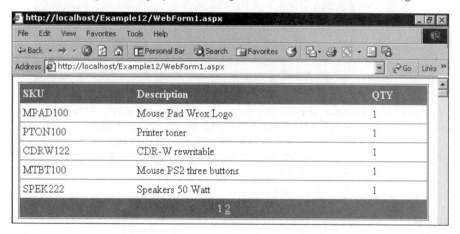

We have to attach some code to the PageIndexChanged event handler in order to manage the navigation. The code is really simple:

```
private void dgBasket_PageIndexChanged(object source,
System.Web.UI.WebControls.DataGridPageChangedEventArgs e)
{
  dgBasket.CurrentPageIndex = e.NewPageIndex;
  dgBasket.DataBind();
}
```

This sets the CurrentPageIndex property of the datagrid to the page index selected by the user.

DataGrid Window Component

The DataGrid window component offers similar features to the web control, but with more flexibility and power.

The big difference is how the data is managed. We no longer need to call the DataBind method repeatedly: the data source changes are reflected in the component immediately. Moreover, every datagrid operation, such as removing or modifying a record, is managed by the DataGrid component automatically. Even the sort operation is executed by the component without the need to write event handler code.

The DataGrid window component provides features that you don't find in the web control, because they cannot be represented in an HTML page. One of these is record navigation, which allows users to navigate among related tables – passing from parent records to child records using buttons provided by the component.

The following figure shows two tables are related in a single dataset object. The datagrid component allows the user to navigate between the tables:

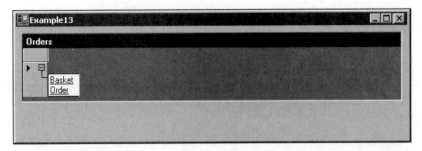

Setting the datagrid's **DataSource** property to a `DataView` allows us to use the **AllowEdit**, **AllowNew**, and **AllowDelete** dataview properties to either enable or disable features in the datagrid component. For example, setting the **AllowNew** property to **False** in the dataview prevents the data grid component from creating a new record in the data source. We can prevent the datagrid from allowing modfications, regardless of whether the data source is a dataview object, by setting the datagrid's **ReadOnly** property to **True**.

Summary

In this chapter we have seen how we can use Visual Studio .NET to create ADO.NET applications quickly and easily. We have found easy ways to implement common database access features into our applications. Using Visual Studio .NET, and very little code, we have learned to:

❑   Connect to a database

❑   Execute commands against a database

❑   Work with `DataAdapters`

❑   Create and use typed datasets

❑   Work with the `DataView` component

❑   Display data using the `DataGrid`

In later chapters we will see how we can use code, as well as visual tools, to give our applications far more flexibility.

Using DataReaders

The `RecordSet` that we used with ADO was a multi-talented beast. In days of yore, when two tiered, connected applications were the norm, the `RecordSet` provided us with connected functionality by utilizing server-side cursors. As application architectures evolved and n-tier, disconnected architectures gained favor, the `RecordSet` also had to evolve to provide for client-side cursors. Although the `RecordSet` coped admirably with its changing role, it was becoming cumbersome in its attempts to be all things to all people.

With ADO.NET, the `RecordSet` is no more. Instead we find ourselves with a whole host of objects that perform database-related tasks. Two of these objects are the `DataTable` and datareaders. The `DataTable` is the ADO.NET equivalent of the `RecordSet` in a disconnected state: it's a snapshot of some data taken at some point in time that can be manipulated as required and then persisted back to the database. The `DataReader` is ADO.NET's equivalent of a connected `RecordSet`: it allows us fast, forward-only, read-only access to a stream of data.

The datareaders in the .NET framework are available in two flavors: we have at our disposal the `SqlDataReader` and the `OleDbDataReader`. These two classes live in the `System.Data.SqlClient` and `System.Data.OleDb` namespaces respectively. If you cannot wait to find out more about these datareaders specifically then refer to the "*ADO.NET DataReaders*" section in this chapter.

The two datareaders vary slightly, but both provide the same things:

- ❑ Connected access
- ❑ High performance
- ❑ Small footprint
- ❑ Strongly typed data access

The datareaders achieve their high performance by utilizing an open connection to the database. It's not possible to create a disconnected `DataReader`. Of course, this high performance depends largely on the quality of our network, but with the advance of high-speed connections at home and in business this is becoming less of an issue.

`Datareaders` deal with a single row at a time; they don't provide bulk data retrieval. Hence this method of retrieving data only requires a very small footprint and won't gobble memory. This contrasts with the `DataTable`, which is stored in-memory and requires a chunk of memory for every single row it contains.

Using methods like `GetSqlInt32` (for SQL Server databases) or `GetInt32` (for other OLE DB databases) means that we can retrieve data from the row in a type safe manner. Gone are the days when we had to retrieve some generic data type and pray while we cast it to the required data type.

In this chapter we will be covering the following features and issues, and a little more along the way:

- ❑   The interfaces of the datareaders
- ❑   When to use the SqlDataReader or OleDbDataReader
- ❑   Retrieving data using both SQL and stored procedures
- ❑   Creating a simple, real-world application using the DataReader
- ❑   Performance issues

We will start with a quick note about the contents of the chapter; this will hopefully help you get the best out of what you are about to read.

A Note About the Chapter Contents

There really isn't a great deal of difference in the way we use the `SqlDataReader` and the `OleDbDataReader`, and because of this we will use both throughout the chapter. You'll see early on in this chapter that it isn't recommended to use `OleDbDataReader` against SQL Server 2000 and in the real world I wouldn't be using `OleDbDataReader` in my code. Nevertheless I think it's helpful to see how we use the `OleDbDataReader` and how similar it is in operation to the `SqlDataReader`.

Sometimes I'll refer simply to datareaders: whenever I do that I'm talking in generic terms, because the topic covers both the `SqlDataReader` and `OleDbDataReader` alike. In situations where there is a difference between the two datareaders, I'll highlight this clearly.

All the code in this chapter is written in C# and SQL Server 2000 was used as the backend. The examples all use the `Northwind` database that comes installed with SQL Server. In some examples I've used stored procedures – these are just standard stored procedures that come with `Northwind`; they haven't been modified in any way. Hopefully, this will make the examples in this chapter accessible to most of you reading this.

All the projects reference the `System.Data` assembly, which is automatically referenced when you create a C# Console project or Windows Application in Visual Studio .NET. The two main namespaces used are `System.Data.SqlClient` and `System.Data.OleDb` for the `SqlDataReader` and `OleDbDataReader` examples respectively. Where we access specific `SqlClient` data types we must also reference the `System.Data.SqlTypes` namespace.

Now we have that out of the way, let's look at the datareaders for real.

The Basics of a DataReader

In ADO.NET there is no base class for implementers of DataReaders to derive from. Instead, a class must implement two interfaces in order to provide the functionality required of a DataReader. These two interfaces are called IDataReader and IDataRecord. The IDataReader interface provides the methods and properties that allow us to traverse the result set(s) and query the DataReader for its state, while the IDataRecord interface provides methods and properties for accessing the data in the DataReader result set(s). Let's have a look at these interfaces in turn.

The IDataReader Interface

This interface defines a number of methods and properties that provide a user with a means of traversing result sets and getting details of the result set being dealt with. The tables below show the contents of the IDataReader interface:

Method	Description
Close	Closes the datareader object.
GetSchemaTable	Returns a DataTable that describes the schema of the datareader's result set.
NextResult	Moves the datareader to the next result set if one exists.
Read	Moves the datareader to the next record.

Property	Description
Depth	Gets a value indicating the depth of nesting for the current row. Although found on both datareaders, this property is only applicable to the OleDbDataReader.
IsClosed	Returns a Boolean indicating whether the datareader is closed.
RecordsAffected	Gets the number of records affected by the execution of the SQL statement. A value of -1 indicates that a select statement was executed. Any other values indicate the number of rows affected by either an update, delete or insert statement being executed.

I won't dwell too much on these methods and properties now, because over the course of the chapter we'll be seeing them quite a lot. Suffice it to say that from the table we should be able to see that the members of the IDataReader interface allow us to traverse, get schema information, and also check various states regarding the result set (or sets). Notice that none of these methods actually manipulate the result set contents; this is because datareaders are read-only.

The IDataRecord Interface

As we've just seen, the IDataReader interface allows us to move over the result set and get information regarding the schema, result set position etc. Once we've got our datareader, it's not much use if we can't actually access the data in the records. This is where the IDataRecord interface comes into play.

Through this interface we can access the column values for the current row in the datareader. The tables below show some of the methods and properties on this interface:

Method	Description
GetBoolean	Gets a Boolean value for a given column.
GetByte	Gets an 8-bit unsigned integer for a given column.
GetInt64	Gets a 64-bit signed integer for a given column.

Property	Description
FieldCount	Gets the number of columns in the current row.
Item	Gets a given column's value.

Generally, the methods on the `IDataRecord` interface take the form of `GetXXX`, where "XXX" is the data type to be retrieved. This provides us with a generic manner of retrieving just about any data type that can be stored in a database.

As well as finding these methods on a datareader, it's also quite likely that the datareader will provide database-specific data types in its implementation. A case in point is the `SqlDataReader`; this provides strongly typed methods for retrieving specific SQL types such as `GetSqlInt64` and `GetSqlMoney`. If we were to use the `OleDbDataReader` we would use the `GetInt64` and `GetDecimal` methods to try to retrieve the same data. Just by looking at the method names we can see that different types are being returned. This is most apparent if we compare the method names `GetSqlMoney` and `GetDecimal`. The `OleDb` provider doesn't have the concept of a "money" type at all so we can only retrieve `decimal` values, where as using the `SqlClient` provider we can retrieve a strongly typed `SqlMoney` type.

Through these interfaces the designers of `ADO.NET` have defined the minimum amount of functionality that `DataReaders` should implement to meet a user's needs. We'll now move on and see how the two `DataReaders` that come with `ADO.NET` both implement these interfaces to provide a standard and reasonably consistent method of retrieving and traversing data.

The ADO.NET DataReaders

With the current incarnation of ADO.NET we find ourselves with two datareaders to play with. These are known as the `SqlDataReader` and the `OleDbDataReader`, which can be found in the `System.Data.SqlClient` and `System.Data.OleDb` namespaces respectively.

The classes that live in these namespaces collectively make up ADO.NET's managed providers. Specifically the classes that make the `SqlClient` managed provider are:

❑   `SqlCommand, SqConnection, SqlDataAdapter, SqlDataReader, SqlParameter`

And the classes that make the `OleDb` managed provider are:

❑   `OleDbCommand, OleDbConnection, OleDbDataAdapter, OleDbDataReader, OleDbParameter`

For more information on the .NET Managed Providers, see Chapter 2.

The fact that these providers are managed means that the runtime will take care of things like memory management and interoperability, leaving us more time to concentrate on providing an elegant solution to a problem.

It's possible to use the `OleDbDataReader` against later versions of SQL Server, but not recommended. The simple reason for this is how the different `DataReaders` use their knowledge of the backend. By this, I mean that the `SqlDataReader` has got very specific knowledge of how best to communicate with the SQL Server, whereas the `OleDbDataReader` has to treat any database connection in the same way. The diagram below illustrates this:

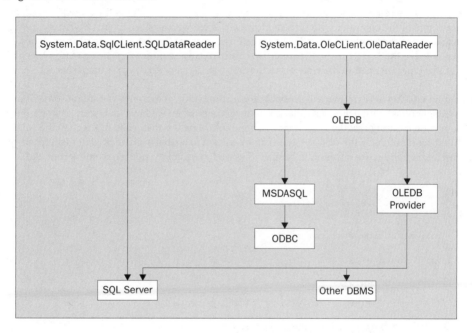

This shows how the `SqlDataReader` maximizes its knowledge of the backend database to efficiently manage data transfers. In this specific case, the `SqlDataReader` directly communicates with the data connection using SQL Server's Tabular Data Stream (TDS) protocol. If we compare this to how the `OleDbDataReader` would access SQL Server, we can see that it has several layers to go through before it reaches the database.

However, it is not only a performance issue: using the correct datareader for the backend can also provide us with strongly typed access to the data. Consider the two examples below:

```
OleDbDataReader reader = command.ExecuteReader();

while ( reader.Read() )
{
    Console.WriteLine ( reader.GetDateTime(2) );
}
```

```
SqlDataReader reader = command.ExecuteReader();

while ( reader.Read () )
{
    Console.WriteLine ( reader.GetSqlDateTime(2) );
}
```

At this point I don't want to get bogged down in the details of the code. For now it's enough to say that both examples create a datareader and then use it to read the results that the command generated. Remember that both datareaders are connected to SQL Server. The piece of code we're most interested in is the `Console.WriteLine` code in the `while` loop. In the first example, we're using `reader.GetDateTime(2)` to retrieve a generic `DateTime` object. This is fine, it works well, and it prints out the contents of the column to the screen. However, since we know we have a SQL Server database, why shouldn't we get at a strongly typed SQL data type? This is what the second code example does. By using the special knowledge the `SqlDataReader` has, we can explicitly request a `SqlDateTime` object. To use objects of this type, we need to have access to the `System.Data.SqlTypes` namespace.

Anyone from a COM background will probably have come into contact with variants at some point. Variants are not strongly typed – there is always that air of uncertainty when we have a variant. It's not unheard of to write more code ensuring that the variant is what we think/hope it is than actually creating the value in the first place! In the world of .NET the `object` type can be treated in a similar manner, with methods or properties that return an `object` we're never entirely sure what we have until we perform some sort of check on it such as:

```
object theValue = GetValue ();

if ( theValue is string )
{
    // do something with a string
}
else if ( theValue is int )
{
    // do something with an int
}
```

In the code above we have a mythical method called `GetValue`, which returns an `object` to us. We then have a series of if statements that use the `is` operator to check the underlying type of the returned `object`. Once we've found the correct type we can then do something with it. This is a prime example of non-type safe access. It leads to untidy, error-prone code. If we knew the method returned an `int` or `string` then the code would be much simpler and safer-this is the main advantage of using type safe methods wherever possible.

DataReader Operations

The next few sections will highlight the main functionality of the datareaders. Among other things we will see how we can traverse results sets, how data can be retrieved, and how to get detailed information about the result set we're working with. To end this section, we'll bring together a number of the most important aspects of the datareader by creating a simple application.

Let's start by looking at the basics of using a datareader.

Creating a DataReader

It is not possible to create a datareader explicitly. The constructors for datareader objects are marked as `public internal`, which means that only objects in the same assembly as the `DataReader` classes can create a `DataReader`. To gain access to a `DataReader` we must first of all have a `Command` object. We can create a useable datareader through the `Command` object.

As we saw in chapter 2, a `command` object represents a SQL statement or a stored procedure. In ADO.NET there are two `Command` objects: these are `SqlCommand` and `OleDbCommand`. All `command` objects in ADO.NET implement the `IDbCommand` interface. The `IDbCommand` interface provides a template for all `Command` objects. Through this interface we can look at the SQL command to be executed, any command parameters, the database connection, and so on. It's through one of the methods on this interface that we can create a datareader. The method in question is called `ExecuteReader`. We'll have a quick look at the `ExecuteReader` method next.

The ExecuteReader Method

This is where it all begins, with a call to `ExecuteReader`. This method executes the SQL or stored procedure that the `Command` object represents and returns a datareader object.

There are two overrides of the `ExecuteReader` method: the first takes no parameters and the second takes an enumerated value of `CommandBehavior` type that is defined in `System.Data`. The table below shows the possible values and their use:

Value	Use
CloseConnection	Closes the connection when the datareader is closed.
KeyInfo	The query returns column and primary key information. Using `KeyInfo` with the SQL Server Managed Provider causes a FOR BROWSE clause to be appended to the statement being executed. This may have side effects, such as interference with the use of SET FMTONLY ON.
SchemaOnly	The query returns column information only and does not affect the database state.
SequentialAccess	The results are read sequentially to the column. This enables applications to read large binary values using methods such as `GetBytes`.
SingleResult	The query returns a single result. Execution of the query may affect the database state.
SingleRow	The query expects to return a single row. This may improve performance because providers can use this information to optimize the command.

So we can either get default behavior by using the parameterless method:

```
OleDbDataReader reader = command.ExecuteReader ();
```

Or we can be more specific in what we want and use the second implementation like this:

```
OleDbDataReader reader = command.ExecuteReader (CommandBehavior.SingleRow);
```

139

We can also use combinations of `CommandBehavior` values. So, for example, we could write:

```
OleDbDataReader reader = command.ExecuteReader
    (CommandBehavior.CloseConnection | CommandBehavior.SingleResult)
```

This particular piece of code would cause the `Connection` object to close when the datareader closes and specifies that only a single result set should be returned regardless of how many result sets are found.

I'm not going to dwell any further on this method or the `Command` objects.

Creating and Using a DataReader

Now, let's have some code. We've already briefly seen an example of a datareader being created, but now we'll go into it in slightly more depth. Here is a simple case using a datareader:

```
OleDbConnection conn = new OleDbConnection
    ( "Provider=SQLOLEDB;Data Source=localhost;Initial Catalog=Northwind;"
    + "Integrated Security=SSPI;" );

OleDbCommand command = new OleDbCommand ( "select * from CUSTOMERS", conn );

conn.Open ();

OleDbDataReader reader = command.ExecuteReader ();

while ( reader.Read () )
{
    // code in here
}

reader.Close ();

conn.Close ();
```

For demonstration purposes, this example uses the `OleDb` managed provider, even though it's accessing a SQL Server 2000 database. The first thing we do is to create an `OleDbConnection` object to give us the connection to the database.

Next we construct the `Command` object that will be used to execute the command. Again, because we're using the `OleDb` provider, we're using the `OleDbCommand` class. We construct the `OleDbCommand` object by passing it the SQL we want executed and the connection. Next, the connection to the database is opened. If the connection isn't opened before we call `ExecuteReader` then an `InvalidOperationException` will be raised. This behavior differs from the data adapter objects. A data adapter will open a connection when executing a command if it's not already open and then close it when finished. The connection **must** always be open before the datareader is created using `ExecuteReader`. Finally, with the connection open we can execute the SQL against the database; this returns us (in this case) an `OleDbDataReader`.

Using the `Read` method on the datareader, we can now traverse the records generated by the SQL. The code example above simply keeps calling `Read` until it returns `false`, at which point there are no more records in the result set. The final two method calls close the datareader and the connection.

It's worth mentioning the `Close` method on the datareader. Unless `CommandBehavior.CloseConnection` was passed to `ExecuteReader`, this doesn't close the connection that the datareader is using: it simply closes the datareader itself. In practical terms, this means that other objects can now use the connection that the datareader was using. The sharing of an existing connection is more desirable than creating a new one. Creating and opening connections is an extensive process that should be avoided wherever possible. If we tried to use the connection without closing the datareader, we'd get an `InvalidOperationException` telling us that the connection was already being used.

Call the `Close` method before trying to use the connection again. An open datareader going out of scope **does not** free the connection. So, to summarize this section, we should note that:

❑ Datareaders can only be created using command objects

❑ The connection must always be open before we call `ExecuteReader`

❑ Use the `ExecuteReader` method to create a datareader

❑ Always call `Close` on the datareader when it's finished with; failing to do so will prevent other objects using the connection

Now we've seen how we go about creating a datareader, we will look at what we can do with the datareader in more detail.

Simple Data Retrieval With the DataReader

Now we'll move on to a fuller example. We're going to create an `OleDbCommand` object that selects all the records from the `Orders` table in the `Northwind` database. Using this `Command` object, we'll create an `OleDbDataReader`, read all the records, and dump them to the console. So, let's have a look at the code (this code is in the `SqlDataRetrieval` and `OleDbDataRetrieval` projects).

```
OleDbConnection conn = new OleDbConnection ("Provider=SQLOLEDB;Data
Source=localhost;Initial Catalog=Northwind;Integrated Security=SSPI;");

OleDbCommand selectCommand = new OleDbCommand("select * from ORDERS", conn);

conn.Open ();

OleDbDataReader reader = selectCommand.ExecuteReader ( );

while ( reader.Read () )
{
    object id = reader["OrderID"];
    object date = reader["OrderDate"];
    object freight = reader["Freight"];

    Console.WriteLine ( "{0}\t{1}\t\t{2}", id, date, freight );
}

reader.Close ();
conn.Close ();
```

As we have seen before, the first thing we do is create a `Connection` object. In this case we're using the `OleDb` managed provider, so we create an `OleDbConnection`. Next, we create the `SqlCommand` object. This represents the Transact-SQL command we wish to execute, and will yield the `OleDbDataReader` to us.

Before we call ExecuteReader, we open the connection; if we fail to do this, the SqlCommand object will raise an exception. Once ExecuteReader is called (assuming everything worked) we're in a position to read directly from the Northwind database.

We traverse over the records by using the Read method on the DataReader. This has the effect of moving the DataReader to the next record. When a DataReader is first returned, it is actually positioned before the first record in the result set. This being the case, we must call Read before trying to access any of the values in the DataReader columns. Failure to do so raises an exception.

> **Read must always be called before any of the data access methods are used.**

Now we are into the while loop. Each time Read is called we advance to the next record. If Read is called and there are no more records left, then false is returned and the while loop terminates.

Let's look at the code in the loop. The first three lines are the most interesting. Using the Item indexer property, we retrieve values for three of the columns in the datareader. Any object that supports an indexer property essentially allows us to treat that object as an array. If we consider how we might retrieve an element from an array:

```
int []values = new int[] {1, 5, 9, 15, 26};

int theValue = values[3];
```

We can see that the syntax values[3] isn't that different to our previous example where we use reader["OrderID"]. The main obvious difference is that when we retrieve the integer from our array we specify the element position, in this case element 3 – which would give us the value 15. But when we use the datareader indexer we specify the column name – OrderID. We could, if wanted to, specify the ordinal value of the column OrderID, which is 0. To do this we'd write:

```
object id = reader[0];
```

It has the same effect as specifying the column name (though as we'll see at the end of chapter it does improve performance). The ordinal values of columns are always zero-based, so the first column in the table has an ordinal value of 0, the next column has a value of 1 and so on.

Note that the indexer has returned us values of type object. Using the datareader indexer always returns object types. This is because an indexer has to be able to return any type of data that can be stored in a database and in .NET the object type is the base class of all objects. By returning an object an indexer is capable of returning anything. In this example, the final line of the loop outputs the values to the console. In many cases we'd probably want to access the data in a type-safe manner, which we will learn more about later.

The final two lines close the datareader and the connection. If we don't close the datareader, no other objects will be able to use the connection. Connections are scarce resources and shouldn't be held on to for a moment longer than they're needed.

> **Always close the `DataReader` as soon as it's finished with.**

If we run the program, the output looks like this:

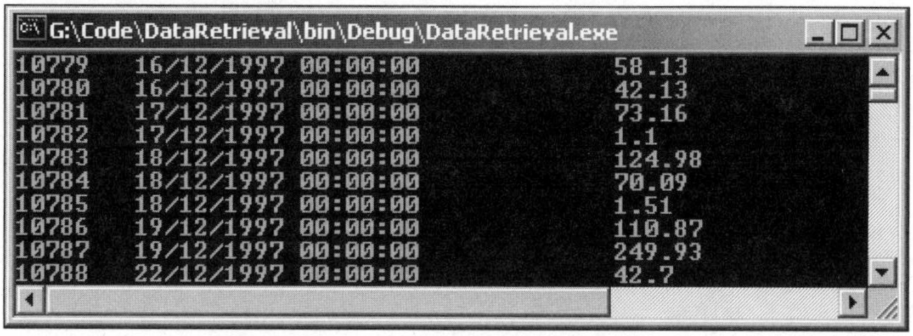

The output shows a list containing three columns. In order, it shows `OrderID`, `OrderDate`, and finally the `Freight` column from the `Orders` table.

That's how we execute SQL statements – as you can see, it's pretty straightforward. Now, we'll move on to executing stored procedures.

Executing Stored Procedures with a DataReader

We have seen how to execute simple SQL statements against the database, so now we're going to look at how we use the command object and the datareader to execute a stored procedure. We'll be using the `CustOrdersDetail` stored procedure that comes with `Northwind` in this example. The stored procedure SQL is shown below; don't worry too much about its contents, all we need to know is that it takes an order ID and returns the details for that order:

```
CREATE PROCEDURE CustOrdersDetail @OrderID int
AS
SELECT ProductName,
    UnitPrice=ROUND(Od.UnitPrice, 2),
    Quantity,
    Discount=CONVERT(int, Discount * 100),
    ExtendedPrice=ROUND(CONVERT(money, Quantity * (1 - Discount) * Od.UnitPrice),
2)
FROM Products P, [Order Details] Od
WHERE Od.ProductID = P.ProductID and Od.OrderID = @OrderID
```

The `Command` object does most of the work when executing stored procedures. We still use the datareader in exactly the same way we normally would. The entire code for the example can be found in the `SqlStoredProcedureExample` project. As usual, the code for the `OleDb` provider is almost identical and this can be found in the `OleDbStoredProcedureExample`. The listing below shows the main method of the `SqlClient` code:

```
SqlConnection conn = new SqlConnection ( "Initial Catalog=Northwind;Data
Source=localhost;Integrated Security=SSPI" );

SqlCommand storedProcCommand = new SqlCommand ( "CustOrdersDetail", conn );
storedProcCommand.CommandType = CommandType.StoredProcedure;
storedProcCommand.Parameters.Add ( "@OrderID", 10248 );
```

```
    conn.Open ();

    ArrayList rowList = new ArrayList ();

    SqlDataReader reader = storedProcCommand.ExecuteReader ( );

    while ( reader.Read () )
    {
        object []values = new object[ reader.FieldCount ];

        // retrieves all the fields values into an array of objects
        reader.GetValues ( values );

        rowList.Add ( values );
    }

    reader.Close ();
    conn.Close ();

    foreach ( object []row in rowList )
    {
        foreach ( object column in row )
            Console.WriteLine ( column );

        Console.WriteLine ( "\n" );
    }
```

Now we'll look at the code in more detail. First we'll have a look at how we create the `Connection` object. In this example we're using the `SqlClient` managed provider, so we'll be creating a `SqlConnection` object:

```
SqlCommand storedProcCommand = new SqlCommand ( "CustOrdersDetail", conn );
storedProcCommand.CommandType = CommandType.StoredProcedure;
storedProcCommand.Parameters.Add ( "@OrderID", 10248 );
```

The first line constructs the `SqlCommand` object, and we pass in two parameters. The second parameter is the usual connection object; it's the first parameter that's more interesting. Instead of a SQL string, we've passed in the name of the stored procedure as it exists in the `Northwind` database – in this case `CustOrdersDetail`. This tells the `SqlCommand` object which stored procedure to execute.

The second line tells the `Command` object that a stored procedure is going to be executed. We do this by setting the `CommandType` property to `StoredProcedure`. If we didn't do this, the `Command` would try to execute as a normal SQL statement and a syntax exception would be raised.

Finally we need to add some parameters to the command. The `CustOrdersDetail` stored procedure expects to receive the ID of a customer order, so we add a new parameter to the `SqlCommand`'s parameter collection. The name of the parameter is `@OrderID` and the order we're interested in is `10248`. Note the use of the @ symbol? Ultimately, all the information in the `Command` object is constructed to make a SQL statement. The @ symbol in a SQL statement is used to denote a parameter.

Now we're ready to create the datareader:

```
ArrayList rowList = new ArrayList ();

SqlDataReader reader = storedProcCommand.ExecuteReader ( );

while ( reader.Read () )
{
    object []values = new object[ reader.FieldCount ];

    reader.GetValues ( values );

    rowList.Add ( values );
}
```

I've introduced a couple of new properties and methods this time, so we'll have a look at them first. The first line in the `while` loop is creating an array of objects. Each object in the array represents a column in the datareader. We know how many columns are in the datareader by using the `FieldCount` property.

Now we have the array of objects we need to get some values. If we wanted, we could get each value individually and add it to the array; another way is to use the `GetValues` method. This method will populate our object array with the column values currently in the datareader. The tradeoff for this ease of use is the fact that we lose the type safety, but, as usual, that's a choice that has to be made in the context of the development situation.

If you've been wondering why we created an `ArrayList` at the top of code sample, you're about to find out! In the last line of code we add the object array to the `ArrayList` object called `rowList`. Why are we doing this? Well, bear in mind that while the datareader is open. It's effectively "blocking" the connection so that no other objects can access it. It is often a good idea to cache away the values retrieved from the datareader and process them after the datareader is closed. The less time we're blocking the data connection the better.

> **Process datareader results after the datareader is closed.**

Finally, after we've closed the datareader and the connection, we can output the retrieved values to the screen. We use the following code to do this:

```
foreach ( object []row in rowList )
{
    foreach ( object column in row )
        Console.WriteLine ( column );

    Console.WriteLine ( "\n" );
}
```

This code is fairly straightforward. By this point, we have an `ArrayList` containing arrays of objects, and each object in the array represents a value from a column in the datareader. So, in the outer loop we get the array of column values, and in the inner loop we iterate over the column values and output them to the `Console`. Finally, we write a blank line to the screen: this just makes the output clearer to see.

If we run the program we get the following results:

```
H:\Code\SqlStoredProcedureExample\bin\Debug\SqlStoredProcedureExample.e...   _ □ ×
Queso Cabrales
14
12
0
168


Singaporean Hokkien Fried Mee
9.8
10
0
98


Mozzarella di Giovanni
34.8
5
0
174
```

If we wanted to execute a slightly more complex stored procedure then the only code we have to modify relates to the Command object. Let's have a quick look at how we modify the code to execute a stored procedure that takes more than one parameter.

For this example we'll use the Sales by Year procedure that we also find in the Northwind database. We can see the modified code below:

```
SqlCommand storedProcCommand =
    new SqlCommand ( "Sales by Year", conn );

storedProcCommand.CommandType = CommandType.StoredProcedure;

SqlDateTime startDate = new SqlDateTime ( 1996, 7, 16 );

SqlDateTime endDate = new SqlDateTime ( 1996, 8, 12 );

storedProcCommand.Parameters.Add ( "@Beginning_Date", startDate );
storedProcCommand.Parameters.Add ( "@Ending_Date", endDate );
```

I've omitted the rest of the code for the sake of brevity. Sales by Year lists all the sales made between the start year and end year. These two values have to be passed in as parameters. The above code shows how we create two SqlDateTime objects – the start date and the end dates between which we want the stored procedure to search. We then have to add these two parameters to the Command's parameter collection. The procedure expects the parameters to be called @Beginning_Date and @Ending_Date.

That's it! No more changes are required to the code to get it to work. I haven't included a code example to show how this is done because it's pretty easy to do. If you've tried this code out then the results should be something like this:

That concludes this section on using datareaders with stored procedures. As we have seen, the datareader is quite versatile, and it's quite easy to use the datareader to traverse a result set and output the records from it without ever having to know what the data is.

We've now covered traversing simple result sets generated by both the execution of SQL and of stored procedures. Sometimes, though, the command we execute may generate numerous result sets. We will now look at how the datareaders are used in these situations.

Navigating Multiple Result Sets

It is generally desirable to avoid making multiple trips to the data layer. The overhead of numerous calls across a network and the increase in network traffic can seriously affect the performance of an application. The effects of unnecessary calls become even more apparent when the amount of data being transferred is sizeable. One of the ways to achieve this is by executing multiple statements in one call to the database. We can do this easily using the Command object.

The code below shows how we'd run multiple statements in one call. This code uses the OleDb provider, but the SqlClient code works in exactly the same way. Note that the SELECT statement we used here is being run against SQL Server and may not be valid against all databases:

```
string select = "select * from Categories; select * from customers";

OleDbCommand command = new OleDbCommand ( select, conn );

conn.Open ();
OleDbDataReader reader = command.ExecuteReader ();
```

We can see that the SELECT statement is selecting data from the Categories and Customers tables. In the case of SQL being run against SQL Server, we separate the two commands with a semi-colon. Up to the point when we call ExecuteReader, the code should look pretty familiar.

The datareader we now have at our disposal has two result sets: the first contains the records from the `Categories` table and the second has the data for the `Customers` table. Now we need to traverse these results; the code below shows how we do this:

```
do
{
   while ( reader.Read () )
   {
      Console.WriteLine ( "{0}\t\t{1}", reader[0], reader[1] );
   }
} while ( reader.NextResult () );
```

Now we have multiple result sets, we need to traverse the data in a slightly different way. To move through the result sets we use the method `NextResult`; this method is defined on the `IDataReader` interface. It works in a similar way to the `Read` method in that once there are no more result sets to navigate it returns `false`. If we look at the code, though, we'll see that we use the `NextResult` method in a do...while, rather than the usual while...do. This is because when datareaders are returned they are already positioned on the first result set. If we were to use the while...do construct, we'd immediately skip over the first result set. It is easy to forget this and try to use the `NextResult` method in the same way we'd use the `Read` method, so if you seem to be missing your first result set, check that you're not calling `NextResult` before you retrieve any data the first time round.

> **Calling `NextResult` immediately on a newly returned DataReader with multiple result sets skips the first result set.**

The inner loop simply advances the datareader over the records in the result set and prints out the first two columns. Once the first result has been traversed we call `NextResult` – in our example this would then move us to the result set for the `Customers` table. We then dump the records for this table. The next time we call `NextResult`, it will return `false` because we've processed all the result sets.

Accessing the Data in a Type-Safe Manner

We have learned a fair amount about datareaders. We know how to traverse single or multiple result sets and how we get a result sets contents via the indexer. So far we haven't explored using any other method of accessing data, like using the type-safe methods that all datareaders implement. This is what we'll look at now.

As we saw earlier, indexers allow us to access columns in the datareader either using the column name or the column ordinal (the zero-based position of the column in the table). The drawback with using the indexer is that the objects returned have to be cast to the data type we require.

We'll now revisit one of the first examples we looked at and convert it so that the code is type safe. Here is the original version:

```
while ( reader.Read () )
{
   object id = reader["OrderID"];
   object date = reader["OrderDate"];
   object freight = reader["Freight"];

   Console.WriteLine ( "{0}\t{1}\t\t{2}", id, date, freight );
}
```

As we can see from the code above, when we access any of these columns we have no idea what's actually being returned. We're completely data-type agnostic. Is this a good thing? Sometimes, but usually not. There are advantages of being type-safe in terms of performance and the maintainability of code.

We now use the other methods of the `IDataRecord` interface. These are the methods that follow the `GetXXX` convention we looked at earlier. Using these methods, we could make the above code type-safe by changing it thus (this code is in the `OleDbTypeSafeDataRetrieval` project):

```
while ( reader.Read () )
{
    int id = reader.GetInt32 ( 0 );
    DateTime date = reader.GetDateTime ( 3 );
    decimal freight = reader.GetDecimal ( 7 );

    Console.WriteLine ( "{0}\t{1}\t\t{2}", id, date, freight );
}
```

And there we have it: nice, type-safe code. Actually, is it that nice? In some ways, but now we have to access the columns using their ordinal values. A simple way round this is to define constant values somewhere in your class to make it clearer what column you're after. So, we might add something like this:

```
private const int OrderID = 0;
private const int OrderDate = 3;
private const int Freight = 7;
```

Now we can use these constant values to access the column values:

```
DateTime date = reader.GetDateTime ( OrderDate );
```

Now that's much clearer. Of course, there's the problem of maintainability isn't there? If it's a new project and your database schema is constantly "evolving" then keeping these values in sync with the schema could be a nightmare.

The `GetOrdinal` method of the datareader provides a great way to work around this. `GetOrdinal` takes the column name as a parameter, and returns that column's ordinal position. We want to define a 'constant' value, but it needs to be the result of the `GetOrdinal` method call. Therefore it cannot be assigned until after the datareader is open. Instead of declaring constants we would declare read-only variables, and not assign a value yet:

```
private readonly int OrderID;
private readonly int OrderDate;
private readonly int Freight;
```

We can then assign a value to the variable in the class's constructor, but nowhere else:

```
OrderID = reader.GetOrdinal("OrderID");
OrderDate = reader.GetOrdinal("OrderDate");
Freight = reader.GetOrdinal("Freight");
```

Now we can use type-safe methods to access the data, without needing to know at design time in what order the columns will appear. As an added bonus, the process of looking up a column by name is quite a resource-intensive operation. Using GetOrdinal, we only do this once. This is slightly slower than using constants, but in many cases might provide the best solution.

There is one issue here though. To assign the ordinal value to a read-only variable, the DataReader needs to be available the class's constructor. There are three ways around this:

❑ Assume that the ordinal won't change and assign at design time, as above

❑ Don't use read-only variables for this purpose, stick with normal ones

❑ Use the datareader in such a way that it can be loaded in a class's constructor

Deciding when to use each solution will depend one weighing up how likely the ordinal position of columns is to change, how important it is to protect the variable from tampering, and whether it is efficient to load the DataReader as soon as the class loads.

Using a variable instead of a constant will impair performance slightly. For really good performance, we could use the read-only variable and GetOrdinal method while the database schema is still changing, and then replace the read-only declaration with a constant once we know that this won't change.

SQL Server Types

There is one final way of accessing this data; so far we've looked at using the indexer and the type safe methods that all DataReaders have by virtue of implementing the IDataRecord interface. Remember that in this example we have been making use of the OleDb managed provider.

Those of us who have SQL Server 7 or later can use the SqlClient providers and access the "real" SQL types.

In order to do this we must now reference some different namespaces:

```
using System.Data.SqlClient;
using System.Data.SqlTypes;
```

The System.Data.SqlClient namespace contains the objects that make up the SqlClient provider and the System.Data.SqlTypes namespace contains the definitions for the SQL data types we will use.

The actual changes to the code itself are not difficult (this code can be found in the SqlTypeSafeDataRetrieval project):

```
SqlConnection conn = new SqlConnection ( "Initial Catalog=Northwind;" +
    "DataSource=localhost;Integrated Security=SSPI" );

SqlCommand selectCommand = new SqlCommand ( "select * from ORDERS", conn );

conn.Open ();

SqlDataReader reader = selectCommand.ExecuteReader ( );

while ( reader.Read () )
{
```

```
    SqlInt32 id = reader.GetSqlInt32 ( OrderID );
    SqlDateTime date = reader.GetSqlDateTime ( OrderDate );
    SqlMoney freight = reader.GetSqlMoney ( Freight );

    Console.WriteLine ( "{0}\t{1}\t\t{2}", id, date, freight );
}
reader.Close ();
conn.Close ();
```

Of course we're now using `SqlConnection`, `SqlCommand`, and `SqlDataReader`, but notice that once we have renamed them they are still used in exactly the same way (also bear in mind the connection string is slightly different).

The really interesting changes are to be found inside our `while` loop. Notice now that we're getting "proper" SQL types and not generic OLE DB types? So, for example, `GetInt32` has been replaced with `GetSqlInt32`. To my mind, the most interesting change is the line where we access the `Freight` column. Previously we wrote:

```
decimal freight = reader.GetDecimal ( Freight );
```

We had to do that because OLE DB doesn't have any concept of the `SQLMoney` type. Now we can write:

```
SqlMoney freight = reader.GetSqlMoney ( Freight );
```

In real terms `SqlMoney` wraps a `decimal` value anyway, but it just further clarifies what types we're dealing with and it's also bullet proof in that any changes that Microsoft makes to the `SqlMoney` type in the future will be picked up automatically. Having specific types enables us to define methods that work with money that would not be relevant for all decimal values, and force these methods to accept only money types.

Getting the Result Set's Schema

It's quite often useful to get the result set's schema. The datareader provides a message that does just this. It's called `GetSchemaTable` and it's defined on the `IDataReader` interface.

In order to illustrate the power of this method we'll have a look at a small Windows application I've created. The sourcecode can be found in the `SqlGetSchemaExample` and `OleDbGetSchemaExample` projects. We'll look at the `OleDb` provider example here.

The application is pretty simple: the main form has a `DataGrid` component and a single `Button` control. I've added an event handler for the button and all the code we require goes in there. Let's have a look at this event handler:

```
private void button1_Click(object sender, System.EventArgs e)
{
    OleDbConnection connection = new OleDbConnection
      ("Provider=SQLOLEDB;Data Source=localhost;Initial "
      + "Catalog=Northwind;Integrated Security=SSPI;");

    OleDbCommand comm = new OleDbCommand ( "ORDERS", connection );

    comm.CommandType = CommandType.TableDirect;
```

```
        connection.Open ();

        OleDbDataReader reader = comm.ExecuteReader (
                            CommandBehavior.SchemaOnly );

        this.dataGrid1.SetDataBinding ( reader.GetSchemaTable (), "" );

        reader.Close ();
        connection.Close ();
    }
```

The basic outline of this is probably starting to look pretty familiar. The first line of interest is creating the OleDbCommand. Note that we pass through the name of a table in Northwind, Orders. On it's own this obviously isn't a valid SQL command, but the next line sets the CommandType property to TableDirect. This means that all the columns for the Orders table will be retrieved: it's the equivalent of writing SELECT * FROM ORDERS. This functionality isn't available to the SqlClient provider, so we'd have to use the full SELECT statement; trying to set TableDirect on a SqlCommand will cause an exception to be raised.

Next we open the connection and call ExecuteReader. This time, though, we're passing through a parameter. The SchemaOnly value tells the command that no result sets are to be returned, we're just interested in the schema that would be generated on executing the SQL or stored procedure. If we were to specify SchemaOnly and then call reader.Read, a value of false would be returned immediately, because there are no results.

Finally we call GetSchemaTable on the datareader. This will return a DataTable that represents the entire schema for the result set (or would-be result in this case, don't forget we have no results) that's returned. We can bind this DataTable directly to the DataGrid component and that's what the SetDataBinding method does. The output from the OleDb example can be seen below:

	ColumnName	ColumnOrdin	ColumnSize	NumericPreci	NumericScale	DataType	ProviderType	IsLong	A
▶	OrderID	1	4	10	255	System.Int32	3	☐	
	CustomerID	2	5	255	255	System.Strin	130	☐	
	EmployeeID	3	4	10	255	System.Int32	3	☐	
	OrderDate	4	16	23	3	System.Date	135	☐	
	RequiredDate	5	16	23	3	System.Date	135	☐	
	ShippedDate	6	16	23	3	System.Date	135	☐	
	ShipVia	7	4	10	255	System.Int32	3	☐	
	Freight	8	8	19	255	System.Deci	6	☐	
	ShipName	9	40	255	255	System.Strin	202	☐	
	ShipAddress	10	60	255	255	System.Strin	202	☐	
	ShipCity	11	15	255	255	System.Strin	202	☐	
	ShipRegion	12	15	255	255	System.Strin	202	☐	
	ShipPostalCo	13	10	255	255	System.Strin	202	☐	
	ShipCountry	14	15	255	255	System.Strin	202	☐	
＊									

Form1

Go

If we were to run the `SqlClient` example we'd get a slightly different output from the `OleDb` example, we'd see some columns ordered slightly differently and a couple of the columns containing different values. This is simply down to how the two providers interpret and present the data they receive; for example the `OleDbDataReader` will return a column size of 16 for `DateTime` types while the `SqlDataReader` will return a column size of 8.

Being able to get the entire schema like this is extremely handy; a simple example of where we might use this can be seen in the application we create later on. Perhaps more importantly it's also extremely fast – far faster than doing something like creating a `DataTable`, selecting data into it, and then trying to work out the schema by enumerating the `DataColumns` on the table. For those of you that are curious how this might be achieved refer to the `SqlEmulateSchemaTable` and `OleDbEmulateSchemaTable` projects.

If we look at the screenshot, we can work out the structure of the `DataTable` that's been returned to us by `GetSchemaTable`. Each row in the `DataTable` represents a column from the result set and each column contains a discrete piece of information about the result set's column schema.

So, for example, if we look at the first row we can see that the column it represents is the `OrderID` column: it's the first column in the table (as denoted by the value 1 in the `ColumnOrdinal` column) and if we look in the `DataType` column we can see that its .NET type is `Int32`.

Given that it's not possible to see all the information available in the schema table on this page, I'd thoroughly recommend running one of the applications to see the kind of information you can retrieve.

We'll now move on and bring all of this datareader functionality together to create a slightly more useful application.

Bringing it all Together

In this section we are going to be looking at an application that lets us browse the orders that are stored in the `Northwind` database. We'll use SQL, stored procedures, and the `GetSchemaTable` method to provide us with a simple and fast way of viewing details for a particular order.

The two projects, `SqlBrowser` and `OleDbBrowser`, have the source code for this application. I won't be showing all the code in these pages simply because a lot of the code generated to create the GUI is of no concern to us. I'll be concentrating on four main methods.

The main GUI for the application looks like this:

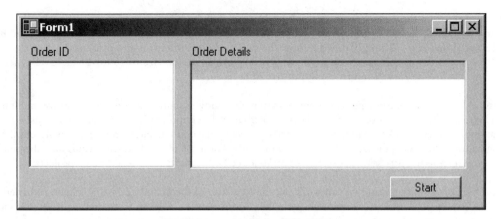

I've added two event handlers: one to handle the **Start** button being clicked, and one for the selection in the **Order ID** column changing. We'll begin by looking at the code for the **Start** button.

```
private void button1_Click(object sender, System.EventArgs e)
{
    SqlCommand command = new SqlCommand ("select OrderID from
                        ORDERS",this.connection);

    this.connection.Open ();

    SqlDataReader reader = command.ExecuteReader ( );

    while ( reader.Read () )
    {
        this.orderIDsList.Items.Add ( reader.GetInt32 ( 0 ) );
    }

    reader.Close ();
    this.connection.Close ();
}
```

This method is pretty straightforward. We create a `SqlCommand` that will select just the `OrderID` column from the `Orders` table. As usual we open the connection and call `ExecuteReader`. By this point we should be quite comfortable with what's happening in the `while` loop. As we read each record in we add the value from the `OrderID` column to the **Order ID** list. We've only selected a single column in this code so we're pretty safe in using `reader.GetInt32(0)` – there are no more columns in the datareader.

Once we have clicked the **Start** button we've populated a listbox with all the order IDs from the `Orders` table. Now we need to add a handler so that as we click on an order ID in the list, the order details appear in the `ListView` (the `ListView` class is located in the `System.Windows.Forms` namespace). The event handler looks like this:

```
private void orderIDsList_SelectedIndexChanged(object sender, System.EventArgs e)
{
    int orderID = Convert.ToInt32 ( this.orderIDsList.SelectedItem );

    SqlCommand storedProcCommand = new SqlCommand ( "CustOrdersDetail",
                        this.connection );
```

```
storedProcCommand.CommandType = CommandType.StoredProcedure;
storedProcCommand.Parameters.Add ( "@OrderID", orderID );

this.connection.Open ();

ArrayList rowList = new ArrayList ();

SqlDataReader reader = storedProcCommand.ExecuteReader ( );

while ( reader.Read () )
{
    object []values = new object[ reader.FieldCount ];

    reader.GetValues ( values );

    rowList.Add ( values );
}

if ( m_columnsSet == false )
{
    DataTable schema = reader.GetSchemaTable ();
    SetColumnHeaders ( schema );
}

reader.Close ();
this.connection.Close ();

PopulateOrderDetails ( rowList );
}
```

This code is almost exactly the same as that covered in the section on stored procedures, so I won't explain all of it. The first line is new: this line gets the currently selected item in the "Order ID" list and converts it to an `int`. This value is then used as the order ID when we add a new parameter to the command object.

As usual we get all the values from the records in the `while` loop and add them to an `ArrayList`. Now, the next bit of code is slightly different. We need to add columns to the `ListView` so that we can view the order details – this isn't something we only want to do once so I've declared a global variable, `m_columnsSet`. If `m_columnsSet` is true then we've already added columns to the `ListView` and there's no need to do it again, otherwise we'll add the columns. In a real-world application I wouldn't put this code here, as it makes no sense to check this every time we select a new order, never mind the fact that we shouldn't be doing any processing of the data while we're still using the `DataReader`. It's here simply because, for this chapter, it makes it easier to explain.

So, assuming we haven't already added the columns to the table, we call the `SetColumnHeader` method. Into this method we pass the `DataTable` containing the schema for the result set. The method looks like this.

```
private void SetColumnHeaders ( DataTable schema )
{
    foreach ( DataRow row in schema.Rows )
    {
        this.orderDetailsList.Columns.Add ( (string) row["ColumnName"],
                    50, HorizontalAlignment.Left );
    }

    m_columnsSet = true;
}
```

We iterate over all the columns in the schema `DataTable` and add a new column for each row. We access the "ColumnName" column in the row to set the name of the column in the `ListView`. The other two values are of no importance: the second value (50) is the width of the column and the third sets the alignment of the column. Before the method exits, it sets the global variable m_columnsSet to `true` to indicate that the columns were added successfully.

Now we return to the **Order ID** listbox event handler. We close both the datareader and the `Connection` and finally call a method called `PopulateOrderDetails`. Into this method we pass the `ArrayList` that contains all the row values that we got from the datareader. This method will now use this information to populate the `ListView`:

```
private void PopulateOrderDetails ( ArrayList rowList )
{
    this.orderDetailsList.Items.Clear ();

    foreach ( object []row in rowList )
    {
        string []orderDetails = new string[ row.Length ];

        int columnIndex = 0;

        foreach ( object column in row )
        {
            orderDetails [columnIndex++ ] = Convert.ToString (column);
        }

        ListViewItem newItem = new ListViewItem ( orderDetails );

        this.orderDetailsList.Items.Add ( newItem );
    }
}
```

The first thing this method does is call `Clear` on the `ListView`: this removes any items that may have been previously added. Now we need to add the column values for each row into the `ListView`. We will do this by creating a `ListViewItem` object and adding that to the `Items` collection of the `ListView`. In order to create a `ListViewItem` we want to create an array of strings, where each string in the array corresponds to a column in the `ListView`. Using the `Length` property of the "row" object enables us to allocate enough strings in the array to hold each column that exists in the row. We then iterate over the columns in the row, convert each one to a `string`, and insert it into the string array. Once we have built the `string` array, we create a new `ListViewItem` and add it the `ListView`.

Phew, that's it – our application is complete. All we need to do now is run it. Fire up the application and click the **Start** button: in the blink of an eye you should see the left-hand list fill up with order numbers. Select an order number and the right-hand list will display the order details. You should see something like this:

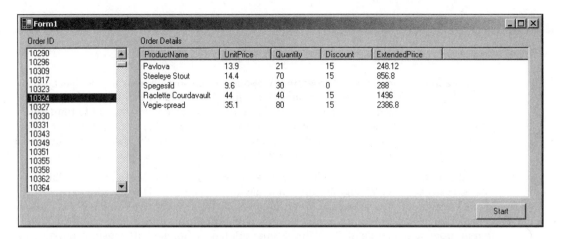

I'll briefly recap what we've done here. To populate the left-hand list with order IDs we used a `SqlCommand` object to execute a `SELECT` statement that retrieved the `OrderID` column from the `Orders` table. In order to populate the right-hand list, we have to select an order from the left-hand list; this order ID is then used to fill out a parameter, which is passed to the `CustOrdersDetail` stored procedure. On executing this stored procedure, we use the `GetSchemaTable` method to return us a `DataTable` containing the schema for the result set; this is then used to set the column headers in the right hand list view. Finally, the order data we cached away is used to populate the right hand view.

This application is a good example of when datareaders should be used. If we took this application a bit further we might use it to generate reports on the orders. We don't need to modify the data to create reports, so the read-only aspect of the datareader isn't an issue.

It would be possible to implement this application using `DataTables` but it would incur more of a performance overhead. Consider the code that populates the `ListView` containing the order IDs. With the datareader we only ever have a single order ID in memory at one time as we add it to the `ListView`, with the `DataTable` implementation we'd have to select all the order IDs in to the table then enumerate over each ID in the table and add it to the `ListView`. This means that before we can populate the **Order ID** `ListView` we'd have to store the entire table in memory for the period that we're enumerating over table, so in this respect a larger memory footprint is required.

Commonly Encountered Exceptions

In this section we'll have a look at some of the exceptions that we may encounter when we use the `DataReader`. The list is in no particular order and isn't meant to be exhaustive. These tend to be the exceptions that are raised by common programming errors:

IndexOutOfBoundsException

This is caused when an attempt to access a column that doesn't exist in the datareader has been made. This will usually be through a method such as `GetXXX` or through the item indexer. For instance, trying to retrieve the fourth column from a datareader that only contains three columns will generate this exception. If the item indexer has been used to find a named column (rather than using an ordinal) the exception message will specify the name of the column it failed to find.

InvalidOperationException

Four datareader associated problems are likely to cause an `InvalidOperationException`:

❑ This exception is thrown when an attempt was made to do something with the object that conflicts with its internal state. For example, closing the datareader and then calling `GetSchemaTable` will throw this exception with the message **Invalid attempt to read data when reader is closed**. Closing the connection and then attempting to access any data from the datareader result will also raise this exception. This is because the datareader requires an open connection to function and if its connection closes so does the datareader.

❑ Care should be taken when we call `ExecuteReader` with a `CommandBehavior` value of `SequentialAccess`. When this mode of behavior is specified, the datareader expects to access the columns in a sequential order; in other words, if you access column 4 you can't then access column 3 as this will cause the exception to be thrown with the message **Invalid attempt to read from column ordinal '3'. With CommandBehavior.SequentialAccess, you may only read from column ordinal '5' or greater.**

❑ Closing the connection while the datareader is still retrieving data will cause this exception to be raised with the message **Invalid attempt to read when reader is closed**.

❑ Another common error resulting in this exception is attempting to call `ExecuteReader` when the connection is closed. Although not an exception thrown by the datareader, the two are closely related and you'll only ever see this exception when you try to create the datareader. The message for this exception reads, **ExecuteReader requires an open and available Connection (state=Closed)**.

DataReader Performance Considerations

Performance is one of the most important aspects of the datareader. In this section we'll look at how to optimize data access through the datareader.

I've tested the performance by creating a simple table in my SQL Server database. This table has two columns. The first is called `ID`, which contains the primary key and stores `int` types. The second column is called `Name` and contains `nvarchar` up to 255 characters long. Into this table I've added one million rows (the IDs are numbered sequentially from 0 to 999999) and to populate the `Name` column I've generated a random number, converted that into a string, and then inserted it into the column.

All results shown are based on the datareader accessing the million rows over ten iterations. In other words, for each test result you see, the rows have been accessed 10 million times. Maybe the chances of you retrieving ten million rows in a single chunk is slim, but I've retrieved so much data in order to try to spread the duration of the work being done. Hopefully this will give more realistic results.

I haven't given code examples for this profiling because it's pretty easy to do. Below is the basic outline for the code I used for profiling:

```
long startTime = DateTime.Now.Ticks;

while ( reader.Read () )
{
    // do your data access here
```

```
    }

    long endTime = DateTime.Now.Ticks;

    TimeSpan timeTaken = new TimeSpan ( endTime - startTime );
```

The first line of code gets the current time represented in 100-nanosecond intervals that have elapsed since the date 1 January 2001 12:00 midnight. We then do our data processing as we usually would in the `while` loop. Once we've finished processing the data we get the current time again. Finally we subtract the start time from the end time to give us a `TimeSpan` object. The `TimeSpan` object represents the number of 100-nanosecond intervals from the point where we started processing the data until the time we finished. If we use the `TotalSeconds` property on the `TimeSpan` object we get the number of seconds it took to process the data.

As you can see, it's not rocket science! If we had more time we could look at some of the performance classes in the `System.Diagnostics` namespace and see how we could use performance counters to time our data access. If I've whet your appetite start by taking a look at the `PerformanceCounter` class.

Column Ordinal Versus Column Name

There are several ways of retrieving data from a datareader: two of these are to use the column ordinal or its name. There are quite serious performance implications to consider when deciding which method to use.

To refresh your memory here are two quick examples:

```
    object name = reader [ "ID" ];
```

```
    object name = reader [ 0 ];
```

The first example shows how to use a datareader to retrieve data using the name of the column; the second example uses the column ordinal to get the data.

I ran the tests, which read each row in turn. One test used the column name, and the other test used the column ordinal. Here are the results:

Provider	Method	Time (for 10 million records) in Seconds
SqlClient	reader["ID"]	64.192304
	reader[0]	48.3995952
OleDb	reader["ID"]	152.5092976
	reader[0]	131.1285536

It's pretty clear that, regardless of which provider we use, the column ordinal is significantly faster. As to be expected, using the `OleDb` provider produces much slower times. Remember, we're working against SQL Server 2000 in all of these tests, so this is always going to be the case. The results for the `OleDb` provider are still valid though: if we were running against another backend we'd still expect to see the ordinal indexer outperform the column name indexer.

Why is this then? Well, when we use the column name indexer, the providers still have to map that column name to the appropriate ordinal value. The current providers do this by calling GetOrdinal, which takes the column name, and returns the column's ordinal; using this they then call GetValue, which returns the column's value.

Which do we use then? In terms of performance there's no contest really: the ordinal indexer is far faster. Problems start to occur if the schema changes; we might reference the wrong column. At least if a column name is removed, we know that we will get an exception. We can get around this by using GetOrdinal once, storing the ordinal in a variable, and from then on referring to it by ordinal using the variable. This is slightly slower than using a literal or constant number, but still faster than using the column name every time. We discussed this in more detail in the *Accessing Data in a Type-Safe Manner* section of this chapter.

Type Safe Access versus Non-Type-Safe Access

As we've just seen, we can access data using indexers. They are very fast but don't care about the data type they're dealing with. Sometimes this is OK; at other times it's nice to be able to access data in a type safe manner (if for no other reason than that it makes you feel good inside!).

Let's have a look at the code below; these examples show some of the ways we can access data in a type-safe manner.

```
SqlInt32 id = reader.GetSqlInt32 ( 0 );

SqlString name = reader.GetSqlString ( 1 );

int id reader.GetInt32 ( 0 );

string name reader.GetString ( 1 );
```

The first two lines above are making use of the SqlClient's knowledge of SQL Server and retrieving proper SQL types. The third and fourth lines are getting the data back in a type-safe manner, but it's also very generic in that when we use GetString we don't really know how that data was being stored in the database. You may have noticed that all these methods use the column ordinal; none of the methods allow you to retrieve a column based on its name.

So, the big question is whether there's any tradeoff between being able to access data like this or using an indexer. As usual, I ran the tests and used both datareaders to read every record in my table. Here are the results.

Provider	Method	Time (for 1 million records) in Seconds
SqlClient	reader.GetString (1)	65.7545504
	reader.GetSqlString (1)	65.6844496
	(string)reader[1]	46.81732
OleDb	reader.GetString (1)	140.1114704
	(string)reader[1]	147.061464

If we look at the `SqlClient` results first, we can see that there's practically no difference in retrieving data from the `Name` column as a `SqlString` or `string` data type. This is to be expected, because if were to delve in to the intermediate language for the `GetString` and `GetSqlString` methods, we'd see that `GetString` actually calls straight through to `GetSqlString`! Look at the indexer though: in comparison with the type-safe access, it's much faster. This is to be expected really: when we call `GetSqlString`, the `SqlClient` jumps through lots of hoops to get us a nice, cuddly `SqlString`. When we use the indexer, we're getting an `object` back and leaving it to the runtime to cast it for us.

We'll now turn our attentions to the `OleDb` provider. Hmm, what do we have here? The typed `GetString` method is actually faster than the indexer. This took me somewhat by surprise – after trawling through Microsoft documentation and looking at the IL for this method, I finally reached this conclusion: I can only presume that this method is far quicker because the `OleDbDataReader` accesses all the data in its native format. In other words, when we use the `GetString` method, the datareader does as little work as possible to coerce the value it has into a `string` object.

Again we have to ask ourselves which one to choose. Yet again the answer is "it depends". If the `SqlDataReader` is being used, and all-out performance is the order of the day, then the indexer is a lot faster. As usual, whether the indexer is used will probably be down to personal preference. If the `OleDbDataReader` is being used then the type-safe access methods are significantly quicker.

When considering performance, always try to think of the "big picture". Don't take the blinkered approach and assume that just because *a* is faster than *b*, *a* is always best. As the scenario above illustrates, this isn't necessarily the case.

Summary

In this chapter we have looked at the `SqlDataReader` and `OleDbDataReader`. We've looked at how we can traverse one or many result sets using `NextResult` and also how we can access data using either indexers or type-safe methods. We've also seen that the `OleDbDataReader` supports hierarchical rows or chapters and how we can navigate these chapters.

To consolidate our new found knowledge we created a simple application that demonstrated the core functionality of the datareaders. To finish with we've also considered the performance implications of accessing data in various ways and looked at suggesting where one method may be better than the next.

5

The DataSet

The DataSet is the centerpiece of a disconnected, data-driven application; it is an in-memory representation of a complete set of data, including tables, relationships, and constraints. The DataSet does not maintain a connection to a data source, enabling true disconnected data management. The data in a DataSet can be accessed, manipulated, updated, or deleted, and then reconciled with the original data source. Since the DataSet is disconnected from the data source, there is less contention for valuable resources, such as database connections, and less record locking.

The DataSet uses eXtensible Markup Language (XML) for transmission and persistence. Moving data across application boundaries no longer incurs the expense of COM data type marshaling, since the data is transmitted in text-based XML format. Any application or object that can handle text can deal with a DataSet in some fashion. If the object does not support ADO.NET, but can parse XML, then it can treat the DataSet as an XML file. If the object supports ADO.NET, then the data can be materialized into a DataSet, which will expose all of the properties and methods of the System.Data.DataSet class. We'll discuss the DataSet and its relationship to XML in Chapter 8.

The DataSet object model will help us understand the power and usefulness of the DataSet. The following is a partial view of this model:

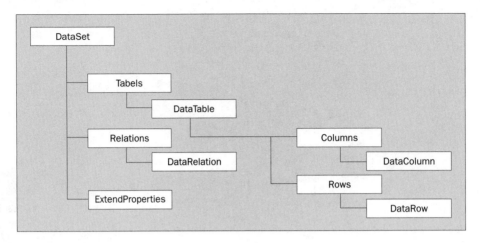

When we look at the `DataSet` object model, we see that it is made up of three collections, `Tables`, `Relations`, and `ExtendedProperties`. These collections make up the relational data structure of the `DataSet`.

❑ **Tables Collection**

The `DataSet.Tables` property is a `DataTableCollection` object, which contains zero or more `DataTable` objects. Each `DataTable` represents a table of data from the data source. Each `DataTable` is made up of a `Columns` collection and a `Rows` collection, which are zero or more `DataColumns` or `DataRows`, respectively.

❑ **Relations Collection**

The `DataSet.Relations` property is a `DataRelationCollection` object, which contains zero or more `DataRelation` objects. The `DataRelation` objects define a parent-child relationship between two tables based on foreign key values.

❑ **ExtendedProperties Collection**

The `DataSet.ExtendedProperties` property is a `PropertyCollection` object, which contains zero or more user-defined properties. The `ExtendedProperties` collection can be used to store custom data related to the `DataSet`, such as the time when the `DataSet` was constructed.

To understand the `DataSet` fully, we first need to understand the `DataTable`. For the first part of this chapter we will be dissecting the `DataTable` class, and understanding how the `DataTable` works and its role in a data-driven application. Once we have worked with `DataTables`, we will begin using `DataTables` in `DataSets`, and building `DataRelations` between two `DataTables`, in the same way we would have a relationship between two tables in a database. Before we finish, we will also discuss how to cache `DataSets` for increased performance in our application.

The DataTable

A `DataTable` stores data in a similar form to a database table: data is stored in a set of fields (columns) and records (rows). The `DataTable` class is a central class in the ADO.NET architecture; it can be used independently, and in `DataSet` objects. A `DataTable` consists of a `Columns` collection, a `Rows` collection, and a `Constraints` collection. The `Columns` collection combined with the `Constraints` collection defines the `DataTable` schema, while the `Rows` collection contains the data.

❑   **Columns Collection**

The `Columns` collection is an instance of the `DataColumnCollection` class, and is a container object for zero or more `DataColumn` objects. The `DataColumn` objects define the `DataTable` column, including the column name, the data type, and any primary key or incremental numbering information.

❑   **Rows Collection**

The `Rows` collection is an instance of the `DataRowCollection` class, and is a container for zero or more `DataRow` objects. The `DataRow` object contains the data in the `DataTable`, as defined by the `DataTable.Columns` collection. Each `DataRow` has one item per `DataColumn` in the `Columns` collection.

❑   **Constraints Collection**

The `Constraints` collection is an instance of the `ConstraintCollection` class, and is a container for zero or more `ForeignKeyConstraint` objects and/or `UniqueConstraint` objects. The `ForeignKeyConstraint` object defines the action to be taken on a column in a primary key/foreign key relationship when a row is updated or deleted. The `UniqueConstraint` is used to force all values in a column to be unique.

DataColumn

A `DataColumn` defines the column name and data type. We can create a new `DataColumn` using the `DataColumn` constructor or by invoking the `Add` method of the `DataTable.Columns` collection property:

```
DataColumn myColumn == new DataColumn("ID", Type.GetType("System.Int32"));
```

Or:

```
productsTable.Columns.Add("ID", Type.GetType("System.Int32"));
```

In the preceding code we use the `Type` class's `GetType` method when we create the `DataColumn`. This method creates a `Type` object based on the string value passed into it. The `DataTable.Columns.Add` method expects two arguments: the name of the `DataColumn` and a `Type` object. This is an overloaded `DataColumnCollection.Add` method; there are other overloaded versions of this method:

❑   `productsTable.Columns.Add();`

Creates and adds a new `DataColumn` to the `DataColumnCollection`. The `DataColumn` is given a default name ("Column1", "Column2", etc.).

❑   `productsTable.Columns.Add(myDataColumn);`

Adds the specified `DataColumn` to the `DataColumnCollection`.

❑   `productsTable.Columns.Add("SubTotal",`
    `Type.GetType("System.Single"), "Sum(Price)");`

Creates and adds a `DataColumn` with the specified name, data type and `Expression` property. The expression can be used to filter rows, calculate the values in a column, or create an aggregate column.

In the following example we create a new `DataTable`, and define its schema by creating three columns in the columns collection:

```
//Create a new DataTable in the DataSet
DataTable productsTable = new DataTable("Products");

//Build the Products schema
productsTable.Columns.Add("ID", Type.GetType("System.Int32"));
productsTable.Columns.Add("Name", Type.GetType("System.String"));
productsTable.Columns.Add("Category", Type.GetType("System.Int32"));
```

This snippet builds a new `DataTable` using the `DataTable` constructor to create a new instance of the `DataTable` class. To build the `DataTable` schema we use the `Add` method of the `DataTable.Columns` collection once for each column we are adding to the `DataTable`. For each `DataColumn`, we pass in arguments for the `ColumnName` and `DataType` properties. The result is a `DataTable` named "Products" made up of three columns: `ProdID`, `Name`, and `Category`.

With the `DataTable` constructed, and the columns defined, we can begin populating the `DataTable` with data. Adding a new `DataRow` object to the `DataTable.Rows` collection for each record we are adding does this.

DataRow

To populate a `DataTable` we add new `DataRow` objects to the `DataTable.Rows` collection. Each `DataRow` can reference each `DataColumn` in the `DataTable` schema. To create a new row in the `DataTable`, we invoke the `DataTable.NewRow` method, which returns a `DataRow` using the `DataTable`'s current schema. Next, we set the value of each column in the `DataRow` and invoke the `DataTable.Rows.Add` method, passing the new `DataRow` in as the only argument:

```
//Create a new DataRow with the same schema as the DataTable
DataRow tempRow;
tempRow = productsTable.NewRow();

//Set the column values
tempRow["ID"] = 1;
tempRow["Name"] = "Caterham Seven de Dion";
tempRow["Category"] = 1;

//Add the DataRow to the DataTable
productsTable.Rows.Add(tempRow);
```

In this example we add one row to `productsTable`. We create a new `DataRow` object (`tempRow`) using the schema from the `DataTable` using the `productsTable.NewRow` method. Next, we set the value for each of the columns defined in the `productsTable.Columns` collection. Lastly we invoke the `productsTable.Rows.Add` method to add the new `DataRow` to the `productsTable.Rows` collection.

Constraints

Relational databases enforce data integrity with constraints, or rules applied to a column that defines what action to take when data in a related column or row is altered. In ADO.NET there are two types of constraints: `ForeignKeyConstraint` and `UniqueConstraint`. The constraint objects are contained in the `Constraints` property of a `DataTable`, which is `ConstraintsCollection` object. We will briefly introduce these objects here, and we will use them a little in this chapter, but constraints will be covered in-depth in Chapter 9.

ForeignKeyConstraint

A `ForeignKeyConstraint` specifies the action to take when a value in a column or columns is deleted or updated. This type of constraint is intended for use in a primary key/foreign key relationship. When a value in a parent column is changed or deleted, a `ForeignKeyConstraint` defines how the child column should react. For example, if a parent record is deleted, we could specify that all child records should be deleted. Alternatively, if a parent record is deleted, we could set the related field in the child columns to null or default values – identifying orphaned records. This is known as a cascading action, where the action is cascaded down from the parent to the child.

The action to be taken is defined in the `ForeignKeyConstraint.DeleteRule` or the `ForeignKeyConstraint.UpdateRule` property and can be set to one of four possible values:

❑ **Rule.Cascade** – deletes or updates related rows; this is the default action

❑ **Rule.SetNull** – sets values in related rows to `DBNull`

❑ **Rule.SetDefault** – sets values in related rows to the `DefaultValue` property value

❑ **Rule.None** – no action is taken on related rows

For example:

```
myForeignKeyConstraint.DeleteRule = Rule.SetDefault;
```

UniqueConstraint

A `UniqueConstraint` enforces unique values in a column. This type of constraint is ideal for primary key columns, which we'll discuss next. If a column has a `UniqueConstraint`, attempting to set the same value for that column in two different rows throws an exception.

We can also set a `UniqueConstraint` over more than one column. In this case setting every constrained column to the same value in two rows will throw an exception.

Primary Key

Since both the `DataSet` and `DataTable` are designed to support all of the basic relational database concepts, a `DataTable` can have a primary key. In a `DataTable`, the primary key is defined as an array of `DataColumns` that provide a unique identifier for the `DataRow` within the `DataTable`. To create a primary key in a `DataTable`, set the `PrimaryKey` property of the `DataTable` to an array of `DataColumns`. When we define a `PrimaryKey`, a `UniqueConstraint` is automatically applied to the `DataColumn` array.

```
//Set up the ID column as the PrimaryKey
DataColumn[] pk = new DataColumn[1];
pk[0] = productsTable.Columns["ID"];
productsTable.PrimaryKey = pk;
```

The `DataColumn` class also exposes properties for defining a column as a read-only, auto-increment column, with the numbering starting from 1:

```
productsTable.Columns["ID"].AutoIncrement = true;
productsTable.Columns["ID"].AutoIncrementSeed = 1;
productsTable.Columns["ID"].ReadOnly = true;
```

Dynamically Constructing a DataTable

In the following code example, we dynamically create a `DataTable`, set the primary key, and set the `AutoIncrement` and `ReadOnly` properties of the `DataColumn`. This example code uses the same code as the previous examples, all put together, to demonstrate how we can dynamically create `DataTables`.

```
//Create the table
DataTable productsTable = new DataTable("Products");

//Build the Products schema
productsTable.Columns.Add("ID", Type.GetType("System.Int32"));
productsTable.Columns.Add("Name", Type.GetType("System.String"));
productsTable.Columns.Add("Category", Type.GetType("System.Int32"));

//Set up the ID column as the PrimaryKey
DataColumn[] pk = new DataColumn[1];
pk[0] = productsTable.Columns["ID"];
productsTable.PrimaryKey = pk;
productsTable.Columns["ID"].AutoIncrement = true;
productsTable.Columns["ID"].AutoIncrementSeed = 1;
productsTable.Columns["ID"].ReadOnly = true;
```

In this example we create a new `DataTable` and define its schema by adding `DataColumns`. We use the `DataTable` constructor to create an empty `DataTable` named `Products`. Next, we add three `DataColumns` to the `DataTable` by invoking the `Add` method of the `Columns` collection. The `Add` method takes two arguments: the `ColumnName` and the `DataType`. We define the primary key column by setting the `DataTable` object's `PrimaryKey` property to a one-dimensional array of `DataColumns` containing only the `ProdID` column. We set the `AutoIncrement` property of the primary key column to `true`, and set the `AutoIncrementSeed` property to 1. Finally we set the primary key column's `ReadOnly` property to `true`.

Once the `DataTable` is constructed, we can populate it with `DataRows`. For this example, we populate the `DataTable` with alternating values. We use the `Math.IEEERemainder` method to do this. The `IEEERemainder` method takes two arguments: a dividend and a divisor. The method returns a double that is the remainder of dividing the dividend by the divisor. We check the returned value to see if it is 0: is the remainder is 0, then the value of `i` is even; if it is anything other than 0, the value of `i` is odd. For even values, we will set the `Name` column of the `DataRow` to "Caterham Seven de Dion" and the `Category` value to 1. For odd rows we will set the `Name` value to "Dodge Viper" and the `Category` value to 2.

```
DataRow tempRow;

//Populate the Products table with 10 cars
for(int i = 0; i < 10; i++)
{
  //Make every even row a Caterham Seven de Dion
  if(Math.IEEERemainder(i,2) == 0)
  {
    tempRow = productsTable.NewRow();
    tempRow["Name"] = "Caterham Seven de Dion #" + i.ToString();
    tempRow["Category"] = 1;
    productsTable.Rows.Add(tempRow);
  }else{
    tempRow = productsTable.NewRow();
    tempRow["Name"] = "Dodge Viper #" + i.ToString();
    tempRow["Category"] = 2;
    productsTable.Rows.Add(tempRow);
  }
}
```

To populate the `DataTable` we create a new `DataRow` object by invoking the `productTable.NewRow` method. This creates a new `DataRow` using the schema defined by the `DataTable`. We then set the value of each column in the `DataRow`. Notice we do not set the `ID` column value, since it is defined as a read-only, auto-increment column. Once the row is filled with values, we invoke the `Add` method of the `DataTable.Rows` collection, which appends the `DataRow` to the end of the collection.

DataTable Events

Like many of the objects in the .NET Framework, the `DataTable` exposes a set of events that can be captured and handled. It can be very useful to handle the `DataTable` event – for instance, we can use the events to update the user interface, or to validate edits, updates, or deletes before they are committed. There are six events, and they all work in nearly the same way; they each have similar arguments, and are invoked when their respective event is fired. The events are:

- **ColumnChanging**
  Occurs when a value is being changed for the specified `DataColumn` in a `DataRow`.

- **ColumnChanged**
  Occurs after a value has been changed for the specified `DataColumn` in a `DataRow`.

- **RowChanging**
  Occurs when a `DataRow` is changing. This event will fire each time a change is made to the `DataRow`, after the `ColumnChanging` event fires.

- **RowChanged**
  Occurs after a `DataRow` has been changed successfully.

- **RowDeleting**
  Occurs when a `DataRow` is about to be deleted.

- **RowDeleted**
  Occurs after a `DataRow` is successfully deleted.

As we can see, these events are paired: one event fires when something is happening, and one fires after the first finishes successfully. We can handle these events by creating an event handler for each event. The event handlers take arguments as specified for the event:

```
private void ColumnChangingHandler(object sender,
  DataColumnChangeEventArgs e)
{
  //Do something to handle this event.
}
```

To add the event handler to an instance of a `DataTable`, create a new event handler object, and pass in the name of the method that will handle the event.

```
//Add ColumnChanging and ColumnChanged Event Handlers
myDataTables.ColumnChanging +=
  new DataColumnChangeEventHandler(ColumnChangingHandler);
```

Each of the `DataTable` events works in the same fashion. The `ColumnChanging` and `ColumnChanged` events take a `DataColumnChangeEventArgs` object, while the other events take a `DataRowChangeEventArgs` object.

The `DataColumnChangeEventArgs` object exposes three properties:

- ❑ **Column**
  Gets the `DataColumn` with the changing value.

- ❑ **ProposedValue**
  Gets or sets the proposed value. This is the new value being assigned to the column. For example, in a `ColumnChanging` event handler we can evaluate the `ProposedValue` and accept or reject the change based on its value. We'll see how to use this in the following `DataTable` Events Example.

- ❑ **Row**
  Gets the `DataRow` with the changing value.

The `DataRowChangeEventArgs` object exposes only two properties:

- ❑ **Action**
  Gets the action that has occurred on the `DataRow`

- ❑ **Row**
  Gets the `DataRow` upon which the action occurred

DataTable Events Example

In the following example we create a `DataTable` and populate it dynamically, as we did in the previous example. We will build an ASP.NET web form interface that will enable updating and deleting rows in the `DataTable`, which will cause each of the aforementioned events to fire and be handled.

The code for this example is rather long, so we'll break down as we go. If you are building this sample, write all the code in the gray boxes continuously as we go through it. The web form we are building will look like this when we have finished:

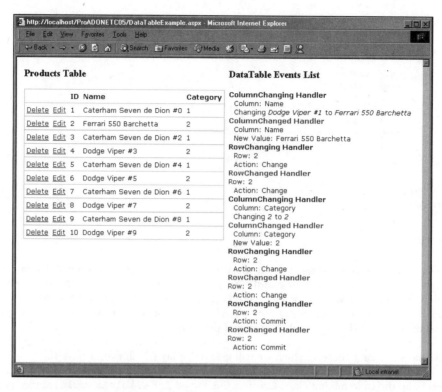

Let's start by building the ASP.NET web form interface. Create a new file in your web application named `DataTableExample.aspx`:

```
<%@ Page Inherits="DataTableExample" Src="DataTableExample.cs" %>
<HTML>
<BODY>
<FORM runat="server">
  <TABLE CellPadding="4" CellSpacing="0" Brider="0">
    <TR>
      <TD VALIGN="TOP">
        <H3>Products Table</H3>
        <asp:DataGrid runat="server" id="productGrid"
          CellPadding="4" CellSpacing="0"
          BorderWidth="1" Gridlines="Horizontal"
          Font-Names="Verdana, Arial, sans-serif"
          Font-Size="x-small"
          HeaderStyle-Font-Bold="True"
          OnEditCommand="DataGrid_OnEditCommand"
          OnCancelCommand="DataGrid_OnCancelCommand"
          OnUpdateCommand="DataGrid_OnUpdateCommand"
          OnDeleteCommand="DataGrid_OnDeleteCommand"
          >
          <Columns>
            <asp:ButtonColumn
              Text="Delete"
              CommandName="Delete"
              />
            <asp:EditCommandColumn
```

```
                    EditText="Edit"
                    CancelText="Cancel"
                    UpdateText="Update"
                    />
              </Columns>
           </asp:DataGrid>
        </TD>
        <TD VALIGN="TOP">
           <H3>DataTable Events List</H3>
           <asp:Label runat="server" id="EventsList"
              Font-Names="Verdana, Arial, sans-serif"
              Font-Size="x-small"
              />
        </TD>
      </TR>
    </TABLE>
  </FORM>
  </BODY>
  </HTML>
```

In the web form we have a `DataGrid` that specifies methods for the Edit, Cancel, Update, and Delete commands. These commands will be handled in the web form code, behind class specified in the `@Page` directive at the top of the web form. The `DataGrid` has two columns prefixed to the `DataGrid.Columns` collection: a `ButtonColumn` that will have a "Delete" link button, and an `EditCommandColumn` that will enable editing of the row.

Lastly we have a `Label` control, which we will use to display which events have fired.

Now, lets build the code-behind class. Create a file named `DataTableExample.aspx.cs` and save it to the same directory as the web form file.

Import the necessary namespaces to use in an ASP.NET code behind class, and the `System.Data` namespace. The namespaces give us access to the basic `System` classes, and the classes associated with a web form, as well as the ADO.NET data classes, such as the `DataTable` and `DataSet` classes. Then declare the class name, `DataTableExample`:

```
using System;
using System.Data;
using System.Web;
using System.Web.UI;
using System.Web.UI.WebControls;

public class DataTableExample : Page
{
```

Declare the `DataTable` at the classlevel. This will allow us to access the `DataTable` object in any of the methods. Also map a code-behind variable to the web form server controls.

```
//Declare the DataTable object at the class level
protected DataTable myDataTable;
//Map the Web Form server controls
protected DataGrid productGrid, categoryGrid;
protected Label EventsList;
```

We are going to create a method to build our `DataTable`. In this method we create a new `DataTable`: `Products`. The `MakeData` method creates a `DataTable` object and assigns it to the class-level `myDataTable` object.

```csharp
private void MakeData()
{
  myDataTable = (DataTable)Cache.Get("myDataTable");

  //If myDataTable is not in the cache, create it
  if(myDataTable == null)
  {
    myDataTable = new DataTable("Products");

    //Build the Products schema
    myDataTable.Columns.Add("ID",
      Type.GetType("System.Int32"));
    myDataTable.Columns.Add("Name",
      Type.GetType("System.String"));
    myDataTable.Columns.Add("Category",
      Type.GetType("System.Int32"));

    //Set up the ID column as the PrimaryKey
    DataColumn[] pk = new DataColumn[1];
    pk[0] = myDataTable.Columns["ID"];
    myDataTable.PrimaryKey = pk;

    myDataTable.Columns["ID"].AutoIncrement = true;
    myDataTable.Columns["ID"].AutoIncrementSeed = 1;
    myDataTable.Columns["ID"].ReadOnly = true;

    DataRow tempRow;

    //Populate the Products table with 10 cars
    for(int i = 0; i < 10; i++)
    {
      //Make every other car a Caterham Seven de Dion
      if(Math.IEEERemainder(i,2) == 0)
      {
        tempRow = myDataTable.NewRow();
        tempRow["Name"] =
          "Caterham Seven de Dion #" + i.ToString();
        tempRow["Category"] = 1;
        myDataTable.Rows.Add(tempRow);
      }else{
        tempRow = myDataTable.NewRow();
        tempRow["Name"] =
          "Dodge Viper #" + i.ToString();
        tempRow["Category"] = 2;
        myDataTable.Rows.Add(tempRow);
      }
    }

    Cache.Insert("myDataTable", myDataTable);
  }
}
```

The `MakeData` method is nearly identical to the previous example, where we created a `DataTable` dynamically. One significant difference is that, at the end of the `MakeData` method, we put the `myDataTable` in the application's cache. This will make the `DataTable` accessible to us after postbacks, so we don't have to recreate it each time.

Next, create a `BindData` method that will invoke the `MakeData` method and bind the `productGrid` `DataGrid` server control to the `myDataTable` object:

```
private void BindData()
{
  //Get the DataSet
  MakeData();

  //Set the DataGrid.DataSource properties
  productGrid.DataSource = myDataTable;

  //Bind the DataGrid
  productGrid.DataBind();
}
```

Now we are going to build the event handlers for the `DataTable` events. Each event handler is similar – they all render the event information in the `EventList Label` server control. For example, in the `ColumnChanging` event handler, we write that the event was fired, the name of the column that is changing, the original value of the column, and the proposed value. Each of the event handlers works in the same way, so we won't look at them all in detail:

```
//********************************************************************//
//******************** DataColumn Event Handlers ********************//
//********************************************************************//
  private void ColumnChangingHandler(object sender,
    DataColumnChangeEventArgs e)
  {
  EventsList.Text += String.Format(
    "<B>ColumnChanging Handler</B><BR>" +
      "  Column: {0}<BR>",
    e.Column.ColumnName);

  string propValue = e.ProposedValue.ToString().ToLower();

  //if the user changed the name of the car to anything with
  //the word "pinto" in it, raise an exception.
  if((e.Column.ColumnName == "Name")
    && (propValue.IndexOf("pinto") > -1))
  {
    throw(new System.Exception(
      "Pintos are not allowed on this list."));
  }
  else
  {
    EventsList.Text += String.Format(
      "  Changing <I>{0}</I> " +
        "to <I>{1}</I><BR>",
      e.Row[e.Column.ColumnName],
      e.ProposedValue);
  }
}
```

In the preceding code we create an event handler for the `DataTable.ColumnChanging` event. In the event handler we can do any number of things, including checking the proposed value and reacting to it. In this example, we prohibit any user from changing a `Name` field value to anything including the word "Pinto" (after all, this is an exotic car list, and the Pinto, while a classic, is far from exotic!). We use the `String` class's `IndexOf` method to check for the word "Pinto" anywhere in the proposed value. If "Pinto" is in the proposed value, the `IndexOf` method will return an integer indicating the starting position of the substring; if the value is not found, `IndexOf` will return −1.

If "Pinto" is in the proposed value, we throw a `System.Exception`: "Pintos are not allowed on this list". By throwing an exception, the change is rejected, and the original values are restored.

The remaining event handlers are similar to the `ColumnChangingHandler` method, although in the rest of them we do not throw any exceptions.

```
private void ColumnChangedHandler(object sender,
  DataColumnChangeEventArgs e)
{
  EventsList.Text += String.Format(
    "<FONT COLOR=\"RED\">" +
      "<B>ColumnChanged Handler</B></FONT><BR>" +
      "  Column: {0}<BR>",
    e.Column.ColumnName);

  EventsList.Text += String.Format(
    "  New Value: {0}<BR>",
    e.ProposedValue);
}

//************************************************************//
//********************* DataRow Event Handlers *********************//
//************************************************************//
private void RowChangingHandler(object sender,
  DataRowChangeEventArgs e)
{
  EventsList.Text += String.Format(
    "<B>RowChanging Handler</B><BR>" +
      "  Row: {0}<BR>",
    e.Row["ID"]);

  EventsList.Text += String.Format(
    "  Action: {0}<BR>",
    e.Action);
}

private void RowChangedHandler(object sender,
  DataRowChangeEventArgs e)
{
  EventsList.Text += String.Format(
    "<FONT COLOR=\"RED\"><B>" +
      "RowChanged Handler</B></FONT><BR>" +
      "Row: {0}<BR>",
    e.Row["ID"]);

  EventsList.Text += String.Format(
    "  Action: {0}<BR>",
    e.Action);
}
```

```
    private void RowDeletingHandler(object sender,
      DataRowChangeEventArgs e)
    {
      EventsList.Text += String.Format(
        "<B>RowDeleting Handler</B><BR>" +
          "Row: {0}<BR>",
        e.Row["ID"]);

      EventsList.Text += String.Format(
        "  Action: {0}<BR>",
        e.Action);
    }

    private void RowDeletedHandler(object sender,
      DataRowChangeEventArgs e)
    {
      EventsList.Text += "<FONT COLOR=\"RED\">" +
        "<B>RowDeleted Handler</B></FONT><BR>";

      EventsList.Text += String.Format(
        "  Action: {0}<BR>",
        e.Action);
    }
```

Since in the web form we are using a DataGrid with methods defined for Edit, Update, Cancel, and Delete events, we need to create those event handlers. In the web form we defined DataGrid_OnEditCommand, DataGrid_OnUpdateCommand, DataGrid_OnCancelCommand, and DataGrid_OnDeleteCommand as the respective event handler methods.

In the DataGrid_OnEditCommand we first clear the EventsList Label server control (so we get a list of only the events on the current postback), and set the EditItemIndex property of the DataGrid to the index of the row that was clicked on. This puts the DataGrid into edit mode, and renders TextBox server controls in each non-read-only column with the row values in the TextBoxes.

```
//***************************************************************//
//******************** DataGrid Event Handlers ******************//
//***************************************************************//
    protected void DataGrid_OnEditCommand(object sender,
      DataGridCommandEventArgs e)
    {
      EventsList.Text = "";
      ((DataGrid)sender).EditItemIndex = e.Item.ItemIndex;
      BindData();
    }
```

In the DataGrid_OnCancelCommand event handler we simply set the DataGrid's EditItemIndex value to -1, which turns off the DataGrid edit mode.

```
    protected void DataGrid_OnCancelCommand(object sender,
      DataGridCommandEventArgs e)
    {
      ((DataGrid)sender).EditItemIndex = -1;
      BindData();
    }
```

The `DataGrid_OnUpdateCommand` event handler is a little more complicated:

```
protected void DataGrid_OnUpdateCommand(object sender,
  DataGridCommandEventArgs e)
{
  EventsList.Text = "";

  //Cast an object as the source DataGrid
  DataGrid senderGrid = (DataGrid)sender;
```

In this event handler, we set the class-level `myDataTable` object to the current instance of the `DataTable` (the one saved in cache) by invoking the `MakeData` method.

```
  //Invoke MakeData() to create the myDataTable object
  MakeData();
```

We create a new `TextBox` object and cast the first control in each column as an instance of the `TextBox` class. These control instances represent the `TextBox`es that rendered in the `DataGrid` edit mode.

```
  //Get the edited item values
  TextBox Name = (TextBox)e.Item.Cells[3].Controls[0];
  TextBox Category = (TextBox)e.Item.Cells[4].Controls[0];
```

We get the primary key value of the row being updated by setting a string object to the value of the text in the third column of the `DataGrid` (the first column is the Delete link button, and the second is the Edit/Update/Cancel link button column).

```
  //Get the PrimaryKey column text
  string item = e.Item.Cells[2].Text;
```

We use the primary key value we captured to invoke the `DataTable.Rows.Find` method. This method will use the primary key value to return the `DataRow` that is being edited.

```
  //Get the DataRow from myDataTable
  DataRow dr = myDataTable.Rows.Find(Int32.Parse(item));
```

In a try/catch block we attempt to change the values in the `DataRow` to the values submitted by the user. If the proposed value includes the word "Pinto" then the `ColumnChangingHandler` method will throw an exception, and the code in the catch block will be executed; otherwise the values will be changed in the `DataRow`.

```
  //Change the DataRow values
  //This will raise the ColumnChanging event
  try
  {
    dr[1] = Name.Text;
    dr[2] = Int32.Parse(Category.Text);

    //Commit the changes to the DataRow
    //This will raise the ColumnChanged event
    dr.AcceptChanges();
  }
```

```
catch(Exception ex)
{
  EventsList.Text +=
    "<FONT COLOR=\"RED\"><B>Error: </FONT>" +
    ex.Message +
    "</B>";
}
```

Lastly, we re-cache the `DataTable`, set the `EditItemIndex` to –1 (to turn off the `DataGrid` edit mode), and invoke the `BindData` method.

```
//Recache the DataTable
Cache.Insert("myDataTable", myDataTable);

      //Bind the DataGrid
senderGrid.EditItemIndex = -1;
BindData();
}
```

In the `DataGrid_OnDeleteCommand` event handler, we place similar functionality to the previous event handler, but instead of updating the row, we use the `DataRowCollection.Remove` method to delete the specified `DataRow` from the `DataTable.Rows` collection.

```
protected void DataGrid_OnDeleteCommand(object sender,
  DataGridCommandEventArgs e)
{
  EventsList.Text = "";

  //Cast an object as the source DataGrid
   DataGrid senderGrid = (DataGrid)sender;

   //Get the Data and create a DataView to filter
   MakeData();

  //Get the PrimaryKey column text
  string item = e.Item.Cells[2].Text;

  //Get the DataRow from myDataTable
  DataRow dr = myDataTable.Rows.Find(Int32.Parse(item));

  //Use the Remove() method to delete the row
  myDataTable.Rows.Remove(dr);

  //Recache the DataSet
  Cache.Insert("myDataTable", myDataTable);

      //Bind the DataGrid
  senderGrid.EditItemIndex = -1;
  BindData();
    }
```

Lastly we create the `Page_Load` event handler, which will fire each time the page is loaded, including on a postback. In the event handler, we evaluate for a postback, and if this is the first request for the page, we use the `Cache.Remove` method to make sure there is no cached version of `myDataTable`.

```
        protected void Page_Load(object sender, EventArgs e)
        {
          if(!Page.IsPostBack)
          {
            //Start with a fresh DataTable
            Cache.Remove("myDataTable");
          }
```

Next we invoke MakeData to create the myDataTable object. On the first request for this page, the MakeData method will create the myDataTable object and insert it into the cache. If this is a postback, then the MakeData method will cast the cached myDataTable object into the myDataSet object class-level object.

```
        //Create a new DataSet by calling the MakeData method
        MakeData();
```

Once the myDataTable object is constructed, we set all of the event handlers that we have created methods for:

```
        myDataTable.ColumnChanging +=
          new DataColumnChangeEventHandler(ColumnChangingHandler);
        myDataTable.ColumnChanged +=
          new DataColumnChangeEventHandler(ColumnChangedHandler);
        //Add RowChanging and RowChanged Event Handlers
        myDataTable.RowChanging +=
          new DataRowChangeEventHandler(RowChangingHandler);
        myDataTable.RowChanged +=
          new DataRowChangeEventHandler(RowChangedHandler);
        //Add RowDeleting and RowDeleted Event Handlers
        myDataTable.RowDeleting +=
          new DataRowChangeEventHandler(RowDeletingHandler);
        myDataTable.RowDeleted +=
          new DataRowChangeEventHandler(RowDeletedHandler);
```

Lastly, if this request is not a postback, we invoke the BindData method to bind the DataGrid. If this is a postback, the BindData method will be invoked in the event handler that is fired on the postback, such as the DataGrid_OnEditCommand event handler.

```
        if(!Page.IsPostBack)
        {
          BindData();
        }
      }
```

With the code all complete, we can test the event handlers by browsing to the page – there is no need to compile the code-behind class because the SRC attribute in the @ Page directive of the web form indicates that the Just-In-Time (JIT) compiler should be used to compile the class.

In the DataGrid, click on the **Edit** link and change a value. When you click the **Update** link, notice that the ColumnChanging and ColumnChanged event handlers get fired twice for one row. This is because they are fired once for each column in the row that changed. Also notice that the RowChanging and RowChanged events fire three times: once with each column change, and once when AcceptChanges is invoked on the DataRow. The AcceptChanges method commits all changes made to the DataRow since the last time AcceptChanges was invoked.

If we try to change the Name value of any row to any string containing the word "Pinto", an exception is thrown (recall that we throw our own exception for any Name value with the substring "Pinto"). Since an exception was thrown, the change fails, and the data is rolled back.

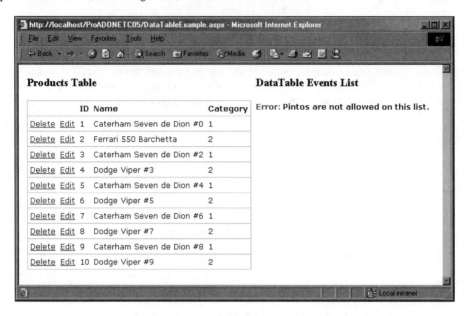

Now that we have an understanding of the DataTable class, let's look at how the DataTable is used in a DataSet, and how we can build relationships between DataTables.

Populating a DataSet

In the previous section we looked at how to dynamically create DataTable objects and populate them with data. However, we will usually be working with a data store and we will be populating a DataSet with table data from that data store. We can, of course, populate a DataSet with these DataTable objects, but more often we will be working with database data.

To populate a DataSet with a dynamically created DataTable, use the DataSet.Tables collection Add method.

```
MyDataSet.Tables.Add(myDataTable);
```

On the other hand, ADO.NET provides an object, the DataAdapter, which is what we use with the DataSet. The DataAdapter is a bridge between a database and the DataSet. The DataAdapter is used to manage a connection to a database, execute a command, and return any data to the DataSet. In Chapter 6 we will learn more about the DataAdapter and how incredibly useful it is in working with DataSets, but for now let's look at how to use a DataAdapter to populate a DataSet.

Constructing a DataAdapter

To use a `DataAdapter`, either a `SqlDataAdapter` or an `OleDbDataAdapter`, we must specify a connection and a command that will be executed. When we execute the command, we specify the `DataSet` that we want to fill. The `DataAdapter` creates `Connection` and `Command` objects, opens the connection to the database, executes the command on the connection, fills the results into a `DataTable` in the `DataSet`, and closes the connection. Note that the management of the connection is a function of the `DataAdapter`, not the `DataSet`.

> To understand the difference between the **SqlDataAdpter** and the **OleDbDataAdapter**, we need to understand the difference between the SQL Server Data Provider and the OLE DB Data Provider. See Chapter 2 for more information on the .NET Data Providers.

We can use one of three `DataAdapter` constructors (we construct `SqlDataAdapter` and `OleDbDataAdapter` in the same way):

❑ `SqlDataAdapter myDataAdapter = new SqlDataAdapter();`

Creates a new `SqlDataAdapter` with no connection or command.

❑ `SqlDataAdapter myDataAdapter = new SqlDataAdapter(myCommand);`

Creates a new `SqlDataAdapter` that uses the specified `SqlCommand`

❑ `SqlDataAdapter myDataAdapter =`
`    new SqlDataAdapter(mySqlStmt, myConnection);`

Creates a new `SqlDataAdapter` that will execute the specified T-SQL command on the specified `SqlConnection`

❑ `SqlDataAdapter myDataAdapter =`
`    new SqlDataAdapter(mySqlStmt, myConString);`

Creates a new `SqlDataAdapter` that will execute the specified T-SQL command using the specified connection string to build a `SqlConnection`

For the `DataAdapter` to work, it must have a valid `SqlCommand` as its `SelectCommand` property. We can construct a `SqlCommand` and assign it to the `SqlDataAdapter.SelectCommand` property:

```
//Define the SQL command and connection string
String mySqlStmt ="SELECT * FROM Customers";
String myConString = "server=localhost;database=Northwind;uid=sa;pwd=;";

//Construct a new SqlDataAdapter
SqlDataAdapter myDataAdapter = new SqlDataAdapter();

//Construct the SqlCommand that will be the DataAdapters SelectCommand
SqlConnection myConnection = new SqlConnection(ConString);
SqlCommand myCommand = new SqlCommand(SqlStmt, myConnection);

//Set the SelectCommand property
myDataAdapter.SelectCommand = myCommand;
```

If we construct the DataAdapter using one of the overloaded constructors, a SqlCommand will be constructed and assigned to the SelectCommand property:

```
String mySqlStmt ="SELECT * FROM Customers";
String myConString = "server=localhost;database=Northwind;uid=sa;pwd=;";
SqlDataAdapter myDataAdapter = new SqlDataAdapter(mySqlStmt, myConString);
```

The preceding code will construct a new SqlDataAdapter, and build a SqlCommand using the specified CommandText (the first argument passed in) and the specified ConnectionString (the second argument passed in).

Invoking Fill

The DataAdapter.Fill method is the trigger that fires the SqlDataAdapter.SelectCommand. To populate a DataSet with a new DataTable we can use the Fill method and pass in a DataSet as an argument. The Fill method will create a DataTable in the DataSet and fill it with the results of the T-SQL command.

When we invoke the Fill method, the following happens:

❑ The connection to the database is opened (if it was not already opened explicitly)

❑ The T-SQL command is executed

❑ A new DataTable is constructed in the DataSet.Tables collection

❑ The DataTable is populated with the results of the command

❑ The connection is closed – unless it was already open before calling Fill

> If a connection is explicitly opened, the **DataAdapter** will leave it open after the command execution. This is useful if we are using one connection to execute several commands. By explicitly opening the connection, the **DataAdapter** will leave it open, allowing us to continue to use the same connection without having to reopen it.

When Fill is invoked, a new DataTable will be added to the DataSet.Tables collection. By default the new DataTable will be given the TableName property value of "Table", and additional tables will be given the TableName values "Table1", "Table2", and so on. Optionally we can pass a string into the Fill method as a table name. The string value will be assigned to the DataTable.TableName property:

```
myDataAdapter.Fill(myDataSet, "Customers");
```

This will create a new DataTable with the name "Customers".

The DataTable is accessible either by its DataSet.Tables collection index value:

```
DataTable myDataTable = ds.Tables[0];  //The first table has an index of 0
```

or by its DataTable.TableName property:

```
DataTable myDataTable = ds.Tables["Customers"];
```

DataAdapter Example

In the following example we use the `SqlDataAdapter`, the `DataAdapter` used for SQL Server connections, to retrieve the first ten records from the `Northwind Customers` table (using the T-SQL `TOP 10` command). This example, like the previous example, uses an ASP.NET web form as the user interface. The resulting page will look like this:

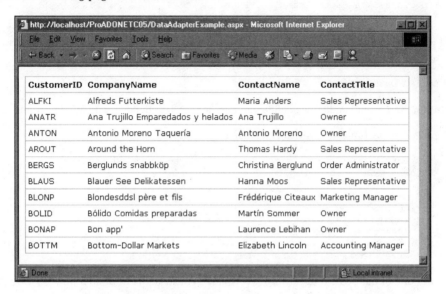

Create a file named `DataAdapterExample.aspx` and add a `DataGrid` to it:

```
<%@ Page Inherits="DataAdapterExample" Src="DataAdapterExample.aspx.cs" %>
<HTML>
<BODY>
<FORM runat="server">
  <asp:DataGrid runat="server" id="myDataGrid"
    CellPadding="4" CellSpacing="0"
    BorderWidth="1" Gridlines="Horizontal"
    Font-Names="Verdana, Arial, sans-serif"
    Font-Size="x-small"
    HeaderStyle-Font-Bold="True"
  />
</FORM>
</BODY>
</HTML>
```

Now create the code-behind class file, named `DataAdapterExample.aspx.cs`, in the same directory as the web form file.

First we import the required namespaces. We use the `System` and `System.Data` namespaces as we did in the previous examples, but we also import the `System.Data.SqlClient` namespace because we are using the SQL Server .NET Data Provider:

```
using System;
using System.Data;
using System.Data.SqlClient;
using System.Web;
using System.Web.UI;
using System.Web.UI.WebControls;

public class DataAdapterExample : Page
{
```

We add a variable that maps to the `DataGrid` in the web form. This gives us programmatic access to the `DataGrid`.

```
protected DataGrid myDataGrid;
```

In the `Page_Load` event handler, we define variables for the T-SQL command and the connection string:

```
protected void Page_Load(object sender, EventArgs e)
{
  //Create a new DataSet with the DataSetName value "Northwind"
  DataSet myDataSet = new DataSet("Northwind");

  //Create the T-SQL and ConnectionString values
  String mySqlStmt =
    "SELECT TOP 10 CustomerID, CompanyName, ContactName, " +
    "ContactTitle FROM Customers";
  String myConString =
    "server=localhost;database=Northwind;uid=sa;pwd=;";
```

Next we use one of the `SqlDataAdapter` overloaded constructors to build a new `SqlDataAdapter`:

```
  //Construct a new SqlDataAdapter with the preceding values
  SqlDataAdapter myDataAdapter =
    new SqlDataAdapter(mySqlStmt, myConString);
```

We then construct a `DataSet`, with the `DataSetName` value of "Northwind" that the returned data will be filled into:

```
  //Create a new DataSet with the DataSetName value "Northwind"
  DataSet myDataSet = new DataSet("Northwind");
```

Once all of the pieces are in place, we invoke the `Fill` method. We specify the `DataSet` and the optional name to apply to the `DataTable` that is constructed:

```
  //Invoke the Fill() method to create a
  //new DataTable in the DataSet
  myDataAdapter.Fill(myDataSet, "Customers");
```

Lastly, we bind the `DataSet` to the `DataGrid` server control. By default, the `DataGrid` will render the data from the `DataTable` with the index value of 0 (the first `DataTable` in the `DataSet`).

```
  myDataGrid.DataSource = myDataSet;
  myDataGrid.DataBind();
  }
}
```

In this example, we displayed the `CustomerID`, `CustomerName`, `ContactName`, and `ContactTitle` of the first ten records from the `Northwind Customers` table by using the T-SQL `TOP 10` command. This was accomplished with out ever having to explicitly create a `SqlConnection`, `SqlCommand`, or `DataTable`. The `DataAdapter` managed the construction of these objects for us based on the data we provided. This, of course, improves our application performance, because resources are constructed at the last possible moment, and released as soon as they are finished with.

While this is useful, the real power of the `DataSet` is in its ability to hold multiple related tables and make data available based on the `DataTable` relationships. To understand how this works, let's start by looking at the `DataSet.Tables` collection.

The Tables Collection

The `DataSet.Tables` property is an instance of the `DataTableCollection` class; it is a collection of `DataTable` objects. In a previous example we indirectly populated a `DataSet` with a `DataTable` using the `DataSet.Tables.Add` method. The `DataAdapter` invokes this method for us, under the covers so to speak, when the `DataAdapter.Fill` method is invoked. As a result, each time we invoke the `Fill` method, a new `DataTable` is added to the `DataSet.Tables` collection.

Populating the Tables Collection with Multiple DataTables

We can populate the `DataSet` with multiple tables in a number of possible ways: we can create a `DataTable` dynamically and use the `DataSet.Tables.Add` method to add the `DataTable` to the `DataSet.Tables` collection; we can use multiple `DataAdapters` to fill the same `DataSet`; or we can use one `DataAdapter` and alter the `DataAdapter.SelectCommand.CommandText` property before invoking `Fill` the second time.

- ❏ Using multiple `DataAdapters` to fill the same `DataSet`:

```
myDataAdapter.Fill(myDataSet, "Customers");
myOtherDataAdapter.Fill(myDataSet, "Employees");
```

- ❏ Using a single `DataAdapter` to fill the same `DataSet` using different T-SQL commands each time:

```
//Invoke the Fill() method
myDataAdapter.Fill(myDataSet, "Customers");

//Reset the SelectCommand.CommandText property
myDataAdapter.SelectCommand.CommandText = "SELECT * FROM Orders";

//Invoke the Fill() method for the second table
myDataAdapter.Fill(myDataSet, "Orders");
```

If no table name is passed into the `Fill` method then the newly constructed `DataTable` will be named "Table", "Table1", "Table2", and so on. This naming rule also applies to T-SQL commands that return multiple result sets.

```
myDataAdapter.SelectCommand.CommandText =
    "SELECT * FROM Customers; SELECT * FROM Orders";
myDataAdapter.Fill(myDataSet);
```

The preceding code will populate the `DataSet` with two `DataTable` objects: "Table" and "Table1".

In the following example we use the `SqlDataAdapter` to fill a `DataSet` with two `DataTables`. The `DataTables` are created automatically for us because the T-SQL command we are using returns two result sets, the `Customers` table and the `Orders` table.

Multiple DataSet Tables Example

In this example we will populate a `DataSet` with multiple `DataTables`, using a single `SqlDataAdapter`. The `DataTables` will be bound to `DataGrid` in an ASP.NET web form.

As with the previous examples, we will be creating an ASP.NET web form to use as the interface. The following example will create a web form that looks like this:

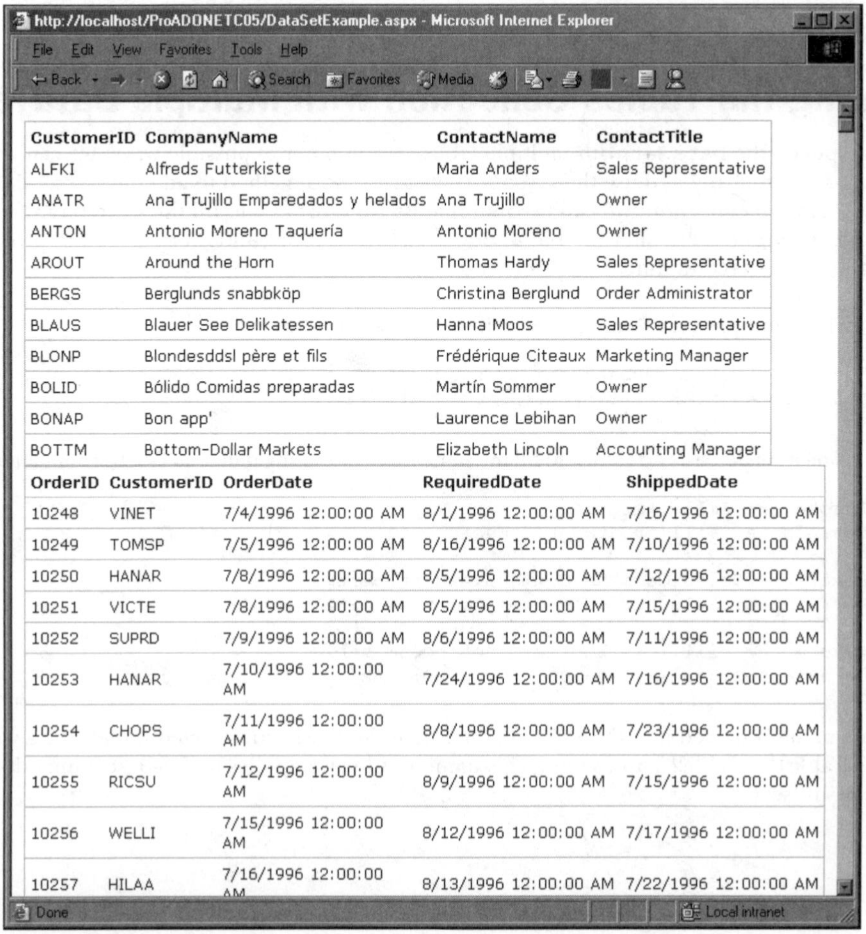

186

To begin, create a file named `DataSetExample.aspx` and add the following code to render two DataGrids:

```
<%@ Page Inherits="DataSetExample" Src="DataSetExample.aspx.cs" %>
<HTML>
<BODY>
<FORM runat="server">
  <asp:DataGrid runat="server" id="customersDataGrid"
    CellPadding="4" CellSpacing="0"
    BorderWidth="1" Gridlines="Horizontal"
    Font-Names="Verdana, Arial, sans-serif"
    Font-Size="x-small"
    HeaderStyle-Font-Bold="True"
  />

  <asp:DataGrid runat="server" id="ordersDataGrid"
    CellPadding="4" CellSpacing="0"
    BorderWidth="1" Gridlines="Horizontal"
    Font-Names="Verdana, Arial, sans-serif"
    Font-Size="x-small"
    HeaderStyle-Font-Bold="True"
  />
</FORM>
</BODY>
</HTML>
```

For the code-behind class file, create a file named `DataSetExample.aspx.cs` in the same directory as the web form. Start by adding the basic namespace declarations that we have been using, declare the class, and create variables that map to the `DataGrid` server controls:

```
using System;
using System.Data;
using System.Data.SqlClient;
using System.Web;
using System.Web.UI;
using System.Web.UI.WebControls;

public class DataSetExample : Page
{
  //Map the Web Form server controls
  protected DataGrid customersDataGrid, ordersDataGrid;
```

Create a `BindData` method that we can invoke to populate a `DataSet` and bind the data from the `DataTables` to the `DataGrids` on the web form:

```
    private void BindData()
    {
      //Create a new DataSet with the DataSetName value "Northwind"
      DataSet myDataSet = new DataSet("Northwind");

      //Create the T-SQL and ConnectionString values
      String mySqlStmt ="SELECT TOP 10 CustomerID, CompanyName, " +
        "ContactName, ContactTitle FROM Customers";
      String myConString =
        "server=localhost;database=Northwind;uid=sa;pwd=;";

      //Construct a new SqlDataAdapter with the preceding values
```

```
    SqlDataAdapter myDataAdapter =
      new SqlDataAdapter(mySqlStmt, myConString);

    //Invoke the Fill() method to create a
    //new DataTable in the DataSet
    myDataAdapter.Fill(myDataSet, "Customers");

    //Change the DataAdapter's SelectCommand
    mySqlStmt = "SELECT OrderID, CustomerID,OrderDate, " +
      "RequiredDate, ShippedDate FROM ORDERS";
    myDataAdapter.SelectCommand.CommandText = mySqlStmt;

    //Invoke the Fill() method to create a
    //new DataTable in the DataSet
    myDataAdapter.Fill(myDataSet, "Orders");

    customersDataGrid.DataSource = myDataSet.Tables["Customers"];
    ordersDataGrid.DataSource = myDataSet.Tables["Orders"];
    Page.DataBind();
  }
```

Lastly, create a `Page_Load` event handler that will invoke the `BindData` method on the first page request:

```
  protected void Page_Load(object sender, EventArgs e)
  {
    if(!Page.IsPostBack)
    {
      //Create a new DataSet by invoking
      //the BindData() method
      BindData();
    }
  }
}
```

When the page is requested, the `BindData` method fires and the `DataSet` is filled with two `DataTables`. Each of the `DataTables` is bound to a `DataGrid` and rendered to the page.

Retrieving the Tables Collection Metadata

The `DataSet.Tables` collection, which is an instance of the `DataTableCollection` class, exposes properties that describe the tables. This 'data about the data' is called metadata. We can access this metadata as individual properties, such as `myDataSet.Tables.Count`, which will return the number of `DataTables` in the collection. The `Tables` collection exposes an `Item` property, which returns a specified `DataTable` (in C# the `Item` property is the indexer). We can also bind the `DataSet.Tables` collection to a `DataGrid` to display all of the `DataTable` metadata.

In the following example we use an ASP.NET web form to display the `DataSet.Tables` metadata. The resulting Web Form will look like this:

Prefix	DesignMode	Namespace	HasErrors	MinimumCapacity	TableName	DisplayExpression	CaseSensitive
	False		False	50	Customers		False
	False		False	50	Orders		False

CustomerID	CompanyName	ContactName	ContactTitle
ALFKI	Alfreds Futterkiste	Maria Anders	Sales Representative
ANATR	Ana Trujillo Emparedados y helados	Ana Trujillo	Owner
ANTON	Antonio Moreno Taquería	Antonio Moreno	Owner
AROUT	Around the Horn	Thomas Hardy	Sales Representative
BERGS	Berglunds snabbköp	Christina Berglund	Order Administrator
BLAUS	Blauer See Delikatessen	Hanna Moos	Sales Representative
BLONP	Blondesddsl père et fils	Frédérique Citeaux	Marketing Manager
BOLID	Bólido Comidas preparadas	Martín Sommer	Owner
BONAP	Bon app'	Laurence Lebihan	Owner
BOTTM	Bottom-Dollar Markets	Elizabeth Lincoln	Accounting Manager

OrderID	CustomerID	OrderDate	RequiredDate	ShippedDate
10248	VINET	7/4/1996 12:00:00 AM	8/1/1996 12:00:00 AM	7/16/1996 12:00:00 AM
10249	TOMSP	7/5/1996 12:00:00 AM	8/16/1996 12:00:00 AM	7/10/1996 12:00:00 AM
10250	HANAR	7/8/1996 12:00:00 AM	8/5/1996 12:00:00 AM	7/12/1996 12:00:00 AM
10251	VICTE	7/8/1996 12:00:00 AM	8/5/1996 12:00:00 AM	7/15/1996 12:00:00 AM
10252	SUPRD	7/9/1996 12:00:00 AM	8/6/1996 12:00:00 AM	7/11/1996 12:00:00 AM
10253	HANAR	7/10/1996 12:00:00 AM	7/24/1996 12:00:00 AM	7/16/1996 12:00:00 AM
10254	CHOPS	7/11/1996 12:00:00 AM	8/8/1996 12:00:00 AM	7/23/1996 12:00:00 AM
10255	RICSU	7/12/1996 12:00:00 AM	8/9/1996 12:00:00 AM	7/15/1996 12:00:00 AM
10256	WELLI	7/15/1996 12:00:00 AM	8/12/1996 12:00:00 AM	7/17/1996 12:00:00 AM
10257	HILAA	7/16/1996 12:00:00 AM	8/13/1996 12:00:00 AM	7/22/1996 12:00:00 AM

To complete this example, we can modify the code from the previous example. Start by adding another `DataGrid` to the web form, before the two existing `DataGrids`:

```
<FORM runat="server">
  <asp:DataGrid runat="server" id="metaDataDataGrid"
    CellPadding="4" CellSpacing="0"
    BorderWidth="1" Gridlines="Horizontal"
    Font-Names="Verdana, Arial, sans-serif"
    Font-Size="x-small"
    HeaderStyle-Font-Bold="True"
  />
  <asp:DataGrid runat="server" id="customersDataGrid"
```

Next, in the code-behind class, bind the `metaDataDataGrid` to the `myDataSet.Tables` collection, not to one of the `DataTables`.

```
ordersDataGrid.DataSource = myDataSet.Tables["Orders"];
metaDataDataGrid.DataSource = myDataSet.Tables;
Page.DataBind();
```

Browsing to the web form renders a table displaying the properties of the `DataTable` objects in the `myDataSet.Tables` collection as seen in the previous screenshot.

The page displays the following properties of each `DataTable` in the `DataSet.Tables` collection:

❑ **Prefix**
The namespace for the XML representation of this `DataTable`. In Chapter 8 we will discuss the `DataSet` and XML, where you will learn that the `DataSet` can be represented in XML. Each `DataTable` can have an XML namespace, which is used to uniquely identify it in the `DataSet`.

❑ **DesignMode**
A Boolean value indicating whether the `DataTable` is currently in design mode.

❑ **Namespace**
The namespace for the XML representation of this `DataTable`. This is the same as the Prefix value.

❑ **HasErrors**
A Boolean value indicating whether there are errors in any row in the `DataTable`.

❑ **MinimumCapacity**
The initial starting size (number of rows) for this `DataTable`.

❑ **TableName**
The name of the `DataTable`.

❑ **DisplayExpression**
The expression that will return a value used to represent this table in UI.

❑ **CaseSensitive**
A Boolean value indicating whether string comparisons within the table are case-sensitive.

The Relations Collection

The `DataSet.Relations` property is an instance of the `DataRelationsCollection` class. The `Relations` collection contains `DataRelation` objects, which are used to create parent-child relations between `DataTables` in the `DataSet`. A primary-key/foreign-key relationship is an example of this type of relation.

We can create a relationship between two tables in a `DataSet` by invoking the `DataSet.Relations.Add` method. There are seven overloaded `Add` methods:

❑ `DataSet.Relations.Add(DataRelation);`

Adds the specified `DataRelation` object to the collection.

❑ `DataSet.Relations.Add(DataColumn, DataColumn);`

Creates a `DataRelation` object in the collection based on the two `DataColumns`. The first argument is the parent column, and the second is the child column. The `DataRelation` is given a default name.

❑ `DataSet.Relations.Add(DataColumn[], DataColumn[]);`

Creates a `DataRelation` object in the collection based on the two `DataColumn` arrays. The first argument is the parent column array, and the second is the child column array. The `DataRelation` is given a default name.

❏   `DataSet.Relations.Add(string, DataColumn, DataColumn);`

Creates a `DataRelation` object in the collection with the specified string as the `DataRelation.RelationName` property. The `DataRelation` is based on the two `DataColumns`. The first argument is the parent column, and the second is the child column.

❏   `DataSet.Relations.Add(string, DataColumn[], DataColumn[]);`

Creates a `DataRelation` object in the collection with the specified string as the `DataRelation.RelationName` property. The `DataRelation` is based on the two `DataColumn` arrays. The first argument is the parent column array, and the second is the child column array.

❏   `DataSet.Relations.Add(string, DataColumn, DataColumn, bool);`

Creates a `DataRelation` object in the collection with the specified string as the `DataRelation.RelationName` property. The `DataRelation` is based on the two `DataColumns`. The first argument is the parent column, and the second is the child column. The Boolean argument indicates whether or not to create constraints.

❏   `DataSet.Relations.Add(string, DataColumn[], DataColumn[], bool);`

Creates a `DataRelation` object in the collection with the specified string as the `DataRelation.RelationName` property. The `DataRelation` is based on the two `DataColumn` arrays. The first argument is the parent column array, and the second is the child column array. The `Boolean` argument indicates whether or not to create constraints.

We can create a relationship in a `DataSet` using any of the overloaded methods. For example, using the fourth overloaded method:

```
//Create a relation ship between Customers and Orders
myDataSet.Relations.Add("CustomersToOrders",
   myDataSet.Tables["Customers"].Columns["CustomerID"],
   myDataSet.Tables["Orders"].Columns["CustomerID"]);
```

In this code we invoke the `Add` method of the `myDataSet.Relations` object. The `Add` method creates a new `DataRelation` object in the `myDataSet.Relations` collection. In this example, the `DataRelation`'s constructor takes three arguments: the name to use for this `DataRelation` object, the parent `DataColumn`, and the child `DataColumn`. When this method is invoked, a `DataRelation` is constructed. This adds a `UniqueConstraint` to the parent `DataTable` and a `ForeignKeyConstraint` to the child `DataTable` (see "*Constraints*" earlier in this chapter). The `UniqueConstraint` ensures that all parent column values are unique in the table, and the `ForeignKeyConstraint` sets up cascading deletes and updates from parent to child records.

We can also construct the `DataRelation` object explicitly, and then add it to the `Relations` collection:

```
//Create two DataColumns
DataColumn parentColumn;
DataColumn childColumn;

//Set the two columns to instances of the parent and child columns
parentColumn = myDataSet.Tables["Customers"].Columns["CustomerID"];
childColumn = myDataSet.Tables["Orders"].Columns["CustomerID"];
```

```
//Create a new DataRelation object
DataRelation CustomersToOrders = new DataRelation("CustomersToOrders",
  parentColumn, childColumn);
//Add the DataRelation to the DataSet.Relations collection
myDataSet.Relations.Add(CustomersToOrders);
```

A `DataRelation` can be constructed using an array of `DataColumns` for both the parent and child columns. For instance, say there is a table of `Employees`, and a table of `Managers`. The `Managers` table contains the data for employees who are also managers (this example assumes that the names of the employees are duplicated in both the `Employees` table and the `Managers` table).

```
//Create arrays of DataColumns for the parent and child columns
DataColumn[] parentArray = new DataColumn[2];
parentArray [0] = myDataSet.Tables["Employees"].Columns["FirstName"];
parentArray [1] = myDataSet.Tables["Employees"].Columns["LastName"];

DataColumn[] childArray = new DataColumn[2];
childArray [0] = myDataSet.Tables["Managers"].Columns["FirstName"];
childArray [1] = myDataSet.Tables["Managers"].Columns["LastName"];

DataRelation EmpToMngr = new DataRelation("EmployeesToManagers",
  parentArray, childArray)

myDataSet.Relations.Add(EmpToMngr);
```

In the preceding code we construct a `DataRelation` using a `DataColumn` array for both the parent and child columns of the relationship. When the relation is constructed, a `UniqueConstraint` is added to the `Employees` table, enforcing a unique combination of first and last names, and a `ForeignKeyConstraint` is added to the `Managers` table, enforcing cascading deletes and updates across the relationship.

DataRelations Example

In the following code example we build a `DataSet` and populate it with two `DataTable` objects, `Customers` and `Orders`. We build a `DataRelation` establishing `Customers` as the parent and `Orders` as the child. In the ASP.NET Web Form we add a **Delete** `ButtonColumn` to the **Customers** `DataGrid`, which will invoke a `DeleteCustomer` method. This method will delete the customer row from the `Customers` `DataTable`. As we have a `DataRelation`, this will cascade the delete to the child table, `Orders`, and delete all orders for the customer we are deleting.

First we will build the ASP.NET Web Form interface. When we have finished, the web form will look like this:

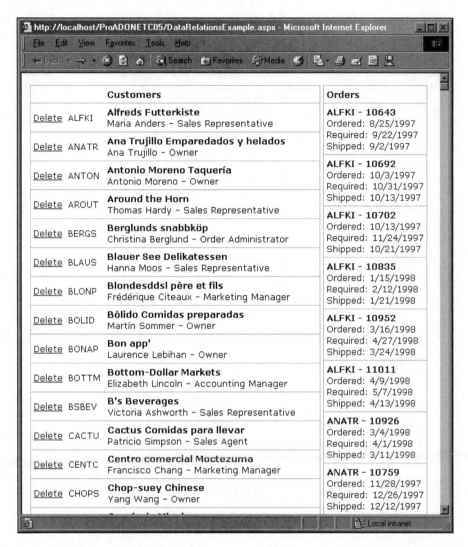

Create a new ASP.NET web form named `DataRelationsExample.aspx` and add the following code:

```
<%@ Page Inherits="DataRelationsExample" Src="DataRelationsExample.aspx.cs" %>
<%@ Import Namespace="System.Data" %>
<HTML>
<BODY>
<FORM runat="server">
 <TABLE Border="0" CellPadding="2" CellSpacing="0">
  <TR>
   <TD valign="top">
    <asp:DataGrid runat="server" id="customersDataGrid"
     CellPadding="4" CellSpacing="0"
     BorderWidth="1" Gridlines="Horizontal"
     Font-Names="Verdana, Arial, sans-serif"
     Font-Size="x-small"
```

```
          HeaderStyle-Font-Bold="True"
          AutogenerateColumns="False"
          OnDeleteCommand="DeleteCustomer">
          <Columns>
           <asp:ButtonColumn Text="Delete" CommandName="Delete" />
           <asp:BoundColumn DataField="CustomerID" />
           <asp:TemplateColumn HeaderText="Customers">
            <ItemTemplate>
             <b>
             <%# DataBinder.Eval(Container.DataItem, "CompanyName") %>
             </b><br>
             <%# DataBinder.Eval(Container.DataItem, "ContactName") %>
             -
             <%# DataBinder.Eval(Container.DataItem, "ContactTitle") %>
            </ItemTemplate>
           </asp:TemplateColumn>
          </Columns>
         </asp:DataGrid>
        </TD>
        <TD valign="top">
         <asp:DataGrid runat="server" id="ordersDataGrid"
          CellPadding="4" CellSpacing="0"
          BorderWidth="1" Gridlines="Horizontal"
          Font-Names="Verdana, Arial, sans-serif"
          Font-Size="x-small"
          HeaderStyle-Font-Bold="True"
          AutogenerateColumns="False">
          <Columns>
           <asp:TemplateColumn HeaderText="Orders">
            <ItemTemplate>
             <b>
             <%# DataBinder.Eval(Container.DataItem, "CustomerID") %>
             -
             <%# DataBinder.Eval(Container.DataItem, "OrderID") %>
             </b><br>
             Ordered:
             <%# DataBinder.Eval(Container.DataItem, "OrderDate", "{0:d}") %>
             <br>
             Required:
             <%# DataBinder.Eval(Container.DataItem, "RequiredDate", "{0:d}") %>
             <br>
             Shipped:
             <%# DataBinder.Eval(Container.DataItem, "ShippedDate", "{0:d}") %>
            </ItemTemplate>
           </asp:TemplateColumn>
          </Columns>
         </asp:DataGrid>
        </TD>
       </TR>
      </TABLE>
     </FORM>
    </BODY>
   </HTML>
```

This web form uses the `DataGrid` `BoundColumn` and `TemplateColumn` objects to create a custom layout of the data. In the `customersDataGrid` we specify the `OnDeleteCommand` method to invoke when the **Delete** link button is clicked.

Now create a code-behind class file named `DataRelationsExample.aspx.cs` in the same directory as the web form. Start by building the class definition, including the `using` statement for the ADO.NET and SQL Server .NET Data Provider namespaces, and variable definitions for the web form server controls, and a class-level `DataSet`.

```
using System;
using System.Data;
using System.Data.SqlClient;
using System.Web;
using System.Web.UI;
using System.Web.UI.WebControls;

public class DataRelationsExample : Page
{
  //Map the Web Form server controls
  protected DataGrid customersDataGrid, ordersDataGrid;
  //Create a new DataSet with the DataSetName value "Northwind"
  DataSet myDataSet = new DataSet("Northwind");
```

Next, build a method to construct a `DataSet`. The `DataSet` contains two `DataTables`: `Customers` and `Orders`. The `DataSet` is filled using the `SqlDataAdapter.Fill` method:

```
  private void MakeData()
  {
    //Create the T-SQL and ConnectionString values
    String mySqlStmt ="SELECT CustomerID, CompanyName, " +
      "ContactName, ContactTitle FROM Customers " +
      "ORDER BY CustomerID";
    String myConString =
      "server=localhost;database=Northwind;uid=sa;pwd=;";

    //Construct a new SqlDataAdapter with the preceding values
    SqlDataAdapter myDataAdapter =
      new SqlDataAdapter(mySqlStmt, myConString);

    //Invoke the Fill() method to create a
    //new DataTable in the DataSet
    myDataAdapter.Fill(myDataSet, "Customers");

    //Change the DataAdapter's SelectCommand
    mySqlStmt = "SELECT OrderID, CustomerID,OrderDate, " +
      "RequiredDate, ShippedDate FROM Orders " +
      "ORDER BY CustomerID";
    myDataAdapter.SelectCommand.CommandText = mySqlStmt;

    //Invoke the Fill() method to create a
    //new DataTable in the DataSet
    myDataAdapter.Fill(myDataSet, "Orders");
```

Identify the `Customers` table `PrimaryKey` by creating a new `DataColumn` array, with only the `CustomerID` `DataColumn` in it, and set the `Customers` table `PrimaryKey` value as the `DataColumn` array:

```
    DataColumn[] pk = new DataColumn[1];
    pk[0] = myDataSet.Tables["Customers"].Columns["CustomerID"];
    myDataSet.Tables["Customers"].PrimaryKey = pk;
```

Define the primary key/foreign key relationship between the Customers and Orders tables:

```
//Create a relation ship between Customers and Orders
myDataSet.Relations.Add("CustomersToOrders",
  myDataSet.Tables["Customers"].Columns["CustomerID"],
  myDataSet.Tables["Orders"].Columns["CustomerID"]);
}
```

Create a BindData method that can be called from anywhere in the class. In the BindData method, bind the DataGrid server controls to their respective DataTables in the DataSet:

```
private void BindData()
{
  customersDataGrid.DataSource = myDataSet.Tables["Customers"];
  ordersDataGrid.DataSource = myDataSet.Tables["Orders"];
  Page.DataBind();
}
```

Create the DeleteCustomers method that will be invoked when the **Delete** LinkButton is clicked:

```
protected void DeleteCustomer(object sender,
  DataGridCommandEventArgs e)
{
  MakeData();
  //Find the DataRow based on the primary key value
  //the CustomerID which is in the second column, index 1
  DataRow myDataRow =
    myDataSet.Tables["Customers"].Rows.Find(
      e.Item.Cells[1].Text
    );
  //Remove the DataRow from the DataSet
  //and Bind the server control
  myDataSet.Tables["Customers"].Rows.Remove(myDataRow);
  BindData();
}
```

Finally, create the Page_Load event handler, which will invoke MakeData and BindData only on the first request for the page:

```
protected void Page_Load(object sender, EventArgs e)
{
  if(!Page.IsPostBack)
  {
    //Create a new DataSet by invoking
    //the MakeData() method
    MakeData();
    //Bind the data to the server controls
    BindData();
  }
}
```

When we browse to this page, we can test the DataRelation by clicking on a **Delete** link for any row. When the form posts, the DeleteCustomer method is invoked, and the specified Customer table row is removed. As we have a parent-child relationship, the delete is cascaded to the child table, Orders, and all of the orders for the specified customer are deleted as well.

Merging DataSets

The DataSet class exposes a Merge method that is used to merge one DataSet into another, a DataTable into a DataSet, or an array of DataRows into a DataSet. This type of action is useful when you have data for the same purpose coming from separate sources, such as inventory data coming from multiple remote locations. Each location can pass a DataSet object to a centralized application where the DataSets can be merged. In a situation like this, the central application may have a DataSet of the most recent inventory data for each remote location, which includes location IDs, product IDs and quantities. A remote location can pass the central application a DataSet filled with the latest inventory data, which may include update inventory quantities, new product IDs and quantities, and possibly a new field that specifies product attributes, such as color, that are not reflected in the product's ID, but are required to specify the product as a different item. The DataSet.Merge method can be used to merge the two DataSets, and arguments can be set to determine how to handle and changes to the data and/or schema.

The DataSet has the following overloaded Merge methods:

❏   Merge(DataRow[]);

Merges an array of DataRow objects into the calling DataSet.

❏   Merge(DataSet);

Merges a DataSet into the calling DataSet.

❏   Merge(DataTable);

Merges a DataTable into the calling DataSet.

❏   Merge(DataSet, bool);

Merges a DataSet into the calling DataSet preserving changes according to the Boolean argument. A value of true indicates changes to the calling DataSet should be maintained. A value of false indicates that changes to the DataSet provided in the parameter take priority.

❏   Merge(DataRow[], bool, MissingSchemaAction);

Merges an array of DataRow objects into the calling DataSet, preserving changes to the DataSet according to the Boolean argument, and handling an incompatible schema according to the MissingSchemaAction argument.

❏   Merge(DataSet, bool, MissingSchemaAction);

Merges a DataSet into the calling DataSet, preserving changes to the calling DataSet according to the Boolean argument, and handling an incompatible schema according to the MissingSchemaAction argument.

❏   Merge(DataTable, Boolean, MissingSchemaAction);

Merges a DataTable into the calling DataSet, preserving changes to the DataSet according to the Boolean argument, and handling an incompatible schema according to the MissingSchemaAction argument.

> The `MissingSchemaAction` argument is an enumeration that specifies how to handle the merge operation if the object being merged has a different schema from the calling `DataSet`. This scenario would occur if a new `DataColumn` were added to the schema in the merging `DataSet`.

Now we will walk through some code snippets demonstrating different ways that the `Merge` method can be used.

Merging Two DataSets

To merge two `DataSets`, we invoke the `Merge` method on the `DataSet` we want to merge the data into, and pass the other `DataSet` into the method as an argument.

```
MyDataSet.Merge(myOtherDataSet);
```

The result of this method execution has all the values from the `myOtherDataSet` object merged into the `myDataSet` object. If both `DataSets` had records with the same primary key value, the values from the `myOtherDataSet` object are set as the values of the `myDataSet` records. Any records not already in the `myDataSet` object are added.

Merging Two DataSets and Maintaining Original Values

We can merge two `DataSets` and ensure that the values of the target `DataSet` are preserved, while new values are added.

```
MyDataSet.Merge(myOtherDataSet, true);
```

The second argument in this `Merge` method is a Boolean value indicating whether the values in the target `DataSet` (`myDataSet`) should be preserved. When set to `true`, the values in `myDataSet` will be preserved, and new records will be added. This allows us to maintain the existing values and add new records at the same time.

Merging Two DataSets with Different Schemas

We can merge two `DataSets` with different schemas, and specify how the schema differences should be handled.

```
MyDataSet.Merge(myOtherDataSet, true, MissingSchemaAction.Add);
```

The `MissingSchemaAction` enumeration is used to specify how schema differences should be handled. The possible values are:

❑   `MissingSchemaAction.Add`

Indicates that additional columns defined in the source `DataSet` (`myOtherDataSet`) should be added to the target `DataSet` (`myDataSet`) schema.

❑   `MissingSchemaAction.AddWithKey`

Indicates that additional columns defined in the source `DataSet` should be added to the target `DataSet` with primary key information.

❑ MissingSchemaAction.Error

Indicates that a System.Exception will be thrown if the target schema and source schema do not match.

❑ MissingSchemaAction.Ignore

Indicates that any additional columns in the source DataSet should be ignored when it is merged into the target DataSet.

You can download the sample code for this chapter from www.wrox.com. Included in the sample code is a web form that demonstrates various Merge() method options. The web form looks like this:

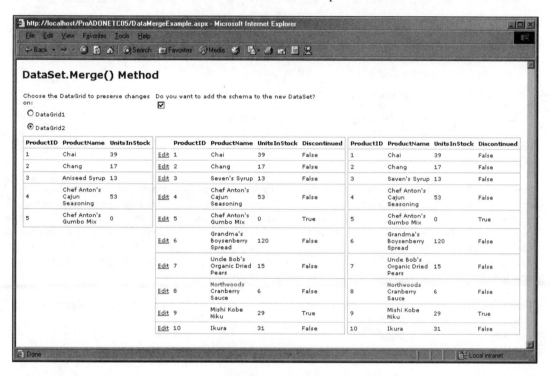

Caching DataSets for Better Performance

In an ASP.NET web application we can cache a DataSet to increase the performance of the application. Rather than going to the database and retrieving the requested data on every request, we can put the DataSet into a memory cache on the server. Each time a request is made we can check the application cache for the DataSet, and only connect to the database if a cached version of the DataSet is not present.

For example, an online retailer will have a catalogue that displays all of the products for sale on its web site. It is unlikely that this data will change frequently, so it is a perfect candidate for storing in application cache. With a cached DataSet, the first web site visitor who makes a request for the catalogue causes the database access to occur, and the data is retrieved and put into a DataSet. The DataSet is then cached so that all future requests can use the cached DataSet, eliminating the need for additional connections to the database.

In many cases it is better to use a **DataReader** object to get data from a database and stream it into the application (see Chapter 4). Since the **DataReader** streams one record at a time, there is a tremendous performance gain over bringing all of the records into a **DataSet**; however, a **DataReader** cannot be cached. So, when using a **DataReader**, we have to go and get the data on each request. What we are looking at here is the tradeoff between bringing more data into our application at once (more memory usage), and reducing the network traffic and database connections by caching the **DataSet** in the application cache. Caching a **DataSet** is not always the best solution to increase performance – you have to weight the pros and cons of using more memory and reducing network traffic and database connections.

Items are stored in the cache as key-value pairs, which makes them easy to work with. An item can be placed in the cache using one of three methods:

❑   `Cache ("CachedDataSet") = myDataSet;`

❑   `Cache.Add("CachedDataSet", myDataSet);`

❑   `Cache.Insert("CachedDataSet", myDataSet);`

The `Add` and `Insert` methods expose optional arguments for creating file dependencies and setting expiration specifics.

In the following web form, we retrieve data from the database on the first request, and add it to the application cache. When we add the `DataSet` to the cache, we set an expiration of five minutes, so that all request in the next five minutes will use the cached `DataSet`. On the first request after the cached `DataSet` expires, the database access will occur again, and a new `DataSet` will be cached. To help prove our point, when the `DataSet` is first created, we add a key-value pair to the `DataSet.ExtendedProperties` collection. This is a collection that can hold user defined key-value pairs. We are going to use it to store the time that the `DataSet` was created, so we can render that on the page.

The ASP.NET web form we are going to create will have one `Label` server control, and one `DataGrid` server control, and will look like this:

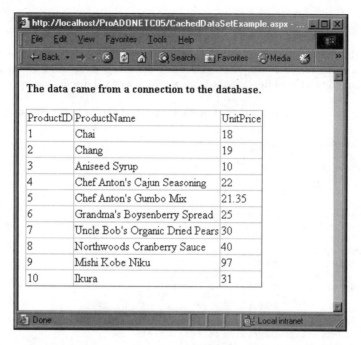

As usual, start by creating the web form file. Create a new file named CachedDataSetExample.aspx, and add the following code:

```
<%@ Page Inherits="CachedDataSetExample" Src="CachedDataSetExample.aspx.cs" %>
<HTML>
<BODY>
  <asp:Label runat="server" id="DataLocation" />
  <asp:DataGrid runat="server" id="myDataGrid" />
</BODY>
</HTML>
```

Now, create a code-behind class file named CachedDataSetExample.aspx.cs. Add the necessary using statements, declare the class, and map variables to the web form Server Controls.

```
using System;
using System.Data;
using System.Data.SqlClient;
using System.Web;
using System.Web.UI;
using System.Web.UI.WebControls;

public class CachedDataSetExample : Page
{
  protected DataGrid myDataGrid;
  protected Label DataLocation;
```

In the Page_Load event handler, construct a new DataSet and set it to the result of the Cache.Get method, which returns an Object instance matching the specified key name. Since this is an Object data type, we must cast the object as a DataSet:

```
        DataSet myDataSet = (DataSet)Cache.Get("CachedDataSet");
```

If the `DataSet` that is taken out of the cache is `null`, then the `DataSet` was not in the cache, and must be created by accessing the database. The `myDataSet` instance will be `null` on the first request for the page, or if the cached version of the `DataSet` has expired, as we'll discuss in a moment.

If the `DataSet` is not `null` then it did exist in the cache, and can be used without any database access:

```
    if(myDataSet == null)
    {
      DataLocation.Text =
        "<P><B>The data came from a connection " +
        "to the database.</B></P>";

      SqlDataAdapter myAdapter = new SqlDataAdapter(
        "SELECT TOP 10 ProductID, ProductName, UnitPrice " +
          "FROM Products;",
        "server=localhost;database=Northwind;uid=sa;pwd=;");
      myDataSet = new DataSet();

      myAdapter.Fill(myDataSet, "Products");

      //Add a key/value pair to the ExtendedProperties
      //specifying what time the DataSet was created.
      myDataSet.ExtendedProperties.Add("CreateTime",
        DateTime.Now.ToLongTimeString());

      //Insert the DataSet object in cache
      //Set a null file dependency
      //(this object does not depend on file changes
      //and a five minute expiration interval
      Cache.Insert("CachedDataSet", myDataSet, null,
        DateTime.Now.AddMinutes(5), TimeSpan.Zero);
    }
    else
    {
      DataLocation.Text =
        "<P><B>The data came from the cache. " +
        "It was created at: " +
        myDataSet.ExtendedProperties["CreateTime"].ToString() +
        "</P><P>The current system time is: " +
        DateTime.Now.ToLongTimeString() +
        "</B></P>";
    }
```

Lastly, we bind the `DataSet` to a `DataGrid`:

```
      myDataGrid.DataSource = myDataSet.Tables["Products"];
      myDataGrid.DataBind();
    }
  }
```

We can test the cache by browsing to this web form. On the first request we see the following:

After waiting a few minutes, if we refresh the page we see this:

Since we specified in the `Cache.Insert` method that the `DataSet` should remain in cache for five minutes, the `DataAdapter` in the `Page_Load` event handler will not try to connect to the database. After five minutes, the cache will automatically expire the `DataSet` and on the next request after it expires, the `DataAdapter` will connect to the database and get fresh data.

Summary

In this chapter we discussed the `DataSet` and its role in a data-driven application. The `DataSet` has the following qualities:

❑ It is a data object that works with the basic relational database concepts

❑ It can contain multiple `DataTables` and `DataRelations`

❑ It can have constraints, such as `UniqueConstraints` and `ForeignKeyConstraints`

❑ Data integrity that is enforced by constraints holds true to the relational data structure, with data changes and deletes cascaded to related `DataTables`

❑ It can be merged with other `DataSets`, `DataTables`, and `DataRows` and their data and schemas can be consolidated

Finally we saw how, in an ASP.NET web application, a `DataSet` can be put into the application cache to reduce connections to the database, and increase application performance.

6

Using the DataAdapter

ADO.NET provides two different ways to retrieve data from a database. The first method is using the `DataReader` object, which retrieves a read-only, forward-only stream of data. The second technique is using an object derived from the `DataAdapter` class, which is strictly tied with the `DataSet` class to create an in-memory representation of the data. The main difference between these two methods is to be found in how they manage the connection with the database. The `DataReader` object retrieves the information from a database by opening a connection, executing the SQL command, going through the retrieved records, and, finally, closing the connection when no more operations are needed. The `DataAdapter` object uses the connection to the database just for the time that is absolutely necessary to fill the `DataSet` object, releasing all the server resources after finishing that operation.

In this chapter we will examine every `DataAdapter` aspect, focusing our attention on these concepts:

❑ Filling a `DataSet` and a `DataTable` object by retrieving data from different databases

❑ Updating the database using SQL statements and stored procedures

❑ Creating XML schemas containing database structures

The DataAdapter Base Class

The .NET Framework class hierarchy contains the `DataAdapter` class. This class is an abstract class that provider-specific data adapters inherit from. The `DataAdapter` class implements the `IDataAdapter` interface, which defines the capabilities that a `DataAdapter` must support. The `DataAdapter` class provides the basic blocks to implement a disconnected data access mechanism to fill the `DataSet` object and to update the data source.

The DbDataAdapter class is the child of the DataAdapter class and it is used to implement more specific functionalities in the derived classes. The DbDataAdapter class implements the IDbDataAdapter interface, so every class inheriting from it must provide the capabilities that the interface defines.

We have seen that there are three different managed providers, so you can imagine that we will have three different data adapter objects:

❑ The SqlDataAdapter is provided to manage Microsoft SQL Server 7.0 (or higher) databases

❑ The OleDbDataAdapter is provided to manage every database for which an OLE DB data provider is available

❑ The OdbcDataAdapter is provided to manage every database for which an ODBC driver has been released

To summarize, the classes inherit from each other as follows:

```
DataAdapter
    DbDataAdapter
        SqlDataAdapter
        OleDbDataAdapter
        OdbcDataAdapter
```

DataAdapter and DbDataAdapter are abstract classes – we cannot instantiate them directly.

It is important to decide which database to use in your application before starting to develop it, because we need to use the related Managed Provider classes. However, changing to a different Managed Provider is not particularly difficult, since all providers work in very similar ways, and many ADO objects are independent of any particular provider.

DataAdapter and DataSet

The DataAdapter works with the DataSet to provide a disconnected data retrieval mechanism. This is ideal for applications where server resources are really important, but client resources can be further exploited. A DataSet object is an in-memory representation of the data returned from a database. The DataAdapter handles the conversion of data between the data source format and the format used by the DataSet. So every time we fill a DataSet from a database, or write DataSet changes to a database, the DataAdapter provides conversion between the two formats.

The code that runs within a .NET application creates a DataAdapter-derived class (for example, SqlDataAdapter class) and uses the SQL query statement specified in the SelectCommand property to retrieve the data from the database. After that operation, the DataAdapter class cuts the connection to the database, freeing database resources for other incoming requests. The DataAdapter object analyzes the result of the query and fills the DataSet object, creating an in-memory data structure that mirrors the database structure.

Let's take a look at how to use the DataAdapter. We will see how to load the authors table from the pubs database available in Microsoft Access and SQL Server, into a DataSet using the DataAdapter. All of the code for the examples in this chapter is available from the Wrox web site. Here is how SQL Server displays the table's properties:

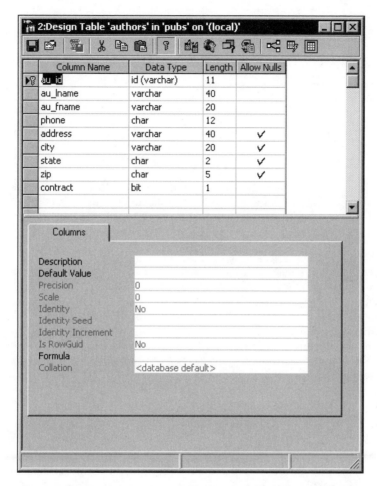

The authors table from the pubs database is formed by nine fields having different data types. Using the DataAdapter class to fill the DataSet object, we will be able to create a similar in-memory table. Let's see how we can accomplish that.

First of all we import the namespaces that contain the classes to use to connect to the chosen database. The System.Data namespace contains the DataSet class description and System.Data.SqlClient contains the data adapter class's references for Microsoft SQL Server database:

```
using System;
using System.Data;
using System.Data.SqlClient;
```

Within the Main function, which is called automatically when the program runs, we create a SqlDataAdapter object. We have provided two parameters in the constructor: a SQL SELECT statement string and a connection string. Internally, the SqlDataAdapter creates a SqlConnection object, passing it the connection string. Moreover, it creates a SqlCommand object that will fill the DataSet object with the SQL statement string provided:

```
namespace Example1
{
    class Class1
    {
        static void Main(string[] args)
        {
            // Create the data adapter object pointing to the authors
            // table
            SqlDataAdapter da = new SqlDataAdapter("SELECT au_id, au_lname,
                    au_fname, phone, address, city, state, zip, contract FROM
                    authors", "Server=localhost;database=pubs;uid=sa;pwd=;");
```

Now we create the DataSet object that will contain the records retrieved by the execution of the SQL statement. The string within the constructor represents the name of the DataSet, which will be used – among other things – if we write the DataSet to XML:

```
            // Create a dataset to contain the records
            DataSet ds = new DataSet("Authors");
```

This is the core of the code, where the DataAdapter object analyzes the SQL statement, retrieves the records from the database, and creates a similar table structure within the DataSet object. As we will see from this program's output, the in-memory table is not identical to the related database table and we need to add some specific properties ourselves. The code uses the two parameters version of the Fill method, where the DataSet to fill is provided as the first parameter, and the name of the table that will be created as the second parameter:

```
            // Fill the dataset creating an internal table called
            // author
            da.Fill(ds, "author");
```

In the final part of the code we add a loop to write some properties from each column to the console. As you can see, we use the table name that we specified as a parameter in the Fill method:

```
            // Loop through the columns created by data adapter
            // printing some properties
            foreach(DataColumn c in ds.Tables["author"].Columns)
            {
                Console.WriteLine("Column name: {0}", c.ColumnName);
                Console.WriteLine("DataType: {0}", c.DataType);
                Console.WriteLine("MaxLength: {0}", c.MaxLength);
                Console.WriteLine("AllowNulls?: {0}", c.AllowDBNull);
                Console.WriteLine
                    ("-=-=-=-=-=-=-=-=-=-=-=-=-=-=-=-=-=-=-=-=-=-=-=-=-");
            }
        }
    }
}
```

Here is the output of the code:

The DataAdapter has retrieved the column name and the data type correctly. However, the MaxLength property has been retrieved with a −1 value, meaning that there is no limit on the length, instead of the maximum length of the text field. And the AllowDBNull property is always true, even when the table columns are defined to not allow null values.

The primary key has not been correctly retrieved by the Fill method. The reason for this is that when we call the Fill method, the DataAdapter looks to see if the DataSet already has a schema that fits the requested data. If not, by default it will add tables and columns but not keys. So we can do one of two things to solve the problem:

❑ Instruct the DataAdapter to add the primary key by setting the MissingSchemaAction property to AddWithKey – the default is just Add

❑ Ensure that the schema – including the key data – already exists by using a typed DataSet

The MissingSchemaAction property will be discussed in Chapter 11 on Mappings, and typed datasets will be covered in Chapter 7 – Strongly Typed DataSets and DataSet Schemas.

Alternatively, of course, we can define columns as primary keys and add constraints after the DataSet has been filled.

More Details for the Fill Method

We have seen how the `Fill` method covers an important role during the record-retrieving phase. This method populates the specified `DataSet` or `DataTable` object, retrieving a set of records from the database. The `Fill` method connects to the database using either the connection string or a connection object. It retrieves the records by executing the SQL statement specified, either using a string parameter or a command object. It then closes the connection, freeing the server's resources.

> **If you use the `Fill` method with an open connection, the method will use that connection without closing it after retrieving the records.**

In the code examined above, we have encountered just one of the `Fill` method's variants exposed by the `DataAdapter`. For example, you can omit the string parameter that defines the table name that is created in the `DataSet` object. Let's see what happens when the second parameter is omitted:

```
// Create the data adapter object pointing to the authors table
OleDbDataAdapter da = new OleDbDataAdapter("SELECT au_id, au_lname, au_fname,
phone, address, city, state, zip, contract FROM authors",
"Provider=Microsoft.Jet.OLEDB.4.0;Password=;User ID=Admin;Data
Source=D:\\PRO.ADO.NET\\DataAdapter\\Samples\\pubs.mdb");

DataSet ds = new DataSet("Authors");

da.Fill(ds);
```

Since we haven't specified the table name in the `Fill` method, after retrieving every record from the table, you can point to the `DataTable` object added by the `DataAdapter`'s `Fill` method in two different ways:

1. Using the index of the table contained in the collection within the `DataSet`

2. Using the default `Table` name created by the `Fill` method

Here follow two examples showing these different methods:

```
// First case
foreach(DataRow r in ds.Tables[0].Rows)
{
    Console.WriteLine("First name: {0}", r["au_fname"]);
    Console.WriteLine("Last name: {0}", r["au_lname"]);
}
```

```
// Second case
foreach(DataRow r in ds.Tables["Table"].Rows)
{
    Console.WriteLine("First name: {0}", r["au_fname"]);
    Console.WriteLine("Last name: {0}", r["au_lname"]);
}
```

The loops above retrieve every record contained in the `DataSet` object displaying the first name and the last name of every author. As you can see, the first case uses an index number to point to the table, while in the second case the default table name is used. The figure below shows the output of the above code:

Using More Complex Queries

Until now we have used really simple queries where data has been retrieved from a single table. In real projects the SQL SELECT statements are more complex, where more than one table is joined to other tables using primary and foreign keys. However, what happens to the `DataSet` object when we specify a more complex query to execute? Well, let's see an example; starting from the following tables contained in the pubs database, we will build the query:

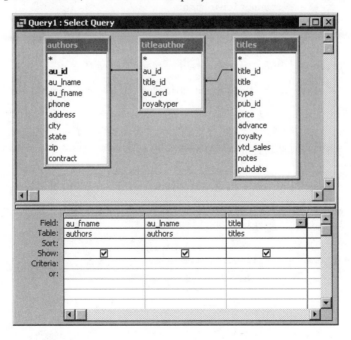

The `authors`, `titleauthor`, and `titles` tables are joined together by the respective primary and foreign keys. The SQL `SELECT` statement has to retrieve the author's first name and last name and the books that they have written.

```
SELECT authors.au_fname, authors.au_lname, titles.title
FROM (authors
INNER JOIN titleauthor ON authors.au_id = titleauthor.au_id)
INNER JOIN titles ON titleauthor.title_id = titles.title_id
```

Executing a `SELECT` query like this will produce a single `DataTable` in the `DataSet` – the database engine handles the relationships to produce a single result set combining data from three tables.

However we can use the `DataAdapter` to obtain the three tables used above, complete with the relationships between them, as separate tables in the `DataSet`. In order to realize a `DataSet` that has the same table structure and the same relations, you can use more than one `DataAdapter` object to fill it, and then you can add the relations and the constraints to the generated `DataSet` structure:

```csharp
using System;
using System.Data;
using System.Data.OleDb;

namespace Example5
{
    /// <summary>
    /// Summary description for Class1.
    /// </summary>
    class Class1
    {
        static void Main(string[] args)
        {
            // Create a connection object
            OleDbConnection dbConn = new OleDbConnection("Provider=Microsoft.
                Jet.OLEDB.4.0;Password=;User ID=Admin;Data Source=
                D:\\PRO.ADO.NET\\DataAdapter\\Samples\\pubs.mdb");

            DataSet ds = new DataSet("AuthorsAndTitles");

            // Create the data adapter object pointing to the authors
            // table
            OleDbDataAdapter daAuthors = new OleDbDataAdapter("SELECT au_id,
                au_fname, au_lname FROM authors",dbConn);

            // Fill the DataSet with author
            daAuthors.Fill(ds,"Author");

            // Create the data adapter object pointing to the titleauthor
            // table
            OleDbDataAdapter daTitleAuthor = new OleDbDataAdapter("SELECT
                au_id, title_id FROM titleauthor", dbConn);

            // Fill the DataSet with titleauthor
            daTitleAuthor.Fill(ds,"TitleAuthor");
```

```
            // Create the data adapter object pointing to the titles
            // table
            OleDbDataAdapter daTitle = new OleDbDataAdapter("SELECT
                title_id,title FROM titles", dbConn);

            // Fill the DataSet with titles
            daTitle.Fill(ds,"Titles");
```

We can define more than one single `DataAdapter` object to fill the same `DataSet`. In that way, we maintain a different `DataTable` object for each table in the database, creating a more complex structure. As you can see from the code below, after defining a `DataAdapter` object for the `authors`, `titleauthor`, and `titles` tables, and filling the `DataSet`, you can complete the in-memory data structure by defining primary keys and foreign key constraints between the tables:

```
            // Define primary keys
            ds.Tables["Titles"].Columns["title_id"].Unique = true;
            ds.Tables["Titles"].Columns["title_id"].AllowDBNull = false;
            ds.Tables["Titles"].PrimaryKey = new DataColumn[]
                {ds.Tables["Titles"].Columns["title_id"]};

            ds.Tables["Author"].Columns["au_id"].Unique = true;
            ds.Tables["Author"].Columns["au_id"].AllowDBNull = false;
            ds.Tables["Author"].PrimaryKey = new DataColumn[]
                {ds.Tables["Author"].Columns["au_id"]};

            ds.Tables["TitleAuthor"].PrimaryKey = new DataColumn[]
                {ds.Tables["TitleAuthor"].Columns["au_id"],
                ds.Tables["TitleAuthor"].Columns["title_id"]};

            // Define constraints
            ForeignKeyConstraint fk1 = new ForeignKeyConstraint(
                "authorstitleauthor",ds.Tables["Author"].
                Columns["au_id"],ds.Tables["TitleAuthor"].Columns["au_id"]);
            ds.Tables["TitleAuthor"].Constraints.Add(fk1);
            ForeignKeyConstraint fk2 = new ForeignKeyConstraint(
                "titlestitleauthor",ds.Tables["Titles"].
                Columns["title_id"],ds.Tables["TitleAuthor"].
                Columns["title_id"]);
            ds.Tables["TitleAuthor"].Constraints.Add(fk2);

            // Write the related XML document representing the DataSet
            ds.WriteXml("D:\\join.xml",XmlWriteMode.WriteSchema);
        }
    }
}
```

At the end of the code, an XML document has been written in order to show you that the `DataSet` now contains the same structure as the database:

```
    <?xml version="1.0" standalone="yes"?>
    <AuthorsAndTitles>
      <xsd:schema id="AuthorsAndTitles" targetNamespace="" xmlns=""
      xmlns:xsd="http://www.w3.org/2001/XMLSchema" xmlns:msdata="urn:schemas-
      microsoft-com:xml-msdata">
```

```
<xsd:element name="AuthorsAndTitles" msdata:IsDataSet="true">
  <xsd:complexType>
    <xsd:choice maxOccurs="unbounded">
      <xsd:element name="Author">
        <xsd:complexType>
          <xsd:sequence>
           <xsd:element name="au_id" type="xsd:string" />
           <xsd:element name="au_fname" type="xsd:string"
           minOccurs="0" />
           <xsd:element name="au_lname" type="xsd:string"
           minOccurs="0" />
          </xsd:sequence>
        </xsd:complexType>
      </xsd:element>
      <xsd:element name="TitleAuthor">
        <xsd:complexType>
          <xsd:sequence>
            <xsd:element name="au_id" type="xsd:string" />
            <xsd:element name="title_id" type="xsd:string" />
          </xsd:sequence>
        </xsd:complexType>
      </xsd:element>
      <xsd:element name="Titles">
        <xsd:complexType>
          <xsd:sequence>
            <xsd:element name="title_id" type="xsd:string" />
            <xsd:element name="title" type="xsd:string" minOccurs="0" />
          </xsd:sequence>
        </xsd:complexType>
      </xsd:element>
    </xsd:choice>
  </xsd:complexType>
```

Every table has been added in the XML schema and every column has been defined with the respective data type. Below, the XML schema defines the constraints among the tables and defines the columns that become the primary keys.

```
<xsd:unique name="Constraint1" msdata:PrimaryKey="true">
  <xsd:selector xpath=".//Author" />
  <xsd:field xpath="au_id" />

</xsd:unique>
<xsd:unique name="TitleAuthor_Constraint1"
msdata:ConstraintName="Constraint1" msdata:PrimaryKey="true">
  <xsd:selector xpath=".//TitleAuthor" />
  <xsd:field xpath="au_id" />
  <xsd:field xpath="title_id" />
</xsd:unique>
<xsd:unique name="Titles_Constraint1"
msdata:ConstraintName="Constraint1" msdata:PrimaryKey="true">
  <xsd:selector xpath=".//Titles" />
  <xsd:field xpath="title_id" />
</xsd:unique>
<xsd:keyref name="titlestitleauthor" refer="Titles_Constraint1"
msdata:ConstraintOnly="true">
  <xsd:selector xpath=".//TitleAuthor" />
  <xsd:field xpath="title_id" />
```

```
        </xsd:keyref>
        <xsd:keyref name="authorstitleauthor" refer="Constraint1"
        msdata:ConstraintOnly="true">
          <xsd:selector xpath=".//TitleAuthor" />
          <xsd:field xpath="au_id" />
        </xsd:keyref>
      </xsd:element>
  </xsd:schema>
```

Working this way has two main advantages. Firstly, it means that we can easily present data to users so that they can see, and work with, the relationships. Secondly it makes updates easier – finding an UPDATE statement to correspond with a SELECT statement containing joins is a complex proposition. But if we have separate, related DataTable objects then each one can be updated by its own simple UPDATE statement.

Filling a DataSet Object with Few Records

Did you note that every query we have executed doesn't present the WHERE condition in the SELECT statement? So, what happens if we have a lot of records in the table? Each time we refresh the DataSet content using the Fill method, a lot of time will be spent on retrieving the records and filling the DataSet object. So, the best solution is a filtered query that extracts just the needed records. However, for some specific operations even the filtered query is not the best solution. For example, if we want to show all the records in the table divided by pages we need to use a variant of the Fill method that expects four parameters:

1. The DataSet object to fill

2. The numeric position of the record to start with

3. The maximum number of records to retrieve

4. The name of the table that will be added in the DataSet

Using this version of the Fill method, we can retrieve just the number of records we want by adding or refreshing the DataSet with new or old records, respectively. In the following figure you can see an application that uses this method to browse between records in the authors and titles tables, retrieving just one record at a time:

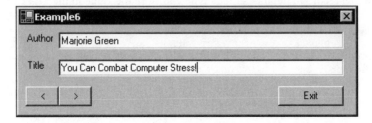

Let's examine the code that allows us to create this application.

```
public class frmMain : System.Windows.Forms.Form
{
    private System.Windows.Forms.Label label1;
    private System.Windows.Forms.TextBox txtAuthor;
```

```
private System.Windows.Forms.Label label2;
private System.Windows.Forms.TextBox txtTitle;
private System.Windows.Forms.Button btnPrev;
private System.Windows.Forms.Button btnNext;
private System.Windows.Forms.Button btnExit;

private OleDbDataAdapter da;
private int iCurr;
private int iMax;
```

First of all we declare class member variables. The `OleDbDataAdapter` will be used to fill a `DataSet` object and it will be created in the `Form_Load` event handler. The `iCurr` integer value represents the number of the current record to display in the application, while the `iMax` integer value contains the maximum number of records that the application can show.

Before the application is shown for the first time, the `Form_Load` event handler is called. This is a good place to add our initialization code:

```
private void frmMain_Load(object sender, System.EventArgs e)
{
    // Create a connection object
    OleDbConnection dbConn = new OleDbConnection("Provider=Microsoft.
        Jet.OLEDB.4.0;Password=;User ID=Admin;Data Source=
        D:\\PRO.ADO.NET\\DataAdapter\\Samples\\pubs.mdb");

    // Retrieve maximum number of records
    dbConn.Open();
    OleDbCommand cmd = new OleDbCommand("SELECT COUNT(authors.au_fname) FROM
        (authors INNER JOIN titleauthor ON authors.au_id = titleauthor.au_id)
        INNER JOIN titles ON titleauthor.title_id = titles.title_id",dbConn);
    iMax = (int) cmd.ExecuteScalar();
    dbConn.Close();
```

The first initialization retrieves the maximum number of records that the application can show. This value is set to the `iMax` variable and it will be used within the navigation bar to avoid an out-of-bound record being retrieved. In the code above, an `OleDbCommand` object is used to execute a scalar query that retrieves just the first record of the specified statement. As we need to retrieve the total number of records, we cast the resulting record to the integer data type and store the value in the `iMax` variable.

```
    // Create the data adapter object pointing to the authors table
    da = new OleDbDataAdapter("SELECT authors.au_fname, authors.au_lname,
        titles.title FROM (authors INNER JOIN titleauthor ON authors.au_id =
        titleauthor.au_id) INNER JOIN titles ON titleauthor.title_id =
        titles.title_id",    dbConn);

    DataSet ds = new DataSet("Authors");

    // Fill the DataSet
    da.Fill(ds,iCurr,1,"AuthorAndTitle");

    FillForm(ds);
}
```

In the last part of the event handler code, the global `DataAdapter` object is created and the SQL statement is specified in order to retrieve the author's first name and last name together with the respective book. The `Fill` method is used to retrieve just the first record and the resulting `DataSet` is passed to the `FillForm` method that displays the record in the application:

```
private void FillForm(DataSet ds)
{
    txtAuthor.Text = ds.Tables["AuthorAndTitle"].Rows[0]["au_fname"] + " " +
        ds.Tables["AuthorAndTitle"].Rows[0]["au_lname"];
    txtTitle.Text = ds.Tables["AuthorAndTitle"].Rows[0]["title"].ToString();
}
```

Finally, the code behind the navigation buttons will create a new `DataSet` object that will be filled either with the previous or the next record. The resulting record will be displayed by the `FillForm` method. See the code below:

```
private void btnNext_Click(object sender, System.EventArgs e)
{
    if (iCurr <= iMax)
    {
        DataSet ds = new DataSet("Authors");

        iCurr++;

        // Fill the DataSet
        da.Fill(ds,iCurr,1,"AuthorAndTitle");

        FillForm(ds);
    }
}

private void btnPrev_Click(object sender, System.EventArgs e)
{
    if (iCurr > 0)
    {
        DataSet ds = new DataSet("Authors");

        iCurr--;

        // Fill the DataSet
        da.Fill(ds,iCurr,1,"AuthorAndTitle");

        FillForm(ds);
    }
}
```

Filling a DataSet Object with Only the Schema

As have seen in the `DataSet` chapter, a `DataSet` is an in-memory representation of data. The data is not always retrieved from a database: the `DataSet` object can be filled with data retrieved from other data sources. A common example is the XML document and schema. The schema contains a definition of the tags that form the document, including data types, field length, and much more. So, the `DataSet` object can easily contain data retrieved from an XML document instead of the database.

With the arrival of Web services, it will be a common task to retrieve data items from an XML document and insert them into a database. With this scenario, none of the Fill versions we have encountered is the best choice to prepare the DataSet object to retrieve the data from an XML document. We need a method that fills just the structure of the DataSet object without retrieving any data from the database. The DataAdapter provides the FillSchema method, which accomplishes this task. Let's see an example where this method is used:

```
<?xml version="1.0" standalone="yes"?>
<Authors>
  <Table>
    <au_id>172-32-1176</au_id>
    <au_lname>White</au_lname>
    <au_fname>Johnson</au_fname>
    <phone>408 496-7223</phone>
  </Table>
  <Table>
    <au_id>213-46-8915</au_id>
    <au_lname>Green</au_lname>
    <au_fname>Marjorie</au_fname>
    <phone>415 986-7020</phone>
  </Table>
  <Table>
    <au_id>238-95-7766</au_id>
    <au_lname>Carson</au_lname>
    <au_fname>Cheryl</au_fname>
    <phone>415 548-7723</phone>
  </Table>
</Authors>
```

The XML document above contains some records that we want to insert in the DataSet object and eventually store in the authors table in the pubs database. So, the first thing we can do is fill a DataSet object with the schema of the authors table and then load the XML document with the ReadXml method of the DataSet:

```
private void Form1_Load(object sender, System.EventArgs e)
{
    // Create the data adapter object pointing to the authors table
    OleDbDataAdapter da = new OleDbDataAdapter("SELECT au_id, au_lname,
        au_fname, phone FROM authors", "Provider=Microsoft.Jet.OLEDB.
        4.0;Password=;User ID=Admin;Data Source=
        D:\\PRO.ADO.NET\\DataAdapter\\Samples\\pubs.mdb");

    // Create a DataSet
    DataSet ds = new DataSet("Authors");

    // Fill the DataSet just with the schema
    da.FillSchema(ds, SchemaType.Source);

    // Load the data from the XML document
    ds.ReadXml("D:\\Example7Data.xml");

    // Display the DataSet data in a DataGrid component
    dg.DataSource = ds.Tables[0];
}
```

In the Form_Load event handler we can add the code to initialize the variables and to display data as soon as the application starts. The code above fills the DataSet object just with the schema retrieved from the authors table and then uses the ReadXml method to store the data in the DataSet object. Finally, the table and its contents are displayed inside a DataGrid data component. Look at the next figure:

The FillSchema method prepares the DataSet object by adding one or more DataTables containing the specified columns. When the ReadXml method is called, the DataSet looks for similar column names to fill with the data.

You will learn that the ReadXml method is able to create the DataSet schema by reading or inferring the schema from the XML document. However the FillSchema method is more useful when:

❑ You need to retrieve only specific columns from an XML document

❑ The elements in the XML document match the columns and tables in the database

❑ You want use the mapping mechanism (see the mapping chapter for more details)

The FillSchema method has four variants, but the following one is most useful:

```
public DataTable[] FillSchema(
    DataSet dataSet,
    SchemaType schemaType,
    string srcTable
);
```

Sometimes you will omit the third parameter, allowing the default name of Table. The interesting parameter is the SchemaType:

❑ The SchemaType.Source value will ignore the mapped columns, retrieving the schema exactly as it has been defined in the data source

❑ The SchemaType.Mapping enumeration value will use the mapped columns when it retrieves the schema from the data source

We will learn more about mapping in Chapter 11. Put simply, it maps column and table names in the data source to different column and table names in the DataSet.

Filling a DataSet Object that Already has a Schema

Until now we have seen how the `Fill` method of the `DataAdapter` fills a `DataSet` object, creating its own in-memory schema. However, sometimes you will have to fill a `DataSet` object that already has a schema, for example when the `DataSet` has been created as a strongly-typed `DataSet` or its schema has been read from the XML schema. When the `Fill` method finds the `DataSet` schema, it fills the `DataSet` columns that are equal to the ones specified in the `SELECT` command. It could happen that the `DataAdapter` retrieves more, or different, columns from the database than the ones defined in the `DataSet` schema. We can choose the action to take when a column is missing in the `DataSet` schema by setting the `MissingSchemaAction` property, which accepts one of the following `MissingSchemaAction` enumeration values:

MissingSchemaAction value	Description
Add	Adds every column that is not present in the `DataSet` object schema. This is the default value.
AddWithKey	Adds all columns that are not present in the `DataSet` object schema, and identifies primary keys.
Error	Raises a `System.Exception` exception when a missing column is missed in the `DataSet`'s schema.
Ignore	Ignores every extra column.

Updating a Database

We have seen that each time we call the `Fill` method exposed by the `DataAdapter` object, a fresh set of records is retrieved, and the `DataSet` content is refreshed. However, what would happen if we change the content of our `DataSet`? We will have an in-memory set of records different from the database counterpart. We need a way to write changes back to the database. ADO.NET offers the `Update` method exposed by the `DataAdapter` object. This method analyzes the `RowState` of each record in the `DataSet` and calls the appropriate `INSERT`, `UPDATE`, and `DELETE` statements.

The same method is used to insert, delete, and modify the records in the database. The `Fill` method associates a `RowState` value with each row retrieved within the `DataSet` object. The starting value is set to `Unchanged` for every row, but when something changes the `RowState` assumes different values from the `DataRowState` enumeration:

❑ The `Added` value is assigned to a new row that has been inserted in the `DataSet` object

❑ The `Deleted` value is assigned to a deleted row within the `DataSet` object

❑ The `Detached` value is assigned to a new row that is not part of the rows contained in the `DataSet` object or that has been removed from it

❑ The `Modified` value is assigned to a modified row within the `DataSet` object

The `Update` method goes through each record within the provided `DataSet` object, analyzing the `RowState` value and calling the respective SQL command when this value is different from the `Unchanged` state. We need SQL commands to perform these updates, inserts, and deletes. We can choose to write our own, or use the `CommandBuilder` object. We will discuss the `CommandBuilder` object next.

Using a CommandBuilder Object

The easiest way to create an application that updates the records in a database is by using a CommandBuilder object, which analyzes the provided SQL SELECT statement and creates the other three statements automatically. We have two constraints when using this object:

1. We have to specify a SELECT command either in the DataAdapter constructor or from the SelectCommand parameter of the DataAdapter that retrieves records from only one table

2. We have to specify at least a primary key or a unique column as a required column within the SELECT command

When these two conditions are satisfied then we can create a CommandBuilder object. We can specify the DataAdapter object in the CommandBuilder constructor:

```
// Create the insert, delete and update
// statements automatically.
OleDbCommandBuilder cb = new OleDbCommandBuilder(da);
```

There are command builders for each data provider. The common ones will be OdbcCommandBuilder, OleDbCommandBuilder, and SqlCommandBuilder.

The UPDATE statement that is created by the CommandBuilder contains a WHERE condition to identify the correct record to update. This WHERE condition updates the record only if none of the column values have changed since the last Fill method call. This is a useful rule in multi-user environments where the changes to the database can occur from various users. It means there is no risk of overwriting a record that has been changed by another user only a few moments before your updating operation.

If the row we want to update has already been updated by another user, the DataAdapter throws a DBConcurrencyException. We can use the Row property of this exception to identify the row that caused the problem.

Let's see an example:

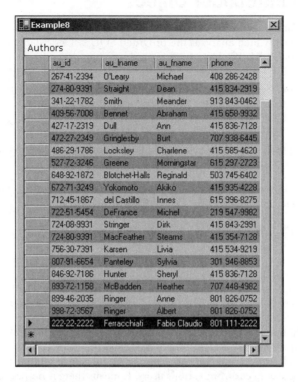

This example uses a `DataGrid` data component. The `DataGrid` enables users to interact with a `DataSet` very easily, and requires very little programming. See the *Visual Studio .NET and ADO.NET* chapter for more information.

In this example, a form loads and allows users to manipulate a `DataSet` loaded from the `pubs` database. When the user has finished editing, they close the form. This gives them the opportunity to save their changes. Here is the form's load event handler:

```
private void Form1_Load(object sender, System.EventArgs e)
{
    // Create a Connection object
    OleDbConnection dbConn = new OleDbConnection("Provider=Microsoft.
      Jet.OLEDB.4.0;Password=;User ID=Admin;Data Source=
      D:\\PRO.ADO.NET\\DataAdapter\\Samples\\pubs.mdb");

    // Create the data adapter object pointing to the authors table
    da = new OleDbDataAdapter("SELECT au_id, au_lname, au_fname, phone FROM
      authors",dbConn);

    // Fill the DataSet
    da.Fill(ds);

    // Display the records in a DataGrid component
    dg.DataSource = ds.Tables[0];
}
```

In the code above, we retrieve the records from the database and fill the `DataGrid` data component. Note that the `SELECT` statement contains the primary key and retrieves data only from the single `authors` table. Here is the event handler for when the form closes:

```
private void Form1_Closing(object sender, System.ComponentModel.CancelEventArgs e)
{
    // Message box to prompt the save request.
    if (MessageBox.Show("Do you want save the changes?",
        "Example8",MessageBoxButtons.YesNo) == DialogResult.Yes)
    {
        try
        {
            // Create the insert, delete and update
            // statements automatically.
            OleDbCommandBuilder cb = new OleDbCommandBuilder(da);

            // Retrieve just the changed rows
            DataSet dsChanges = ds.GetChanges();

            if (dsChanges != null)
            {
                // Update the database
                da.Update(dsChanges);

                // Accept the changes within the
                // DataSet
                ds.AcceptChanges();
            }
        }
        catch(Exception ex)
        {
            // Error occurs, show the message
            MessageBox.Show(ex.Message);
        }
    }
}
```

The form's `Closing` event handler is used to prompt the user to update the database with the changes made to the `DataSet`. If the user presses the **Yes** button from the message box, an `OleDbCommandBuilder` object is created and the `DataAdapter` object, a class member, is filled with the SQL commands. Finally, the `Update` method is called and a new `DataSet` object containing just the changed rows is provided to it. In this case there is little advantage in using the `GetChanges` method. But it is very useful when the `DataAdapter` and `Connection` objects exist on another server, because it means only changed records get passed back over the network – reducing network traffic.

Using SQL Commands

When we have a more complex query that retrieves records from different tables, or don't want the `UPDATE` command to check for changes in the database before updating it, we can specify our own SQL commands. We do this by assigning commands to the `DataAdapter` properties `InsertCommand`, `UpdateCommand`, and `DeleteCommand`.

The `Command` objects allow developers to specify parameters dynamically at run time. When defining the SQL statement we use a **placeholder** instead of a particular value. Then we use the `Parameters` collection of the `Command` object to define the dynamic column value. We use the @ placeholder for `SqlCommand` objects and the ? placeholder for the other providers. The following code shows how to do this using the `OleDb` provider:

```
//
// cmmInsert
//
OleDbCommand cmmInsert = new OleDbCommand();
cmmInsert.CommandText =
    "INSERT INTO authors(au_id, au_fname, au_lname, phone) " +
    "VALUES (?, ?, ?, ?)";

cmmInsert.Connection = this.dbConn;
cmmInsert.Parameters.Add(new OleDbParameter("id", OleDbType.Char, 11,
    ParameterDirection.Input, false, ((System.Byte)(0)), ((System.Byte)(0)),
    "au_id", DataRowVersion.Current, null));

cmmInsert.Parameters.Add(new OleDbParameter("fname", OleDbType.Char, 20,
    ParameterDirection.Input, false, ((System.Byte)(0)), ((System.Byte)(0)),
    "au_fname", DataRowVersion.Current, null));

cmmInsert.Parameters.Add(new OleDbParameter("lname", OleDbType.Char, 40,
    ParameterDirection.Input, false, ((System.Byte)(0)), ((System.Byte)(0)),
    "au_lname", DataRowVersion.Current, null));

cmmInsert.Parameters.Add(new OleDbParameter("phone", OleDbType.Char, 12,
    ParameterDirection.Input, false, ((System.Byte)(0)), ((System.Byte)(0)),
    "phone", DataRowVersion.Current, null));

// Define the insert command in the DataAdapter
da.InsertCommand = cmmInsert;
```

And here we use the SQL Server provider:

```
//
// cmmInsert
//
SqlCommand cmmInsert = new SqlCommand();
cmmInsert.CommandText = "INSERT INTO authors(au_id, au_fname, au_lname,"
    + "phone) VALUES (@au_id, @au_fname, @au_lname, @phone)";

cmmInsert.Connection = this.dbConn;
cmmInsert.Parameters.Add(new SqlParameter("@au_id", SqlType.Char, 11,
    ParameterDirection.Input, false, ((System.Byte)(0)),
    ((System.Byte)(0)), "au_id", DataRowVersion.Current, null));

cmmInsert.Parameters.Add(new SqlParameter("@au_fname", SqlType.Char, 20,
    ParameterDirection.Input, false, ((System.Byte)(0)),
    ((System.Byte)(0)), "au_fname", DataRowVersion.Current, null));

cmmInsert.Parameters.Add(new SqlParameter("@au_lname", SqlType.Char, 40,
    ParameterDirection.Input, false, ((System.Byte)(0)), ((System.Byte)(0)),
    "au_lname", DataRowVersion.Current, null));

cmmInsert.Parameters.Add(new SqlParameter("@phone", SqlType.Char, 12,
    ParameterDirection.Input, false, ((System.Byte)(0)), ((System.Byte)(0)),
    "phone", DataRowVersion.Current, null));

// Define the insert command in the DataAdapter
da.InsertCommand = cmmInsert;
```

The code above accomplishes the same task using different .NET data providers. It starts by defining the INSERT statement where some placeholders are inserted as values of the command. Then, four parameters are added to the Parameters collection. These parameters will contain the values of the respective columns to insert in the database when the Update method is called. To define a new parameter you have to create a new Parameter object, specifying the following values:

❑ parameterName – the parameter's name. The SQL Server provider uses this to identify which parameter you are setting. Other providers use the order in which you define the parameters.

❑ dbType – the parameter's data type.

❑ size – the width of the parameter

❑ direction – whether the parameter is an input value or an output value. If you provide the value to the command use ParameterDirection.Input value; if you expect a returning value from the command use ParameterDirection.Output.

❑ isNullable – a Boolean value indicating whether the parameter can be null (true) or not (false).

❑ precision – the total number of digits to the left and to the right of the decimal point (zero if the parameter is not a number).

❑ scale – the total number of decimal places.

❑ sourceColumn – the name that the column has in the DataTable object.

❑ sourceVersion – which version of the DataRow to use when performing the update.

❑ value – the parameter's default value.

It is very important that you specify the correct value for sourceColumn. Otherwise the DataAdapter will not be able to identify how the in-memory column names correspond with the database column names. Once we have created a parameter and assigned it to the InsertCommand property of the DataAdapter, we can use it using the following code:

```
private void button1_Click(object sender, System.EventArgs e)
{
    DataRow r = ds.Tables[0].NewRow();
    r["au_id"] = "222-22-2222";
    r["au_fname"] = "Fabio Claudio";
    r["au_lname"] = "Ferracchiati";
    r["phone"] = "801 111-2233";
    ds.Tables[0].Rows.Add(r);

    da.Update(ds);

    this.Close();
}
```

In the button's Click event handler, shown above, a new row is added to the DataSet object. Finally, the code calls the Update method in order to insert the new record in the database. The Update method goes through each record looking for a RowState that is different from the Unchanged value. It finds the row with the Added value, so it calls the InsertCommand statement stored in its property. It looks for the first parameter associated with the au_id column, finds it, and sets the specified value. The same processing occurs for the other parameters. If you don't specify the source column, or you make a mistake during parameter specification, an exception will be thrown:

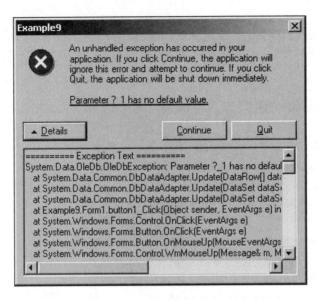

The message is not really clear because it says that no default value has been assigned to the parameter. This is because the parameter associated with the source column has not been found and, since we haven't declared a default value for the parameter, we receive the error.

Making Updates Using Stored Procedures

A stored procedure is a sort of SQL function that is compiled and stored in the database. It is a great idea to use them in your application, for two main reasons:

❑ They remove every SQL statement from the applications code, making the code more readable and maintainable.

❑ They run faster, because they are already compiled into the database. If we embed SQL in our applications, the SQL string is passed to the database and re-compiled every time we run it.

Let's see a simple Microsoft SQL Server stored procedure retrieving an author specified by their identification column value:

```
CREATE PROCEDURE spRetrieveAuthor
    @au_id integer
AS
    SELECT *
    FROM authors
    WHERE au_id = @au_id
```

Microsoft Access also supports stored procedures to some extent. We can create a query in the database by selecting the **Create query in Design view** item, as illustrated opposite:

Switching to the SQL view you can add the following SQL statement:

```
SELECT *
FROM authors
WHERE (((authors.au_id) Like [?]));
```

Calling a stored procedure from the code is similar to what we have seen before. The main difference consists in declaring the type of the command we are going to execute. It is easy to learn how to use stored procedures by example:

```
oleDbSelectCommand1.CommandText = "spRetrieveAuthor";
oleDbSelectCommand1.CommandType = CommandType.StoredProcedure;
oleDbSelectCommand1.Connection = oleDbConnection1;
oleDbSelectCommand1.Parameters.Add(new OleDbParameter("au_id", OleDbType.Char, 11,
ParameterDirection.Input, true, ((System.Byte)(0)), ((System.Byte)(0)), "au_id",
DataRowVersion.Current, null));
```

As shown above, we have to specify the name of the stored procedure in the CommandText property. Moreover, we set the CommandType property to CommandType.StoredProcedure to inform the DataAdapter that it has to execute a stored procedure instead of a SQL statement. Finally, the code provides a value for every parameter expected by the stored procedure. In this case, the code declares just the author identification column, au_id.

```
private void button1_Click(object sender, System.EventArgs e)
{
    // Create a DataSet
    DataSet ds = new DataSet("Author");

    // Specify an au_id to retrieve just one record
    // da is a class member DataAdapter
    da.SelectCommand.Parameters[0].Value = "172-32-1176";
```

```
        // Fill the DataSet
        da.Fill(ds);

        // Show a message box with the author's last name
        if (ds != null)
            MessageBox.Show("Hi, author: " +
                    ds.Tables[0].Rows[0]["au_lname"].ToString());
}
```

The code above illustrates a simple example, showing how easy it is to pass parameters to the stored procedure. You can specify all the parameters' values pointing to the items in the collection by either their index or their name. The code fills the DataSet with a specific author retrieved by specifying their identification number and shows a message box reporting the author's last name.

The DataAdapter's Events

The DataAdapter exposes two useful events that you can catch to manage the updating process. The RowUpdating and RowUpdated events are fired when the DataAdapter Update method is going to update the DataSet object and when it has updated the record, respectively. You can define an event handler in your code to change the default behavior of the Update method. For example, you can insert the following code to check that another user has not already updated the record you want to update:

```
da.RowUpdating += new OleDbRowUpdatingEventHandler(OnRowUpdating);
...
```

First of all, the code adds the OnRowUpdating event handler for the RowUpdating event. Here is the code for the handler:

```
private void OnRowUpdating(object sender, OleDbRowUpdatingEventArgs e)
{
    // Enter in the if only when it is an UPDATE statement
    if (e.StatementType == StatementType.Update)
    {
        // Check that the original record is not changed
        string strSQL = "SELECT au_id, au_lname, au_fname, phone FROM authors
            WHERE au_id='";
        strSQL = strSQL + e.Row["au_id",DataRowVersion.Original] + "' AND
            au_lname='";
        strSQL = strSQL + e.Row["au_lname",DataRowVersion.Original] + "' AND
            au_fname='";
        strSQL = strSQL + e.Row["au_fname",DataRowVersion.Original] + "' AND
            phone='";
        strSQL = strSQL + e.Row["phone",DataRowVersion.Original] + "'";
```

Within the event handler, the code checks that the SQL statement that is going to update the current row is the UPDATE command. Then, a SELECT command is built to check that the current record has not been changed after the last Fill operation. As you can see, the OleDbRowUpdatingEventArgs parameter, provided by the event handler, is used to retrieve the original row values that are concatenated to the SELECT command.

```
        // Open the connection
        dbConn.Open();

        // Create a command to retrieve the number of record affected
        OleDbCommand cmm = new OleDbCommand(strSQL, dbConn);

        // If the number of records retrieved are zero
        // the record has changed
        if (cmm.ExecuteNonQuery() == 0)
        {
```

The code goes on retrieving the number of records affected by the query. If the value is equal to zero then the row has already been changed by another user.

```
        // Display the confirm message
        if (MessageBox.Show("The record you are attempting to modify has
            already changed by another user. Do you want overwrite
            it?","Example12",MessageBoxButtons.YesNo) == DialogResult.No)
        {
            // Skip the update for the current row
            e.Status = UpdateStatus.SkipCurrentRow;
        }
    }

    // Close the connection
    dbConn.Close();
    }
}
```

In this case, a message box is displayed that asks the user to confirm the record overwrite. If the user chooses to not overwrite the current row, the UpdateStatus.SkipCurrentRow value is specified in the Status property. In this way, the record will be skipped and no updating will be accomplished.

The OleDbRowUpdatingEventArgs event handler parameter, like the SqlRowUpdatingEventArgs and OdbcRowUpdatingEventArgs event handler parameters, is really useful when you use the RowUpdating event. In the following table you can see the properties exposed by the parameter:

Property	Description
Command	Get or set the command object to execute when the Update method has been called.
Errors	Get the errors generated by the command object when the Update method is executed.
Row	Get the row that is going to be updated.
StatementType	Get the type of the SQL statement to execute.
Status	Get the UpdateStatus value of the command object.
TableMapping	Get the DataTableMapping object used during the Update execution. We will learn more about mapping in Chapter 11.

The OleDbRowUpdatedEventArgs event handler parameter, like the SqlRowUpdatedEventArgs and OdbcRowUpdatedEventArgs event handle parameters, is similar to the parameter seen above. It has just one more property and, naturally, is passed to the RowUpdated event that is fired when the row has been updated.

Property	Description
RecordsAffected	Get the number of records that have been affected by the Update method execution.

Summary

In this chapter we have seen how the DataAdapter holds a fundamental role in the new in-memory data representation mechanism introduced by the ADO.NET framework. We have seen how the Fill method is able to retrieve the record from a data source, and create DataTable objects in a DataSet. We have seen that the created DataTable has a similar structure to the database counterpart, including primary keys and constraints. We have seen how the Update method accomplishes SQL command tasks, such as inserting, deleting, and updating operations.

7

Typed DataSets and DataSet Schemas

So far, we have looked at how to use the DataSet class provided by the System.Data namespace. We have learned about the Rows collection, the Columns collection, and how to access individual rows and columns of data within the DataSet. For example, in a typical DataSet in C#, you might access the first name of a customer like so:

```
myRow = MyDataSet.Tables["Customers"].Rows[0];
Console.WriteLine( myRow["FirstName"] );
```

By the time we're done with this chapter, you'll be able to get access to your data in a much more programmer-friendly, and reader-friendly, fashion:

```
Console.WriteLine( CustomerDataSet.Customers[0].FirstName );
```

As you can see, the second method is far easier to understand and write. The functionality we just described is made possible by a convention in the .NET framework known as **Strongly Typed DataSets**.

Strongly Typed DataSets are made possible through inheritance and an **XML Schema Definition** (XSD). This schema provides a rich description of the data types, relations, keys, and constraints within the DataSet. We will discuss how the XSD fits into the DataSet and how to create Typed DataSets later in this chapter. First, however, we will run through a brief overview of some of the basic elements of XSD and how they apply to Strongly Typed DataSets.

At the end of this chapter, you should be able to:

❑   Create an XSD schema, either manually or with the aid of Visual Studio .NET

❑   Identify the benefits and drawbacks of using Strongly Typed DataSets

❑   Create a fully functional, annotated Strongly Typed DataSet

❑   Manipulate Strongly-Typed DataSets based on relational data such as SQL Server tables

Overview of XSD

Before you start double-checking the title of this chapter, we should explain why we're covering XSD here. Relational database servers like SQL Server and Oracle all have their own internal and proprietary formats for defining the structure of stored data. An Oracle table definition looks nothing like an internal SQL Server table definition. DataSets, on the other hand, store their own internal structure in a standardized, widely-used format called XSD. If you're not at all familiar with XSD, you might want to refer to the Wrox *Professional XML Schemas* ISBN 1-861005-47-4 book or skip to the other sections of this chapter and come back to review XSD later.

The **XML Schema Definition** (XSD) language is a dialect of XML for describing data structures. It is particularly useful because it allows applications to read and use schema information when handling data. Strongly Typed DataSets use an XSD data schema to generate a subclass of DataSet that is tailored to that particular schema.

The following overview of XSD should give you enough information to create and use Strongly-Typed DataSets. However, this is only a small portion of what XSD can do.

If you are already familiar with XML Schemas and their use, you may want to skip directly to the *DataSet Schemas* section later in the chapter. However, you should still at least skim the information provided in this next section as a refresher so that XSD will be foremost in your mind when we start to go into more detail on how XSD impacts on the DataSet.

Simple Types

As we said, XSD is an XML dialect used to describe data types, relationships, and other rules that constrict or constrain the information that can be contained by an XML document that conforms to the schema. XSD elements control how various elements and attributes can appear in the related XML document. A simple type is an XSD type that defines data that contains no child elements, no attributes, and only a basic data type as its contents within the instance document.

Basic Data Types

The XSD standard comes with several built-in data types. The following table lists many of the data types for which the XSD standard already contains definitions:

Primitive XML Data Type	Description
String	Character strings.
Boolean	Represents a true or false value.
Decimal	Numbers of arbitrary precision.
Float	Single-precision, 32-bit floating-point number.
Double	Double-precision 64-bit floating-point number.
Duration	Represents a span of time.
dateTime	Represents a specific point in time.
Time	Represents a given time of day.
Date	Represents a calendar date.
gYearMonth	A Gregorian month and Gregorian year.
gYear	A Gregorian year.
gMonthDay	A Gregorian month and Gregorian day. Specific date that occurs once a year.
gDay	A Gregorian day of the month.
gMonth	A Gregorian month.
hexBinary	Represents hex-encoded binary data.
Base64Binary	Base64-encoded arbitrary binary data.
anyURI	Any URI as defined by RFC 2396; may be absolute or relative.
QName	Qualified name. Composed of a prefix and a local name separated by a colon. The prefix must be a namespace prefix defined by the namespace declaration.
NOTATION	Represents a set of QNames.

The following is an example of an XSD schema file that utilizes a couple of the primitive types described above. Some of the syntax may not make all that much sense, but we'll describe that shortly. For now, just take a look at the attribute declarations and their associated data types.

```xml
<?xml version="1.0" encoding="utf-8" ?>
<xsd:schema targetNamespace="http://tempuri.org/XMLSchema.xsd"
elementFormDefault="qualified" xmlns="http://tempuri.org/XMLSchema.xsd"
xmlns:xsd="http://www.w3.org/2001/XMLSchema">
  <xsd:element name="MyElement">
   <xsd:complexType>
    <xsd:sequence />
    <xsd:attribute name="MyString" type="xsd:string" />
    <xsd:attribute name="MyTime" type="xsd:time" />
    <xsd:attribute name="MyBool" type="xsd:boolean" />
```

```
      <xsd:attribute name="MyDecimal" type="xsd:decimal" />
    </xsd:complexType>
  </xsd:element>
</xsd:schema>
```

This schema indicates that an element called `MyElement` can exist in the XML document, and that it will have four attributes of varying data types. The following XML indicates a document that conforms to the above schema:

```
<MyElement MyString="Hello"
  MyTime="12:00"
  MyBool="true"
  MyDecimal="3.851"/>
```

We'll learn more about `sequence`, `complexType`, and `element` later in this section.

Attributes

As shown in the above example, attributes provide additional information about a given element. Attributes can only exist within the context of an element that they give additional information about – they cannot contain child elements of their own. Attributes can be defined as any of the above listed primitive XML data types, or derived simple types such as a `Currency` type.

The syntax for declaring an attribute in XSD is:

```
<xsd:attribute
  form = "qualified | unqualified"
  id = "(ID)"
  name = "(Name)"
  ref = "(reference qualified name)"
  type = "(data type, qualified name)"
  use = "( default | fixed | prohibited | required )"
  value = "…"
>
</xsd:attribute>
```

The element declaration in the sample schema above also showed how we could nest attribute declarations to assign them to a given element. We won't go into much more detail about the intricacies of attribute declarations, but we will look at a few of the more important attributes of the `attribute` element in XSD:

- ❏ **Form** – indicates whether the attribute needs to have a valid namespace prefix in the instance document.

- ❏ **Type** – the name of one of the primitive XML data types listed above.

- ❏ **Use** – indicates how the attribute can be used. The default value is **optional**, which indicates that the attribute is optional and can have any value. You can also use this attribute to indicate that the attribute in the instance document has a **default** value, has a **fixed** value, or is **required** to appear once.

Enumerations

Enumerations provide a way for you to restrict the values available for the XML document to only those that you select. You can only provide enumerations for primitive data types such as strings, etc. You define an enumeration by defining an `<xsd:simpleType>` containing an `<xsd:restriction>` with a `base` attribute.

The `base` attribute of the `<xsd:restriction>` tag is the primitive data type on which the restriction is placed. In the case of our sample, we're creating an enumeration of strings. So, at this point your XSD fragment might look like this:

```
<xsd:simpleType name="TestEnumeration">
  <xsd:restriction base="xsd:string">

  </xsd:restriction>
</xsd:simpleType>
```

So far, so good. From here we can define any number of restrictions on the value that this new simple data type can accept. Keep in mind that the above XSD portion is defining a simple data type that we're going to want to use as the data type of an attribute later.

For our example, we're going to define an enumeration restriction that looks like this:

```
<xsd:enumeration value="red"/>
<xsd:enumeration value="white"/>
<xsd:enumeration value="blue"/>
```

Our final schema, which indicates that our XML document can contain a "MyElement" element, with a `MyEnum` attribute and a `MyString` attribute, looks like this:

```
<?xml version="1.0" encoding="utf-8" ?>
<xsd:schema targetNamespace="http://tempuri.org/XMLSchema.xsd"
elementFormDefault="qualified" xmlns="http://tempuri.org/XMLSchema.xsd"
xmlns:xsd="http://www.w3.org/2001/XMLSchema">
 <xsd:element name="MyElement">
  <xsd:complexType>
   <xsd:sequence />
   <xsd:attribute name="MyEnum" type="MyEnumeration" />
   <xsd:attribute name="MyString" type="xsd:string" />
  </xsd:complexType>
 </xsd:element>

 <xsd:simpleType name="MyEnumeration">
  <xsd:restriction base="xsd:string">
   <xsd:enumeration value="red" />
   <xsd:enumeration value="white"/>
   <xsd:enumeration value="blue"/>
  </xsd:restriction>
 </xsd:simpleType>
</xsd:schema>
```

Note the `type="MyEnumeration"` portion of the XSD, indicating that the `MyEnum` attribute can take only values of red, white, or blue.

So, if we attempted to validate the following XML against the above schema, the validation would fail because the MyEnum attribute in the XML below contains a value of "purple", which isn't allowed by the enumeration we defined.

```
<MyElement MyEnum="purple" MyString="Hello"/>
```

User-Defined Types

A user-defined type within the context of an XSD document is a restriction that is placed on the content of an element or attribute. As we saw above, the enumeration is actually a user-defined type, as it places a restriction on the values that the primitive type xsd:string can use. The user-defined simple type will always restrict the contents of the element or attribute to which it is applied to a subset of the base type from which it is derived. What that all boils down to is that, when you create a user-defined simple type, you create a restriction on a primitive type. You can also create user-defined complex types, but that is slightly beyond the scope of this chapter.

The way in which individual restrictions are placed on primitive types for the purpose of defining user-defined simple types is through XSD elements called **facets**.

Facets

Facets are elements that are used to define a set of legal values for a simple type (which can be a user-defined simple type or a primitive type like string or float). Constraining facets appear as child elements of an <xsd:restriction> node, which is in turn a child of an <xsd:simpleType> node. The following is a list of the constraining facets that can be applied to a simple type (either built-in or user-defined):

❑ **enumeration** – as we've already seen, this facet constrains the value of the simple type to a specified list of values.

❑ **fractionDigits** – specifies the maximum number of allowable digits in the fractional portion of the value.

❑ **length** – specifies the number of units of length. The units are determined by the base type of the simple type to which the facet is being applied. All values must be *exactly* this length.

❑ **maxExclusive** – maximum value. All values must be less than this value to qualify.

❑ **maxInclusive** – maximum value. All values must be less than *or equal to* in order to qualify.

❑ **maxLength** – maximum number of units of length. Units are determined by data type.

❑ **minExclusive** – minimum value. All values must be greater than this to qualify.

❑ **minInclusive** – minimum value. All values must be greater than *or equal to* this to qualify.

❑ **minLength** – minimum allowed length of the value. Units of length depend on the data type.

❑ **pattern** – specifies a regular expression that all values must match. A favorite!

❑ **totalDigits** – value must have a specific maximum number of total digits.

❑ **whiteSpace** – indicates whether the element should **preserve**, **replace**, or **collapse** whitespace.

Complex Types

Complex Types in XML Schemas are used to declare the attributes that can be placed on an element, as well as the behavior of an element's child nodes (if any). If an element in our instance document is going to be anything other than simple (meaning that it contains no child elements, no attributes, and only a basic data type as its contents) then you must declare it as a complex type in the schema.

Let's take a look at a fairly simple XML document with just a two-level hierarchy:

```
<Book>
  <Title>Professional ADO.NET</Title>
  <Publisher>Wrox Press Ltd</Publisher>
</Book>
```

The top-level element (DocumentElement for those used to DOM programming) is the Book element. It has two child elements: Title and Publisher. Based on our definition of a complex type, the Book element is complex, but both the Title and Publisher elements are simple (they are based on basic data types and have no attributes or child elements).

Let's create a portion of a schema that represents the hierarchy above. Whenever we declare a complex type, we need to use the complexType XSD element. Let's take a look at the schema:

```
<?xml version="1.0"?>
<xsd:schema xmlns:xsd = "http: //www.w3.org/2001/XMLSchema">
 <xsd:element name="Book">
  <xsd:complexType>
   <xsd:sequence>
    <xsd:element name="Title" type="string"/>
    <xsd:element name="Publisher" type="string"/>
   </xsd:sequence>
  </xsd:complexType>
 </xsd:element>
</xsd:schema>
```

Mixed Attribute

The mixed attribute allows the content of a given element (so long as the complexType element is a child node) to contain a mixture of simple character data and child nodes. This attribute is extremely helpful in mixing markup tags with standard prose, such as defining reference links and information within the context of a magazine article, a book review, or any other form of content.

If we make a slight change to our above schema (SimpleBooks.xsd in the downloadable samples) and modify the complexType element to include the mixed="true" attribute, we can then write a valid XML document that contains mixed content and looks like this:

```
<Book>
  The title of this book is <Title>Professional ADO.NET</Title> and
  the publisher of the book is <Publisher>Wrox Press Ltd</Publisher>.
</Book>
```

Mixed content is very often seen in Business to Business (B2B) document exchanges between business partners or content providers. For example, if a media provider provided movie reviews to dozens of online movie retailers, they could provide those reviews with mixed content, marking up the portions of those reviews that contained data that could be accessed or programmed for, such as the rating or the title of the movie. In general, mixed content is avoided if possible, due to the complexities it adds to code responsible for parsing mixed elements.

Element Groups

There are only a few more things left to cover before we can get into the specifics of how schemas affect `DataSets`. One of those things is element groupings. Any time a set of more than one element appears as a child of another element, it is considered an element grouping. There are four main XSD elements for declaring the behavior of element groups:

- ❏ `all`
- ❏ `choice`
- ❏ `sequence`
- ❏ `group`

all Element

The `all` element indicates that all child elements declared beneath it can exist in the instance document in any order. Here's a quick example of our book schema that indicates that all of the child elements of the `Book` element exist in the instance document in any order:

```xml
<?xml version="1.0"?>
 <xsd:schema xmlns:xsd="http://www.w3.org/2001/XMLSchema">
  <xsd:element name="Book">
   <xsd:complexType>
    <xsd:all>
     <xsd:element name="Title" type="string"/>
     <xsd:element name="Publisher" type="string"/>
    </xsd:all>
   </xsd:complexType>
  </xsd:element>
 </xsd:schema>
```

choice Element

The `choice` element indicates that one and only one of its child elements can exist in the instance document. Therefore, if we modify our book schema to use a `choice` element, we can either have a `Title` element or a `Publisher` element, but validation will fail if we have both.

```xml
<?xml version="1.0"?>
 <xsd:schema xmlns:xsd="http://www.w3.org/2001/XMLSchema">
  <xsd:element name="Book">
   <xsd:complexType>
    <xsd:choice>
     <xsd:element name="Title" type="string"/>
     <xsd:element name="Publisher" type="string"/>
    </xsd:choice>
```

```
    </xsd:complexType>
  </xsd:element>
</xsd:schema>
```

sequence Element

The sequence element indicates that the order in which the child elements are declared must be the same as the order in which those elements appear in the instance document. The following is our modified book schema using the sequence element:

```
<?xml version="1.0"?>
<xsd:schema xmlns:xsd="http://www.w3.org/2001/XMLSchema">
  <xsd:element name="Book">
   <xsd:complexType>
    <xsd:sequence>
      <xsd:element name="Title" type="string"/>
      <xsd:element name="Publisher" type="string"/>
    </xsd:sequence>
   </xsd:complexType>
  </xsd:element>
</xsd:schema>
```

This means that if we validate this schema against the following XML document, the validation will fail, because our instance document contains the child elements in the wrong order:

```
<Book>
  <Publisher>Wrox Press Ltd</Publisher>
  <Title>Professional ADO.NET</Title>
</Book>
```

group Element

The group XSD element provides a method for naming a grouping of either elements or attributes. This becomes exceedingly useful if the same grouping of child elements will appear in more than one place. For example, if you have an instance document that contains both customers and contacts, then you might want a re-usable group of elements for the name, address, and phone number. The group element can contain an all element, a choice element, or a sequence element. Here's an example portion of a schema that utilizes a group element:

```
<xsd:group name="ContactInfo">
 <xsd:all>
  <xsd:element name="Address1" type="xsd:string"/>
  <xsd:element name="Address2" type="xsd:string"/>
  <xsd:element name="City" type="xsd:string"/>
  <xsd:element name="State" type="xsd:string"/>
 </xsd:all>
</xsd:group>

<xsd:element name="Contact">
 <xsd:complexType>
   <xsd:group ref="ContactInfo"/>
    <xsd:element name="Company" type="string"/>
 </xsd:complexType>
</xsd:element>
```

```
    <xsd:element name="Customer">
     <xsd:complexType>
      <xsd:group ref="ContactInfo"/>
       <xsd:element name="Status" type="string"/>
     </xsd:complexType>
    </xsd:element>
```

You can see how the ContactInfo grouping of elements was reused for two different parent elements without having to type the information twice.

Attribute Groups

This same idea of grouping reuse can be applied to attributes just as easily as it can be applied to elements. If, for example, we wanted to convert our small book description XML document so that the Title and Publisher become attributes of the Book element, we could group those attributes as follows, allowing them to be reused throughout the schema:

```
<?xml version="1.0"?>
<schema xmlns:xsd="http://www.w3.org/2001/XMLSchema"/>

 <xsd:attributeGroup name="BookDetails">
  <xsd:attribute name="Title" type="xsd:string"/>
  <xsd:attribute name="Publisher" type="xsd:string"/>
 </xsd:attributeGroup>

 <xsd:element name="Book">
  <xsd:attributeGroup ref="BookDetails"/>
 </xsd:element>
</xsd:schema>
```

So, our XML instance document for the new schema looks like this:

```
<Book Title="Professional ADO.NET" Publisher="Wrox Press Ltd"/>
```

XSD Annotation

One of the biggest benefits of XML Schemas is that they are written in a human-readable form. Compilers and applications can interpret them for use in data manipulation scenarios, and the programmers using those schemas can read them.

Often, schemas will be sent to business partners to ensure that everyone is formatting their data properly. At other times, schemas are generated by an application architect and then provided to the programmers who write the actual code. No matter what the reason, it is extremely helpful to have the ability to embed documentation and additional information into the schema itself rather than having the programmers search elsewhere.

XML Schemas provide two ways of annotating a schema. You can either annotate your schema with documentation designed to be read by a human examining the XSD, or you can provide annotation designed to provide additional detailed information to the program or process that is interpreting the XML Schema. All annotation for an XML Schema occurs within the annotation element. The two different types of annotations allowed occur as child elements within the annotation. The annotation element should occur as the first child of the element to which the annotation applies.

documentation Element

The documentation element contains human-readable information provided for the intended audience of the XML Schema file. Here is a quick example of a modified schema for our book document that contains some documentation:

```
<?xml version="1.0"?>
<schema xmlns:xsd = "http://www.w3.org/2001/XMLSchema">
 <xsd:element name="Book">

  <xsd:annotation>
   <xsd:documentation>
    This book element contains information about a single book.
    It should contain the full title and the official name of
    the publisher.
   </xsd:documentation>
  </xsd:annotation>

  <xsd:complexType>
   <xsd:sequence>
    <xsd:element name="Title" type="xsd:string"/>
    <xsd:element name="Publisher" type="string"/>
   </xsd:sequence>
  </xsd:complexType>
 </xsd:element>
</xsd:schema>
```

appinfo Element

The appinfo element provides a way for the schema author to supply additional information to an application interpreting the schema. This kind of information might include actual script code, filenames, switches, or flags of some kind indicating parameters for processing. As with the documentation element, the appinfo element occurs within an annotation element. For a more thorough examination of the appinfo element and other XSD details, check out Wrox's *Professional XML Schemas,* ISBN:1-861005-47-4.

XmlSchema Class

One of the biggest disadvantages of using DTDs for constraining the behavior of instance documents was that the DTD syntax was not XML, so not only did the programmer have to learn a new syntax for DTDs, but validating XML parsers had to know how to parse the DTD syntax as well as XML.

XML Schemas are actually a dialect of XML, therefore an XML parser can actually interpret schema information. The System.XML namespace in the .NET Framework SDK includes a class called XmlSchema. This class can be used to programmatically create and load XML Schemas. We won't go into too much detail, but it was important to mention its existence. You can always peruse the MSDN documentation for a detailed reference of the class.

To demonstrate the principal functionality of the XmlSchema class, we've cooked up a console application called SchemaGen (found in the **SchemaGen** directory in the code sample downloads).

> *As with all of the sample code in this chapter, the sample assumes that it is using the Visual Studio.NET solution file and the executable is in the obj\debug directory beneath the main project directory. The downloadable code samples are all in this format.*

This application programmatically creates the same schema as we defined earlier in this chapter. Here is the source to the `SchemaGenerator.cs` file:

```csharp
using System;
using System.Xml;
using System.Xml.Schema;
using System.IO;

namespace Wrox.ProADONET.Chapter6.SchemaGen
{
class SchemaGenerator
{
static void Main(string[] args)
{
  // Create a new instance of an XML schema.
  XmlSchema Schema = new XmlSchema();

  // Produce the following XSD in the document:
  // <element name="Book">
  XmlSchemaElement ElementBook = new XmlSchemaElement();
  Schema.Items.Add( ElementBook );
  ElementBook.Name = "Book";

  // <complexType>
  XmlSchemaComplexType CType = new XmlSchemaComplexType();
  ElementBook.SchemaType = CType;

  XmlSchemaSequence Sequence = new XmlSchemaSequence();
  CType.Particle = Sequence;

  // <element name="Title" ...
  XmlSchemaElement ElementTitle = new XmlSchemaElement();
  ElementTitle.Name = "Title";
  // indicate that the data type of the Title element is not just
  // "any" string, but the string as defined by the W3C's namespace
  ElementTitle.SchemaTypeName = new XmlQualifiedName("string",
    "http://www.w3.org/2001/XMLSchema");

  XmlSchemaElement ElementPublisher = new XmlSchemaElement();
  ElementPublisher.Name = "Publisher";
  ElementPublisher.SchemaTypeName = new XmlQualifiedName("string",
    "http://www.w3.org/2001/XMLSchema");

  Sequence.Items.Add( ElementTitle );
  Sequence.Items.Add( ElementPublisher );

  // Just because we used code to create all the nodes, doesn't
  // mean that they're automatically valid schemas. We need to
  // compile the schema before we write it to make sure it is
  // valid.
  Schema.Compile( new ValidationEventHandler( ValidationHandler ));
  Schema.Write( Console.Out );
}

public static void ValidationHandler( object sender, ValidationEventArgs args)
{
  Console.WriteLine("Schema Validation Failed.");
  Console.WriteLine( args.Message );
}
}
}
```

If this looks similar to building an XML document via the DOM interface, then you've been paying attention. It looks similar because the hierarchical nature of element and attribute building is inherent in all XML generating tools, including those that generate XSD. If your application must generate XML Schemas on the fly, then this class will come in extremely handy. If it must generate very similar schemas on the fly, you might want to consider deriving from the XmlSchema class yourself, adding in functionality intrinsic to your own application.

The above code sample uses the Console class's Out stream as the destination for the new schema. This allows us to either see the schema on the screen, or, using the old DOS re-direction operator (you do remember that, don't you?) '>', we can actually re-direct this application's output to a .XSD file with the following command line:

```
SchemaGen > SimpleBooks.XSD
```

This generates the following XML Schema file (SimpleBooks.XSD):

```
<?xml version="1.0" encoding="IBM437"?>
<schema targetNamespace="" xmlns="http://www.w3.org/2001/XMLSchema">
 <element name="Book">
  <complexType>
   <sequence>
    <element name="Title" type="string" />
    <element name="Publisher" type="string" />
   </sequence>
  </complexType>
 </element>
</schema>
```

The class we used to generate this schema has a default encoding format of IBM437. This could easily be changed to UTF-8 or any other character encoding format supported by the schema generation class.

DataSet Schemas

At this point, you might be wondering when we're actually going to start talking about Strongly Typed DataSets. It would be unnecessarily confusing to rush into a discussion of the Typed DataSet without a thorough discussion of how DataSets store their internal data structures. As such, a discussion of the internal structure of a DataSet would never be complete without having first provided an overview of XML Schemas.

This next section is going to cover XML Schemas as they apply to DataSets, covering the XSD elements and structures that relate directly to various DataSet behaviors and configurations.

Schema Translation

This next section will provide a thorough coverage of how XSD schemas are translated into entities that the DataSet exposes to clients, such as Tables, Rows, Columns, Relationships, Keys, and Constraints. While it is theoretically possible for you to accomplish everything you need by simply dragging a table from a database connection in Visual Studio.NET onto a new DataSet class and never looking at the underlying XSD, it may not be practical. There are many times when the structure in a database does not necessarily reflect the structure you want in your DataSet. If the tables you are dragging from a database to Visual Studio.NET's designer do not contain all the appropriate primary keys, foreign keys, unique constraints and more, the Strongly Typed DataSet you generate might not even compile (this has happened countless times in Beta 2, and may be something that is corrected in the final release version).

It is always a good idea to know as much about a technology you plan to utilize as you possibly can. XSD and `DataSets` are no exception. Having a thorough knowledge of which elements in XSD produce which behaviors in a `DataSet` can save you time, effort, redundant code, and the always annoying problem of wizard-generated code getting close to your desired results, but not exactly. The same can apply to the use of wizards when programming. Wizards make excellent starting points, but you should never assume that code entirely generated by wizards will always suit all of your needs. It is a good defensive programming concept to only assume that a wizard is a starting point, and that any wizard-generated code will have to be modified before it is ready to use. Dragging a table definition from SQL server onto the designer surface of the Visual Studio.NET `DataSet` designer might be sufficient to get the job done, but you can accomplish quite a bit more with some knowledge of the underlying details.

Generating Tables and Columns

In this next section, we're going to cover how to indicate `Tables`, `Rows`, and `Columns` with XSD. Every `DataSet` must have a single root element, which indicates the `DataSet` itself. It is beneath this root element that you can supply your definitions for `Tables` and `Columns` for your `DataSet`.

Tables occur as complex elements beneath the root element. Columns appear as child elements of the complex element indicating the table.

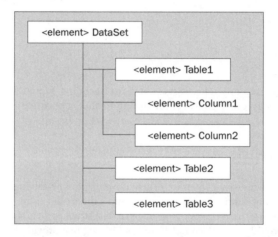

Let's take our simple book schema from earlier in the chapter and make it into a `DataSet` schema. The first thing we need to do is define the outermost element, the `DataSet`. In our case, we'll call it `BookDataSet`. Beneath that, we'll create an element called `Books`. And lower still beneath that, we will create two elements, `Title` and `Publisher`. Let's take a look at our XSD modified to produce a working `DataSet` (`BookDataSet.XSD`):

```
<?xml version="1.0" encoding="utf-8" ?>
<xsd:schema id="BookDataSet"
      targetNamespace="urn:wrox-proadonet-chapter6-BookDataSet.xsd"
      elementFormDefault="qualified"
      xmlns="urn:wrox-proadonet-chapter6-BookDataSet.xsd"
      xmlns:xsd="http://www.w3.org/2001/XMLSchema"
      xmlns:msdata="urn:schemas-microsoft-com:xml-msdata">

  <xsd:element name="BookDataSet" msdata:IsDataSet="true">
    <xsd:complexType>
      <xsd:choice maxOccurs="unbounded">
```

```
      <xsd:element name="Books">
       <xsd:complexType>
        <xsd:sequence>
         <xsd:element name="Title" type="xsd:string" minOccurs="0" />
         <xsd:element name="Publisher" type="xsd:string" minOccurs="0" />
        </xsd:sequence>
       </xsd:complexType>
      </xsd:element>
     </xsd:choice>
    </xsd:complexType>
   </xsd:element>
</xsd:schema>
```

There are a couple of differences that might immediately jump out at you. The first is that we've assigned an ID to our schema. Also, you'll see that there is an elementFormDefault with the value of "qualified". This means that, by default, all elements within the schema must be qualified with their appropriate namespace prefix (in our case, all of our elements are prefixed with XSD, the default that DataSets use for the XMLSchema namespace. You'll also notice that we've defined a target namespace for the instance documents of this XML schema. While we can get away with leaving this blank, it is always a good idea to fill in all the available information to avoid any potential confusion when transferring DataSet contents between AppDomains or even machines or platforms.

Looking deeper into the schema, we notice that we have an unlimited number of Books elements, which then contain a sequence of elements called Title and Publisher, in that order. We create a Books.XML document for our sample application to read that looks like this:

```
<BookDataSet xmlns="urn:wrox-proadonet-chapter6-BookDataSet.xsd">
 <Books>
  <Title>Professional ADO.NET</Title>
  <Publisher>Wrox Press Ltd</Publisher>
 </Books>
 <Books>
  <Title>Professional .NET Framework</Title>
  <Publisher>Wrox Press Ltd</Publisher>
 </Books>
</BookDataSet>
```

We've built a little console application that creates a standard DataSet, reads the XSD (BookDataSet.XSD) file, loads our Books.XML file, and then prints to the console the information in the XML file using the relational paradigm of Tables, Columns, and Rows. The source code for the DSSample1 example, DSSchemaSample1.cs, is listed below. You can find all of this code in the DSSample1 directory supplied with the code downloads. The BookDataSet.XSD and Books.XML file are both in the obj\debug directory beneath the project.

```
using System;
using System.Data;

namespace Wrox.ProADONET.Chapter6.DSSample1
{
class DSSchemaSample1
{
static void Main(string[] args)
{
  DataSet BookDataSet = new DataSet();
```

```
      BookDataSet.ReadXmlSchema( "BookDataSet.XSD" );
      BookDataSet.ReadXml( "Books.XML" );
      Console.WriteLine("Recent Books:");
      Console.WriteLine("-------------");
      foreach (DataRow xRow in BookDataSet.Tables["Books"].Rows)
      {
         Console.WriteLine(" {0} by {1}", xRow["Title"], xRow["Publisher"] );
      }
   }
 }
 }
```

Constraints

Constraints are rules enforced on the contents of the DataSet. It is entirely possible to use nothing but the DataSet methods to create, modify and enforce constraints on your DataSet; you should also know what constraints look like in the underlying XSD that your DataSet works with. There are several constraint types that you can enforce on the data contained within a DataSet via its associated schema.

Keys

You can use the <xsd:key> element in an XML Schema to enforce key constraints on data contained within the DataSet. A key constraint must be unique throughout the schema instance, and cannot have null values.

The following addition to our BookDataSet.XSD schema creates a key on the Title column.

```
<xsd:key name="KeyTitle">
 <xsd:selector xpath=".//Books"/>
 <xsd:field xpath="Title"/>
</xsd:key>
```

The selector element contains an xpath attribute, which indicates to the DataSet the selector XPath query to run in order to locate the table on which the key applies. The next element, field, also contains XPath, which indicates to the DataSet how to locate the field on which the key applies (relative to the table's element).

Unique Constraints

A unique constraint is slightly more forgiving than a key constraint. A unique constraint requires only that data should be unique, if it exists. Of course, individual columns can specify whether or not they allow nulls, overriding some of the default behavior of the unique constraint. We could just as easily have indicated a unique constraint on our Title column with the following XSD fragment:

```
<xsd:unique name="KeyTitle">
   <xsd:selector xpath=".//Books"/>
   <xsd:field xpath="Title"/>
</xsd:key>
```

Foreign Keys (Keyrefs) and Relationships

keyref elements within an XML Schema provide a facility for declaring links within the document. The functionality they establish is similar in nature to that of foreign key relationships in relational databases like SQL Server. If a keyref element is encountered by the DataSet when loading a schema, the DataSet will create an appropriate foreign key constraint. It will also create a parent-child relationship (discussed shortly).

For this schema example, we're going to create a new table in our DataSet called BookReviews. Then, we'll use the keyref element to create a foreign key relationship between the BookReviews table and the Books table. To make things easier (and more realistic) we'll also add a BookID column. All of the code for this sample can be found in the DSSample2 directory of the code download for this chapter.

The new BookDataSet.XSD for DSSample2:

```
<?xml version="1.0" encoding="utf-8" ?>
<xsd:schema id="BookDataSet"
     targetNamespace="urn:wrox-proadonet-chapter6-BookDataSet.xsd"
     elementFormDefault="qualified"
     xmlns="urn:wrox-proadonet-chapter6-BookDataSet.xsd"
xmlns:xsd="http://www.w3.org/2001/XMLSchema"

xmlns:msdata="urn:schemas-microsoft-com:xml-msdata">

 <xsd:element name="BookDataSet" msdata:IsDataSet="true">
  <xsd:complexType>
   <xsd:choice maxOccurs="unbounded">

    <xsd:element name="Books">
     <xsd:complexType>
      <xsd:sequence>
       <xsd:element name="BookID" type="xsd:integer" minOccurs="1" />
       <xsd:element name="Title" type="xsd:string" minOccurs="1" />
       <xsd:element name="Publisher" type="xsd:string" minOccurs="1" />
      </xsd:sequence>
     </xsd:complexType>
    </xsd:element>
```

Up until this point everything looked pretty similar. You'll notice that we've added the BookID column, an integer column that must appear any time a Books element appears (minOccurs=1). Next, we create a new definition for a table. Remembering that a table in XSD is nothing more than an element that contains more elements, it is pretty easy to declare a new table.

```
    <xsd:element name="BookReviews">
     <xsd:complexType>
      <xsd:sequence>
       <xsd:element name="BookID" type="xsd:integer" minOccurs="1" />
       <xsd:element name="Rating" type="xsd:integer" minOccurs="1" />
       <xsd:element name="Review" type="xsd:string" minOccurs="0" />
      </xsd:sequence>
     </xsd:complexType>
    </xsd:element>

   </xsd:choice>
  </xsd:complexType>
```

This should look familiar. We went over the key element earlier. The xpath for the selector indicates the Books table, while the xpath for the field indicates the BookID column.

```
   <xsd:key name="KeyTitle">
    <xsd:selector xpath=".//Books"/>
    <xsd:field xpath="BookID"/>
   </xsd:key>
```

Now we use a `keyref` element to indicate that we are creating a foreign key originating from the `BookID` column of the `BookReviews` tag, referring to the key element named `KeyTitle`.

```
<xsd:keyref name="KeyTitleRef" refer="KeyTitle">
 <xsd:selector xpath=".//BookReviews" />
 <xsd:field xpath="BookID" />
</xsd:keyref>


</xsd:element>
</xsd:schema>
```

The code listing for `SchemaSample2.cs`:

```
using System;
using System.Data;

namespace Wrox.ProADONET.Chapter6.DSSample2
{
class SchemaSample2
{
static void Main(string[] args)
{
  DataSet BookDataSet = new DataSet();

  BookDataSet.ReadXmlSchema( "BookDataSet.XSD" );
  BookDataSet.ReadXml( "Books.XML" );
```

Programmers like proof. To prove that a relationship in the `DataSet` has been created with exactly the same name as the `keyref` element in the XSD, we iterate through the `Relations` collection, printing out the name of the relationship. You'll see in the output shortly that there is indeed a relationship called `KeyTitleRef` in the `DataSet` immediately after the schema is loaded.

```
Console.WriteLine("Relations Created:");
foreach (DataRelation xRelation in BookDataSet.Relations)
{
  Console.WriteLine( xRelation.RelationName );
}

Console.WriteLine("\nWrox Books");
Console.WriteLine("----------");
Console.WriteLine();
```

So far its pretty straightforward; just iterate through each of the rows in the `DataSet` and print out the value in the "`Title`" column for each of the rows.

```
foreach (DataRow xRow in BookDataSet.Tables["Books"].Rows)
{
  Console.WriteLine( xRow["Title"] );
  // obtain child rows using the KeyTitleRef relation
```

The GetChildRows function obtains a list of child rows of a given row utilizing a relationship. You can either specify the name of the relationship or a DataRelation object. You can optionally specify a row version to further filter the results returned by querying the relation. Remember that, in our source XML document, the information was stored flat, in two separate tables. With the use of the GetChildRows, we're actually forcing a hierarchical traversal of the information in the DataSet.

```
        foreach (DataRow zRow in xRow.GetChildRows( "KeyTitleRef" ) )
        {
            Console.WriteLine("\t{0}", zRow["Rating"] );
        }
    }

}
}
}
```

When we're all done, we're presented with console output like the following, showing each of the titles and the rating of each review indented to help display the hierarchy of the row relationships.

```
Relations Created:
KeyTitleRef

Wrox Books
----------

Professional ADO.NET
    5
    1
Professional .NET Framework
    4
    2
```

So that you can see where the numbers are coming from, let's take a look at our updated Books.XML file that now contains information for the BookReviews table:

```
<BookDataSet xmlns="urn:wrox-proadonet-chapter6-BookDataSet.xsd">
  <Books>
    <BookID>1</BookID>
    <Title>Professional ADO.NET</Title>
    <Publisher>Wrox Press Ltd</Publisher>
  </Books>
  <Books>
    <BookID>2</BookID>
    <Title>Professional .NET Framework</Title>
    <Publisher>Wrox Press Ltd</Publisher>
  </Books>
```

The books table information should look pretty familiar. Below, we list the contents of the BookReviews table. Each row in the BookReviews table is surrounded by the <BookReviews> tag.

```
<BookReviews>
  <BookID>1</BookID>
  <Rating>5</Rating>
```

```
          <Review>This book was by far one of the best books on .NET ever
                written!</Review>
     </BookReviews>
     <BookReviews>
       <BookID>1</BookID>
       <Rating>1</Rating>
       <Review>I'm not sure this could be classified as a technical manual. It
               is worth more as a paperweight</Review>
     </BookReviews>
     <BookReviews>
       <BookID>2</BookID>
       <Rating>4</Rating>
       <Review>Top Notch! Excellent book! I especially liked the chapter on
               Strongly-Typed DataSets and XSD schemas!</Review>
     </BookReviews>
     <BookReviews>
       <BookID>2</BookID>
       <Rating>2</Rating>
       <Review>I liked the introduction. Thats it.</Review>
     </BookReviews>

</BookDataSet>
```

> Even though foreign keys and relationships in a **DataSet**'s schema can indicate a hierarchical relationship, the data does not have to appear to be nested in the instance document.

Typed DataSets

We've walked through a brief overview of the more commonly used features available to us in XSD and we've learned how various elements in XML Schemas affect the way in which DataSets behave. We've learned how to control data types of individual columns, and represent multiple tables, columns, indices, and constraints within a DataSet. A lot of what we've covered with regards to XSD and DataSet schemas you could theoretically survive without, but knowing the internals of how your tools are working is always an incredibly helpful thing. While most of our examples so far and throughout this chapter deal with using DataSets and XML data, all of this information can be applied to DataSets used in conjunction with relational databases. The essential point to remember is that whether the data came from an XML document, a relational database, or some other provider, the XSD schemas still have the same format, and you can still utilize all of the features of the DataSet.

Now we'll put all of that knowledge together and get to the real meat of this chapter, Strongly Typed DataSets. You may remember that one of the first things the chapter showed was how we were going to be able to turn the following lines of code:

```
myRow = MyDataSet.Tables["Customers"].Rows[0];
Console.WriteLine( myRow["FirstName"] );
```

into this short easy-to-read line of code:

```
Console.WriteLine( CustomerDataSet.Customers[0].FirstName );
```

This is all made possible by the incredibly strong support in the .NET framework itself for inheritance and clear, easy-to-follow, and logical object hierarchies. The essential concept behind a Strongly Typed `DataSet` is that a new class is created that derives from the `DataSet` class. It implements properties and methods that are *strongly typed* based on the schema used to generate that class.

Therefore, when this class is derived, it will provide logically named properties of integer type if your schema called for integer columns, logically named properties that appear as arrays of strongly-typed rows. So, rather than dealing with `DataRows` and `DataTables`, we end up dealing with task-specialized concepts such as a `CustomersRow` and a `CustomersTable`, which may contain columns called `FirstName` or `LastName`, rather than forcing us to provide hard-to-use array indexes.

There are two (equally valid) approaches toward creating Strongly Typed `DataSets`: you can either create them graphically through the tools provided within Visual Studio.NET, or you can use command line utilities and compiler arguments to incorporate your Strongly Typed `DataSets`. We will cover both approaches here, and you can pick the one that best fits your skills, style, and preferences.

Building Strongly Typed DataSets in Visual Studio .NET

Visual Studio.NET provides an incredibly easy, point-and-click approach to creating Strongly Typed `DataSets`. It is actually such a natural extension of Visual Studio.NET that if you're using it to develop your application, it can actually be very hard to avoid using Visual Studio NET to create your Strongly Typed `DataSets`.

To start out, we'll take the concept from our books and book reviews example, and develop a Strongly Typed `DataSet` for it in Visual Studio.NET. As usual, we're going to start out by creating a new Console application and calling it `TypedDS_VS1`. We'll change the namespace of our default class to `Wrox.ProADONET.Chapter6.TypedDS_VS1`, and rename the main class to `TypedSetDemo`.

Next, right-click the Project, choose **Add**, then **Add Class**, and then select the `DataSet` icon and type in `BookDataSet.XSD` as the filename. Using the Toolbox, drag two elements into open areas of the designer surface. From there, we can use the visual interface to add child elements (for the columns) to each of the elements we dropped onto the surface. Create the elements according to the columns we used in the `DSSample2` example (`Books` and `Book Reviews`). Then, finish it off by creating a primary key on the `BookID` column in the `Books` table, and your designer should look something like this:

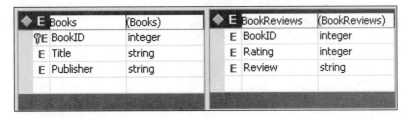

At this point, what we have is two completely disjointed and unrelated tables. These tables, remember, are being created by nesting the appropriate `<element>` tags in the XSD hierarchy as we saw in our hierarchy diagram earlier.

Now for the fun stuff: the relation. Open up the Toolbox and drag a relation onto the designer, hovering over any of the elements (or whitespace) in the `BookReviews` element (table). When you let go, you'll see a dialog prompting you for more information about the relation (`keyref`). Change the name of the `keyref` to KeyBookIDRef. As there is already a key on a table, and there are two equally named columns in each table, the dialog has automatically populated all of the information you need to form the parent-child relationship. Go ahead and confirm that, and take a look at the XSD for your visually designed Strongly Typed `DataSet`:

```xml
<?xml version="1.0" encoding="utf-8" ?>
<xsd:schema id="BookDataSet"
  targetNamespace="urn:wrox-proadonet-chapter6-bookdataset.xsd"
  elementFormDefault="qualified"
  xmlns="urn:wrox-proadonet-chapter6-bookdataset.xsd"
  xmlns:xsd="http://www.w3.org/2001/XMLSchema"
  xmlns:msdata="urn:schemas-microsoft-com:xml-msdata">

<xsd:element name="BookDataSet" msdata:IsDataSet="true">
<xsd:complexType>
<xsd:choice maxOccurs="unbounded">
<xsd:element name="Books">
 <xsd:complexType>
  <xsd:sequence>
   <xsd:element name="BookID" type="xsd:integer" minOccurs="0" />
   <xsd:element name="Title" type="xsd:string" minOccurs="0" />
   <xsd:element name="Publisher" type="xsd:string" minOccurs="0" />
  </xsd:sequence>
 </xsd:complexType>
</xsd:element>
<xsd:element name="BookReviews">
 <xsd:complexType>
  <xsd:sequence>
   <xsd:element name="BookID" type="xsd:integer" minOccurs="0" />
   <xsd:element name="Rating" type="xsd:integer" minOccurs="0" />
   <xsd:element name="Review" type="xsd:string" minOccurs="0" />
  </xsd:sequence>
 </xsd:complexType>
</xsd:element>
</xsd:choice>
</xsd:complexType>

<xsd:key name="KeyBookID">
 <xsd:selector xpath=".//Books" />
 <xsd:field xpath="BookID" />
</xsd:key>

<xsd:keyref name="KeyBookIDRef" refer="KeyBookID">
 <xsd:selector xpath=".//BookReviews" />
 <xsd:field xpath="BookID" />
</xsd:keyref>

</xsd:element>
</xsd:schema>
```

It should come as no surprise to you that this looks remarkably similar to the `DataSet` document that was built manually during the schema overview.

Now we'll enter some code into the main class of the Console application to generate the same output as our previous example, but we'll fully utilize the features of a class that we actually did nothing to generate except define the schema. Before we proceed, make sure that you've set the default namespace for your project (right-click the project, choose **Properties**) to `Wrox.ProADONET.Chapter6.TypedDS_VS1`. This will make the dynamically generated Strongly Typed `DataSet` will be part of the same namespace as the rest of your project. One other thing you **must** keep in mind is that the namespace of the data in the XML you're reading into the `DataSet` absolutely must be the same as the namespace of the schema you used to create the `DataSet`. This is also case-sensitive. I say this because I personally spent an hour pondering the meaning of life looking at an empty `DataSet` until I realized that I had created my `DataSet` in Visual Studio.NET with an entirely lowercase target namespace!

Source listing for `TypedSetDemo.cs`:

```
using System;
using System.Data;

namespace Wrox.ProADONET.Chapter6.TypedDS_VS1
{
  class TypedSetDemo
  {
    static void Main(string[] args)
    {
```

Notice here that we're not instantiating a `DataSet`, but a class named `BookDataSet`.

```
      BookDataSet myDS = new BookDataSet();
      myDS.ReadXml( "Books.XML" );
```

Just like last time, we'll dump to the console the relations defined in the `DataSet`. For our example, we have one relation called `KeyBookIDRef`.

```
      Console.WriteLine( "Relations Found:" );
      foreach ( DataRelation xRelation in myDS.Relations )
      {
        Console.WriteLine( xRelation.RelationName );
      }

      Console.WriteLine( "Wrox Books and Reviews" );
      Console.WriteLine( "---------------------" );
```

This is where it gets downright enjoyable to write the code. Instead of iterating through the rows of a particular ordinal index table object, we're indexing through each of the "`BooksRow`" objects in our Strongly Typed `DataSet`'s "`Books.Rows`" collection. It is much easier to read and much easier for the programmer to write.

```
      foreach ( BookDataSet.BooksRow Book in myDS.Books.Rows )
      {
```

As we said, the code generator for the Strongly Typed `DataSet` will actually generate properly typed properties for each of the columns. Here you can see that we're actually printing out the value of "`Book.Title`" rather than `Tables["Books"].Rows[0]["Title"]` or something equally complex. Also, note that instead of invoking the `GetChildRows` function, we're actually calling a function called `GetBookReviewsRows`, which our Strongly Typed `DataSet` coded for us. This function returns an array of `BookReviewsRow` objects.

257

```
            Console.WriteLine( Book.Title );
            foreach ( BookDataSet.BookReviewsRow Review in
              Book.GetBookReviewsRows() )
            {
              Console.WriteLine( "\t{0}", Review.Rating );
            }
          }
        }
      }
    }
```

After you've placed all the code into your solution (or you've loaded the TypedDS_VS1 solution from the TypedDS_VS1 directory in the code downloads), rebuild the entire solution. Then, from the Project menu, make sure that Show All Files is selected. You should then see that the BookDataSet.XSD file has some child items. Click the plus sign to expand it and you should then see that a BookDataSet.cs file has been generated for you automatically! This is the actual class that you will be using as your Strongly Typed DataSet.

Let's take a look at the console output generated by this sample. It should look extremely similar to our previous sample, but the key thing to remember is that this DataSet isn't generic, it has been derived and specialized to work *only* with Books and Book Reviews according to our schema. As I said above as a caution, this particular sample is also specialized to work only on data from our specific namespace.

Relations Found:
KeyBookIDRef
Wrox Books and Reviews

Professional ADO.NET
    5
    1
Professional .NET Framework
    4
    2

The code for the BookDataSet.cs is too long to look at here in its entirety (though it is available in the downloads for this chapter), but we will take a look at a few key points. The first thing we'll look at is the Books property. This property is a strongly typed wrapper around some inherent DataSet functionality. Here is the BookDataSet's definition for the Books property:

```
public BooksDataTable Books {
get {
  return this.tableBooks;
}
}
```

It's actually a wrapper around a private member variable. The key thing to note here is the data type of the property. It is actually a nested class called BooksDataTable, which is another dynamically generated class deriving from the DataTable class.

Now let's take a look at the other piece of "magic" that the Typed DataSet is performing on our behalf: the invocation of GetChildRows through the GetBookReviewsRows function.

```
public BookReviewsRow[] GetBookReviewsRows() {
  return ((BookReviewsRow[])
    (this.GetChildRows(this.Table.ChildRelations["KeyBookIDRef"])));
}
```

This function locates a `DataRelation` object by pulling the `KeyBookIDRef` item out of the `ChildRelations` collection. It then pulls the child rows by passing the relation object to the `GetChildRows` function, typecasting the resulting array of `DataRow` objects to an array of `BookReviewsRow` objects. As with all of the items on the Typed `DataSet`, this function is visible through IntelliSense in Visual Studio.NET, dramatically reducing your chances of mistyping the name of the child row's relation name.

One more useful feature of the Typed `DataSet` is the strongly typed properties. Let's take a look at the `Title` property of the `BooksRow` class:

```
public string Title {
  get {
    try {
      return ((string)(this[this.tableBooks.TitleColumn]));
    }
    catch (InvalidCastException e) {
      throw new StrongTypingException(
        "Cannot get value because it is DBNull.", e);
    }
  }
  set {
    this[this.tableBooks.TitleColumn] = value;
  }
}
```

This property is made possible by an override in C# for the indexer on the `BooksRow` class. It allows an actual column object to be supplied, rather than an ordinal or a string as a field identifier on which to set and get values.

Building Typed DataSets Manually

Now that we've looked at how to make Typed `DataSets` through Visual Studio .NET, which automatically makes those `DataSets` available to the rest of the project, let's look at how to do it "the hard way". Of course, that's a misnomer, because there's nothing hard about using command-line tools to create your own Typed `DataSets`.

You should not confuse "manually" with the process of writing all of the code for the `DataSet` class yourself. Even without Visual Studio.NET, there is still a tool that automates the generation of the class file. For our "manual" sample, we'll build the same code sample we built under Visual Studio.NET, though all of the compilation, code editing, and `DataSet` generation will be done from the command line and from Notepad (or whatever your favorite text editor is). This is mostly an exercise to prove to you that you can actually write useful code without Visual Studio.NET.

The first thing we'll do is create a new directory (we used `TypedDS_NoVS`). Into this directory, we'll copy the `BookDataSet.XSD` that we built containing the definitions for the `Books` table, the `BookReviews` table, the keys and the `keyref` parent-child relationship. This file should be called `BookDataSet.XSD`. Also, we'll copy the `Books.XML` file from the previous example so we can test that our `DataSet`s are going to function identically.

With almost no changes to our `TypedSetDemo.cs` file (renamed to `TypedSetDemo2.cs` and the `TypedSetDemo` class renamed to `TypedSetDemo2`) we went ahead and wrote a batch file to illustrate the command-line arguments to build our Typed `DataSet` and associated Console application:

The `BuildAll.bat` file:

```
xsd /n:Wrox.ProADONET.Chapter6.TypedDS_NoVS /d /l:C# BookDataSet.xsd
csc /r:System.data.dll typedsetdemo2.cs bookdataset.cs
```

The first line of the batch file invokes a utility called `XSD.EXE`. This utility is used to generate schema or class files from a given source. It can take a schema and convert it to classes or create a Typed `DataSet` from it (the `/d` argument). As well, it can create an XSD file from an XDR file to upgrade the schema definition. The second line invokes the C# compiler to compile the `bookdataset.cs` file and the `typedsetdemo2.cs` file with a reference to the `System.Data` DLL.

Running the `BuildAll.bat` file and then running the `TypedSetDemo2.EXE` file, we get the following screen output, which is exactly the same as the output generated by the Visual Studio .NET version:

```
Relations Found:
KeyBookIDRef
Wrox Books and Reviews
----------------------
Professional ADO.NET
     5
     1
Professional .NET Framework
     4
     2
```

Strongly Typed DataSets and Relational Data

We've spent a lot of time covering how XSD is used to define the internal structure (schema) of a `DataSet`. We've also spent a lot of time dealing with `DataSets` that read and write XML documents. While it's very handy to know how to use XML with Strongly Typed DataSets, the reality is that most people are going to be using them to store data obtained from an RDBMS such as Oracle or SQL Server.

To demonstrate this, we're going to create a Strongly Typed `DataSet` called `CustomerOrders`. This `DataSet` will contain schema information for the `Customers` table and for the `Orders` table, as well as a relation linking the two in a parent-child relationship.

To get started, create a new Visual Studio.NET Console application (C#), making sure you have the necessary reference to `System.Data.dll`. Right-click the project and click **Add** then **Add Class**. Choose the `DataSet` template and call the new `DataSet CustomerOrders.xsd`. Once you get the designer surface, you should then be able to establish a connection to your `Northwind` table (this example is using SQL Server 2000 locally, which has a `Northwind` database).

Modify your project so that the default namespace is `Wrox.ProADONET.TypedDS_Northwind` (right-click your project and choose **Properties** and modify the default namespace item). With your `Northwind` database visible in the Server Explorer, left-click and drag the `Customers` and `Orders` tables onto the surface of the designer. Then drag a **Relation** item anywhere into the `Orders` table. Accept all of the defaults here and just click **OK**. Now you can **Build** your solution, and if you click **Show All Files**, you'll see the `CustomerOrders.cs` file that Visual Studio .NET has generated on your behalf.

Enter in the following code for your main class (`Class1.cs`), which will display all of the freight charges for the first Customer retrieved:

```
using System;
using System.Data;
using System.Data.SqlClient;

namespace Wrox.ProADONET.TypedDS_Northwind
{
class Class1
{
static void Main(string[] args)
{
  SqlConnection Connection =
    new SqlConnection("Server=localhost; Initial Catalog=Northwind;
        Integrated Security=SSPI;");
  Connection.Open();
  SqlDataAdapter CustomersDA = new SqlDataAdapter("SELECT * FROM Customers",
      Connection);
  SqlDataAdapter OrdersDA = new SqlDataAdapter("SELECT * FROM Orders",
      Connection);
  CustomerOrders CustOrders = new CustomerOrders();

  CustomersDA.Fill( CustOrders, "Customers" );
  OrdersDA.Fill( CustOrders, "Orders" );

  CustomerOrders.CustomersRow FirstCustomer = CustOrders.Customers[0];
  Console.WriteLine("{0}'s Freight Charges To Date:",
      FirstCustomer.ContactName);
  foreach (CustomerOrders.OrdersRow _Order in FirstCustomer.GetOrdersRows() )
  {
    Console.WriteLine("Order: Freight: {0:C}, Date: {1}",
      _Order.Freight,
      _Order.OrderDate.ToShortDateString());
  }

}
}
}
```

The important thing to keep in mind about this sample is foreign key relationships. When we created the Relation, we created a foreign key. This means that an Order cannot exist without a parent Customer. In other words, if you try to `Fill` the `Orders` table before you `Fill` the `Customers` table, an exception will be thrown. Here's the console output of the above program:

```
Maria Anders's Freight Charges To Date:
Order: Freight: $29.46, Date: 8/25/1997
Order: Freight: $61.02, Date: 10/3/1997
Order: Freight: $23.94, Date: 10/13/1997
Order: Freight: $69.53, Date: 1/15/1998
Order: Freight: $40.42, Date: 3/16/1998
Order: Freight: $1.21, Date: 4/9/1998
```

Typed DataSet Performance

So far we've shown you all of this great stuff about how Typed DataSets make the job of the DataSet creator and consumer both far easier. The Typed DataSets are easier to maintain, have strongly typed accessors, providing rigid data validation, and, because they are still serializable components, they can be exposed as the return type of Web Service function calls.

You might be wondering, however, Are these things any faster or slower than regular DataSets? Well, the answer is unfortunately somewhat vague. You may already know by now that exception throwing incurs a slight overhead from the Runtime, as does typecasting. All of the properties and functions in a Typed DataSet are wrapped in exception handling calls, and a great many are wrapped with typecasting code. This leads some people to believe that they are slightly less efficient than standard DataSet s

Also, consider the case of schema loading or schema inference. When a regular DataSet loads XML directly from an XML source, that XML is parsed and traversed *twice* in order first to obtain an inferred schema, and second to actually populate the data. A Typed DataSet knows its schema ahead of time, so no matter where it loads its data from, it will only have to traverse that data once to populate its internal data. Just remember the following tip and you should be in good shape with regard to the performance argument:

> In any production-scale application, you will be wrapping your **DataSet** calls in exception handling and typecasting code anyway, so the fact that the Typed **DataSet** does this for you should be considered an advantage, and not a performance drain.

Annotating Typed DataSets

Earlier in the chapter, during the overview of some of the commonly used features of XSD, we covered schema annotation. We saw that annotation can take two forms: one form is through the <documentation> element, which is targeted at human audiences for informational purposes; the other form is through the <appinfo> element. Providing annotations on schemas for DataSets allows you to customize the names and behaviors of the elements in your Typed DataSet (covered shortly) without having to change the underlying schema structure. Keep in mind, however, that the annotations we're discussing on a DataSet are done through attributes and not annotation tags.

As you've seen in the previous examples, when you create a Typed DataSet using the standard methods, either Visual Studio .NET or XSD.EXE will generate the names of all of that DataSet class's properties, methods, relations, and constraints for you. If you're going to be using a lot of Typed DataSets, or you plan on having them available for several other programmers or programming teams, you'll be pleased to know that you can actually obtain fine-grained control over the naming conventions and automated facilities of the code generator for Typed DataSet classes.

This is accomplished by supplying attributes from two XML namespaces provided by Microsoft: the first is the codegen namespace (defined by xmlns:codegen="urn:schemas-microsoft-com:xml-msprop") and the second is the msdata namespace (defined by xmlns:msdata="urn:schemas-microsoft-com:xml-msdata").

codegen

The codegen namespace is one provided by Microsoft that contains a set of attributes that directly affect the code generation of a DataSet. You apply the codegen attributes to the various elements of an XSD file, which then gives fine-grained instructions to either XSD.EXE or the VS.NET compiler on exactly how to generate the new DataSet. We'll build a sample of a new, Visual Studio annotated, DataSet using these new attributes at the end of this section.

Of course, all of this functionality can be controlled by programmatically modifying the properties of the DataSet later. However, if the functionality and control is built into the schema in a human-readable form, as well as the derived Typed DataSet, there can be no mistake about how the class creator intended it to function.

typedName

The typedName attribute will indicate the name of the object as it appears in the new DataSet. This attribute can apply to DataTables, DataRows, Properties, and DataSet events.

typedPlural

The typedPlural attribute will indicate the name of the object when a plurality of the object is needed, such as in the DataRowCollection or DataTableCollection.

typedParent

The typedParent attribute indicates the name of the object when it is referred to in a parent relationship. Typed DataSets automatically generate accessor functions for retrieving parents and children. For example, in our previous example, the GetBookReviewsRows function was a child accessor.

typedChildren

The typedChildren attribute indicates the name of the object when it is referred to in a child relationship. As stated above, Typed DataSets generate both parent and child accessors, usually with confusing or unwieldy names. Providing the typedChildren and typedParent attributes generally makes for a much easier user experience for your Typed DataSet.

nullValue

The nullValue attribute is an incredibly useful one. It allows you to define what action will be taken in the DataSet when a **DBNull** value is encountered. The following is a list of the valid values for the nullValue attribute:

- ❏ *Replacement* – rather than indicating a behavior, you can simply indicate what value your DataSet will store rather than DBNull.

- ❏ **_throw** – throws an exception any time a DBNull is encountered on the related element in the DataSet.

- ❏ **_null** – returns a null, or if a primitive type is encountered, throws an exception.

- ❏ **_empty** – returns an object created from an empty constructor. For strings, it will return String.Empty. For any other primitive type it will throw an exception.

msdata

The `msdata` namespace is another namespace used by Microsoft to further control the behavior of the `DataSet`. The `msdata` namespace of attributes is primarily concerned with the definition, naming, and control of keys and constraints. Again, even though these are considered "DataSet Annotations", they do not appear in an `<annotation>` tag like standard XSD annotations.

ConstraintName

This is the name of the constraint as it will appear in the `DataSet`. This can apply to any kind of constraint defined in XSD, such as a `key` or a `unique` constraint.

ConstraintOnly

The default behavior of the code generator is to create a relationship whenever a foreign key constraint is found. You can override this behavior and not create the relationship automatically by using the `ConstraintOnly` flag. The syntax looks like this:

```
<element msdata:ConstraintOnly="true" />
```

UpdateRule

This attribute controls the behavior of related parent/child rows when an update is made to a row. The default if it is not supplied is set to `Cascade`. Otherwise, it can be set to `None`, `SetDefault`, or `SetNull`.

- ❑ **Cascade** – cascades the update across to all related rows

- ❑ **None** – no action will be taken on related rows

- ❑ **SetDefault** – all of the related rows affected by the update action will be set to their default values as indicated by their `DefaultValue` property

- ❑ **SetNull** – all related rows will be set to `DBNull` as a result of the update action

DeleteRule

The value of this attribute functions identically to that of the `UpdateRule` attribute, with the exception that its rule is only applied when a delete action takes place. All available options for the rule value are identical as well.

PrimaryKey

Indicates whether or not the constraint on which this attribute exists is to be treated as a primary key. If it is `true`, then the `DataSet` will treat the constraint as a primary key constraint and enforce appropriate restrictions on related values.

Relationship

There is one exception to the statement mentioned earlier about these annotations not actually being in an `annotation` tag. The `Relationship` tag appears within an `appinfo` annotation tag. You can use the `msdata:Relationship` to explicitly define a parent-child relationship as an alternative to using the key/keyref syntax. It is really a matter of preference and many staunch XSD purists prefer to use the key/keyref syntax, as it is not application-specific.

The syntax for specifying the relationship using this tag looks like this:

```
<xsd:annotation>
 <xsd:appinfo>
  <msdata:Relationship name="KeyBookIDRef"
   msdata:parent="Books"
   msdata:child="BookReviews"
   msdata:parentkey="BookID"
   msdata:childkey="BookID" />
 </xsd:appinfo>
</xsd:annotation>
```

Annotated Typed DataSet Example

Now that we've covered how to annotate our `DataSet` to control how its code is generated, and to gain a finer grained control over its behavior, constraints, and rules, let's take a look at one in action. For this example, we're going to create a Windows Forms (C#) application. Create a new C# Windows application and call this project `TypedBindingAnnotated`. (It can also be found in the `TypedBindingAnnotated` directory of the code sample downloads.) Add a new class to the project and choose **DataSet** as the class type. Call the `DataSet` `BookDataSet.xsd`. Paste the following annotated XSD into your new `DataSet` class XSD file:

```
<?xml version="1.0" encoding="utf-8" ?>
<xsd:schema id="BookDataSet" targetNamespace="urn:wrox-proadonet-chapter6-
bookdataset.xsd"
 elementFormDefault="qualified"
 xmlns="urn:wrox-proadonet-chapter6-bookdataset.xsd"
 xmlns:xsd="http://www.w3.org/2001/XMLSchema"
```

This is new. We've already seen that Visual Studio.NET puts the `msdata` namespace declaration into our `DataSet` schemas for us, but we have to manually enter the one below to gain access to the `codegen` namespace prefix.

```
 xmlns:codegen="urn:schemas-microsoft-com:xml-msprop"
 xmlns:msdata="urn:schemas-microsoft-com:xml-msdata">

<xsd:element name="BookDataSet" msdata:IsDataSet="true">
<xsd:complexType>
<xsd:choice maxOccurs="unbounded">
```

Here's a look at our first use of the `codegen` namespace. We're indicating that the `typedName` of the `Books` element (matches `<Books>` tags in our XML instance document) is going to be called `Book`, and the `typedPlural` will be called `Books`. What we've done is place some human-logical plurality (or lack thereof) onto the `<Books>` tags in our instance document.

```
<xsd:element name="Books" codegen:typedName="Book"
 codegen:typedPlural="Books">
 <xsd:complexType>
  <xsd:sequence>
   <xsd:element name="BookID" type="xsd:integer" minOccurs="1" />
   <xsd:element name="Title" type="xsd:string" minOccurs="1" />
   <xsd:element name="Publisher" type="xsd:string" minOccurs="1" />
```

```
      </xsd:sequence>
    </xsd:complexType>
  </xsd:element>
```

As with the `<Books>` tags, we're placing some logical naming conventions onto the individual items. A single row of the `BookReviews` table will now be considered a `BookReview`, rather than "a BookReviews".

```
<xsd:element name="BookReviews" codegen:typedName="BookReview"
codegen:typedPlural="BookReviews">
  <xsd:complexType>
    <xsd:sequence>
      <xsd:element name="BookID" type="xsd:integer" minOccurs="0" />
      <xsd:element name="Rating" type="xsd:integer" minOccurs="0" />
      <xsd:element name="Review" type="xsd:string" minOccurs="0" />
    </xsd:sequence>
  </xsd:complexType>
</xsd:element>

</xsd:choice>
</xsd:complexType>

<xsd:key name="KeyBookID">
 <xsd:selector xpath=".//Books" />
 <xsd:field xpath="BookID" />
</xsd:key>
```

Here we've got a couple of really interesting things going on. The first is that in our last sample, we discovered that the `DataGrid` uses the name of the relationship to provide a visual link to the child tables. Therefore, we tidied up the name of our relationship so it looks good in the UI. As well, we've effectively renamed the `GetBookReviewsRows` function that previous samples generated to `Reviews`.

```
<xsd:keyref name="Reviews" refer="KeyBookID"
 codegen:typedParent="Book"
 codegen:typedChildren="Reviews">
  <xsd:selector xpath=".//BookReviews" />
  <xsd:field xpath="BookID" />
</xsd:keyref>

</xsd:element>
</xsd:schema>
```

To save your eyes some strain, we'll skip past the designer variable portions of our `frmMain.cs` code and only show you the form's constructor, where all the real action is taking place. To prove that, even though we've done some annotation to our `DataSet`, we can still use data binding techniques like before, here is the constructor for `frmMain`:

```
public frmMain()
{
  //
  // Required for Windows Form Designer support
  //
  InitializeComponent();
  //
```

```
      // TODO: Add any constructor code after InitializeComponent call
      //
      _Books = new BookDataSet();
      _Books.ReadXml( "../../Books.XML" );
      dgBooks.DataSource = _Books.Books;
}
```

We've declared the _Books variable as a private member of the frmMain class. Also, to show you how incredibly straightforward our new annotated class is, we've rigged up a button that displays a message box containing the sum of all of the scores of the reviews. We could just iterate through the Reviews table, but instead we'll use the foreach syntax to demonstrate just how close the code syntax is to how we might describe the functionality out loud to another programmer.

```
private void btnSumScores_Click(object sender, System.EventArgs e)
{
    int sum = 0;
```

This right here is the true beauty of Typed DataSets. Not only do we have accessors without using array indexes (visibly) or collections, but also everything is named appropriately, and everything is strongly typed, so if we attempt to use the wrong data type, an exception will be thrown. Iterating through a hierarchy of data has never been this easy.

```
      foreach (BookDataSet.Book Book in _Books.Books)
      {
         foreach (BookDataSet.BookReview Review in Book.Reviews())
         {
            sum += (int)Review.Rating;
         }
      }
      MessageBox.Show(this, "Score Total: " + sum.ToString() );
}
```

The following screenshot shows just how much nicer everything looks when things have been annotated and given human (and programmer)-readable names:

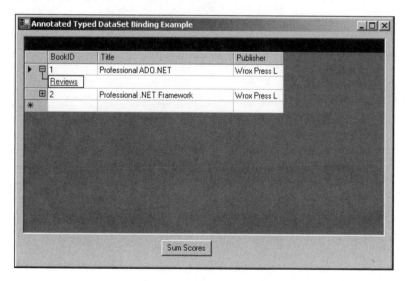

Summary

In this chapter we spent a little time giving a brief overview of the most common features of XML Schema (XSD). We discovered the importance of this review of XSD as we delved into the internal structure of the DataSet, and how it interprets XSD to form its internal data structure of columns, tables, constraints, keys, and relations.

Once we got comfortable with how the DataSet interacts directly with the XSD schema information, we used this same schema to derive our own DataSet sub-class that provides a strongly typed object model on top of our specific data structure.

At last, we got to bind our derived Strongly Typed DataSet class to the DataGrid control and see how the control handles the embedded hierarchical structure of the DataSet. Last, but certainly not least, we learned how to provide additional information and instructions to the code generator that allow us fine-grained control over the generation of the DataSets.

In short, the DataSet is a core component within ADO.NET, and understanding its symbiotic relationship with XML Schema is essential to harnessing the true power of the DataSet and creating strongly typed derivatives, Typed DataSets.

8

XML and the DataSet

Many of us may be getting tired of hearing about how important XML is to the future of computing: how it will revolutionize the way companies do business; how it will make the lives of all programmers easier; how embracing XML will make the world a happier place. Surprisingly, quite a few facts and solid examples help justify this euphoric vision. Many people believe that the .NET framework is the ideal platform to exploit XML, carrying programmers and users into the next stage of computing.

Examination of just about every aspect of the framework reveals an inner dependence on XML or a related technology. XML configuration files can configure managed applications (those .NET applications managed by the CLR) on the fly. XML files can override publisher policy components in the Global Assembly Cache. The configuration files for remoted Assemblies are based on XML. ASP.NET uses XML files for web site configurations. The list goes on and on.

Web services are a high-profile use of XML. Web services advertise their functionality over the Internet using an XML dialect called **Web Services Description Language** (**WSDL**). Clients can use these services. The Web service and the client communicate using **SOAP** (**Simple Object Access Protocol**) – and XML based technology – over HTTP.

The entire .NET framework is built upon and relies upon XML and related technologies. The ADO.NET `DataSet` is particularly dependent on XML. The `DataSet` uses XML as its internal storage format. We saw in the previous chapter that the dataset's internal data structures are defined by XML Schemas.

As we will soon see, XML deserves as much attention when discussing .NET data access as the `DataSet` or any other ADO.NET component. Before discussing the use of XML in the `DataSet`, we will take a look at XML documents in the .NET framework and how to query XML documents using **XPath**.

In this chapter, we will cover the following:

- Using the `XmlDocument` class

- XPath queries

- How `DataSet` schema inference works

- XML document validation

- The relationship between datasets and XML documents

- Marshaling and serializing datasets

- Filtering `DataSets` and using `DataViews`

- Using the `XmlDataDocument`

- Using XSLT transformations

XmlDocument (W3C DOM)

This chapter assumes that you have a passing familiarity with XML and the W3C Document Object Model (DOM) specification. If not, you might want to check out the XML specification on the W3C's website at http://www.w3.org/TR/1998/REC-xml-19980210. There is also a very good tutorial approach to the XML DOM at http://www.devguru.com/Technologies/xmldom/quickref/xml/dom_intro.html. Also, MSDN and the .NET framework documentation are full of information and samples regarding XML and XML document manipulation.

The `XmlDocument` class is in the `System.Xml` namespace of the .NET framework. `XmlDocument` is an in-memory representation of an XML document that conforms to the W3C Core DOM Level 1 and Core Level 2 standards. Knowing how to deal with data in an `XmlDocument` is very useful when working with `DataSets`, because `DataSets` hold their data internally in a binary format that is optimized for translation into XML for `DataSet` marshaling and persistence.

Knowing how to manipulate XML in DOM form is extremely useful information for mastering datasets and ADO.NET. For more detail and reference on working with XML documents in your favorite language, consult either of Wrox's new language-specific .NET books, *Professional C#* ISBN1-861004-99-0 or *Professional VB.NET* ISBN 1-861004-97-4.

When an XML document is loaded, it is loaded into a tree representation as a grouping of `XmlNode` objects. Each `XmlNode` object can have many child `XmlNode` objects, but only a single parent.

Before going into any more detail, we will look at a simple example of manipulating an XML document. We will use the `XmlDocument` and related classes to create an XML document from scratch. Then we will save it to disk and traverse the document, displaying each of the nodes created. This will demonstrate both reading and writing with the document object.

We will create a C# Console Application called `XmlDocumentDemo`. Here is the source code listing for the `XmlDocumentDemo.cs` file:

```
using System;
using System.Xml;

namespace Wrox.ProADONET.Chapter7.XmlDoc
```

```
{

  class XmlDocumentDemo
  {
  static void Main(string[] args)
  {
    int FakeQuantity;
    System.Xml.XmlDocument Doc = new XmlDocument();
    XmlAttribute newAtt;
    XmlElement TempNode;

    // Use the XmlDeclaration class to place the
    // <?xml version="1.0"?> declaration at the top of our XML file
    XmlDeclaration dec = Doc.CreateXmlDeclaration( "1.0", null, null);
    Doc.AppendChild( dec );
    XmlElement DocRoot = Doc.CreateElement( "Orders" );
    Doc.AppendChild( DocRoot );

    // generate a couple of phony orders.
    for (int x=0; x<12; x++)
    {
      XmlNode Order = Doc.CreateElement( "Order" );
      newAtt = Doc.CreateAttribute( "Quantity" );
      FakeQuantity = 10 * x + x;
      newAtt.Value = FakeQuantity.ToString();
      Order.Attributes.Append( newAtt );
      DocRoot.AppendChild( Order );
    }

    // saves the XML document. We can use a filename or an XmlTextWriter
    // as the parameter.
    Doc.Save( "../../OutDocument.XML" );

    // this effectively wipes the document and re-loads
    // it with the data just generated.
    Doc.Load( "../../OutDocument.XML" );
    Console.WriteLine("Orders Loaded:");

    for (int x=0; x< DocRoot.ChildNodes.Count; x++)
    {
      TempNode = (XmlElement)DocRoot.ChildNodes[x];
      Console.WriteLine("Order Quantity: {0}", TempNode.GetAttribute(
        "Quantity" ) );
    }
  }
  }
}
```

In the example above, we are using the XmlDocument class (as well as other related classes) to create a new XML document and provide some feedback to the users. The first thing we do after creating the actual document instance (the Doc variable above) is to create an instance of an XmlDeclaration. This is the header of an XML document that defines the appropriate version and optionally defines some additional header information. The declaration is then appended to the existing document. We then create our root node (Orders), and then use a for loop to create twelve artificial Order nodes. Once we've saved the new XML document to disk, we can then iterate through all of the Order nodes that we've created, displaying to the console the values of the Quantity attribute.

This example generates the following XML file (OutDocument.XML):

```
<?xml version="1.0"?>
<Orders>
  <Order Quantity="0" />
  <Order Quantity="11" />
  <Order Quantity="22" />
  <Order Quantity="33" />
  <Order Quantity="44" />
  <Order Quantity="55" />
  <Order Quantity="66" />
  <Order Quantity="77" />
  <Order Quantity="88" />
  <Order Quantity="99" />
  <Order Quantity="110" />
  <Order Quantity="121" />
</Orders>
```

It writes the following to the console:

Orders Loaded:
Order Quantity: 0
Order Quantity: 11
Order Quantity: 22
Order Quantity: 33
Order Quantity: 44
Order Quantity: 55
Order Quantity: 66
Order Quantity: 77
Order Quantity: 88
Order Quantity: 99
Order Quantity: 110
Order Quantity: 121

Obviously there are hundreds of different things we can do with the various XML-related classes. All we are looking at here is how to create and navigate XML documents using the W3C Document Object Model, treating the contents of the document as nodes of a tree and not as relational data.

XPath

The **XML Path Language** (**XPath**) is a general-purpose query notation that is used to query and address elements and text within XML documents. Even if you're already familiar with the XML DOM, you may not be familiar with XPath. Many people refer to XPath as the SQL of the Internet. XPath notation declaratively uses patterns called expressions, which indicate a hierarchical relationship between elements, as well as specify further limitations on each node that can appear in your result set. To put it simply, your result set begins initially with nothing, and you then form your XPath expression to allow nodes following a specific hierarchical relationship and matching certain conditions to appear in your result set.

All XPath queries have what is called a **context**. A context is a specific node within the document tree of the document you are searching. You can think of it as a starting point. If you ask for all of the nodes named "Order" from the root of a document tree, you'll get a different set of results if you ask for all of the nodes named "Order" from a branch nested deep in the tree. When building your XPath expressions, you should always keep in mind the context from which the expression is being evaluated.

The following is a list of some of the strings you can place in your XPath expressions that indicate the context from which the rest of the expression should be evaluated. We'll take a look at the structure of a full expression shortly.

❑   `./` – A pattern that begins with `./` indicates that it should be evaluated from the current context. The current context in this case might be the XML node from which you are running the XPath expression.

Example:

`./Order` will find all elements named Order within the current context.

❑   `/` – A pattern that begins with a forward slash indicates that the remainder of the expression should be evaluated using the root of the document tree as a context.

Example:

`/Order` will find all elements named Order at the root of the document tree.

❑   `//` – A pattern that begins with the double forward-slash indicates that the remainder of the expression should be evaluated without regard to the depth at which matching elements can be found.

Example:

`//Order` will find all elements named Order anywhere in the document tree, regardless of depth or hierarchical structure.

> **XPath expressions are made up of location steps, formed by specifying an axis, a node test, and optionally a list of predicates. We form "Location paths" by concatenating multiple location steps with forward slashes, yielding sets of nodes as a result.**

Forward slashes are used in forming XPath expressions, in a similar way to navigating into sub-directories in Unix or on the Web:

```
/Books/book/title
```

The forward-slash in a location path indicates the child axis. The above example requests all `title` elements that are children of a `book` element that is a child of a `Books` element. You can mix the simple child axis steps in a location path with additional filters, as in the following example:

```
/Books/book[@Price<21.99]/title
```

This example will return all of the `title` elements that are children of a `book` element with a `Price` attribute < 21.99, where those `book` elements are children of a `Books` element, and that `Books` element is at the root of the document (technically the first forward slash in a location path indicates 'child of the root').

As usual, the canonical source for the reference on W3C standards is the W3C itself. The XPath 1.0 recommendation is available for your perusal at http://www.w3c.org/TR/xpath.

The above expression defines a subset (often referred to as Infoset subset) of `title` nodes that are children of nodes named `book` that are children of the root node named `Books`. Each of the expressions above separated by the forward slash is called a **location step**.

The format of a location step within a location path is as follows:

```
axis :: node-test [predicate][predicate]...
```

We will examine each part of this expression in detail and then show some examples of putting the XPath expressions to use. These contain many shorthand characters: for example, the immediate child axis is represented in the location path with a forward slash.

Axis

An axis is a portion (or perspective) of the document relative to the **context node**. It defines a set of nodes that have a specific hierarchical relationship to the current node. The following is a list of some of the axes available when building a location step.

- ❑ `self`
- ❑ `child`
- ❑ `parent`
- ❑ `descendent[-or-self]`
- ❑ `ancestor[-or-self]`
- ❑ `attribute`
- ❑ `namespace`
- ❑ `following[-sibling]`
- ❑ `preceding[-sibling]`

Let's take a look at a couple of examples.

```
child::Customer
```

This indicates that the node test ("Customer") should be performed on the child axis. In English, this means that the Infoset returned should contain all those Customer elements that are child elements of the current (or context) node.

```
descendent::OrderItem
```

The above location step selects all descendents (of the context node) that match the node name "OrderItem". Note the difference between descendent and child – child always means immediate child, but descendent goes deeper (a grandchild is a descendent of a grandfather, but not a child).

Node Test

The node test can be any expression used to indicate the set of nodes that are considered valid at that position in the location path. The node test filters the initial result subset by either name or type. We've already seen how you can filter by name, so let's look at how you can filter by type:

```
child::text()
```

This selects all of the child text nodes of the context node. The types available for you to filter are the types in the XPath tree model: **text**, **node**, **comment**, and **processing-instruction**. What this means is that, in addition to being able to filter on nodes that have certain names (as we saw above in our previous examples), you can also filter on nodes that are of a certain type.

Predicate

To additionally filter the Infoset returned by the given location step, the use of **predicates** is required. The predicate portion of the location step is an assertion of a fact that, when evaluated within the current context node (or node set), is either true or false. If a node evaluates to true for all of the predicates then it will be included.

In predicates, we can use expressions to further limit the results. Let's look at some location step expressions that involve the use of predicates.

The following expression returns the list of child nodes of the context node named book that have the publisher attribute equal to the value of 'Wrox Press Ltd':

```
child::book[attribute::publisher = 'Wrox Press Ltd']
```

The above location step expression may look more familiar to you using the shorthand that most code accepts:

```
book[@publisher='Wrox Press Ltd']/*
```

The next expression is a bit more complicated. It uses the count function to retrieve all descendent book nodes that have more than five chapters:

```
descendent::book[count(child::chapter) > 5]
```

The following example uses the `starts-with` function to retrieve all of those child `book` nodes whose `publisher` attribute starts with 'Wr':

```
child::book[starts-with(attribute::publisher, 'Wr')]
```

XPath enables us to filter data to obtain meaningful subsets. It also provides a very fast way to access any node within an XML document immediately. If you know a given element's XPath location, you can access it immediately, regardless of its depth in the tree. XPath enables us to select fine-grained subsets of nodes from XML documents, and it is also used in XSLT transformations, which use XPath syntax to transform XML documents into other XML documents, HTML, etc. By matching patterns using XPath location paths, those matches can then be transformed according to rules defined in XSLT. When we get to discussing XSLT and transformations, you will find more uses for XPath. You will also see XPath expressions crop up in our discussion of `DataSet` schemas.

Here's a quick sample written in VB.NET that illustrates how to use XPath on an `XmlDocument` class to obtain a relevant subset of information. We'll start it off with the source listing (`XPDemo.vb`). The project was created by creating a new VB .NET Console Application.

```
Imports System.Xml
Namespace Wrox.ProADONET.Chapter7
    Module XPathDemo

    Sub Main()
        Dim XDoc As Xml.XmlDocument
        Dim XNodes As XmlNodeList
        Dim XNode As XmlNode

        XDoc = New XmlDocument()
        XDoc.Load("../../Orders.Xml")

        '** Essentially, the following XPath translates to:
        '** For all those Customers whose Name Attribute begins with 'A',
        '** select all Order nodes beneath.
        XNodes = XDoc.DocumentElement.SelectNodes("//Customer
            [starts-with(@Name, 'A')]/Order")

        '** here's the above using the XPath notation without shorthand.
        'XNodes = XDoc.DocumentElement.SelectNodes(
            "descendant::Customer[starts-with(attribute::Name,
            'A')]/child::Order")

        Console.WriteLine("Found {0} Nodes", XNodes.Count)
        For Each XNode In XNodes
            Console.WriteLine("Customer {0} ordered {1} {2}", _
            XNode.ParentNode.Attributes.GetNamedItem("Name").Value, _
            XNode.Attributes.GetNamedItem("Quantity").Value, _
            XNode.InnerText)
        Next

    End Sub
```

```
      End Module
   End Namespace
```

One thing you'll notice here is that we use the shorthand syntax, since that is what a lot of programmers are familiar with. However, to use the longhand, just uncomment the appropriate line. The Axis names in this function are abbreviated. In this case, the `//` symbol indicates the descendent axis, and the `@` symbol indicates the attribute axis. Other abbreviations include `'.'` for self, as well as `'..'` for parent.

If we run this example against the following file:

```xml
<?xml version="1.0"?>
<Orders>
  <Customer Name='Albert'>
    <Order Quantity="12">
      Roast Duck
    </Order>
    <Order Quantity="5">
      Red Wine
    </Order>
  </Customer>
  <Customer Name='John'>
    <Order Quantity="3">
      French Fries
    </Order>
    <Order Quantity="4">
      Coffee
    </Order>
  </Customer>
  <Customer Name='Stephen'>
    <Order Quantity="5">
      Milk
    </Order>
  </Customer>
  <Customer Name='Alice'>
    <Order Quantity="18">
      Frozen Pizza
    </Order>
    <Order Quantity="3">
      Potato Chips
    </Order>
  </Customer>
</Orders>
```

We get the following console output:

```
Found 4 Nodes
Customer Albert ordered 12
    Roast Duck

Customer Albert ordered 5
    Red Wine

Customer Alice ordered 18
    Frozen Pizza
```

Customer Alice ordered 3
    Potato Chips

Notice that the whitespace (and CR/LF codes) surrounding the text of each of the `Order` nodes is completely preserved, displaying a new line and indentation. This is an important feature to note for later in the chapter. What we have essentially done is selected all of the orders made by people whose names start with the letter 'A'. Many people feel that the hierarchical, path paradigm of XPath actually allows much more sophisticated queries than SQL does.

DataSet Schemas

In Chapter 7 we spent a good deal of time discussing how the XSD schema affects the `DataSet`. We covered everything from defining simple type restrictions on data through to defining foreign key relationships that established a hierarchical structure within the `DataSet`. We discussed how to create the data structure using XSD files and typed `DataSet`s.

In this chapter we will create data structures in a different way – inferring schemas from existing XML documents.

> *Some versions of ADO used the XDR (XML Data Reduced) standard for schemas. This specification is similar to XSD, but is not quite so fully featured. The* XSD.EXE *tool that ships with the framework can perform conversions between XDR and XSD for you.*

Schema Inference

Schema inference is a process that is performed when a `DataSet` object without an existing data structure attempts to load data from an XML document. The `DataSet` will make an initial pass through the XML document to infer the data structure, and then a second pass to actually load the `DataSet` with the information contained in the document.

There is a set of rules for inferring `DataSet` schemas that is always followed. Therefore, we can accurately predict what the schema inferred from a given XML document will look like.

Inference Rules

When inferring a schema from an XML document, the dataset follows the following rules:

❑ Elements with attributes become `Table`s.

❑ Elements with child elements become `Table`s.

❑ Repeating elements become a single `Table`s.

❑ If the document (root) element has no attributes and has no child elements that can be inferred as columns, it is inferred as a `DataSet`. Otherwise the document element becomes a `Table`.

❑ Attributes become columns.

❑   For elements inferred as `Tables` that have no child elements and contain text, a new column called `Tablename_Text` is created for the text of each of the elements. If an element with both child nodes and text is inferred as a table, the text is ignored.

❑   For elements that are inferred as `Tables` nested within other elements inferred as `Tables`, a nested `DataRelation` is created between the two tables.

Inference Rules in Action

Let's take a look at a couple of sample XML documents and see what kind of schema the `DataSet` will infer from them.

This is done using a simple program called `InferIt`. This program takes two arguments: the filename of an input XML file and the filename of an output schema. It loads the XML into a `DataSet`, which automatically infers the schema. It then uses the `DataSet` to write the schema to an XSD file. The full source code to this utility is available in the download for this chapter. The syntax of `InferIt` is as follows:

```
Inferit.EXE Input.XML Output.XSD
```

Let's load the following XML document into a `DataSet`:

```xml
<?xml version="1.0"?>
<WroxBooks>
  <Book ISBN="1861005474" Title="Professional XML Schemas"/>
  <Book ISBN="1861004990" Title="Professional C#"/>
  <Book ISBN="1861005563" Title="Professional .NET Framework"/>
</WroxBooks>
```

The `DataSet` will infer from this that there is a single table, `Book`, with two columns: `ISBN` and `Title`. The `DataSet` will set its name to `WroxBooks`.

If we use the `DataSet` to generate an XSD file, we will get the following:

```xml
<?xml version="1.0" standalone="yes"?>
<xsd:schema id="WroxBooks" targetNamespace="" xmlns=""
xmlns:xsd="http://www.w3.org/2001/XMLSchema" xmlns:msdata="urn:schemas-microsoft-
com:xml-msdata">
  <xsd:element name="WroxBooks" msdata:IsDataSet="true">
    <xsd:complexType>
      <xsd:choice maxOccurs="unbounded">
        <xsd:element name="Book">
          <xsd:complexType>
            <xsd:attribute name="ISBN" type="xsd:string" />
            <xsd:attribute name="Title" type="xsd:string" />
          </xsd:complexType>
        </xsd:element>
      </xsd:choice>
    </xsd:complexType>
  </xsd:element>
</xsd:schema>
```

281

For our second example, we're going to infer a schema from a more complex XML document. In this XML document we have a nesting three levels deep. Let's take a look at the XML and see if we can figure out the inferred structure before we test it with our program:

```xml
<?xml version="1.0"?>
<WroxBooks>
  <Book ISBN="1861005474" Title="Professional XML Schemas" >
    <Chapter Number="1" Title="Getting Started with XML Schemas">
      <Review Rating="5">
        One of the best introductory chapters ever written.
      </Review>
    </Chapter>
    <Chapter Number="2" Title="Datatype Basics">
      <Review Rating="2">
        A decent chapter. Could spice it up with more violence and
        bloodshed.
      </Review>
    </Chapter>
  </Book>
  <Book ISBN="1861004990" Title="Professional C#">
    <Chapter Number="1" Title=".NET Architecture">
      <Review Rating="3">
        I thought it was a splendid chapter.
      </Review>
      <Review Rating="5">
        Top notch intro. Two thumbs up.
      </Review>
    </Chapter>
  </Book>
  <Book ISBN="1861005563" Title="Professional .NET Framework">
    <Chapter Number="10" Title="Working with Data in the .NET Framework">
      <Review Rating="0">
        This chapter was so horrible I dare not discuss the details.
      </Review>
    </Chapter>
  </Book>
</WroxBooks>
```

We have some repeating elements. At the top level, we have a repeating Book element that has both attributes and child nodes. This should qualify for becoming a table. Underneath the book element, there is a Chapter element that also has both attributes and child elements. It should qualify to become a table as well. Finally, beneath the Chapter elements there is a Review element. This will become a table as well. Because of the nesting, what relationships do you think are going to be inferred?

Inference Tester.
Inferred Relational Structure:
Table Book
        Book_Id
        ISBN
        Title
Table Chapter
        Chapter_Id
        Number
        Title

        Book_Id
Table Review
    Rating
    Review_Text
    Chapter_Id

Inferred Relations:
Chapter_Review
Book_Chapter

Our inference tester indicates that it inferred three tables, Book, Chapter, and Review, just as we expected. However, what's with those extra columns? They weren't included in the original XML document, so where'd they come from?

The truth is that the XSD inference is doing some of the work for us. As our XML file nested a couple of tables, the DataSet needs a way of relating a row from one table to a row in another table. To do this, it creates a couple of auto-numbering ID columns.

You can also see from the above output that two relations were created. The first, Chapter_Review, is the master-detail relationship between Chapters and Reviews. The other is the Book_Chapter relation, a master-detail relationship between Books and Chapters.

Let's take a look at the XSD generated by the above inference. The first thing we may notice is that it is considerably more complicated than the previously inferred schemas.

```xml
<?xml version="1.0" standalone="yes"?>
<xsd:schema id="WroxBooks" targetNamespace="" xmlns=""
xmlns:xsd="http://www.w3.org/2001/XMLSchema" xmlns:msdata="urn:schemas-microsoft-
com:xml-msdata">
  <xsd:element name="WroxBooks" msdata:IsDataSet="true">
    <xsd:complexType>
      <xsd:choice maxOccurs="unbounded">
```

The Book table's definition starts here. You'll see that even the definitions in the schema are nested in the same hierarchy as the XML in the test document we provided:

```xml
<xsd:element name="Book">
  <xsd:complexType>
    <xsd:sequence>
```

This starts the definition of the Chapter table:

```xml
<xsd:element name="Chapter" minOccurs="0"
                            maxOccurs="unbounded">
  <xsd:complexType>
    <xsd:sequence>
```

Here's the start of the Review table:

```xml
<xsd:element name="Review" minOccurs="0"
                           maxOccurs="unbounded">
  <xsd:complexType>
    <xsd:simpleContent msdata:ColumnName="Review_Text"
```

```
                                      msdata:Ordinal="1">
                  <xsd:extension base="xsd:string">
                    <xsd:attribute name="Rating" type=
                                   "xsd:string" />
                    <xsd:attribute name="Chapter_Id" type="xsd:int"
                                   use="prohibited" />
                  </xsd:extension>
                </xsd:simpleContent>
              </xsd:complexType>
            </xsd:element>
          </xsd:sequence>
```

You may have noticed that, even though all the data in the XML document is inferred as a string, the artificially generated ID columns to support parent-child relationships are all based on xsd:int.

```
              <xsd:attribute name="Chapter_Id"
                    msdata:AutoIncrement="true" type="xsd:int"
                    msdata:AllowDBNull="false" use="prohibited" />
              <xsd:attribute name="Number" type="xsd:string" />
              <xsd:attribute name="Title" type="xsd:string" />
              <xsd:attribute name="Book_Id" type="xsd:int"
                    use="prohibited" />
            </xsd:complexType>
          </xsd:element>
        </xsd:sequence>
        <xsd:attribute name="Book_Id" msdata:AutoIncrement="true"
              type="xsd:int" msdata:AllowDBNull="false"
              use="prohibited" />
        <xsd:attribute name="ISBN" type="xsd:string" />
        <xsd:attribute name="Title" type="xsd:string" />
      </xsd:complexType>
    </xsd:element>
  </xsd:choice>
</xsd:complexType>
```

Here the XSD defines all of the relationships. You can see that primary keys have been created, and the parent-child relationships have been created on the newly created ID columns.

```
<xsd:unique name="Chapter_Constraint1" msdata:ConstraintName=
      "Constraint1" msdata:PrimaryKey="true">
  <xsd:selector xpath=".//Chapter" />
  <xsd:field xpath="@Chapter_Id" />
</xsd:unique>
<xsd:unique name="Constraint1" msdata:PrimaryKey="true">
  <xsd:selector xpath=".//Book" />
  <xsd:field xpath="@Book_Id" />
</xsd:unique>
<xsd:keyref name="Book_Chapter" refer="Constraint1"
      msdata:IsNested="true">
  <xsd:selector xpath=".//Chapter" />
  <xsd:field xpath="@Book_Id" />
</xsd:keyref>
<xsd:keyref name="Chapter_Review" refer="Chapter_Constraint1"
```

```
        msdata:IsNested="true">
      <xsd:selector xpath=".//Review" />
      <xsd:field xpath="@Chapter_Id" />
    </xsd:keyref>
  </xsd:element>
</xsd:schema>
```

You may have noticed that one of the limitations of schema inference is that it will not automatically detect data types for you. For instance, the Number field in the Chapter table is obviously designed to be numeric, but the schema inferred will only be of type xsd:string. What this means for people inferring schemas is that, unless you go into the inferred schema and convert it into a supplied schema later by saving it to disk, you will gain no benefit from type checking, as every piece of data in your DataSet will be a string. Also, with a little playing around with the XML file, you can try to add columns of the same name to related tables, and the inference will not use those columns in the generated relationships; the DataSet will still create new columns and create relationships between those new columns. There is, of course, nothing limiting you from modifying the inferred schema to suit your needs later.

Supplied Schemas

As well as allowing the DataSet to infer the schema, we can supply schemas to the DataSet explicitly. As we saw, schema inference can only go so far before it deviates from how we wanted the data organized. It cannot infer proper data types, nor will it infer existing column relationships (it will create new columns and new relationships).

There are a two ways in which you can supply schemas to your DataSet. You can either supply an XSD file (or XmlSchema class) to the DataSet, or you can leave the responsibility of generating the internal relational structure to a DataAdapter.

We can supply existing schemas on disk (typically in the form of .XSD files) to your DataSet by calling the ReadXmlSchema method on the DataSet. The result of this operation is that the DataSet will take on the data structure and characteristics as defined by the XSD file indicated. For example, rather than inferring the data structure a second time for the samples above, we could take the files that the InferIt program generated and supply them directly to the DataSet via the ReadXmlSchema method.

The DataAdapter contains a method called FillSchema. This method pulls the schema information for the command specified in its SelectCommand property from the associated connection and configures the DataSet accordingly. In fact, every time we call the Fill method on a DataAdapter, it calls the FillSchema method automatically.

Let's look at how we can supply a schema from an XSD file to a DataSet. To do this, we will create a C# Console project called SupSchemaDisk. We will supply the following code for the main class file, SuppliedSchema.cs:

```
using System;
using System.Data;

namespace Wrox.ProADONET.Chapter7.SupSchemaDisk
{
class SuppliedSchema
{
```

```
static void Main(string[] args)
{
DataSet MyDS = new DataSet();
MyDS.ReadXmlSchema( "BooksComplex.XSD" );

Console.WriteLine("Supplied Relational Structure:");
foreach( DataTable _Table in MyDS.Tables )
{
  Console.WriteLine( "Table {0}", _Table.TableName );
  foreach( DataColumn _Column in _Table.Columns )
  {
    Console.WriteLine( "\t{0}", _Column.ColumnName );
  }
}
}
}
}
```

We will load the XSD file generated by our second schema inference example, `BooksComplex.XSD`. We will need to copy the file to the location of our new application. As we know enough about how the `DataSet` works, we know that when we run this program, we'll see exactly the same relational structure as we saw in the structure that the `DataSet` inferred from the XML document.

The benefit here is that a `DataSet`'s data structure is portable, reusable, and transmissible. We can publish reusable data structures and data structure standards to development teams across an organization.

We can also embed the structure used to validate an XML document within the document itself. We will take a look at how to do this next.

Document Validation with Schemas

In playing with the `DataSet`, you may have been able to produce enough typos to cause the `DataSet` to complain about improperly formed XML data. While it's true that you can try to load XML into a structured `DataSet`, this only applies to data intended for a `DataSet`. What this means is that, unless the structure of an XML document meets some minimum standards that a `DataSet` expects, you will either be unable to load the data into the `DataSet`, or the data will appear very strange. There is a way of validating XML documents against schemas that may or may not be for `DataSets`. This allows you to validate a document intended for a `DataSet` against its schem.

XmlValidatingReader

`XmlValidatingReader` is a class that provides a forward-only, read-only, fast method for traversing an XML document. In addition to providing traversal over the document, the `XmlValidatingReader` provides definitions for events to be thrown when a validation failure occurs. The `XmlValidatingReader` can also take as a constructor argument a stream representing a fragment of XML to validate, rather than requiring an entire document.

We'll create another C# Console project and call it `ValidatingReader`. The first thing we'll do is copy the `BooksComplex.XSD` and `BooksComplex.XML` files from the second inference example so that we can play with them for our sample. We'll modify both the XML and the XSD files so that the XML file indicates the location of its validating schema, and the XSD file properly identifies the namespace to which it applies.

Here's the header of our modified XSD file:

```
<?xml version="1.0" standalone="yes"?>
<xsd:schema id="WroxBooks" targetNamespace="xsdBooksComplex"
  xmlns="xsdBooksComplex"
  xmlns:xsd="http://www.w3.org/2001/XMLSchema"
  xmlns:msdata="urn:schemas-microsoft-com:xml-msdata" >
```

and the change to the header of our XML file to point to the validating schema:

```
<?xml version="1.0"?>
<wb:WroxBooks xmlns:wb='xsdBooksComplex'
  xsi:schemaLocation='xsdBooksComplex BooksComplex.xsd'
  xmlns:xsi='http://www.w3.org/2001/XMLSchema-instance'>
```

The change to the above header of our XML file includes a couple of new pieces of information that we didn't have before. We use the `xsi:schemaLocation` directive to tell the XML parser the namespace of the schema, as well as the file in which the validating schema is contained. Now let's take a look at the sourcecode to our validating reader sample (`ReaderSample.cs`):

```
using System;
using System.IO;
using System.Xml;
using System.Xml.Schema;

namespace Wrox.ProADONET.Chapter7.ValidatingReader
{
class ReaderSample
{
static void Main(string[] args)
{
```

Here we open a new `XmlValidatingReader` "on top of" an existing `XmlTextReader`.

```
XmlTextReader xtr = new XmlTextReader( "../../BooksComplex.XML" );
XmlValidatingReader xvr = new XmlValidatingReader( xtr );

xvr.ValidationType = ValidationType.Schema;
```

We've set the `ValidationType` here to `ValidationType.Schema`. The `XmlValidatingReader` class can handle many different types of validation, including `Auto` (detects validation type based on the document itself), `DTD`, `XDR`, or `Schema`. Here we wire up an event handler that will be triggered if any of our element traversals encounters a validation failure:

```
xvr.ValidationEventHandler += new ValidationEventHandler(
    ValidationErrorHandler );
```

```
// traverse the entire document. If something is wrong, an event
// will be thrown and we'll display it. Note that we don't stop
// traversing, so one error could cascade and cause dozens more
// after it.
while (xvr.Read())
{
```

Here we'll display some information about the document we're traversing.

```
if (xvr.SchemaType is XmlSchemaComplexType )
{
   Console.WriteLine("{0} - {1}", xvr.NodeType, xvr.Name );
}
while (xvr.MoveToNextAttribute())
{
   Console.WriteLine("\t{0} - {1}: {2}", xvr.NodeType, xvr.Name,
        xvr.Value );
}
}
}


/// <summary>
/// Event thrown by the validating reader class in the event of a validation
/// failure. args here will contain both the severity and the message
/// of the validation failure
/// </summary>
/// <param name="sender">sender object (thrower)</param>
/// <param name="args">validation failure args</param>
public static void ValidationErrorHandler( object sender, ValidationEventArgs args
)
{
  Console.WriteLine( "XML Document Validation Failure\n");
  Console.WriteLine( "The ValidatingReader Failed with Severity : {0}",
        args.Severity );
  Console.WriteLine( "The failure message was: {0}", args.Message );
}
}
}
```

When we first run this against our new XML file, we shouldn't encounter any problems. To test and see if we really are validating our document against the schema, we'll modify the schema so that the Number attribute of all Chapter elements must be numeric by changing the definition of the attribute to the following:

```
<xsd:attribute name="Chapter_Id" msdata:AutoIncrement="true" type="xsd:int"
msdata:AllowDBNull="false" use="prohibited" />
<xsd:attribute name="Number" type="xsd:int" />
<xsd:attribute name="Title" type="xsd:string" />
```

Now we'll go back to our XML file and cause some damage by changing one of the chapter numbers to the string "ABC". Let's look at the output of our program after we make that change:

Element - Book
    Attribute - ISBN: 1861005563
    Attribute - Title: Professional .NET Framework
XML Document Validation Failure

The ValidatingReader Failed with Severity : Error
The failure message was: The 'Number' attribute has an invalid value according to its data type. An error occurred at file:///C:/Documents and Settings/Kevin S Hoffman/My Documents/Wrox/Professional ADO.NET/Chapter 7/ValidatingReader/BooksComplex.XML(28, 13).
Element - Chapter
    Attribute - Number: ABC
    Attribute - Title: Working with Data in the .NET Framework
Element - Review
    Attribute - Rating: 0

You can see from this partial output that we can see at what point in our traversal we got the failure. The message supplied with the failure is quite verbose and has lots of useful information that we can use to troubleshoot our validation failure.

As an exercise to work with your schema and XML skills, you might want to try doing various kinds of damage to your XML file and see what kinds of errors you can produce in the validating reader program. The more you learn about what will violate a schema, the more you learn how to avoid violating it in the first place.

DataSets and XML Data

So far in this chapter, we've seen how you can locate data within an XML document using XPath queries and we've seen how you can control the data structure of a `DataSet` with an XML Schema. In addition, we've seen how you can validate an XML document with an XSD schema and the `XmlValidatingReader` object.

As you already know, the `DataSet` is an in-memory cache of relational data that can be populated from or expressed as XML. In this next section, we'll show how to populate a `DataSet` with XML data from an XML document, as well as how to save the contents of a `DataSet` into XML.

Loading XML

There are quite a few ways in which you can populate a `DataSet` with XML. Loading XML into the `DataSet` is generally done by using one of the many overrides of the `ReadXml` method. The `ReadXml` method has eight overrides. The first four are:

❑   `ReadXml(Stream)` – this will load the `DataSet` with the XML indicated by the stream. This stream can be any object that inherits from `Stream`. One of the most common uses here is a `System.IO.FileStream`. However, it could just as easily be a stream of data coming down from a web site, etc.

❑   `ReadXml(string)` – this will load the `DataSet` with the XML stored in the given disk file. The filename of the disk file is the string argument passed to the function.

❑   `ReadXml(TextReader)` – loads the `DataSet` with the XML processed by the given `TextReader`.

❑ ReadXml(XmlReader) – loads the DataSet with the XML processed by the given XmlReader. As we've seen, the XmlValidatingReader inherits from the XmlReader, meaning that you could pass an XmlValidatingReader to this function.

The remaining four overrides correspond to those above, but with an additional XmlReadMode parameter. We will now look at how to use this parameter.

XmlReadMode

The XmlReadMode enumeration is used to determine the behavior of the XML parser when loading documents from various sources. The following is a list of some of the possible values of the enumeration and what impact they have on the DataSet and how it loads the XML:

❑ **DiffGram** – a **DiffGram** is an XML representation of a *before* and *after* state. The DataSet will load a DiffGram, applying the changes indicated by the DiffGram to the DataSet. Input being supplied for a DiffGram operation should only be supplied by the results of an output operation via WriteXml on a previous DataSet state. If the schema of the source DiffGram is not the same as the schema of the target DataSet, the merge operation will fail and an exception will be thrown. We will be covering a bit more on DiffGrams later on in this chapter.

❑ **InferSchema** – this option will force the DataSet to infer the schema from the XML document, ignoring any in-line schema in the document and extending any schema already in place in the DataSet.

❑ **ReadSchema** – this option will load any in-line schema supplied by the DataSet and then load the data. If any schema information exists in the DataSet prior to this operation, the schema can be extended by the in-line XML schema. However, if new table definitions exist in the in-line schema for tables that already exist in the DataSet, an exception will be thrown.

❑ **Auto** – this is the default. It attempts to select one of the above options automatically. If the data being loaded is a DiffGram, then the XmlReadMode is set to **DiffGram**. If the DataSet has already been given a schema through some means, or the XML document has an in-line schema defined, then the XmlReadMode is set to **ReadSchema**. If the DataSet does not contain a schema, and there is no in-line schema defined, and the XML document is not a DiffGram, then the XmlReadMode is set to **InferSchema**. Depending on how much decision-making needs to take place, using the default Auto mode may perform more slowly than explicitly setting the read mode. A good rule of thumb is to explicitly supply the read mode whenever you know what it will be ahead of time.

Now that we have some information on the ReadXml function and how to process XML when loading data, let's load some XML data into a DataSet. In the following source listing, we take a slightly modified Books.xsd and Books.xml file and load them both into a DataSet, supplying both an XML schema and XML document. Nothing is special about the class declaration:

```
using System;
using System.Data;

namespace Wrox.ProADONET.Chapter8.XmlDataSet_Read
{
class XmlReader
{
  static void Main(string[] args)
  {
```

This section should also look familiar. We have already shown the methods used for supplying schema to `DataSets` from disk files:

```
DataSet MyDS = new DataSet();
MyDS.ReadXmlSchema( "../../Books.XSD" );
Console.WriteLine("Schema Loaded.");

foreach (DataTable _Table in MyDS.Tables)
{
  Console.WriteLine("Table {0}, {1} Columns", _Table.TableName,
        _Table.Columns.Count );
}
// by not supplying an XmlReadMode, we're choosing "Auto".
// since there's already a schema loaded, it won't try and infer one
// from the XML document.
```

Now load the `Books.XML` file into the `DataSet`. We use `XmlReadMode.IgnoreSchema` to indicate that we're using the current schema defined within the `DataSet`:

```
MyDS.ReadXml( "../../Books.XML", XmlReadMode.IgnoreSchema );
Console.WriteLine("Data Loaded.\n");
foreach (DataRow _Book in MyDS.Tables["Book"].Rows )
{
  Console.WriteLine( "{0} : {1} - ${2}", _Book["ISBN"], _Book["Title"],
        _Book["Price"] );
}
  }
 }
}
```

Running the program will write the following to the console:

```
Schema Loaded.
Table Book, 3 Columns
Data Loaded.

1861005474 : Professional XML Schemas - $59.99
1861004990 : Professional C# - $59.99
1861005563 : Professional .NET Framework - $59.99
```

Writing XML

It is just as easy to write XML from a `DataSet` as it is to read XML into it. We can write XML to `Streams`, `XmlWriters`, `TextWriters`, and disk files.

We are going to take the XML and XSD files from the previous example and use them to programmatically add a new row to the `DataSet`. We will then write an XML document containing the new `DataSet`. We will also write an XML document containing a `DiffGram` indicating only the changes to the `DataSet` since we loaded it.

As usual, we create a new C# Console project called `XmlDataSet_Write`. We call the main class `DataSetWriter` within the `ProADONET.Chapter8.XmlDataSet_Write` namespace. Here is the source listing for the `DataSetWriter.cs` file:

```
using System;
using System.Data;

namespace Wrox.ProADONET.Chapter7.XmlDataSet_Write
{
class DataSetWriter
{
  static void Main(string[] args)
  {
    DataSet MyDS = new DataSet();
    MyDS.ReadXmlSchema( "../../Books.XSD" );
    MyDS.ReadXml( "../../Books.XML" );

    // if we don't call AcceptChanges, the DataSet thinks
    // that -all- data read from disk is "new". We only want
    // the row that we add programmitically to appear as "new"
    MyDS.AcceptChanges();

    Console.WriteLine( "Data Loaded From Disk." );
```

Here we have loaded some information that conforms to our schema from disk into our DataSet. Next we will append a new row to the Book table. Finally, we will write the information back to disk both as a DiffGram (XML change description) and as a complete XML document.

```
    DataRow NewBook = MyDS.Tables["Book"].NewRow();
    NewBook["ISBN"] = "186100527X";
    NewBook["Title"] = "Professional ADO.NET";
    NewBook["Price"] = 49.99;
    MyDS.Tables["Book"].Rows.Add( NewBook );
    // with the new row added, the DataSet is storing
    // "change" data. We can store this change as a DiffGram.

    MyDS.WriteXml( "../../Books_Changes.XML", XmlWriteMode.DiffGram );

    // now commit the changes and write the entire DataSet.
    MyDS.AcceptChanges();
    MyDS.WriteXml( "../../Books_New.XML", XmlWriteMode.IgnoreSchema );

    Console.WriteLine( "Changes and entire DS have been written." );
  }
}
}
```

The DiffGram resulting from the above operation looks as follows:

```
<?xml version="1.0" standalone="yes"?>
<diffgr:diffgram xmlns:msdata="urn:schemas-microsoft-com:xml-msdata"
xmlns:diffgr="urn:schemas-microsoft-com:xml-diffgram-v1">
  <WroxBooks>
    <Book diffgr:id="Book1" msdata:rowOrder="0" ISBN="1861005474"
         Title="Professional XML Schemas" Price="59.99" />
    <Book diffgr:id="Book2" msdata:rowOrder="1" ISBN="1861004990"
```

```
            Title="Professional C#" Price="59.99" />
        <Book diffgr:id="Book3" msdata:rowOrder="2" ISBN="1861005563"
            Title="Professional .NET Framework" Price="59.99" />
        <Book diffgr:id="Book4" msdata:rowOrder="3" diffgr:hasChanges="inserted"
            ISBN="186100527X" Title="Professional ADO.NET" Price="49.99" />
    </WroxBooks>
  </diffgr:diffgram>
```

And the final XML document, resulting from loading the three books and the programmatic addition of a fourth, looks like this:

```
<?xml version="1.0" standalone="yes"?>
<WroxBooks>
  <Book ISBN="1861005474" Title="Professional XML Schemas" Price="59.99" />
  <Book ISBN="1861004990" Title="Professional C#" Price="59.99" />
  <Book ISBN="1861005563" Title="Professional .NET Framework"
        Price="59.99" />
  <Book ISBN="186100527X" Title="Professional ADO.NET" Price="49.99" />
</WroxBooks>
```

Fidelity Loss and DataSet Schemas

In our previous example, we read data from an XML document and then wrote data back out. Everything was fine and we didn't have any trouble. This will not always be the case. The DataSet is very strict about the rules it follows when reading and writing XML.

When a DataSet already has a schema and it is not inferring schema from the document, it will only load data defined by the schema. For example, the DataSet would ignore XML attributes of a book that were not defined in the DataSet's schema. If we change the DataSet and then save to XML, the saved XML would not contain the attributes that were not in the schema. In addition, characters, formatting, and whitespace that might be desired or meaningful in the original document will cease to exist in the DataSet-generated document. The following example demonstrates this.

We will add an attribute to our document called "Category". This attribute is just a regular string attribute. There's also formatting and whitespace in the original to further demonstrate the point. We will look at the XML document before and after running the following program against it, to see how it destroys the fidelity of our original:

```
using System;
using System.Data;

namespace Wrox.ProADONET.Chapter8.FidelityLoss
{
class FidelityTester
{
  static void Main(string[] args)
  {
    DataSet MyDS = new DataSet();
    // load the schema (important, inferring it won't
    // demonstrate fidelity loss.)
    MyDS.ReadXmlSchema( "../../Books.XSD" );
```

```
    // load the original document Data.
    MyDS.ReadXml( "../../Books.XML" );

    // we're not going to do a single thing to the data,
    // just simply write the data back out to a new XML
    // file (so we can compare before and after)
    MyDS.WriteXml( "../../Books_After.XML" );
  }
}
}
```

We are loading an XML document and then saving it back to disk. We might expect, therefore, that the saved XML document will be no different from the original one. It doesn't work that way, though. Let's take a look at the source XML file:

```
<?xml version="1.0"?>
<WroxBooks>
  <Book ISBN="1861005474" Title="Professional XML Schemas" Price="59.99"
      Category="XML">
  </Book>


  <Book ISBN="1861004990" Title="Professional C#" Price="59.99"
      Category="C#"/>


  <Book ISBN="1861005563" Title="Professional .NET Framework" Price="59.99"
      Category=".NET General"/>

</WroxBooks>
```

The `DataSet` removes the non-standard whitespace, and does not even read the `Category`. This is because the schema we supplied does not define them. Here is this XML file after being run through the `DataSet`:

```
<?xml version="1.0" standalone="yes"?>
<WroxBooks>
  <Book ISBN="1861005474" Title="Professional XML Schemas" Price="59.99" />
  <Book ISBN="1861004990" Title="Professional C#" Price="59.99" />
  <Book ISBN="1861005563" Title="Professional .NET Framework"
      Price="59.99" />
</WroxBooks>
```

Just like we said, the document has not been fully preserved. It is not the same document that we loaded. It is not only missing whitespace and formatting, but data that might have been essential to our program.

Our real problem here isn't the `DataSet`. The issue is that we're trying to enforce a relational view on a hierarchical XML document. While this usually works, if we want the XML document to maintain the same structure it had when we opened it, we need to insert a layer between our relational view and the actual XML document. This is accomplished using the `XmlDataDocument`.

DataSet Marshaling

The `DataSet` class inherits from the `MarshalByValueComponent` class, and implements the `ISerializable` interface.

In the traditional COM world, when you transferred an ADO Recordset between processes, it would have to be marshaled. I'm sure everyone has heard by now that COM marshaling is a slow and expensive process, and that it should be avoided wherever possible. In fact, many C++ programmers make it their mission to write as much code as possible without having to marshal objects.

The difference between COM marshaling and marshaling the ADO.NET `DataSet` is that standard COM marshaling is marshal by reference, in which case a pointer to a chunk of memory is passed around, and the memory chunk is copied from stack to stack with a protocol interface in the middle. However, with the `DataSet` (and, consequently, the `DataTable`), its contents are marshaled by value. When a `DataSet` is marshaled, it is serialized onto an XML stream, which is less expensive in network latency terms than requiring type conversions.

DataSet Serialization

Serialization is a term with which many programmers working in OOP languages like Java and C++ are very familiar. Serialization takes an object's internal data and converts it to a stream of bytes. The stream can then be stored on disk or transmitted over a network. There are other objects in the .NET framework that marshal by value, possibly making the performance of marshaling on those objects considerably faster than traditional marshaling.

The serialization of a `DataSet` is typically because the `DataSet` is being passed across the process boundary. This could be to pass data to/from a Web Service, an out-of-process component on the same machine, or a remoted component somewhere on the Internet. As .NET marshaling runs over XML and HTTP, serialized `DataSet` objects can pass through firewalls easily. The `DataSet` will serialize onto an XML stream and completely reconstitute itself on the other side of the function call without losing any data integrity, if a `DataSet` class is available on the client.

Transferring DataSet XML Between Applications

We are going to walk through a simple example that demonstrates how `DataSets` are serialized and marshaled across boundaries. For the first section of the example, we will create and populate a `DataSet` and hand it off to another object in another process. (This other process could be another application, a remoted component, or a Web Service).

The second section will involve that other process of modifying the `DataSet` and returning it to the caller. This will prove that the `DataSet` is actually being passed by value and not by reference.

Let's take a look at the code. Our sample consists of three files: `DSecho.cs`, `Server.cs`, and `Client.cs`. `DSecho.cs` is a class that provides some functionality that will take a `DataSet` and return a `DataSet`, making a slight modification in the process. For this sample, everything is compiled and run from the command line with C# programs and the `CSC` compiler.

Here's the source listing for `DSecho.cs`:

```
namespace Wrox.ProADONET.Chapter8
{
  using System;
  using System.Data;
```

This is hardly the place for a primer on .NET remoting, but we should mention this here, as it applies to our sample. This class inherits from `MarshalByRefObject` because, when the server is holding an instance of it, the client should be expected to be able to *reference* the *same* instance, and not just a copy of it. With `DataSets`, we can use a value copy because they are just in-memory caches capable of being serialized.

```
public class DSEcho : MarshalByRefObject
{
```

We've put some console output in the constructor just so you can see *where* the object is constructed (on the server rather than the client).

```
DSEcho()
{
  Console.WriteLine("DSECHO: Constructed.");
}
```

Here we have a simple function that will echo the incoming `DataSet` to the console (that is, the console of whatever process is currently running this instance), create a new row, and then send the `DataSet` back. When the `DataSet` is transferred across process boundaries, it is serialized in XML, rather than marshaled by reference.

```
public DataSet EchoDataSet(DataSet inDS)
{
  Console.WriteLine("Echoing DS (pre-modify):");
  Console.WriteLine( inDS.GetXml() );
  DataRow newRow = inDS.Tables["Book"].NewRow();
  newRow["Title"] = "New Book";
  newRow["ISBN"] = "11111111";
  newRow["Price"] = 12.99;
  inDS.Tables["Book"].Rows.Add(newRow);
  inDS.AcceptChanges();

  return inDS;
  }
 }
}
```

For our example, we're going to have a server host the `DSEcho` component. A client program will then instantiate that component via remoting and call the `EchoDataSet` function. Let's take a look at the code for the server, then we'll look at the client code and console output.

```
using System;
using System.Runtime.Remoting;
```

```
using System.Runtime.Remoting.Channels;
using System.Runtime.Remoting.Channels.Tcp;

namespace Wrox.ProADONET.Chapter7
{
  public class DSEchoServer
  {
    public static void Main(string[] args)
    {
```

Here we tell the application that it is going to be using the TCP channel (port) 7011. It uses the RemotingConfiguration class to register channel the DSecho component on that TCP. This is done by telling the RemotingConfiguration class the exact type of the component being hosted. In our case, we use the typeof(DSEcho) line of code to provide this information.

```
      TcpServerChannel channel = new TcpServerChannel(7011);
      ChannelServices.RegisterChannel(channel);
      RemotingConfiguration.RegisterWellKnownServiceType(
              typeof(DSEcho),
              "DSEcho",
              WellKnownObjectMode.SingleCall);
      Console.WriteLine("Hit Enter to Exit");
      Console.ReadLine();
    }
  }
}
```

As long as this program is running in memory, it is using the TCP remoting channel 7011 to host the remoting component DSEcho. The following is the code for the client application that accesses it.

```
using System;
using System.Runtime.Remoting.Channels;
using System.Runtime.Remoting.Channels.Tcp;
using System.Data;

namespace Wrox.ProADONET.Chapter7
{
  public class DSEchoClient
  {
    public static void Main(string[] args)
    {
```

This is where the code gets a little fancy. Rather than just instantiating our DSEcho class via the new operator (that would be still in the same process and AppDomain – dependent on the application's config file – and would be quite boring, wouldn't it?) we actually instantiate the object by providing the URI for the object. In our case, that would be tcp://localhost:7011/DSEcho. DSEcho is the name the server used to register the type, while the rest of the URI indicates the host, port number, and protocol (channel).

```
      ChannelServices.RegisterChannel(new TcpClientChannel());
      DSEcho dsEcho = (DSEcho)Activator.GetObject(
              typeof(DSEcho),
```

```
            "tcp://localhost:7011/DSEcho" );

    if (dsEcho == null) {
      Console.WriteLine( "Could not locate DSEcho Server" );
    }
```

Here we build the `DataSet` that we're going to send to the remote object. One of the purposes of this little exercise is to prove to you that the object is truly remote and executing in an entirely different process.

```
    DataSet MyDS = new DataSet();
    MyDS.ReadXml( "Books.XML" );
```

Now, invoke the `EchoDataSet` method on our remote object. This should echo the original contents of the `DataSet` to a console (we'll see which one in a minute), and then return the contents with an extra row.

```
    DataSet MyOtherDS = new DataSet();
    MyOtherDS = dsEcho.EchoDataSet( MyDS );
    Console.WriteLine("DataSet After Remote Modification:");
    Console.WriteLine( MyOtherDS.GetXml() );

    }
  }
}
```

The following screenshot shows the server process being run from the command line. You can see that the output from the `DSEcho` object's constructor and `EchoDataSet` function are all going to the server's console. You can also see that the `DataSet` contents transferred just fine:

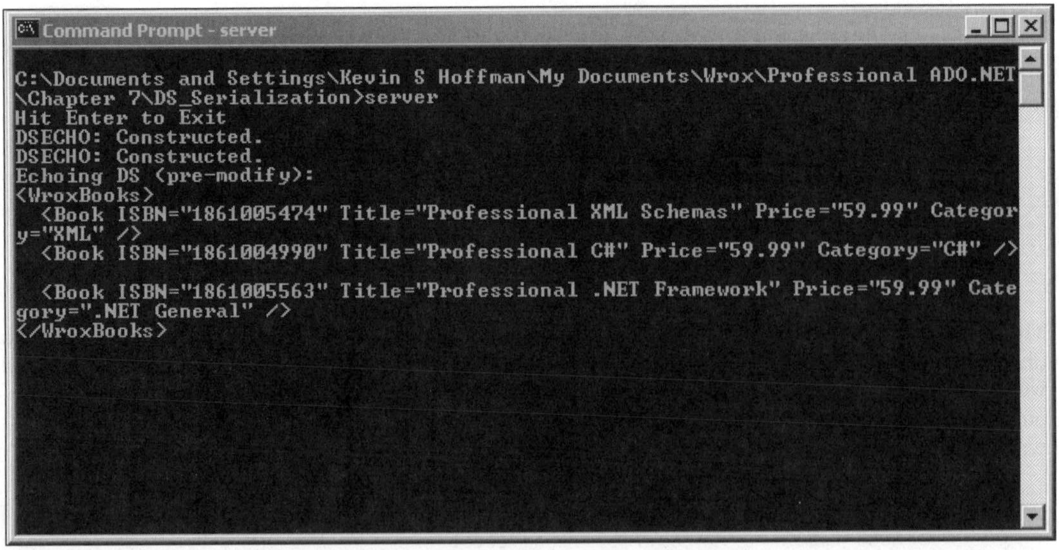

Now let's take a look at the output on the client process's console. Remember that the code for the client displays the contents of the DataSet *after* returning from the EchoDataSet method. Here we can clearly see that a remoted component hosted by a TCP Channel Host actually modified the contents of the DataSet and shipped them back via XML serialization to the calling client process.

As the DataSet can be serialized, it can be streamed to disk, or across a network to a Web service or a Remoting component. We do not need to write any code to give these abilities to the DataSet – they are already there for us to use. A DataSet can also hold complex relationships, keys, hierarchical data, constraints, and more. For these reasons, the DataSet is a very powerful way of managing data.

Picture this brief example of DataSet serialization: a Windows client program has a DataSet that it is using to maintain some bank account information. When connecting with an online banking institution, the client program could simply transfer the DataSet to the server to be populated with new transactions. Once the remoting call is done on the server, not only will the client have access to the new transactions, but because of the versioning support in DataTable rows, the client application will know exactly which rows were modified by the bank and which rows were modified by the end user. This is just one example of hundreds where transferring a DataSet between applications or processes can be an incredibly useful, powerful, and time-saving technology.

Data Filtering

So far we've seen how to populate DataSets with XML, and in an earlier chapter we learned about filling DataSets by using DataAdapters. Once you've got your data in the DataSet, you might occasionally want to work with a smaller portion of that data.

For various reasons, your program or component may want to deal with only a smaller portion of the data contained within the DataSet. There are two main ways of accomplishing this. The first method might seem familiar to classic ADO programmers – filtering the rows in a table by providing a filter string. The second method is to use a Data View. We will discuss and illustrate both methods for filtering data below.

Select Method

The select method is actually very simple and easy to use. It returns an array of DataRow objects that match the criteria you specify in your query. In addition to supplying traditional filter expressions (such as 'Column = 5' or 'Date < '01/01/2001'), you can also supply a DataRowViewState, allowing you to select all rows that not only match given criteria, but have a specific version (such as added, original, deleted, etc.). We'll illustrate this in our example.

The first thing we need to do is create some sample data. We'll use this data for our Data View example as well. To break away from the "Book" examples we've been using, we'll use an XML document containing a list of students, shown below.

```xml
<?xml version="1.0" encoding="utf-8" ?>
<Students>
  <Student ID="1">
    <Name>John Doe</Name>
    <Age>18</Age>
    <GPA>3.95</GPA>
    <LockerCombination>10-12-35</LockerCombination>
  </Student>
  <Student ID="2">
    <Name>Albert Morris</Name>
    <Age>17</Age>
    <GPA>4.0</GPA>
    <LockerCombination>5-17-15</LockerCombination>
  </Student>
  <Student ID="3">
    <Name>Rupert Howard</Name>
    <Age>19</Age>
    <GPA>1.5</GPA>
    <LockerCombination>35-12-20</LockerCombination>
  </Student>
  <Student ID="4">
    <Name>Esteban Colon</Name>
    <Age>17</Age>
    <GPA>3.75</GPA>
    <LockerCombination>20-14-7</LockerCombination>
  </Student>
  <Student ID="5">
    <Name>Julia Jones</Name>
    <Age>18</Age>
    <GPA>2.86</GPA>
    <LockerCombination>10-34-8</LockerCombination>
  </Student>
  <Student ID="6">
    <Name>Kelly Norton</Name>
    <Age>18</Age>
    <GPA>3.01</GPA>
    <LockerCombination>15-13-24</LockerCombination>
  </Student>
  <Student ID="7">
    <Name>Boy Genius</Name>
    <Age>14</Age>
```

```
      <GPA>4.01</GPA>
      <LockerCombination>1-2-3</LockerCombination>
    </Student>
</Students>
```

One thing you should keep in mind is that anything you do to a DataSet that was loaded from an XML document, you can also do to a DataSet that was populated by a SQL query and a DataAdapter.

To create our sample, we created a new C# Console project called SelectFilter. After renaming the main class to FilterSample, we created the following source code:

```
class FilterSample
{
static void Main(string[] args)
{
  DataSet StudentDS = new DataSet();

  // as usual, read files from two levels up so the EXE can run
  // from the obj/debug directory.
  StudentDS.ReadXmlSchema( "../../Students.XSD" );
  StudentDS.ReadXml( "../../Students.XML" );

  // Accept changes now so that original data from the XML file
  // is considered "original".
  StudentDS.AcceptChanges();

  Console.WriteLine("Students With Failing GPAs (<2)");
  Console.WriteLine("------------------------------");
```

Here's our first select statement. You can see that it follows the same syntax that ADO Recordset filtering followed with ADO 2.6, etc. This expression is a simple one, but be aware that ADO.NET filters can be far more complex and finer-grained than classic ADO filters. This particular expression requests all rows where the GPA column is less than 2.0 from the Student table. The GPA (Grade Point Average) is the average of a student's scores, with a 4.0 being perfect.

```
  DataRow[] SelectRows = StudentDS.Tables["Student"].Select( "GPA < 2.0" );
```

We treat the resulting array of DataRow objects just like we would any other array, and iterate through them with a for loop.

```
  for (int i=0; i< SelectRows.Length; i++)
  {
    Console.WriteLine( SelectRows[i]["Name"] );
  }

  SelectRows = StudentDS.Tables["Student"].Select( "Age > 16" );
  Console.WriteLine("\nStudents Over 16:");
  Console.WriteLine("-----------------");

  for (int i=0; i<SelectRows.Length; i++)
```

```
      {
         Console.WriteLine( SelectRows[i]["Name"] );
      }
```

The code below will create new student rows and add those rows to the `Student` table in our `DataSet`. This will give us some rows that we can use to test our version-specific select statements.

```
      DataRow NewRow = StudentDS.Tables["Student"].NewRow();
      NewRow["ID"] = 8;
      NewRow["Name"] = "The New Kid";
      NewRow["Age"] = 17;
      NewRow["GPA"] = 3.99;
      NewRow["LockerCombination"] = "5-9-30";
      StudentDS.Tables["Student"].Rows.Add( NewRow );

      NewRow = StudentDS.Tables["Student"].NewRow();
      NewRow["ID"] = 9;
      NewRow["Name"] = "Girl Genius";
      NewRow["Age"] = 12;
      NewRow["GPA"] = 4.15;
      NewRow["LockerCombination"] = "3-2-1";
      StudentDS.Tables["Student"].Rows.Add( NewRow );

      // important here not to AcceptChanges, so the DataSet still knows
      // which rows are "new".

      Console.WriteLine("\nStudents Just Added to the DataSet, Over 16");
      Console.WriteLine("-------------------------------------------");
```

This is where we get a little fancy. Not only are we requesting all the students older than 16, but from that result set, we only want those rows where `RowState` is `Added`. This allows us to query only recently added rows, rather than the entire `DataSet`.

```
      SelectRows = StudentDS.Tables["Student"].Select("Age > 16", "",
                     DataViewRowState.Added );
      for (int i=0; i<SelectRows.Length; i++)
      {
         Console.WriteLine( SelectRows[i]["Name"] );
      }
   }
}
```

All this code generates the following output at the console:

Students With Failing GPAs (<2)

Rupert Howard

Students Over 16:

John Doe
Albert Morris
Rupert Howard

Esteban Colon
Julia Jones
Kelly Norton

Students Just Added to the DataSet, Over 16

The New Kid

If you go back and compare our original XML document with the results of the filters displayed above, you can verify that they are accurate. Also, pay special attention to the fact that even though we added *two* records programmatically, only one of them is returned. This is because we only added one new student whose age is greater than 16. Neither of the child geniuses appear anywhere in our output.

Data Views

The second way in which we can limit the data that we work with from our DataSet is by using a DataView. A DataView is a bindable, customized view of a given DataTable. You can customize this view so that you control what DataViewRowState the view is allowed to see. As well, you can supply the filter expression so that you can control which rows are accessible to the view. In addition to allowing you to view limited data, you can also use the view to modify data in the original table, so long as the modifications conform to the view restrictions.

Our Data View example is fairly simple. It takes the data from the previous example and creates a couple of views of that data. Here is the source code to the FilterSample.cs file in the ViewFilter project:

```
using System;
using System.Data;

namespace Wrox.ProADONET.Chapter8.ViewFilter
{
class FilterSample
{
static void Main(string[] args)
{
  DataSet StudentDS = new DataSet();

  // load the data from the previous filtering example.
  StudentDS.ReadXmlSchema( "../../../SelectFilter/Students.XSD" );
  StudentDS.ReadXml( "../../../SelectFilter/Students.XML" );

  // again, accept the changes so the dataset has an "original" state.
  StudentDS.AcceptChanges();
```

Firstly, we create a new DataView, indicating that this new view is based on the Student table in the StudentDS DataSet. The next line after that tells the view to limit its visibility to only those rows whose DataRowViewState is set to Added. At the start of the program, this view will be empty since no rows are added (because we called AcceptChanges above).

```
      DataView AddedStudents = new DataView( StudentDS.Tables["Student"] );
      AddedStudents.RowStateFilter = DataViewRowState.Added;

      PrintStudents(AddedStudents, "Added Students Listing (Program Start)");
```

Now we'll create another view on the same table, only this time the criteria are that the student's GPA must be greater than 3.90 and the student's age must be less than 15. Looking back at our original XML document, we see that this only includes the student "Boy Genius".

```
      DataView Prodigies = new DataView( StudentDS.Tables["Student"] );
      Prodigies.RowFilter = "(GPA > 3.90) AND (Age < 15)";

      PrintStudents( Prodigies, "Prodigies Student Listing (Program Start)");

      // now modify the original table (not the views).
      DataRow NewRow = StudentDS.Tables["Student"].NewRow();
      NewRow["ID"] = 8;
      NewRow["Name"] = "The New Kid";
      NewRow["Age"] = 17;
      NewRow["GPA"] = 3.99;
      NewRow["LockerCombination"] = "5-9-30";
      StudentDS.Tables["Student"].Rows.Add( NewRow );

      NewRow = StudentDS.Tables["Student"].NewRow();
      NewRow["ID"] = 9;
      NewRow["Name"] = "Girl Genius";
      NewRow["Age"] = 12;
      NewRow["GPA"] = 4.15;
      NewRow["LockerCombination"] = "3-2-1";
      StudentDS.Tables["Student"].Rows.Add( NewRow );

      PrintStudents( AddedStudents, "Added Students Listing (After Update)");
      PrintStudents( Prodigies, "Prodigy Student Listing (After Update)");
   }
```

This is just a simple little routine that prints out all of the students for a given `DataView`. It avoids having to re-type the same `for` loop over and over again, and illustrates some principals of iterating through a `DataView`.

```
   private static void PrintStudents(DataView dv, string Caption)
   {
     Console.WriteLine("\n{0}", Caption);
     Console.WriteLine("-------------------------------");
     for (int i=0; i<dv.Count; i++)
     {
       Console.WriteLine("\t{0}", dv[i]["Name"]);
     }
     Console.WriteLine("\t\t{0} Students.", dv.Count);
   }
   }
   }
```

The above code produces the following console output:

Added Students Listing (Program Start)
```
-------------------------------
        0 Students.
```

Prodigies Student Listing (Program Start)
```
-------------------------------
    Boy Genius
        1 Students.
```

Added Students Listing (After Update)
```
-------------------------------
    The New Kid
    Girl Genius
        2 Students.
```

Prodigy Student Listing (After Update)
```
-------------------------------
    Boy Genius
    Girl Genius
        2 Students.
```

This should give you enough information to whet your appetite for using DataViews. As you can see, they are a powerful tool, not only for limiting the amount of data that is visible to a given object, but also for simplifying code access to a particular logical subset of data and allowing you to bind visual controls to a sub-set of data.

The DataSet and the XmlDataDocument

So far, we've talked about how to filter DataSets, how to use XML with the DataSet object, and how to provide views of relational data with the DataView class. Earlier in the chapter, we also mentioned that, if you use a DataSet to manipulate an XML document, the fidelity of that document might not be preserved when changes are written to disk. This is due to the fact that the DataSet conforms *only* to its schema, to the exclusion of all else.

So, what do you do if you want to have a relational view of XML data, and you don't want to destroy extraneous data? For example, what do you do if you have an XML document containing Orders and Customers, and you want a DataSet to only manipulate the Orders? Well, if you used a schema detailing Orders to load this XML document, the first change you committed to disk would completely wipe out the Customer information, because the DataSet won't read or write anything that isn't defined by its schema.

The answer to all of these questions is to use the XmlDataDocument. The XmlDataDocument allows structured XML data to be stored, retrieved, and manipulated through a DataSet. More importantly, the XmlDataDocument will preserve the fidelity of the XML document being used to populate the associated DataSet. The XmlDataDocument and the DataSet are synchronized so that when a change is made to one object, the other object is informed of the change.

Relational Projection of DOM View via XSD

The DataSet acts as a flashlight, illuminating a specific part of an XmlDataDocument. The illuminated region is the parts described by the XML Schema on which the DataSet is based. To demonstrate this "projection" of relational data from an XML document to a DataSet, we'll take our previous example and add some extra data. First, we'll add some child nodes beneath each of our students (Classes). Let's say that the intended user of our new DataSet is someone we don't think should have access to the locker combinations of the students. To "hide" this information from the DataSet without clearing it from the source XML document, all we have to do is remove the definition of that information from our XSD file.

Let's take a look at the data we'll be working with and then we can move on to the schema that defines the structure of this data:

```xml
<?xml version="1.0" encoding="utf-8" ?>
<Students>
  <Student ID="1">
    <Name>John Doe</Name>
    <Age>18</Age>
    <GPA>3.95</GPA>
    <LockerCombination>10-12-35</LockerCombination>
    <Class Title="Biology" Room="100" />
    <Class Title="English Lit" Room="101" />
  </Student>
</Students>
```

We removed a few of the actual students from the listing above to keep things clear and simple. The full XML document is available in the code downloads. Here is the new StudentClasses.XSD file:

```xml
<?xml version="1.0" standalone="yes"?>
<xsd:schema id="Students" targetNamespace="" xmlns=""
xmlns:xsd="http://www.w3.org/2001/XMLSchema" xmlns:msdata="urn:schemas-microsoft-
com:xml-msdata">
  <xsd:element name="Students" msdata:IsDataSet="true">
    <xsd:complexType>
      <xsd:choice maxOccurs="unbounded">
        <xsd:element name="Student">
          <xsd:complexType>
            <xsd:sequence>
              <xsd:element name="Name" type="xsd:string" minOccurs="0"
                  msdata:Ordinal="0" />
              <xsd:element name="GPA" type="xsd:float" minOccurs="0"
                  msdata:Ordinal="2" />
              <xsd:element name="Class" minOccurs="0" maxOccurs="unbounded">
                <xsd:complexType>
                  <xsd:attribute name="Title" type="xsd:string" />
                  <xsd:attribute name="Room" type="xsd:string" />
                  <xsd:attribute name="StudentID" type="xsd:int"
                      use="prohibited" />
                </xsd:complexType>
              </xsd:element>
            </xsd:sequence>
            <xsd:attribute name="ID" type="xsd:int" />
```

```
        </xsd:complexType>
      </xsd:element>
    </xsd:choice>
  </xsd:complexType>
  <xsd:unique name="StudentID" msdata:PrimaryKey="true">
    <xsd:selector xpath=".//Student" />
    <xsd:field xpath="@ID" />
  </xsd:unique>
  <xsd:keyref name="StudentClasses" refer="StudentID"
      msdata:IsNested="true">
    <xsd:selector xpath=".//Class" />
    <xsd:field xpath="@StudentID" />
  </xsd:keyref>
  </xsd:element>
</xsd:schema>
```

The element declarations for both `LockerCombination` and `Age` have been removed to protect that information from the `DataSet`.

We can see from our XML that each student has a class roster, an `Age`, a `GPA`, and a `LockerCombination`. The following example demonstrates displaying that information with the use of an `XmlDataDocument`. The commented out code tries to access an element not included in the schema, so uncommenting it will throw an exception. Here is the code:

```
using System;
using System.Xml;
using System.Data;

namespace Wrox.ProADONET.Chapter8.XmlDataDocument1
{
class DataDocumentSample
{
static void Main(string[] args)
{
  DataSet DSStudentClasses = new DataSet();
  XmlNode tmpNode;

  DSStudentClasses.ReadXmlSchema( "../../StudentClasses.XSD" );
  XmlDataDocument XDocStudents = new XmlDataDocument( DSStudentClasses );
  XDocStudents.Load( "../../Students.XML" );

  Console.WriteLine("Students in DataSet:");
  foreach (DataRow _Row in DSStudentClasses.Tables["Student"].Rows )
  {
  // if we try to access the locker combination or age, we'll
  // throw an exception!
  Console.WriteLine("{0}:{1}", _Row["Name"], _Row["GPA"]);

    tmpNode = XDocStudents.GetElementFromRow( _Row );
  Console.WriteLine(
        "\tLocker Combination (from XML, not DataSet): {0}",
        tmpNode.SelectSingleNode("LockerCombination").InnerText );
```

```
    // uncomment the following lines to generate an exception
    //Console.WriteLine(
    //    "\tLocker Combination (from DS): {0}",
    //    _Row["LockerCombination"] );

    foreach (DataRow _Class in _Row.GetChildRows("StudentClasses") )
    {
      Console.WriteLine("\t{0}", _Class["Title"] );
    }
    }

}
}
}
```

The following line, reproduced from above, shows how we can access data that isn't in the schema through the XmlDataDocument:

```
tmpNode = XDocStudents.GetElementFromRow( _Row );
Console.WriteLine(
        "\tLocker Combination (from XML, not DataSet): {0}",
        tmpNode.SelectSingleNode("LockerCombination").InnerText );
```

The first line returns the XmlNode that corresponds to a DataRow in a table of the associated DataSet. We can use this node to access elements and attributes not included in the schema. Doing this has a downside though: we need to know ahead of time the exact hierarchical structure of the XML document. A benefit of the DataSet is that we always deal with columns, rows, and tables. We don't need to know whether a given column came from an element or an attribute.

The application's output looks like this:

```
Students in DataSet:
John Doe:3.95
      Locker Combination (from XML, not DataSet): 10-12-35
      Biology
      English Lit
Albert Morris:4
      Locker Combination (from XML, not DataSet): 5-17-15
      Computer Science
      .NET Basics
      Moral Values and Ethics in Classic Cartoons
Rupert Howard:1.5
      Locker Combination (from XML, not DataSet): 35-12-20
      Biology
Esteban Colon:3.75
      Locker Combination (from XML, not DataSet): 20-14-7
      Biology
      .NET Basics
Julia Jones:2.86
      Locker Combination (from XML, not DataSet): 10-34-8
      Influence of Porky Pig on Modern Language
      An exploration of Hubris and Daffy Duck
```

Biology
Kelly Norton:3.01
    Locker Combination (from XML, not DataSet): 15-13-24
    Computer Science
    .NET Basics
    Moral Values and Ethics in Classic Cartoons
Boy Genius:4.01
    Locker Combination (from XML, not DataSet): 1-2-3
    Intro to Scooby Doo Mystery Solving

If we uncomment a line of code that attempts to access the locker combination directly from the DataSet, we get the following console output:

Students in DataSet:
John Doe:3.95
    Locker Combination (from XML, not DataSet): 10-12-35

Unhandled Exception: System.ArgumentException: Column 'LockerCombination' does not belong to table Student.
   at System.Data.DataRow.get_Item(String columnName)
   at Wrox.ProADONET.Chapter7.XmlDataDocument1.DataDocumentSample.Main(String[] args) in c:\documents and settings\kevin s hoffman\my documents\wrox\professiona l ado.net\chapter 7\xmldatadocument1\datadocumentsample.cs:line 27

Relational Projection Views with a Typed DataSet

We've just been looking at how to use the XmlDataDocument and its ability to synchronize and project XML to a standard DataSet with a supplied schema. We discussed typed DataSets in the previous chapter. If you know the schema at application design time, it might be a good idea to use a typed DataSet.

Let's see how we can do this when using an XmlDataDocument. We will use the same data and the same XSD file to generate a C# console project that uses a typed DataSet called Students, generated from our StudentClasses.XSD file. (See Chapter 7 for how to generate a typed DataSet.) Here is the source code:

```
using System;
using System.Data;
using System.Xml;

namespace Wrox.ProADONET.Chapter8.XmlDataDocument2
{
class ClassMain
{
static void Main(string[] args)
{
   Students StudentClasses = new Students();
   XmlDataDocument XDocStudents = new XmlDataDocument( StudentClasses );
   XDocStudents.Load( "../../Students.XML" );

   Console.WriteLine("Students in Typed DataSet:");
   foreach (Students.StudentRow _Student in StudentClasses.Student.Rows )
   {
     Console.WriteLine("{0}:{1}", _Student.Name, _Student.GPA );
```

```
      foreach (Students.ClassRow _Class in _Student.GetClassRows() )
      {
      Console.WriteLine( "\t{0} in Room {1}", _Class.Title, _Class.Room );
      }
    }
    Console.WriteLine("\nStudents who have classes in Room 100:");
    Console.WriteLine("------------------------------------");
    XmlNodeList tmpNodes = XDocStudents.SelectNodes
              ("//Student/Class[@Room='100']");
    for (int i=0; i<tmpNodes.Count; i++)
    {
      Console.WriteLine("{0}", tmpNodes[i].
            ParentNode.SelectSingleNode("Name").InnerText);
    }
  }
 }
 }
 }
```

The following lines, reproduced from above, uses XPath to select specific nodes from the XmlDataDocument:

```
XDocStudents.SelectNodes("//Student/Class[@Room='100']");
  for (int i=0; i<tmpNodes.Count; i++)
  {
    Console.WriteLine("{0}", tmpNodes[i].
          ParentNode.SelectSingleNode("Name").InnerText);
  }
```

The nodes we select are the Class nodes that are children of Student nodes and have the Room attribute set to 100. (So we are requesting all students who have classes in Room 100).

Except for displaying the two students who have classes in Room 100, the console output of this example is identical to the previous one.

Using XSL and XSLT Transformations

Earlier in the chapter, we saw a quick overview of XPath statements. In addition, we saw how to use DataSets with well-formed XML documents and how to validate those documents. Then, we went through filtering data and creating dynamic, programmable views to our data.

Rather than creating a dynamic view of our relational data, we might want to transform the XML that we have into some other text format. Transformations like this use XSL (eXtensible Stylesheet Language) to define pattern matches. An XSL transformation consists of finding or selecting a pattern match by selecting a result set using XPath, and then, for each item in that result set, defining the resulting output for each of those matches. Obviously, this is an over-simplification. For more information about XSLT, check out Wrox's *Professional XSL (ISBN:1-861003-57-9)*.

We are going to use the XML documents that we have been playing with throughout this chapter and XSL to produce a very professional-looking HTML report. To do this, we've created a C# Console project called XslTransform. The source code to the main .cs file is listed opposite:

```
using System;
using System.Xml;
using System.Data;

namespace Wrox.ProADONET.Chapter7.XslTransform
{
class Transformer
{
static void Main(string[] args)
{
  System.Xml.Xsl.XslTransform xslt = new System.Xml.Xsl.XslTransform();
  xslt.Load( "../../StudentsToHTML.xsl" );

  System.Xml.XPath.XPathDocument XDoc = new System.Xml.XPath.XpathDocument
          ( "../../Students.XML" );
  XmlWriter writer = new XmlTextWriter( "Students.HTML",
          System.Text.Encoding.UTF8 );
  xslt.Transform( XDoc, null, writer );
}
}
}
```

Firstly we create an `XslTransform` object and then load our XSL transformation file into it. We'll see the contents of this file shortly.

Then we create an `XpathDocument` and load the `Students.XML` file that we've been using throughout the chapter. The reason for using an `XPathDocument` is that it is highly optimized for rapid traversal, enabling very fast XSLT operations.

Next, we create an XML writer to write to the `Students.HTML` file. Finally, we use the `XslTransform` object to transform the XML document, and save the result using the `XmlWriter`.

The resulting HTML page looks as shown overleaf:

Student Listing		
Student	**GPA**	**Age**
John Doe	**3.95**	**18**
Biology		Room 100
English Lit		Room 101
Albert Morris	**4.0**	**17**
Computer Science		Room 102
.NET Basics		Room 103
Moral Values and Ethics in Classic Cartoons		Room 104
Rupert Howard	**1.5**	**19**
Biology		Room 200
Esteban Colon	**3.75**	**17**
Biology		Room 100
.NET Basics		Room 103
Julia Jones	**2.86**	**18**
Influence of Porky Pig on Modern Language		Room 105
An exploration of Hubris and Daffy Duck		Room 106
Biology		Room 200
Kelly Norton	**3.01**	**18**
Computer Science		Room 102
.NET Basics		Room 103
Moral Values and Ethics in Classic Cartoons		Room 104
Boy Genius	**4.01**	**14**
Intro to Scooby Doo Mystery Solving		Room 205

The C# code is obviously very simple. The real work goes into the XSL file, so let's take a look at that now. It combines specific XPath statements to match patterns and insert information into the output file:

```
<?xml version="1.0"?>
<xsl:stylesheet xmlns:xsl="http://www.w3.org/1999/XSL/Transform" version="1.0">

<xsl:template match="/">
  <html>
  <head>
    <title>Students Listing</title>
  </head>
  <body>
    <!-- Table Header -->
    <table width="750" border="0" cellspacing="0" cellpadding="3"
         style="border:1px; border-style:solid; border-color:#000000;">
      <tr bgcolor="#E6E6FA">
        <td align="middle" colspan="3">
          <font face="Arial,Helvetica" size="2"><b>Student
               Listing</b></font>
        </td>
      </tr>
      <tr bgcolor="#E6E6FA">
        <td>
          <font face="Arial,Helvetica" size="2"><b>Student</b></font>
        </td>
```

```
        <td>
          <font face="Arial,Helvetica" size="2"><b>GPA</b></font>
        </td>
        <td>
          <font face="Arial,Helvetica" size="2"><b>Age</b></font>
        </td>
      </tr>
```

The following `<xsl:for-each>` statement will iterate over each student node obtained from the source document, placing into the destination document all of the text contained within the `<xsl:for-each>` tag.

```
<xsl:for-each select="//Student">
  <tr>
    <td>
      <font face="Arial,Helvetica" size="2">
```

The `<xsl:value-of>` statement will insert into the destination (transformed) document the value returned by the XPath statement supplied for the select attribute. In this case, it will place the value of the Name element. Our context node for this XPath statement is going to be whatever Student element we are accessing from the outer for-each XPath query.

```
        <b><xsl:value-of select="Name" /></b>
      </font>
    </td>
    <td>
      <font face="Arial,Helvetica" size="2">
        <b><xsl:value-of select="GPA" /></b>
      </font>
    </td>
    <td>
      <font face="Arial,Helvetica" size="2">
        <b><xsl:value-of select="Age" /></b>
      </font>
    </td>
  </tr>
  <tr bgcolor="#eff7de">
    <td colspan="3">
      <table width="100%" border="0" style="border:1px; border-
            style:solid; border-color:#c0c0c0;" cellspacing="0"
            cellpadding="3">
        <xsl:for-each select="Class">
          <tr>
            <td width="75%">
              <font face="Arial,Helvetica" size="2"><xsl:value-of
                    select="@Title" /></font>
            </td>
            <td align="right" width="25%">
              <font face="Arial,Helvetica" size="2">Room <xsl:value-of
                    select="@Room" /></font>
            </td>
          </tr>
        </xsl:for-each>
```

```
            </table>
          </td>
        </tr>
      </xsl:for-each>

    </table>
  </body>
  </html>
</xsl:template>
</xsl:stylesheet>
```

XSL is a powerful tool for taking XML and transforming it into any format we want. The format could be HTML, tab-delimited text files, or even snippets of script or programming language code – the possibilities are virtually limitless. Using XSLT gives us a way of creating meaningful, user-viewable information from an XML document (or portion of a document). It is a great report-generating tool. Another powerful use for XSLT is to take `DataSets` linked to `XmlDataDocuments`, and perform an XSLT transformation on the `DataSet`'s XML representation.

Another use for XSL is to convert between different XML schemas. The BizTalk server uses XSLT to convert from one document format to another, allowing automated exchange of business-to-business data and information.

Summary

This chapter has covered many of the things that you can do with `DataSets` and XML. We have seen how XML and the `DataSet` are interrelated, and how applications can benefit from using XML, `DataSets`, or both. It should be apparent that there are many tasks that can be simplified or automated by using these techniques, and you should now have enough information to decide if any of these techniques are right for you.

Throughout reading this chapter, you should have gained the following:

❑ An introduction to using the `XmlDocument` class

❑ An overview of XPath queries

❑ A good understanding of how `DataSet` schema inference works

❑ An overview of XML document validation

❑ A good understanding of the relationship between `DataSets` and XML documents

❑ An understanding of `DataSet` marshaling and serialization

❑ An overview of how to filter `DataSets` and use `DataViews`

❑ An understanding of how to use the `XmlDataDocument`

❑ An introduction to using XSLT transformations

9

Constraints, Relations, and Views

We have seen in previous chapters that DataSets enable us to work with data while disconnected from the data source. We have seen the advantages of disconnected data access, particularly in multi-user and Internet systems. In this chapter we will extend this knowledge using three ADO.NET features: constraints, relations, and DataViews.

We will start by looking at **constraints**, which force data to obey certain rules. Usually these rules are derived from business rules. For example, we might have a business rule that each account needs a unique account number. If data breaks this rule, the database will quickly cease to be very useful. We can use a constraint called a UniqueConstraint to ensure that this doesn't happen. We will also look at using a ForeignKeyConstraint to ensure that the relations between tables are not violated, and creating our own custom constraints to ensure, for example, that string values obey certain formatting rules.

Next we will go on to look at **relations**. Relations represent the way in which tables within a dataset link together. If we have a table of *store* information for our business, and a table of *regions*, the store table would have a region ID to identify the region that the store is in – a **foreign key**. The ADO.NET DataRelation object would make it easy to navigate between the *store* table and the *regions* table.

In the past, application developers have relied on the database server to do this kind of work. However datasets encourage us to work with data without being connected to the database server. Using these ADO.NET features means that we can detect problems as they happen, rather than waiting until we try to update the data source.

Relations and constraints make it easier for us to edit data, and reduce the risk of damaging the data's integrity. This is particularly important when we are allowing users of our applications to manipulate data themselves. The final object we will look at is designed specifically for letting users view or edit data in a controlled way, the DataView. The DataView allows us to present a DataTable in a particular way, perhaps only showing a subset of the records, for example. Users can edit a DataView, and the changes will be made to the underlying table. However, DataViews are particularly useful because we can control what editing operations are allowed – perhaps we can allow users to edit existing records but not add new ones, or allow them to add new ones but not edit existing ones.

Finally we will show how constraints, relations, and DataView objects can work together by developing two applications: one using Windows Forms, the other using Web Forms.

Constraints

Constraints restrict the data allowed in a data column or set of data columns. For example, in SQL Server, a constraint might be created to ensure that a value for a column or set of columns is not repeated within a table. If data is entered that does not meet this constraint, an error is thrown. ADO.NET provides this functionality to client-side code.

Constraints in ADO.NET work primarily with DataTables and DataColumns to enforce data integrity. There are two constraint classes in the System.Data namespace: UniqueConstraint and ForeignKeyConstraint. The UniqueConstraint class allows for ensuring that a given column or set of columns contain a unique value in each row. The ForeignKeyConstraint constrains values in two different data tables and provides for cascading updates and deletes of related values. We will look at each of these in more detail in the sections that follow.

There are several things to note about constraints in general before we get into the details. Firstly, constraints are only enforced when the EnforceConstraints property of the DataSet is set to true. This is the default value of this property, so it should not need to be modified to allow for enforcing constraints. However, if a method is receiving a DataSet as a parameter then it should ensure that this property is set to true if its code relies on constraints.

If the EnforceConstraints property is set to false and changes are made to the data that violate the constraint, and then the EnforceConstraints property is set to true, an attempt will be made to enable all of the constraints for the table. Those values that violate the constraint will cause an exception to be raised.

When merging DataSets, constraints are applied after all of the data has been merged, rather than as each item is being merged. This makes the merge process faster, as the entire set of new data can be merged without each row of data being checked.

Constraints are enforced any time data is edited or added to a data table. Specifically, the following methods initiate a check of constraints:

- ❑ DataSet.Merge
- ❑ DataTable.LoadDataRow
- ❑ DataRowCollection.Add
- ❑ DataRow.EndEdit
- ❑ DataRow.ItemArray

There are two primary exception classes to be concerned with when working with constraints: `ConstraintException` and `InvalidConstraintException`. If a constraint is violated at the time it is checked, a `ConstraintException` will be thrown. We can catch these exceptions in order to instruct the user how they should change their input to meet the constraints. Keep in mind that exceptions should only be used for exceptional circumstances. If we think there's a good chance that a constraint will be violated, we should try to check the values first.

At the time that a constraint is created, if the values in the data table do not meet the criteria for the constraint, an `InvalidConstraintException` will be thrown. For example, trying to create a `UniqueConstraint` on a `DataColumn` that does not contain unique values will throw an `InvalidConstraintException`. This exception can also occur when setting the `EnforceConstraints` property to `true`. When loading data into a dataset, where we don't know if the values will meet the local constraints, it is important to catch this exception to ensure that the constraint can be applied.

Unique Constraint

As mentioned above, the `UniqueConstraint` class provides a mechanism for constraining the data in a column or columns to be unique values. This can be helpful if the column in question is a key value, or if you have a requirement that this value should be unique. Keep in mind that, while the values must be unique, if you allow null values in this column then several rows can have `null`. Essentially, this constraint keeps the values, when set, from duplicating each other.

If you want to ensure that the values in your column are both unique and non-null, then you have two options. The first option is to set up that column or columns as the primary key for the data table. If a primary key already exists, or if the column or columns to be constrained are not a primary key, then the second option is to apply a unique constraint and be sure to set the `AllowDBNull` property of the column or columns to `false`.

Let's take a look at an example of a `UniqueConstraint` in action. The following example creates a unique constraint on the `Customers` table to ensure that the customer phone number is unique:

```
//Connect and fill dataset with three tables of data
SqlConnection nwindConnection = new SqlConnection(connectionString);
SqlDataAdapter nwindAdapter = new SqlDataAdapter("select * from customers; select
* from orders; select * from [order details]",nwindConnection);

DataSet constraintDS = new DataSet();

//we use this to get the primary key for the tables
nwindAdapter.MissingSchemaAction = MissingSchemaAction.AddWithKey;
nwindAdapter.Fill(constraintDS);

//name the tables to match the source
constraintDS.Tables[0].TableName = "Customers";
constraintDS.Tables[1].TableName = "Orders";
constraintDS.Tables[2].TableName = "OrderDetails";

//create the unique constraint passing in the columns to constrain
UniqueConstraint uniqueContact = new
  UniqueConstraint(constraintDS.Tables["Customers"].Columns["Phone"]);
```

```
//add the constraint to the constraints collection of the table
constraintDS.Tables["Customers"].Constraints.Add(uniqueContact);
```

We first load up some data from the Northwind database and name the tables to match the table names in the database. We then create a new instance of the UniqueConstraint class, passing in the phone column of the Customers table. Just creating the constraint is not enough – we also need to add it to the collection of constraints for the table. Only after we add it does the constraint become active.

As mentioned before, we can also create a unique constraint and indicate that we will not allow null values in this column. In order to do this, we simply modify the PhoneNumber data column such that it will not allow nulls. In addition, we can use a shortcut to create the constraint. By simply setting the Unique property of a DataColumn to true, a UniqueConstraint is automatically created on the column for us. In the example below, we use this shorthand method of creating the constraint, as well as restrict the column such that it does not allow null values.

```
//Connect and fill dataset with three tables of data
SqlConnection nwindConnection = new SqlConnection(connectionString);
SqlDataAdapter nwindAdapter = new SqlDataAdapter("select * from customers; select
* from orders; select * from [order details]",nwindConnection);

DataSet constraintDS = new DataSet();

//we use this to get the primary key for the tables
nwindAdapter.MissingSchemaAction = MissingSchemaAction.AddWithKey;
nwindAdapter.Fill(constraintDS);

//name the tables to match the source
constraintDS.Tables[0].TableName = "Customers";
constraintDS.Tables[1].TableName = "Orders";
constraintDS.Tables[2].TableName = "OrderDetails";

//create the unique constraint by using the Unique property
constraintDS.Tables["Customers"].Columns["Phone"].Unique=true;

//do not allow null values in the phone column
constraintDS.Tables["Customers"].Columns["Phone"].AllowDBNull = false;
```

Finally, we can create a unique constraint that involves more than one column. This comes in handy when we need the combination of two or more columns to be unique. For example, we might need to constrain a table of order details by having a unique combination of the customer ID and the order ID. This allows the detail records to be uniquely identified for a given order and customer. Since no two customers should have the same order number, this constraint will prevent users assigning the wrong customer to an order. The only difference in creating a constraint with multiple columns is that, in the constructor, we pass an array of data columns instead of a single column:

```
DataColumn[] columns = new DataColumn[2];
columns[0] = constraintDS.Tables["orderdetails"].Columns["orderid"]; columns[1] =
constraintDS.Tables["orderdetails"].Columns["customerid"];
UniqueConstraint multiUniqueConstraint = new UniqueConstraint(columns);
```

The unique constraint is extremely helpful in managing client-side data and maintaining integrity between the data on the client and the data on the server.

ForeignKeyConstraint

When working with relational data, one of the ways in which data is constrained is by defining relationships between tables and creating a `ForeignKeyConstraint`. This constraint ensures that items in one table have a matching item in the related table. For example, if we have an `Orders` table that is related to a `Customers` table, it is important that an order does not exist without a customer. The diagram below shows what this might look like:

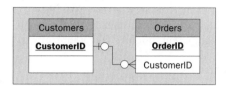

A given order is connected to a customer by the `CustomerID` field. If we put a foreign key constraint on this relationship, then an order cannot be inserted or updated unless it has a customer ID that is a valid customer ID. This type of constraint is extremely useful in maintaining data integrity. In this situation, the `Customers` table is considered to be the parent table and the `Orders` table is the child. While the parent table has to have a valid `CustomerID` for every record, the `Customers` table can have `CustomerID` values that do not appear in the `Orders` table. However, a row in the parent table that is referenced from the child table cannot be deleted. This prevents us, in our example, from removing customers who have orders, which would then leave an order without customer information.

In order to use a `ForeignKeyConstraint` in a `DataSet`, we specify the `DataColumn` or columns from the respective `DataTable` objects that will be constrained. The example below loads a `DataSet` with data from the `Northwind` database's `Customers` and `Orders` table and creates a `ForeignKeyConstraint` on these tables. This constraint is then added to the `Constraints` collection of the child table:

```
//Connect and fill dataset with three tables of data
SqlConnection nwindConnection = new SqlConnection(connectionString);
SqlDataAdapter nwindAdapter = new SqlDataAdapter("select * from customers; select
* from orders; select * from [order details]",nwindConnection);

DataSet constraintDS = new DataSet();

//we use this to get the primary key for the tables
nwindAdapter.MissingSchemaAction = MissingSchemaAction.AddWithKey;
nwindAdapter.Fill(constraintDS);

//name the tables to match the source
constraintDS.Tables[0].TableName = "Customers";
constraintDS.Tables[1].TableName = "Orders";
constraintDS.Tables[2].TableName = "OrderDetails";

//create a new foreign key constraint between the customers
//and orders tables on the customer id field
DataColumn Parent = constraintDS.Tables["Customers"].Columns["CustomerID"];
DataColumn Child = constraintDS.Tables["Orders"].Columns["CustomerID"];
```

```
ForeignKeyConstraint customerIDConstraint = new ForeignKeyConstraint(Parent,
    Child);

//add the constraint to the child table
constraintDS.Tables["Orders"].Constraints.Add(customerIDConstraint);
```

The process of creating a `ForeignKeyConstraint` is much like that for the `UniqueConstraint`, except that we pass in two `DataColumnObjects`, the first representing the column in the parent table, and the second representing the related column in the child table. Once we have created this constraint, we add it to the child table's collection of constraints. It might seem odd that we add the foreign key constraint to the child and not the parent, but let's take a look at what actually happens under the covers when we add this constraint.

First of all, when we look at a `ForeignKeyConstraint`, we are really trying to ensure that the child data can be related to the parent data. In light of this alone, it begins to make more sense that the child table contains the constraint. It is when those rows that are in the child table are changed that we need to be concerned about the integrity of our data. As we mentioned before, the parent table might have rows that have no corresponding data in the child table and this is acceptable. However, it is not acceptable for the child table to have rows that do not have a companion in the parent table.

Another important fact to consider is what happens to the parent table when the foreign key constraint is added to the child table. The parent table also gets a constraint added to its constraint collection – a `UniqueConstraint`. This ensures that the parent table has unique values for the column that relates to the child table. If this were not the case, then there would be no way to know which row of the parent table a row in the child table was related to. This is similar to the function the primary key plays in many relational database systems. If the column has already been identified as the primary key of the `DataTable`, then it will already have this `UniqueConstraint` applied.

In addition to being able to constrain relations based on a single column in each data table, the `ForeignKeyConstraint` can be applied to a range of columns. This is useful when the key for a table is a multi-column key. For example, perhaps an order is unique by virtue of the combination of the order number and the store number where this order was taken. This way, order numbers can be reused through out the company, but because the key value for orders involves the store ID as well, orders can be uniquely identified. We might then have an `OrderDetails` table that relates to the order table by way of this multi-column key. The figure below shows this relationship:

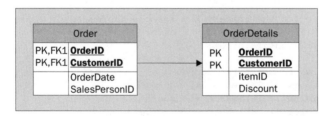

The `ForeignKeyConstraint` can also be created on these multiple columns in a `DataSet`. The following example creates a `ForeignKeyConstraint` on the `Order` and `OrderDetails` tables using a multi-column key:

```
//create the array of columns for the parent table
DataColumn[] parentColumns = new DataColumn[2];
parentColumns[0]=simpleForeign.Tables["Orders"].Columns["OrderID"];
parentColumns[1]=simpleForeign.Tables["Orders"].Columns["CustomerID"];

//create the array of columns for the child table
DataColumn[] childColumns = new DataColumn[2];
childColumns[0]=simpleForeign.Tables["OrderDetails"].Columns["OrderID"];
childColumns[1]=simpleForeign.Tables["OrderDetails"].Columns["CustomerID"];

//create the constraint
ForeignKeyConstraint customerIDConstraint = new
ForeignKeyConstraint(parentColumns, childColumns);
//add the constraint to the child table
simpleForeign.Tables["Orders"].Constraints.Add(customerIDConstraint);
```

Here we have used the hypothetical situation where the `OrderDetails` table contains a customer ID to help identify the detail records. When we create this constraint, the `OrderDetails` table gets the `ForeignKeyConstraint` placed on the `OrderID` and `CustomerID` columns, while the `Orders` table gets a `UniqueConstraint` created on its `OrderID` and `CustomerID` columns. Notice that we add the constraint to the `Constraints` property of the child table and not the parent. Attempting to assign the constraint to the parent table will generate an exception.

One concept that goes along with foreign key constraints is referential integrity. This is the concept described above where the integrity of the data in the two related tables is maintained. One mechanism that helps with this process is known as cascading deletes, a new feature in SQL Server 2000, but one that has existed in Microsoft Access since version 2.0. This mechanism works so that, in our scenario of customers and orders, if I delete a customer, the related rows in the `Orders` table are also deleted automatically instead of raising an exception.

This same mechanism of cascading changes from one table to another is available in the ADO.NET framework, but it provides more flexibility than simply cascading deletes. We use the `AcceptRejectRule` enumeration to identify the actions to take when a value is updated or deleted in the parent table and the `DataTable`, `DataSet`, or `DataRow` objects' `AcceptChanges` or `RejectChanges` methods are called. Similarly, we use the `Rule` enumeration to identify the actions to take on the related rows when a value in a column is updated or deleted.

The `AcceptRejectRule` is applied, as mentioned above, when the `AcceptChanges` or `RejectChanges` method is called on the `DataTable`, `DataRow`, or `DataSet` objects. This means that this rule will not be put into effect during the editing process; rather, it will only get applied when the changes made to the database are either accepted or rejected based on the values that would result from this action. There are two possible values for the `AcceptRejectRule` property as defined in the `AcceptRejectRule` enumeration. These two options are presented in the table overleaf, along with the resulting outcome of using each:

Enumerated Value	Result
Cascade	The change made in the parent table is cascaded to all related rows in the child table.
None	No action is taken on the related rows. An exception will result if there is a violation of the constraint and this value has been chosen for the `AcceptRejectRule` of the `ForeignKeyConstraint`.

The `Cascade` option duplicates the actions taken in the parent table to the related rows in the child table. So, if the parent row is deleted, the child rows are deleted as well. If the column that is acting as part of the foreign key constraint in the parent table was updated, the change would be cascaded to the related rows in the child table, changing its key value to match the new key value in the parent. When the "None" option is selected, none of these changes propagate to the child rows.

Here we set up a cascading update rule:

```
//Load data into dataset
...
//create a new foreign key constraint on the customer id columns
DataColumn Parent = simpleForeign.Tables["Customers"].Columns["CustomerID"];
DataColumn Child = simpleForeign.Tables["Orders"].Columns["CustomerID"];
ForeignKeyConstraint customerIDConstraint = new ForeignKeyConstraint(Parent,
Child);

//indicate that on accept or reject, the changes should cascade
//to the related child rows
customerIDConstraint.AcceptRejectRule = AcceptRejectRule.Cascade;

//add the constraint to the child table
simpleForeign.Tables["Orders"].Constraints.Add(customerIDConstraint);
```

By defining this rule, we are indicating that, when a parent row is deleted, the corresponding child rows should also be deleted. Or, when a parent row has a column that is involved in this constraint updated, then the change should propagate to the child rows as well, updating their key value. The default value for this property is `None`, which means that by default no changes will be cascaded.

In addition to acting on changes when the changes are applied to a `DataTable`, we can apply rules to indicate what actions should be taken on the child rows when the value in the parent table is actually changed. We use the `UpdateRule` and `DeleteRule` properties of the `ForeignKeyConstraint` to identify the action to be taken on the child rows using an item in the `Rule` enumeration. The table opposite shows the various values of the `Rule` enumeration and their impact on the actions taken:

Enumerated Value	Result
Cascade	The change made in the parent table is cascaded to all related rows in the child table. For rows that are deleted in the parent, the related rows in the child are also deleted. For rows where the key value is updated, the related rows in the other table are updated with the new value for the key. This is the default setting for both the UpdateRule and DeleteRule property.
None	No action is taken on the related rows. An exception will result if there is a violation of the constraint and this value has been chosen for the DeleteRule or UpdateRule.
SetDefault	The related rows will have their key value set to the default value for the column. If no default value has been specified, the child rows will be set to NULL.
SetNull	The related rows will have their key value set to DBnull. This will generate an exception if the data column does not allow null values.

Like the AcceptRejectRule, we have the options to cascade changes or take no action. In addition, we have the ability to indicate that the child rows should have their key value set to null or set to the default value for the column. This provides greater flexibility than just cascading or doing nothing. We can take an action that sets the key for our child rows, but not to a value that will correspond to a parent row. This leaves our child rows in a state of flux, as they have no relation to the parent table at this time. Or we can set the default to the manager's ID, so that all "floating" child records are automatically assigned to the manager.

Here's an example of using the Delete and Update rules:

```
//Load data into dataset
...

//create a new foreign key constraint on the customer id columns
DataColumn Parent = simpleForeign.Tables["Customers"].Columns["CustomerID"];
DataColumn Child = simpleForeign.Tables["Orders"].Columns["CustomerID"];
ForeignKeyConstraint customerIDConstraint = new
ForeignKeyConstraint(Parent,Child);

//indicate that on accept or reject, the changes should cascade
//to the related child rows
customerIDConstraint.AcceptRejectRule = AcceptRejectRule.Cascade;

//indicate that when an item in the parent is deleted, the
//related child records should have their key value set to null
customerIDConstraint.DeleteRule = Rule.SetNull;

//indicate that when the parent is updated, the child rows
//should also be updated to match
customerIDConstraint.UpdateRule = Rule.Cascade;

//add the constraint to the child table
simpleForeign.Tables["Orders"].Constraints.Add(customerIDConstraint);
```

Here we have expanded on our previous example to specify the delete and update rules for the constraint. In this case, when a row in the parent table is deleted, the child row will have its key value set to null. When the parent has its key value updated, that change will cascade to the child rows to keep the two tables in synch.

`DeleteRule` and `UpdateRule` are acted upon when the constraint is enforced, which is when the value is actually changed. The `AcceptRejectRule`, however, is acted upon when the changes to the table are accepted or rejected, using the `AcceptChanges` or `RejectChanges` methods found on the `DataRow`, `DataTable`, and `DataSet` objects. Therefore, if the update or delete rule conflicts with the `AcceptRejectRule`, the outcome may not be as expected. As the update and delete rules will be acted upon first, these changes will override those defined in the `AcceptRejectRule`. For example, if the `UpdateRule` is set to `SetNull` and the `AcceptRejectRule` is set to `Cascade`, when the parent value is updated the child rows will have their key value set to null. When the `AcceptRejectRule` is applied, the child columns will have already been updated, so no action will be taken.

The foreign key constraint is extremely useful when working with multiple, related tables of data in a `DataSet`. As we will see later, this functionality is enhanced when we use data relations in conjunction with the foreign key constraint.

Custom Constraint

The `ForeignKeyConstraint` and `UniqueConstraint` both derive from the abstract `Constraint` class. This class defines much of the base functionality of the constraint classes. However, several of the abstract methods in the `Constraint` class that need to be overridden in derived classes have assembly level protection, which means that only classes in the `System.Data` assembly can appropriately override these abstract methods. Therefore, at this time it is not possible to derive from the `Constraint` class in our own code. Microsoft has indicated that this may be possible in future versions of the .NET framework, but for now we have some limited options.

While we cannot derive a class from `System.Data.Constraint` to create our own custom constraints, we can create a custom constraint that provides a good deal of the functionality of the included constraint classes. As an example, we'll create a custom constraint to ensure that phone numbers entered into the phone number column of a `DataTable` are in the following format: (123) 456-7890.

When a constraint is created, either unique or foreign key, it registers for change events on the `DataTable` so that it can check the values of the data and throw an exception if the value does not meet the constraint. We can use this same mechanism in creating our constraint to listen for new or changed values in the column constrained.

We start by importing the necessary namespaces, including the `System.Data` namespace for access to object related to the `DataSet` and `DataTable`, as well as the `System.Text.RegularExpressions` namespace, which contains the classes we will use to validate the column value. We identify a namespace for our class and wrap the entire contents of the code in this namespace. This helps to uniquely identify our class. Next we define variables to hold the state information we will need, including a reference to the column that should be constrained, the constraint name, and a Boolean value that will indicate if the constraint is violated. Finally, we create a default constructor:

```
using System;
using System.Data;
using System.Text.RegularExpressions;
```

```
namespace Wrox.ProfessionalADODotNet
{
  public class USPhoneNumberConstraint
  {

    //the column we are interested in
    private DataColumn ConstrainedColumn;

    //the name of our constraint
    private string m_ConstraintName;

    //a test to see if the constraint is currently violated
    private bool IsViolated;

    //a static definition of the regular expression that defines
    //the format required for a value to meet this constraint
    private const string comparisonValue = @"\(\d{3}\) \d{3}-\d{4}";


    public USPhoneNumberConstraint()
    {    }
  }
}
```

The other thing to notice about our initial setup is that we have created a constant representing the pattern that values must match in order to meet the constraint. The comparisonValue constant holds a regular expression that matches a phone number with the area code in parentheses. We have used the C# "@" syntax to indicate that the C# compiler should ignore escape sequences, because regular expressions use these same escape sequences. The expression is broken down in the following table:

Pattern	Meaning
\(\d{3}\)	Three numeric characters surrounded by parentheses
\d{3}	A space followed by three numeric characters
-\d{4}	A hyphen followed by four numeric characters

Next, we will add some other constructors to our class to indicate the column constrained and a constraint name. We will create a constructor that just takes the column, and one that takes the column and a name.

```
public USPhoneNumberConstraint(DataColumn
constrainedColumn):this("USPhoneNumberConstraint",constrainedColumn)
{    }

public USPhoneNumberConstraint(string constraintName, DataColumn
constrainedColumn)
{
//make sure the column isn't null
if(constrainedColumn == null)
{
```

```
      throw new InvalidConstraintException("Constraints cannot be applied to
        DataColumns with Null value");
    }

    //make sure our column is in a table
    if (constrainedColumn.Table == null)
    {
      throw new InvalidConstraintException("US Phone Number constraint can only
        be applied to columns which are in a table.");
    }

    //set our local variable to the passed in column
    ConstrainedColumn = constrainedColumn;

    //set the constraint name
    ConstraintName = constraintName;

    //make sure the existing values meet the criteria
    CheckExistingValues();

    //hook up to the dataColumn change event if we have a valid column
    if(ConstrainedColumn!=null)
    {
      ConstrainedColumn.Table.ColumnChanged += new
    DataColumnChangeEventHandler(this.DataColumn_OnChange);
    }

    }
```

Our first constructor simply passes the DataColumn parameter on to the second constructor, along with a default name. In the second constructor we do a lot of work to ensure that we can successfully create the constraint. We check that the column is not null and that it belongs to a DataTable and throw an InvalidConstraintException if neither of these conditions is met.

We then set our local variables for the constrained column and the constraint name and check that the values currently in the table meet the constraint. We will take a look at the CheckExistingValues method shortly. Finally, we attach an event handler to the ColumnChanged event of the table to which our column belongs:

```
    //checks the values in the data table associated with
    //the constrained column and throws an exception if they
    //don't all meet the criteria
    private void CheckExistingValues()
    {
      foreach(DataRow row in ConstrainedColumn.Table.Rows)
      {
        if(Regex.IsMatch(row[ConstrainedColumn,
          DataRowVersion.Current].ToString(),comparisonValue)==false)
        {
          throw new InvalidConstraintException("The existing values in the data
            table do not meet the US Phone Number constraint.");
```

```
      }
    }
  }
```

First we create the `CheckExistingValues` method, which uses `foreach` to iterate through the rows in the table, and check the current value in the constrained column against our regular expression pattern. If we come upon any rows that do not match, we throw a new `InvalidConstraintException`. We use the static `IsMatch` method of the `RegEx` class to test the value against our pattern. This method returns a Boolean indicating whether the value matches the pattern we specify.

```
//check any values that occur when the data column we are
//constraining is changed
public void DataColumn_OnChange(object sender, DataColumnChangeEventArgs
  eArgs)
{
  //check to see that it is the column we are interested in and that
  //constraints are being enforced for the data set
  if(eArgs.Column == ConstrainedColumn &&
    ConstrainedColumn.Table.DataSet.EnforceConstraints==true)
  {
    //if it is the constrained column, check the value
    if(Regex.IsMatch(eArgs.Row[ConstrainedColumn,
      DataRowVersion.Proposed].ToString(),comparisonValue)==false)
    {
    //if we did not find a match, indicate that the constraint is violated
    //and throw an exception
    IsViolated = true;
    throw new ConstraintException("The value in column " +
      ConstrainedColumn.ColumnName + " violates the US Phone Number
      Constraint.");
    }
  }
}
```

Then, as you can see above, we create our event handler for the `ColumnChanged` event. In the event handler, we need to first check to see that the changing column is the one we are interested in. If it is, then we check the proposed value with the regular expression's `IsMatch` method, as we did in the previous method. If there isn't a match, we set the `IsViolated` field to `true` so that we can now query our constraint to see if it is violated. Finally, we throw a `ConstraintException`, which will indicate that the constraint has been violated.

These two methods provide the bulk of the functionality for our constraint. The first ensures that the table can be constrained when we create the constraint. The second manages enforcing the constraint as the data is edited.

Next, we add some property accessors to allow a user to set the constraint name and the `DataColumn`, as well as getting the associated `DataTable`.

```
//public accessor for the constraint name
public string ConstraintName
{
  get{return m_ConstraintName;}
  set{m_ConstraintName=value;}
}

//public read-only accessor for the data table
//of the constrained column
public DataTable Table
{
  get
  {
    if(ConstrainedColumn!=null)
      return ConstrainedColumn.Table;
    else
    {
      return null;
    }
  }
}

//property to access the data column
//being constrained. Allows for setting the column
//after the constraint has been created
public DataColumn Column
{
  get{return ConstrainedColumn;}
  set
  {
    //if the column is a new column then
    //check the constraint for the new column
    if(value!= ConstrainedColumn)
    {
      ConstrainedColumn = value;
      CheckExistingValues();
    }
  }
}
```

The property accessor for the constraint name is a simple accessor for the private field. The property get for the table first checks to make sure the DataColumn is not null, and if not, returns the DataTable for the constrained column. In the property for the DataColumn, we add a check on the set accessor, such that if the column is not the current column we check the existing values to ensure that the existing values can be constrained. Using these properties, calling code can now set the column to be constrained and the name of the constraint outside the constructor.

Now that we have our constraint, we can use it in our code much like we use the predefined constraints. The example below is a simple Console application that shows our constraint in action using data from the authors table of the pubs database.

We start by adding a using statement that includes the Wrox.ProfessionalADODotNet namespace to which our custom constraint belongs:

```
using System;
using System.Data;
using System.Data.SqlClient;
using Wrox.ProfessionalADODotNet;

namespace ConstraintTest
{
  class Class1
  {
```

Next we load up a DataSet with data from the authors table of the pubs database:

```
    static void Main(string[] args)
    {
      //connecto to local sql server and fill the dataset
      //with data from the authors table of the pubs database
      SqlConnection cnn = new
        SqlConnection("server=(local);database=pubs;uid=sa;pwd=;");
      SqlDataAdapter da = new SqlDataAdapter("select * from authors",cnn);

      DataSet ds = new DataSet();
      da.Fill(ds, "Authors");
```

We create our constraint, passing in the column to be constrained – in this case the "phone" column of the table – and give it a name. So far, this is much like the process we have used for the predefined constraints, but this is where it begins to differ. Notice that we do not add our constraint to the constraints collection of the data table. As this collection can only hold items that derive from System.Data.Constraint, we will get an exception if we try to add our class to the collection. However, we see that trying to enter a value in this column that does not meet the criteria will throw an exception.

```
      //indicate to the output that we are starting
      Console.WriteLine("Creating Constraint");

      //create a new instance of our constraint passing in the
      //phone column of the table as the data column to be constrained
      //and a name for our constraint
      USPhoneNumberConstraint phoneConstraint = new
        USPhoneNumberConstraint("phoneConstraint",
        ds.Tables["Authors"].Columns["phone"]);

      //indicate that we are changing the number to an incorrect format
      Console.WriteLine("Changing number to incorrect format");

      try
      {
        ds.Tables["Authors"].Rows[0].BeginEdit();
        ds.Tables["Authors"].Rows[0]["Phone"] = "123 222-4568";
        ds.Tables["Authors"].Rows[0].EndEdit();

      }
      catch(ConstraintException e)
```

```
        {
          Console.WriteLine("Constraint Exception encounetered");
          Console.WriteLine(e.ToString());
        }

        Console.WriteLine("\nPress the enter key to exit");
        Console.ReadLine();
      }
    }
  }
```

As we are not deriving from the base `Constraint` class, there are some limitations to our custom constraint. Since it is not included in the constraints collection of the data table, a check of this collection could indicate that there are no constraints violated when our constraint is in fact violated. One way to work around this is to use the `SetColumnError` method of the `DataRow` object to indicate that there is a problem with the value the user has entered. This allows us to use the `HasErrors` method of the `DataRow` or `DataTable` objects to determine if there are errors with our data. We can see how this shortcoming manifests itself if we try to use our constraint in a `DataGrid` on a Windows form. The constraint does not prevent a user from changing the value to one that does not meet the constraint parameters. The `DataGrid` catches the exception we raise, but it is not able to get at the information about our constraint to raise a message to the user, or stop the change from happening. If we set an error, the grid displays a red marker indicating that there is an error in the row.

To enhance our constraint, we will add a few lines of code to make it work more effectively. We will enhance our event handler for the column changed event in such a way that we do not allow values to be entered that violate our constraint. In this way, a user of our constraint cannot catch our exception and ignore it to put an invalid value in our column.

```csharp
public void DataColumn_OnChange(object sender, DataColumnChangeEventArgs eArgs)
  {
  //check to see that it is the column we are
  //interested in and that constraints
  //are being enforced for the data set
  if(eArgs.Column == ConstrainedColumn &&
     ConstrainedColumn.Table.DataSet.EnforceConstraints==true)
  {
    //if it is the constrained column, check the value
    if(Regex.IsMatch(eArgs.Row[ConstrainedColumn,
      DataRowVersion.Proposed].ToString(),comparisonValue)==false)
    {
    //if we did not find a match, indicate that the constraint is
    //violated
      //and throw an exception
      IsViolated = true;
  //reset the value to the original value-we don't let the value change
    eArgs.Row[ConstrainedColumn]=eArgs.Row[ConstrainedColumn,DataRowVersion
      .Original];
  throw new ConstraintException("The value in column " +
    ConstrainedColumn.ColumnName + " violates the US Phone Number
    Constraint.");
    }
  }
}
```

By resetting the value in the column, we ensure that the value cannot be changed to a value that does not meet our criteria. In this way, we do not have to keep track of the column or row state after the constraint is violated. We still throw the exception, so that a program using our constraint can be notified that the constraint was violated, and take an appropriate action, such as notify the user.

When loading our data, we are already throwing an exception if the data does not match our criteria and we do not set the event handler for the column changed event, so we do not have to worry about a user creating our constraint when the data is already invalid.

This code sample is intended to provide a starting point for creating a custom constraint and give more insight into the workings of the constraint mechanism in ADO.NET. As it has some limitations, this solution is best suited to creating common constraints that can be used in many different projects and in an environment with some guidance on how to best use these custom constraints.

DataRelations

A `DataRelation` defines the relationship between two different `DataTable` objects. This should not be confused with the `ForeignKeyConstraint`, which constrains the data in two tables. However, we will see that the `DataRelation` and `ForeignKeyConstraint` work closely together. We use the `DataRelation` primarily for navigating between data tables. Thus, using a specific row in the parent table, we can access all of the related data rows in the related table.

We will start by creating a simple relation between two `DataTable` objects. The example below creates a new `DataRelation`, identifying the data columns to use for the relationship, and adds this new relation to the `DataRelation` collection of the `DataSet` class.

```
//Connect and fill dataset with three tables of data
SqlConnection nwindConnection = new SqlConnection(connectionString);
SqlDataAdapter nwindAdapter = new SqlDataAdapter("select * from customers; select
* from orders; select * from [order details]",nwindConnection);

DataSet relationData = new DataSet();

//we use this to get the primary key for the tables
nwindAdapter.MissingSchemaAction = MissingSchemaAction.AddWithKey;
nwindAdapter.Fill(relationData);

//name the tables to match the source
relationData.Tables[0].TableName = "Customers";
relationData.Tables[1].TableName = "Orders";
relationData.Tables[2].TableName = "OrderDetails";

//create a new relation giving it a name and identifying the columns
//to relate on
DataColumn Parent=relationData.Tables["Customers"].Columns
  ["Customerid"];
DataColumn Child = relationData.Tables["Orders"].Columns["customerid"];
DataRelation customerRelation = new DataRelation
  ("customerRelation",Parent,Child);

//add the relation to the dataset's relation property(DataRelationCollection)
relationData.Relations.Add (customerRelation);
```

As you can see, the creation of a data relation is very similar to that of a constraint. We create the relation, identifying the columns to use, and then add it to the collection. Creating a `DataRelation` will also, by default, create corresponding constraint `objects`, because we have not specified otherwise. There are alternative constructors that allow for preventing the constraints from being created.

We are starting to see how the `DataRelation` and the `Constraints` work together. By allowing the `DataRelation` to create constraints, we end up with a `UniqueConstraint` on the parent column, such that the values are required to be unique, and a `ForeignKeyConstraint` on the child table to ensure integrity between the two tables. We can avoid the creation of constraints by using a different version of the `DataRelation` constructor:

```
DataRelation(string Name, DataColumn parent, DataColumn child, bool
createConstraints)
```

By specifying `False` for the last parameter, we instruct the `DataRelation` not to create the constraints on the tables. This allows for the data to be related, but not constrained. So, we can navigate using the relationship, but we can also do things like delete rows from the parent table without receiving an exception. Likewise, the `GetParentRows` method now becomes more powerful as we can use it to get at multiple rows in the parent table with the same key value.

As mentioned above, the primary use for the `DataRelation` is to allow for navigation between related rows in different data tables. This is accomplished by using the `GetChildRows` and `GetParentRows` methods of the `DataRow` object. In using these methods, we must specify the data relation to use to find the related rows. We are able to setup multiple relations on a table and find only those rows that we need based on a specific relationship. The example below shows how we extract a set of rows from a related table using a defined `DataRelation`. `childrenData` is a `DataTable` in a dataset:

```
DataRow[] rows = childrenData.Rows[0].GetChildRows("customerRelation");
```

We use the `GetChildRows` method of the `DataRow` object to get an array of `DataRow` objects. We can pass in the name of the relation, as we have here, or pass in a reference to the relation itself. For a better understanding of how this can be applied, the example below is based on a Windows Forms application and uses this method in a master-detail situation. We have two data grids on a form and the first grid contains the customers' information. The second grid will be updated automatically to reflect the selected row in the master table.

We first load some data into the dataset and create our `DataRelation` between the `Customers` and `Orders` tables:

```
//load the dataset -relationData (code omitted)

//create the relation and add it to the collection
//for the dataset
DataColumn[] parentColumns = new DataColumn[1];
parentColumns[0]=relationData.Tables["Customers"].Columns["Customerid"];

DataColumn[] childColumns = new DataColumn[1];
childColumns[0]=relationData.Tables["Orders"].Columns["customerid"]

DataRelation customerRelation = new DataRelation("customerRelation",
parentColumns, childColumns);
```

```
//add the relation to the dataset
relationData.Relations.Add (customerRelation);

//set the datasource of the grid to the customers table
Grid1.DataSource = childrenData.Tables["customers"].DefaultView;

//hook up the event handler so we can update the
//child grid when a new row is selected
Grid1.CurrentCellChanged += new EventHandler(this.CurrentCellChangedEventHandler);
```

We then add an event handler for the `CurrentCellChanged` event. In this handler, we extract the current row from the arguments passed into the handler. We use this data, along with the `Find` method of the `DataRowCollection` class, to identify the parent row selected. We then call `GetRows` on this row, passing in the name of the relation we created:

```
private void CurrentCellChangedEventHandler(object sender, System.EventArgs
    e)
{
    //instance values
    DataRow[] rows;
    int rowIndex;

    //get the row number of the selected cell
    rowIndex = ((DataGrid)sender).CurrentCell.RowNumber;

    //use the row number to get the value of the key (customerID)
    string Key = ((DataGrid)sender)[rowIndex, 0].ToString();

    //use the key to find the row we selected in the data source
    DataView sourceView = ((DataView)((DataGrid)sender).DataSource);
    DataRow row=sourceView.Table.Rows.Find(Key);
    rows = row.GetChildRows("customerRelation");
```

Next, we use this array of rows as the data source to the second grid by merging it into a new, empty, dataset and using the default view of the table created.

```
    //merge the child rows into a new dataset and set the source of the
    //child table to the default view of the initial table
    DataSet tmpData = new DataSet();
    tmpData.Merge(rows);
    Grid2.DataSource=tmpData.Tables[0].DefaultView;
}
```

This is one simple example of using the `GetChildRows` method to update a User Interface element, but there are many other situations in which it is important to get at the related child rows. Similarly, it is often useful to get the parent row for the current child row. We can access the parent row that is related to the current child row in much the same way as we access the child rows. We use the `GetParentRow` or `GetParentRows` methods of the `DataRow` class.

```
DataRow[] rows =
childrenData.Table["orders"].Rows[0].GetParentRows("customerRelation");
```

We have seen how to fetch the related parent and child rows. We can further define the rows we wish to retrieve by calling an overloaded version of the `GetChildRows` or `GetParentRows` method to get a specific version of the `DataRow` in the related table.

The `DataRowVersion` enumeration allows for identifying a specific version of the row. As the data in a row is updated, the original row values are maintained and each version of this row is kept in memory. The versions available at any given time depend on what editing steps have been taken on the row. The table below shows the different `DataRowVersion` enumeration values, their definition, and when they are available.

DataRowVersion	Description	Availability
Current	The row contains the current value	Always available
Default	The row contains its default value	Available if a default value is specified for the column and the value has been entered by default
Original	The row contains the original value	After calling `AcceptChanges` on the `DataRow` object
Proposed	The row contains a proposed value	After editing the value and before calling the `AcceptChanges` method on the `DataTable` or `DataSet` containing the row.

An example of when we might want to use this version information could be that the business requirements for our application call for checking all proposed values before they were applied. We could use the `GetChildRows` method, specifying that we want proposed values so that we can check only those values that will be applied when changes are accepted.

Be aware that if the version requested in the `GetChildRows` method is not available, an exception of type `VersionNotFoundException` will be thrown. In order to avoid this, we can check for the version to see if it is available. We can use the `HasVersion` method of the `DataRow` to determine if the row has the version we are looking for. In the example below, `customerRelation` is the `DataRelation` used to query for the child rows. We first check to see that the row we are interested in has a particular version, and then query for that version.

```
//get the child rows as an array
DataRow[] rows;
rows=ds.Tables["Customers"].Rows[0].GetChildRows(customerRelation);

//check to see if the first item has a proposed value
if(rows[0].HasVersion(DataRowVersion.Proposed))
  {
    //if so, then we'll get the proposed values for the children
    //and print out the first column from the first row.
    rows=ds.Tables[0].Rows[0].GetChildRows(r,DataRowVersion.Proposed);
    Console.WriteLine(rows[0][0].ToString());
  }
```

XML and DataRelations

`DataSets` have many built in capabilities relating to XML. Several methods of the `DataSet` allow for serializing and deserializing the data in the `DataSet` to and from XML. When creating `DataRelationObjects`, it is possible to affect the format of the XML representation of the data by using the `Nested` property of the `DataRelation`. Using the `GetXml` method of the `DataSet`, we can see that the typical XML output of a `DataSet` with multiple tables is structured such that each table is represented independently with its contained rows. A simple example of this is shown below.

The code used to generate the XML simply loads a dataset with data from the `Customers`, `Orders`, and `Order Details` tables of the `Northwind` database and creates relations between them. The `GetXml` method of the `DataSet` is called to get the XML.

```
//load data into dataset: nested
...

//create a data relation using customers and orders
DataColumn[] parentColumns = new DataColumn[1];
parentColumns[0]=nested.Tables["customers"].Columns["customerid"];

DataColumn[] childColumns = new DataColumn[1];
childColumns[0]=nested.Tables["orders"].Columns["customerid"];

DataRelation customerIDrelation = new DataRelation("CustomerOrderRelation",
parentColumns, childColumns);

//create a data relation using orders and order details
DataColumn[] parentColumns = new DataColumn[1];
parentColumns[0]=nested.Tables["orders"].Columns["orderid"];

DataColumn[] childColumns = new DataColumn[1];
childColumns[0]=nested.Tables["orderdetails"].Columns["orderid"];

DataRelation orderDetailsRelation = new
  DataRelation("OrderDetailsRelation",parentColumns, childColumns);

//add the relations to the dataset collection of relations
nested.Relations.Add(customerIDrelation);
nested.Relations.Add(orderDetailsRelation);

Console.WriteLine(nested.GetXml());
```

Once we have created the two relations that connect the customers' records to the orders, and the orders to the order details, we retrieve the XML with the `GetXml` method of the `DataSet`, and see the XML output below.

```
<NewDataSet>
  <Customers>
    <CustomerID>ALFKI</CustomerID>
    <CompanyName>Alfreds Futterkiste</CompanyName>
    <ContactName>Maria Anders</ContactName>
    <ContactTitle>Sales Representative</ContactTitle>
```

```
      <Address>Obere Str. 57</Address>
      <City>Berlin</City>
      <PostalCode>12209</PostalCode>
      <Country>Germany</Country>
      <Phone>030-0074321</Phone>
      <Fax>030-0076545</Fax>
   </Customers>
   <Customers>
      <CustomerID>ANATR</CustomerID>
      <CompanyName>Ana Trujillo Emparedados y helados</CompanyName>
      <ContactName>Ana Trujillo</ContactName>
      <ContactTitle>Owner</ContactTitle>
      <Address>Avda. de la Constitución 2222</Address>
      <City>México D.F.</City>
      <PostalCode>05021</PostalCode>
      <Country>Mexico</Country>
      <Phone>(5) 555-4729</Phone>
      <Fax>(5) 555-3745</Fax>
   </Customers>
...
   <Orders>
      <OrderID>10248</OrderID>
      <CustomerID>VINET</CustomerID>
      <EmployeeID>5</EmployeeID>
      <OrderDate>1996-07-04T00:00:00.0000000-05:00</OrderDate>
      <RequiredDate>1996-08-01T00:00:00.0000000-05:00</RequiredDate>
      <ShippedDate>1996-07-16T00:00:00.0000000-05:00</ShippedDate>
      <ShipVia>3</ShipVia>
      <Freight>32.38</Freight>
      <ShipName>Vins et alcools Chevalier</ShipName>
      <ShipAddress>59 rue de l'Abbaye</ShipAddress>
      <ShipCity>Reims</ShipCity>
      <ShipPostalCode>51100</ShipPostalCode>
      <ShipCountry>France</ShipCountry>
   </Orders>
   <Orders>
      <OrderID>10249</OrderID>
      <CustomerID>TOMSP</CustomerID>
      <EmployeeID>6</EmployeeID>
      <OrderDate>1996-07-05T00:00:00.0000000-05:00</OrderDate>
      <RequiredDate>1996-08-16T00:00:00.0000000-05:00</RequiredDate>
      <ShippedDate>1996-07-10T00:00:00.0000000-05:00</ShippedDate>
      <ShipVia>1</ShipVia>
      <Freight>11.61</Freight>
      <ShipName>Toms Spezialitäten</ShipName>
      <ShipAddress>Luisenstr. 48</ShipAddress>
      <ShipCity>Münster</ShipCity>
      <ShipPostalCode>44087</ShipPostalCode>
      <ShipCountry>Germany</ShipCountry>
   </Orders>
...
   <OrderDetails>
      <OrderID>10248</OrderID>
      <ProductID>11</ProductID>
```

```
        <UnitPrice>14</UnitPrice>
        <Quantity>12</Quantity>
        <Discount>0</Discount>
      </OrderDetails>
      <OrderDetails>
        <OrderID>10248</OrderID>
        <ProductID>42</ProductID>
        <UnitPrice>9.8</UnitPrice>
        <Quantity>10</Quantity>
        <Discount>0</Discount>
      </OrderDetails>
  ...
  </NewDataSet>
```

One of the benefits of XML is that it can easily represent hierarchical data. In order to represent the data in the most logical hierarchical way, we set the `Nested` property of the `DataRelation` objects to `true`. This causes the data to be output such that each element representing a row from the parent table has the child rows as nested elements. The example below shows the same data as the previous example, but with the related child rows nested within their respective parent rows. To generate this output, we simply add the following two lines of code to the last sample, just before the last line where we call `GetXml`.

```
//add the relations to the dataset collection of relations
nested.Relations.Add(customerIDrelation);
nested.Relations.Add(orderDetailsRelation);
```

```
//indicate that the relation should be nested and show the XML
customerIDrelation.Nested = true;
orderDetailsRelation.Nested = true;
```

```
Console.WriteLine(nested.GetXml());
```

Here is the output:

```
<NewDataSet>
  <Customers>
    <CustomerID>ALFKI</CustomerID>
    <CompanyName>Alfreds Futterkiste</CompanyName>
    <ContactName>Maria Anders</ContactName>
    <ContactTitle>Sales Representative</ContactTitle>
    <Address>Obere Str. 57</Address>
    <City>Berlin</City>
    <PostalCode>12209</PostalCode>
    <Country>Germany</Country>
    <Phone>030-0074321</Phone>
    <Fax>030-0076545</Fax>
    <Orders>
      <OrderID>10643</OrderID>
      <CustomerID>ALFKI</CustomerID>
      <EmployeeID>6</EmployeeID>
      <OrderDate>1997-08-25T00:00:00.0000000-05:00</OrderDate>
      <RequiredDate>1997-09-22T00:00:00.0000000-05:00</RequiredDate>
```

```
            <ShippedDate>1997-09-02T00:00:00.0000000-05:00</ShippedDate>
            <ShipVia>1</ShipVia>
            <Freight>29.46</Freight>
            <ShipName>Alfreds Futterkiste</ShipName>
            <ShipAddress>Obere Str. 57</ShipAddress>
            <ShipCity>Berlin</ShipCity>
            <ShipPostalCode>12209</ShipPostalCode>
            <ShipCountry>Germany</ShipCountry>
            <OrderDetails>
               <OrderID>10643</OrderID>
               <ProductID>28</ProductID>
               <UnitPrice>45.6</UnitPrice>
               <Quantity>15</Quantity>
               <Discount>0.25</Discount>
            </OrderDetails>
            <OrderDetails>
               <OrderID>10643</OrderID>
               <ProductID>39</ProductID>
               <UnitPrice>18</UnitPrice>
               <Quantity>21</Quantity>
               <Discount>0.25</Discount>
            </OrderDetails>
            <OrderDetails>
               <OrderID>10643</OrderID>
               <ProductID>46</ProductID>
               <UnitPrice>12</UnitPrice>
               <Quantity>2</Quantity>
               <Discount>0.25</Discount>
            </OrderDetails>
         </Orders>
         <Orders>
   ...
   </Customers>
</NewDataSet>
```

In the first instance, each table is represented by separate and distinct elements and no relations are apparent. In the second, each customer element has its related orders nested beneath it and each order, in turn, has all of the order details nested beneath it. This simple change can make the data more readable for humans and applications.

DataRelationObjects are extremely helpful when working with multi-table DataSetObjects to manage and navigate the relationships between the tables. We will see some other examples shortly about how DataRelationObjects can be even more useful when used in conjunction with some of the other tools.

DataViews

Often, data retrieved from a data source is not in exactly the same form as you would like to present it. The DataView, along with the DataTable, provides an implementation of the popular Model-View design pattern. This pattern defines a model of the data, and different views that provide different representations of the data in the model. By using this design pattern, we are able to have a DataTable that contains our data and various DataViews that provide different views of the data.

A `DataView` provides us with several useful mechanisms for working with data:

❑ Sorting – the view of the data can be sorted based on one or more columns in ascending or descending order

❑ Filtering – the data visible through the view can be filtered with expressions based on one or more columns

❑ Row version filtering – the data visible through the view can be filtered based on the version of the rows

These abilities provide much of the real power when working with data in a `DataTable` and we'll see how each of them can make working with data easier. In order to use this functionality, we must first create a `DataView`.

There are three ways to create a `DataView`:

❑ Retrieve the default view of a `DataTable` by using its `DefaultView` property

❑ Create a new instance of a `DataView` that can than be associated with a `DataTable`

❑ Use a `DataViewManager` to create a `DataView` for a `DataTable`

We will examine each of these methods as we look at how to work with `DataViews`.

Sorting

The `DataView` provides the means to sort and filter the representation of the data in a `DataTable`. Sorting a view orders rows based on the values in particular columns. After setting the sort criteria on a `DataView`, the rows will be accessed in the order specified. So if the data view is used to present data to the user, it will appear in the sorted order.

When applying the sort criteria, the column and direction are specified. For example, if we want to sort data by the `DateOfBirth` column in descending order, we would use the following:

```
DataView.Sort = "DateOfBirth DESC"
```

The example below shows sorting a view based on the `Region` field of the data table. It also shows one of the mechanisms for creating a data view:

```
SqlConnection nwindConnection = new SqlConnection(connectionString);
SqlDataAdapter nwindAdapter = new SqlDataAdapter("select * from customers; select
* from orders; select * from [order details]",nwindConnection);

DataSet firstSort= new DataSet();

nwindAdapter.MissingSchemaAction = MissingSchemaAction.AddWithKey;
nwindAdapter.Fill(firstSort);

firstSort.Tables[0].TableName = "Customers";
firstSort.Tables[1].TableName = "Orders";
```

```
firstSort.Tables[2].TableName = "OrderDetails";

//create the data view object and set the table to the
//customers table by passing it in the constructor
DataView tableSort = new DataView(firstSort.Tables["customers"]);

//set the sort criteria for the view
tableSort.Sort = "Region DESC";
```

The creation of the dataset is a familiar task. After we have filled the dataset, we create a new object of type DataView and pass in a DataTable to the constructor. We then set the sort criteria for the DataView to sort the items in descending order by the Region field. Setting the Sort property of the view causes the DataView to reorder its view of the data to match the criteria. Keep in mind that this does not change the order of the rows in the DataTable itself, only the data as viewed through this interface. This allows us to have multiple views of the same DataTable, with different sort criteria.

Setting DataView sorts should be familiar to programmers who have worked with Structured Query Language (SQL). And, as in SQL, we can specify multiple columns to sort on, providing a direction for each column. Thus, we could sort addresses in a data table by the region in descending order, followed by the city in ascending order. We can expand our previous sample to sort on both columns by simply adding the extra criteria to the sort property as shown below:

```
//create the data view object and set the table to the
//customers table by passing it in the constructor
DataView tableSort = new DataView(firstSort.Tables["customers"]);

//set the sort criteria for the view
tableSort.Sort = "Region DESC, City ASC";
```

We can specify any number of columns to sort on, providing a direction for each. The default direction for the sort is ascending, so it is only necessary to specify the direction explicitly when we want to sort in descending order. However, explicitly identifying the sort order can make your code more readable.

It is important to remember that the sort order of a data view is dependent on the data type of the data column. For example, a column with a string data type with numeric values in it will not sort as a number, but in the alphabetic precedence. The example data below shows this:

```
1
10
100
11
```

Things work fine for the first two values, but when we get to the third value we see that the 11 should have come after the 10, but instead, because it is not being treated as a number, it comes after 100. In order to ensure that the data in the view is sorted as you expect, be sure you know the data type of the column you are sorting on and the effect of sorting on that type.

Filtering

In addition to sorting the data in a `DataView`, we can also filter out records to show only those rows that meet criteria we specify. There are two ways to filter the rows in a `DataView`: by values in the rows, or by the version of the row data. We will look first at filtering based on values, but we will cover filtering by row version next. We filter records in the `DataView` based on their values by setting the `RowFilter` property to a Boolean expression that can be evaluated against each row. Only those rows meeting the criteria will be visible in the view. Below is an example of filtering the rows in a `DataView`:

```
//load data
...

//create a new data view based on the customers table
DataView tableFilter = new DataView(dataFilter.Tables["customers"]);

//set the row filter property of the view to filter the
//viewable rows
tableFilter.RowFilter = "Country='UK'";
```

Once we have set the `RowFilter` property of the view, only those rows matching the criteria will appear in the view. Developers familiar with the Structured Query Language (SQL) will notice many similarities in the syntax for filtering data in a `DataView` and filtering queries run against a database. This familiarity should simplify your programming. We can change this property as needed to expose the rows we need to work with. As it is simply a view of the data, this operation is more flexible than working directly with the data, because less information needs to be moved around and the original data is still available to be viewed in other ways. Notice that we put the test case in single quotation marks: this is required when working with the `RowFilter` property and specifying a string value; if we are specifying a date, we surround the value with the # symbol.

Like the `Sort` property, the `RowFilter` property also allows for specifying multiple columns and expressions upon which to filter the data. However, rather than using a comma to separate the criteria, we use `AND` and `OR` to build up the criteria. Below we filter the data based on the values in both the country and the city:

```
//create a new data view based on the customers table
DataView tableFilter = new DataView(dataFilter.Tables["customers"]);

//set the row filter property of the view to filter the
//viewable rows
tableFilter.RowFilter = "Country='UK' AND City='Cowes'";
```

The expressions allowed for the `RowFilter` property are the same as those for the `Expression` property of the `DataColumn`. The syntax is similar to SQL, which should make things easier, as working with data on the client and server is very similar. We have the ability to use the following operators, aggregate functions, and expressions:

Operators

These operators can be used in the filter statement to combine or modify values used in the expression.

Operator	Meaning
AND	
OR	
NOT	
<	Less than
>	Greater than
<=	Less than or equal to
>=	Greater than or equal to
<>	Not equal to
=	Equal to
IN	Values are in the specified set. Usage: In(a,b,c)
LIKE	Tests if a given value is like the test case. Used with text values, this is similar to '='
+	Addition with numeric values or string concatenation
–	Subtraction
*	Multiplication with numeric values or wildcard (single character) for string comparisons
/	Division
%	Modulus with numeric values or wildcard (multiple characters) for string comparisons

Using the comparisons with string values, we can also specify wildcard characters in our comparison. The example below shows a comparison for values using the LIKE operator and a wildcard:

```
DataView.RowFilter = "City LIKE 'Map*'";
```

We can use the wildcard characters at the end or beginning of the text, but not in the middle. We can also use parentheses to indicate precedence in our expressions, as shown below:

```
DataView.RowFilter = "(city='Milan' OR city='Paris') AND category='Fashion'";
```

Relationship Referencing

An expression can use the relationships that exist between the table behind the view and other tables in the DataSet. In this way, the parent table can be filtered based on the values in the child table, or vice versa.

Reference	Meaning
`Child.ColumnName`	References the specified column in the child table
`Child(RelationshipName). ColumnName`	References the specified column in the child table as determined by the relationship specified

If there is more than one relationship, the second syntax needs to be used to specify the specific relation to use. We can also reference parent columns in the same way using `Parent.ColumnName`. This syntax is most often used with the Aggregate functions identified below. For example, we might want to filter the view to show all records where the sum of the price of the child records is greater than $50.

Aggregate Functions

Aggregate functions provide a means for operating on multiple rows of data to return a value. They are often used with related tables, as described above.

Function	Meaning
`Sum`	Sum of the column(s) specified
`Avg`	Average value of the column specified
`Min`	Minimum value of the column specified
`Max`	Maximum value of the column specified
`Count`	Count of the rows in the column specified
`StDev`	Standard deviation
`Var`	Statistical Variance

Aggregates can be used on the table to which the `DataView` applies, or they can be computed on the data in related rows. When working with a single table, the value of this expression would be the same for all rows. For example, if we calculate the total of the price column, all rows will have the same value. This does not lend itself well to filtering the data based on the outcome. However, when working with related tables, we can choose to show only those rows in the parent table where the related rows in the child table meet our criteria. A simple example is shown below:

```
DataView.RowFilter="Sum(Child. UnitPrice)>100";
```

The above example gets those rows from the current view where the related child rows have a sum of `UnitPrice` that is greater than 100.

Functions

Functions provide some flexibility in creating expressions by allowing the developer to substitute or manipulate a given column value in order to test it. For example, we might want all rows where the description column starts with "Exclusive", so we could use the SubString function for our test.

Function	Meaning	Syntax
Convert	Converts the given value to the specified type	Convert(value, type)
Len	Returns the length of the specified value	Len(value)
IsNull	Returns the replacement value if the expression provided evaluates to null	IsNull(expression, replacement)
IIF	Returns the trueResult if the expression evaluates to true, or the falseResult if the expression evaluates to false	IIF(expression, trueResult, falseResult)
SubString	Returns the portion of the string specified starting at startingPoint and continuing for length characters	SubString(string, startingPoint, length)

Filtering on Row State

Finally, we can filter the data in a DataView based on the version of the row. Using the RowStateFilter property, we identify the rows to be visible in the view based on the status of the data in the rows. This status changes as the data in the table is edited, which means that not all versions are always available for every row. We set the RowStateFilter property to one of the DataViewRowState enumeration values. These values and their meanings are shown below:

Value	Meaning
Added	Includes only new rows
CurrentRows	Current rows, which includes those that have not been changed, new rows, and modified rows
Deleted	Rows that have been deleted
ModifiedCurrent	A current version of a row that has been modified
ModifiedOriginal	The original version of a modified row
None	None
OriginalRows	Original rows which includes unchanged and deleted rows
Unchanged	A row that has not been changed

In addition to filtering the data based on a single version, we can use the Boolean Or operator (the '|' character in C#) to indicate multiple row states. For example, we can use the following code to get both the added rows and the original rows:

```
DataView.RowStateFilter = DataViewRowState.Added | DataViewRowState.OriginalRows;
```

Using these values, we can limit the rows in a DataView to a particular set based on the edited state of the data. Using this filter, we can have different DataViews filtering on different RowStates. For example, we can have two different views: one showing the current data, and another showing the original values of those rows that have been modified. The example below shows this in action:

```
//load data into dataset:filterVersion (code omitted)
...

//create two new views on the customers table
DataView currentView = new DataView(filterVersion.Tables["customers"]);
DataView originalView = new DataView(filterVersion.Tables["customers"]);

//set the rowstatefilter property for each view
currentView.RowStateFilter = DataViewRowState.CurrentRows;
originalView.RowStateFilter = DataViewRowState.ModifiedOriginal;
```

If we used these views in a Windows form with the DataGrid control, we would see output similar to this:

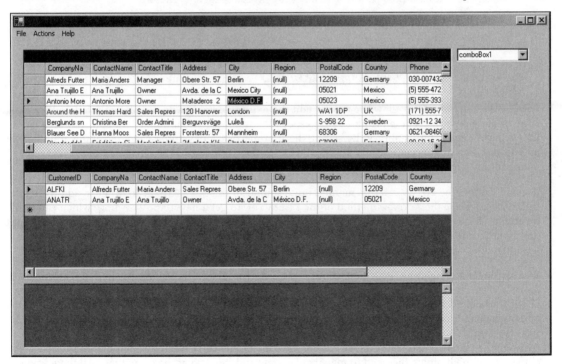

Only those items that have been edited in the top grid show up in the bottom grid. This behavior is especially useful for working with UI elements as shown, but can also be useful for keeping track of the different values that a column contains during the editing process. Let's take a look now at how to use the `DataView` to help us edit data.

Editing Data in the DataView

The `DataView` not only allows for viewing data, but can also be used to edit the data in a data table. There are three properties of the `DataView` that dictate its editing behavior: the `AllowNew`, `AllowEdit`, and `AllowDelete` properties, which each hold Boolean values that indicate whether the respective actions can be taken. For example, if the `AllowNew` property is set to `False` then an attempt to add a new row to the `DataView` using the `AddNew` method will throw an exception. The default value for all of these properties is `true`.

An example of constraining the user's ability to edit the data is shown below. When this is applied to the `DataGrid` in a Windows form, the user is simply not allowed to perform the action, but no error is displayed if they try:

```
//load data into dataset: viewEditSet
...

//indicate that the user cannot delete items
viewEditSet.Tables["Orders"].DefaultView.AllowDelete = false;

//indicate that the user cannot add new items
viewEditSet.Tables["Orders"].DefaultView.AllowNew = false;

//indicate that the user can edit the current items
viewEditSet.Tables["Orders"].DefaultView.AllowEdit = true;
```

Using the setup above, we allow the user to edit the existing data, but do not allow them to either delete rows or add new rows. These properties are especially useful when building client applications that utilize the Windows forms library. By setting these properties, a developer can control the ability of the user to edit data in a `DataGrid` that has the `DataView` as its data source. The `DataGrid` will automatically pickup and apply rules set in the `DataView`.

We add rows to the `DataView` in a manner quite similar to the `DataTable`. In order to add rows to a `DataView`, we use the `AddNew` method of the `DataView` to get a new `DataViewRow`, which can then be edited. We do not need to add the row to the view or the table as we do when adding a row straight to a `DataTable`. We delete a row by calling the `Delete` method, passing in the index of the row we wish to delete, as it appears in the view. To edit data, we simply change the values of the row.

It is important to remember that the `DataView` is simply a view of the data contained in its associated `DataTable`. Therefore, when we refer to adding or editing data in the view, we are actually talking about working with the data in the table. The actions we take on the view are applied to the data in the table. Similarly, any constraints put on the data table will continue to be enforced even if we are working with the `DataView`. We cannot, therefore, add or edit data in such a way as to violate these constraints without an exception being raised. The operations carried out through the `DataView` are a convenience to eliminate the need to manage the view and the data at the same time. All the editing actions can be taken directly on the table or the row without having to use the view. The following example shows each of the editing actions:

```
//load dataset
...

//create new dataview
DataView editingView = new DataView(ds.Tables["customers"]);

//add new row to the view
DataRowView newRow = editingView.AddNew();

//edit the new row
newRow["CompanyName"] = "Wrox Press";

//edit the first row in the view
editingView[0]["CompanyName"] = "Wrox Press";

//Delete the second record in the view
editingView.Delete(1);
```

Being able to edit using the `DataView` is extremely helpful. Considering that this is the mechanism by which we will often present the data to our user, it would be much more difficult to have to manually coordinate the actions on the data in the view with the actual data in the data table. Being able to indicate the actions the user can take only further refines this ability.

DataViewManager

As mentioned above, one of the ways in which a `DataView` can be created is by using a `DataViewManager`. A `DataViewManager` is associated with a `DataSet` and is used to manage and gain access to `DataViewObjects` for each of the `DataTableObjects` in the `DataSetObject`. The `DataViewManager` makes working with multi-table `DataSetObjects` much easier by providing a single object to manage the collection of `DataViewObjects` for the entire `DataSetObject` and is more powerful because it can also use the relationships that have been defined between tables. The `DataViewManager` also allows for easy data binding, as we will see later in this chapter.

In order to use a `DataViewManager`, we create and fill a `DataSet` and then create a new `DataView Manager` and set its `DataSet` property to the filled `DataSet`. We can then use the `DataView Settings` collection to gain access to a specific `DataView`. Alternately, we can create a new `DataView Manager`, passing in the `DataSet` to the constructor. The code below provides an example of creating a `DataViewManager` and accessing the `DataViewObjects` for specific `DataTable` objects in the `DataSet`.

```
//load dataset: ManagerData
...

//create a new dataviewmanager based on the dataset
DataViewManager manager = new DataViewManager(ManagerData);

//sort the data in the view for the orders table based on the
//order date in ascending order
manager.DataViewSettings["Orders"].Sort="OrderDate DESC";
```

We create and fill a `DataSet` and then create a `DataViewManager`, passing in the `DataSet` to the constructor. We then set the sort criteria for the `DataView` on the `Orders` table by using the `DataViewSettings` property of the `DataViewManager`. We simply specify the name of the table in the indexer (or the `Item` property in VB), and then set the `Sort` property for a `DataView`.

Another method for accessing `DataViews` with the `DataViewManager` is to use the `CreateView` method to create a new view based on a given table. This provides us with a direct reference to a specific view of the data. This same method is used when accessing the `DefaultView` property of the `DataTable`. The example below creates a `DataView` of the `Customers` table using this method.

```
//load dataset "customerData"
. . .

DataTable customerTable = customerData.Tables[0];
DataView custView =
    customerData.DefaultViewManager.CreateView(customerTable);
```

When working with `DataTables`, it is possible to get a `DataView` using the `DefaultView` property. We can also obtain a `DataViewManager` using the `DefaultViewManager` property of the `DataSet` class. These default views and managers are created the first time they are accessed. For example, if we create a `DataSet` and then access the `DefaultView` property of a `DataTable` in that `DataSet`, the `DataTable` object will attempt to get a reference to the default `DataViewManager` for the `DataSet` and use it to create the `DataView`. If the `DefaultViewManager` is null, one will be created and then used to create the `DataView` needed. Similarly, when we access a `DataView` for the `DataSet` by using the `DataViewSettings` property of the `DataViewManager`, the `DataViewManager` creates the `DataView` the first time we access it.

This "create-on-access" methodology is important to understand for performance reasons. If there is no need to create a `DataView` for a particular operation, then it should not be created at all to avoid the creation of the extra objects on the heap.

As the `DataViewManager` has access to `DataViewObjects` for all of the tables in a `DataSet`, it is most useful in situations when working with multiple tables in the `DataSet`. For example, when a `DataSet` contains multiple tables and `DataRelationObjects`, we can use the `DataViewManager` to more easily manage the many views.

Databinding

One of the main reasons for using a `DataView` is to bind the data represented by the view in a user interface (UI) element. The `DataGrid` is a common control to which `DataViews` are bound. The act of binding data to a UI element for display is a common practice for both Windows-based and Web-based applications. When working in a Windows Forms application, the power of the `DataView`, `Constraints`, and `DataRelations` can be fully realized. Users interact with the data, while the `DataGrid` enforces properties set on the `DataView` and the `Constraints` set on the `DataTable`.

`DataRelations` also become very powerful in the Windows Forms environment. The Windows Forms `DataGrid` can display an entire `DataSet`, allowing the user to navigate the relationships between tables. When a `DataRelation` exists, a given row can be expanded and a specific relation selected. The related child rows then fill the grid and the parent rows optionally appear at the top of the grid. A user can then navigate back to the parent table using a button on the grid. The figure opposite shows a `DataGrid` with a data relation expanded. The parent row is shown in gray above the child rows:

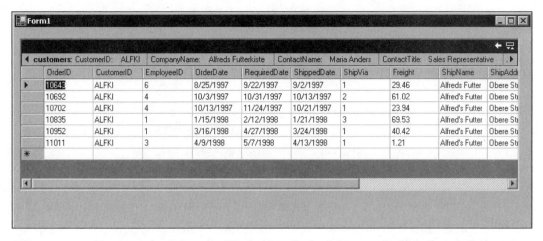

There are several ways to bind data to a UI element. Each of these methods deals with the `DataSource` property of the element, and at times the `DataMember` property. The easiest way to bind data in a `DataSet` to a UI control is to set the `DataSource` property of the element to a `DataView`. In the example below, we bind a `DataGrid` to a `DataView`:

```
//bind the grid to the default view of the customers table
Grid1.DataSource = bindingData.Tables["customers"].DefaultView;
```

As mentioned above, the `DataMember` property often comes into play when binding data to a UI element. The need for this will depend on the element being used and the mechanism for identifying the source. For example, when working with a `ListBox` control, we have to set a display member and a value member. We might, when working with a `DataGrid`, set the `DataSource` to a `DataViewManager` object and set the `DataMember` to the name of a table in the `DataSet`. The examples below show both of these binding mechanisms in action.

Binding a `DataView` to a `ListBox`. – the list displays the `CompanyName`, but the underlying value is the selected record's `CustomerID`:

```
//set the datasource of the list to the default view
//of the customers table
BoundCombo.DataSource = listSet.Tables["Customers"].DefaultView;

//now we identify the item to be displayed
BoundCombo.DisplayMember = "CompanyName";

//and identify the item to maintain as
//the value of the item
BoundCombo.ValueMember = "CustomerID";
```

Binding a `DataSet` to a `DataGrid`, and displaying the `Customers` table from that `DataSet`:

```
//set the datasource to the dataset
Grid1.DataSource = MemberSet;

//provide the name of a data table to indicate the item
```

351

```
//within the source to use for the data
Grid1.DataMember = "Customers";
```

We can also use this same syntax with a `DataViewManager` and the name of a `DataTable`, as shown below:

```
//create a new dataviewmanager based on the dataset
DataViewManager manager = new DataViewManager(ManagerData);

//sort the data in the view for the orders table based on the
//order date in ascending order
manager.DataViewSettings["Orders"].Sort="OrderDate DESC";

//set the grid source to be the manager and the member
//to be the orders table
Grid1.DataSource = manager;
Grid1.DataMember = "Orders";
```

`DataViewObjects` provide a very flexible and powerful mechanism for working with the data in a `DataTable` and presenting that data to users. `DataViewObjects` can also be very helpful in a web environment by allowing for the view to be cached on the server using the new caching functionality built into ASP.NET and reused on subsequent requests. An example of this is shown in the web example in the next section.

Bringing it Together

While each of the classes we have discussed is useful on its own, the true power of working with client-side data comes when we use these classes together. This section provides several quick pointers to handy functionality achieved using these classes together, followed by examples of a Windows Forms and Web Forms application.

We have shown how we can use a `DataRelation` to navigate between related `DataTableObjects`. In addition, an example we gave showing a master-detail relationship on a Windows form. One nice feature of the data grid control is that we can use a relationship to have the master-detail relationship managed for us automatically. Assuming we have a `DataSet`, `CustomerData`, with the following characteristics:

❑ customers and orders data tables

❑ a data relation between the two tables named `CustomerOrderRelation`

❑ a Windows form with two `DataGrids` named `Grid1` and `Grid2`

we can use the following code to setup our master-detail relationship.

```
Grid1.DataSource = CustomerData;
Grid1.DataMember = "Customers";
Grid2.DataSource = CustomerData;
Grid2.DataMember = "Customers.CustomerOrderRelation";
```

The first grid is set up as described in the data binding section. However, for the second grid, we set the data source to the DataSet and then identify the data member as a string representing the parent table concatenated, by a period, with the name of a DataRelation to use. When we use this syntax, the data grid automatically sets up event handlers to manage updating the detail grid when an item in the master row is selected.

Another helpful capability is being able to create a DataView for the child rows involved in a relationship. This allows us to start with a given row in a view of the parent table and retrieve a view that only contains the related rows from the child table. With this view, we can further manipulate the representation of the child rows using all of the familiar properties of the DataView class. The code below provides an exsample of how to use this functionality. After loading a DataSet and creating a DataRelation between the two tables, we use the DataView of the parent table to access the related rows in the child table in a DataView that we can then sort before presenting it to the user.

```
//load dataset
SqlConnection cnn = new
   SqlConnection("server=(local);database=northwind;uid=sa;pwd=;");
SqlDataAdapter da = new SqlDataAdapter("Select * from customers;select *
   from orders order by customerid",cnn);
DataSet ds = new DataSet();

da.Fill(ds,"Customers");
ds.Tables[1].TableName="Orders";

//create the data relation
DataColumn Parent = ds.Tables["customers"].Columns["customerid"];
DataColumn Child = ds.Tables["orders"].Columns["customerid"];

DataRelation customerRelation = new
   DataRelation("CustomerRelation",Parent, Child);

//create the parent view
DataView customers = ds.Tables["customers"].DefaultView;

//loop through the parent data view
foreach(DataRowView rowView in customers)
{
   Console.WriteLine(rowView["ContactName"]);

//for each row, get the related child rows in a view
DataView orders = rowView.CreateChildView(customerRelation);

//sort the related child rows by order date
orders.Sort="OrderDate desc";

//loop through the child rows and print out their value
foreach(DataRowView orderRowView in orders)
{
Console.WriteLine(orderRowView["OrderDate"] + " " +
   orderRowView["ShipName"]);
}
}
```

These two examples show how powerful these classes can be when used in conjunction with one another. This power continues to grow as we take advantage of more and more of the features of the various classes in ADO.NET. For example, we can combine the previous two examples if we use a `DataViewManager` to work with the views in related tables. When not working with a `DataViewManager`, but two separate `DataViewObjects`, it may happen that if we have sorted the child table, when we access the related records using `GetChildRows`, they may not be sorted properly. However, if we use the `DataViewManager` and access those child records, they will be sorted and filtered appropriate to the view for that child table. It is through combining the features that we have covered here, and in the rest of the book, that we are able to fully utilize the power and flexibility of ADO.NET.

Examples

The two following examples pull together what we have learned in this chapter. The first is a Windows Forms application that allows the user to edit data from the Pubs database. It uses `DataRelationObjects` and `ConstraintObjects` to constrain the data, and the `DataView` to manage the presentation of the data. The second example is a web application that shows many of the same concepts in a web model.

Example 1

We start by extending the form class and adding two data grid controls named `Grid1` and `Grid2` in a file named `Form1.cs`. The form is shown in the following figure:

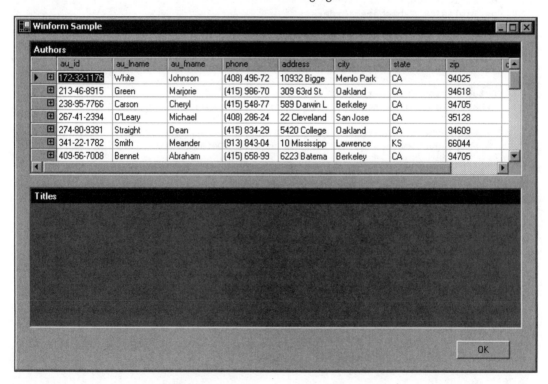

In the constructor, we connect to the pubs database and load a dataset with the data from the `authors`, `titleauthor`, and `titles` tables:

```
public class Form1 : System.Windows.Forms.Form
{
  private System.Windows.Forms.DataGrid Grid1;
  private System.Windows.Forms.Button OKButton;
  private System.Windows.Forms.DataGrid Grid2;

  private System.ComponentModel.Container components = null;

  public Form1()
  {
    InitializeComponent();

    //load the data into a data set
    SqlConnection PubsConnection = new
      SqlConnection("server=(local);database=pubs;uid=sa;pwd=;");
    SqlDataAdapter PubsAdapter = new SqlDataAdapter("Select * from
      authors; Select * from titles; select * from
      titleauthor",PubsConnection);
    DataSet PubsDataSet = new DataSet();

    //identify that we want the primary key
    PubsAdapter.MissingSchemaAction = MissingSchemaAction.AddWithKey;
    PubsAdapter.Fill(PubsDataSet);
```

We name the `DataTables` and then create two data relations to connect the tables, which automatically creates corresponding constraints:

```
    //name tables
    PubsDataSet.Tables[0].TableName = "Authors";
    PubsDataSet.Tables[1].TableName = "Titles";
    PubsDataSet.Tables[2].TableName = "TitleAuthor";

    //create two new data relations allowing the constraints to
    //be created as well
    DataRelation AuthorTitleParent = new
      DataRelation("AuthorTitleParent",PubsDataSet.Tables["Authors"].
      Columns["au_id"], PubsDataSet.Tables["TitleAuthor"].
      Columns["au_id"]);
    DataRelation AuthorTitleChild = new DataRelation("AuthorChildParent",
      PubsDataSet.Tables["Titles"].Columns["title_id"],
      PubsDataSet.Tables["TitleAuthor"].Columns["title_id"]);

    //add the relations to the dataset
    PubsDataSet.Relations.Add(AuthorTitleParent);
    PubsDataSet.Relations.Add(AuthorTitleChild);
```

Finally, we create a view of the data and set the appropriate properties to allow the records to be edited, but not deleted:

```
        //create a dataview of the data
        DataView AuthorView = new DataView(PubsDataSet.Tables["Authors"]);

        //restrict the access to the authors table
        AuthorView.AllowDelete=false;
        AuthorView.AllowEdit = true;
        AuthorView.AllowNew = true;

        //set the grid source to the author view
        Grid1.DataSource = AuthorView;

        //hook up the event handler
        Grid1.CurrentCellChanged+= new EventHandler(this.Grid1_CellChanging);


    }
```

In the event handler for the CellChanging event, we make sure that this is not a new row. Next, we get the child rows of the current author. This gets us the rows in the intermediate table, TitleAuthor, but we need to get the rows in the Title table. To do that, we iterate over the rows in the intermediate table and get the parent rows using the relationship:

```
    private void Grid1_CellChanging(object sender, EventArgs eArgs)
    {
      if(((DataGrid)sender).CurrentCell.RowNumber <
        ((DataView)((DataGrid)sender).DataSource).Table.Rows.Count)
      {
        //instance values
        DataRow[] rows;
        int rowIndex;

        //get the row number of the selected cell
        rowIndex = ((DataGrid)sender).CurrentCell.RowNumber;

        //use the row number to get the value of the key (customerID)
        string Key = ((DataGrid)sender)[rowIndex, 0].ToString();

        //use the key to find the row we selected in the data source
        rows =
          ((DataView)((DataGrid)sender).DataSource).Table.Rows.Find(Key).
          GetChildRows("AuthorTitleParent");

        DataSet tmpData = new DataSet();
```

We then merge each of these sets of rows into a temporary dataset, create a view from the initial table if it exists, set up the editable properties of the view, sort it, and set it as the data source of the second grid:

```
        foreach(DataRow row in rows)
        {
          //tmpData.Merge(new DataRow[]{row});
          tmpData.Merge(row.GetParentRows("AuthorChildParent"));
```

```
        }

        //if there is no data to be displayed, then don't display
        //the data in the grid. If there is, create a view and display it
        if(tmpData.Tables.Count >0)
        {
          DataView TitleView = new DataView(tmpData.Tables[0]);
          TitleView.AllowDelete = false;
          TitleView.AllowEdit = true;
          TitleView.AllowNew = true;

          TitleView.Sort = "Title ASC";

          Grid2.DataSource=tmpData.Tables[0].DefaultView;
        }
        else
        {
          Grid2.DataSource = null;
        }
      }
    }
```

Example 2

We have two pieces to our code, which includes the web form or ASP.NET page and the code behind it.

In the web form, `WebForm1.aspx`, we define the layout for our page including two drop-down lists, which will be filled with the names of the columns in the data table:

```
<%@ Page language="c#" Codebehind="WebForm1.aspx.cs" AutoEventWireup="false"
Inherits="Chapter10WebSample.WebForm1" %>
<!DOCTYPE HTML PUBLIC "-//W3C//DTD HTML 4.0 Transitional//EN" >
<HTML>
 <HEAD>
 </HEAD>
 <body ms_positioning="GridLayout">
  <form id="Form1" method="post" runat="server">
   <table>
    <tr>
     <td valign="top">
      <table>
       <tr>
        <td valign="top">
         <b>Sort & Filter</b>
         <br>
         Sort Field
         <br>
         <asp:dropdownlist id="SortList" runat="server"></asp:dropdownlist>
        </td>
       </tr>
       <tr>
        <td>
         Sort Direction
         <br>
```

We also use a radio button list to allow the user to indicate the sort direction and a textbox to specify the filter criteria:

```
<asp:radiobuttonlist id="SortDirection" runat="server">
 <asp:ListItem value="ASC" text="Asc"
      selected="True"></asp:ListItem>
 <asp:ListItem value="DESC" text="Desc"></asp:ListItem>
 </asp:radiobuttonlist>
 </td>
</tr>
<tr>
 <td>
 Filter Field
 <br>
 <asp:dropdownlist id="FilterList"
      runat="server"></asp:dropdownlist>
 </td>
</tr>
<tr>
 <td>
 Filter Criteria
 <br>
 <asp:textbox id="FilterCriteria" runat="server"></asp:textbox>
 </td>
</tr>
<tr>
 <td>
```

Finally, we have a grid for displaying the results and a button to submit the form:

```
 <asp:button id="submit" runat="server" text="Update"></asp:button>
 </td>
 </tr>
 </table>
 </td>
 <td valign="top">
 <asp:datagrid id="Authors" runat="server"></asp:datagrid>
 </td>
 </tr>
 </table>
 </form>
 </body>
</HTML>
```

The resulting page will look like this:

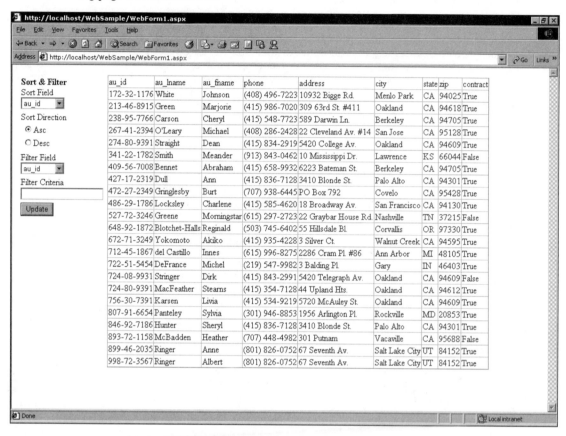

Let's take a look at the code behind this page – which we have called `Webform1.aspx.cs`. We start with namespace and variable declarations:

```
using System;
using System.Collections;
using System.ComponentModel;
using System.Data;
using System.Data.SqlClient;
using System.Drawing;
using System.Web;
using System.Web.SessionState;
using System.Web.UI;
using System.Web.UI.WebControls;
using System.Web.UI.HtmlControls;

namespace Chapter10WebSample
{

  public class WebForm1 : System.Web.UI.Page
  {
```

```
      //variables for our controls
      protected System.Web.UI.WebControls.DropDownList SortList;
      protected System.Web.UI.WebControls.RadioButtonList SortDirection;
      protected System.Web.UI.WebControls.DropDownList FilterList;
      protected System.Web.UI.WebControls.TextBox FilterCriteria;
      protected System.Web.UI.WebControls.Button submit;
      protected System.Web.UI.WebControls.DataGrid Authors;

      public WebForm1()
      {
        Page.Init += new System.EventHandler(Page_Init);
      }
```

Next, we put the bulk of our code in the page_load event handler. We first attempt to retrieve a DataView and DataColumnCollection object from the cache. If they are not present in the cache, we connect to the database and load a dataset:

```
      private void Page_Load(object sender, System.EventArgs e)
      {
        //if there is no view or columns are in the cache then create them
        DataView AuthorView = (DataView)Cache["Authors"];
        DataColumnCollection Columns = (DataColumnCollection)Cache["Columns"];

        if(AuthorView==null || Columns==null)
        {
          //load the data into the dataset
          SqlConnection AuthorConnection = new
            SqlConnection("server=(local);database=pubs;uid=sa;pwd=;");
          SqlDataAdapter AuthorAdapter = new SqlDataAdapter("Select * from
            authors", AuthorConnection);
          DataSet AuthorDataSet = new DataSet();

          AuthorAdapter.Fill(AuthorDataSet);
```

We then set variables for the columns and view and insert them in the cache so they will be available to us next time:

```
        //set the view and columns variables
        Columns = AuthorDataSet.Tables[0].Columns;
        AuthorView = AuthorDataSet.Tables[0].DefaultView;

        //insert the items into the cache setting a 20 minute time out
        Cache.Insert("Authors",AuthorView,null,System.DateTime.
          Now.AddMinutes(20),System.TimeSpan.Zero);
        Cache.Insert("Columns",AuthorDataSet.Tables[0].Columns,
          null,System.DateTime.Now.AddMinutes(20), System.TimeSpan.Zero);

      }
```

We then apply any filters and sorts to the view:

```
//if we are posting back, then filter and sort the view
if(IsPostBack)
{
  //sort the view
  AuthorView.Sort = SortList.SelectedItem + " " +
    SortDirection.SelectedItem;

  //set the filter if one exists, or set it to nothing
  if(FilterCriteria.Text != String.Empty)
  {
    AuthorView.RowFilter = FilterList.SelectedItem + "= '" +
      FilterCriteria.Text + "'";
  }
  else
  {
    AuthorView.RowFilter = "";
  }
}
```

Then we set the drop-down lists to use the columns collection and the grid to use the view:

```
  //set the source of the drop down lists to be the columns
  SortList.DataSource = Columns;
  FilterList.DataSource = Columns;

  //set the source of the datagrid to be the view
  Authors.DataSource = AuthorView;

  //databind all of the controls.
  DataBind();
}

private void Page_Init(object sender, EventArgs e)
{
  InitializeComponent();
}

private void InitializeComponent()
{
  this.Load += new System.EventHandler(this.Page_Load);

}
  }
}
```

Summary

In this chapter we have examined the items in ADO.NET that allow us to have a rich client experience and maintain data integrity. We then used `DataRelationObjects`, `DataViewObjects`, and `ConstraintObjects` together to make working with data on the client side a much easier experience.

In this chapter we covered the following:

- ❏ Constraints, including the `UniqueConstraint` and `ForeignKeyConstraint`
- ❏ Defining cascading changes in a parent table and the result in the child table
- ❏ Creating a custom constraint to further constrain the data in our dataset
- ❏ `DataRelationObjects` and navigating to related data
- ❏ `DataViewObjects`, including filtering and sorting
- ❏ `DataViewManager`
- ❏ Data binding

10

Transactions

We have so far covered ADO.NET fundamentals and various objects such as `Connection`, `Command`, and `DataSet`. In this chapter we are going to look at one of the important aspects of any business application – Transactions. In this chapter we will cover:

❑   The basics of database transactions

❑   How ADO.NET provides transaction support

❑   How to write database applications that make use of ADO.NET transaction features

What is a Transaction?

A transaction is a set of operations where either all of the operations must be successful or all of them must fail. Let's look at the traditional example of a transaction.

Suppose we need to transfer $1000 from account A to account B. This operation involves two steps:

1. $1000 should be deducted from account A

2. $1000 should be added to account B

Suppose that we successfully completed step 1, but, due to some error, step 2 failed. If we do not undo Step 1, then the entire operation will be faulty. Transactions help to avoid this. Operations in the same transaction will only make changes to the database if *all* the steps are successful. So in our example, if Step 2 fails, then the changes made by Step 1 will not be committed to the database.

Transactions usually follow certain guidelines known as the ACID properties, which ensure that even complex transactions will be self-contained and reliable. We will look at these in the next section.

ACID Properties

Transactions are characterised by four properties popularly called ACID properties. To pass the ACID test, a transaction must be **Atomic**, **Consistent**, **Isolated**, and **Durable**. While this acronym is easy to remember, the meaning of each word is not obvious. Here is a brief explanation:

❑   **Atomic** – all steps in the transaction should succeed or fail together. Unless *all* the steps from a transaction complete, a transaction is not considered completed.

❑   **Consistent** – the transaction takes the underlying database from one stable state to another.

❑   **Isolated** – every transaction is an independent entity. One transaction should not affect any other transaction running at the same time.

❑   **Durable** – changes that occur during the transaction are permanently stored on some medium, typically a hard disk, before the transaction is declared successful. That is, logs are maintained on a drive, so that should a failure occur, the database can be reconstructed so as to retain transactional integrity.

Note that, even though these are ideal characteristics of a transaction, practically we can alter some of them to suit our requirements. In particular, we can alter the isolation behavior of a transaction, as we will discuss later. Also, constructs such as nested transactions, which we will also look at later, allow us to control the atomicity of a transaction.

However, we should only change from these behaviors after careful consideration. The following sections will include discussion of when and how to change them.

Database Transactions

Transactions are frequently used in many business applications. Typically, when we develop a software system, some RDBMS is used to store the data. In order to apply the concept of transactions in such software systems, the RDBMS must support transactions. Modern databases such as SQL Server 2000 and Oracle 8 provide strong support for transactions. For instance, SQL server 2000 provides support for Transaction SQL (T-SQL) statements such as BEGIN TRANSACTION, COMMIT TRANSACTION, and ROLLBACK TRANSACTION (T-SQL is SQL Server's own dialect of structured query language).

Data access APIs, such as ODBC, OLE DB, and ADO.NET, enable developers to use transactions in their applications. Typically, RDBMSs and data access APIs provide transaction support, as long as we are working with a single database. In many large applications, more than one database is involved, and we need to use Microsoft Distributed Transaction Coordinator (MSDTC). Microsoft Transaction Server (MTS) and COM+, which are popular middle wares, also use MSDTC internally to facilitate multi-database transactions. It should be noted that .NET provides access to COM+ functionality via the System.EnterpriseServices namespace.

> **ADO.NET transactions are not the same as MTS or COM+ transactions. ADO.NET transactions are connection-based, and span only one database at a time. COM+ transactions use MSDTC to facilitate transactions, and can span multiple databases.**

Transaction Vocabulary

There are some commands that are used frequently in the context of database transactions. They are BEGIN, COMMIT, and ROLLBACK. These are the basic building blocks used in implementing transactions. Before going any further, let's take a quick look at what these commands do.

❏   BEGIN – before executing any queries under a transaction, a transaction must be initiated; to do this, we use BEGIN

❏   COMMIT – a transaction is said to be committed when all the changes that occurred during the transaction are written successfully to the database; we achieve this with the COMMIT command

❏   ROLLBACK – a rollback occurs when all changes made to the transaction are undone because some part of the transaction has failed

Now that we know the basics of transactions, let us see how ADO.NET provides support for them.

ADO.NET Transaction Support

ADO.NET provides strong support for database transactions. As we've already seen, transactions covered under this support are single database transactions. Here, transactions are tracked on a per connection basis. Transaction functionality is provided with the connection object of ADO.NET. However, there is some difference in implementation of transaction support in ADO.NET as compared to ADO.

If you have worked with ADO, you will recollect that it provides methods such as BeginTrans, CommitTrans, and RollbackTrans for the connection object itself. In the case of ADO.NET, the connection object is used simply to start a transaction. The commit or rollback of the transaction is taken care of by a dedicated object, which is an implementation of the transaction class. This enables us to associate different command objects with a single transaction object, so that those commands participate in the same transaction.

ADO.NET provides connected as well as disconnected data access, and provides support for transactions in both the modes. In connected mode, the typical sequence of operations in a transaction will be as follows:

❏   Open a database connection

❏   Begin a transaction

❏   Fire queries directly against the connection via the command object

❏   Commit or Rollback the transaction

❏   Close the connection

The following figure shows how transactions are handled in connected mode:

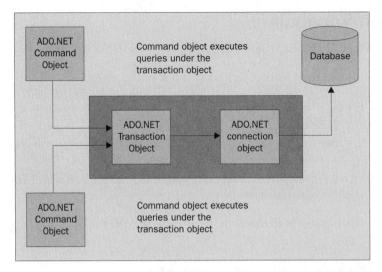

In disconnected mode, we generally first fetch data (generally one or more tables) into a DataSet object, manipulate it as required, and then update data back in the database. In this mode, the typical sequence of operations will be as follows:

- ❏ Open a database connection
- ❏ Fetch required data in a DataSet object
- ❏ Close the database connection
- ❏ Manipulate the data in the DataSet object
- ❏ Again open a connection with the database
- ❏ Start a transaction
- ❏ Update the database with changes from the DataSet
- ❏ Close the connection

The following diagram illustrates this sequence of events:

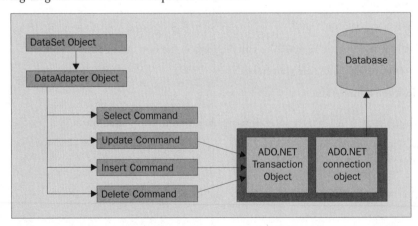

Implementing transactions in connected mode is relatively simple, as we have everything happening live. However, in disconnected mode, while updating the data back into the database, some care should be taken to allow for concurrency issues.

In the following section, we will look at the transaction class. We will also look at the commonly used methods of the transaction class, and typical ways of using these methods.

Transaction Class

There are currently three .NET data providers: OleDB, SQLClient, and ODBC. Each of these providers has their own implementation of the transaction class: the OleDB data provider has the OleDbTransaction class, which resides in the System.Data.OleDb namespace; the SQLClient data provider has the SqlTransaction class, which resides in the System.Data.SqlClient namespace; and the ODBC data provider has the ODBCTransaction class, which resides in the System.Data.ODBC namespace.

All of these classes implement the IDbTransaction interface, from the System.Data namespace. Most of the properties and methods of these classes are identical. However, each has some specific methods of its own, as we will see later.

Methods of the Transaction class

The transaction classes have two methods that we will use most frequently while working with them.

They are:

❑ Commit – this method identifies a transaction as successful. Once we call this method, all the pending changes are written permanently to the underlying database.

❑ Rollback – this method marks a transaction as unsuccessful, and pending changes are discarded. The database state remains unchanged.

Typically, both of these methods are used together. The following code snippet shows how they are used in the most common way:

```
MyConnection.Open()
MyTransaction = MyConnection.BeginTransaction()
MyCommand1.Transaction = MyTransaction
MyCommand2.Transaction = MyTransaction
Try
    MyCommand1.ExecuteNonQuery()
    MyCommand2.ExecuteNonQuery()
    MyTransaction.Commit()
Catch
    MyTransaction.Rollback()
Finally
    MyConnection.Close()
End Try
```

The transaction class also has other properties and methods, which we will look at later in the chapter.

Now we will move on to actually developing applications that use the transactional features of ADO.NET.

Writing Transactional Database Applications

Implementing a basic transaction using ADO.NET in an application can be fairly straightforward. The most common sequence of steps that would be performed while developing a transactional application is as follows:

❑ Open a database connection using the Open method of the connection object.

❑ Begin a transaction using the BeginTransaction method of the connection object. This method provides us with a transaction object that we will use later to commit or rollback the transaction. Note that changes caused by any queries executed before calling the BeginTransaction method will be committed to the database immediately after they execute.

❑ Set the Transaction property of the command object to the above mentioned transaction object.

❑ Execute the SQL commands using the command object. We may use one or more command objects for this purpose, as long as the Transaction property of all the objects is set to a valid transaction object.

❑ Commit or roll back the transaction using the Commit or Rollback method of the transaction object.

❑ Close the database connection.

Note that once we have started a transaction on a certain connection, all the queries that use that particular connection must fall inside the boundary of the transaction. For example, we could execute two INSERT queries and one UPDATE query inside a transaction. If we execute a SELECT query without the transaction, we will get an error indicating that a transaction is still pending. Also, one connection object can have only one pending transaction at a time. In other words, once we call the BeginTransaction method on a connection object, we cannot call BeginTransaction again, unless we commit or roll back that transaction. In such situations, we will get an error message stating that parallel transactions are not supported. To overcome this error, we may use another connection to execute the query.

Let us put our knowledge about transactions into practice by developing an application that uses ADO.NET transaction features.

Implementing Transactions

In this section, we will develop a small Console Application that illustrates how to develop transactional applications with ADO.NET.

For our example we will use the Northwind database that ships with SQL server. Our application operates in the following way:

❑ We want to place new orders against the customer ID, 'ALFKI', for product ids 1,2 and 3.

❑ We will supply quantities for product IDs from the command line. This will allow us to violate business rules for testing purpose.

❑ We will then place the order by inserting records into the Orders table and the Order Details table.

❑ We will then check if the requested quantity of any product is greater than the available quantity. If it is, the entire transaction is rolled back. Otherwise, the transaction is committed.

Here is the complete code for the application:

```
using System;
using System.Data;
using System.Data.SqlClient;

namespace Wrox
{
class TransactionDemo
{
    static void Main(string[] args)
    {
        SqlConnection myconnection;
        SqlCommand mycommand;
        SqlTransaction mytransaction;
        string ConnectionString;
        int stock;
        int qty1,qty2,qty3;
        if(args.Length<3)
        {
            Console.WriteLine(
            "Please enter required quantities for product ids 1,2 and 3");
            Console.ReadLine();
            return;
        }
        else
        {
            qty1 = int.Parse(args[0]);
            qty2 = int.Parse(args[1]);
            qty3 = int.Parse(args[2]);
        }
```

As usual, we declare various database objects such as connection, command, and transaction. We then open a connection with the database. The code following this simply opens a connection with the `Northwind` database:

```
ConnectionString =
    "User ID=sa;Initial Catalog=Northwind;Data Source=.";
myconnection=new SqlConnection(ConnectionString);
myconnection.Open();
```

We begin the transaction by calling the `BeginTransaction` method of the connection object. The `BeginTransaction` method returns an instance of the transaction object, which we will hold in a `SqlTransaction` variable called `mytransaction`.

```
mytransaction = myconnection.BeginTransaction();
//configure command object to use tansaction
mycommand = new SqlCommand();
mycommand.Connection = myconnection;
```

The next step is to set the `SqlCommand` object's `Transaction` property so that all the SQL statements fired through it will participate in the transaction.

```
mycommand.Transaction = mytransaction;
```

We then execute various SQL statements. We are now ready to fire our queries using the `SqlCommand` object.

We may change the `CommandText` property of the same object to fire different queries, or create new command objects. Remember that if you use new command objects, their `Transaction` property needs to be set. Typically, we would place the appropriate code in a `try` ... `catch` block, so that if an error occurs, the transaction may be rolled back. You may also check for any business validations here, and decide whether to commit or rollback the transaction:

```
try
{
    //insert into orders table
    mycommand.CommandText = "INSERT INTO " +
        "orders(customerid,orderdate,requireddate) " +
        "values('ALFKI',GetDate(),DATEADD(d,15,GetDate()))";
    mycommand.ExecuteNonQuery();

    //store identity value for further queries
    mycommand.CommandText = "SELECT @@identity FROM orders";
    string id = mycommand.ExecuteScalar().ToString();

    //insert product details
    mycommand.CommandText = " INSERT INTO [order details]" +
        "(orderid,productid,unitprice,quantity)" +
        "values(" + id + ",1,18," + args[0] + ")";
    mycommand.ExecuteNonQuery();
    mycommand.CommandText = " INSERT INTO [order details]" +
        "(orderid,productid,unitprice,quantity)" +
        "values(" + id + ",2,19," + args[1] + ")";
    mycommand.ExecuteNonQuery();
    mycommand.CommandText = " INSERT INTO [order details]" +
        "(orderid,productid,unitprice,quantity)" +
        "values(" + id + ",3,10," + args[2] + ")";
    mycommand.ExecuteNonQuery();
    //rollback if ordered quantity exceeds stock quantity
    mycommand.CommandText = " SELECT unitsinstock FROM products " +
        "WHERE productid=1";
```

Once we are done with our operations, we must call either the `Commit` or `Rollback` method of the transaction object:

```
    stock = int.Parse(mycommand.ExecuteScalar().ToString());
    if(stock < qty1)
    {
        mytransaction.Rollback();
        Console.WriteLine("Quantity for Product ID 1 exceeds " +
            "available stock");
        Console.ReadLine();
        return;
    }
    mycommand.CommandText = "SELECT unitsinstock FROM products " +
        "WHERE productid=2";
    stock = int.Parse(mycommand.ExecuteScalar().ToString());
    if(stock < qty2)
    {
        mytransaction.Rollback();
        Console.WriteLine("Quantity for Product ID 2 exceeds " +
            "available stock");
```

```
            Console.ReadLine();
            return;
        }
        mycommand.CommandText = "SELECT unitsinstock FROM products " +
            "WHERE productid=3";
        stock = int.Parse(mycommand.ExecuteScalar().ToString());
        if(stock < qty3)
        {
            mytransaction.Rollback();
            Console.WriteLine("Quantity for Product ID 3 exceeds " +
                "available stock");
            Console.ReadLine();
            return;
        }
        mytransaction.Commit();
        Console.WriteLine("Your order has been successfully placed!");
        Console.WriteLine("Order ID :" + id);
        Console.ReadLine();

    }
    catch(Exception e)
    {
        Console.WriteLine(e.Message);
        Console.ReadLine();
    }
    finally
    {
        myconnection.Close();
    }
}
}
}
```

Running the Application

Compile the application using Visual Studio .NET's Build menu option. Try running the application with various command-line argument values for product quantities. In order to test rollback, supply some values that are greater than stock quantity (say 115, for ProductID 3).

> A transaction should be completed as soon as possible. An active transaction puts locks on various resources involved, so, it is always a good practice to keep transactions as small as possible. If you are selecting data within a transaction, then you should only SELECT the rows you really require.

Examining the Effect of Isolation Level

Now that we know how to implement basic transactions, let's go into some more detail. In this section, we will investigate **isolation levels**, and how they affect our application. In doing so, we will encounter some terms that are frequently used while discussing isolation level. Finally, we will see how to set isolation levels in our code.

What are Isolation Levels?

The isolation level is measure of the extent to which changes made outside a transaction are visible inside that transaction. For example, by default, if two transactions are running independently of one another, then records inserted by one transaction are not visible to the other transaction, unless the first transaction is committed.

We may wish to alter the behavior of the transactions so that the second transaction can view records inserted by first one. We can achieve this through setting isolation levels appropriately. For an ADO.NET programmer, the isolation level can be set via isolation level enumerated values. We will see shortly how these are used.

Some Related Terms

Before going any further it is important to understand some terms that are used frequently when discussing isolation levels.

- **Dirty read** – a dirty read is a condition when a transaction reads data that has yet to be committed. Consider a case where transaction A inserts some records into the table, but is pending. Transaction B reads these records. Now, if transaction A rolls back, transaction B will refer to data that is invalid.

- **Non-repeatable read** – consider a case where transaction A reads a record from a table. Transaction B then alters or deletes the records, and commits the changes. Now, if transaction A wants to re-read the record, it will either be a different version, or will not be available at all. Such a condition is called a non-repeatable read.

- **Phantom read** – suppose that transaction A has some criteria for record selection. Initially, transaction A has, say, 100 rows matching these criteria. Now transaction B inserts some rows that match the selection criteria of transaction A. If transaction A executes the selection query again, it will receive a different set of rows than in the previous case. The rows added in this way are called phantom rows.

Possible Isolation Levels in ADO.NET

Let us now look at the different isolation level values that we can implement with ADO.NET. As stated earlier, these values are accessible via the `IsolationLevel` enumeration.

- `Chaos` – the pending changes from more highly isolated transactions cannot be overwritten. This setting is not supported by SQL Server.

- `ReadUncommitted` – in this case, a dirty read is possible. This means that no shared locks are placed, and no exclusive locks are honored. This type of isolation level is appropriate when we want to work with all the data matching certain conditions, irrespective of whether it's committed or not.

- `ReadCommitted` – shared locks are held while the data is being read by the transaction. This avoids dirty reads, but the data can be changed before a transaction completes. This may result in non-repeatable reads or phantom rows. This type of isolation level is appropriate when we want to work with all the data that matches certain conditions, and is committed.

  Shared locks are locks that are placed when a transaction wants to read data from the database, and no exclusive lock is already held on that data item. No other transactions can modify the data while shared locks exist on a table, or tables. Exclusive locks are the locks that prevent two or more transactions modifying data simultaneously. An exclusive lock is issued when a transaction needs to update a table, or tables, and no other locks are already held on the respective tables.

- ❏ RepeatableRead – in this case, shared locks are placed on all data that is used in a query. This prevents others from modifying the data. This also prevents non-repeatable reads. However, phantom rows are possible. This type of isolation level is appropriate when we want the records that are read to retain the same values for future reads.

- ❏ Serializable – in this case, a range lock is placed on the data set, preventing other users from updating or inserting rows into the data set until the transaction is complete. This type of isolation level is appropriate when you want all the data you are working with to be exactly the same until you finish the processing.

- ❏ Unspecified – in this type, a different isolation level than the one specified is being used; however, the level cannot be determined.

These isolation level values can be supplied while initiating a transaction through the BeginTransaction method of the OleDbConnection or SqlConnection object. We may read the current value of isolation level using the IsolationLevel property of the transaction object.

Changing Isolation Levels

We will now develop a small application that changes the default isolation level of a SQL Server database from Read Committed to Read Uncommitted. The application works in the following way:

- ❏ We will open a connection with Northwind database and begin a transaction. The isolation level for this transaction will be the default – ReadCommitted.

- ❏ We will open another connection with the database and begin another transaction. However, we will set the isolation level to ReadUncommitted.

- ❏ From the first transaction, we will then insert two rows into the Orders table.

- ❏ Without committing the first transaction, we will fetch the last two order IDs in the second transaction, and output the results on the console. This will prove that, even though the first transaction is yet to be finished, the second transaction reads records inserted by it.

- ❏ We will roll back the first transaction, and output the last two orders again from the second transaction, in order to show that they are different.

Here is the complete code of the application:

```
using System;
using System.Data;
using System.Data.SqlClient;

namespace Wrox
{
    class TransactionExample3
    {
        static void Main(string[] args)
        {
            SqlConnection myconnection1,myconnection2;
            SqlCommand mycommand1,mycommand2;
            SqlTransaction mytransaction1,mytransaction2;
            SqlDataReader myreader;
            string ConnectionString;

            //open a database connection
            ConnectionString =
```

```
                      "User ID=sa;Initial Catalog=Northwind;Data Source=.";
myconnection1 = new SqlConnection(ConnectionString);
myconnection2 = new SqlConnection(ConnectionString);
myconnection1.Open();
myconnection2.Open();

//start a transaction
mytransaction1 = myconnection1.BeginTransaction();
mytransaction2 = myconnection2.BeginTransaction
   (IsolationLevel.ReadUncommitted);

//configure command object to use tansaction
mycommand1=new SqlCommand();
mycommand1.Connection=myconnection1;
mycommand1.Transaction=mytransaction1;

mycommand2=new SqlCommand();
mycommand2.Connection=myconnection2;
mycommand2.Transaction=mytransaction2;

//execute various sql statements
try
{
   mycommand1.CommandText = "INSERT INTO orders DEFAULT VALUES";
   mycommand1.ExecuteNonQuery();
   mycommand1.CommandText = " INSERT INTO orders DEFAULT VALUES";
   mycommand1.ExecuteNonQuery();

   mycommand2.CommandText =
      "SELECT TOP 2 orderid FROM orders ORDER BY orderid DESC";
   myreader = mycommand2.ExecuteReader();
   Console.WriteLine("Last 2 Orders - Transaction is pending");
   while (myreader.Read())
   {
      Console.WriteLine(myreader.GetInt32(0));
   }
   myreader.Close();
   Console.ReadLine();

   mytransaction1.Rollback();
   mycommand2.CommandText =
      "SELECT TOP 2 orderid FROM orders ORDER BY orderid DESC";
   myreader = mycommand2.ExecuteReader();

   Console.WriteLine("Last 2 Orders - Transaction rolled back");

   while (myreader.Read())
   {
      Console.WriteLine(myreader.GetInt32(0));
   }
   Console.ReadLine();
}

catch(Exception e)
{
   Console.WriteLine(e.Message);
   Console.ReadLine();
}
finally
{
   myconnection1.Close();
```

```
            myconnection2.Close();
        }
      }
    }
}
```

Here, note how we have initiated the second transaction by passing the `IsolationLevel` enumeration value to the `BeginTransaction` method.

```
mytransaction2 = myconnection2.BeginTransaction
    (IsolationLevel.ReadUncommitted);
```

Here is the result from a test run of the application:

> Isolation level is the measure of the extent to which changes made outside a transaction are visible inside that transaction. The default isolation level for SQL Server is **ReadCommitted**.
>
> Changing the default isolation level is a tricky issue that depends on the level of consistency and concurrency you want. Generally, you will find that the higher the isolation level, thehigher the consistency will be, but the lower the concurrency will be.

When to Use Transactions

Even though ADO.NET provides good support for transactions, it is not necessary that you should always use transactions. In fact, every time you are using a transaction you are actually carrying some overhead. Also, transactions involve some kind of locking of table rows. Thus, unnecessary use of transactions may cause performance penalties. So, as a rule of thumb, use a transaction only when your operation requires one. For example, if you are simply selecting records from a database, or firing a single query, then most of the time you will not need a transaction.

Transactional features are provided by underlying RDBMS as well as ADO.NET. The choice between the two actually depends on what you are trying to accomplish. For example, suppose that you are using a stored procedure that performs a certain operation that requires a transaction. You may find that, instead of starting an ADO.NET transaction and calling the stored procedure in that transaction, it is much easier and more efficient to initialize the transaction in the stored procedure itself. On the other hand, if you are firing multiple SQL statements – inserts, for example – that require a transaction, then using ADO.NET transaction capabilities will be very easy. Also, if the commit or rollback depends on some factor external to the database, then using ADO.NET transactions would be preferable.

Transactions and Performance

Always keep in mind that a lengthy transaction that performs data modification to many different tables can effectively block the work of all other users in the system. This may cause serious performance problems. While implementing a transaction, the following practices can be followed in order to achieve acceptable results:

❑ Keep transactions as short as possible.

❑ Avoid returning data with a SELECT in the middle of a transaction, unless your statements depend on the data returned.

❑ If you use the SELECT statement, fetch only the rows that are required.

❑ Wherever appropriate, try to write transactions within stored procedures instead of always using ADO.NET transactions.

❑ Avoid transactions that combine multiple independent batches of work. Put such batches in individual transactions.

Default Behavior for Transactions

One point that is also to be noted is the default behavior of transactions. By default, if you do not explicitly commit the transaction, then the transaction is rolled back. Even though default behavior allows the rolling back of a transaction, it is always a good programming practice to explicitly call the rollback method. This will not only release any locks from data, but also make code much more readable, and less error prone.

Transactions and User Confirmation

When developing applications that deal with transactions interactively, some care must be taken in order to avoid locking issues. Consider a case in which we are developing an application that transfers money from one account to another. We develop a user interface, in the form of a typical message box, which requires confirmation about the money transferred. Now, consider that our application conforms to the following sequence of operations:

1. Open a connection

2. Begin a transaction

3. Execute various queries

4. Ask the user for confirmation of the transaction using a messagebox

5. On confirmation, commit the transaction

6. In the absence of confirmation, roll back the transaction

If, after Step 4, the user is unable to confirm the transaction (perhaps walk out for lunch or a meeting) the locks will still be maintained on the rows under consideration. Also, a live connection is maintained with the database. This might cause problems for other users. In such cases, we can perform Steps 1, 2, and 3 after getting confirmation from the user.

Note that in the above example, since we wanted to obtain user confirmation, we opted for altering the sequence. If we are simply displaying the transaction status in some user interface component, such as a status bar, or a label, that does not require any user interaction, the steps mentioned above can be used without any alterations. Also, you should notify the user of any changes – an account balance, for instance – just before committing the changes, otherwise another transaction might alter the balance for the second time, and the notification would be wrong.

Simultaneous ADO.NET and DBMS Transactions

Although rare, we might encounter cases where we are using ADO.NET transactions as well as DBMS transactions. Suppose that we have one stored procedure that uses transactions internally, and you are calling this stored procedure as a part of your own ADO.NET transaction. In such cases, both the transactions work as if they are nested. In such cases, the ADO.NET commit or rollback decides the outcome of the entire process. However, there are chances of getting into errors if you rolled back from the stored procedure, or placed improper nesting levels.

> **Transactions can generate considerable overhead and affect performance if used without thought. While developing the user interfaces of applications that deal with transactions, some care should be taken to reduce locks.**

Advanced Techniques

Up to now we have seen how to implement transactions using ADO.NET. We also saw how to change a transaction's isolation level. Now it's time to move on to some advanced topics. These topics include save points, nested transactions, and using transactions with disconnected data access techniques.

Savepoints

Whenever we roll back a transaction, it nullifies the effects of every statement from that transaction. In some cases, we may not want to roll back each and every statement. We can implement this through the use of **savepoints**.

Savepoints are markers that act like a bookmark: you may mark a certain point in the flow of transaction, and then roll back up to that point, rather than completely rolling back the transaction. We can accomplish this using `Save` method of the transaction object. Note that the `Save` method is available only for the `SqlTransaction` class, and not for the `OleDbTransaction` class.

We will now develop a simple example that illustrates the use of the Save method.

Here is the complete code for the example:

```csharp
using System;
using System.Data;
using System.Data.SqlClient;

namespace Wrox
{
    class TransactionSavePoint
    {
        static void Main(string[] args)
        {
            SqlConnection myconnection;
            SqlCommand mycommand;
            SqlTransaction mytransaction;
            SqlDataReader myreader;

            //open a database connection

            myconnection = new SqlConnection(
                "User ID=sa;Initial Catalog=Northwind;Data Source=.");
            myconnection.Open();

            //start a transaction
            mytransaction=myconnection.BeginTransaction();

            //configure command object to use transaction
            mycommand = new SqlCommand();
            mycommand.Connection=myconnection;
            mycommand.Transaction=mytransaction;

            //execute various sql statements
            try
            {
                //insert into orders table
                mycommand.CommandText = "INSERT INTO orders DEFAULT VALUES";
                mycommand.ExecuteNonQuery();
                mytransaction.Save("firstorder");
                mycommand.CommandText = " INSERT INTO orders DEFAULT VALUES";
                mycommand.ExecuteNonQuery();
                mycommand.CommandText = " INSERT INTO orders DEFAULT VALUES";
                mycommand.ExecuteNonQuery();
                mytransaction.Rollback("firstorder");

                mycommand.CommandText = " INSERT INTO orders DEFAULT VALUES";
                mycommand.ExecuteNonQuery();
                mycommand.CommandText = " INSERT INTO orders DEFAULT VALUES";
                mycommand.ExecuteNonQuery();
                mytransaction.Commit();

                mycommand.CommandText =
                    "SELECT TOP 3 orderid FROM orders ORDER BY orderid DESC";
                myreader = mycommand.ExecuteReader();
                Console.WriteLine("Last 3 Orders");

                while (myreader.Read())
                {
                    Console.WriteLine(myreader.GetInt32(0));
```

```
                }
            }
            catch(Exception e)
            {
                Console.WriteLine(e.Message);
            }
            finally
            {
                myconnection.Close();
            }
        }
    }
}
```

Here, we have executed a total of five queries that insert orders. After inserting the first order, we have put a savepoint by using the following statement:

```
mytransaction.Save("firstorder");
```

We then insert two more rows and roll back up to the savepoint called `firstorder`. Note how the same `Rollback` method is used with the savepoint name as a parameter. We then insert another two rows and, finally, commit the transaction. We then display the last three order IDs to confirm that the effect of the first insert is indeed committed to the database.

The following figure shows a sample run of this application:

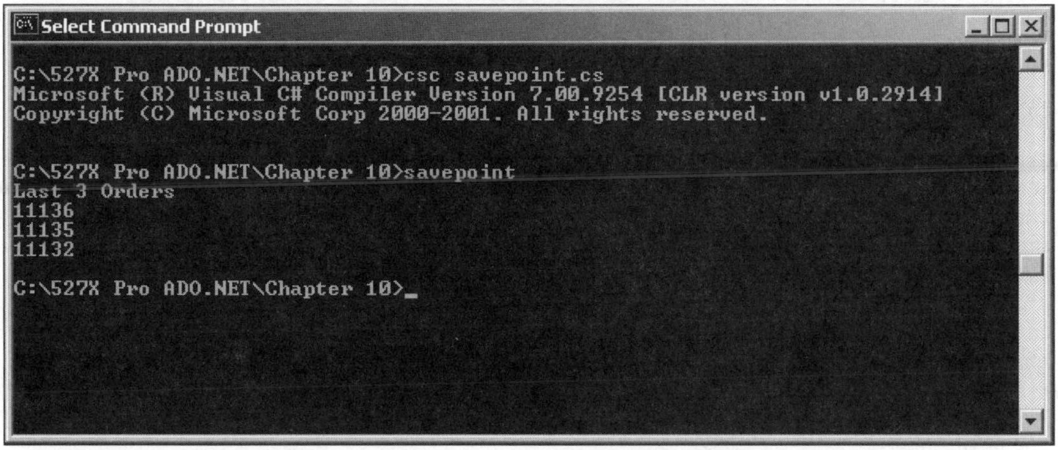

Note that the missing order IDs are due to the fact we rolled back some inserts.

There are a couple of things that can make savepoints messy. One of the common mistakes novice programmers make while working with savepoints is to forget calling either `Commit` or `Rollback` after rolling back to a certain savepoint. Savepoints can be thought of as bookmarks: we still need to explicitly call `Commit` or `Rollback`. Another point to be noted is that once we rollback to a savepoint, all the savepoints defined after that save point are lost. We must set them again if they are needed.

Nested Transactions

As we saw in the previous section, savepoints allow a transaction to be arranged as a sequence of actions that can be rolled back individually. Nesting, on the other hand, allows a transaction to be arranged as a hierarchy of such actions. In cases of nested transactions, one transaction can contain one or more other transactions. To initiate such nested transactions, the `Begin` method of the transaction object is used. This method is available only for `OleDbTransaction` class, not for the `SqlTransaction` class. Note that the `OleDb` managed providers for SQL Server and MS-Access do not support nested transactions. The following code snippet illustrates the usage of the `Begin` method:

```
Mytransaction = myconnection.BeginTransaction();
myanothertransaction = mytransaction.Begin();
```

The `Begin` method returns an instance of another transaction object, which we can use just like the original transaction object. However, rolling back this transaction simply rolls back the current transaction, and not the entire transaction.

> Savepoints and nested transactions provide a means of dividing a transaction into multiple 'sub-transactions'. The `SqlCLient` data provider supports savepoints, whereas the `OleDb` data providers do a similar thing by using the `Begin` method of the transaction object.

Using Transactions with a DataSet and DataAdapter

In the examples above, we used the command object directly to fire queries against the database. However, we can also use the `DataSet` and `DataAdapter` objects. We might want to do this, for instance, if we had bound data in a `DataSet` to controls, and wanted to implement batch updates.

We would first fetch all the records needed, place them in the `DataSet`, and then manipulate them as required. Finally, we might send new values back to the database. Since the `DataAdapter` uses command objects, internally, to update changes back to the database, we would, essentially, be using the same techniques that we discussed above. The following example illustrates how we can use transactions with the `DataSet` and `DataAdapter` objects.

In this example, we want to fetch order details for an order ID into a dataset. We then change the order quantity for various products, and update the data source from the `DataSet`, via the `DataAdapter`:

```
using System;
using System.Data;
using System.Data.SqlClient;

namespace Wrox
{
    class TransactionDataSet
    {
        static void Main(string[] args)
        {
            string ConnectionString;
            SqlConnection myconnection;
            SqlTransaction mytransaction;
            SqlCommand mycommand1;
```

```
SqlParameter myparam;
SqlDataAdapter da;

DataSet ds=new DataSet();

ConnectionString
    = "User ID=sa;Initial Catalog=Northwind;Data Source=.";
myconnection=new SqlConnection(ConnectionString);
myconnection.Open();

da = new SqlDataAdapter
    ("SELECT * FROM [order details] WHERE orderid=11116",
    myconnection);
da.Fill(ds,"orderdetails");
myconnection.Close();

ds.Tables[0].Rows[0]["Quantity"] = args[0];
ds.Tables[0].Rows[1]["Quantity"]= args[1];
ds.Tables[0].Rows[2]["Quantity"] = args[2];

mycommand1=new SqlCommand
    ("UPDATE [order details] SET quantity=@qty " +
    "WHERE orderid=@ordid AND productid=@prdid",myconnection);
myparam = new SqlParameter("@qty",SqlDbType.SmallInt);
myparam.SourceColumn = "Quantity";
myparam.SourceVersion = DataRowVersion.Current;
mycommand1.Parameters.Add(myparam);

myparam = new SqlParameter("@ordid",SqlDbType.Int);
myparam.SourceColumn = "OrderID";
myparam.SourceVersion = DataRowVersion.Current;
mycommand1.Parameters.Add(myparam);

myparam = new SqlParameter("@prdid",SqlDbType.Int);
myparam.SourceColumn = "ProductID";
myparam.SourceVersion = DataRowVersion.Current;
mycommand1.Parameters.Add(myparam);

myconnection.Open();
mytransaction = myconnection.BeginTransaction();
mycommand1.Transaction=mytransaction;
da.UpdateCommand = mycommand1;
try
{
    da.Update(ds,"orderdetails");
    mytransaction.Commit();
    Console.WriteLine("Order modified successfully !");
    Console.ReadLine();
}
catch(Exception e)
{
    mytransaction.Rollback();
    Console.WriteLine(e.Message);
    Console.ReadLine();
}
finally
{
```

```
            myconnection.Close();
        }

    }
  }
}
```

The program works as follows:

❑ We first establish a connection with the database and fetch order details for order ID 11116 into a DataSet. Note that you may have to change this order ID to suit data from your database.

❑ The connection with the database is closed.

❑ We then modify the order quantities in the DataSet.

❑ We again open a connection with the database and begin a transaction.

❑ We then set the UpdateCommand property of the SqlDataAdapter to run within this transaction.

❑ We finally call the Update method of the DataAdapter. Since the update command is running within a transaction, we must call the Commit method of the transaction object to save the changes.

The following figure shows a sample run of the above application:

Summary

In this chapter, we started with a general discussion about transactions and how ADO.NET supports them. We also looked at the details of implementing transactions: using Commit, Rollback, and savepoints. We also saw how to initialize a transaction using the BeginTransaction method, and how to use the transaction object that is returned. In order to commit a transaction, we would call the Commit method of a transaction object, whereas in order to roll back a transaction, we would call the Rollback method of a transaction object. We then looked at isolation levels, and how they affect the data read within a transaction.

11

Mapping

Frequently, the names that objects in a database have are inappropriate for a particular application. For example, we might want to provide a Web service for English-speaking Americans using a database with Spanish table and column names. In this chapter we will see how we can **map** different names to one another – so that our code can refer to objects by the name we choose, regardless of the names they have in the database.

SQL has a built in feature for mapping column names – the AS keyword. Many of us will be familiar with this method, and in some cases it can be the simplest solution. We will discuss how to use this in our ADO.NET applications, and identify its shortcomings.

We will then look at using the DataTableMapping and DataColumnMapping objects, which provide a far more comprehensive solution.

Finally we will apply our knowledge to building an XML Web service. We will use mapping objects so that the table and column names provided by our service will be clearer and more consistent than the names in the underlying database.

Using the SQL AS Keyword

Before we look at the mapping facilities provided by ADO.NET, let's have a look at the traditional mapping methods provided by the SQL language.

In the following code we load a DataSet with data from an imaginary database with very terse column names. We use the SQL AS keyword to map these short names to longer, more meaningful names for use in our application. We then write the rows to the console, using these mapped names:

```
using System;
using System.Data;
using System.Data.OleDb;
using System.Data.Common;

namespace Example5
{
    /// <summary>
    /// Summary description for Class1.
    /// </summary>
    class Class1
    {
        static void Main(string[] args)
        {
            try
            {
```

Initially, we define a connection object:

```
OleDbConnection dbConn = new
    OleDbConnection("Provider=Microsoft.Jet.OLEDB.4.0;Password=;
    User ID=Admin;Data Source=
    F:\\PRO.ADO.NET\\Mapping\\Example2\\db.mdb");
```

We then create a data adapter to retrieve records from the database:

```
string strSELECT = "SELECT ID AS UserID, fn AS FirstName, ln AS
    LastName, cty AS City, st AS State FROM tabUsers";
OleDbDataAdapter daUsers = new OleDbDataAdapter(strSELECT,
    dbConn);
DataSet dsUsers = new DataSet("User");
```

We then fill the `DataSet`:

```
daUsers.Fill(dsUsers);

// Go through the records and print them using the mapped names
foreach(DataRow r in dsUsers.Tables[0].Rows)
    Console.WriteLine("ID: {0}, FirstName: {1}, LastName: {2},
        City: {3}, State: {4}",r["UserID"],r["FirstName"],
        r["LastName"],r["City"],r["State"]);
}
catch (Exception ex)
{
    // An error occurred. Show the error message
    Console.WriteLine(ex.Message);
}
        }
    }
}
```

This method has succeeded in giving us new column names, which in many cases will be enough. However it does not automatically map table names. We can do that ourselves, using the `DataTable` `TableName` property.

The `Fill()` method provided by the `DataAdapter` object doesn't create mapping classes when it encounters the aliased column names. In fact, the database software, not .NET, handles the mapping.

The ADO.NET Mapping Mechanism

Now let's take a look at the new mapping mechanisms provided by ADO.NET. We will introduce the objects by using mappings when filling a `DataSet`. Then we will move on to using mappings when making updates to the data source.

There is a big difference between the SQL method and the ADO.NET method. The mapping objects allow developers to manage `DataSet` data and schemas that have been created using XML documents and XML schemas. With the SQL `AS` keyword, we can use the aliased column names only when we deal with the database and records.

Using Mapping when Retrieving Data

When we fill a `DataSet`, the `DataAdapter` looks at its own `TableMappings` property to see if the developer has defined mapping rules. By default, the `TableMappings` property is empty, so the same column names used in the database are used in the dataset table.

Let's take a look at how we would use the ADO.NET mapping mechanism to rename very terse column names in a `DataSet` to more meaningful alternatives. We will use the same Microsoft Access database that we used in the previous example.

To use ADO.NET mappings, we create a `DataTableMapping` object. This object enables us to map between two names for the same table, and also contains the `ColumnMappings` property – a collection of `DataColumnMapping` objects that map between names of the column in the table. Once we have created this object, and added all of the required column mappings, we add it to the `DataAdapter` object's `TableMappings` property.

Let's look at an example that puts this into practice.

The following is just a class outline. To keep the new code clear, we will use a separate method to handle the mapping – DoDataMappings. Notice that we introduce the System.Data.Common namespace, which we need to use the mapping classes:

```
using System;
using System.Data;
using System.Data.OleDb;
using System.Data.Common;

namespace Example2
{
    /// <summary>
    /// Summary description for Class1.
    /// </summary>
    class Class1
    {
        static void Main(string[] args)
        {
            // implemented later
        }

        static void DoDataMappings(DataAdapter da)
        {
            // implemented later
        }
    }
}
```

The `Main` method looks like this:

```
static void Main(string[] args)
{
    try
    {
        // Define a connection object
        OleDbConnection dbConn = new
            OleDbConnection("Provider=Microsoft.Jet.OLEDB.4.0;Password=;"
            + "User ID=Admin;Data Source=" +
            "F:\\PRO.ADO.NET\\Mapping\\Example2\\db.mdb");

        // Create a data adapter to retrieve records from db
        OleDbDataAdapter daUsers = new OleDbDataAdapter("SELECT " +
            "ID,fn,ln,cty,st FROM tabUsers", dbConn);
        DataSet dsUsers = new DataSet("User");

        // Call method to create data mappings
        DoDataMappings(daUsers);

        // Fill the dataset
        daUsers.Fill(dsUsers);

        // Go through the records and print them using the mapped names
        foreach(DataRow r in dsUsers.Tables[0].Rows)
            Console.WriteLine("ID: {0}, FirstName: {1}, LastName: {2}," +
                " City: {3}, State: {4}",r["UserID"],r["FirstName"],
                r["LastName"],r["City"],r["State"]);
    }
    catch (Exception ex)
    {
        // An error occurred. Show the error message
        Console.WriteLine(ex.Message);
    }
}
```

Notice the call to `DoDataMappings`, which comes before calling the `DataAdapter Fill` method. This method means that although we have retrieved columns from the database with names like `ln` and `cty`, we can refer to them as `LastName` and `City`. Let's take a look at the `DoDataMappings` method now.

We start by declaring `DataColumnMapping` objects. We create a new `DataColumnMapping` object for each database column that we want to map to a `DataSet` column:

```
static void DoDataMappings(DataAdapter da)
{
    try
    {
        // Define each column to map
        DataColumnMapping dcmUserID = new
            DataColumnMapping("ID","UserID");
        DataColumnMapping dcmFirstName = new
            DataColumnMapping("fn","FirstName");
        DataColumnMapping dcmLastName = new
            DataColumnMapping("ln","LastName");
        DataColumnMapping dcmCity = new DataColumnMapping("cty","City");
        DataColumnMapping dcmState = new
            DataColumnMapping("st","State");
```

The `DataColumnMapping` object contains the relation between the column within the database and the column inside the `DataSet`. We construct it by providing two strings. The first specifies the column name in the data source; the second defines the column name that will appear in the `DataSet`.

Once we have created these `DataColumnMapping` objects, we create a `DataTableMapping` object and add the `DataColumnMapping` objects to it:

```
// Define the table containing the mapped columns
DataTableMapping dtmUsers = new
    DataTableMapping("Table","tabUsers");
dtmUsers.ColumnMappings.Add(dcmUserID);
dtmUsers.ColumnMappings.Add(dcmFirstName);
dtmUsers.ColumnMappings.Add(dcmLastName);
dtmUsers.ColumnMappings.Add(dcmCity);
dtmUsers.ColumnMappings.Add(dcmState);
```

The `DataTableMapping` object has a constructor that takes two strings. The first specifies the name of the source table, and is case sensitive. This name must correspond to the table name used during the filling or updating process accomplished by the `DataAdapter` object. If you do not specify a source table name you must use the default name assigned by the `DataAdapter` object: `Table`.

The second parameter is the `DataTable` object's name in the `DataSet`. The `DataTableMapping` object exposes the `ColumnMappings` collection property that must contain every column you want to map from the database to the `DataSet`.

Finally, we add the `DataTableMapping` object to the `TableMappings` property of the `DataAdapter`. Now when we fill the `DataSet`, the `DataAdapter` will find the `DataTableMapping` in its `TableMappings` collection, and use it:

```
        // Activate the mapping mechanism
        da.TableMappings.Add(dtmUsers);
    }
    catch (Exception ex)
    {
        // An error occurred. Show the error message
        Console.WriteLine(ex.Message);
    }
} // End of the DoDataMappings method.
```

This has taken quite a bit more code than just using the SQL `AS` keyword. The good news is that there is a shorter way to use the data mapping objects – we've just looked at the longer version to get a better idea of what is happening. The bad news is that it is still not quite as short as using the `AS` keyword. Let's look at a shortened version of the `DoDataMappings` method:

```
static void DoDataMappings(DataAdapter da)
{
    try
    {
        // Define an array of column to map
        DataColumnMapping[] dcmMappedColumns = {
            new DataColumnMapping("ID","UserID"),
            new DataColumnMapping("fn","FirstName"),
            new DataColumnMapping("ln","LastName"),
            new DataColumnMapping("cty","City"),
```

```
        new DataColumnMapping("st","State")};

        // Define the table containing the mapped columns
        DataTableMapping dtmUsers = new
            DataTableMapping("Table","tabUsers",dcmMappedColumns);

        // Activate the mapping mechanism
        da.TableMappings.Add(dtmUsers);
    }
    catch (Exception ex)
    {
        // An error occurred. Show the error message
        Console.WriteLine(ex.Message);
    }
}
```

This time we create an array of DataColumnMapping objects, instead of declaring them all separately. We then use another DataTableMapping constructor that accepts an array of DataColumnMapping objects in the constructor, rather than adding each DataColumnMapping separately.

There are no substantial differences between using one method over the other. The first case requires more code, but it is slightly more readable than the second one. However with a few clear comments, the shorter version is perfectly understandable.

The MissingMappingAction and MissingSchemaAction Properties

We have seen that when the DataAdapter fills a DataSet, it checks to see what table mappings have been specified. If none have been specified, then it uses the original names. However, this is only the default. We can choose how we want the DataAdapter to react if it meets columns that we have no specified mappings for. The MissingMappingAction property of the DataAdapter has three settings:

❑ Passthrough (the default) – if a mapping is not specified, the data adapter will assume the name is the same in the data source and the DataSet

❑ Error – if a mapping is not specified, the DataAdapter will raise a SystemException

❑ Ignore – if a mapping is not specified, the DataAdapter object will ignore that column

Moreover, when we use the Fill() and the Update() method, we can choose what the DataAdapter should do when a DataSet schema that does not meet expectations. The MissingSchemaAction property of the DataAdapter can accept four values:

❑ Add (default option) – when the schema is missing for the current column, the DataAdapter will create it and add it to the DataSet object without creating information on primary keys or unique columns.

❑ AddWithKey – the same as the Add option, but with the difference that primary keys and unique columns will be created. Remember that the identity column will be created without identity seed and identity increment values. You should add them after the Fill() or the Update() calls.

❑ Ignore – when the schema is missing for the current column, the DataAdapter will ignore it and continue analyzing the other columns.

❑ Error – when the schema is missing for the current column, the DataAdapter will raise a SystemException exception.

These settings also apply when using the `DataAdapter` to update a data source, which we will go on to look at now.

Inserting Records Using Mapped Names

Until now, we have focused our attention on retrieving records. But mapping makes even the database's other operations, such as inserting a new record or updating an existing one, easier to write and manage. After mapping column names, we can use them throughout our code to accomplish every kind of database access. Let's see an example of adding a new record inside the Microsoft Access DB.MDB database:

```
using System;
using System.Data;
using System.Data.Common;
using System.Data.OleDb;

namespace Example7
{
    /// <summary>
    /// Summary description for Class1.
    /// </summary>
    class Class1
    {
        static void DoDataMappings(DataAdapter da)
        {
          // same implementation as above
        }

        static void Main(string[] args)
        {
            DataSet dsUsers = new DataSet("Users");

            try
            {
                // Define a connection object
                OleDbConnection dbConn = new
                    OleDbConnection("Provider=Microsoft.Jet.OLEDB.4.0;Password=;"
                    + "User ID=Admin;Data Source=" +
                    "F:\\PRO.ADO.NET\\Mapping\\Example2\\db.mdb");

                // Create a data adapter to retrieve records from db
                OleDbDataAdapter daUsers = new OleDbDataAdapter("SELECT" +
                    "ID,fn,ln,cty,st FROM tabUsers", dbConn);

                // call the same DoDataMappings method as we've used before
                DoDataMappings(daUsers);

                // Fill the dataset
                daUsers.Fill(dsUsers);

                // Declare a command builder to create SQL instructions
                // to create and update records.
                OleDbCommandBuilder cb = new OleDbCommandBuilder(daUsers);

                // Insert a new record in the DataSet
                DataRow r = dsUsers.Tables[0].NewRow();
                r["FirstName"] = "Eddie";
                r["LastName"] = "Robinson";
                r["City"] = "Houston";
                r["State"] = "Texas";
```

```
                    dsUsers.Tables[0].Rows.Add(r);

                    // Insert the record even in the database
                    daUsers.Update(dsUsers.GetChanges());

                    // Align in-memory data with the data source ones
                    dsUsers.AcceptChanges();

                    // Print successfully message
                    Console.WriteLine("A new record has been added to the " +
                        "database.");
                }
                catch (Exception ex)
                {
                    // An error occurred. Show the error message
                    Console.WriteLine(ex.Message);

                    // Reject DataSet changes
                    dsUsers.RejectChanges();
                }
            }
        }
    }
```

In the highlighted snippet of code above a new row has been created and filled using the mapped column names. Below, we update a column using the mapping mechanism:

```
using System;
using System.Data;
using System.Data.Common;
using System.Data.OleDb;

namespace Example8
{
    /// <summary>
    /// Summary description for Class1.
    /// </summary>
    class Class1
    {
        static void DoDataMappings(DataAdapter da)
        {
            // same implementation as above
        }

        static void Main(string[] args)
        {
            DataSet dsUsers = new DataSet("Users");

            try
            {
                // Define a connection object
                OleDbConnection dbConn = new
                    OleDbConnection("Provider=Microsoft.Jet.OLEDB.4.0;Password=;"
                    + "User ID=Admin;Data Source=" +
                    "F:\\PRO.ADO.NET\\Mapping\\Example2\\db.mdb");

                // Create a data adapter to retrieve records from db
                OleDbDataAdapter daUsers = new OleDbDataAdapter("SELECT " +
                    "ID,fn,ln,cty,st FROM tabUsers", dbConn);
```

```csharp
        // call the same DoDataMappings method as we've used before
        DoDataMappings(daUsers);

        // Fill the dataset
        daUsers.Fill(dsUsers);

        // Set the primary key in order to use the Find() method
        // below.
        DataColumn[] dcaKey = { dsUsers.Tables[0].Columns["UserID"] };
        dsUsers.Tables[0].PrimaryKey = dcaKey;

        // Declare a command builder to create SQL instructions
        // to create and update records.
        OleDbCommandBuilder cb = new OleDbCommandBuilder(daUsers);

        // Find the row that we want to update
        DataRow r = dsUsers.Tables[0].Rows.Find(3);

        if (r != null)
        {
            r["FirstName"] = "Venus";
            r["LastName"] = "Williams";
            r["City"] = "Houston";
            r["State"] = "Texas";

            // Update the record even in the database
            daUsers.Update(dsUsers.GetChanges());

            // Align in-memory data with the data source ones
            dsUsers.AcceptChanges();

            // Print successfully message
            Console.WriteLine("The record has been updated " +
                "successfully.");
        }
        else
        {
            Console.WriteLine("No record found...");
        }
    }
    catch (Exception ex)
    {
        // Reject DataSet changes
        dsUsers.RejectChanges();

        // An error occurred. Show the error message
        Console.WriteLine(ex.Message);
    }
  }
 }
}
```

In the code above we can see how the `Find` method retrieves the `DataRow` object reference that is used in the updating process. The code has to define a primary key within the `DataSet` in order to use the `Find` method, which needs a valid primary key value as a parameter to retrieve the correct record.

Web Services with Mapping

We have seen how mapping classes help us to create more easily readable code by allowing us to use the preferred column names throughout our code. However, mapping classes are even more useful when we need to deal with XML documents and XML schemas. We might often receive an XML document containing different elements from the related table in your database, or from the necessary names used by the parser to analyze the document. We can use the ADO.NET mapping mechanisms to solve all these problems.

In this section of the chapter we will analyze a typical scenario that will be common in the next few years: exchanging documents between different companies.

Imagine a big company that over the years has spent a lot of money on implementing electronic systems and software applications to automate its own bureaucracy. Now try telling them that they have to change some of their systems because other big companies use different systems. Faxes, mails, and couriers would remain the most used systems to exchange documents between companies.

Fortunately, the .NET framework offers a better solution based on XML document exchange, using TCP/IP protocols such as HTTP, FTP, and SMTP. In this scenario, the big company has only to develop a new system to produce a text file that contains XML elements describing its own document, and then use the preferred TCP/IP protocol to send its data. With .NET, we don't even need to worry about the XML or the transmission protocol. Using Web services we can transmit objects such as `DataSets` over the Web with almost no effort, as the following example shows.

Our "big company", called Pet Lovers, supplies pet materials to affiliated pet shops. The pet shops order the supplies from Pet Lovers by phone. Pet Lovers communicates with its supplier using a Web service. This Web service has a method that will return a list of items along with the available quantity. Moreover, the supplier will provide a web method that accepts incoming orders from its customers. This diagram should help to clarify what happens:

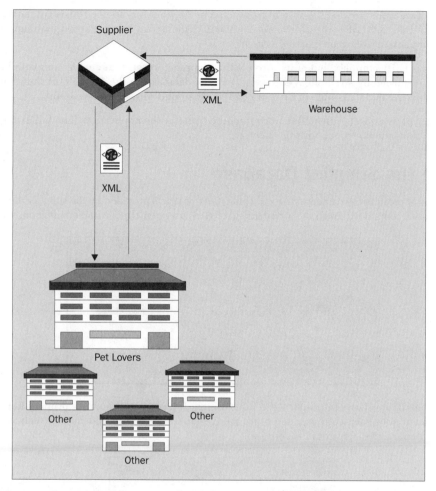

The supplier provides a method that returns a complete list of products within an XML document. The Pet Lovers Company, as with as every affiliated company, retrieves the document and sends back a new one having the same XML elements describing the required goods. Another scenario could be where XML documents are exchanged between the Supplier and its warehouse to retrieve the quantities of the available items.

We will focus our attention on the document exchange between supplier and customer. Let's see the steps we are going to undertake:

1. Create the Supplier's database containing the products, the orders, and the customers

2. Create the Web service providing two methods: one for retrieving the list of products and one for storing the order

3. Create the Pet Lovers application that retrieves the products list and submits the order

4. Map the columns between the Supplier XML document and Pet Lovers database to store the order's information

Of course, if we were creating the system from scratch, we would try to use consistent names for the databases and the XML. However this case study will demonstrate how we could use mapping to provide compatibility between existing systems.

The system is fairly complex, but at its core are the mapping objects that enable compatibility between a `DataSet`, returned by a remote Web service, and the database on the client. This shows how the mapping objects can, in a couple of lines of code, make applications far more useful.

This chapter presents a representative portion of the code for the application. The full example is included in the code download for this chapter.

Creating the Supplier Database

The first task is creating the database that will contain the products provided by the supplier, the orders done by the affiliated companies, and a table containing a list of customers. In our implementation, we will have three tables:

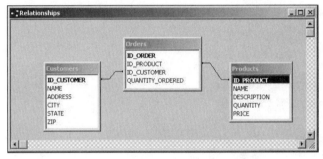

The following figure shows the Customers table design. It has an auto-number primary key containing the identification for each customer and other fields containing generic information such as the customer's name and the customer's address:

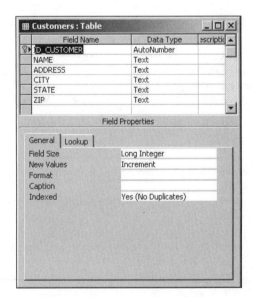

The next figure shows the **Products** table structure. It has an auto-increment primary key to identify each product in the table, plus text fields that describe it:

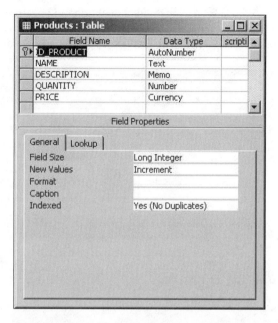

Orders is the last table, illustrated below. It contains each order submitted by the customers. It has an auto-number primary key that identifies the order and the primary keys from the other tables to identify the product and the customer. Finally, it has a field to store the quantity ordered by the customer:

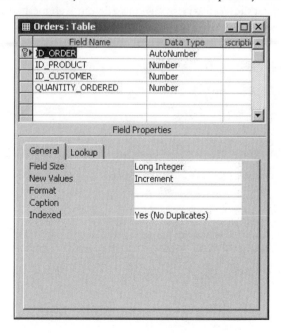

Creating the Supplier Web Service

The Supplier will provide a Web service containing a method used to retrieve an update list of products available, along with their related stock level. Creating a web service in Visual Studio .NET is easy: just choose the Visual C# Projects | ASP.NET Web Service option from the New Project menu:

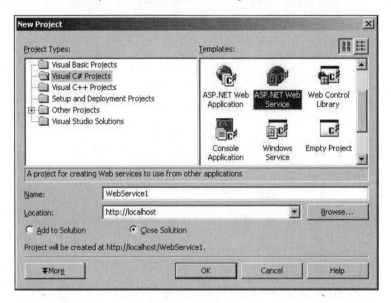

After choosing a valid name and selecting the OK button, Visual Studio .NET generates all the necessary code to implement the Web service. We just add our web method, which retrieves the product list from the respective table in the database:

```
[WebMethod]
public DataSet RetrieveList()
{
    // Create a data set that will contain the list of products
    DataSet ds = new DataSet("Products");

    try
    {
        // Create the connection object
        OleDbConnection dbConn = new
            OleDbConnection("Provider=Microsoft.Jet.OLEDB.4.0;Password=;User
            ID=Admin;Data Source=F:\\pets.mdb");

        // Create the data adapter specifying the SQL
        // statement used to fill the dataset
        OleDbDataAdapter da = new OleDbDataAdapter("SELECT ID_PRODUCT, NAME,
            DESCRIPTION, QUANTITY, PRICE FROM Products", dbConn);

        // fill the dataset
        da.Fill(ds);
    }
    catch
    {
```

```
        // Error, returning a null dataset
        ds = null;
    }

    // return the dataset
    return ds;
}
```

Eventually the Web service will contain a second method called Order, which we will see later.

Creating the Pet Lovers Application

We will now look at the construction of the code for the Pet Lovers application. The full application may be downloaded from the Wrox web site at **www.wrox.com**. Initially, we'll look at that section which is concerned with ordering materials from the supplier.

In the following figure you can see the application running:

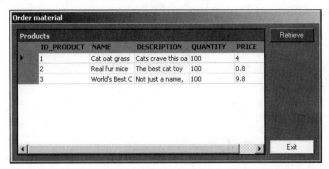

It is composed of a DataGrid data component that shows the products, quantities, and prices retrieved directly from the supplier Web service and two buttons, one to exit from the application and one to retrieve the available products from the supplier. Pressing the **Retrieve** button calls the web method and fills the list using the retrieved DataSet object. Double-clicking on the selected record within the list causes the product details to be shown on screen:

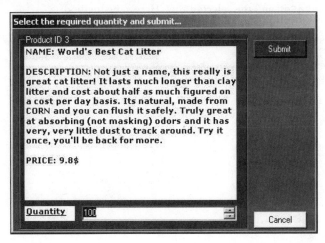

After selecting the quantity to order and pressing the **Submit** button, the `Order` web method is called and a `DataSet` object containing the product and quantity ordered is passed to the supplier. We will see how the `Order` method works later. The `Order` method will return a `DataSet` containing the order information as the quantity and the product identifier. This information will be stored in the local `PetLovers` database, which contains a similar `Orders` table, only with different column names. The application will use the mapping mechanism to update the table.

Let's see some code for the `PetLovers` Windows application. The following code illustrates how the **Retrieve** button click event is managed by the application. First of all, the mouse pointer changes to the wait cursor and then an object pointing to the Web service is created. The `RetrieveList()` web method returns the `DataSet` object reference that is used as the data source for the `DataGrid` component (see *the Visual Studio .NET and ADO.NET* chapter for more information on the `DataGrid`). Finally, the mouse pointer returns to the default cursor.

```
private void btnRetrieve_Click(object sender, System.EventArgs e)
{
    // Change mouse pointer to wait cursor
    this.Cursor = Cursors.WaitCursor;

    // create an object from the web service
    localhost.PetGoodsDistribution service = new localhost.PetGoodsDistribution();

    // Retrieve the product list
    ds = service.RetrieveList();

    // Fill the data grid with the dataset content
    dgProducts.DataSource = ds.Tables[0];

    // Restore the original cursor
    this.Cursor = Cursors.Default;
}
```

The next snippet shows what happens when the user double-clicks the selected item within the `DataGrid` component. The first operation retrieves the index of the selected row. The `DataGrid` will return the −1 value when the user has made a wrong selection. The code checks this value and continues only when the user selects a valid row. We then load `frmSubmit`, and set member variables in that form to the `DataSet` and the selected row. Here's the method:

```
private void dgProducts_DoubleClick(object sender, System.EventArgs e)
{
    // Retrieve the current row index selected
    int iIndex = ((DataGrid)sender).CurrentRowIndex;

    // If the row is valid
    if (iIndex != -1)
    {
        // Create an object from the Submit form
        frmSubmit dialog = new frmSubmit();

        // Pass to submit form some parameters
        dialog.iIndex = iIndex;
        dialog.dsSubmit = ds;
        // Show the modal submit form
        dialog.ShowDialog();
```

```
        // Refresh the product list
        btnRetrieve_Click(sender,e);
    }
}
```

When we call the ShowDialog method, before the **Submit** form is shown, the Load() event is called and you can see the code within its handler, below. After retrieving the content of the record from the DataSet using the index of the DataGrid selected row, the code fills a label with the name, description, and price of the selected product. Moreover, a NumericUpDown control is filled with the product's quantity and the maximum quantity purchasable:

```
private void frmSubmit_Load(object sender, System.EventArgs e)
{
    // Retrieve the selected row
    DataRow drSubmit;
    drSubmit = dsSubmit.Tables[0].Rows[iIndex];

    // Add the Product ID to the group box label
    groupBox.Text = groupBox.Text + drSubmit["ID_PRODUCT"];

    // Fill the label with the product name, description and price
    string txt = "NAME: " + drSubmit["NAME"] + "\n\nDESCRIPTION: " +
        drSubmit["DESCRIPTION"] + "\n\nPRICE: " + drSubmit["PRICE"] + "$";
    lbText.Text = txt;

    // Set the maximum and the value of the field
    // to the current quantity value.
    txtQuantity.Maximum = (int) drSubmit["QUANTITY"];
    txtQuantity.Value = (int) drSubmit["QUANTITY"];
}
```

The code below executes when the user presses the **Submit** button. At the beginning, a new object is created to manage the Supplier service. Then, the quantity value contained in the DataSet object is updated with the required product quantity. The modified DataSet object is passed back to the Web service, which will use it to update the database:

```
private void btnSubmit_Click(object sender, System.EventArgs e)
{

    // Create an object to use the web services
    localhost.PetGoodsDistribution service = new
                    localhost.PetGoodsDistribution();

    // Update the quantity with the required product quantity
    dsSubmit.Tables[0].Rows[iIndex]["QUANTITY"] = txtQuantity.Value;
    // Submit the updated dataset to the web method.
    // 1 is the Customer ID assigned by the supplier
    DataSet ds = service.Order(dsSubmit.GetChanges(DataRowState.Modified),
                    1);

    // If everything goes well insert the order in the local database
    if (ds != null)
    {
        InsertOrder(ds);
        this.Close();
    }
```

```
      else
      {
         MessageBox.Show("Error occurred during order processing.");
      }
   }
```

The `Order()` web method will return a new `DataSet` containing order information. We will use the `InsertOrder()` method to update the local database with this `DataSet`. Let's see what the `Order()` web method contains. A new `DataSet` object has been created to contain the orders stored in the `Orders` table. Naturally, this is an example, but when you work in real situations you rarely retrieve all the records contained in the table. You should filter the `SELECT` statement with an ad hoc `WHERE` condition. Here's the code:

```
[WebMethod]
public DataSet Order(DataSet d, int iCustomerID)
{
    // Create a dataset to contain the orders
    DataSet ds = new DataSet("Orders");

    try
    {
        // Create a connection object
        OleDbConnection dbConn = new
        OleDbConnection("Provider=Microsoft.Jet.OLEDB.4.0;Password=;User
            ID=Admin;Data Source=F:\\pets.mdb");

        // Create a data adapter object to fill the dataset
        OleDbDataAdapter da = new OleDbDataAdapter("SELECT ID_ORDER,
            ID_PRODUCT, ID_CUSTOMER, QUANTITY_ORDERED FROM Orders", dbConn);
        da.Fill(ds);
```

In the following loop, every new row contained in the source `DataSet` object is used to create a new row in the `Orders` table of the `Supplier` database:

```
        // Go through each row that has to be inserted
        foreach (DataRow r in d.Tables[0].Rows)
        {
            DataRow newRow = ds.Tables[0].NewRow();
            newRow["ID_PRODUCT"] = r["ID_PRODUCT"];
            newRow["QUANTITY_ORDERED"] = r["QUANTITY"];
            newRow["ID_CUSTOMER"] = iCustomerID;
            ds.Tables[0].Rows.Add(newRow);
        }
```

Finally, the code creates a `CommandBuilder` object that automatically generates every SQL statement to insert, update, and delete records from the table. Then the `DataAdapter` object is used to update the database with the `DataSet` changes that will be returned to the calling application if no errors occur. Before that, the private `UpdateQuantity()` method is used to update the quantity of the product, subtracting the required quantity to obtain the available one:

```
        // Update the database with new records
        OleDbCommandBuilder cm = new OleDbCommandBuilder(da);
        da.Update(ds.GetChanges());

        // Update the available quantity
```

```
            UpdateQuantity(d);

            // Return
            return ds.GetChanges();

      }
      catch
      {
            return null;
      }
}
```

We now arrive at the main code where the mapping mechanism is used to map DataSet columns to the Orders table contained in the PetLovers database. As you can see from the following figure, the field names of the Orders table are different from those contained in the DataSet returned from the Web service. This is a typical case where the mapping mechanism is useful to store the information without changing the table structure:

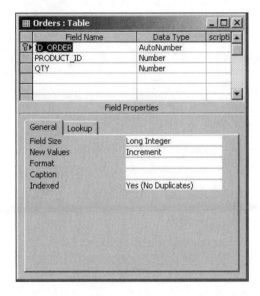

The code starts by creating a connection object pointing to the local database, and a DataAdapter object that will be used to update the database. Here we use the SELECT statement to inform the DataAdapter about the DataSet structure, but not to fill it:

```
private void InsertOrder(DataSet d)
{
    // Create a new connection object pointing to PetLovers DB
    OleDbConnection dbConn = new
        OleDbConnection("Provider=Microsoft.Jet.OLEDB.4.0;Password=;User
            ID=Admin;Data Source=F:\\PetLovers.mdb");

    // Create a data adapter used to store the information in the DB
    OleDbDataAdapter da = new OleDbDataAdapter("SELECT
        ID_ORDER,PRODUCT_ID,QTY FROM Orders",dbConn);
```

The code goes on to create the mapped columns that will be used by the `Update()` method during the database updating process. The first parameter of the `DataColumnMapping` object's constructor is equal to the physical table's column in the local database. The second parameter is equal to the column of the `DataSet` retrieved from the Web service. The `DataTableMapping` object is then created, using the constructor that accepts an array of mapped columns:

```
// Map table columns to the dataset columns
DataColumnMapping[] dcm = { new
    DataColumnMapping("PRODUCT_ID","ID_PRODUCT"),
    new DataColumnMapping("QTY","QUANTITY_ORDERED")};

// Create a new table mapping object
DataTableMapping dtm = new DataTableMapping("Table","Table",dcm);
```

The `DataAdapter` class contains two properties, `MissingMappingAction` and `MissingSchemaAction`, that are useful to inform the code about the action to take when there is either a mapping column or an element in the XML schema that cannot be found in the `DataSet` object. In the code below, every column not declared as a mapped column will be ignored.

```
// Inform the application about the action to undertake
// whether a missing mapped column or a missing schema
// is found in the dataset
da.MissingMappingAction = MissingMappingAction.Ignore;
da.MissingSchemaAction = MissingSchemaAction.Ignore;
```

Finally, the code starts the mapping mechanism before calling the `Update` method, which will insert the new record in the local database:

```
// Start the mapping mechanism
da.TableMappings.Add(dtm);

// Update the database
OleDbCommandBuilder cm = new OleDbCommandBuilder(da);
da.Update(d);
}
```

Summary

In this chapter we have seen how to use mapping to make code easier to read and modify, and how to map column and table names so that data can be passed easily between different data sources.

We started by reviewing how to use the `AS` keyword in SQL, which is a simple but inflexible way to achieve column mappings.

We then moved on to looking at the ADO.NET mapping objects, with the `DataAdapter` object's `ColumnMappings` property, and the `DataColumnMapping` and `DataTableMapping` classes.

Finally we built a client-server application using a Web service and windows forms application to demonstrate mapping in action.

12

Making a Data
Services Component

Here we are again, another chapter on making a Data Services component, sometimes called a Data Application Layer (DAL) component. If you are reading this book you are probably all too familiar with what a DAL component is and have probably contributed to or developed an entire one by yourself.

If you are not familiar with them, here's a summary: it is one layer within an n-tier (multi-tier) application that encapsulates data access. We will not be going into great detail on what the Data Layer is or n–tier architecture, but we will be showing you how to create a DAL component for .NET applications.

The coming of .NET has made the development, organization, and distribution of DAL components a very simple process because of features like the common language runtime (CLR), base class libraries (BCL), and the "all-in-one" development environment, Visual Studio .NET!

In this chapter you will learn how to develop, compile, deploy, and use a DAL component using .NET – specifically we will be covering the following topics:

❑ What is a DAL and why use one?

❑ How to build a DAL component

❑ How to deploy a DAL component

❑ How to use the DAL in a Web Form and a Web Service

❑ Performance and optimization tips through Object Pooling and Database Transactions

By the end of this chapter you will have a firm grasp on how to develop Data Service components in a .NET development environment. The following list contains everything you will need and need to do to complete this chapter. You will notice that you should have Microsoft SQL Server, Microsoft Access, and a System DSN. We'll be using all three of these so that you will see how to connect to a data store using all three of the present .NET Data Providers: `Sql`, `OleDb`, and `Odbc`.

Things you will need for this chapter:

❑ Microsoft SQL Server with the `Northwind` sample database installed, for the `SqlClient` examples.

❑ Microsoft Access `Northwind` database, for the `OleDb` examples.

❑ A System DSN setup going to the SQL Server Northwind database, for `ODBC` examples.

❑ ODBC .NET Data Provider Installed – after you download and install the ODBC .NET Data Provider please read the next section and follow the directions to add a reference to the new provider in the `machine.config` file. You can download the ODBC .NET Data Provider from http://msdn.microsoft.com/downloads/default.asp?
URL=/code/sample.asp?url=/MSDN–FILES/027/001/668/msdncompositedoc.xml – if for some reason this link doesn't work, just go to the Microsoft download center and search for ODBC .NET.

❑ ASP.NET installed and configured on a .NET-compatible operating system.

Installing ODBC .NET

Once you have finished downloading and installing ODBC .NET, open up your `machine.config` file, found at `C:\WINNT\Microsoft.NET\Framework\v1.0.2914\CONFIG` – note: you might have more than one directory with a version number – you'll want to use the newest version. In this example I am using version V1.0.2914

Once you have the `machine.config` file open, go to the following section and add a reference to the `System.Data.Odbc` assembly as seen in the following XML:

```
<configuration>
    <system.web>
        <compilation debug="false" explicit="true" defaultLanguage="vb">
            <assemblies>
                <add assembly="mscorlib"/>
                <add assembly="System, Version=1.0.2411.0, Culture=neutral,
                    PublicKeyToken=b77a5c561934e089"/>
                <add assembly="System.Web, Version=1.0.2411.0, Culture=neutral,
                    PublicKeyToken=b03f5f7f11d50a3a"/>
                <add assembly="System.Data, Version=1.0.2411.0, Culture=neutral,
                    PublicKeyToken=b77a5c561934e089"/>
                <add assembly="System.Data.Odbc, Version=1.0.2411.0,
                    Culture=neutral, PublicKeyToken=b77a5c561934e089"/>
                <add assembly="System.Web.Services, Version=1.0.2411.0,
                    Culture=neutral, PublicKeyToken=b03f5f7f11d50a3a"/>
                <add assembly="System.Xml, Version=1.0.2411.0, Culture=neutral,
                    PublicKeyToken=b77a5c561934e089"/>
```

```
            <add assembly="System.Drawing, Version=1.0.2411.0,
                Culture=neutral, PublicKeyToken=b03f5f7f11d50a3a"/>
            <add assembly="*"/>
        </assemblies>
    </compilation>
  </system.web>
</configuration>
```

Now save and close the file.

What is a Data Service Component and Why Use It?

Many "new generation" developers have not being developing for a large number of years and can't develop in assembly code. This fact comes with many problems, but also many benefits. A big benefit is that systems designers develop solutions that solve the problem in a logical way, rather than tying the solution tightly to the system architecture. Object Orientation and n-tier development are ways of solving problems in a solution-centered way. In this section we will introduce a high level look at what n-tier architecture is, where DAL components fit into the picture, and some of the benefits of using DAL components.

There are a few things that have been introduced over the years that have been really exciting: n–tier software architecture getting more robust, newer and better Windows operating systems to run programs on, XML, and now .NET – the logical next step – and in this chapter we are going to be using each one of these ... how convenient!

We often assume that most developers know what a "Data Services" or "Data Layer" component is. However, NOT everyone knows what one is or they might have heard of it, but don't really have a firm grasp of the concept – to this end, here is a short section to give you an overview of what a DAL component is and some of its many benefits. By no means will this section tell you everything you should know, but it will get you going in the right direction.

What is the Data Service Component?

The Data Service Components is a third+ tier object that encapsulates data access for any application that needs to access data from a data store. What does this mean? As the following diagram illustrates, you will have one or more DAL components that one or more applications use for all data access, resulting in absolute control over how data is accessed. The diagram consists of three levels or tiers. The first is the "Presentation Layer", which would be the user interfaces – for example, a Console Application GUI or a Web Application's web page. The next layer contains business rules, which would consist of routines that do things like data validation or formatting. Then comes the "Data Services Layer", which consists of routines to manipulate data from backend data stores such as a Microsoft SQL Server database. An important thing to note is that this model can be on a single machine (known as logical layers) or multiple machines (known as physical layers):

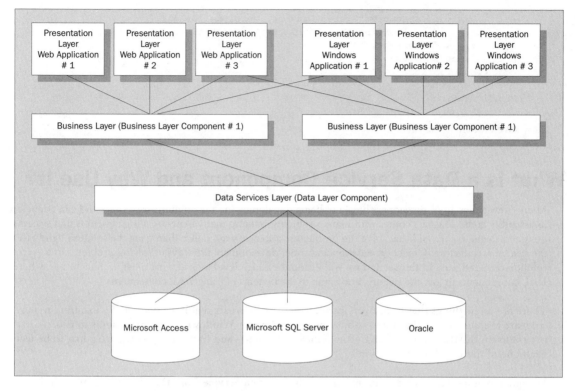

As the proceeding diagram illustrates the Data Services Layer is completely separated from both the business layer and presentation layer. What this means to you as a developer and designer is that you can have one DAL component that is used by multiple business layer objects and in turn can be used by many different applications.

What are the Benefits?

DAL components are located in a centralized location and one or more applications use them. This is of great benefit, because there is now a centralized place for application updates. For instance, say that your company decides to switch the backend database from Oracle to Microsoft SQL Server 2000 to take advantage of its vast XML support. As all of your data access is done in one place, you will only have to change, edit, or add features in the DAL component, rather than every application that connects to this database as long as the DAL component's interface doesn't change

Another benefit is your ability to control all database activity. Instead of 15 applications all connecting to your database from different locations and in different ways, you can create one component that connects to your database and control what type of data can be returned to clients. For instance, in this chapter we are going to make a component that will only return a DataSet, DataReaders, or an XmlDataDocument, and nothing else. Some benefits of using a DAL component are:

❑ Centralized code – if you need to make a code change you only make it in one place

❑ Security – you control how connections are made to a database and what type of data can be returned from the data store

❑ Performance – one way it improves performance is by ensuring that components use specific technologies such as object pooling and connection pooling

❑ Ease of maintenance

Creating a Data Service Component

In this section we are going to jump right into building our Data Application Layer component, but first let's see a description of the component. Our DAL component encapsulates all classes used for data access into one place. The component is universal and can be used to connect to any database supported by .NET – SQL, OleDb, ODBC (still in beta so database support is limited). There are two classes in this example and two enumerations – the following diagram illustrates the basic structure of the DataLayer namespace:

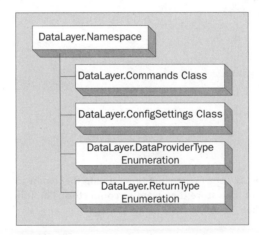

❑ ConfigSections – This class is used to set up configuration data used by the Commands class to execute database commands. For example, a connection string for database access.

❑ Commands– used to execute commands against the database.

❑ DataProviderType enumeration – used to set what type of data provider to use.

❑ ReturnType enumeration – used to set what type of data object to return from queries.

The Data Service Component

Before we jump into making our DAL component, let's go over its features. Many enterprise-level applications these days need access to many types of data store (for example, databases). For this reason our DAL component will have features that enable it to connect to not only SQL Server using the SQL .NET Data Provider, but also any database supported by the OleDb .NET Data Provider and Odbc .NET Data Provider. As you will see in the code example this is easily accomplished by taking advantage of the IDbConnection interface.

The second feature we need is the ability for the client (any object that uses the DAL component) to execute not only stored procedures, but also straight SQL text. To accommodate this we will take advantage of constructor overloading – creating multiple constructors of a class with different arguments (parameters).

The third feature we needed was the ability for the DAL component to return multiple types of data. For instance, in one situation the client may need a `DataSet` and in another a `DataReader` object (`SqlDataReader`).

So now that you have an overview of the component, let's take a look at the code for the component. The following are our enumerations for the component – we are going over these first because they are used in the other two classes:

The DataLayer Namespace – Public Enumerators

File – `\CSharp\DataLayer\codebase\DataLayer_Enums.cs`:

```csharp
public enum ReturnType {

  DataSetType,
  DataReaderType,
  XmlDocumentType

}

public enum DataProviderType {

  Sql,
  OleDb,
  Odbc

}
```

These enumerators enable the user to set what type of data they want to return from a database query and to indicate what type of data store they want to connect to. The following two tables list all the enumeration values and their descriptions:

`ReturnType` enumeration:

Enumeration Value	Type Returned	Description
IDataReaderType	DataReader	A `SqlDataReader`, `OleDbDataReader`, or `OdbcDataReader` will be returned
XmlDocumentType	XmlDataDocument	An `XmlDataDocument` will be returned
DataSetType	DataSet	A `DataSet` will be returned

`DataProviderType` enumeration:

Enumeration Value	Provider Used	Description
Sql	SQL Data Provider	The SQL Data Provider will be used
OleDb	OleDb Data Provider	The OleDb Data Provider will be used
Odbc	ODBC Data Provider	The ODBC Data Provider will be used

The ConfigSettings Class – Public Properties

The ConfigSettings class is used to configure the DAL components settings and must be initialized before any methods are called in this component, because it is used by the other classes' methods to create database connections and execute commands. The client uses this class to set connection strings that should be used, and SQL commands to execute. The following is the code for this class:

File – \CSharp\DataLayer\codebase\DataLayer_Initializer.cs:

```
using System;
using System.Data;
using System.Data.OleDb;
using System.Data.Odbc;
using System.Data.SqlClient;

namespace DataLayer {

 public class ConfigSettings {

  private string _ConnectionString;
  private object _DBCommand;
  private DataProviderType _DataStore;

  public string ConnectionString { // Used by Commands class to create
                                   // connection object

   set {
    _ConnectionString = value;
   }

   get {
    return _ConnectionString;
   }

  }

  public object DBCommand { // Command object to execute against database

   set {
    _DBCommand = value;
   }

   get {
```

```
      return _DBCommand;
    }

  }

  public DataProviderType DataStore { // Used by Commands class to determine
                                      //  .NET Data Provider to use

   set {
    _DataStore = value;
   }

   get {
    return _DataStore;
   }

  }
```

There are three properties in this class:

❑   ConnectionString – used to set the connection string that should be used to connect to a database – its value should be a string.

❑   DBCommand – used to set the SQL Statement or Command to execute against the database. The DBCommand is of the type object: a valid command object such as a SqlCommand, or a string value with the SQL statement can be used.

❑   DataStore – indicates what type of database to connect to. The value for DataStore will be one of the DatabaseType enumeration values that we saw previously.

The ConfigSettings Class – Public Constructors

```
  public ConfigSettings(string ConnectionString, object CommandObject,
DataProviderType DataStore) {

   _ConnectionString = ConnectionString;
   _DBCommand = CommandObject;
   _DataStore = DataStore;

  } // end DataLayer.ConfigSettings.ConfigSettings Constructor 1

  public ConfigSettings(string ConnectionString, string CommandText,
DataProviderType DataStore) {

   _ConnectionString = ConnectionString;

   switch (DataStore) {

    case DataProviderType.Sql:
     _DBCommand = new SqlCommand(CommandText);
     break;

    case DataProviderType.OleDb:
```

```
        _DBCommand = new OleDbCommand(CommandText);
        break;

    case DataProviderType.Odbc:
        _DBCommand = new OdbcCommand(CommandText);
        break;

    }

    _DataStore = DataStore;

    } // end DataLayer.ConfigSettings.ConfigSettings Constructor 2

    } // end DataLayer.ConfigSettings

} // end DataLayer
```

As previously mentioned the `ConfigSettings` class has two public constructors. The only difference between the two is the second parameter. The following table describes each overload, the parameter list, and a description of that particular constructor's modus operandi.

`ConfigSettings` Overload 1:

public ConfigSettings (string ConnectionString, object CommandObject, DatabaseType DataStore)	
string ConnectionString	The connection string that should be used to connect to the data store. Example: server=localhost;trusted_connection=true;database= northwind
object CommandObject	A valid command object (SqlCommand, OleDbCommand, OdbcCommand)
DataProviderType DataStore	A value from the DataProviderType enumeration. (See DataLayer_Enums.cs.)

`ConfigSettings` Overload 2:

public ConfigSettings(string ConnectionString, string CommandText, DatabaseType DataStore)	
string ConnectionString	The connection string that should be used to connect to the data store. Example: server=localhost;trusted_connection=true;database= northwind
string CommandText	A valid SQL Statement: SELECT * FROM Products. Within the constructor it is converted to the appropriate Command object based on the DataBaseType value.
DataProviderType DataStore	A value from the DataProviderType enumeration. (See DataLayer_Enums.cs.)

The Commands Class – Public ExecuteQuery Method

The Commands class is where all database activity happens and is completely dependent on the ConfigSettings class for execution. Remember that the ConfigSettings class contains the connection string that should be used to connect to the database, and what type of database to connect to. The following code example contains the method that is used to return data back to the client and is called the ExecuteQuery method.

File – \CSharp\DataLayer\codebase\DataLayer_Commands.cs:

```csharp
using System;
using System.Data;
using System.Data.OleDb;
using System.Data.SqlClient;
using System.Data.Odbc;
using System.Xml;
using System.Web;


namespace DataLayer {

 public class Commands {

   private IDbConnection GenericConnection;
   private IDbDataAdapter GenericDataAdapter;
   private DataSet DSQueryReturn = new DataSet();

   public object ExecuteQuery(ConfigSettings Configuration,
     ReturnType ReturnType)
   {

    try {

     Connection(Configuration);
     ((IDbCommand)Configuration.DBCommand).Connection = GenericConnection;

     switch (ReturnType) {

      case ReturnType.DataSetType:

       switch (Configuration.DataStore) {

        case DataProviderType.Sql:

         GenericDataAdapter = new
           SqlDataAdapter((SqlCommand)Configuration.DBCommand);
         break;

        case DataProviderType.OleDb:

         GenericDataAdapter = new
           OleDbDataAdapter((OleDbCommand)Configuration.DBCommand);
         break;

        case DataProviderType.Odbc:
```

```
            GenericDataAdapter = new
              OdbcDataAdapter((OdbcCommand)Configuration.DBCommand);
            break;
        }

        GenericDataAdapter.Fill(DSQueryReturn);
        GenericConnection.Close();
        return DSQueryReturn;

      case ReturnType.DataReaderType:

        return ((IDbCommand)Configuration.DBCommand).ExecuteReader
          (CommandBehavior.CloseConnection);

      case ReturnType.XmlDocumentType:

        switch (Configuration.DataStore) {

          case DataProviderType.Sql:
            GenericDataAdapter = new SqlDataAdapter
              ((SqlCommand)Configuration.DBCommand);
            break;

          case DataProviderType.OleDb:
            GenericDataAdapter = new OleDbDataAdapter
              ((OleDbCommand)Configuration.DBCommand);
            break;

          case DataProviderType.Odbc:
            GenericDataAdapter = new OdbcDataAdapter
              ((OdbcCommand)Configuration.DBCommand);
            break;

        }

        GenericDataAdapter.Fill(DSQueryReturn);
        XmlDataDocument XmlDDoc = new XmlDataDocument(DSQueryReturn);
        GenericConnection.Close();
        return XmlDDoc;

      }

      throw new ApplicationException("Parameter Types Are Incorrect");

    } catch (Exception E) {

      HttpContext.Current.Trace.Write("An Exception Occurred in the"
        + "ExecuteQuery Method: ", E.Message.ToString());
      return E;

    }

  }
```

The ExecuteQuery method has two parameters and is used to execute queries that return data. The first parameter is the ConfigSettings object we discussed in the previous section, and the second is a value from the ReturnType enumeration. Recall that the ReturnType value can be a DataSet, DataReader, or an XmlDataDocument. The first thing that happens in this method is that the Connection method is invoked, which makes the connection to the desired database – this method will be discussed in the next section. After a valid connection has been made, a switch statement is executed based on the ReturnType value. We'll go over each individual case next.

Case DataSet

When the client requests a DataSet as the data object that the ExecuteQuery method should return, the following code is executed:

```
switch (ReturnType) {

 case ReturnType.DataSetType:

  switch (Configuration.DataStore) {

   case DataProviderType.Sql:

    GenericDataAdapter = new SqlDataAdapter
      ((SqlCommand)Configuration.DBCommand);
    break;

   case DataProviderType.OleDb:

    GenericDataAdapter = new OleDbDataAdapter
      ((OleDbCommand)Configuration.DBCommand);
    break;

   case DataProviderType.Odbc:

    GenericDataAdapter = new OdbcDataAdapter
      ((OdbcCommand)Configuration.DBCommand);
    break;
  }

  GenericDataAdapter.Fill(DSQueryReturn);
  GenericConnection.Close();
  return DSQueryReturn;
```

We will use a DataAdapter to create the DataSet to return, so the first thing to do is a SELECT CASE statement based on the Configuration.DataStore value (recall that this value is going to be a value of the DatabaseType enumeration) and, depending on the data store, a corresponding DataAdapter is created. After the SELECT CASE statement, we invoke the Fill method to populate the DataSet; next we invoke the Close method for our active connection (in order to take advantage of connection pooling always close your connection objects); finally, we return the DataSet.

Case DataReader

When the client requests a DataReader as the data object to return, the following code is executed:

```
case ReturnType.DataReaderType:
```

```
return ((IDbCommand)Configuration.DBCommand).ExecuteReader
   (CommandBehavior.CloseConnection);
```

This one was easy: invoke the `ExecuteReader` method of the `Command` object.

You will notice that there is a parameter passed into this method
(`CommandBehavior.CloseConnection`) – this behavior closes our active connection after the
`Reader` has finished executing. For more information on other `CommandBehavior` values, see the
`CommandBehavior` enumeration found in the `System.Data` namespace

Case XmlDataDocumrnt

The final object that can be returned in this component is an `XmlDataDocument`. We might use the
`XmlDataDocument` because it enables us to store structured data in it, it can be loaded with either
relational data from a database or XML data, and it can be manipulated using the W3C Document
Object Model. This is important if the client needs to manipulate data on their tier:

```
case ReturnType.XmlDocumentType:

switch (Configuration.DataStore) {

  case DataProviderType.Sql:
   GenericDataAdapter = new
    SqlDataAdapter((SqlCommand)Configuration.DBCommand);
   break;

  case DataProviderType.OleDb:
   GenericDataAdapter = new
    OleDbDataAdapter((OleDbCommand)Configuration.DBCommand);
   break;

  case DataProviderType.Odbc:
   GenericDataAdapter = new
    OdbcDataAdapter((OdbcCommand)Configuration.DBCommand);
   break;

 }

 GenericDataAdapter.Fill(DSQueryReturn);
 XmlDataDocument XmlDDoc = new XmlDataDocument(DSQueryReturn);
 GenericConnection.Close();
 return XmlDDoc;

 }

 throw new ApplicationException("Parameter Types Are Incorrect");

} catch (Exception E) {

 HttpContext.Current.Trace.Write("An Exception Occurred in the ExecuteQuery"+
  Method: ", E.Message.ToString());
 return E;

 }
```

Again, a `DataAdapter` is created and a `DataSet` is created. Next we instantiate a new `XmlDataDocument` object and pass in the `DataSet` as a parameter. Then we close the active connection and return the `XmlDataDocument` object to the caller.

That's it! Can it get much easier? You can add any number of data return types; for instance, if you use a custom XML schema, you can dynamically create XML documents here, or you can return the data as an array. The possibilities are (almost) endless.

The Commands Class – Public ExecuteNonQuery Method

The `ExecuteNonQuery` method is used to execute SQL that doesn't return data. Here is the code for this method:

```
public bool ExecuteNonQuery(ConfigSettings Configuration) {

  try {

   Connection(Configuration);
   ((IDbCommand)Configuration.DBCommand).Connection = GenericConnection;
   ((IDbCommand)Configuration.DBCommand).ExecuteNonQuery();
   GenericConnection.Close();
   return true;

  } catch (Exception E) {

   HttpContext.Current.Trace.Write
     ("An Exception Occured: ", E.Message.ToString());
   return false;

  }

} // end ExecuteNonQuery
```

Again, the first thing to do is create an active connection using the `Connection` method. Next, because we haven't wired the active connection and the command object together yet, we have to set the command's `Connection` property to the active connection. All there is to do now is invoke the command object's `ExecuteNonQuery` method and close the connection. This method returns a Boolean value – true if no exceptions occurred and the SQL statement executed properly, and false if it didn't.

The Commands Class – Private Connection Method

The final method in the `Commands` class is the `Connection` method. The `Connection` method is used to create an active connection for all other methods to use to execute commands against the database. The following is the code for this method:

```
private void Connection(ConfigSettings Configuration) {

  switch (Configuration.DataStore) {

   case DataProviderType.Sql:
    GenericConnection = new SqlConnection(Configuration.ConnectionString);
    break;
```

```
        case DataProviderType.OleDb:
          GenericConnection = new
            OleDbConnection(Configuration.ConnectionString);
          break;

        case DataProviderType.Odbc:
          GenericConnection = new OdbcConnection(Configuration.ConnectionString);
          break;

      }


      try {

        GenericConnection.Open();

      } catch (Exception E) {

        HttpContext.Current.Trace.Write
          ("An Exception Occured: ", E.Message.ToString());

      }

    } // end Connection
  } // end DataLayer.Commands
} // end DataLayer
```

Again, we use the value of `Configuration.DataStore` to create a `Connection` object based on the database type. Then the connection object's `Open` method is invoked and the routine is finished.

Creating an Assembly Information File

An assembly information file can be used to create an identity or Evidence of an assembly. Evidence is information that the CLR uses to make decisions on security policies. As you will see in the following code example there are many different types of evidence, for example a strong name, publisher, or the application directory. Assembly information files can also be used to set assembly characteristics or attributes such as culture, title, version, and copyright information. For more assembly attributes see the `System.Reflection` namespace.

The following code is one way – create a new file named
`\CSharp\DataLayer\codebase\DataLayer_AssemblyInfo.cs` and add the following code:

```
using System;
using System.Reflection;
using System.Runtime.InteropServices;

[assembly: AssemblyTitle("DataLayer")]
[assembly: AssemblyDescription("DAL Component")]
[assembly: AssemblyCompany("M7")]
[assembly: CLSCompliant(true)]
[Assembly: AssemblyVersion("1.0.*")]
```

If you are using Visual Studio .NET you can add a new Assembly Information File by going to Project | Add New File | Assembly Information File – all of the classes listed are members of the System.Reflection namespace. The main attribute we are concerned with here is AssemblyVersion – this is how we will distinguish one DataLayer assembly from another. I used the value 1.0.0.*, where 1 is the major version, 0 is the minor version, 0 is the build, and * is the revision. Using * will cause the build to be equal to the number of seconds since midnight that day.

Compiling the Data Service Component

If you wish to compile this code as is and test it, you can use the following code either directly in the command prompt or by creating a .bat file and placing it in the same directory as the class files for this project:

File – \CSharp\DataLayer\codebase\make.BAT:

```
csc.exe /target:library /out:..\..\bin\Wrox.DataLayer.CSharp.DLL *.cs
/r:System.dll /r:System.Data.dll /r:System.Xml.dll /r:System.Web.dll
/r:System.Data.Odbc.Dll /r:System.EnterpriseServices.DLL
pause

@ REM We'll use this in a moment to put the assembly in the GAC
@ REM gacutil.exe /i ..\..\bin\Wrox.DataLayer.CSharp.DLL
@ REM pause
```

Wrox.DataLayer.CSharp.dll will be created in the application's /bin directory.

Recall that, in the previous section, we created an Assembly Information File: let's take a look at what that did. Locate Wrox.DataLayer.CSharp.dll in the application's /bin directory, right-click on it, and go to the Version tab of the dialog box. You'll see something similar to the following:

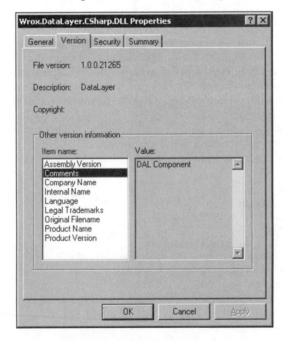

You'll notice in the previous figure that there is a version and description for the DAL component. Also note that the last set of numbers in the version number were automatically generated using the number of seconds since midnight the day it was compiled.

Even though we have compiled our DAL component into an assembly you can use by placing it into an application's /bin directory, it isn't accessible machine-wide yet. In the next section, we'll be illustrating how to deploy this component into the Global Assembly Cache, or GAC, which enables any application on the machine to access the same assembly.

Deploying a Data Service Component

Deploying a solution developed by utilizing the .NET framework is a very easy task, due to the very nature of .NET – the use of self–describing components and a Common Language Runtime (CLR). We aren't going to go into every aspect of packaging and deploying a .NET application, because all we are concerned with is deploying our DAL component.

There are two categories of assemblies with regards to distribution: Private and Shared. A private assembly will be located within an application's directory structure: the /bin directory. However, what is the use of this if multiple applications need to use the object, as with our component? This is where the Global Assembly Cache, or GAC, and shared assemblies come into play.

The Global Assembly Cache – (GAC)

The GAC is an assembly cache that is accessible machine-wide. What this means is that it is accessible from an ASP.NET application, a Windows Form application, a Web Service, or any other .NET application running on the machine. There are several advantages to installing assemblies in the GAC:

❑ Components are located in a centralized location

❑ Components are secure – you must be an administrator on the machine to install or manipulate any assemblies in the GAC

❑ Side-by-Side Versioning – you can have multiple versions of the same assembly running side by side

Before you can install a component into the GAC, there are some things you must do and attributes that your component must possess. Your assembly must be a Strong-Named assembly. A Strong-Name is essentially your assembly's identity – that is, what distinguishes it from all other assemblies. No two assemblies can have the same name. A strong name can include information about your assembly's name, version, public key, and a digital signature.

A public and private key pair is used to create an assembly's strong name and this key-pair file is used during the component's compilation to create its strong name. Microsoft has included a utility with the .NET SDK that you can use to generate a key-pair file that will be used to sign an assembly. This tool is called the Strong Name Utility, sn.exe.

Strong Name Utility – sn.exe

We use the Strong Name tool to create a file containing a cryptographic key pair. You should be able to use sn.exe directly from the command line. It will usually be in the C:\Program Files\Microsoft.NET\FrameworkSDK\Bin folder.

The following table contains some of the more widely used features of this tool. For a complete list of features, please see the .NET SDK Help files section on "Strong Name Tool (sn.exe)" or type sn.exe /? at the command prompt:

Switch	Description
- k OutFile	Generates a new Key Pair and writes it to the specified file.
- v Assembly	Verifies the strong name for an assembly.
- e Assembly OutFile	Extracts the public key from an assembly and stores it in the specified file.
- ?	Displays all command syntax for sn.exe.

The following code snippet will automatically generate the .snk file we will be using in our example. .snk is Microsoft recommended extension-naming convention for these files.

Create and run the file \CSharp\DataLayer\codebase\strongnamemake.bat:

```
sn.exe -k C:\OurKeyPair.snk
```

Now that we have our .snk file, we have to add an attribute to our assembly to use the specified file. This is done using the AssemblyKeyFileAttribute class, as illustrated in the following code:

```
[assembly: AssemblyKeyFileAttribute("OurKeyPair.snk")]
```

Put this code in the DataLayer_AssemblyInfo.cs file and re – compile the assembly – now we are ready to install the assembly in the GAC.

Global Assembly Cache Utility – gacutil.exe

The Global Assembly Cache Utility (gacutil.exe) is used to manipulate the contents of the Global Assembly Cache (GAC) – to install, uninstall, and list.

> The GAC is usually located at C:\WINNT\assembly – be careful with this directory, because once it is lost, the only way to get it back is to reinstall the framework.

The following table contains some of the more often used commands:

Switch	Description
/i Assembly	Installs an assembly into the GAC
/u Assembly	Uninstalls an assembly from the GAC
/l	Lists the contents of the GAC
/cdl	Deletes the contents of the download cache
/?	Displays all commands

Now let's install our `DataLayer` component into the GAC. Use the following code in the command prompt window or in a `.bat` file to install it.

File – `\CSharp\DataLayer\codebase\make.BAT`:

```
csc.exe /target:library /out:..\..\bin\Wrox.DataLayer.CSharp.DLL *.cs
/r:System.dll /r:System.Data.dll /r:System.Xml.dll /r:System.Web.dll
/r:System.Data.Odbc.Dll /r:System.EnterpriseServices.DLL
pause

@ REM We'll use this in a moment to put the assembly in the GAC
gacutil.exe /i ..\..\bin\Wrox.DataLayer.CSharp.DLL
pause
```

If you are simply running the `make.bat` file then you will have to open it up in a text editor and remove `@ REM` from the last two lines, to bring it in line with the example above.

As you can see in the following figure, the assembly was added to the GAC:

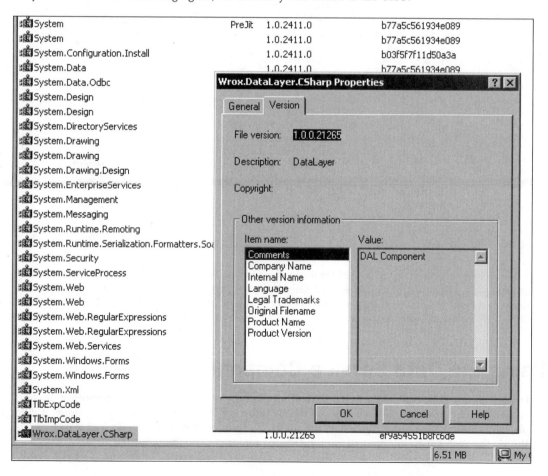

Making a Reference to DataLayer in machine.config

The final step to make before the assembly is available machine-wide is to register it by making a new entry in the `machine.config` file. The `machine.config` file can be compared to the `web.config` file found in ASP.NET applications. But the `machine.config` file includes configuration settings for an entire machine, whereas a `web.config` file includes configuration settings unique to that application.

Go ahead and open up the `machine.config` file we looked at earlier when installing the ODBC .NET Data Provider that is found in `C:\WINNT\Microsoft.NET\Framework\v1.0.2914\CONFIG`. Once you have the `machine.config` file open, go to the following section and add the highlighted entry:

```
<configuration>
    <system.web>
        <compilation debug="false" explicit="true" defaultLanguage="vb">
            <assemblies>
                <add assembly="mscorlib"/>
                <add assembly="System, Version=1.0.2411.0, Culture=neutral,
                    PublicKeyToken=b77a5c561934e089"/>
                <add assembly="System.Web, Version=1.0.2411.0, Culture=neutral,
                    PublicKeyToken=b03f5f7f11d50a3a"/>
                <add assembly="System.Data, Version=1.0.2411.0, Culture=neutral,
                    PublicKeyToken=b77a5c561934e089"/>
                <add assembly="System.Data.Odbc, Version=1.0.2411.0,
                    Culture=neutral, PublicKeyToken=b77a5c561934e089"/>
                <add assembly="System.Web.Services, Version=1.0.2411.0,
                    Culture=neutral, PublicKeyToken=b03f5f7f11d50a3a"/>
                <add assembly="System.Xml, Version=1.0.2411.0, Culture=neutral,
                    PublicKeyToken=b77a5c561934e089"/>
                <add assembly="System.Drawing, Version=1.0.2411.0,
                    Culture=neutral, PublicKeyToken=b03f5f7f11d50a3a"/>
                <add assembly="DataLayer, Version=1.0.0.21265, Culture=neutral,
                    PublicKeyToken=ef9a54551b8fc6de"/>
                <add assembly="*"/>
            </assemblies>
        </compilation>
    </system.web>
</configuration>
```

You can find the information needed for this section in the `C:\WINNT\assembly` by right-clicking on the assembly and going to properties. The `machine.config` file contains much more than what is illustrated here, but this is all that we are concerned with for this example. Notice that our added entry, `DataLayer`, includes the assembly name, `Version`, `Culture`, and `PublicKeyToken` attributes.

Using the Data Service Component

Using this new DAL component is the same from one type of .NET application to another. In this section of the chapter we will demonstrate this by using the DAL component from a couple of different places. There is code illustrating how to use the DAL component in a Web Form and a Web Service. Within the Web Form code we will use the DAL component to do the following tasks:

❏ Executing SQL INSERT, UPDATE, SELECT, and DELETE commands using SQL statements using the Sql, OleDb, and Odbc .NET Data Providers

❏ Executing SQL Stored Procedures

❏ Returning different types of data objects: DataSet, DataReader, and XmlDataDocument

You can find all the web form files (.aspx and .cs) in the CSharp\DataLayer\WebFormCode folder along with a .bat file you can use to compile the files. The compilation code can be found in the following code example:

File – \CSharp\DataLayer\WebFormCode\make.bat:

```
csc.exe /target:library /out:..\bin\Wrox.DataLayer.DLL  *.cs /r:System.dll
/r:System.Data.dll /r:System.Xml.dll /r:System.Web.dll /r:System.Data.Odbc.Dll
/r:..\bin\Wrox.DataLayer.CSharp.DLL
pause
```

Using the DAL Component in a ASP.NET Web Form

The first example illustrates how to use the DAL component from a Web Form environment. This first example illustrates how to execute a SELECT, UPDATE, DELETE, and INSERT statement using the DAL component. You must have all the requirements for the chapter as explained in the introduction for this example to work properly:

Executing SQL Text

Web Form – \CSharp\DataLayer\WebFormCode\webform.aspx:

```
<%@ Page Language="cs" TRACE="false" AutoEventWireup="true"
Codebehind="webform.aspx.cs" Inherits="Wrox.CSharp.webform"%>
<html>
  <head>
    <title></title>
  </head>
  <body>
    <form method="post" runat="server">
      <table cellpadding="4" cellspacing="0" border="0">
        <tr>
          <td>
            <asp:DropDownList ID="ddlSqlType" runat="server">
              <asp:ListItem Selected="True" Text="Pick Function" />
              <asp:ListItem Text="SELECT" Value="SELECT" />
              <asp:ListItem Text="INSERT" Value="INSERT" />
              <asp:ListItem Text="EDIT" Value="EDIT" />
              <asp:ListItem Text="DELETE" Value="DELETE" />
            </asp:DropDownList>
            <asp:DropDownList ID="ddlDataSource" runat="server">
              <asp:ListItem Selected="True" Text="Pick Data Store" />
              <asp:ListItem Text="SQL Server" Value="SqlClient" />
              <asp:ListItem Text="OleDb - Access" Value="OleDb" />
              <asp:ListItem Text="ODBC - SQL Server" Value="Odbc" />
```

```
          </asp:DropDownList>
          <asp:Button Text="Submit" Runat="server" />
        </td>
      </tr>
      <tr>
        <td>
          <asp:Label ID="lblMessage" Runat="server" font-Size="10" />
        </td>
      </tr>
      <tr>
        <td>
          <asp:DataGrid ID="DGProducts" Runat="server" Font-Size="10" />
        </td>
      </tr>
    </table>
  </form>
  </body>
</html>
```

This web form contains five server controls:

❑ A DropDownList named ddlSqlType that is used to pick what type of function to execute – SELECT, DELETE, UPDATE, or INSERT

❑ A DropDownList named ddlDataSource that is used to pick a data store – SQL Server, Access, ODBC

❑ A Button that is used to POST the page back to the server

❑ A Label that is used to display messages to users

❑ A DataGrid that is used to display the contents of the Product table – the table we are manipulating

The code behind for this page can be found in the following code example:

Code Behind – \CSharp\DataLayer\WebFormCode\webform.cs:

```
using DataLayer;
using System;
using System.Web;
using System.Web.UI.WebControls;

namespace Wrox.CSharp {

public class webform : System.Web.UI.Page {

  protected DropDownList ddlSqlType;
  protected DropDownList ddlDataSource;
  protected Label lblMessage;
  protected DataGrid DGProducts;

  protected string SqlConString =
  "server=localhost;trusted_connection=true;database=northwind";
```

```csharp
  protected string OleDbConString = "Provider=Microsoft.Jet.OLEDB.4.0;" +
"Data Source=" + HttpContext.Current.Server.MapPath("../../data/nwind.Mdb");
  protected string OdbcConString = "DSN=NorthWind;UID=Sa";

  protected string SelectCmdString = "SELECT * FROM Products";
  protected string EditCmdString = "UPDATE Products SET ProductName = 'new &
Improved ' + ProductName WHERE ProductID = 1";
  protected string InsertCmdString = "INSERT INTO Products (ProductName) VALUES
('Macks Fried Chicken')";
  protected string DeleteCmdString = "DELETE FROM Products WHERE ProductID = 87";

  protected ConfigSettings DLConfig;
  protected Commands DLCommands = new Commands();

  protected void Page_Load(object sender, EventArgs e) {

    switch (ddlSqlType.SelectedItem.Value) {

      case "SELECT":
        Show_Products();
        break;

      case "INSERT":
        Insert_Products();
        break;

      case "DELETE":
        Delete_Products();
        break;

      case "EDIT":
        Edit_Products();
        break;

      default:
        Show_Products();
        break;

    }

  } // end Page_Load

  protected void Show_Products() {

    switch (ddlDataSource.SelectedItem.Value) {

      case "SqlClient":
        DLConfig = new ConfigSettings(SqlConString, SelectCmdString,
DataProviderType.Sql);
        break;

      case "OleDb":
        DLConfig = new ConfigSettings(OleDbConString, SelectCmdString,
DataProviderType.OleDb);
```

```
      break;

   case "Odbc":
     DLConfig = new ConfigSettings(OdbcConString, SelectCmdString,
DataProviderType.Odbc);
     break;

   default:
     DLConfig = new ConfigSettings(SqlConString, SelectCmdString,
DataProviderType.Sql);
     break;

   }

   //      DATASET()
   DGProducts.DataSource = DLCommands.ExecuteQuery(DLConfig,
ReturnType.DataSetType);
   //      DATAREADER
   //      DGProducts.DataSource = DLCommands.ExecuteQuery(DLConfig,
ReturnType.DataReaderType);
   //      XMLDATADOCUMENT
   //      DGProducts.DataSource = DLCommands.ExecuteQuery(DLConfig,
ReturnType.XmlDocumentType).DataSet;
   DGProducts.DataBind();

   } // end Show_Products

   private void Edit_Products() {

   switch (ddlDataSource.SelectedItem.Value) {

    case "SqlClient":
     DLConfig = new ConfigSettings(SqlConString, EditCmdString,
DataProviderType.Sql);
     break;

    case "OleDb":
     DLConfig = new ConfigSettings(OleDbConString, EditCmdString,
DataProviderType.OleDb);
     break;

    case "Odbc":
     DLConfig = new ConfigSettings(OdbcConString, EditCmdString,
DataProviderType.Odbc);
     break;
    }

   lblMessage.Text = "The Row Was Updated: " +
DLCommands.ExecuteNonQuery(DLConfig).ToString();
   Show_Products();

   } // end Edit_Products

   protected void Insert_Products() {
```

```csharp
    switch (ddlDataSource.SelectedItem.Value) {

      case "SqlClient":
       DLConfig = new ConfigSettings(SqlConString, InsertCmdString,
DataProviderType.Sql);
       break;

      case "OleDb":
       DLConfig = new ConfigSettings(OleDbConString, InsertCmdString,
DataProviderType.OleDb);
       break;

      case "Odbc":
       DLConfig = new ConfigSettings(OdbcConString, InsertCmdString,
DataProviderType.Odbc);
       break;

     }

     lblMessage.Text = "The Row Was Inserted: " +
DLCommands.ExecuteNonQuery(DLConfig).ToString();
     Show_Products();

   } // end Insert_Products

  protected void Delete_Products() {

    switch (ddlDataSource.SelectedItem.Value) {

      case "SqlClient":
       DLConfig = new ConfigSettings(SqlConString, DeleteCmdString,
DataProviderType.Sql);
       break;

      case "OleDb":
       DLConfig = new ConfigSettings(OleDbConString, DeleteCmdString,
DataProviderType.OleDb);
       break;

      case "Odbc":
       DLConfig = new ConfigSettings(OdbcConString, DeleteCmdString,
DataProviderType.Odbc);
       break;

     }

     lblMessage.Text = "The Row Was Deleted: " +
DLCommands.ExecuteNonQuery(DLConfig).ToString();
     Show_Products();

   } // end Delete_Products
 } // end webform
} // end Wrox.CSharp
```

In the code behind for this web form, variables containing connection strings are created for all three data stores and SQL statements are created for each of the SQL commands that are going to be executed. Within the `Page.Load` event handler there is a SELECT CASE statement that is used to invoke a particular method within the class. There are a total of four methods: `Show_Products`, `Edit_Products`, `Insert_Products`, and `Delete_Products`.

❑ `Show_Products`
The `Show_Products` method determines what type of database to connect to. It initializes a new instance of the `ConfigSettings` class with the proper parameters, SQL command, and connection for the chosen database type. Next, the `DataGrid.DataSource` is set to the result of the `Commands.ExecuteQuery` method. You'll notice that there is code there for each of the three types of data objects that can be returned by the method – I recommend trying all three.

❑ `Edit_Products`
Again, a new instance of `ConfigSettings` is created with the proper parameters and then the `Commands.ExecuteNonQuery` method is invoked; recall that this method returns a Boolean value – `true` or `false`. The `Label` control named `lblMessage` is used to display a message of whether or not the edit was successful.

The SQL UPDATE statement used inserted "New And Improved" in front of the value of the `ProductName` field for the row within the `Products` table with a `ProductID` value of 1. You may have to change the `ProductID` value in your database before executing this. After executing this SQL statement you might want to change the value back to its original form.

❑ `Insert_Products`
We need to insert a product before we can delete one, because we don't want to delete one of the example products. The `Insert_Products` method inserts a new row into the `Products` table with a `ProductName` of "Mack's Fried Chicken". Because the `ProductID` column is an auto-generated value, we don't have to worry about it.

The code in this method is identical to the `Edit_Products` method, except for the value of the `CommandText` parameter (the SQL statement).

❑ `Delete_Products`
The final method is `Delete_Products` and it is used in this example to delete the row that was inserted using the `Insert_Products` method. You will have to get the value of the `ProductID` column of that row and insert it in the SQL statement found as the value of the `DeleteCmdString` variable. For example:

```
Protected DeleteCmdString As String = "DELETE FROM Products WHERE
ProductID = new ProductID Value"
```

Everything else in this method is exactly the same as the previous two methods.

The following figure is an illustration of this page after a postback doing an INSERT using SQL Server as a database. Notice the new row added:

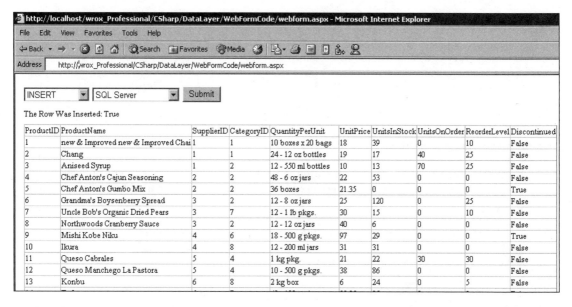

Now that you have seen how to use the DAL component to execute SQL statements using text-based SQL statements, let's see how to execute stored procedures using command objects – `SqlCommand`, `OleDbCommand`, and `OdbcCommand`.

Executing Stored Procedures

The following code example illustrates how to use the DAL component to execute stored procedures.

File – \CSharp\WebFormCode\WebFormStoredProcedure.aspx.aspx:

```
<%@ Page Language="c#" trace="false" AutoEventWireup="true"
Codebehind="WebFormStoredProcedure.aspx.cs"
Inherits="Wrox.CSharp.WebFormStoredProcedure"%>
<html>
  <head>
    <title></title>
  </head>
  <body>
    <form method="post" runat="server">
      <table cellpadding="4" cellspacing="0" border="0">
        <tr>
          <td>
            <asp:DropDownList ID="ddlDataSource" runat="server">
            <asp:ListItem Selected="True" Text="Pick Data Store" />
            <asp:ListItem Text="SQL Server" Value="SqlClient" />
            <asp:ListItem Text="OleDb - Access" Value="OleDb" />
            <asp:ListItem Text="ODBC - SQL Server" Value="Odbc" />
          </asp:DropDownList>
          <asp:Button Text="Submit" Runat="server" ID="Button1" />
        </td>
        <tr>
```

```
        <td>
            <asp:DataGrid Runat="server" ID="dgProducts" font-size="8" />
        </td>
    </tr>
  </table>
 </form>
</body>
</html>
```

In this web form there are three server controls:

❑ A `DropDownList` named `ddlDataSource`, which is used to pick what type of database to use – the same three data stores are used in this example that were used in the first example

❑ A `Button` that is used to submit the form back to the server

❑ A `DataGrid` that is used to display the results of the stored procedures

Let's take a look at the code behind for this web form:

File – `\CSharp\WebFormCode\WebFormStoredProcedure.aspx.cs`:

```
using DataLayer;
using System;
using System.Web;
using System.Web.UI.WebControls;
using System.Data;
using System.Data.SqlClient;
using System.Data.Odbc;
using System.Data.OleDb;

namespace Wrox.CSharp {

 public  class WebFormStoredProcedure : System.Web.UI.Page {

   protected DropDownList ddlDataSource;
   protected DataGrid dgProducts;

   protected string SqlConString =
"server=localhost;trusted_connection=true;database=northwind";
   protected string OleDbConString = "Provider=Microsoft.Jet.OLEDB.4.0;" +
"Data Source=" + HttpContext.Current.Server.MapPath("../../data/nwind.Mdb");
   protected string OdbcConString = "DSN=NorthWind;UID=Sa";

   protected ConfigSettings DLConfig;
   protected Commands DLCommand = new Commands();

   protected void Page_Load(object sender, EventArgs e) {

     switch (ddlDataSource.SelectedItem.Value) {

       case "SqlClient":
        Sql_StoredProcedure();
```

```
      break;

    case "OleDb":
     OleDb_StoredProcedure();
      break;

    case"Odbc":
     Odbc_StoredProcedure();
      break;
    }
  } // end Page_Load

  protected void OleDb_StoredProcedure() {

    OleDbCommand cmd = new OleDbCommand();
    cmd.CommandText = "[Invoices Filter]";
    cmd.CommandType = CommandType.StoredProcedure;
    cmd.Parameters.Add("@OrderID", OleDbType.Integer).Value = "10895";
    DLConfig = new ConfigSettings(OleDbConString, cmd, DataProviderType.OleDb);

    dgProducts.DataSource = DLCommand.ExecuteQuery(DLConfig,
ReturnType.DataReaderType);
    dgProducts.DataBind();

  } // end OleDb_StoredProcedure

  protected void Odbc_StoredProcedure() {

    OdbcCommand cmd = new OdbcCommand();
    cmd.CommandText = "{ call CustOrderHist(?) }";
    cmd.CommandType = CommandType.StoredProcedure;
    cmd.Parameters.Add("@CustomerID", OdbcType.VarChar, 200).Value = "ALFKI";
    DLConfig = new ConfigSettings(OdbcConString, cmd, DataProviderType.Odbc);

    dgProducts.DataSource = DLCommand.ExecuteQuery(DLConfig,
ReturnType.DataReaderType);
    dgProducts.DataBind();

  } // end Odbc_StoredProcedure

  protected void Sql_StoredProcedure() {

    SqlCommand cmd = new SqlCommand();
    cmd.CommandText = "CustOrderHist";
    cmd.CommandType = CommandType.StoredProcedure;
    cmd.Parameters.Add("@CustomerID", SqlDbType.VarChar, 200).Value = "ALFKI";
    DLConfig = new ConfigSettings(SqlConString, cmd, DataProviderType.Sql);

    dgProducts.DataSource = DLCommand.ExecuteQuery(DLConfig,
ReturnType.DataReaderType);
    dgProducts.DataBind();

  } // end Sql_StoredProcedure
 } // end Wrox.CSharp.WebFormStoredProcedure
} // end Wrox.CSharp
```

There are three methods used to execute the stored procedures against the designated database: `OleDb_StoredProcedure`, `Odbc_StoredProcedure`, and `Sql_StoredProcedure`. The `SELECT CASE` statement found in the `Page.Load` event handler determines which one to invoke. Let's look at them:

❑ `OleDb_StoredProcedure`

In this method, a new `OleDbCommand` is initialized and its properties set. Notice that there is a syntax change in the naming of the stored procedure. This is because there is a space in the name. (Note: syntax rules apply for different databases, even when using the command objects. This will be even more evident in the next section.) After the creation of the `OleDbCommand` object, using the DAL component is exactly the same as in the `Sql_StoredProcedure` method (see section later).

❑ `Odbc_StoredProcedure`

In this method, a new `OdbcCommand` is created. Notice the syntax of the `OdbcCommand.CommandText` property is that of traditional ODBC commands – these commands are specific to ODBC and are not likely to change soon and must be used, but as you see, setting the values for the parameters is exactly the same as with the rest of the code for this method compared to the other two methods.

❑ `Sql_StoredProcedure`

A new `SqlCommand` object is initialized and its properties set – stored procedure name, and parameters. Then a new `ConfigSettings` object is initialized using the `SqlCommand` object as the second parameter – `CommandObject` – and the `Commands.ExecuteQuery` method is invoked and set as the `DataGrid.DataSource`. Note: you can use a `SqlCommand` or any of the other command objects for any type of query!

The following figure illustrates this page using the **OleDb – Access** option from the `DropDownList`:

Using the DAL Component in a Web Service

As previously mentioned, now that we have registered the DAL component in the GAC, it can be used from anywhere without the need to put the `.dll` file in the `/bin` directory of the application. In this section, we'll illustrate this through a simple Web Service example:

File – `\CSharp\DataLayer\WebServiceCode\WSDAL.asmx`:

```
<%@ WebService Language="C#"  Class="WSDAL" %>
```

```
using System.Web.Services;
using System.Data;
using System.Data.SqlClient;
using DataLayer;

public class WSDAL : WebService {

  protected ConfigSettings DLConfig;
  protected Commands DLCommand = new Commands();
  protected string SqlConString =
    "server=localhost;trusted_connection=true;database=northwind";

  [WebMethod]
  public DataSet GetProducts(string CustomerID ) {

    if (CustomerID.Length > 0) {

    SqlCommand cmd = new SqlCommand();
    cmd.CommandText = "CustOrderHist";
    cmd.CommandType = CommandType.StoredProcedure;
    cmd.Parameters.Add("@CustomerID", SqlDbType.VarChar,
      200).Value = CustomerID;
    DLConfig = new ConfigSettings(SqlConString, cmd, DataProviderType.Sql);
    return (DataSet)DLCommand.ExecuteQuery(DLConfig,
      ReturnType.DataSetType);

    } else {

    return new DataSet();

    }
  } // END GetProducts
} //END WSDAL Class
```

Save the preceding code example as WSDAL.asmx. This Web Service has one web method, GetProducts. GetProducts expects a CustomerID as a parameter – you can use ALFKI. Notice that there is some logic included to make sure that the caller of this web method actually passed a CustomerID in as a parameter – this saves an additional call being made to the database to retrieve the ID. The DAL component is created and executed identically to that of the web form examples. In fact, no matter what application you are creating, the DAL component will be created and executed in the same way. The following figure illustrates the result from the execution of this web method:

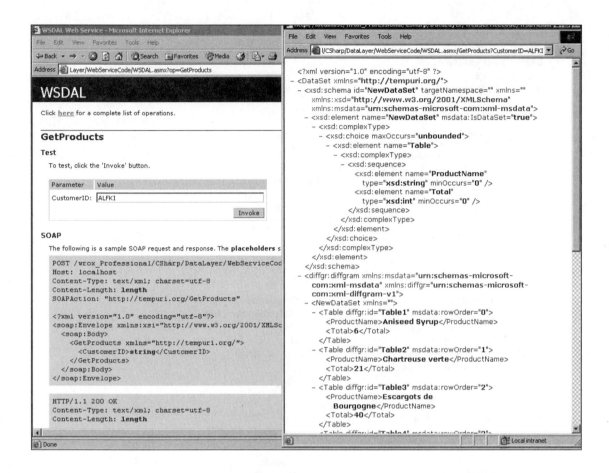

Performance and Optimization Tips

In this last section we will be going over a few optimization and performance tips with regards to creating business and data service components. We will cover object pooling and transactions.

Object Pooling

Before .NET arrived on the scene object pooling in COM+ was only available to the Visual C++ developer so programmers who used Visual Basic or FoxPro were out of luck. Object pooling in .NET is still utilized as a COM+ service. For those who aren't familiar with object pooling it is technology that enables you to create one or more objects and put them in a pool. Once these objects are in the pool clients can use them without having to create them from scratch. For example, say there is component named `CheckOut` and it is used often in your applications. You can enable object pooling for the `CheckOut` component and when an application needs to use the object it simply requests the object from the pool, uses it, and then releases back into the pool so it can be used by another application later.

When you enable object pooling you have control over such things as the size of the pool. You can set both a minimum and maximum size for the pool. The minimum size of the pool is how many objects are created and ready for use as soon as the pool is activated, and the maximum number is the maximum number of objects that can be in the pool. Once the maximum is met clients, requests for the objects are automatically queued up and objects are served to the clients as they become available – you can also set a timeout for clients' queue times. The best thing about object pooling is the performance gain client applications see because they rarely need to create an object from scratch.

If you want a component to take advantage of object pooling it must be derived from the ServicedComponent class – a member of the System.EnterpriseServices class. This enables you to use ObjectPoolingAttribute to enable and configure object pooling for the component. The ObjectPoolingAttribute contains the following properties that you can use to configure object pooling for components:

❑ CreationTimeout – sets the length of time, in milliseconds, to wait for an object to become available. After that an exception is thrown.

❑ Enabled – a Boolean value indicating whether object pooling is enabled.

❑ MaxPoolSize – the maximum number of objects that can be in the pool.

❑ MinPoolSize – the minimum number of objects that can be in the pool.

Additionally your component must possess the following attributes:

❑ Must be strong named (sn.exe)

❑ Must be registered in the Windows registry (regsvcs.exe – we'll talk about this soon)

❑ Type library definitions must be registered and installed in the application (regsvcs.exe)

The following example will illustrate how to develop and deploy a pooled object. This object is used as a "Hit Tracker". It contains only two methods; the first is used to update a database with unique web site hits and the second is used to update every web site hit. The reason I chose this example is because it isn't economical to put an object in the pool if it isn't used that often. If your web site is anything like mine, http://www.dotnetjunkies.com/, it gets hit quite often so pooling the tracking component just makes sense. The pooled object in this example is used by the global.asax file because there are events that you can handle within this file that are fired for both unique requests and every request for the documents in a web application.

Building a Hit Tracker Component

There will be three aspects to this example: the database, which we will create in SQL Server; the code for the pooled component; and the global.asax file.

Creating a Database

The first thing we need to do is create a new database to use with our example. This example uses SQL Server, but the code can be adapted to use any other database. The following script can be used to generate the needed database.

File – \CSharp\ObjectPooling\codebase\SqlScript.SQL:

```
CREATE TABLE [dbo].[PageViews] (
    [HitDate] [datetime] NULL ,
```

```
        [TotalHits] [float] NULL
) ON [PRIMARY]
GO

CREATE TABLE [dbo].[Unique] (
     [HitDate] [datetime] NOT NULL ,
     [TotalHits] [float] NOT NULL
) ON [PRIMARY]
GO

SET QUOTED_IDENTIFIER OFF
GO
SET ANSI_NULLS ON
GO

CREATE PROCEDURE [dbo].[HitsTotal]
@todaysdate datetime
AS
DECLARE @TOTAL int
SET @TOTAL = (SELECT COUNT(*) FROM [PageViews] WHERE HitDate = @todaysdate)

IF @TOTAL > 0
     BEGIN
          UPDATE PageViews
               SET TotalHits = ((SELECT TotalHits FROM PageViews WHERE HitDate
= @todaysdate) + 1)
               WHERE HitDate = @todaysdate
     END
ELSE
     BEGIN
          INSERT INTO PageViews
               (
                     HitDate,
                     TotalHits
               )
               VALUES
               (
                     @todaysdate,
                     1
               )
     END
GO
SET QUOTED_IDENTIFIER OFF
GO
SET ANSI_NULLS ON
GO

SET QUOTED_IDENTIFIER OFF
GO
SET ANSI_NULLS ON
GO

CREATE PROCEDURE [dbo].[HitsUnique]
@todaysdate datetime
```

```
AS
DECLARE @TOTAL int

SET @TOTAL = (SELECT COUNT(*) FROM [Unique] WHERE HitDate = @todaysdate)

IF   @TOTAL > 0
     BEGIN
           UPDATE [Unique]
                 SET
                 TotalHits =
           ((SELECT TotalHits FROM [Unique] WHERE HitDate = @todaysDate ) +1)
                 WHERE HitDate = @todaysdate
     END
ELSE
     BEGIN
           INSERT INTO [Unique]
                 (
                       HitDate,
                       TotalHits
                 )
                 VALUES
                 (
                       @todaysdate,
                       1
                 )
     END
GO
SET QUOTED_IDENTIFIER OFF
GO
SET ANSI_NULLS ON
GO
```

Creating the Component

Let's take a look now at the Hit Tracker component:

File: \CSharp\ObjectPooling\codebase\objectpooling.cs:

```csharp
using System;
using System.EnterpriseServices;
using System.Web;
using System.Data;
using System.Reflection;
using System.Data.SqlClient;
using System.Web.UI.WebControls;
using System.Runtime.InteropServices;

[assembly: ApplicationName("Object Pooling Sample")]
[assembly: AssemblyVersion("1.0.0.1")]
[assembly: ApplicationActivation(ActivationOption.Server)]
[assembly: AssemblyKeyFile("C:\\CSHARP\\ObjectPooling\\codebase\\OurKeyPair.snk")]
```

In this example, instead of building an additional file to hold our assembly information, we include it all in one file. Whichever way you do it has the same end result. Typically, if I have only one class in a project I'll include it all in one file and if I have more than one class I'll create a separate file.

An attribute you may not have seen before is included here – the `ApplicationActivation` attribute. The `ApplicationActivation` attribute is used to specify whether the component should run in the creator's process or in a system process. The constructor expects one parameter, a value from the `ActivationOption` enumeration. If you want a component to run in COM+ you must use `ActivationOption.Server` – the other possible value is `ActivationOption.Library`.

```
namespace Wrox.ObjectPoolingServer {

[ObjectPooling(MinPoolSize=1, MaxPoolSize=5, CreationTimeout=90000)]
[JustInTimeActivation(true)]
[ClassInterface(ClassInterfaceType.AutoDual)]

public class HitTracker : ServicedComponent {
```

The class we are creating is named `HitTracker` and it is derived from `ServicedComponent`. Three additional attributes are used to describe this class: `ObjectPooling`, controls the object pooling attributes for the component; `JustInTimeActivation`, also a member of the `EnterpriseServices` namespace, enables or disables Just in Time activation (JIT); `ClassInterface` identifies what type of interface should be generated for the class. The value for this constructor must be a member of the `ClassInterfaceType` enumeration. The available values are as follows:

❑   `AutoDispatch` – Only a `IDispatch` interface is generated for the class

❑   `AutoDual` – A dual interface is generated for the class

❑   `None` – No class interface is generated

The rest of the code is exactly the same as any other class you may create with one exception: the `AutoCompleteAttribute` found before each method. The `AutoCompleteAttribute` indicates that the object should automatically return to the pool after the object is finished with.

```
protected SqlConnection SqlCon = new SqlConnection
    ("server=localhost;trusted_connection=true;database=localhits");
protected SqlCommand SqlCmd;
protected DateTime HitDateTime = DateTime.Today;

[AutoComplete] //Automatically returns object to the pool when done. Invokes
SetComplete()
public void AddUnique() { //Updated on every new session

  try {

    SqlCmd = new SqlCommand("HitsUnique", SqlCon);
    SqlCmd.CommandType = CommandType.StoredProcedure;
    SqlCmd.Parameters.Add("@todaysdate", SqlDbType.SmallDateTime)
        .Value = HitDateTime;
    SqlCon.Open();
    SqlCmd.ExecuteNonQuery();
```

```
        SqlCon.Close();

    } catch (Exception Ex) {

        HttpContext.Current.Trace.Write("An exception has occured in: " +
            Ex.Message.ToString());

    }

} // end AddUnique

[AutoComplete] //Automatically returns object to the pool when done. Invokes
SetComplete()
public void AddPageView() { // Updated on every page view

    try {

        SqlCmd = new SqlCommand("HitsTotal", SqlCon);
        SqlCmd.CommandType = CommandType.StoredProcedure;
        SqlCmd.Parameters.Add("@todaysdate", SqlDbType.SmallDateTime).Value
            = HitDateTime;
        SqlCon.Open();
        SqlCmd.ExecuteNonQuery();
        SqlCon.Close();

    } catch (Exception Ex) {

        HttpContext.Current.Trace.Write("An exception has occured in: "
            + Ex.Message.ToString());

    }

} // end AddPageView

public override bool CanBePooled() {

    return true;

} // end CanBePooled

} // end HitTracker

} // end Wrox.ObjectPoolingServer
```

There are three methods in the class: CanBePooled, AddUnique, and AddPageView. The AddUnique method is used to execute the HitsUnique stored procedure and the AddPageView method is used to execute the HitsTotal method. The last method is CanBePooled and this is a member of the base class ServicedComponent and is used to specify whether or not the object can be pooled.

The following compilation code compiles the code into an assembly, registers it in COM+, and adds it to the GAC so it can be used machine-wide.

File – \CSharp\ObjectPooling\codebase\make.bat:

```
csc.exe /target:library /out:..\..\bin\Wrox.CSharp.ObjectPoolingServer.DLL  *.cs
/r:System.dll /r:System.Data.dll /r:System.Xml.dll /r:System.Web.dll
/r:System.Data.Odbc.Dll /r:System.EnterpriseServices.DLL
pause
regsvcs.exe ..\..\bin\Wrox.CSharp.ObjectPoolingServer.DLL
pause
gacutil.exe /i ..\..\bin\Wrox.CSharp.ObjectPoolingServer.DLL
pause
```

Now let's take a look at how to use the component:

File – \CSharp\global.asax.cs:

```csharp
using System;
using System.Web;
using System.Web.SessionState;
using System.EnterpriseServices;
using System.Reflection;
using System.ComponentModel;
using Wrox.ObjectPoolingServer;
using System.Runtime.Remoting;

namespace Wrox {

 public class Global : System.Web.HttpApplication {

   public HitTracker hitTrak = new HitTracker();

   public void Application_OnBeginRequest(object sender, EventArgs e) {

    hitTrak.AddPageView();

   }

   public void Session_Start(object sender, EventArgs e) {

    hitTrak.AddUnique();

   }
 }
```

File – \CSharp\global.asax:

```
<%@ Application Inherits="Wrox.Global" %>
```

File – \CSharp\make.bat:

```
csc.exe /target:library /out:bin/Wrox.DLL  *.cs  /r:System.dll /r:System.Web.dll
/r:bin\Wrox.CSharp.ObjectPoolingServer.DLL /r:System.EnterpriseServices.DLL
pause
```

After you have all the above set up, execute any page within the web application. Verify that data was added to the `PageViews` and `Unique` tables within the `localhits` database and then do the following:

❑ Go to: Start | Settings | Control Panel | Administration Tools | Component Services.

❑ Open up **Component Services**.

❑ Open up **Computers**.

❑ Open up and select the folder **COM+ Applications**.

❑ Notice in the right pane **Object Pooling Sample** is there with the spinning ball. This is our component.

❑ Now open up "**Object Pooling Sample**" on the left pane.

❑ Open up components, right-click, and go to properties on `Wrox.ObjectPoolingServer.HitTracker`.

❑ Click on the activation tab – notice the minimum and maximum pool size are there along with the creation time-out.

That's it, our object is now pooled and ready for use. The following figure shows our object happily spinning in COM+:

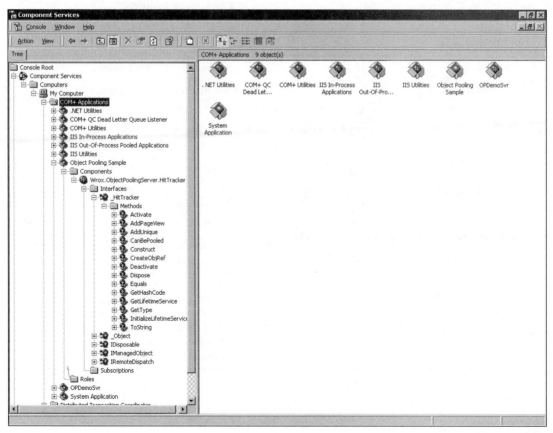

Transactions

Transactional functionality has been important for some time now for many reasons. For instance, if you are executing INSERT statements into multiple tables and all the inserted data is inter-dependent you would want to abort all of them if one INSERT failed. In this section we'll be demonstrating how to enable transactional processing for SQL execution from within your components. When you see how easy it is to do in .NET you will be astonished!

Before we get into a code example let's look at the objects that we'll be using. This example is using the SQL Server .NET Data Provider, but the technology used can be used with other .NET Data Providers in exactly the same way. The primary class we'll be introducing in this section is the SqlTransaction class (see Chapter 10). Once created, the SqlTransaction object controls all database operations (whether they are committed or rolled back). You have control over whether or not a database execution is completed, aborted, or partially done. The following tables contain a description of the more important properties and methods of the SqlTransaction class:

Public Properties	
IsolationLevel	Specifies the locking behavior for the connection. The value must be a member of the IsolationLevel enumeration found in the System.Data namespace.

Public Methods	
Commit	Commits the database transaction.
Rollback	Rolls-back or cancels the database transaction.
Save	Saves all database transactions that have successfully occurred up to the point the save method is invoked.

We create an SqlTransaction object using the SqlConnection.BeginTransaction method. There are four overloads available for the BeginTransaction method:

SqlConnection.BeginTransaction Overloads	
SqlConnection.BeginTransaction()	Begins a new transaction and returns an object representing the new transaction.
SqlConnection.BeginTransaction (IsolationLevel)	Begins a new transaction, returns an object representing the new transaction, and sets the isolation level at which the transaction should run. (See the IsolationLevel enumeration for possible values.)

SqlConnection.BeginTransaction Overloads	

`SqlConnection.BeginTransaction`
 	
 `(string)`
	Begins a new transaction, returns an object representing the new transaction, and specifies the transactions name.

`SqlConnection.BeginTransaction`
 	
 `(IsolationLevel, string)`
	Begins a new transaction, returns an object representing the new transaction, sets the isolation level for the transaction, and gives the transaction a name.

The following simple example illustrates how to use the `SqlTransaction` object to perform a SQL `INSERT` statement. This example inserts a new product into the `Products` table of the `Northwind` database. If there isn't a `ProductName` present then the transaction is aborted.

File – `\CSharp\Transactions\codebase\ConnectionTransaction.cs`:

```
using System;
using System.Data;
using System.Data.SqlClient;
using System.Web;

namespace Wrox.CSharp {

 public class Transactions {

  public bool Add(string ProductName) {

   SqlConnection SqlConn = new
SqlConnection("server=localhost;trusted_connection=true;" +
             "uid=sa;database=northwind");
   SqlConn.Open();
   SqlTransaction SqlTrans;
   SqlTrans = SqlConn.BeginTransaction(IsolationLevel.ReadCommitted,
"ProcessTransaction");
```

Invoking the `BeginTransaction` method creates the `SqlTransaction` object:

```
   SqlCommand SqlCmd = new SqlCommand("INSERT INTO Products(ProductName) VALUES
(@ProductName)", SqlConn);
   SqlCmd.Parameters.Add("@ProductName", SqlDbType.VarChar, 200).Value =
ProductName;
   SqlCmd.Transaction = SqlTrans;

   try {

    if (ProductName.Length <= 0) throw new NullReferenceException();
```

The above `if` statement throws a new `NullReferenceException` if the length of `ProductName` is 0. Once the `NullReferenceException` is thrown, code execution jumps to the catch statement. If the length is more than 0 characters then the `SqlCommand.ExecuteNonQuery` method is executed, the `SqlTransaction.Commit` method is invoked, and finally the `Connection` object is closed:

```
      SqlCmd.ExecuteNonQuery();
      SqlTrans.Commit();
      SqlConn.Close();
      return true;

   } catch (Exception Ex) {

      HttpContext.Current.Trace.Write("Exception", Ex.Message.ToString());
```

Within the catch block the `SqlTransaction.Rollback` method is executed:

```
      SqlTrans.Rollback("ProcessTransaction");
      return false;

   }

   } // end Add

   } // end Transactions

} // end Wrox.CSharp
```

The following code will build this example and place the assembly in the application /bin directory:

File – \CSharp\Transactions\codebase\make.bat:

```
csc.exe /target:library /out:..\..\bin\Wrox.CSharp.TransactionServer.DLL *.cs
/r:System.dll /r:System.Data.dll /r:System.Web.dll
pause
```

The following web form code will be used to demonstrate how to use the
`Wrox.CSharp.Transactions` class. This web form contains one `TextBox` and one Button. When the
page is submitted by clicking the button, the value of the textbox will inserted into the `Products` table
as a new `Product`.

File – \CSharp\Transactions\ConnectionTransaction.aspx:

```
<%@ Page Language="c#" TRACE="TRUE" AutoEventWireup="true"
Codebehind="ConnectionTransaction.aspx.cs"
Inherits="Wrox.ConnectionTransaction" %>
<html>
  <head>
    <title>Database Transactions</title>
  </head>
  <body>
    <form runat="server">
      enter product name (or not) -
      <asp:TextBox id="txtProductName" Runat="Server" />
      <asp:Button Text="Submit" Runat="Server" OnClick="Submit_Click" />
    </form>
  </body>
</html>
```

File – \CSharp\Transactions\ConnectionTransaction.aspx.cs:

```csharp
using System;
using Wrox.CSharp;
using System.Web.UI.WebControls;

namespace Wrox {

  public class ConnectionTransaction : System.Web.UI.Page {

    protected TextBox txtProductName;

    protected void Submit_Click(object sender, EventArgs e) {

    Transactions trans = new Transactions();

    if (trans.Add(txtProductName.Text.Trim())) {

      Response.Write("The Transaction Succeeded");

    } else {

      Response.Write("The Transaction Was Aborted");

    }

    }

  }

}
```

File – \CSharp\Transactions\make.bat:

```
csc.exe /target:library /out:..\bin\Wrox.CSharp.TransactionClient.DLL
*.cs /r:System.DLL /r:System.Web.DLL
/r:..\bin\Wrox.CSharp.TransactionServer.DLL
pause
```

Once you have browsed to ConnectionTransaction.aspx enter a value in the textbox and submit the page – you'll get a message "The Transaction Succeeded". Now submit the page without entering a value in the textbox – you'll get a message "The Transaction Was Aborted ". The following figure is this page after it is submitted without a value in the textbox:

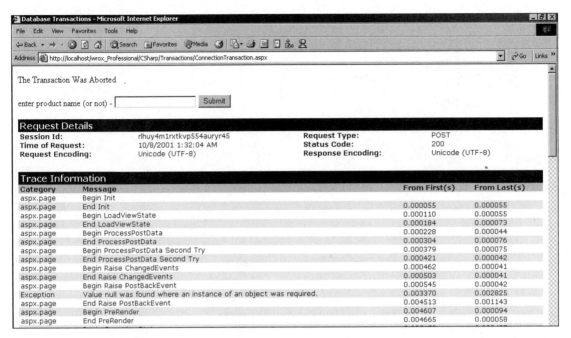

There are two things that you should notice here. First, the message that the transaction was aborted – the message written out to the user is determined by whether or not the `Wrox.CSharp.Transactions.Add` method returns true or false. If it returns true then the transaction succeeded and if it returns false it failed. The second thing you should notice is found within the Trace Information section. There is one line that has Exception as the Category and an error message as the Message. This is from the catch block within the `Add` method. This information is good for debugging your applications.

A final note: In this example I threw my own exception to simulate a database-thrown exception. In real life you will not be able to plan for everything. For instance, all of your data may pass validation and the commands to the database may be executed, but if your database doesn't agree with the data and an exception is thrown the transaction would still roll back.

Uninstalling the Components

The following code will uninstall all the sample components we made in this chapter.

File Name – `\CSharp\Uninstalling\unmake.bat`:

```
@ REM - Uninstall Object Pooling Sample

regsvcs.exe /u ..\bin\Wrox.CSharp.ObjectPoolingServer.DLL
gacutil.exe /u Wrox.CSharp.ObjectPoolingServer

@ REM - Uninstall DataLayer Sample

gacutil.exe /u Wrox.DataLayer.CSharp
```

```
@echo.
@echo All components have been uninstalled successfully! Have a good day!
@echo.

Pause
```

Summary

In this chapter you learned how easy it is to make and distribute a Data Application Layer (DAL) component using .NET. We discussed how to make a component that supports three different Data Providers, how to execute different types of SQL statements using both text and Command objects such as SqlCommand, and finally how to return different types of data object. Next, we discussed how to create a Strong-Named assembly so that it can be installed in the Global Assembly Cache. Finally, we went over how to use the DAL component from a Web Form and from a Web Service.

In the second part of the chapter we looked at some performance and optimization tips. We looked at how you can use object pooling to reduce costly object creation by keeping ready-made objects in an object pool within COM+. Then we looked at how to use transactions to optimize database activity by controlling whether or not data is manipulated in the database. By using transactions we demonstrated how to roll back costly mistakes such as invalid data and how to commit transactions.

In this chapter you were introduced to quite a few different aspects of development and deployment using .NET and ADO.NET. Some were covered in more details than others. The following list contains some recommended topics for you to look at further:

- ❏ N–Tier Architecture Concepts
- ❏ IDbConnection Interface
- ❏ IDbDataAdapter Interface
- ❏ SqlCommand, OleDbCommand, OdbcCommand, and the IDbCommand Interface
- ❏ ODBC .NET Provider
- ❏ Strong Name Tool (sn.exe)
- ❏ Global Assembly Cache Tool (gacutil.exe)
- ❏ Machine.Config
- ❏ Assembly Information Files
- ❏ SqlTransaction class
- ❏ ServicedComponent class
- ❏ .NET Services Installation Tool (regsvcs.exe)

13

ADO.NET and Web Services

In this day and age it is nearly inconceivable to think of building a new enterprise application that does not include the Internet in its architectural diagram. Whether the Internet is used to transfer data from clients to a central processing application, or to link multiple servers in separate geographic locations, the Internet has become an integral part of application architecture, and it is only becoming more critical.

Enter the Web Service.

A Web Service is a piece of application logic that is publicly exposed and available to any number of potentially disparate systems through the use of common Internet standards, such as HTTP, XML, and SOAP. Essentially, a Web Service is code that we expose in an application that can be accessed locally, over an intranet, or over the Internet. We have the option of allowing any number of possible clients to access our Web Service, or restricting the access to authenticated clients only.

Web Services rely heavily on the acceptance of XML in the public arena. Web Services use XML as the means for serializing data to receive from, or return to the client. Any client that can parse XML can use the data returned, regardless of whether the client and the Web Service host are using the same operating system, or the applications are written in the same language. In the same manner, if the Web Service expects complex data to be passed into it, the client can pass that data as an XML document, in a SOAP message.

Web Services provide a high level of abstraction between the application logic, or the provider, and the client that uses, or consumes, the Web Service. The only thing the provider and the consumer need to know about each other is what inputs the consumer needs to provide, and what outputs the provider will return. The simplicity of this "contract" frees the consumer from any need to be concerned with the application logic itself. As long as the Web Service interface – the input and output definition – doesn't change, the provider can make code changes to the Web Service, and the consumer never needs to know about it, and never needs to be given any code to implement the updated service.

As we will discover in this chapter, Web Services are opening the door to a newer and simpler distributed application-programming model. The documentation that is provided with the .NET Framework SDK says it best:

"As the next revolutionary advancement of the Internet, Web Services will become the fundamental structure that links together all computing devices." – Web Services Overview, Microsoft .NET Framework SDK documentation.

In this chapter you will learn:

❑   What a Web Service is

❑   How to build a Web Service

❑   How to build a Web Service consumer in Visual Studio .NET

❑   How to build a Web Service consumer using a proxy client

❑   How to work with datasets in Web Services

❑   How to work with custom objects in Web Services

❑   How to secure a Web Service

Setting Up the Code Samples

In this chapter we will build a three projects: two ASP.NET Web applications named `CSharpProvider` and `CSharpConsumer`, and one Windows Forms project named `CsharpWinFormsConsumer`. The sample code available at www.wrox.com has all three projects as Visual Studio .NET projects.

To set up the projects on your system, do the following:

> **Note: skip Steps 5 – 8 if you will be building all of the examples. Steps 5 – 8 add the sample code to the project so you do not have to build it yourself. In this chapter I will assume you are building the project, and give explicit instruction on what file types and names to add.**

1. Create a new directory named `C:\Inetpub\wwwroot\ProADONET\`.

2. Launch Visual Studio .NET and create a new Blank Solution.

3. In the New Project dialog window, create a new C# ASP.NET Web Application in the `http://localhost/ProADONET` location, named `CsharpProvider`.

4. Next, create a New Project in the Solution named `CSharpConsumer` (be sure to select C# ASP.NET Application and check the Add to Solution radio button).

5. Copy the contents of the `CSharpProvider` folder into the `C:\Inetpub\wwwroot\ProADONET\CSharpProvider` folder that was created by Visual Studio .NET (choose the "Yes to All" in the Confirm File Replace dialog box).

6. In Visual Studio .NET you will be prompted with a dialog indicating that the project/solution was changed outside of Visual Studio .NET. Choose the Discard button to discard your changes, and update the project with the files you copied into the directory.

7. Copy the contents of the `CSharpConsumer` folder into the `C:\Inetpub\wwwroot\ProADONET\CSharpConsumer` folder that was created by Visual Studio .NET (choose the "Yes to All" in the Confirm File Replace dialog box).

8. In Visual Studio .NET you will be prompted with a dialog indicating that the project/solution was changed outside of Visual Studio .NET. Choose the Discard button to discard your changes, and update the project with the files you copied into the directory.

9. Finally, create a new C# Windows Application project in the solution, named `CsharpWinFormsConsumer`.

10. *Do not* copy the files into this project directory as you did with the others. We will be building this project later in this chapter.

You should have three projects in the Solution Explorer: `CSharpProvider`, `CSharpConsumer`, and `CsharpWinFormsConsumer`:

This chapter refers to some command-line utilities included with the .NET Framework. If you have installed only the .NET Framework SDK these should work fine. If you have installed Visual Studio .NET you must execute these from the Visual Studio .NET Command Prompt. Open this by clicking on **Start** | **Programs** | **Microsoft Visual Studio .NET 7.0** | **Visual Studio .NET Tools** | **Visual Studio .NET Command Prompt**.

Web Services – The New DCOM

Creating applications that enable multiple servers to communicate and exchange information is not new; the advent of Web Services didn't bring this about. Most of us have had some involvement in building an application that required two systems to exchange data, whether via Microsoft's Distributed Component Object Model (DCOM) or Sun's Remote Method Invocation (RMI). The difference between using DCOM or RMI and .NET Web Services is how much time you get to enjoy your social life. You see, Web Services make the process of enabling data exchange between disparate systems easier, enabling you to get the job done more quickly.

Are Web Services the new DCOM? The answer lies in how Web Services work – in how Web Services enable data exchange between disparate systems. A Web Service exposes an interface for invoking a method on one system, from another. A call to this method can be made using one of three Internet protocols: HTTP GET, HTTP POST, or SOAP. Once the Web Service method is invoked, any data that needs to be returned is serialized as XML and returned, either as raw XML, or as XML in the body of a SOAP message. This data exchange model allows for any object that can be serialized as XML – strings, integers, arrays, ADO.NET `DataSets`, or even custom objects – to be exchanged between the provider and the consumer. While Web Services may not work the same way DCOM does, they certainly are a likely candidate to replace DCOM in the near future.

Common Standards

There was nearly nothing worse than trying to get a Java-based system to exchange data with a COM-based system in the pre-Web Services era. Data type marshaling and the incompatibilities of the two systems made this a hassle to implement. Since Web Services rely on a set of common standards, such as HTTP, XML and SOAP, this task becomes child's play – almost.

The use of common standards ensures that any number of disparate systems can exchange data easily and flawlessly, enabling true multi-platform, distributed applications. Following is a short description of the five technologies that Web Services make use of: XML, SOAP, WSDL, DISCO, and UDDI.

❑ **XML**
XML (Extensible Markup Language) has become an accepted Internet standard for data description and exchange, much as HTML became a standard for information display many years ago. Behind the scenes, Web Services use XML as the data transmission format. When a Web Service method is invoked, the data returned, whether it is a string, an integer, a `DataSet`, or a custom object, is serialized as XML and sent back to the consumer.

❑ **SOAP**
SOAP (Simple Object Access Protocol) is an XML-based message protocol. Web Services can use SOAP as the carrier for the XML data that is being exchanged between the Web Service provider and the Web Service consumer. If a Web Service method expects a complex object, such as a custom object that defines a product with properties that describe it, as part of its input, a SOAP message is required to carry that object, serialized as XML in the SOAP message body.

❑ **WSDL**

WSDL (Web Service Description Language) is an XML-based description of a Web Service. For all intents and purposes, the WSDL is the contract that a provider and a consumer agree on. The WSDL describes the interfaces of a Web Service, and how the messages are to be formatted when using HTTP GET, HTTP POST, or SOAP protocols.

❑ **DISCO**

DISCO (Web Service Discovery) is the process of locating (discovering) the WSDL file associated to a Web Service. The discovery process identifies a Web Service and its location. The discovery process is primarily used by tools, such as Visual Studio .NET, to locate a WSDL file, and build proxy clients that can remotely invoke the Web Service methods (proxy clients are covered later in this chapter).

❑ **UDDI**

UDDI (Universal Description, Discovery, and Integration) is an industry effort to enable businesses to quickly, easily, and dynamically find Web Services and interact with one another. UDDI is a distributed directory, or registry of businesses and Web Services. UDDI enables a business to describe itself and its services, discover other businesses offering desired services, and integrate with them. The UDDI community includes Microsoft, IBM, Sun Microsystems, Ariba, and many others, and is lead by a committee of these industry leaders.

Supply and Demand – Web Service Providers and Consumers

Web Services work by exchanging data between two primary entities: the Web Service provider and the Web Service consumer. The Web Service provider is an application that exposes a piece of functionality, which other applications – Web Service consumers – will access. The provider application exposes the WSDL that the consumer must comply with to use the Web Service.

The consumer discovers the Web Service, either by finding it in the UDDI registry, or some other means of discovery. Once the consumer understands the Web Service, via the WSDL document, a method can be invoked, using any of the three acceptable protocols, HTTP GET, HTTP POST, or SOAP. When the Web Service method is invoked, the provider returns the data to the consumer in the form of an XML document, either as a Web response, or embedded in a SOAP message. The data exchange can be protected either with SSL, or by encrypting the XML payload.

In the following sections we will build a few different Web Services, and make use of the different protocols, varied data types, and security options. For simplicity purposes we will not be doing very much database access, since what is really important here is that we understand how Web Services can be used to exchange any data, not just how to exchange data from a database. We will work with data, however: data from an XML file and objects serialized to XML. The concepts demonstrated here can easily be implemented with data from a database as well.

Building a Basic Web Service

Building a Web Service is not drastically different to building any public class and method. A Web Service takes a typical method and exposes it via Internet protocols. We can build a Web Service by adding a few lines of code to any public method in a public class; provide, if there is data returned it is as an XSD compliant data type.

The steps to building a Web Service are show here, and we explore each of them in this section:

1. Build a public class that inherits from `System.Web.Services.WebService`

2. Create a public method

3. Apply the `WebMethod` attribute to the method

4. Create a Web Service file using the `.asmx` extension (we will call ours `MyWebService.asmx`)

5. Add the `@ WebService` attribute to the `.asmx` file and inherit from the class defined in Step 1

The following code shows a basic class that exposes one method, the `RandomNumberGenerator` method:

```
using System;
using System.Web;

namespace CSharpProvider
{
  public class TrivialFunTools
  {
    public int RandomNumberGenerator(int LowNumber, int HighNumber)
    {
      Random RandNumber = new Random();
      return RandNumber.Next(LowNumber, HighNumber);
    }
  }
}
```

The `RandomNumberGenerator` method uses the `System.Random` class to create a random number between the two values passed into the method. A new instance of the `Random` class is constructed and a value between the `LowNumber` and the `HighNumber` is returned. To convert the `RandomNumberGenerator` method to a Web Service requires only a few lines of code.

Create a new Web Service file in the `CSharpProvider` project named `TrivialFunTools.asmx`. Open the `TrivialFunTools.asmx.cs` code-behind file by clicking the click here to switch to code view link.

> **Visual Studio .NET inserts additional code in the class file that the Integrated Design Environment (IDE) needs. In the code samples in this chapter I have excluded most of it, as it is not pertinent to building a Web Service. I will note anywhere that it is important.**

The `using` statement for the `System.Web.Services` namespace is automatically added by Visual Studio .NET so that we don't have to use fully qualified names when referencing a class in this namespace:

```
using System;
using System.Collections;
using System.ComponentModel;
using System.Data;
using System.Diagnostics;
using System.Web;
using System.Web.Services;

namespace CSharpProvider
{
```

The optional `WebService` attribute can be used in the class declaration to add a description, namespace, and so on to the Web Service. This attribute is optional, but using it you can provide greater value to your Web Service by including a brief description, a unique namespace, and more. The .NET Framework SDK Documentation provides a full list of options for the `WebService` attribute class. The .NET Framework will automatically generate an information and test page for the Web Service, and the information passed into the `WebService` attribute will be used on this page. Here's an example of how to use the `WebService` attribute:

```
[WebService(Description="This is a collection of silly Web Services " +
    "that demonstrate various Web Service capabilities.",
    Namespace="http://www.dotnetjunkies.com")]
```

The class itself inherits from the `System.Web.Services.WebService` class, so our class will have all of the same capabilities as the `WebService` class, plus whatever properties, methods, or events we create.

```
[WebService(Description="This is a collection of silly " +
    "Web Services that demonstrate various " +
    "Web Service capabilities.",
    Namespace="http://www.dotnetjunkies.com")]
public class TrivialFunTools : System.Web.Services.WebService
{
```

The `WebMethod` attribute is used preceding any public method that we want to expose as a Web Service method. Like the `WebService` attribute, the `WebMethod` attribute enables us to add a description of the Web Service method for display in the automatically generated information and test page. The `WebMethod` attribute enables our public method as a Web Service method, giving it the ability to be invoked over the Internet using HTTP GET, HTTP POST, or SOAP.

Not all methods in a Web Service need to be Web Service methods – we can create methods in the Web Service that will not be exposed via the Internet. Any method, `public`, `private`, or `protected`, will not be accessible via the Internet unless it has the `WebMethod` attribute applied to it; only `public` methods may have the `WebMethod` attribute.

Add the following method to the `TrivialFunTools` class:

```
[WebMethod(Description="Generate a random number between " +
  "two values.<br>This Web Service demonstrates how a " +
  "basic Web Service works.")]
public int RandomNumberGenerator(int LowNumber, int HighNumber)
{
  Random RandNumber = new Random();
  return RandNumber.Next(LowNumber, HighNumber);
}
```

> **In Visual Basic .NET the format for adding the attributes is:**
>
> ```
> <WebService(Namespace:=http://www.dotnetjunkiescom)> _
> Public Class MyClass
>   Inherits System.Web.Services.WebService
>
> <WebMethod(Description:="My Web method")> _
> Public Function MyWebMethod() As Object
> ```

Methods that we are exposing as `WebService` methods (using the `WebMethod` attribute) must be declared publicly and must be in a public class.

We can build the project by clicking the **Build** option in the **Build** menu. If you are building this project with a text editor, you can use the `CSC.exe` (C# Compiler) command-line compiler with the following statement:

```
csc.exe /t:library TrivialFunTools.asmx.cs /r:System.dll,System.Web.dll
```

If we open the `TrivialFunTools.asmx` file in a text-editor other than Visual Studio .NET (you cannot view this type of file in Visual Studio .NET, only the code-behind class file), we will see the following code:

```
<%@ WebService Language="c#" Codebehind="TrivialFunTools.asmx.cs"
  Class="CSharpProvider.TrivialFunTools" %>
```

The `@ WebService` directive identifies the class that implements the Web Service. When the `TrivialFunTools.asmx` page is browsed to, the .NET Framework will create the information and test page. To do this, right-click on the `TrivialFunTools.asmx` file in the Solution Explorer, and choose **Set as Start Page**.

Next, click the Start button in the top menu bar of Visual Studio .NET. The application will compile, and a browser will open with the following page:

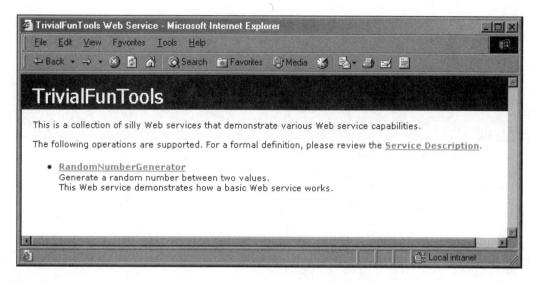

The information and test page provides a link to the Service Description (WSDL), and a link to test any Web Service methods in the Web Service. Clicking the link to the Service Description will show you the actual XML-based WSDL document:

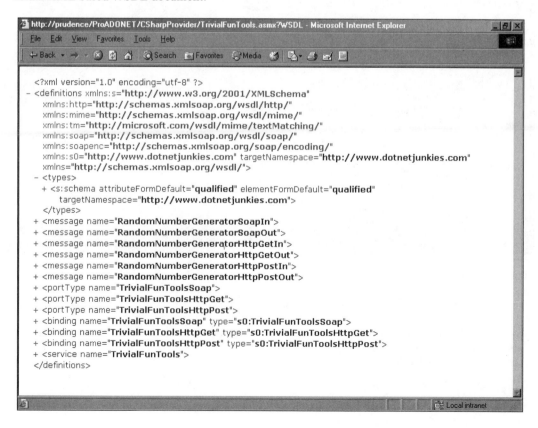

Clicking the Web Service method link on the Web Service information page will bring you to a test interface for the Web Service method:

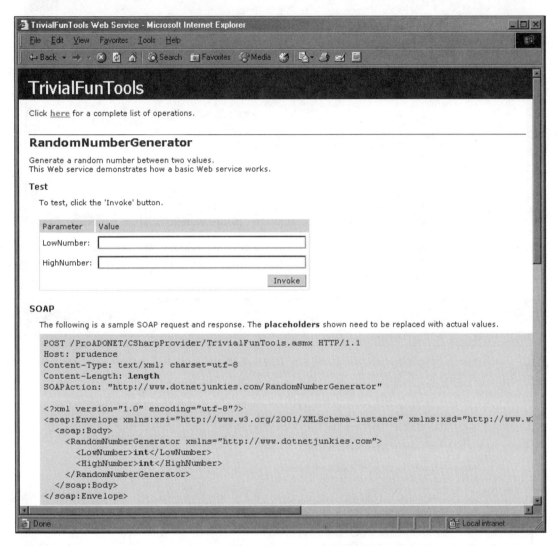

The test interface provides a textbox for each input argument, and a button to invoke the Web Service method. Below the test interface is a list of the acceptable protocols for this Web Service method, and sample requests and responses for the Web method.

We can test this Web Service method by entering values into the textboxes and clicking Invoke. The Web Service method is invoked, and the return data is displayed in a new window, formatted as XML data:

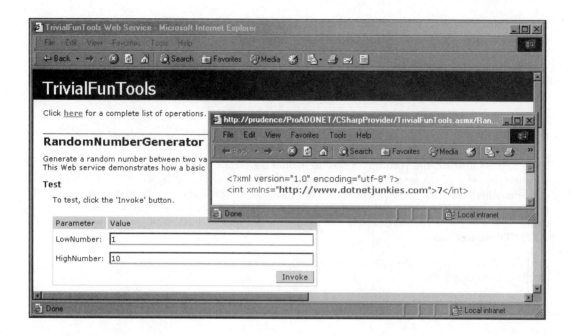

Building a Basic Consumer

A consumer application can access the Web Service in any of three protocols, HTTP GET, HTTP POST, or SOAP. Each protocol has advantages and disadvantages, some of which are listed below:

Protocol	Advantages	Disadvantages
HTTP GET	Easy to implement	Any input values are passed in the query string Cannot exchange complex data types
HTTP POST	Easy to implement	Cannot exchange complex data types
SOAP	Can exchange complex data types	Uses more bandwidth

Web Services enable the consumer application to have any type of user interface necessary, including a Web or a desktop (Windows) application interface. The Web Service will be accessed in code, and the return data can then be formatted and displayed as appropriate. We can build a consumer using a text editor, and if necessary a command-line compiler, or a tool such as Visual Studio .NET.

Building an HTTP Consumer

We can build a consumer that accesses the Web Service using HTTP GET or HTTP POST by simply adding a `<form>` tag to an HTML web page, using `Get` or `Post` as the `Method` and the Web Service URL as the `Action`:

```
<form method="Get" action="http://webserver/webservice.asmx/WebMethod">
```

or:

```
<form method="Post" action="http://webserver/webservice.asmx/WebMethod">
```

The `form` tag instructs the Web server how to handle the form when a user submits it. The `Method` attribute indicates which protocol should be used, HTTP GET or HTTP POST. The `Action` attribute indicates where the Web server should redirect the action. In the first example above, the form will be redirected to the URL in the `Action` attribute as an HTTP GET, with any submitted values as query string parameters. The second example will redirect to the specific URL with any submitted values in the HTTP request header.

Add the following page to the `CSharpConsumer` project as an HTML page named `HttpGetConsumer.htm`:

```html
<!DOCTYPE HTML PUBLIC "-//W3C//DTD HTML 4.0 Transitional//EN" >
<html>
 <head>
  <META NAME="GENERATOR" Content="Microsoft Visual Studio 7.0">
  <title></title>
 </head>
 <body>
  <form method="GET"
action="http://localhost/ProADONET/CSharpProvider/
        TrivialFunTools.asmx/RandomNumberGenerator" ID="Form1">
   <H3>
   Random Number Consumer
   </H3>
   <P>
    To get a random number, enter your number range and click Go.
   </P>
   <B>Low Number:</B>
   <BR>
   <INPUT TYPE="text" NAME="LowNumber" ID="Text1">
   <BR>
   <B>High Number:</B>
   <BR>
   <INPUT TYPE="text" NAME="HighNumber" ID="Text2">
   <BR>
   <BR>
   <INPUT TYPE="submit" VALUE="Go" ID="Submit1" NAME="Submit1">
  </FORM>
 </body>
</html>
```

When the preceding HTML page is filled out and the Go button is clicked, the Web site visitor sees the raw XML returned from the Web Service. We can test this by right-clicking in the IDE and choosing View In Browser.

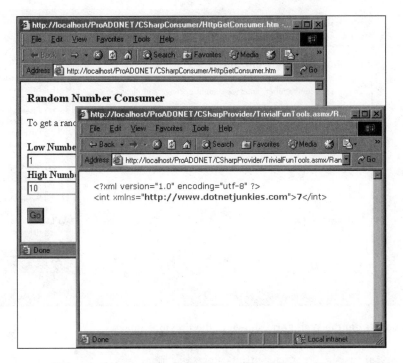

In the preceding example, the browser is simply redirected to the Web Service, and the result of the Web Service method is shown in the browser as an XML document. What would be better (and what Web Services are intended for) is if we invoked the Web Service in code, and captured the returned value to display to the visitor.

To invoke a Web Service method using HTTP GET and capture the return value, first build a Web Form that will be the consumer's interface to the Web Service. Create a new Web Form in the CSharpConsumer project named HttpConsumer.aspx, and model its layout after the screenshot overleaf.

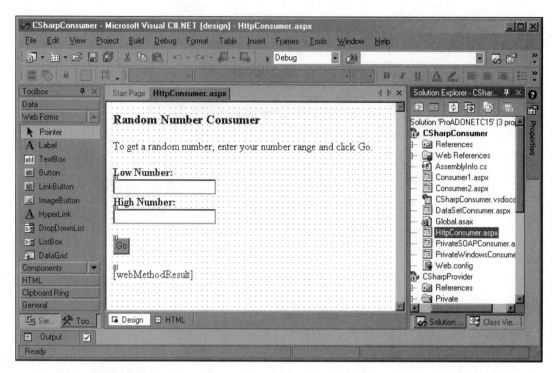

Here is the code from the Web Form shown in the previous image:

```
<%@ Page language="c#" Codebehind="HttpConsumer.aspx.cs"
  AutoEventWireup="false" Inherits="CSharpConsumer.HttpConsumer" %>
<!DOCTYPE HTML PUBLIC "-//W3C//DTD HTML 4.0 Transitional//EN" >
<HTML>
  <HEAD>
    <meta name="GENERATOR" Content="Microsoft Visual Studio 7.0">
    <meta name="CODE_LANGUAGE" Content="C#">
    <meta name="vs_defaultClientScript" content="JavaScript (ECMAScript)">
    <meta name="vs_targetSchema"
      content="http://schemas.microsoft.com/intellisense/ie5">
  </HEAD>
  <body MS_POSITIONING="GridLayout">
    <form id="HttpConsumer" method="post" runat="server">
      <h3>
        Random Number Consumer
      </h3>
      <p>
        To get a random number, enter your number
        range and click Go.
      </p>
      <b>Low Number:</b>
      <br>
      <asp:TextBox Runat="server" ID="lowNumber" />
      <br>
```

```
      <b>High Number:</b>
      <br>
      <asp:TextBox Runat="server" ID="highNumber" />
      <br>
      <p>
        <asp:Button Runat="server" Text="Go" id="Button1" />
      </p>
      <asp:Label Runat="server" ID="webMethodResult" />
    </form>
  </body>
</HTML>
```

What we want to do is invoke the RandomNumberGenerator Web Service method when the Go button is clicked – in the Button.Click event handler – and capture the result to display in the webMethodResult Label control. This will enable the user to enter the low and high values, and post the form. Behind the scenes, we will invoke the Web Service, capture the return value, and display it for the user.

Capturing the Data in an XmlDocument

We can capture the returned XML with an XmlDocument object, and pull the value out of the appropriate child node of the object. The XmlDocument class represents an XML document in code, as an object. The XmlDocument class exposes several methods and properties for traversing the XML node tree and extracting the inner and outer XML values, specifically the ChildNodes property, which is a collection of XmlNode objects in the form of an XmlNodeList object. Using the XmlDocument class will enable us to capture the data returned from the Web Service (which is returned as an XML document), and render only the data in the consumer application, rather than the entire XML document.

Following is the Button1_Click event handler for the previous Web Form. While in the design view of the HttpConsumer.aspx Web Form you can double-click the button control and Visual Studio .NET will set up a Button1_Click event handler in the code-behind class, and display it in the IDE. Add the following code:

```
private void Button1_Click(object sender, System.EventArgs e)
{
    //Add the TextBox values into the HTTP GET query string
    string httpGetUrl =
      "http://localhost/ProADONET/CSharpProvider/" +
      "TrivialFunTools.asmx/RandomNumberGenerator?LowNumber=" +
      lowNumber.Text.Trim() +
      "&HighNumber=" +
      highNumber.Text.Trim();
    //Use an XmlDocument to load the XML returned from the Web Service method
    System.Xml.XmlDocument xmlDoc = new System.Xml.XmlDocument();
    xmlDoc.Load(httpGetUrl);

    //Pull the value out of the second node
    //   1st Node: <?xml version="1.0" encoding="utf-8" ?>
    //   2nd Node: <int xmlns="http://www.dotnetjunkies.com">7</int>
    webMethodResult.Text = "<hr><b>Your number is: </b>" +
      xmlDoc.ChildNodes[1].InnerText;
}
```

After the Web Form has been built, and the `Button1_Click()` event handler is in place, we can run the project to test the code. First, set the `CSharpConsumer` project as the startup project by right-clicking on the `CSharpConsumer` item in the Solution Explorer, and select **Set As StartUp Project**. Next, set the `HttpConsumer.aspx` Web Form as the start form, as we did previously, and click the Start button:

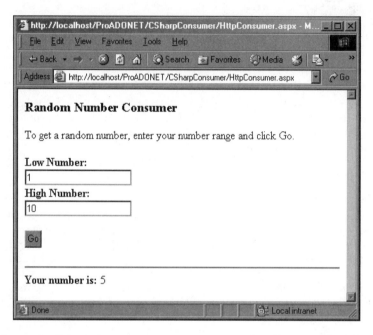

When the **Go** button is clicked, the `Button1_Click()` event handler is invoked. In the event handler we create a string that is the Web Service method URL, with the input arguments as query string values. Using the `XmlDocument` class, we create an object that is a representation of the XML file returned by the `RandomNumberGenerator` Web Service method. The first node of the XML file is:

```
<?xml version="1.0" encoding="utf-8" ?>
<int xmlns="http://www.dotnetjunkies.com">5</int>
```

In the second element, `int` refers to the XML data type of the element – an integer in this case – and `xmlns` refers to the XML namespace – defined in the `WebService` attribute in the `TrivialFunTools` Web Service.

The return value of the Web Service method is the `InnerText` of the `<int>` element (the text between the opening and closing `<int>` tags). Since the `XmlDocument.ChildNodes` property is a zero-based collection, the ordinal "1" references the second node – `xmlDoc.ChildNodes[1].InnerText` refers to the value returned by the Web Service method – the integer 5 in this example.

Build a SOAP Consumer in Visual Studio .NET

While we can consume a Web Service using HTTP GET and HTTP POST, either by setting the `<form>` action and method, or by invoking the Web Service method in code and capturing the return value, we can also consume a Web Service using SOAP. One of the easiest ways to implement a SOAP consumer is by using a tool, such as Visual Studio .NET. Tools such as this may provide wizards or utilities that abstract the process of building a SOAP consumer away from the developer, making it very easy to implement. The consumer can be any application that can access the Internet (or an intranet in the case of private Web Services).

> **Later in this chapter we will use some of the command-line utilities provided by the .NET Framework to create a consumer without using Visual Studio .NET.**

Before writing the code for consuming the Web Service, build the user interface – you can copy the HTML between the opening and closing `<form>` tags in the Web Form created previously, `HttpConsumer.aspx`, to a new Web Form named `Consumer1.aspx`:

```
<%@ Page language="c#" Codebehind="Consumer1.aspx.cs"
  AutoEventWireup="false" Inherits="CSharpConsumer.Consumer1" %>
<!DOCTYPE HTML PUBLIC "-//W3C//DTD HTML 4.0 Transitional//EN" >
<html>
  <head>
    <meta name="GENERATOR" Content="Microsoft Visual Studio 7.0">
    <meta name="CODE_LANGUAGE" Content="C#">
    <meta name="vs_defaultClientScript" content="JavaScript (ECMAScript)">
    <meta name="vs_targetSchema"
      content="http://schemas.microsoft.com/intellisense/ie5">
  </head>
  <body MS_POSITIONING="GridLayout">
    <form id="Consumer1" method="post" runat="server">
      <h3>
        Random Number Consumer
      </h3>
      <p>
        To get a random number, enter your number
        range and click Go.
      </p>
      <b>Low Number:</b>
      <br>
      <asp:TextBox Runat="server" ID="lowNumber" />
      <br>
      <b>High Number:</b>
      <br>
      <asp:TextBox Runat="server" ID="highNumber" />
      <br>
      <p>
        <asp:Button Runat="server" Text="Go" id="Button1" />
      </p>
      <asp:Label Runat="server" ID="webMethodResult" />
```

```
        </form>
      </body>
    </html>
```

With the Web interface constructed, we can begin building the code-behind class that will connect to the Web Service and invoke the `RandomNumberGenerator` method. In the previous examples we have assumed we knew exactly where the Web Service was located; we knew the URL to the `TrivialFunTools.asmx` page. For this example, we will use some discovery tools to find the Web Service.

Discovering Web Services

As a consumer we would know the Web Service URL by either getting it directly from the provider company, or discovering it in the UDDI registry (http://www.uddi.org or http://uddi.microsoft.com). In the UDDI registry we can search for Web Services that are publicly available in many ways, including by business name, location, or classification.

Additionally, if we know the location of the `.disco` or `.vsdisco` discovery files, we can discover available Web Services with either the **Add Web Reference** functionality in Visual Studio .NET, or with a discovery tool, such as `DISCO.exe`.

Using DISCO.exe to Discover Web Services

If we know the URL for the discovery file (`.disco`, `.vsdisco`, `.discomap`) or the WSDL file (`.wsdl` or `.xsd`), we can use the `DISCO.exe` utility to discover what Web Services are available.

The `DISCO.exe` utility allows the following optional arguments:

❑ **/nologo:**
Suppresses the banner (the text that displays in the command window before the results are displayed).

❑ **/nosave:**
Does not save the discovered documents or results (`.wsdl`, `.xsd`, `.disco`, and `.discomap` files) to disk. The default is to save these documents.

❑ **/out:** (shorthand is `/o:`)
Specifies the output directory in which to save the discovered documents. The default is the current directory.

❑ **/username:** (shorthand is `/u:`)
Specifies the user name to use when connecting to a proxy server that requires authentication.

❑ **/password:** (shorthand is `/p:`)
Specifies the password to use when connecting to a proxy server that requires authentication.

❑ **/domain:** (shorthand is `/d:`)
Specifies the domain name to use when connecting to a proxy server that requires authentication.

❑ **/proxy:**
Specifies the URL of the proxy server to use for HTTP requests. The default is to use the system proxy setting.

- ❑ **/proxyusername:** (shorthand is /pu:)
  Specifies the user name to use when connecting to a proxy server that requires authentication.

- ❑ **/proxypassword:** (shorthand is /pp:)
  Specifies the password to use when connecting to a proxy server that requires authentication.

- ❑ **/proxydomain:** (shorthand is /pd:)
  Specifies the domain to use when connecting to a proxy server that requires authentication.

- ❑ **/?**
  Displays command syntax and options for the tool.

In a command window, execute the following command:

```
disco.exe /nosave http://localhost/ProADONET/CSharpProvider/CSharpProvider.vsdisco
```

The result should look similar to the following screenshot:

When this command is executed, the DISCO.exe utility reads the DISCO file, and the Web Service information is returned. Visual Studio .NET automatically generates a .vsdisco file for every Web Application or Web Service project. The .vsdisco file is a dynamic discovery file, which checks the root directory and all sub-directories of the Web application for Web Services.

Adding a Web Reference in Visual Studio .NET

When we make a Web reference in Visual Studio .NET, a lot more is done that just discovery of the Web Service. When we complete the steps to add a Web reference a proxy client class is automatically generated for us. The proxy client is created based on the WSDL provided by the Web Service. The proxy client exposes the Web Service interfaces to the consumer application as if the Web Service was a local class in the consumer application. The proxy client class will be used to invoke the methods of the Web Service.

> **Proxy client classes are explored in detail later in this chapter.**

To create a Web Reference in Visual Studio .NET, click on Project | Add Web Reference.

Then, in the Add Web Reference dialog window we can enter either the Web Service URL or the discovery file URL into the Address textbox, or click on one of the UDDI links to search the Microsoft UDDI:

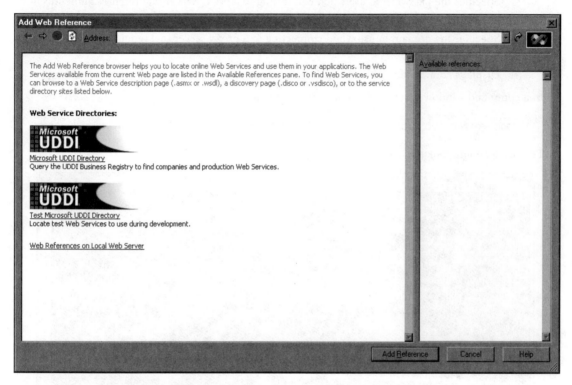

If we type in the URL of the .vsdisco file we will see an XML document that lists all of the available Web Services from this Web application:

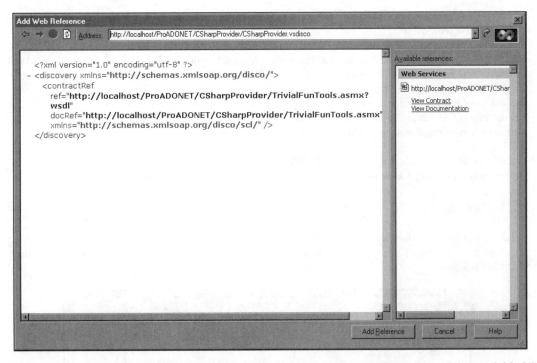

From here we can either click the **Add Reference** button, or type the URL to one of the available Web Services into the **Address** box, and view the Web Service information page:

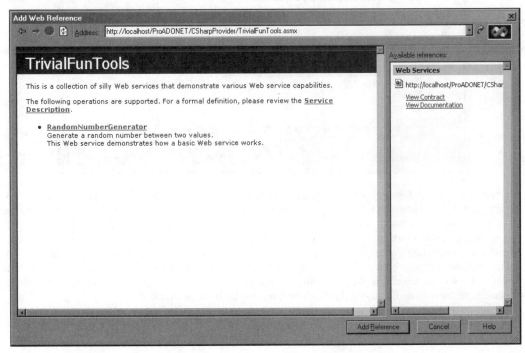

If we decide that this is the Web Service we want, we simply click the **Add Reference** button at the bottom of the window.

When a Web reference is added, behind the scenes Visual Studio .NET uses the Web Service's WSDL to create a proxy client class, which includes the URL of the Web Service, and interfaces for invoking the Web Service methods, both synchronously and asynchronously. Synchronous execution is the typical invoke and wait for a response type of method execution. Asynchronous execution is similar to fire-and-forget; the method is invoked, but the caller does not wait for a response. The proxy client is automatically created with methods for both types of execution.

If we build the project (click on **Build | Build**), we can view the project assembly in the Microsoft Intermediate Language Disassembler (`ILDASM.exe`). From the command line, type:

```
ILDASM.exe
```

When the utility launches, drag the project DLL – found at `C:\Inetpub\wwwroot\ProADONET\CSharpConsumer\bin\CSharpConsumer.dll` – into the **ILDASM** window:

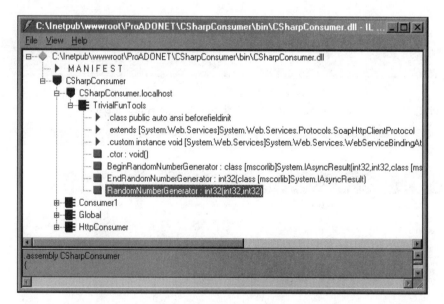

We can see, in the preceding screenshot, that a new namespace was added to our project, the `CSharpConsumer.localhost` namespace, which has one class, `TrivialFunTools`. The class has three public methods, `BeginRandomNumberGenerator`, `EndRandomNumberGenerator`, and `RandomNumberGenerator`. The first two methods are used for invoking the Web Service method asynchronously, while the latter is used for synchronous invocation of the Web Service method. The proxy methods do not contain any of the logic that the Web Service has, they are just an interface for the Web Service method. An object instance of the proxy client class can be constructed, and the proxy methods can be invoked, causing the Web Service methods to be invoked.

The namespace created for the proxy client class is based on the URL that was used to create the Web reference. For example, creating a Web reference to `http://www.dotnetjunkies.com/services/TrivialFunTools.asmx` creates a proxy client class with `CSharpConsumer.com.dotnetjunkies.www` as the namespace.

Building the Consumer Code-Behind Class

In the code-behind class we instantiate the `CSharpConsumer.localhost.TrivialFunTools` class, and invoke the `RandomNumberGenerator` method on a postback – any time the page is posted from a button click. Most of the code in the code-behind class will be added by Visual Studio .NET. Add the highlighted code to the `Consumer1.aspx` code behind class:

```csharp
using System;
using System.Collections;
using System.ComponentModel;
using System.Data;
using System.Drawing;
using System.Web;
using System.Web.SessionState;
using System.Web.UI;
using System.Web.UI.WebControls;
using System.Web.UI.HtmlControls;
using CSharpConsumer.localhost;

namespace CSharpConsumer
{
  /// <summary>
  /// Summary description for Consumer1.
  /// </summary>
  public class Consumer1 : System.Web.UI.Page
  {
    protected System.Web.UI.WebControls.TextBox lowNumber;
    protected System.Web.UI.WebControls.TextBox highNumber;
    protected System.Web.UI.WebControls.Button Button1;
    protected System.Web.UI.WebControls.Label webMethodResult;

    public Consumer1()
    {
      Page.Init += new System.EventHandler(Page_Init);
    }

    private void Page_Load(object sender, System.EventArgs e)
    {
      if(Page.IsPostBack)
      {
        //Create two integer objects to hold
        //the low and high values
        int low = Int32.Parse(lowNumber.Text.Trim());
        int high = Int32.Parse(highNumber.Text.Trim());

        //Create an instance of the
```

```
        //TrivialFunTools proxy client class
        TrivialFunTools tft = new TrivialFunTools();

        //Invoke the Web Service method and catch
        //the return value
        int result = tft.RandomNumberGenerator(low, high);
        //Set the return value to the Label.Text property
        webMethodResult.Text =
          "<hr><b>Your number is: </b>" +
          result.ToString();
      }
    }

    private void Page_Init(object sender, EventArgs e)
    {
      //
      // CODEGEN: This call is required by the
      //ASP.NET Web Form Designer.
      //
      InitializeComponent();
    }

    #region Web Form Designer generated code
    /// <summary>
    /// Required method for Designer support - do not modify
    /// the contents of this method with the code editor.
    /// </summary>
    private void InitializeComponent()
    {
      this.Load += new System.EventHandler(this.Page_Load);

    }
    #endregion
  }
}
```

In the `Consumer1.aspx` code-behind class we add a `using` statement to include the proxy client's namespace, `CSharpConsumer.localhost`, so that we do not have to use fully qualified class names. Visual Studio .NET added variable instances that map to the server controls on the Web Form that we need programmatic access to – the `lowNumber` and `highNumber` TextBoxes, and the `webMethodResult` label.

In the `Page_Load` event handler we evaluate for a page postback. If the current request is the result of a page postback (the Go button was clicked), we invoke the Web Service method. This is done by creating an instance of the `CSharpConsumer.localhost.TrivialFunTools` class, and invoking the `RandomNumberGenerator` method.

When the `RandomNumberGenerator` proxy client method is invoked, a SOAP message is created, and it is sent to the Web Service URL that was used when creating the Web Reference. The method in the Web Service executes on the provider server, and the return data is sent back to the consumer as a SOAP message, where the proxy client returns the data to the calling component as if the method executed locally.

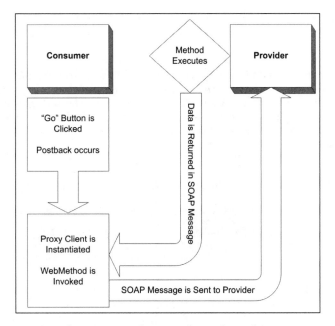

The SOAP message structure that is sent to the provider is shown here:

```xml
<?xml version="1.0" encoding="utf-8"?>
<soap:Envelope xmlns:xsi="http://www.w3.org/2001/XMLSchema-instance"
  xmlns:xsd="http://www.w3.org/2001/XMLSchema"
  xmlns:soap="http://schemas.xmlsoap.org/soap/envelope/">
  <soap:Body>
    <RandomNumberGenerator xmlns="http://www.dotnetjunkies.com">
     <LowNumber>1</LowNumber>
     <HighNumber>10</HighNumber>
    </RandomNumberGenerator>
  </soap:Body>
</soap:Envelope>
```

The Web Service receives the SOAP message and extracts the bold `<LowNumber>` and `<HighNumber>` values from the SOAP message body. The `RandomNumberGenerator` method in the Web Service is invoked, using the `<LowNumber>` and `<HighNumber>` values, and a random number is returned in a SOAP message to the consumer.

```xml
<?xml version="1.0" encoding="utf-8"?>
<soap:Envelope xmlns:xsi="http://www.w3.org/2001/XMLSchema-instance"
  xmlns:xsd="http://www.w3.org/2001/XMLSchema"
  xmlns:soap="http://schemas.xmlsoap.org/soap/envelope/">
  <soap:Body>
    <RandomNumberGeneratorResponse xmlns="http://www.dotnetjunkies.com">
     <RandomNumberGeneratorResult>5</RandomNumberGeneratorResult>
    </RandomNumberGeneratorResponse>
  </soap:Body>
</soap:Envelope>
```

The SOAP message is received, and de-serialized into a .NET object – an integer in this example. The object then has all the functionality provided by its class definition.

> **All error handling for the Web Service execution is the responsibility of the consumer application. The provider has clearly defined, in the WSDL, what is expected and returned by this Web Service – the interfaces. Since this has been clearly defined by the provider, it is expected that the consumer will abide by it. Any incorrect values entered, for instance, will cause the Web Service to return an exception that must be handled by the consumer.**

Below is the Web Form interface after the `RandomNumberGenerator` method is invoked:

What is a Proxy Client?

In the previous example we used Visual Studio .NET to create a Web Service proxy client class, by adding a Web Reference to our project. A proxy client class can also be created using a command-line utility that ships with the .NET Framework – the `WSDL.exe` utility. Before we investigate the `WSDL.exe` utility, let's look at what a proxy client class is.

A proxy client is a local object that simulates the functionality of a remote object. For instance, in the previous example, a proxy client class is created for us by Visual Studio .NET. This proxy client class is a local representation of the remote class. The proxy client class contains all of the method declarations that the remote class has, but the proxy does not include the functionality. Instead, the proxy client is a surrogate class for us to use when implementing the remote object.

Let's take a look at the proxy client class that was created by Visual Studio .NET when we made a Web Reference. This class file can be found at `C:\Inetpub\wwwroot\ProADONET\` `CSharpConsumer\Web References\localhost\TrivialFunTools.cs`.

```
//-------------------------------------------------------------------------
// <autogenerated>
//      This code was generated by a tool.
//      Runtime Version: 1.0.2914.16
//
//      Changes to this file may cause incorrect behavior and will be lost if
//      the code is regenerated.
// </autogenerated>
//-------------------------------------------------------------------------

namespace CSharpConsumer.localhost {
  using System.Diagnostics;
  using System.Xml.Serialization;
  using System;
  using System.Web.Services.Protocols;
  using System.Web.Services;


  [System.Web.Services.WebServiceBindingAttribute(
    Name="TrivialFunToolsSoap", Namespace="http://www.dotnetjunkies.com")]
  public class TrivialFunTools :
  System.Web.Services.Protocols.SoapHttpClientProtocol {

    [System.Diagnostics.DebuggerStepThroughAttribute()]
    public TrivialFunTools() {
```

The proxy class includes a specification of what URL was used when creating the proxy. This is the URL that will be used each time a Web Service method is invoked. In this example the URL property specifies `http://localhost` as the domain where this Web Service is. That is because making a Web Reference to a Web Service on the local machine created the proxy client. The URL property will have whatever URL was used to create the proxy class, for example,
`http://www.dotnetjunkies.com/services/TrivialFunTools.asmx`.

```
      this.Url =
          "http://localhost/ProADONET/CSharpProvider/TrivialFunTools.asmx";
    }
```

> If you create a proxy client using the WSDL for a Web Service on a development server whose URL will change on a production server, you can create a proxy client that gets the URL from a configuration file **<appSetting>**. See *The WSDL.exe Utility* section of this chapter for information on creating proxy client classes.

The RandomNumberGenerator method is included, using SoapDocumentMethodAttribute. This attribute specifies how the SOAP message should be formatted:

```
    [System.Diagnostics.DebuggerStepThroughAttribute()]
    [System.Web.Services.Protocols.SoapDocumentMethodAttribute(
      "http://www.dotnetjunkies.com/RandomNumberGenerator",
      RequestNamespace="http://www.dotnetjunkies.com",
      ResponseNamespace="http://www.dotnetjunkies.com",
      Use=System.Web.Services.Description.SoapBindingUse.Literal,
```

```
    ParameterStyle=
      System.Web.Services.Protocols.SoapParameterStyle.Wrapped)]
    public int RandomNumberGenerator(int LowNumber, int HighNumber) {
      object[] results = this.Invoke("RandomNumberGenerator", new object[] {
      LowNumber,
      HighNumber});
    return ((int)(results[0]));
    }
```

Also included in the proxy client class are methods for invoking the Web Service method asynchronously. The proxy generator (WSDL.exe or Visual Studio .NET) adds these methods to enable asynchronous calls to the Web Service:

```
    [System.Diagnostics.DebuggerStepThroughAttribute()]
    public System.IAsyncResult BeginRandomNumberGenerator(int LowNumber,
      int HighNumber, System.AsyncCallback callback, object asyncState) {
        return this.BeginInvoke("RandomNumberGenerator", new object[] {
        LowNumber,
        HighNumber}, callback, asyncState);
    }

    [System.Diagnostics.DebuggerStepThroughAttribute()]
    public int EndRandomNumberGenerator(System.IAsyncResult asyncResult) {
      object[] results = this.EndInvoke(asyncResult);
      return ((int)(results[0]));
    }
  }
}
```

While the proxy client class provides an interface for invoking the Web Service methods, the code for the Web Service method's functionality remains on the provider server. The proxy client class enables us to construct an object in our code that represents the remote object.

The WSDL.exe Utility

We can use the WSDL.exe utility that is shipped with the .NET Framework to create a proxy client class without Visual Studio .NET. We may want to do this in situations where we will be reading the Web Service URL from the configuration file, or if we are not using Visual Studio .NET to build our application. The WSDL.exe utility includes a number of optional arguments that can be used to customize the proxy client class when it is generated. As we go through the rest of this chapter, we will discover and use many of the optional arguments. For an entire list of WSDL.exe arguments, open a command window and execute the following command:

```
wsdl.exe /?
```

To create a proxy client class for the TrivialFunTools Web Service using the WSDL.exe utility, open a command window, and execute the following command:

```
wsdl.exe http://localhost/ProADONET/CSharpProvider/TrivialFunTools.asmx?WSDL
```

The previous command indicates that a proxy client class should be created using the WSDL document at the specified URL. By default proxy classes generated by the `WSDL.exe` utility are in C#. We can use the `/l:` argument to specify the language we would like the proxy client to be created with – possible values are CS (C#), VB (Visual Basic .NET), JS (Jscript .NET), or we can also specify the fully qualified name of a class that implements the `System.CodeDom.Compiler.CodeDomProvider` class (see the .NET Framework SDK documentation for more information on the `CodeDomProvider` class).

Executing the previous command creates a file named `TrivialFunTools.cs`; the file is named after the Web Service class name. We can create a file using any name we specify by adding the `/out:` argument to the `WSDL.exe` command:

```
wsdl.exe http://localhost/ProADONET/CSharpProvider/TrivialFunTools.asmx?WSDL
/out:TrivialFunToolsProxy.cs
```

The proxy client class, by default, is generated without a specified .NET namespace. We can create the class in a specified namespace by adding the `/n:` argument (shorthand for `/namespace:`).

```
wsdl.exe http://localhost/ProADONET/CSharpProvider/TrivialFunTools.asmx?WSDL
/out:TrivialFunToolsProxy.cs /n:CSharpConsumer.Proxies
```

The resulting proxy client class is nearly identical to the proxy client class created previously by Visual Studio .NET. The only difference is the namespace (`CSharpConsumer.localhost` versus. `CSharpConsumer.Proxies`)

This proxy class can be compiled into our application assembly by including the assembly in our Visual Studio .NET project and rebuilding it.

1. Copy the `TrivialFunTools.cs` file into the `CSharpConsumer` directory

2. Click the **Show All Files** button in the Solution Explorer:

3. Right click on the `TrivialFunTools.cs` file and choose **Include In Project**

4. Build the Project

The Web Service methods of the new namespace can be invoked in the same way as the previous example.

Following is the code for the `Page_Load` event handler of the `Consumer1.aspx` Web Form's code-behind class using the proxy we just built:

```
private void Page_Load(object sender, System.EventArgs e)
{
  if(Page.IsPostBack)
  {
```

```
        //Create two integer objects to hold
        //the low and high values
        int low = Int32.Parse(lowNumber.Text.Trim());
        int high = Int32.Parse(highNumber.Text.Trim());

        //Create an instance of the
        //TrivialFunTools proxy client class
        CSharpConsumer.Proxies.TrivialFunTools tft =
          new CSharpConsumer.Proxies.TrivialFunTools();

        //Invoke the Web Service method and catch the return value
        int result = tft.RandomNumberGenerator(low, high);

        //Set the return value to the Label.Text property
        webMethodResult.Text = "<hr><b>Your number is: </b>" +
          result.ToString();
    }
}
```

There is no functional difference between the proxy client class we created with Visual Studio .NET using a Web Reference and the proxy client class we created using the WSDL.exe utility.

Storing a Web Service URL in a Configuration File

The WSDL.exe utility enables creating a proxy client class that will check the application configuration file for the URL. This is useful when we will have different URLs for the Web Service while our consumer application is in development versus in production. When creating the proxy client class, we can provide the /appsettingurlkey: argument, which identifies the key name of an <appSettings> key-value pair in the configuration file.

```
wsdl.exe http://localhost/ProADONET/CSharpProvider/TrivialFunTools.asmx?WSDL
/out:TrivialFunToolsProxy.cs /n:CSharpConsumer.Proxies
/appsettingurlkey:TrivialFunToolsUrl
```

The preceding command will create a proxy client class like that we created in the previous example; however, the constructor for the class will have an evaluator to check the <appSettings> section of the configuration file for the specified key-value pair. If a pair is found with the specified key name, the value will be used as the URL to connect to when invoking the Web Service; if no pair is found with the specified key name, the URL that was used when creating the proxy client will be used.

```
[System.Diagnostics.DebuggerStepThroughAttribute()]
public TrivialFunTools() {
  string urlSetting = System.Configuration.ConfigurationSettings.
       AppSettings["TrivialFunToolsUrl"];
  if ((urlSetting != null)) {
    this.Url = urlSetting;
  }else {
    this.Url =
      "http://www.dotnetjunkies.com/services/TrivialFunTools.asmx";
  }
}
```

The format for including an `<appSettings>` key-value pair is shown here:

```xml
<?xml version="1.0" encoding="utf-8" ?>
<configuration>
 <appSettings>
  <add key="TrivialFunToolsURL"
   value="http://www.dotnetjunkies.com/services/TrivialFunTools.asmx"
  />
 </appSettings>
</configuration>
```

Using a `<appSetting>` key-value pair for the Web Service URL enables us to use one URL while in development, and another while in production, without having to recompile the proxy client class.

Exchanging Data in Web Services

In the previous examples, we built and consumed a Web Service that took two integer objects as input arguments, and returned a third integer object. Web Services are capable of working with several data types, both simple types – like string and integer – and complex types – like `DataSets` and serialized custom classes. A Web Service can have the following data types as input arguments, or returned results:

XML Schema Definition	C++ Data Type	CLR Data Type
boolean	bool	Boolean
byte	char, __int8	
double	double	Double
datatype	struct	
decimal		Decimal
enumeration	enum	Enum
float	float	Single
int	int, long, __int32	Int32
long	__int64	Int64
Qname		XmlQualifiedName
short	short, __int16	Int16
string	BSTR	String
timeInstant		DateTime
unsignedByte	unsigned __int8	
unsignedInt	unsigned __int32	UInt32
unsignedLong	unsigned __int64	UInt64
unsignedShort	unsigned __int16	UInt16

> **The protocol being used to invoke a Web Service is directly related to the data types . that the Web Service is using. HTTP GET and HTTP POST both use key-value string pairs, which limits the data types that can be passed into a Web Service to simple data types, such as strings. If complex data types, such as DataSets or custom classes, are being passed into the Web Service, SOAP must be used, as the objects can be serialized to XML and transmitted in the body of a SOAP message.**

Working with DataSets

DataSets are a terrific container for exchanging data in Web Services. Using DataSets, we can exchange tremendous amounts of data in a structured, relational data format. .NET consumers can work with the DataSet in its ADO.NET format, while non-.NET consumers can use the DataSet in its XML format, or deserialize it to a proprietary format.

Building a Pre-populated DataSet-Derived Class

To demonstrate how to make a Web Service that returns a DataSet, we'll add a new Web Service method to the TrivialFunTools Web Service. This Web Service method, GetAllMovieQuotes, will return a DataSet that is an instance of a custom class, MovieQuotesDataSet. The custom class derives from the DataSet class, but it is populated from an XML file in the constructor. We are creating this custom class because other Web Service methods we will be creating are going to be using the same data:

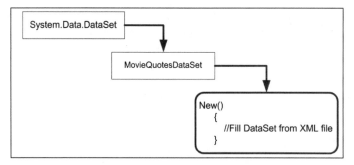

First we create the MovieQuotesDataSet class. This class derives from the DataSet class, and uses the FileStream and StreamReader classes in its constructor to populate the DataSet from an XML file (MovieQuotes.xml).

Create a new class file in the CSharpProvider project, named MovieQuotesDataSet.cs, and add the highlighted code:

```
using System;
using System.Web;
using System.IO;

namespace CSharpProvider
{
    /// <summary>
```

```
/// MovieQuotesDataSet - Derives from DataSet
/// The constructor reads MovieQuotes.xml file and populates itself.
/// </summary>
public class MovieQuotesDataSet : System.Data.DataSet
{
    //In the constructor, read the XML file
    public MovieQuotesDataSet()
    {
        //Open a FileStream to stream in the XML file
        FileStream fs = new FileStream(
          HttpContext.Current.Server.MapPath(
            "MovieQuotes.xml"),
          FileMode.Open, FileAccess.Read);
        StreamReader xmlStream = new StreamReader(fs);
        //Use the ReadXml() method to create a
        //DataTable that represents the XML data
        this.ReadXml(xmlStream);
    }
}
```

In the preceding code we create a custom class, `MovieQuotesDataSet`, which derives from the `System.Data.DataSet` class. In the constructor for the custom class we create a new `System.IO.FileStream` object, passing in the path to the `MovieQuotes.xml` file, and the enumeration arguments to open and grant read access to the file. Using a `System.IO.StreamReader` we create an object to read the characters from the `FileStream`. The `DataSet.ReadXml` method uses the `StreamReader` object to read the XML data into the `DataSet`, creating a new `DataTable` to hold the data. As a result, any time we create an instance of the `MovieQuotesDataSet`, the object is automatically populated with the data from the `MovieQuotes.xml` file.

The `MovieQuotes.xml` file is formatted as follows:

```
<?xml version="1.0" ?>

<MovieQuotes>
  <MovieQuote>
    <Quote>Honestly, this isn't really a brains kind of operation.</Quote>
    <Movie>The Way of the Gun</Movie>
    <ActorOrCharacter>Benicio del Toro</ActorOrCharacter>
  </MovieQuote>

  <MovieQuote>
    <Quote>I've got to return some video tapes.</Quote>
    <Movie>American Psycho</Movie>
    <ActorOrCharacter>Patrick Bateman (Christian Bale)</ActorOrCharacter>
  </MovieQuote>
<MovieQuotes>
```

> The code download includes the entire **MovieQuotes.xml** file.

Building the Web Service Method

The GetAllMovies Web Service method creates and returns an instance of the MovieQuotesDataSet. This is a simple method, since all we need to do is create a new instance of the class, which is populated when it is constructed, and return it to the consumer.

Add this Web Service method to the TrivialFunTools.asmx.cs file (the code-behind file for the TrivialFunTools Web Service).

```
/// <summary>
/// GetAllMovieQuotes - Get all movie quotes.
/// This Web serives shows how you can return a DataSet.
/// </summary>
[WebMethod(Description="Get all movie quotes.<br>" +
  "This Web Service shows how you can return a DataSet.")]
public DataSet GetAllMovieQuotes()
{
  MovieQuotesDataSet myDataSet = new MovieQuotesDataSet();
  return myDataSet;
}
```

In the GetAllMovieQuotes Web Service method, we simply create an instance of the MovieQuotesDataSet class, and return it to the consumer. We can test this Web Service method using the automatically generated test page that is created when we run the project. First set the CSharpProvider project as the startup project and the TrivialFunTools.asmx file as the start page, then click the Start button.

In the Web Service information page, click on the GetAllMovieQuotes link, and click the Invoke button:

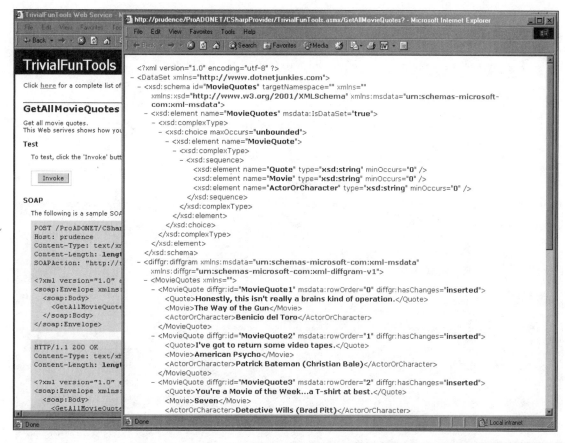

To consume this Web Service, we can follow the same steps as we did when consuming the `RandomNumberGenerator` Web Service method. Of course, Web Service consumers don't have to be .NET applications only: they can be any application that can access the Web Service URL and read the returned XML data. But .NET does make it easy! We will be using a .NET Windows application.

Building a Windows Form Consumer with Visual Studio .NET

A Windows Forms application can consume a Web Service just as an ASP.NET application can – provided the application will always have access to the Web Service URL. As far as the Web Service is concerned, there is no difference between an ASP.NET consumer and a Windows Forms consumer. Both consumers invoke the Web Service method by making a call using one of the three protocols, so the platform, architecture, and language used are irrelevant. As long as the consumer can use one of the protocols, and understand the data returned to it, the Web Service can be used – Windows, Linux, Solaris, Macintosh, and so on are all valid.

To build the Windows Form consumer, follow these steps:

1. In the `CsharpWinFormsConsumer` project, add a Web Reference to the `TrivialFunTools` WSDL file (see *Build a Consumer in Visual Studio .NET* previously in this chapter).

2. By default Visual Studio .NET creates a Windows Form named `Form1`. In the Properties Explorer, change the File Name value to `GetAllMovieQuotesConsumer.cs`.

3. Change the `Text` property of the form to Get All Movie Quotes.

4. Add `GroupBox`, `DataGrid`, and `Button` controls to the Windows Form.

5. Change the `Text` property of the `Button` control to &Get Movie Quotes.

6. Change the `Text` property of the `GroupBox` to Movie Quotes.

The Windows Form should look like the form shown here:

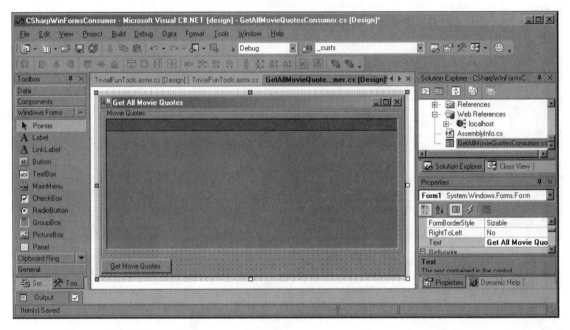

7. Double-click the `Button` in the Windows Form Designer view. This will open up the code view where you can add the following code:

```
private void button1_Click(object sender, System.EventArgs e)
{
    CSharpWinFormsConsumer.localhost.TrivialFunTools tft =
        new CSharpWinFormsConsumer.localhost.TrivialFunTools();
    DataSet ds = tft.GetAllMovieQuotes();
    dataGrid1.DataSource = ds.Tables[0];
}
```

In this code we create an instance of the proxy client class for the Web Service, and invoke the `GetAllMovieQuotes` method. The returned data is instantiated as an instance of the `System.Data.DataSet` class (since our `MovieQuotesDataSet` class is really just a pre-populated `DataSet`). The `dataGrid1.DataSource` is set to the first (and only) `DataTable` in the `DataSet`.

490

Running the Windows Form Project

Build the project, and run it by setting the `CSharpWinFormsConsumer` project as the startup project and clicking the Start button.

When you run the application, the Windows Form will launch. When you click the **Get Movie Quotes** button on the Windows Form, the `button1_Click` event handler will fire. When the `TrivialFunTools` object is created, and the `GetAllMovieQuotes()` method is invoked, a SOAP message is created and sent to the provider, the `GetAllMovieQuotes()` Web Service method is invoked, and a `DataSet` is returned to the consumer in a SOAP message. The first `DataTable` in the `DataSet` is set as the `dataGrid1.DataSource` property, and the movie quotes are displayed in the `DataGrid`:

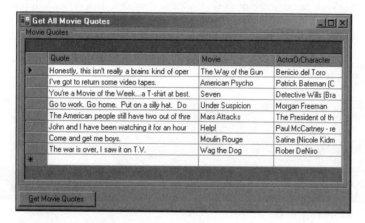

DataSets as Input Arguments

`DataSets` can also be used as input arguments for a Web Service method, much like we used integers as input arguments in the `RandomNumberGenerator` Web Service method previously. In the following example we create a new Web Service method, `AddMovieQuotes`, in the `TrivialFunTools` Web Service, which takes a `DataSet` as an input argument, merges it with the existing `MovieQuotesDataSet` object, and returns the merged `DataSet`.

In the `TrivialFunTools` code behind class, add the following Web Service method:

```
/// <summary>
/// AddMovieQuotes - Adds a DataSet of MovieQuotes to the existing DataSet.
/// This Web serives shows how you can use a DataSet as an input argument.
/// </summary>
[WebMethod(Description="Add movie quotes.<br>" +
   "This Web serives shows how you can use a DataSet " +
   "as an input argument.")]
public DataSet AddMovieQuotes(DataSet MovieQuotes)
{
  MovieQuotesDataSet myDataSet = new MovieQuotesDataSet();
  myDataSet.Merge(MovieQuotes, false, MissingSchemaAction.Add);
  return myDataSet;
}
```

When we declare the method, the input argument is defined with its data type. In the preceding sample code we define a `DataSet` (`MovieQuotes`) as an input argument, and use the `DataSet.Merge()` method to merge the input `DataSet` into the existing `DataSet` (`MovieQuotesDataSet`).

> **For more information on the `DataSet` and the `Merge` method, see Chapter 5, *The DataSet*.**

Web Service methods that accept complex data types, such as `DataSets` and bytes, as input arguments cannot be invoked in all the same ways as Web Service methods that use simple data types, such as strings and integers. Web Service methods that require complex data types as input arguments cannot be invoked using HTTP GET or HTTP POST, since the complex data types cannot be passed in the query string (HTTP GET) or in the request body (HTTP POST). SOAP is the only protocol that can be used when invoking a Web Service method that requires complex data type input arguments. As a result, the information and test page generated by the .NET Framework does not include test mechanisms for HTTP GET and HTTP POST:

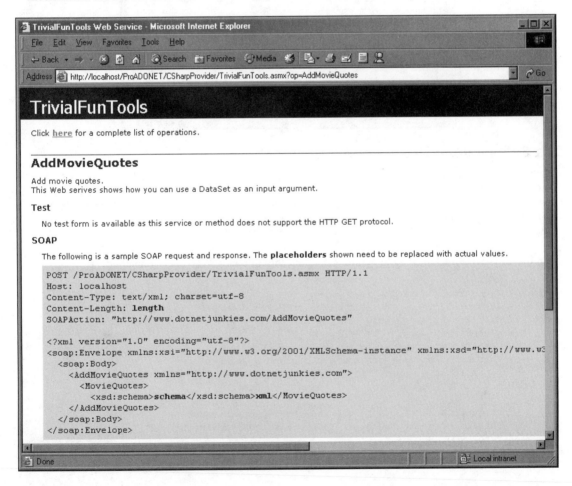

Building a Web Form Consumer

To demonstrate how the AddMovieQuotes Web Service method works, we can build another consumer in the CSharpConsumer project. For this example we will build an ASP.NET Web Form consumer. The Web Form, named DataSetConsumer.aspx, will invoke the GetAllMovieQuotes Web Method to populate a DataGrid server control and load another XML file (MovieQuotes2.xml) to populate a DataSet and another DataGrid. When the AddMovieQuotes Web Service method is invoked, the DataSet created from MovieQuotes2.xml will be passed as the input argument, and the merged DataSet will be used to populate a third DataGrid.

Before creating the Web From, right-click on localhost, under the Web References directory in the Solution Explorer. Choose Update Web Reference. This will rebuild the proxy client class with the newly added Web Service methods:

The Web Form should look like this:

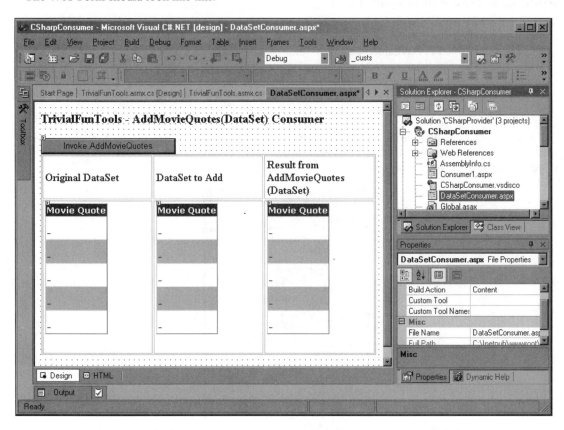

The `DataGrid` objects all use a `TemplateColumn` to customize the output. All three `DataGrid` objects should have the same layout. Use the following `DataGrid` layout for all three `DataGrid` objects in the Web Form:

```
<asp:DataGrid id="OriginalDataGrid" runat="server" AutoGenerateColumns="False"
  Font-Names="Verdana, Arial, sans-serif" Font-Size="x-small"
  HeaderStyle-BackColor="Maroon" HeaderStyle-ForeColor="White"
  HeaderStyle-Font-Bold="True" AlternatingItemStyle-BackColor="Tan">
  <Columns>
    <asp:TemplateColumn HeaderText="Movie Quote">
      <ItemTemplate>
        <%# DataBinder.Eval(Container.DataItem, "Quote") %>
        <br>
        <%# DataBinder.Eval(Container.DataItem, "ActorOrCharacter") %>
        -
        <%# DataBinder.Eval(Container.DataItem, "Movie") %>
      </ItemTemplate>
    </asp:TemplateColumn>
  </Columns>
</asp:DataGrid>
```

In the code-behind file for the Web Form, we will populate the first `DataGrid` by invoking the `GetAllMovieQuotes` Web Service method, and populate the second `DataGrid` by loading a new `DataSet` with data from the `MovieQuotes2.xml` file. Let's build a `GetData` method to encapsulate this functionality.

Open the code-behind class in Visual Studio .NET and add a using statement for the `System.IO` namespace, and declare a class-level `DataSet` object to work with:

```csharp
using System;
using System.Collections;
using System.ComponentModel;
using System.Data;
using System.Drawing;
using System.Web;
using System.Web.SessionState;
using System.Web.UI;
using System.Web.UI.WebControls;
using System.Web.UI.HtmlControls;
using System.IO;

namespace CSharpConsumer
{
  /// <summary>
  /// Summary description for DataSetConsumer.
  /// </summary>
  public class DataSetConsumer : System.Web.UI.Page
  {
    protected System.Web.UI.WebControls.Button Button1;
    protected System.Web.UI.WebControls.DataGrid OriginalDataGrid;
    protected System.Web.UI.WebControls.DataGrid DataToAddGrid;
    protected System.Web.UI.WebControls.DataGrid ResultGrid;
    private DataSet myDataSet;
```

Now build the `GetData` method. In the method, construct a new instance of `myDataSet`, and populate it with the `MovieQuotes2.xml` file. Then construct an instance of the `TrivialFunTools` proxy client class and set the `OriginalDataGrid.DataSource` property to the `DataSet` returned by the `GetAllMovies` Web Service method:

```csharp
    public DataSetConsumer()
    {
      Page.Init += new System.EventHandler(Page_Init);
    }

    private void GetData()
    {
      myDataSet = new DataSet();

      //Open a FileStream to stream in the XML file
      FileStream fs = new
        FileStream(
        HttpContext.Current.Server.MapPath(
          "MovieQuotes2.xml"),
        FileMode.Open, FileAccess.Read);
```

```
        StreamReader xmlStream = new StreamReader(fs);
        //Use the ReadXml() method to create a
        //DataTable that represents the XML data
        myDataSet.ReadXml(xmlStream);
        xmlStream.Close();

        CSharpConsumer.localhost.TrivialFunTools tft = new
          CSharpConsumer.localhost.TrivialFunTools();

        OriginalDataGrid.DataSource = tft.GetAllMovieQuotes();
        DataToAddGrid.DataSource = myDataSet;
    }
```

In the `Page_Load()` event handler, invoke the `GetData` method, then use the `Page.DataBind()` method to data bind all of the server controls in the `Page.Controls` collection only on the first request (not on a postback):

```
    private void Page_Load(object sender, System.EventArgs e)
    {
      if(!Page.IsPostBack)
      {
        GetData();
        Page.DataBind();
      }
    }
```

At this point, when the page is first requested, the `Page_Load()` event handler will be invoked and the first two `DataGrids` will be populated:

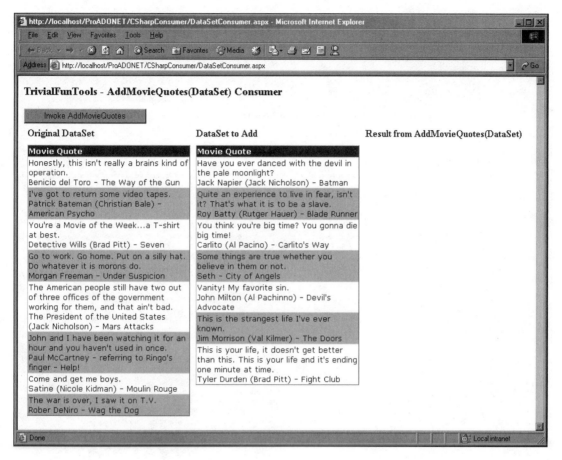

In the `Button1_Click` event handler we want to invoke the `AddMovieQuotes` Web Service method. Since the page is reloaded when the postback occurs, we first call `GetData` to create the `myDataSet` object, then declare a new `DataSet`, `myMergedDataSet`, and instantiate it by invoking the `AddMovieQuotes` Web Service method with `myDataSet` as the input argument:

```
private void Button1_Click(object sender, System.EventArgs e)
{
    //Populate myDataSet
    GetData();
    //Create the TrivialFunTools object
    CSharpConsumer.localhost.TrivialFunTools tft =
        new CSharpConsumer.localhost.TrivialFunTools();
    //Invoke the AddMovieQuotes() method, passing in myDataSet
    //Put the returned DataSet into the myMergedDataSet object
    DataSet myMergedDataSet = tft.AddMovieQuotes(myDataSet);
    //Set the DataSource of the third DataGrid
    ResultGrid.DataSource = myMergedDataSet;
    //Bind all of the controls
    Page.DataBind();
}
```

497

When the button is clicked, and the `Button1_Click` event handler is invoked, the `AddMovieQuotes` Web Service method is invoked, and a merged `DataSet` is returned and bound to the third `DataGrid`:

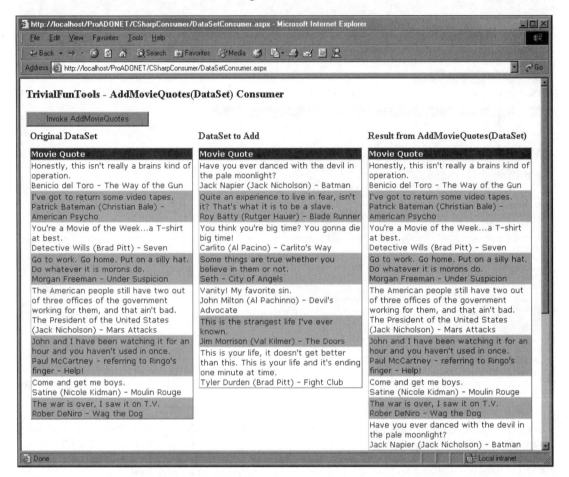

Using XML with Web Services

As we previously discussed, Web Services use XML as their transmission format. In the previous Web Service examples, `RandomNumberGenerator` and `GetAllMovieQuotes`, we saw how the return values of the Web Service methods were serialized as XML before being returned to the consumer. The .NET Framework also enables serializing custom classes that can be returned from a Web Service method. We can create a custom class in the Web Service, and set the return type of a Web Service method as that custom class:

```
[WebMethod()]
public MyClass MyMethod(){
  MyClass obj = new MyClass();
  Return obj;
}
```

Working with Custom Classes as XML

We can create a custom class that our Web Service can use. The proxy client that we create, either with a Web Reference in Visual Studio .NET or using the WSDL.exe utility, can have proxy classes for our custom class as well as for the Web Service class. This enables the consumer to create an instance of the custom class in their application and use as if it were a resident class.

The provider application can define a class. By including this class as either a return data type, or an input data type, this class's interfaces will be included in the Web Service proxy class that is created by the consumer. This enables the consumer to instantiate this class and use the object as if it were resident, when in fact it is a remote object.

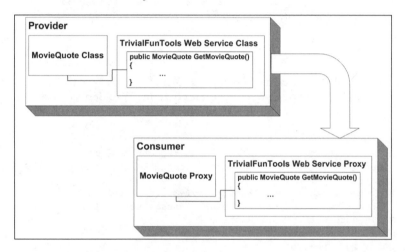

Exposing a Custom Class with a Web Service

To demonstrate this, let's start by building a custom MovieQuote class in the CSharpProvider project. This class will be used to represent a random <MovieQuote> element from the MovieQuotes.xml file – it will expose Quote, ActorOrCharacter, and Movie properties.

Create a new class file in the CSharpProvider project, named MovieQuote.cs:

```
using System;

namespace CSharpProvider
{
  /// <summary>
  /// MovieQuote
  /// Basic MovieQuote object, with three properties.
  /// </summary>
  public class MovieQuote
  {
    public string Quote;
    public string ActorOrCharacter;
    public string Movie;

    public MovieQuote()
    {
```

499

```
        MovieQuotesDataSet ds = new MovieQuotesDataSet();
        //Create a random number to select one of the quotes
        Random RandNumber = new Random();
        //The random number should be between 0 and
        //the number of rows in the table
        int RandomRow =
          RandNumber.Next(0, ds.Tables[0].Rows.Count);
        //Set the MovieQuote properties using the
        //RandomRow as the DataRow index value
        Quote = ds.Tables[0].Rows[RandomRow]["Quote"].ToString();
        ActorOrCharacter =
      ds.Tables[0].Rows[RandomRow]["ActorOrCharacter"].ToString();
        Movie = ds.Tables[0].Rows[RandomRow]["Movie"].ToString();
      }
    }
  }
```

Next, we create a new Web Service method in the TrivialFunTools class, named GetMovieQuote. The Web Service method's return type is MovieQuote. In the Web Service method we construct a new instance of MovieQuote, and return it to the consumer:

```
/// <summary>
/// GetMovieQuoteObject - Get a random MovieQuote object.
/// This Web serives shows how you can return a custom object as XML.
/// </summary>
[WebMethod(Description="Get a random MovieQuote object.<br>" +
  "This Web serives shows how you can return a custom object as XML.")]
public MovieQuote GetMovieQuoteObject()
{
  MovieQuote mq = new MovieQuote();
  return mq;
}
```

Make CSharpProvider the startup project, and TrivialFunTools.asmx the Start Page. Click the Start button to run the applications and test the Web Service method from the test page:

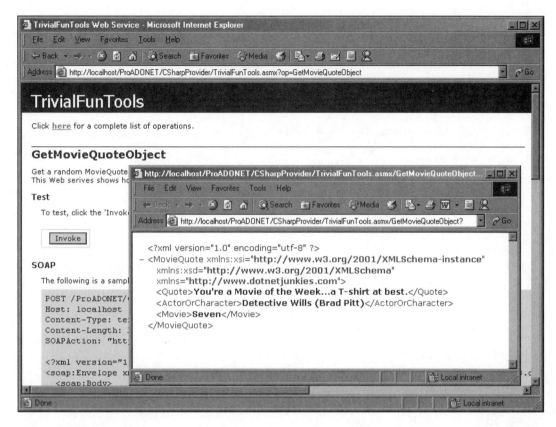

When the Web Service method is invoked, the custom object is automatically serialized as XML. Each of the properties becomes an element in the XML node tree. At the consumer application we can construct an instance of the MovieQuote custom class, using the proxy client, and have full access to its properties.

Consuming a Custom Class from a Web Service

In the CSharpConsumer project we can consume the TrivialFunTools Web Service, and use a proxy MovieQuote object in our application.

We start by updating the Web reference again, by right-clicking on it in the Solution Explorer and choosing **Update Web Reference**. Next we create the consumer Web Form, Consumer2.aspx, in the CSharpConsumer project:

```
<%@ Page language="c#" Codebehind="Consumer2.aspx.cs"
  AutoEventWireup="false" Inherits="CSharpConsumer.Consumer2" %>
<!DOCTYPE HTML PUBLIC "-//W3C//DTD HTML 4.0 Transitional//EN" >
<html>
  <head>
    <meta name="GENERATOR" Content="Microsoft Visual Studio 7.0">
    <meta name="CODE_LANGUAGE" Content="C#">
    <meta name="vs_defaultClientScript"
        content="JavaScript (ECMAScript)">
    <meta name="vs_targetSchema"
```

```
            content="http://schemas.microsoft.com/intellisense/ie5">
      </head>
      <body MS_POSITIONING="GridLayout">
        <form id="Consumer2" method="post" runat="server">
          <h3>
            TrivialFunTools - GetMovieQuoteObject() Consumer
          </h3>
          <b>Movie:</b>
          <asp:Label id="Movie" runat="server" />
          <br>
          <b>Quote:</b>
          <asp:Label id="Quote" runat="server" />
          <br>
          <b>Actor or Character:</b>
          <asp:Label id="ActorOrCharacter" runat="server" />
        </form>
      </body>
    </html>
```

In the code behind class for the Web Form we can instantiate the `MovieQuote` custom class and invoke the `GetMovieObject` Web Service method.

```
private void Page_Load(object sender, System.EventArgs e)
{
    CSharpConsumer.localhost.TrivialFunTools tft =
        new CSharpConsumer.localhost.TrivialFunTools();
      CSharpConsumer.localhost.MovieQuote myMovieQuote =
          new CSharpConsumer.localhost.MovieQuote();
    myMovieQuote = tft.GetMovieQuoteObject();
    Movie.Text = myMovieQuote.Movie;
    Quote.Text = myMovieQuote.Quote;
    ActorOrCharacter.Text = myMovieQuote.ActorOrCharacter;
}
```

The resulting consumer Web Form is shown here:

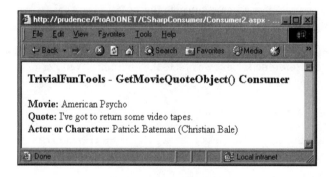

Working with XML Attributes

The `System.Xml.Serialization` namespace includes a set of classes that can be used to control how an object is serialized or deserialized. Controlling how an object is serialized or deserialized can be very beneficial particularly in B2B applications, where a specific XML schema is required. For instance, you may build an application that exchanges customer information with a vendor, and for business reasons it is required to have the `ID` value as an attribute of the root element, and the address as a child element, with the address detail as child elements of the address element.

```
<?xml version="1.0" encoding="utf-8" ?>
<Customer
  xmlns:xsi="http://www.w3.org/2001/XMLSchema-instance"
  xmlns:xsd="http://www.w3.org/2001/XMLSchema"
  ID="DNJCOM"  xmlns=http://www.dotnetjunkies.com>
  <Address>
    <Street>123 Main</Street>
    <City>Seattle</City>
    <State>WA</State>
  </Address>
</Customer>
```

The first of the "attribute" classes that we will look at is the `XmlAttributeAttribute` class. This attribute specifies that the class member that it is applied to should be serialized as an XML attribute.

We can create another custom class, `MovieQuoteWithAttributes`, in the `CSharpProvider` project, which represents one random movie quote, with the `Quote`, `ActorOrCharacter`, and `Movie` values as XML attributes of the `<MovieQuote>` element.

Create a new class file named `MovieQuoteWithAttributes.cs` and add the highlighted code:

```
using System;
using System.Xml.Serialization;

namespace CSharpProvider
{
  /// <summary>
  /// MovieQuoteWithAttributes
  /// MovieQuote object with attributes instead of elements.
  /// </summary>
  public class MovieQuoteWithAttributes
  {
    [XmlAttributeAttribute()]
    public string Quote;
    [XmlAttributeAttribute()]
    public string ActorOrCharacter;
    [XmlAttributeAttribute()]
    public string Movie;

    public MovieQuoteWithAttributes()
    {
      MovieQuote mq = new MovieQuote();
      Quote = mq.Quote;
      ActorOrCharacter = mq.ActorOrCharacter;
```

```
      Movie = mq.Movie;
    }
  }
}
```

If we build a Web Service method to return this custom object, the XML document that is generated looks like this:

```
<?xml version="1.0" encoding="utf-8" ?>
<MovieQuoteWithAttributes
  xmlns:xsi="http://www.w3.org/2001/XMLSchema-instance"
  xmlns:xsd="http://www.w3.org/2001/XMLSchema"
  Quote="Come and get me boys."
  ActorOrCharacter="Satine (Nicole Kidman)"
  Movie="Moulin Rouge"
  xmlns="http://www.dotnetjunkies.com" />
```

The properties of the object are still exposed as properties in the proxy client class. The only thing we have done here is change how the XML representation of this object appears.

Working with XML Elements and Attributes

Another of the XML attribute classes is the XmlTextAttribute. This attribute specifies that the class member that it is applied to should be serialized as XML text:

```
/// <summary>
/// Movie
/// An object that has elements and attributes.
/// </summary>
public class Movie
{
  [XmlTextAttribute()]
  public string Title;
  [XmlAttributeAttribute()]
  public string Quote;
  [XmlAttributeAttribute()]
  public string ActorOrCharacter;

  public Movie()
  {
    MovieQuote mq = new MovieQuote();
    Quote = mq.Quote;
    ActorOrCharacter = mq.ActorOrCharacter;
    Title = mq.Movie;
  }
}
```

The Title property has the XmlTextAttribute class applied to it, specifying that this property should be serialized as the XML text value of the <Movie> element, while the Quote and ActorOrCharacter properties are to be serialized as attributes of the <Movie> element:

```
<?xml version="1.0" encoding="utf-8" ?>
<Movie xmlns:xsi="http://www.w3.org/2001/XMLSchema-instance"
  xmlns:xsd="http://www.w3.org/2001/XMLSchema"
  Quote="You're a Movie of the Week...a T-shirt at best."
  ActorOrCharacter="Detective Wills (Brad Pitt)"
  xmlns="http://www.dotnetjunkies.com">Seven</Movie>
```

Working with Multiple Custom Classes as XML

We can also build a custom class that has another custom class as one of its properties. Both classes can have XML attribute classes applied to them to specify how they should be serialized. In the following code we create a custom Quote class that has one property, MovieQuote, that has the XmlTextAttribute class applied to it, and another property, ActorOrCharacter, that has the XmlAttributeAttribute class applied to it:

```
/// <summary>
/// Quote
/// Only the quote element of a Movie object.
/// </summary>
public class Quote
{
  [XmlTextAttribute()]
  public string MovieQuote;
  [XmlAttributeAttribute()]
  public string ActorOrCharacter;
}
```

By itself, this class would be serialized like this:

```
<?xml version="1.0" encoding="utf-8" ?>
<Quote ActorOrCharacter="Robert DeNiro">The war is over, I saw it on T.V.</Quote>
```

Of course, we want to know what great movie this fabulous quote came from, so we create another class, to act as a parent class, which will have a property whose type is Quote. For this, we build another custom class, Movie. The ComplexMovie class has a MovieQuote property and a Movie property:

```
/// <summary>
/// ComplexMovie
/// An object with an attribute, and an element that also has an attribute.
/// </summary>
public class ComplexMovie
{
  [XmlElementAttribute(ElementName="Quote")]
  public Quote MovieQuote;
  [XmlAttributeAttribute()]
  public string Movie;

  public ComplexMovie()
  {
    MovieQuote mq = new MovieQuote();
    Quote q = new Quote();
    q.MovieQuote = mq.Quote;
    q.ActorOrCharacter = mq.ActorOrCharacter;
```

```
      MovieQuote = q;
      Movie = mq.Movie;
  }
}
```

The `MovieQuote` property has the `XmlElementAttribute` class applied to it, specifying that this property should be serialized as a XML element – a child element of the `<ComplexMovie>` element. We use the `ElementName` property to specify that in the XML document, this element should be named `<Quote>` even though the property's name is `MovieQuote`. Effectively we are overriding the property name and applying a name that is more appropriate for what we are doing.

The XML document created by this class is shown here:

```
<?xml version="1.0" encoding="utf-8" ?>
<ComplexMovie xmlns:xsi="http://www.w3.org/2001/XMLSchema-instance"
  xmlns:xsd="http://www.w3.org/2001/XMLSchema"
  Movie="Wag the Dog" xmlns="http://www.dotnetjunkies.com">
  <Quote ActorOrCharacter="Robert DeNiro">The war is over, I saw it on
    T.V.</Quote>
</ComplexMovie>
```

Through the use of the attribute classes in the `System.Xml.Serialization` namespace we can completely customize the XML output generated by a Web Service. This enables, for example, two businesses to agree on a standard format for data exchange, such as customer information, or a product order, and automate a business process using Web Services. Changing the XML serialization does not affect the use of a proxy client at all. The properties exposed by a class are still exposed in the proxy class; the only thing that has changed is the XML format of the object while it is in transit between the provider and the consumer.

Web Service Security

In many cases we may want to create a Web Service that we want to expose for our business partners to consume, but we don't want everyone to have access to it. In much the same way that we may secure a Web application so that only a predefined set of users are granted access to some or all of the resources, we can secure Web Services using a couple of different security schemas.

The two most likely candidates for securing a Web Service are Windows Authentication and SOAP-based Authentication:

❑   Windows Authentication uses Windows account credentials to grant access to resources. We can secure our application, or a part of our application, to allow only users with valid accounts on our Windows domain access to the resources. This, of course, requires that every user we want to grant access to be given a user account on our domain. This type of authentication is mainly intended for intranets and extranets, where the users are likely to have accounts in our network.

❑   With SOAP-based authentication, we can secure our Web Services at a very granular level: secure each Web Service method individually. Additionally, we can enable access based on usernames, passwords, customer ID number, or any combination of any data we want. The required authentication data is sent in the SOAP message header when the Web Service method is invoked. The credentials can be validated at the method level, allowing anonymous access to some methods and restricting access to others.

Using Windows Authentication

ASP.NET applications can implement Windows Authentication to prevent unauthenticated users from accessing resources. In an application that implements Windows Authentication, the user's Windows login credentials are evaluated to determine if the user should be granted access to the resource. The same type of authentication can be implemented in a Web Service.

To implement Windows Authentication in an ASP.NET application, set the <authentication> configuration setting in the root web.config file:

```
<authentication mode="Windows">
```

We can then restrict access to our Web Service in one of two ways:

1. Use a <location> element in the root web.config file that includes a <deny> element. This is useful when you only want to restrict access to a single resource. This will restrict access to only the specified file:

```
<location path="Private/SuperPrivateServices.asmx">
  <system.web>
    <authorization>
      <deny users="?" />
    </authorization>
  </system.web>
</location>
```

2. Put the Web Service file in a sub-directory with a web.config file that includes a <deny> element. This is useful when you will have multiple resources you are restricting access to. This will restrict access to all .NET managed files in the sub-directory:

```
<?xml version="1.0" encoding="utf-8" ?>
<configuration>
  <system.web>
    <authorization>
      <deny users="?" />
    </authorization>
  </system.web>
</configuration>
```

The <deny> element specifies what type of users or roles to deny access to. Setting the users attribute to ? indicates that all unauthenticated users should be denied access.

Adding Credentials to a Consumer

In order for a consumer application to be granted access to a Web Service that is restricted using Windows Authentication, the consumer application must supply the appropriate Windows credentials. Normally, as a user accessing a restricted resource, we would be prompted with a login window, where we could supply our username, password, and possibly the domain name that our Windows account belongs to. Since we want the consumer application to access the resource without any user intervention, we can supply appropriate credentials to the proxy client when we attempt to invoke the Web Service method.

The proxy client class that we create to access the Web Service derives from the
`SoapHttpClientProtocol`. This class exposes a `Credentials` property (inherited from the
`WebClientProtocol` class) that takes an instance of a class that implements the `ICredentials`
interface, such as `NetworkCredential` or `CredentialCache`.

The `NetworkCredential` class is used to provide credentials for password-based authentication
schemes such as basic, digest, NTLM, and Kerberos authentication, while `CredentialCache` provides
a storage mechanism for multiple credentials.

We can use the `NetworkCredential` class to supply Windows credentials to our proxy object before
invoking the Web Service method.

```
CSharpConsumer.SuperPrivate.SuperPrivateServices sps =
  new CSharpConsumer.SuperPrivate.SuperPrivateServices();
sps.Credentials =
  new System.Net.NetworkCredential("myUserName", "myPassword");
string Result = sps.GetMySuperSecret();
```

In the preceding code, an instance of the `SuperPrivateServices` proxy class is constructed, and the
`Credentials` property is set to an instance of the `NetworkCredential` class. In the constructor for
the `NetworkCredential` class we pass in the username and password for our Windows account.

> The **NetworkCredential** class has an overloaded constructor that takes a domain
> name as a third argument, if it is necessary in your application:
>
> **sps.Credentials = new System.Net.NetworkCredential("myUserName",
> "myPassword", "myDomain");**

When the Web Service method is invoked, the credentials are passed to the provider in the SOAP
message. If the credentials are valid, the Web Service method is invoked and the appropriate data is
returned; if the credentials are invalid, a `System.Net.WebException` is raised:

System.Net.WebException: The request failed with HTTP status 401: Access Denied.

We can add error-handling code in the consumer to catch and handle this error – the key here is that
this error is up to the consumer to handle. If the consumer does not provide valid credentials, then the
consumer is never being granted access to the Web Service. The provider never has the option of
handling the exception – the exception happens in the consumer application (in the proxy client object)
and the provider has no knowledge of it.

Using SOAP-based Authentication

Another means of securing a Web Service is by implementing restrictions with custom headers in a
SOAP message. We can use a class attribute, the `SoapHeaderAttribute`, to specify a SOAP message
header that we are expecting in the incoming request to invoke the Web Service method. For example,
we can create a Web Service method that requires a SOAP header containing a username and
password. We can use the data passed in the SOAP header to authenticate the request.

This type of authentication opens up a broad range of authentication possibilities, including authenticating users from a database or XML document.

To implement this type of authentication, we create a custom class that derives from the `System.Web.Services.Protocols.SoapHeader` class. This class represents the data that will be passed in the SOAP header – the username and password. The values passed in the SOAP header are clear text. The values can be encrypted before being put in the SOAP headers, and decrypted when pulled out. Encryption is out of the scope of this chapter, but I will demonstrate how the authentication works.

Building a Private Web Service

Create a new Web Service file in the `CSharpProvider` project, named `PrivateServices.asmx`. Add the highlighted code to the Web Service code behind class:

```csharp
using System;
using System.Collections;
using System.ComponentModel;
using System.Data;
using System.Diagnostics;
using System.Web;
using System.Web.Services;
using System.Web.Services.Protocols;

namespace CSharpProvider
{
  /// <summary>
  /// Summary description for PrivateServices.
  /// </summary>
  [WebService(Description="This is a Web Service that demonstrates " +
    "SOAP Authentication.",
    Namespace="http://www.dotnetjunkies.com")]
  public class PrivateServices : System.Web.Services.WebService
  {
    public PrivateServices()
    {
      //CODEGEN: This call is required by the
      //ASP.NET Web Services Designer
      InitializeComponent();
    }

    #region Component Designer generated code
    /// <summary>
    /// Required method for Designer support - do not modify
    /// the contents of this method with the code editor.
    /// </summary>
    private void InitializeComponent()
    {
    }
    #endregion

    /// <summary>
    /// Clean up any resources being used.
    /// </summary>
    protected override void Dispose( bool disposing )
```

```
      {
      }

      //Create a property of the Web Service that is
      //the SOAP Header class
      public mySoapHeader Header;

      [WebMethod(Description="Get a secret that no " +
        "one else can get.")]
      [SoapHeader("Header")]
      public string GetMySecret()
      {
        if(Header.ValidUser())
        {
          return "This is my secret.";
        }
        else
        {
          return "The username or password was incorrect.";
        }
      }
    }

    public class mySoapHeader : SoapHeader
    {
      public string Username;
      public string Password;

      public Boolean ValidUser()
      {
        if(Username == "WillyWonka" && Password == "GoldenTicket")
        {
          return true;
        }
        else
        {
          return false;
        }
      }
    }
  }
```

In the preceding code we create two things, a Web Service method called GetMySecret, and a class that derives from the SoapHeader class called mySoapHeader.

In the mySoapHeader class we declare two properties, Username and Password. Additionally, we create a method for validating the user. While in the example we validate the user against a hard-coded username/password pair, we could add logic in the ValidUser method to validate the credentials against a data store.

In the Web Service, we declare a property, Header, whose data type is that of the derived SoapHeader class we just created.

In the Web Service method declaration we apply the `SoapHeaderAttribute`, providing the name of the Web Service member that represents the SOAP header contents (the `Header` property). The `SoapHeaderAttribute` class has three properties we can set to specify how the SOAP header should be used.

- ❑ **Direction** – gets or sets whether the SOAP header is intended for the Web Service, or the Web Service client, or both. `SoapHeaderDirection.In` is the default – `InOut` and `Out` are the other possible enumeration values.

- ❑ **MemberName** – gets or sets the member of the Web Service class representing the SOAP header contents. There is no default value.

- ❑ **Required** – gets or sets a value indicating whether the SOAP header must be understood and processed by the recipient Web Service or Web Service client. The default value is `true`.

In the Web Service method we can evaluate the SOAP header contents – in this example we can invoke the `mySoapHeader.ValidUser` method to see if the credentials are valid – if they are, we execute the code and return the appropriate data to the consumer. If the credentials are invalid, we can return a message, a `null` value, or exit the method without returning a value.

> By applying the **`SoapHeaderAttribute`** to the Web Service method, we eliminate support for HTTP GET or HTTP POST protocols – SOAP is the only allowed protocol for accessing Web Service methods that use the **`SoapHeaderAttribute`**.

Building the Consumer

The consumer application is responsible for adding the username and password credentials to the SOAP header before invoking the Web Service method. Since the `mySoapHeader` class is part of the Web Service, the proxy client has a `mySoapHeader` class.

Build the `CSharpProvider` project. If you built the Web Reference in the `CSharpConsumer` project against the `.vsdisco` discovery file, you can update the Web Reference and a new proxy client class called `PrivateServices.cs` will be added. If you built the Web Reference against the `TrivialFunTools` WSDL file, you need to add a new Web Reference for the `PrivateServices` WSDL file.

Create a new Web Form in the `CSharpConsumer` project, named `PrivateSoapConsumer.aspx`. Add the highlighted code in the Web Form.

```
<%@ Page language="c#" Codebehind="PrivateSoapConsumer.aspx.cs"
AutoEventWireup="false" Inherits="CSharpConsumer.PrivateSoapConsumer" %>
<!DOCTYPE HTML PUBLIC "-//W3C//DTD HTML 4.0 Transitional//EN" >
<HTML>
  <HEAD>
    <meta name="GENERATOR" Content="Microsoft Visual Studio 7.0">
    <meta name="CODE_LANGUAGE" Content="C#">
    <meta name="vs_defaultClientScript"
      content="JavaScript (ECMAScript)">
    <meta name="vs_targetSchema"
```

```
              content="http://schemas.microsoft.com/intellisense/ie5">
    </HEAD>
    <body MS_POSITIONING="GridLayout">
      <form id="PrivateSoapConsumer" method="post" runat="server">
        <h3>
          PrivateServices - GetMySecret() SOAP Authentication
        </h3>
        <P>
          User Name:
          <BR>
          <asp:TextBox id="Username" runat="server" />
        </P>
        <P>
          Password:
          <BR>
          <asp:TextBox id="Password" runat="server" />
        </P>
        <P>
          <asp:Button id="Button1" runat="server"
            Text="Get Secret!" />
        </P>
        <P>
          <asp:Label id="Result" runat="server" />
        </P>
      </form>
    </body>
</HTML>
```

With the Web Form in design view, double-click on the Button control to add a Button1_Click
event handler. In the code-behind class, add the highlighted code:

```csharp
using System;
using System.Collections;
using System.ComponentModel;
using System.Data;
using System.Drawing;
using System.Web;
using System.Web.SessionState;
using System.Web.UI;
using System.Web.UI.WebControls;
using System.Web.UI.HtmlControls;

namespace CSharpConsumer
{
  /// <summary>
  /// Summary description for PrivateSoapConsumer.
  /// </summary>
  public class PrivateSoapConsumer : System.Web.UI.Page
  {
    protected System.Web.UI.WebControls.TextBox Username;
    protected System.Web.UI.WebControls.TextBox Password;
    protected System.Web.UI.WebControls.Button Button1;
    protected System.Web.UI.WebControls.Label Result;
```

```csharp
      public PrivateSoapConsumer()
      {
        Page.Init += new System.EventHandler(Page_Init);
      }

      private void Page_Load(object sender, System.EventArgs e)
      {
        // Put user code to initialize the page here
      }

      private void Page_Init(object sender, EventArgs e)
      {
        //
        // CODEGEN: This call is required by the
        // ASP.NET Web Form Designer.
        //
        InitializeComponent();
      }

      #region Web Form Designer generated code
      /// <summary>
      /// Required method for Designer support - do not modify
      /// the contents of this method with the code editor.
      /// </summary>
      private void InitializeComponent()
      {
        this.Button1.Click += new
          System.EventHandler(this.Button1_Click);
        this.Load += new System.EventHandler(this.Page_Load);

      }
      #endregion

      private void Button1_Click(object sender, System.EventArgs e)
      {
        CSharpConsumer.Private.mySoapHeader header =
          new CSharpConsumer.Private.mySoapHeader();
        header.Username = Username.Text.Trim();
        header.Password = Password.Text.Trim();
        CSharpConsumer.Private.PrivateServices ps =
          new CSharpConsumer.Private.PrivateServices();
        ps.mySoapHeaderValue = header;

        Result.Text = ps.GetMySecret();
      }
    }
  }
```

The mySoapHeader class exposes two public properties, Username and Password – these properties are accessible in the proxy client. For this example we are setting the Username and Password properties of the mySoapHeader proxy object to the values input by the user in the Web Form.

Once the `mySoapHeader` object is constructed and the properties are set, we construct the Web Service proxy class – `PrivateServices` – and set the `mySoapHeader` object as its `mySoapHeaderValue` property.

The SOAP message is constructed with the `mySoapHeader` object serialized in the `<soap:Header>` element:

```
<?xml version="1.0" encoding="utf-8"?>
<soap:Envelope xmlns:xsi=http://www.w3.org/2001/XMLSchema-instance
  xmlns:xsd=http://www.w3.org/2001/XMLSchema
  xmlns:soap="http://schemas.xmlsoap.org/soap/envelope/">
  <soap:Header>
    <mySoapHeader xmlns="http://www.dotnetjunkies.com">
      <Username>WillyWonka</Username>
      <Password>GoldenTicket</Password>
    </mySoapHeader>
  </soap:Header>
  <soap:Body>
    <GetMySecret xmlns="http://www.dotnetjunkies.com" />
  </soap:Body>
</soap:Envelope>
```

As I mentioned previously, the username and password values are passed in the SOAP header as clear text. Encryption can be used before setting the values, and when the SOAP message is received they can be decrypted. Another security option is having the Web Service method call go across SSL for encryption of the entire SOAP message.

Summary

In this chapter we discussed Web Services and how we can use them to exchange data in a variety of formats. Web Services are entities of application programming logic that are exposed to remote consumers via standard Internet protocols, such as HTTP, XML, SOAP, and WSDL.

We can use Web Services with three protocols:

❑   HTTP GET

❑   HTTP POST

❑   SOAP

With Web Services we can exchange simple data types, like strings and integers, as well as more complex data types, like ADO.NET `DataSet` objects, images, and custom-defined classes. The data objects are serialized to XML and transmitted from the provider to the consumer. This enables disparate systems to exchange data regardless of platform or programming language.

We looked at several ways of customizing the XML output from a Web Service, and finally, we looked at two different schemas for providing security to our Web Services – Windows Authentication and SOAP-based Authentication.

ADO.NET

14

SQL Server Native XML Support

As of SQL Server 2000, a suite of new XML-related features is available. These XML-related features of SQL Server can readily be exploited by an ADO.NET application. Within this chapter we will investigate two of the key SQL Server 2000 XML feature:

❑   FOR XML – the FOR XML clause of a SQL SELECT statement allows a rowset to be returned as an XML document. The XML document generated by a FOR XML clause is highly customizable with respect to the document hierarchy generated, per-column data transforms, representation of binary data, XML schema generated, and a variety of other XML nuances.

❑   OPENXML – the OPENXML extension to Transact-SQL allows a stored procedure call to manipulate an XML document as a rowset. Subsequently, this rowset can be used to perform a variety of tasks such as SELECT, INSERT, DELETE, and UPDATE.

SQL Server's XML extensions enhance ADO.NET's ability to generate and consume XML data. SELECT's FOR XML clause facilitates the precise generation of XML documents from SQL Server tables and columns. Using FOR XML, it is possible to generate XML documents that conform to the schema requirements of applications outside SQL Server.

To take a particularly illustrative example, SELECT queries containing FOR XML clauses could be used to generate an XML document using tables such as, for instance, Doctors, Pharmacies, and Medications. The results of such a query (an XML document) could correspond with a properly formed medical prescription. This could be utilized by both an insurance company and the pharmacy that will ultimately dispense the prescription. In such a case, the XML document corresponding to a prescription has been generated to the appropriate form using FOR XML, and hence did not require programmatic massaging, such as that supported by the classes found in System.Xml. Furthermore, such an XML document will not require transformation facilities such as those provided by XSLT, and those in the System.Xml.Xsl namespace.

As mentioned previously, OPENXML is utilized in the consumption of XML. Imagine a pharmacy that receives prescriptions in the form of XML documents. These prescriptions (XML documents) could be used in order to update the underlying SQL server database. These XML documents could be used in conjunction with SQL INSERT, UPDATE, and DELETE commands. There is not need to manually parse the XML document, and from this parsing generate the appropriate SQL command. The XML document is included as part of the SQL command, and can therefore specify the prescriptions to insert, delete, or update.

What is elegant about the XML-specific features of SQL Server is that no overtly intricate steps are required by ADO.NET in order to exploit this functionality. For example, OPENXML is specified in a stored procedure call, so no special steps must be taken in ADO.NET in order to use this SQL Server 2000 feature. Queries containing a FOR XML clause require no intricate extra ADO.NET coding in order to execute such queries, but we do need to be aware that the query contains a FOR XML clause when the query is executed. A SqlCommand object is used to execute such a query. The ExecuteXmlReader method of this class is used to explicitly execute a FOR XML-type query. Other types of query are executed using the ExecuteNonQuery, ExecuteReader, and ExecuteScalar methods. The ExecuteXmlReader method entirely sums up the extra step required to execute such a query with ADO.NET.

In this chapter, we will investigate the construction of two console applications (both C# and VB.NET implementations) that demonstrate these SQL Server XML features being exploited using ADO.NET:

❑   WroxForXMLDemo – demonstrates each style of FOR XML query (RAW, AUTO, and EXPLICIT)

❑   WroxOpenXMLDemo – demonstrates using OPENXML to INSERT, DELETE, and UPDATE a table using data provided via an XML document

We will also look at a variety of ways of constructing SQL script files. These scripts demonstrate FOR XML and OPENXML. In some instances, these scripts must be run before either the WroxForXMLDemo or WroxOpenXMLDemo application can be run. For those not so familiar with using SQL Server, the Query Analyzer or the OSQL command-line application can be used to run these scripts. Query Analyzer is by far the easiest way to execute these scripts and view the results.

> **SQL Server XML support is explored in far more detail in *Professional SQL Server 2000 XML*, ISBN 1-861005-46-6, also from Wrox Press.**

FOR XML

The Transact-SQL extension to the SELECT statement, FOR XML, is defined in the following way:

```
FOR XML mode [, XMLDATA] [, ELEMENTS][, BINARY BASE64]
```

The permissible FOR XML modes are RAW, AUTO, and EXPLICIT, listed in order from the least sophisticated to the most sophisticated. These modes generate SQL as follows:

❑   RAW – generates a two dimensional grid of XML where every row returned by the query is contained in an element named row. The value of each column returned by the query is represented by an attribute with each pair of row tags.

❑   AUTO – generates a potentially hierarchal XML document where the value returned for every column is contained in an element or an attribute.

❑   EXPLICIT – the precise form used to contain the value of each column returned by the FOR XML EXPLICIT query can be specified. The values of columns can be returned as attributes or elements. This distinction can be specified on a per-column basis. The exact data type used to represent a column can be specified, as can the precise XML document hierarchy generated by the query.

The optional components of a FOR XML query (XMLDATA, ELEMENTS, and BINARY BASE64) will be discussed in conjunction with the detailed overview of each mode (RAW, AUTO, and EXPLICIT).

A FOR XML RAW query is the most basic form of a FOR XML query. The XML document generated by this query contains one type of element, named row. Each row element corresponds to a row returned by the query.

This simplicity can lead to a great deal of replicated data, since there is no hierarchy within the XML document generated. The values of each column within the query are contained in the attributes of each row element. There is very little customization of the XML document generated by a FOR XML RAW query.

An example of a FOR XML RAW query (alias a SQL query with FOR XML RAW appended to the query) executed against SQL Server's Northwind database, is as follows:

```
SELECT Region.RegionID, Territories.TerritoryID
FROM   Region
INNER JOIN  Territories ON Region.RegionID = Territories.RegionID
ORDER BY Territories.TerritoryID
FOR XML RAW
```

The XML document generated by the previous query contains dozens of elements named row – one row element per row of data returned by the query's rowset. True to form, the FOR XML RAW query generates duplicate data, since every element shown contains the attribute RegionID. The value of a certain RegionID attribute is the same for each different row elements. The XML generated by the aforementioned query is as follows, and illustrates duplicate RegionID attribute values:

XML_F52E2B61-18A1-11d1-B105-00805F49916B

<row RegionID="1" TerritoryID="01581"/>
<row RegionID="1" TerritoryID="01730"/>
<row RegionID="1" TerritoryID="01833"/>
<row RegionID="1" TerritoryID="02116"/>
<row RegionID="1" TerritoryID="02139"/>
...

The output from the previous FOR XML RAW query was generated using SQL Server's Query Analyzer. The results of each FOR XML query are returned in a rowset containing a single row and a single column. The column in this case is arbitrarily named XML_F52E2B61-18A1-11d1-B105-00805F49916B, but the value stored in this single column/row is the XML document. You may notice that the column name is actually the prefix, XML_, affixed to a GUID. This column name is identical for every FOR XML query; so noting the GUID portion of the column name is simply an antidotal observation, as the GUID portion of the column name provides no addition information with regards to the query or how it will be used.

By default, Query Analyzer displays the results of a query to a grid. The previous XML snippet was not generated in grid form. To better view the results of FOR XML queries, select **Query | Results in Text**.

A FOR XML query of type AUTO exploits the hierarchal nature of certain SQL queries. Each table associated with a FOR XML AUTO query is represented as an XML element (for example, the Region table corresponds to the XML element, Region). The values of each column within the query are contained within each table-specific element (for example, the columns of the Region table retrieved by the query are contained in attributes of the XML element Region). The per-table elements are nested within the XML hierarchy in the order in which they appear in the query. For example, the Territories table would be a sub-element of the Region element if the FROM clause of the FOR XML AUTO query were to be:

```
FROM Region, Territories
```

The values of each of the columns of each table are represented as attributes (by default), or elements, if ELEMENTS is specified as an option to the FOR XML AUTO clause. The ELEMENTS option applies to all column attributes returned by the query and cannot be applied to only a few selected column attributes returned by the query. Swapping the FOR XML RAW for a FOR XML AUTO in the initial query results in the following FOR XML AUTO query (SQL script ForXMLAutoRegTer.sql):

```
SELECT Region.RegionID, TerritoryID FROM Region, Territories
WHERE Region.RegionID = Territories.RegionID ORDER BY TerritoryID
FOR XML AUTO
```

The data generated by this query is as follows:

```
<Region RegionID="1">
 <Territories TerritoryID="01581"/>
 <Territories TerritoryID="01730"/>
 <Territories TerritoryID="01833"/>
 ...
</Region>
<Region RegionID="3">
 <Territories TerritoryID="03049"/>
 ...
</Region>
```

A FOR XML EXPLICIT query is the most complicated and the most customizable form of the FOR XML query. Using this form of FOR XML query, the specific position within the XML data hierarchy can be specified for each table/column pairing. FOR XML EXPLICT queries use per-column **directives** to control the form of XML data generated. Directives dictate whether or not the data of a table/column pairing is represented as XML elements or attributes. This means that one column from a table may generate an XML element, while another column may generate an attribute. The following snippet for a FOR XML EXPLICIT query's SELECT clause demonstrates how the RegionID from Northwind's Region table could be specified as both an attribute and an element within the same XML document (SQL script ForXMLExplicitSimple.sql):

```
SELECT 1 AS Tag,
       0 AS Parent,
       RegionID AS [Region!1!RegionIDAsAttrbute],
```

```
            RegionID AS [Region!1!RegionIDAsElement!element]
    FROM Region
    FOR XML EXPLICIT
```

In the previous SQL, the alias following the first instance of RegionID contains no directive and so is treated as an attribute (the default). The directive element in the alias following the second RegionID ([Region!1!RegionIDAsElement!element]) is what causes the RegionID to be represented as a element. Clearly more infrastructure is required for a FOR XML EXPLICIT query (Tag column, Parent column, etc.) and this infrastructure will be presented in a section dedicated to this flavor of FOR XML query (we will investigate this later). A portion of the XML generated by the previous SQL is as follows:

```
<Region RegionIDAsAttrbute="1">
  <RegionIDAsElement>1</RegionIDAsElement>
</Region>
<Region RegionIDAsAttrbute="2">
  <RegionIDAsElement>2</RegionIDAsElement>
</Region>
...
```

With FOR XML EXPLICIT queries, data transforms can also be specified for each table/column pairing using directives. The types of data transforms possible include disabling the entity encoding of data, generating column data of type ID, treating column data as type CDATA, using columns to specify rowset order without including the column in the XML document generated, and so on.

FOR XML – Optional Arguments

The following optional arguments can be used in conjunction with a FOR XML query:

❑ ELEMENTS – only applicable to a FOR XML AUTO query, this specifies that the column value for each column returned in the rowset will be represented as an element within the XML document and not as an attribute (the default). This option is not valid for FOR XML RAW, since the only element generated by such a FOR XML query is named row. The ELEMENTS option is also not valid FOR XML EXPLICIT queries, since this style of query can specify that the data for certain columns should be contained in elements, while the data for other columns should be contained in attributes.

❑ BINARY BASE64 – this option causes binary data within the XML document to be represented as base-64 encoding. Such data is found in columns of type BINARY, VARBINARY, or IMAGE. The BINARY BASE64 option must be specified in order for FOR XML RAW and FOR XML EXPLICIT queries to retrieve binary data. By default, a FOR XML AUTO query handles binary data by creating a reference within the XML document to the location of the binary data. References make an XML document more readable and reduce the size of a document. The major disadvantage of using references to binary data is that it limits an XML document's portability. When BINARY BASE64 is specified for a FOR XML AUTO query, the XML document generated contains the binary data encoded in base-64 format.

❑ XMLDATA – generates an XML Data schema for the XML document generated by the FOR XML query. This schema is pre-pended to the XML document.

The following SQL is identical to a query previously shown save that this query contains XMLDATA optional FOR XML option:

```
SELECT Region.RegionID, TerritoryID FROM Region, Territories
WHERE Region.RegionID = Territories.RegionID ORDER BY TerritoryID
FOR XML AUTO, XMLDATA
```

A portion of the XML document generated by the previous query (including the pre-pended schema) is as follows:

```
<Schema name="Schema1" xmlns="urn:schemas-microsoft-com:xml-data"
  xmlns:dt="urn:schemas-microsoft-com:datatypes">
  <ElementType name="Region" content="eltOnly" model="closed" order="many">
    <element type="Territories" maxOccurs="*"/>
    <AttributeType name="RegionID" dt:type="i4"/>
    <attribute type="RegionID"/>
  </ElementType>
  <ElementType name="Territories" content="empty" model="closed">
    <AttributeType name="TerritoryID" dt:type="string"/>
    <attribute type="TerritoryID"/>
  </ElementType>
</Schema>
<Region xmlns="x-schema:#Schema1" RegionID="1">
  <Territories TerritoryID="01581"/>
  <Territories TerritoryID="01730"/>
...
```

To put XMLDATA into perspective, it is important to note that this is an XML-Data style of schema. A popular subset of this schema variant also exists, XDR (XML-Data Reduced). An XML-Data schema is not a Document Type Definition (DTD) or a standard W3C XML schema. An XML-Data schema is a proprietary Microsoft schema, proposed in January 1998, three years before the W3C ultimately adopted the W3C schema specification. An XDR schema is used to validate XML documents in environments that are homogeneously Microsoft (for example an e-commerce site developed complete with Microsoft servers and technology).

The major limitation of the XML-Data schema is that it can only be used in applications developed with applications such as SQL Server, Biztalk, and Internet Explorer 5.0 and later. By no means is the XML-Data schema a universal standard and it is not supported on most non-Microsoft systems. Microsoft has committed to supporting the W3C XML schema specification. This means that FOR XML's XMLDATA option may ultimately be altered or superseded in a future version of SQL Server.

FOR XML RAW

Here is an example of a FOR XML RAW query is (see SQL script file FORXMLRawEmployee.sql):

```
SELECT FirstName, LastName, Photo
FROM Employees
ORDER BY LastName, FirstName
FOR XML RAW, BINARY BASE64
```

After the `FOR XML RAW` in the previous query is the optional argument `BINARY BASE64`. This argument causes the binary data (the `Photo` column of type `IMAGE`) to be encoded as BASE64 and placed within the XML document generated. Actually, although `BINARY BASE64` is classified as an optional argument, it is required for queries of type `RAW` and `EXPLICIT` when the query contains a column that is of a binary type (`BINARY`, `VARBINARY`, or `IMAGE`). The `BINARY BASE64` argument is truly optional only when used with `FOR XML AUTO` queries.

A portion of the output generated by this query is as follows, where each row in the result set generates an XML element named `row`:

```
<row FirstName="Steven" LastName="Buchanan" Photo="FRwv ... atBf4="/>
<row FirstName="Laura" LastName="Callahan" Photo="FRwvA ... +tBf4="/>
<row FirstName="Nancy" LastName="Davolio" Photo="FRwvAA ... StBf4="/>
<row FirstName="Anne" LastName="Dodsworth" Photo="FRwv  ... 6tBf4="/>
...
```

Notice that each `Photo` attributed in the previous XML document contains what appear to be "just some characters". This is the employee's photo encoded in base-64. Had `BINARY BASE64` not been specified, then the previous query would have thrown an error, since this argument is required when using `FOR XML RAW` queries. The error thrown is rather specific in this regard:

```
Server: Msg 6829, Level 16, State 1, Line 1
FOR XML EXPLICIT and RAW modes currently do not support addressing binary data
as URLs in column 'Photo'. Remove the column, or use the BINARY BASE64 mode,
or create the URL directly using the 'dbobject/TABLE[@PK1="V1"]/@COLUMN' syntax.
```

Using FOR XML RAW with ADO.NET

The query executed as part of this example is nearly identical to our previous `FOR XML RAW` example:

```
SELECT FirstName, LastName
FROM Employees
ORDER BY LastName, FirstName
FOR XML RAW, XMLDATA
```

The `Photo` column was excluded because it generates too much data, and should only be used when the employee's photograph is needed. Since the `Photo` column (type, `IMAGE`) was not specified, the `BINARY BASE64` option was not required as part of this query. The `XMLDATA` option was used in order to generate a schema for the XML document generated by the previous query. The rationale for generating such a schema will be introduced later in this example.

To execute this query, a `System.Data.SqlClient.SqlCommand` instance is created and associated with an instance of SQL Server containing a `Northwind` database. At the same time, the previously demonstrated `FOR XML RAW` query is specified as a parameter to the `SqlCommand`'s constructor. This is demonstrated in the following excerpt from the C# source file `WroxForXMLDemo.cs`:

```
string strQuery = "SELECT FirstName, LastName FROM Employees " +
    "ORDER BY LastName, FirstName FOR XML RAW, XMLDATA";
```

```
string strConnection =
       "UID=sa;PWD=sa;DATABASE=northwind;SERVER=(local);";

SqlCommand forXMLCommand = new SqlCommand(strQuery,
                             new SqlConnection(strConnection));

forXMLCommand.Connection.Open();
```

The last line of code in the previous snippet ensured that the connection to the specified database is open. The `Open` method exposed by `SqlCommand`'s `Connection` property is used to open the connection to the data source. Once the `SqlCommand` instance has been created, and the connection opened, the `SqlCommand`'s `ExecuteXmlReader` method can be called. The prototype for this method is as follows:

VB.NET

```
Public Function ExecuteXmlReader() As XmlReader
```

C#

```
public XmlReader ExecuteXmlReader();
```

The `ExecuteXmlReader` method executes a query containing a `FOR XML` clause and returns an instance of type `XmlReader` from the `System.Xml` namespace. The `DataSet` class reviewed in previous chapters exposes the `ReadXml` method that can consume an instance of `XmlReader`. The `DataSet` class also exposes the `WriteXml` method that can persist an XML data set to a file. An instance of type `DataSet` can be used in conjunction with our `FOR XML` example in order to persist the XML document as follows:

```
DataSet ds = new DataSet();

ds.ReadXml(forXMLCommand.ExecuteXmlReader(), XmlReadMode.Fragment);
ds.WriteXml("DemoForXMLRaw.xml");
```

When the `ReadXml` method was executed, the `XmlReadMode`'s `Fragment` was specified. When `Fragment` is specified then `ExecuteXmlReader` assumes that the data read into the `DataSet` contains XML documents that include an inline schema. This schema is assumed to be of type XDR (XML-Data Reduced). The `XMLDATA` option was specified in the query's `FOR XML RAW` clause in order to ensure that `ReadXml` can correctly interpret the XML generated by the query. The `FOR XML RAW` demo in its entirety is as follows, as demonstrated by the VB.NET file, `WroxForXMLDemo.vb`:

```
Dim strQuery As String = "SELECT FirstName, LastName FROM Employees " & _
    "ORDER BY LastName, FirstName " & _
    "FOR XML RAW, XMLDATA"
Dim strConnection As String = _
    "UID=sa;PWD=sa;DATABASE=northwind;SERVER=(local);"

Dim forXMLCommand As SqlCommand = _
    New SqlCommand(strQuery, _
    New SqlConnection(strConnection))
Dim ds As DataSet = New DataSet()
```

```
forXMLCommand.Connection.Open()
ds.ReadXml(forXMLCommand.ExecuteXmlReader(), XmlReadMode.Fragment)
ds.WriteXml("DemoOutRaw.xml")
```

FOR XML AUTO

FOR XML's AUTO mode supports the user of BINARY BASE64, but does not require this option to be specified. When the BINARY BASE64 option is specified, references to the binary data will be included in the XML document. In order to demonstrate such references, consider the following SQL (SQL script file, ForXMLAutoBinaryData.sql):

```
SELECT EmployeeID, FirstName, LastName, Photo
FROM Employees
ORDER BY LastName, FirstName
FOR XML AUTO
```

The previous FOR XML AUTO query deliberately contained the EmployeeID column of the Employees table. The EmployeeID column is the primary key of the Employees table and will be used to specify the reference to the employee's Photo. The XML generated using the previous query is as follows:

```
<Employees EmployeeID="5" FirstName="Steven" LastName="Buchanan"
    Photo="dbobject/Employees[@EmployeeID='5']/@Photo"/>
<Employees EmployeeID="8" FirstName="Laura" LastName="Callahan"
    Photo="dbobject/Employees[@EmployeeID='8']/@Photo"/>
<Employees EmployeeID="1" FirstName="Nancy" LastName="Davolio"
    Photo="dbobject/Employees[@EmployeeID='1']/@Photo"/>
...
```

In the previous XML snippet, each photo is referenced by an XPATH query:

```
Photo="dbobject/Employees[@EmployeeID='5']/@Photo"
```

An entire chapter could be dedicated to XPATH, but it suffices to say that each photo reference is specified by a dbobject that is a reference to the Employees table (dbobject/Employees) and within that table a row specified by the primary key, EmployeeID (for example @EmployeeID='5'). Within this row the Photo column is referenced (for example, @Photo).

Referencing XML data is clearly more readable than including BASE64-encoded binary data. The downside to references is that they are only supported in conjunction with SQL Server and Internet Information Server. A drawback to XML documents containing references to binary data is that such documents are not self-contained since the binary data is not contained in the XML document. Simply copying the XML document to another location results in an XML document that is incomplete since the references can no longer be resolved. References to binary data are not portable. One of the alleged benefits of XML is that it is portable since the standards used should be open standards. Once truly portable XML is achieved in the real world (at some future time once the paint is dry on the W3C XML standards) Microsoft-specific references to binary data should be avoided unless the environment deployed under is Microsoft-homogeneous.

Within the `Northwind` database, the `Region` table contains a primary key, `RegionID`. The `RegionID` is a foreign key in the `Territories` table (as there can be multiple territories per region). If a `FOR XML RAW` query were used to retrieve data from `Region` and `Territories`, SQL such as the following would be executed:

```
SELECT R.RegionID, RTRIM(R.RegionDescription) AS RegionDesc,
       T.TerritoryID, RTRIM(T.TerritoryDescription) AS TerritoryDesc
FROM Region AS R, Territories AS T
WHERE R.RegionID = T.RegionID
ORDER BY R.RegionID, T.TerritoryID
FOR XML RAW
```

Executing the previous `FOR XML RAW` query would generate a grid of data such as the following:

```
<row RegionID="1" RegionDesc="Eastern" TerritoryID="01581" TerritoryDesc="Westboro"/>
<row RegionID="1" RegionDesc="Eastern" TerritoryID="01730" TerritoryDesc="Bedford"/>
<row RegionID="1" RegionDesc="Eastern" TerritoryID="01833 "TerritoryDesc="Georgetow"/>
...
<row RegionID="4" RegionDesc="Southern" TerritoryID="78759" TerritoryDesc="Austin"/>
```

Notice that in the XML document that we generated, values of `RegionID` and `RegionDesc` are repeated for each entry in the `Territories` table. The `FOR XML RAW` query was unable to take advantage of the hierarchal relationship between regions and territories because it only returns a rigid "grid" of data. If we want to exploit hierarchies between tables with a `FOR XML` query, we must use `AUTO`. An example of a `FOR XML AUTO` query that accesses the `Region` and `Territories` is found as follows in the stored procedure called `WroxRegionTerritory`:

```
CREATE PROCEDURE WroxRegionTerritory AS
SELECT R.RegionID, RTRIM(R.RegionDescription) AS RegionDesc,
       T.TerritoryID, RTRIM(T.TerritoryDescription) AS TerritoryDesc
FROM Region AS R, Territories AS T
WHERE R.RegionID = T.RegionID
ORDER BY R.RegionID, T.TerritoryID
FOR XML AUTO, XMLDATA
```

A portion of the output generated by this query without the prefixed schema (courtesy of the `XMLDATA` option) is as follows:

```
<R RegionID="1" RegionDesc="Eastern">
  <T TerritoryID="01581" TerritoryDesc="Westboro"/>
  <T TerritoryID="01730" TerritoryDesc="Bedford"/><T TerritoryID="01833"
  ...
  <T TerritoryID="27511" TerritoryDesc="Cary"/><T TerritoryID="40222" TerritoryDesc="Louisville"/>
</R>
<R RegionID="2" RegionDesc="Western">
  <T TerritoryID="60179" TerritoryDesc="Hoffman Estates"/>
  <T TerritoryID="60601" TerritoryDesc="Chicago"/>
  ...
```

Notice that this XML document exploits the relationship between `Region` and `Territories`. There is no repeated data for each region (one region to many territories) as we saw with a `FOR XML RAW` query.

Each Region (element R) contains sub-elements corresponding to the region's Territories (element T). The R (Region) element corresponds to the R query alias name (Region AS R). The columns of the Region table are represented by attributes. The attribute names are RegionID, which corresponds to the column name, and RegionDesc, which corresponds to the query alias name, RegionDesc (RTRIM(R.RegionDescription) AS RegionDesc). The rows of the Territories table are contained in a sub-element, T, which corresponds to the query alias name, T. The columns of the Territories table are represented by the attributes TerritoryID, which corresponds to the column name, and TerritoryDesc, which corresponds to the query alias name, TerritoryDesc.

The ELEMENTS option can be used with FOR XML AUTO queries. This option is specified as follows:

```
,FOR XML AUTO, ELEMENTS, XMLDATA
```

If ELEMENTS had been specified for our previous FOR XML AUTO query, the attributes used to contain per-column data would be replaced by elements. An example of this is as follows:

```
<R>
   <RegionID>1</RegionID>
   <RegionDesc>Eastern</RegionDesc>
   <T>
     <TerritoryID>01581</TerritoryID>
     <TerritoryDesc>Westboro</TerritoryDesc>
   </T>
   <T>
     <TerritoryID>01730</TerritoryID>
...
```

One thing that should be clear from the previous XML snippets is that single letter element names (R and T) fail the test when it comes to self-description. So how much flexibility does FOR XML AUTO afford? The FOR XML AUTO's exploitation of the data hierarchy is a useful feature, as is the ability to choose between elements or attributes. Still, a choice has to be made between using all attributes or all elements. There is no way to indicate that certain columns should specify that their data be contained in attributes while other columns specify that their data be contained in elements. Yes, the configurability that is lacking is the ability for each column to explicitly declare its representation within the XML document (attribute or element, in which level of the hierarchy it is placed, etc.). The next FOR XML mode presented, EXPLICIT, will address this level of XML generation sophistication.

FOR XML AUTO and ADO.NET

We previously demonstrated that a FOR XML RAW query could be executed using ADO.NET. In that example, the query was in the form of SQL placed directly within the source code. With respect to FOR XML AUTO, a stored procedure call, WroxRegionTerritory, has already been presented that can be used in conjunction with ADO.NET to retrieve an XML document This stored procedure is executed in the VB.NET source file, WroxForXMLDemo.vb, by first establishing an optional connection to a SQL Server database:

```
Dim strConnection As String = _
    "UID=sa;PWD=sa;DATABASE=northwind;SERVER=(local);"
Dim sqlConnection As SqlConnection = New SqlConnection(strConnection)

sqlConnection.Open()
```

Once a connection has been set up, the `SqlCommand` instance, `forXMLCommand`, can be created. This SQL command is associated with the `WroxRegionTerritory` stored procedure and the command type for this instance is set to a `CommandType` of `StoredProcedure`. The `forXMLCommand SqlCommand` instance is also associated with the open SQL connection (instance, `sqlConnection`). This setting up of the `SQLCommand` in VB.NET is performed as follows:

```
Dim forXMLCommand As SqlCommand = _
    New SqlCommand("WroxRegionTerritory")

forXMLCommand.CommandType = CommandType.StoredProcedure
forXMLCommand.Connection = sqlConnection
```

Once the stored procedure call has been set up, it can be executed using the `SqlCommand`'s `ExecuteXmlReader` method. The `XmlReader` returned by this method is again associated with a `DataSet` instance. The `DataSet`'s `WriteXml` method is used to write the XML generated to `Console.Out` (of type `TextWriter`). Execution of the stored procedure call and retrieving the SQL Server generated XML document is as follows using VB.NET:

```
Dim ds As DataSet = New DataSet()

ds.ReadXml(forXMLCommand.ExecuteXmlReader(), XmlReadMode.Fragment)
ds.WriteXml("DemoOutAuto.xml", XmlWriteMode.IgnoreSchema)
```

A complete example in C# where the `WroxRegionTerritory` stored procedure is used to retrieve an XML document is as follows (source file, `WroxForXMLDemo.cs`):

```
string strConnection =
    "UID=sa;PWD=sa;DATABASE=northwind;SERVER=(local);";
SqlConnection sqlConnection = new SqlConnection(strConnection);

sqlConnection.Open();

SqlCommand forXMLCommand = new SqlCommand("WroxRegionTerritory");

forXMLCommand.Connection = sqlConnection;
forXMLCommand.CommandType = CommandType.StoredProcedure;

DataSet ds = new DataSet();

ds.ReadXml(forXMLCommand.ExecuteXmlReader(),
           XmlReadMode.Fragment);
ds.WriteXml(Console.Out);
```

The XML document displayed to `Console.Out` in the previous C# code snippet has already been presented. What is important to recognize that the only difference between the previous code and executing any stored procedure call is the use of `SqlCommand`'s `ExecuteXmlReader` method, since the data retrieved is XML generated by SQL Server.

FOR XML EXPLICIT

FOR XML RAW and FOR XML AUTO are simple to use, but are limited with respect to the XML they generate. The EXPLICIT mode of FOR XML provides a tremendous amount of flexibility when it comes to the generation of XML documents, but the tradeoff is a fair amount of complexity with respect to the writing of such queries. To fully understand this we will present an intricate FOR XML EXPLICT query. This query will demonstrate a significant portion of the functionality associated with using the EXPLICIT mode of FOR XML. The query demonstrated is executed against the following set of tables that can be created on your RDBMS using the SQL Script called ForXMLExplicit.sql:

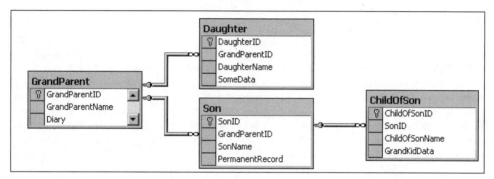

These tables are not meant to be realistic, but are intended to demonstrate how to represent a relational hierarchy as an XML hierarchy. In subsequent code examples, we have assumed that these tables have been created in a database called FamilyDB; however, you can create them in any database you like, so long as you make the appropriate changes to the code. The tables are related as follows:

❏ GrandParent contains a primary key, GrandParentID

❏ Daughter contains a primary key, DaughterID, and a foreign key, GrandParentID, which refers to an entry in the GrandParent table

❏ Son contains a primary key, SonID, and a foreign key, GrandParentID, which refers to an entry in the GrandParent table

❏ ChildOfSon contains a primary key, ChildOfSonID, and a foreign key, SonID, which refers to an entry in the Son table

Using FOR XML EXPLICIT and this hierarchy of relational database tables, we would like to generate an XML document with the following, rather explicit, format:

❏ A root element named GParent, which will contain each row of the GrandParent table and all the grandparent's children and grandchildren. This root element will contain the data retrieved from the GrandParent table by the FOR XML EXPLICIT query.

❏ At the level below the GParent element will exist elements named Daughter and Son. Each of these elements will contain the data retrieved from their respective tables, Daughter and Son.

❏ At the level below the Son element will exist the ChildOfSon element. This element contains the data retrieved from the ChildOfSon table.

The mechanism that FOR XML EXPLICIT uses to support the generation of a specific hierarchy is to assign a tag number to each element within the XML hierarchy. Each element within the hierarchy declares a tag value and the value of its parent. For our hierarchy this is as follows:

Level	Tag	Parent
Gparent	1	0
Son	2	1
Daughter	3	1
ChildOfSon	4	2

The GParent is at the level associated with Tag=1 and contains a parent value of 0. When the parent of a level in the XML hierarchy is set to zero, this indicates that the element is at the root of the XML document. Notice that both Son (Tag=2) and Daughter (Tag=3) have a parent value of 1 (the GParent level of the XML hierarchy). Daughter may have a Tag=3, but it is not at the third level of the hierarchy. Daughter is at the second level because its parent's value is Tag=1 (an element at the first level of the XML hierarchy). The ChildOfSon is assigned a Tag=4 and is associated with a parent whose tag value is 2 (a Son).

Within our FOR XML EXPLICT query, the Tag numbers of our elements (1, 2, 3, and 4) are specified as follows:

```
GrandParentID AS [GParent!1!]
0 AS [Son!2!SonID]
0 AS [Daughter!3!DaughterID!element]
0 AS [GrandKid!4!ChildOfSonID!element]
```

The previous snippet of XML showed how the encoding for each column is specified (for example, [Son!2!SonID]), but is certainly not a complete explanation of how columns are explicitly described using FOR XML EXPLICIT. Each column of the FOR XML EXPLICIT query specifies a per-column encoding that includes a Tag value. The form this per-column encoding takes is as follows:

```
columnName AS [ContainedElementName!Tag!AttributeOrElementName!Directive]
```

The sub-components that make up the explicit declaration of a column are:

- ❑ ContainedElementName – the name of an element in which a column (element/attribute and data) is contained. For example, each column of the GrandParent table is contained in the GParent element. The data within each column of the GrandParent table may be associated with an element or an attribute. Regardless, these elements and attributes will be contained in the GParent element.

- ❑ Tag – the tag value associated with a column. For example, each column of the Son table is associated with Tag=2, while each column of the Daughter table is associated with Tag=3.

- ❑ AttributeOrElementName – name of the element or attribute that contains a column's data:

❏   If no `Directive` is specified then this is the name of the attribute (for example, `[Son!2!SonName]` where the attribute containing the data is named `SonName`)

❏   If the `Directive` specified is `xml`, `element`, or `CDATA`, then `AttributeOrElementName` specifies the name of the element containing the column's data (for example, `[GrandKid!4!GrandKidData!xml]` where the element containing the data is named `GrandKidData`)

❏   If a `Directive` is specified, then `AttributeOrElementName` is optional

❏   If no `AttributeOrElementName` is specified, then the column's data is contained in the element specified by `ContainedElementName`

❏   Directive – used to specify the format that data (hide, element, xml, xmltext, and CDATA) should take, and to specify references between columns (XML data types ID, IDREF, and IDREFS and hence directives: ID, IDREF, and IDREFS). Specifying a directive for a column is optional. We will review the directives in full a little later

FOR XML EXPLICIT – Two-Level Example

Before presenting our "show every features" example, we will digress and demonstrate a simpler (two level) query. This query (see below) is designed to demonstrate how the FOR XML EXPLICIT hierarchy is created using UNION ALL to combine the results of multiple queries (see SQL script `ForXmlExplicitStoredProc.sql`):

```
-- SubQuery1 -- This sub-query retrieves the columns of
-- interest from the GrandParent table
SELECT 1 As Tag,
       0 As Parent,
       GrandParentID AS [GrandParent!1!GrandParentID],
       0 AS [Son!2!SonID]
FROM GrandParent

UNION ALL


-- SubQuery2 -- This sub-query retrieves the columns of
-- interest from the Son table
SELECT 2, -- Tag
       1, -- Parent=1, the grandparent is the parent
       0,
       SonID
FROM GrandParent G, Son S
WHERE g.GrandParentID=S.GrandParentID

FOR XML EXPLICIT
```

The previous SQL query is composed of two sub-queries labeled `SubQuery1` and `SubQuery2`. `SubQuery1` retrieves the columns of interest from the `GrandParent` table. For this example, there is only one column of interest, `GrandParentID`. This sub-query specified a value of `Tag=1` and `Parent=0`. This means that the `GrandParent` data retrieved will be at the root of the XML document because `Parent=0`. The children of `GrandParent` use this tag value (`Tag=1`) in order to indicate who their parent is in the XML hierarchy.

SubQuery2 retrieves the column of interest from the Son table: column, SonID. This sub-query specified Tag=2 and Parent=1. It should be recognized that Parent=1 specifies that the elements of this sub-query are to be stored in a sub-element of the <GrandParent> element.

The sub-queries of our FOR XML EXPLICIT query are combined using UNION ALL. Using a SQL union means that every sub-query must contain the columns of every other sub-query. Notice that SubQuery1 (the GrandParent sub-query) contained a value of the Son table's SonID:

```
0 AS [Son!2!SonID]
```

The value for SonID in each row returned by SubQuery1 is 0. This 0 is not displayed because its tag value is specified as Tag=2. The data associated with this column only appears at tag level 2. The Son's sub-query, SubQuery2, contains a 0 representing the ParentID column. This value is never displayed because the data displayed for the Son table is at tag level 2 and ParentID is at tag level 1.

The XML document generated by the query found in ForXmlExplicitStoredProc.sql is as follows:

```
<GrandParent GrandParentID="1"/>
<GrandParent GrandParentID="2"/>
<GrandParent GrandParentID="3">
  <Son SonID="1"/>
  <Son SonID="2"/>
  <Son SonID="3"/>
</GrandParent>
```

This XML document could have been generated using FOR XML AUTO. The reason for this is that *every* column retrieved (GrandParentID and SonID) is represented as an attribute. FOR XML could be used to store the data for every column in an attribute (default) or an element (for which the ELEMENTS option for FOR XML is specified). FOR XML EXPLICIT is used when the level in the hierarchy or data format of specific columns must be dictated. The directives portion of the per-column encoding dictates the representation used by XML for each column. It would have been possible to specify that the data in the GrandParentID column be contained in an attribute and the data in the SonID column to be contained in an element (using the element directive). Directives are optional, and the previous query contained no directives, hence the data associated with every column was contained in an attribute.

Entity Encoding

Before delving into the tantalizing world of FOR XML EXPLICIT directives, an equally important concept must be introduced: **entity encoding**. The concept of entity encoding is the means by which XML special characters can be included in data. What do we mean by special characters? The less-than character is special because it is used to start each element within an XML document. However, how would an XML parser handle data of the following form?

```
<CompareThis> MassOfEarth < MassOfJupiter </CompareThis>
```

This is not actually XML, because the '<' character inside the element's data leads to parsing ambiguity. In this XML-like snippet, the less-than character indicates the start of each element tag, CompareThis, and is also part of the data associated with the element: MassOfEarth < MassOfJupiter. Entity encoding is the means by which XML treats special characters so that they are not placed literally inside the XML document. The previous XML-like snippet could be properly written using an entity encoding to change how the less-than character is represented:

```
<CompareThis> MassOfEarth &lt; MassOfJupiter </CompareThis>
```

The < in the legitimate XML snippet above is the entity-encoded form of the less-than character, hence there is no ambiguity for XML parsers. The characters deemed as special by XML include: &, ', >, <, and ". These characters are represented within an XML document using the following alternative representation:

Character Name	Character Literal	Entity Encoding Representation
Ampersand	&	&amp;
Apostrophe	'	&apos;
Greater-Than	>	&gt;
Less-Than	<	&lt;
Quotation Mark	"	&quot;

The concept of entity encoding is pertinent to the next section's discussion of the FOR XML EXPLICIT directive xml.

Directives

The previous SQL query demonstrated was a just an aside, designed to demonstrate how FOR XML EXPLICIT can be used to generate a specific hierarchy. Our true goals are far loftier and will be presented using a query that is designed to exercise the majority of directives. The FOR XML EXPLICIT directives presented in this section include:

❏ element – causes a particular column in the query to be represented an element rather than an attribute.

❏ hide – causes a column found in the SELECT clause of the query not generate XML, and therefore, this column is not included in the XML document generated.

❏ xml – causes the data associated with a column to be included in the XML document, but not to be entity-encoded.

❏ xmltext – causes the data associated with a column to be included in the XML document as XML. This is correct a column can contain XML and this XML is included in the XML document generated by the query.

❏ CDATA – causes the data associated with a column to be included in the XML document generated as data type CDATA.

❏ ID – causes the data associated with a column to be included in the XML document generated as data type ID.

❏ IDREF – causes the data associated with a column to be included in the XML document generated as data type IDREF.

❏ IDREFS – causes the data associated with a column to be included in the XML document generated as data type IDREFS.

Recall that an extensive sample query is going to be presented, and that this query will contain a significant number of the directives discussed in this section. The directives presented by this sample query include element. The data associated with the column specified using the element directive is contained within an XML element. An example of this is as follows:

```
[GrandKid!4!ChildOfSonName!element]
```

In the previous example of per-column encoding, the column's data is contained in the ChildOfSonName element. An example of the XML generated by this directive is as follows:

<ChildOfSonName>Kyle</ChildOfSonName>

The xml directive causes the data contained in a column that contains the xml directive not to be entity-encoded when placed in the XML document. For example, this means that the < characters are not converted to <. An example of such a column is:

```
[GrandKid!4!GrandKidData!xml]
```

The XML generated by this directive is as follows, where quote and question-mark characters are not entity encoded, even though they are classified as special characters within XML:

<GrandKidData>"/?%#</GrandKidData>

When the xmltext directive is specified for a column, the data associated with this column is assumed to be well formed XML. The data associated with such a column is displayed at the beginning of the element containing the column. An example using the xmltext directive is:

```
Diary AS [GParent!1!!xmltext]
```

The output generated by this per-column directive is completely dependent on the data contained in the Diary column. For the case of the GrandParent named Olivia, the Diary column contains XML corresponding to the chapters of a diary. The <Chapter> elements in the following XML snippet are not generated by SQL Server, but are instead data extracted from the Diary column of the GrandParent table, courtesy of the xmltext directive:

<GParent GParentName="Olivia">
    <Chapter> ChapNum="1" Body="It was the best of times"</Chapter>
    <Chapter> ChapNum="2" Body="If is a far, far"</Chapter>

The CDATA directive causes the data of the column associated with the directive to be contained in an XML CDATA section. The data associated with the Son table's PermanentRecord column is associated with per-column encoding, [Son!2!!CDATA]. An example of the XML generated by this directive is as follows:

<![CDATA[<Book><Chapter> ChapNum="1" Body="Bye, Bye Yoda"</Chapter><Chapter> ChapNum="2" Body="Yet another Death Star, boom boom"</Chapter></Book>]]>

When the hide directive is specified for a column, the column is not included in the XML document generated. Such hidden columns can be used to order the data without having the column's data appearing in the XML document. Such columns will ultimately be included in an ORDER BY clause, because they are typically used to order data. Since a union joins each sub-query, the columns in the ORDER BY clause must correspond to column in the SELECT clause of each query. This is not a restriction on FOR XML EXPLICIT, but a restriction on SQL's UNION keyword.

When the columns in the ORDER BY clause are not in the SELECT clause, SQL Server generates an error. To demonstrate this, consider the following SQL:

```
SELECT G.GrandParentID, 0 FROM GrandParent G, Son S

UNION ALL

SELECT 0, SonID FROM Son AS S, GrandParent G
WHERE S.GrandParentID = G.GrandParentID

ORDER BY G.GrandParentID, S.SonID
```

When the above SQL is executed, the following error is thrown, because the SQL contains the UNION keyword:

ORDER BY items must appear in the select list if the statement contains a UNION operator.

An example of a hidden column is:

```
[GParent!1!OrderByGrandParentName!hide]
```

There is no example XML to show for the previous column due to the hide directive. This is because this directive deliberately specifies that no XML should be generated for the column associated with the hide directive. What is relevant to the hide directive is the ORDER BY clause of our query. Each sub-query separated by a UNION ALL of our FOR XML EXPLICIT query contains a column corresponding to GrandParentName, aliased to OrderByGrandParentName. This column is not displayed because of the hide directive.

The ORDER BY clause of our sample query is as follows, where four columns, which are not displayed, are used to specify the order of the data generated:

```
ORDER BY [GParent!1!OrderByGrandParentName!hide],
         [Son!2!OrderBySonName!hide],
         [Daughter!3!OrderByDaughterName!hide],
         [GrandKid!4!OrderByChildOfSonName!hide]
```

The directives not discussed in this text include ID, IDREF, and IDREFS. Features such as combining directives and full usage of xmltext were not addressed. For a complete review of every feature of every directive, see *Professional SQL Server 2000 XML* from Wrox Press, ISBN 1-861005-46-6.

The directives alone do not fully control per-column encoding. To understand this, consider the following portion of a query:

```
        GrandParentID AS [GParent!1!],
        GrandParentName AS [GParent!1!OrderByGrandParentName!hide],
        RTRIM(GrandParentName) AS [GParent!1!GParentName],
        Diary AS [GParent!1!!xmltext],
```

The values retrieved from the `GrandParent` table will all be contained in the XML element, `GParent`. The data associated with the `GrandParentName` column is contained in the attribute `GParentName`. For the `GrandParentID` column, there is no attribute name specified, and therefore there is no attribute to contain this column's data. Under these circumstances, the data associated with the `GrandParentID` column is contained directly in the `GParent` element. A sample of the XML generated by this portion of our query is as follows:

```
<GParent GParentName="Jeb">
  <Chapter> ChapNum="1" Body="They call me Ishmael"</Chapter>
  <Chapter> ChapNum="2" Body="Whale sinks"</Chapter>
  1
</GParent>
```

In the previous XML snippet, the data associated with the `GrandParentName` column is contained in the `GParentName` attribute. The `<Chapter>` elements and their corresponding attributes are retrieved from the `Diary` column (the literal data of the `Diary` column). Notice that, in this snippet of XML, the "1" is not associated with an attribute. This "1" is the value of the `GrandParentID` column.

FOR XML EXPLICIT – Three-Level Example

So far, each directive has been presented in piecemeal fashion. Each `FOR XML EXPLICIT` directive presented so far is actually part of a larger query – a query that generates a three-level XML hierarchy in the following form:

```
<GParent> contains Sons and Daughter elements
  <Son> contains GrandKid elements
    <GrandKid> </GrandKid>
  </Son>
  <Daughter> </Daughter>
</GParent>
```

The query that generates this three-level hierarchy is a union of four separate queries combined using `UNION ALL`. These sub-queries perform the following tasks in generating the XML document:

❑ Retrieve grandparent data at level 1 of the hierarchy

❑ Retrieve the son data at level 2 of the hierarchy

❑ Retrieve the daughter data at level 2 of the hierarchy

❑ Retrieve the grandchild (child of son) data at level 3 of the hierarchy

The query that generates this three-level data hierarchy, and at the same time demonstrates the majority of `FOR XML EXPLICIT`'s directives, is as follows:

```
-- Generate the Grandparent level of the hierarchy
SELECT 1 AS Tag,
       0 AS Parent,
       GrandParentID AS [GParent!1!],
       GrandParentName AS [GParent!1!OrderByGrandParentName!hide],
       RTRIM(GrandParentName) AS [GParent!1!GParentName],
       Diary AS [GParent!1!!xmltext],
       0 AS [Son!2!SonID],
       '' AS [Son!2!OrderBySonName!hide],
```

```
                '' AS [Son!2!SonName],
                '' AS [Son!2!!CDATA], -- PermanentRecord
                0 AS [Daughter!3!DaughterID!element],
                '' AS [Daughter!3!OrderByDaughterName!hide],
                '' AS [Daughter!3!DaughterName!element],
                '' AS [Daughter!3!SomeData!element],
                0 AS [GrandKid!4!ChildOfSonID!element],
                '' AS [GrandKid!4!OrderByChildOfSonName!hide],
                '' AS [GrandKid!4!ChildOfSonName!element],
                '' AS [GrandKid!4!GrandKidData!xml]

FROM GrandParent

UNION ALL

-- Generated the Son level of the hierarchy
SELECT 2 AS Tag,
        1 AS Parent,
        0, -- GrandParent.GrandParentID
        G.GrandParentName AS [GParent!1!OrderByGrandParentName!hide],
        '', -- GrandParent.Name
        '', -- GrandParent.Diary
        SonID,
        RTRIM(SonName),
        RTRIM(SonName),
        PermanentRecord,
        0, -- Daughter.DaughterID
        '', -- Daughter.OrderByDaughterName
        '', -- Daughter.DaughterName
        '', -- Daughter.SomeData,
        0, -- ChildOfSon.ChildOfOnID,
        '', -- ChildOfSon.OrderByChildOfSonName
        '', -- ChildOfSon.ChildOfSonName
        '' -- ChildOfSon.GrandKidData
FROM GrandParent AS G, Son AS S
WHERE G.GrandParentID=S.GrandParentID

UNION ALL

-- Generate the Daughter level of the hierarchy
-- that is in the same level as the Son's data
SELECT 3 AS Tag,
        1 AS Parent,
        0, -- GrandParent.GrandParentID
        G.GrandParentName AS [GParent!1!OrderByGrandParentName!hide],
        '', -- GrandParent.Name
        '', -- GrandParent.Diary
        0, -- Son.SonID
        '', -- Son.SonName (hidden)
        '', -- Son.SonName
        '', -- Son.PermentRecord
        DaughterID,
        RTRIM(DaughterName),
        RTRIM(DaughterName),
```

```
            SomeData,
            0, -- ChildOfSon.ChildOfOnID,
            '', -- ChildOfSon.OrderByChildOfSonName
            '', -- ChildOfSon.ChildOfSonName
            '' -- ChildOfSon.GrandKidData

FROM GrandParent AS G, Daughter AS D
WHERE G.GrandParentID=D.GrandParentID

UNION ALL

-- Execute grandchild (child of son) level of the query
SELECT 4 AS Tag,
       2 AS Parent,
       0, -- GrandParent.GrandParentID
       G.GrandParentName AS [GParent!1!OrderByGrandParentName!hide],
       '', -- GrandParent.Name
       '', -- GrandParent.Diary
       0, -- Son.SonID
       RTRIM(S.SonName),
       '', -- Son.SonName
       '', -- Son.PermentRecord
       0, -- Daughter.DaughterID
       '', -- Daughter.OrderByDaughterName
       '', -- Daughter.DaughterName
       '', -- Daughter.SomeData,
       CS.ChildOfSonID,
       RTRIM(CS.ChildOfSonName),
       RTRIM(CS.ChildOfSonName),
       CS.GrandKidData

FROM GrandParent AS G, Son AS S, ChildOfSon AS CS
WHERE G.GrandParentID=S.GrandParentID AND
      S.SonID=CS.SonID

ORDER BY [GParent!1!OrderByGrandParentName!hide],
         [Son!2!OrderBySonName!hide],
         [Daughter!3!OrderByDaughterName!hide],
         [GrandKid!4!OrderByChildOfSonName!hide]

FOR XML EXPLICIT
```

A portion of output generated by the query is as follows:

```
<GParent GParentName="Jeb">
  <Chapter> ChapNum="1" Body="They call me Ishmael"</Chapter>
  <Chapter> ChapNum="2" Body="Whale sinks"</Chapter>
  1
  <Daughter>
    <DaughterID>1</DaughterID>
    <DaughterName>Sade</DaughterName>
    <SomeData>abcd&lt;&gt;&apos;</SomeData>
  </Daughter>
  <Son SonID="3" SonName="Han">
```

```
<![CDATA[<Book><Chapter> ChapNum="1" Body="Bye, Bye Yoda"</Chapter><Chapter>
ChapNum="2" Body="Yet another Death Star, boom boom"</Chapter></Book>]]>
  <GrandKid>
   <ChildOfSonID>3</ChildOfSonID>
   <ChildOfSonName>Kyle</ChildOfSonName>
   <GrandKidData>?????"""???</GrandKidData>
  </GrandKid>
 </Son>
</GParent>
```

FOR XML EXPLICIT – ADO.NET

Our example query could be executed using ADO.NET. In the section on FOR XML RAW, ADO.NET was used to execute a FOR XML RAW query that contained the source code. In the section on FOR XML AUTO, ADO.NET was used to execute a stored procedure call containing a FOR XML AUTO query. With respect to FOR XML EXPLICIT, either a query placed in source code, or within a stored procedure call, could have been used in conjunction with ADO.NET. There is nothing unique to FOR XML EXPLICIT that requires any coding that has not already been demonstrated.

In recognition that ADO.NET and FOR XML is ground already trodden, a comparison will be made between specifying a FOR XML EXPLICIT query inside source code and executing the identical query when specified in a stored procedure call. The query executed is that rather lengthy FOR XML EXPLICIT query that retrieves from grandparent through grandchild in a three-level data hierarchy. The SQL script that creates the stored procedure call is ForXMLExplicitStoredProcFull.sql and the stored procedure executed is WroxForXMLExplicitDemo.

The methods that execute the FOR XML EXPLICIT query will not be shown, as they have already been demonstrated. These methods are:

❑   WroxShowOffForXMLExplicitInSourceSQL – demonstrates ADO.NET being used to execute a FOR XML EXPLICIT query. The source code for this method is fundamentally the same as the code used to demonstrate FOR XML RAW being executed.

❑   WroxShowOffForXMLExplicitInStoredProc – demonstrates ADO.NET being used to call a stored procedure call containing a FOR XML EXPLICIT query. The source code is fundamentally the same as the code used to demonstrate FOR XML AUTO being executed from within a stored procedure call.

The method that calls the previously discussed methods and handles the timing computation is called WroxCompareExplicit. This method creates a SqlConnection object that is used for each query executed. Reusing the query makes the timing of database actions more accurate: because setting up the connection can take a significant amount of time, it is best not factored in as part of execution time. The DataTime structure is used to determine the start and stop time after executing each style of query ten thousand times. A TimeSpan structure is used to compute the difference in the start and stop time for each style of query execution. A single execution of either direct SQL containing FOR XML EXPLICIT or a stored procedure call is far from accurate. Ten thousand provides a more accurate representation of the execution time differences between the two styles' execution. This process of executing both styles of FOR XML EXPLICIT ten thousand times, and determining the time taken to perform this action, is repeated five times for increased accuracy.

The code associated with the WroxCompareExplicit method is as follows:

```
static string strConnectionForDBWhereFamilyResides =
        "UID=sa;PWD=;DATABASE=FamilyDB;SERVER=(local);";
static void WroxCompareExplicit()
{
    SqlConnection connection = null;
    DateTime dateTimeStart;
    TimeSpan timeSpanSQLInSource, timeSpaceStoredProc;
    int innerCount;
    const int maxInnerCount = 10000;

    try
    {
        try
        {
            connection = new
                SqlConnection(strConnectionForDBWhereFamilyResides);
            connection.Open();
            for (int outerCount = 0; outerCount < 5; outerCount++)
            {
                dateTimeStart = DateTime.Now;
                for (innerCount = 0; innerCount < maxInnerCount;
                    innerCount++)
                {
                    WroxShowOffForXMLExplicitInSourceSQL(connection);
                }

                timeSpanSQLInSource = DateTime.Now.Subtract(dateTimeStart);
                dateTimeStart = DateTime.Now;
                for (innerCount = 0; innerCount < maxInnerCount;
                    innerCount++)
                {
                    WroxShowOffForXMLExplicitInStoredProc(connection);
                }

                timeSpaceStoredProc = DateTime.Now.Subtract(dateTimeStart);
                Console.WriteLine("{0}: SQL in src: {1}, Stored Proc: {2}",
                    outerCount, timeSpanSQLInSource, timeSpaceStoredProc);
            }
        }
        finally
        {
            if (null != connection)
            {
                connection.Close();
                connection = null;
            }
        }
    }

    catch(Exception ex)
    {
        Console.Error.WriteLine(ex);
    }
}
```

Most database developers recognize the importance of using stored procedures over SQL queries placed directly within source code. Stored procedure calls should yield significantly higher performance, because their SQL has already been parsed and partially prepared for execution by SQL Server. Furthermore, stored procedure calls place SQL code in a central location (the database itself) rather having the code spread to each application that is implemented using embedded SQL. As it turns out, the stored procedure call executing our complicated FOR XML EXPLICIT query executes seven percent faster than the same query placed directly in source code. Seven percent might seem like a far from significant performance gain, but in some contexts, this type of difference could be significant.

FOR XML EXPLICIT – Conclusion

Our FOR XML EXPLICIT query is quite a monster. FOR XML EXPLICIT is powerful, and can produce highly customized XML documents. Our extremely complicated FOR XML EXPLICT query could be used to generate exactly the data needed for consumption by a third-party application with explicit needs when it comes to data format. For my corporation's web site, FOR XML EXPLICIT is used to generate XML hierarchies based on university (top level of XML), course (middle level of XML), and instructor (bottom level of XML). It is also used to generate XML documents containing publication, article, and author information. The XML generated in the previous two examples is used to display course and publications information.

Using FOR XML EXPLICIT to generate this data makes sense in a development environment that is SQL Server savvy. Development shops that primarily use high-level languages such as VB.NET should consider using a simpler type of query (ADO.NET DataSet generated XML, FOR XML RAW, or FOR XML AUTO) in conjunction with the XML-shaping functionality exposed by the System.Xml and System.Xml.Xsl namespaces.

OPENXML

The OPENXML function of SQL Server's Transact SQL allows an XML document to be viewed as a rowset. This rowset, once opened, can then be manipulated using SQL statements such as SELECT, INSERT, UPDATE, and DELETE. For example, it would be possible to parse an XML document using classes found in the System.Xml namespace, and subsequently dynamically generate a SQL INSERT statement in order to add the contents of the XML document to a SQL Server database. A simpler alternative to manually parsing the XML document would be to use OPENXML to treat the XML document as a rowset, and then insert the rowset (the XML document) directly into a SQL Server database using an INSERT statement with OPENXML specified in the statement's FROM clause.

A classic scenario in which OPENXML is used is when the business tier and the data tier communicate via an API that is defined using XML. The business objects of such an application are implemented using C# and VB.NET. These business objects receive external XML documents or generate XML documents. These documents are passed to the data tier. The data tier is also written in C# and VB.NET and uses ADO.NET to execute stored procedure calls containing OPENXML statements. This means that the C# and VB.NET code never has to consciously transform XML documents to SQL Server rowsets and from SQL Server rowsets. The transformation from XML document to rowset is handled by each stored procedure call containing a command that calls OPENXML.

This tying of SQL Server to an XML document using OPENXML results in certain complexities. For example, what happens if the XML document inserted into a SQL Server table contains extra elements or attributes not taken into account by the OPENXML command specified? In the case of a table update, extra elements and attributes can also exist in the XML document. We refer to this as **overflow**. This overflow results in the elements and tags in question being **unconsumed**. The OPENXML mechanism has the ability to handle unconsumed XML generated due to overflow (as will be demonstrated) by placing such unconsumed XML in a designated column. Remember that the FOR XML EXPLICIT directive xml determines if entity encoding was disabled for a column. The column in which unconsumed XML is placed by OPENXML is what FOR XML EXPLICIT's xml directive was designed to handle.

The OPENXML function of Transact SQL is defined as follows, where parameters surrounded by square brackets (for example, [flags byte[in]]) are optional, and clauses surrounded by square brackets are also optional (for example, [WITH (SchemaDeclaration | TableName)]):

```
OPENXML(idoc int [in],rowpattern nvarchar[in], [flags byte[in]])
    [WITH (SchemaDeclaration | TableName)]
```

The parameters to OPENXML are defined as follows:

❏   idoc (input parameter of type int) – a document handle referring to the parsed XML document. This document handle is created using the stored procedure call sp_xml_preparedocument.

❏   rowpattern (input parameter of type nvarchar) – an XPATH pattern specifying the node of the XML document to be processed as a rowset. The following row pattern indicates that node Region is the level of the XML document to be interpreted: N'/Top/Region'.

❏   flags (input parameter of type byte) – this flag parameter indicates how the type of XML node is to be interpreted as columns of the rowset: 0, 1 indicate that attributes represent the columns, and 2 indicates that elements represent columns. This flag can also be used to specify that data not consumed by the rowset can be placed in an overflow column. By using a value of 8, added to one of the permissible flag values, we can indicate that any unconsumed XML is to be placed in an overflow column. A value of 9 (8 + 1) indicates that attributes will be treated as columns, and unconsumed XML will be place in an overflow column. A value of 10 (8 + 2) indicates that elements will be treated as columns, and unconsumed XML will be place in an overflow column.

Two forms of WITH clause can be specified with OPENXML. These WITH clause variants are as follows:

❏   WITH SchemaDeclaration – this type of OPENVIEW's optional WITH clause allows a schema (a specific mapping of XML document nodes to rowset columns) to be specified.

❏   WITH TableName – this type of OPENVIEW's optional WITH clause indicates that the schema associated with a specified table should be used to interpret the XML document specified. This is the simplest variant of the WITH clause to use with OPENXML.

The steps required to utilize OPENXML are demonstrated using the RegionInsert stored procedure call. This stored procedure call contains an INSERT statement that calls OPENXML. The steps followed in the creation of the RegionInsert stored procedure are as follows:

❑ Call the system-provided stored procedure call, sp_xml_preparedocument, passing it an input parameter of the XML document to be processed (parameter, @xmldoc). The sp_xml_preparedocument stored procedure call parses the XML document and returns a handle (an integer, @docIndex in the following SQL snippet). This handle is used by OPENXML to process the parsed XML document. The following code shows a way of creating the RegionInsert stored procedure call, which receives an XML document as input (@xmlDoc), and in turn calls sp_xml_preparedocument:

```
CREATE PROCEDURE RegionInsert @xmlDoc NVARCHAR(4000) AS
DECLARE @docIndex INT
EXECUTE sp_xml_preparedocument @docIndex OUTPUT, @xmlDoc
```

❑ Call OPENXML to shred the XML document and create a rowset: that is, to parse it and use it to create a rowset. This rowset created by OPENXML can be processed by any applicable SQL command. The following INSERT statement demonstrates OPENXML creating a rowset using the schema associated with the Region table, (WITH Region), and this rowset being used to insert data into a table, the Region table:

```
-- 1 is ATTRIBUTE-centric mapping
INSERT Region
SELECT RegionID, RegionDescription
FROM OPENXML(@docIndex, N'/Top/Region', 1) WITH Region
```

❑ Call the system-provided stored procedure, sp_xml_removedocument, in order to clean up the handle to the XML document. Calling this stored procedure is performed as follows:

```
EXECUTE sp_xml_removedocument @docIndex
```

The creation of the RegionInsert stored procedure in its entirety is as follows:

```
CREATE PROCEDURE RegionInsert @xmlDoc NVARCHAR(4000) AS

DECLARE @docIndex INT

EXECUTE sp_xml_preparedocument @docIndex OUTPUT, @xmlDoc
-- 1 is ATTRIBUTE-centric mapping
INSERT Region
SELECT RegionID, RegionDescription
FROM OPENXML(@docIndex, N'/Top/Region', 1) WITH Region

EXECUTE sp_xml_removedocument @docIndex
```

Before an example can be demonstrated the RegionInsert stored procedure must be created by first executing the OpenXMLSP.sql SQL script. An example of SQL (including the XML document with data to insert) that executes the RegionInsert stored procedure is as follows (SQL script file, OpenXMLDemo.sql):

```
DECLARE @newRegions NVARCHAR(2048)

SET @newRegions = N'
<Top>
```

```
    <Region RegionID="11" RegionDescription="Uptown"/>
    <Region RegionID="22" RegionDescription="DownTown"/>
</Top>'

EXEC RegionInsert @newRegions
```

The SQL above called `RegionInsert` to add two rows to the `Region` table (one with `RegionID` 11 and one with `RegionID` of 22). Remember that XML is case-sensitive, while SQL Server's SQL is not. When `OPENXML` was specified (`OPENXML(@docIndex, N'/Top/Region', 1)`) in the `RegionInsert` stored procedure call, the row pattern was `/Top/Region`. The XML document's elements must match this row pattern's case (`<Top>` and `<Region>`). If `<TOP>` or `<top>` had been specified as the root element name, then the insertion would have failed, as there would have been a case mismatch.

OPENXML Stored Procedures: Deletion and Updates

The SQL script, `OpenXML.sql`, also demonstrates `OPENXML` being used in conjunction with SQL `DELETE` (stored procedure, `RegionDelete`). This SQL that creates this stored procedure is as follows:

```
CREATE PROCEDURE RegionDelete @xmlDoc NVARCHAR(4000) AS

    DECLARE @docIndex INT

    EXECUTE sp_xml_preparedocument @docIndex OUTPUT, @xmlDoc

    DELETE Region
    FROM OPENXML(@docIndex, N'/Top/Region', 1) WITH Region AS XMLRegion
    WHERE Region.RegionID=XMLRegion.RegionID

    EXECUTE sp_xml_removedocument @docIndex
```

The `FROM` clause of the `DELETE` statement above uses the `OPENXML` function to generate a rowset named `XMLRegion` (where `AS XmlRegion` assigns the alias name, `XmlRegion`, to the rowset):

```
OPENXML(@docIndex, N'/Top/Region', 1) WITH Region AS XMLRegion
```

The `OpenXML.sql` script also includes a stored procedure, `RegionUpdate`, which uses an XML document to provide the data used to update the `Region` table. The `RegionUpdate` stored procedure is as follows:

```
CREATE PROCEDURE RegionUpdate @xmlDoc NVARCHAR(4000) AS

    DECLARE @docIndex INT

    EXECUTE sp_xml_preparedocument @docIndex OUTPUT, @xmlDoc

    UPDATE Region
      SET Region.RegionDescription = XMLRegion.RegionDescription
    FROM OPENXML(@docIndex, N'/Top/Region',1) WITH Region AS XMLRegion
    WHERE Region.RegionID = XMLRegion.RegionID

    EXECUTE sp_xml_removedocument @docIndex
```

The `RegionUpdate`'s `UPDATE` statement contains a `FROM` clause that uses `OPENXML`. The `OPENXML` function uses an XML document to generate a rowset, and this rowset contains the entries in the `Region` table to be updated. The values updated in the `Region` table are matched to the values specified in the `OPEMXML`-generated rowset, `XmlRegion`, using the `UPDATE` statement's `WHERE` clause: `WHERE Region.RegionID = XMLRegion.RegionID`.

OPENXML ADO.NET: Insertion, Deletion, and Updates

Thus far, three stored procedures have been created that use `OPENXML`: `RegionInsert`, `RegionUpdate`, and `RegionDelete`. The `WroxOpenXMLDemo` Console application uses ADO.NET to demonstrate each of these stored procedure calls being executed. This Console application is implemented separately in VB.NET and again in C#. The basic objectives of this application are to:

❑ Create rows in the `Region` table using stored procedure, `RegionInsert`

❑ Update the rows just created in the `Region` table using stored procedure, `RegionUpdate`

❑ Delete the rows just updated from the `Region` table using stored procedure, `RegionDelete`

The VB.NET implementation of `WroxOpenXMLDemo` contains the `DemoOpenXML` method. This method creates a `SqlCommand` instance, `openXMLCommand`. The command is constructed using a SQL connection passed in via a parameter to the method and by specifying the name of the first stored procedure to execute, `RegionInsert`.

```
Sub DemoOpenXML(ByVal sqlConnection As SqlConnection)
    Dim openXMLCommand As SqlCommand = _
            New SqlCommand("RegionInsert", sqlConnection)
```

The `CommandType` property of the `SqlCommand` instance, `openXMLCommand`, is set be of type stored procedure. A parameter is then created for this command's `Parameters` collection and the value of this parameter is set to the XML document (`strXMLDoc`) that will be inserted using the `InsertRegion` stored procedure:

```
Dim xmlDocParm As SqlParameter = Nothing
Dim strXMLDoc As String = _
      "<Top>" & _
        "<Region RegionID=""11"" RegionDescription=""UpTown""/>" & _
        "<Region RegionID=""22"" RegionDescription=""DownTown""/>" & _
      "</Top>"

openXMLCommand.CommandType = CommandType.StoredProcedure
xmlDocParm = openXMLCommand.Parameters.Add("@xmlDoc", _
                                    SqlDbType.NVarChar, _
                                    4000)
xmlDocParm.Value = strXMLDoc
```

The `strXMLDoc` variable contains two regions (one with `RegionID=11` and the other with `RegionID=12`). These regions are what the `RegionInsert` stored procedure will ultimately insert into the `Regions` table using `OPENXML`.

The `ExecuteNonQuery` method of the `openXMLCommand` instance can now be called to insert the data specified in the XML document, `strXMLDoc`. The `ExecuteNonQuery` method is called because the `InsertRegion` stored procedure only inserts data and does not return the results of a query. This method is executed as follows in the `WroxOpenXMLDemo` application:

```
openXMLCommand.ExecuteNonQuery()
```

The next stored procedure call to demonstrate is `RegionUpdate`. To facilitate this, the data associated with the parameter (the XML document) is tweaked by changing each instance of the word "Town" to "City" (for region description "UpTown" becomes "UpCity" and "DownTown" becomes "DownCity"). This change is courtesy of the `String` class's `Replace` method. Once the data is tweaked, the command's text is set to `RegionUpdate` and the command is executed using `ExecuteNonQuery` as follows:

```
xmlDocParm.Value = strXMLDoc.Replace("Town", "City")
openXMLCommand.CommandText = "RegionUpdate"
openXMLCommand.ExecuteNonQuery()
```

The remainder of the `DemoOpenXML` subroutine sets the command's text to the stored procedure that handles deletion, `RegionDelete`. Once this is set, the `RegionDelete` stored procedure is executed again using `ExecuteNonQuery` as follows:

```
openXMLCommand.CommandText = "RegionDelete"
openXMLCommand.ExecuteNonQuery()
End Sub
```

The source code associated with the C# implementation of the `OpenXMLDemo` method in its entirety is as follows:

```
static void OpenXMLDemo(SqlConnection sqlConnection)
{
    SqlCommand openXMLCommand = new SqlCommand();
    SqlParameter xmlDocParm = null;
    string strXMLDoc =
        "<Top>" +
        "<Region RegionID=\"11\" RegionDescription=\"UpTown\"/>" +
        "<Region RegionID=\"22\" RegionDescription=\"DownTown\"/>" +
        "</Top>";

    sqlConnection.Open();
    openXMLCommand.Connection = sqlConnection;
    openXMLCommand.CommandText = "RegionInsert";
    openXMLCommand.CommandType = CommandType.StoredProcedure;
    xmlDocParm = openXMLCommand.Parameters.Add("@xmlDoc",
        SqlDbType.NVarChar,
        4000);
    xmlDocParm.Value = strXMLDoc;
    openXMLCommand.ExecuteNonQuery();
    openXMLCommand.CommandText = "RegionUpdate";
    xmlDocParm.Value = strXMLDoc.Replace("Town", "City");
    openXMLCommand.ExecuteNonQuery();
    openXMLCommand.CommandText = "RegionDelete";
    openXMLCommand.ExecuteNonQuery();
}
```

The true elegance in both the C# and VB.NET implementation of the WroxOpenXMLDemo application is that neither implementation language was aware of how the XML document passed to the stored procedure calls is written to SQL Server. The stored procedure calls ultimately use OPENXML, but ADO.NET is blissfully unaware that this OPENXML SQL Server function is called to massage an XML document into a rowset that can ultimately by used be a SQL statement.

Summary

Before the advent of SQL Server's FOR XML and OPENXML, a large amount of time was spent on translating the results of queries to XML documents (the service provided by FOR XML) and translating XML documents to SQL statements (the services provided by OPENXML). Both the FOR XML and OPENXML features of SQL Server are remarkable time savers to the development process.

With respect to FOR XML three modes of operation were presented:

- ❑ FOR XML RAW – provides basic XML manipulation where each row returned in the rowset is placed in a fixed-named element (row) and each column returned is represented by an attribute named for the said column or its alias.

- ❑ FOR XML AUTO – provides a more sophisticated approach to the generation of XML documents by representing data in hierarchal fashion that takes advantage of foreign key relationships. The elements at each level of the hierarchy correspond to the table names or their alias names found in the FROM clause of the query. The value of each column returned by the query is found by default in an attribute named for the column or its alias name. When the ELEMENT option is used with the FOR XML AUTO, the value of each column returned by the query is found in an element named for the column or its alias name. The limitation here is that every column and its value must be represented by attributes or every column and its value must be represented by elements.

- ❑ FOR XML EXPLICIT – this form of for FOR XML query allows the precise format for of each column returned by the query to be specified.

The per-column explicitness exposed by FOR XML EXPLICIT includes:

- ❑ The form used to represent each column and its data includes the type of XML tag used to contain the data. By default, attributes represent column/data pairs, but if the element directive is used, the column/data pairs are contained in elements.

- ❑ The level in the XML hierarchy in which the column/data pair resides is specified using a tag corresponding to each level. This tag is placed in each column's alias.

- ❑ The precise data type of the column/data pair can be specified. The data types supported include CDATA, ID, IDREF, and IDREFS. Each of the aforementioned data types corresponds to a directive named for that data type (CDATA, ID, IDREF, and IDREFS respectively).

- ❑ The way XML contained within the column is presented can also be controlled. The CDATA directive causes the XML contained in column data to be preserved by representing the XML as type CDATA. The xml directive causes data contained in a column/data pairing not to be entity-encoded. The xmltext directive causes the data contained in a column/data pairing to be treated as XML. This data is then placed directly within the XML document generated.

❑   The hide directive causes a column/data pair returned by FOR XML EXPLICITY query not to be included in the XML document generated. Each column used by the query must be specified as part of the SELECT clause including columns whose sole purpose is to order the data. The hide directive allows a column to be specified in the SELECT clause. This column can then be used in the ORDER BY clause and its data will not be placed in the XML document generated.

It is also possible to further control each style of FOR XML query using configuration options such as:

❑   ELEMENT – this option applies only the FOR XML AUTO queries. The ELEMENT option causes each column in the query to generate an element. This is as opposed to the default where each column in the query generates an attribute.

❑   BINARY BASE64 – this option causes binary data to be included within the XML document is represented in base-64.

❑   XMLDATA – when this option is used, an XDR-style schema is included at the front of the XML document generated by the query.

OPENXML dramatically simplifies the process of making an XML document usable by SQL Server. This function very simply exposes the elements (flag parameter value of 2) or attributes (flag parameter value of 0 or 1) of an XML document as the columns of a rowset. Once exposed – the XML document is exposed as a rowset – conventional SQL means can be used to access and utilize the data (INSERT, UPDATE, and DELETE). The elegance of OPENXML is that ADO.NET developers never need be aware of how XML documents are being utilized by SQL Server.

It is important for VB.NET and C# developers to recognize how FOR XML and OPENXML can greatly simplify development. FOR XML or OPENXML may appear to be a bit of SQL magic, but by following the straightforward examples provided in this chapter, and with a bit of practice, you'll find that there will be more time to spend on the golf course and less time spent in development. Then again if you do not play golf (like the author of this text), you'll just end up spending more time writing other code.

15

Performance and Security

Once we've become accustomed to the basics of working with ADO.NET – using the `DataSet`, `DataAdapter`, SQL Client and OLE DB data providers, and so on – we can focus more on some of the details generally left out of most overview texts on the subject. Among such details are performance and security issues.

In this chapter, we'll discuss the issues surrounding creating high-performance applications and components for use with ADO.NET in the .NET framework, as well as issues concerning code and data security. Performance is a problem that plagues even the most well-designed and well-programmed solutions. In this chapter, we will see how to take ADO.NET solutions and make them faster and more secure by using some optimization techniques, asynchronous execution, connection pooling, and various security technologies. By the time this chapter is complete, you should have a thorough understanding of the following topics:

- ❑ Various methods to optimize data access
- ❑ Connection Pooling
- ❑ Message Queuing
- ❑ Security issues and tradeoffs concerning Data Access.

Optimizing Data Access

We all want our applications to run fast. That much should be a given for any programmer on any project. Not too many of us have ever sat in on a design meeting in which people said, "Our application is fine the way it is, there's really nothing to be gained by making it faster." However, the unfortunate fact of life is that many of us have been in meetings where it was decided that it was too expensive in terms of time or money to improve an application's performance.

Traditionally, optimizing applications for the highest performance possible has often been a black art left to programmers who disappear into the basement for weeks at a time. However, this is changing with some of the features of ADO.NET and the .NET Framework. In the past, optimizing ADO for performance has been difficult, because so many of its components were multi-faceted; using a component for one purpose often incurred performance overhead from another purpose not currently being used. This is most obvious when looking at the classic ADO `RecordSet`, which performs so many tasks that you often incur performance overhead from completely unrelated code just by using the `RecordSet`.

This next section should give you some insight on some techniques and tips you can incorporate into your applications that will help speed them up, and keep the code easy to read and maintain.

DataReader or DataSet?

The choice of whether to use a `DataReader` or a `DataSet` should be a fairly straightforward decision, provided we know enough about the type of data we need to access, and the ways in which we intend to process it. Unlike many multi-faceted ADO components, both of those components have well defined roles. As long as we know which roles each of these are designed for, we can choose the most effective solution for our needs. There are a number of major differences between these two components.

An important thing to keep in mind is that, regardless of which solution is *faster*, it doesn't necessarily mean that either component is *better*. Each is suited to a particular task, and each will excel at that task. Conversely, each will perform poorly (if at all) when used to perform a task it isn't suited for.

Memory Consumption

One of the main differences between the `DataReader` and the `Dataset` is that the `DataReader` consumes less memory than a `DataSet`. Depending on the amount of data, and the memory resources available, the performance advantages associated with using less memory can be enormous. We will look at how best to handle large result sets later in the chapter.

A `DataReader` is an object that contains information on only *a single row of data* at a given time. What this means is that, regardless of the size of a result set, traversing this result set with a `DataReader` will only ever have a single record loaded in memory at a given time.

A `DataSet`, on the other hand, is designed specifically to be an in-memory cache of large amounts of data. In this regard, the `DataSet` will consume more memory than the `DataReader`.

To summarize, if we are tight on memory, then we should consider using a `DataReader` rather than a `DataSet`. However, if memory concerns are not at the top of our list of priorities, the increased functionality of an entirely disconnected in-memory data cache may suit our needs better.

Traversal Direction

Whenever we plan on traversing data for a particular task, we need to consider the direction of the traversal. Just as with ADO, we can reap enormous performance benefits if we know in advance exactly how we will need to access data.

If we plan on accessing data to do something simple, such as display all of the records in a result set in HTML form through an ASP.NET page, for instance, then a choice is simple. The `DataReader` is a read-only, forward-only component designed specifically for the task of reading and traversing data rapidly in a single direction. So, when looking at what an application is going to need to do with the data, if we don't need to be able to write changes to an in-memory cache, or if we won't need to have indexed access to any row at any given time, then the `DataReader` will definitely gain us some performance benefits.

> If you don't need to modify data, or access rows in random order, then you can probably gain a considerable performance advantage by using a **`DataReader`**.

Multiple Result Sets

Both the `DataReader` and the `DataSet` support the notion of multiple result sets. The `DataSet` supports this through using tables. The `DataReader` enables us to access additional result sets by providing the `NextResult` method. Just as with row access with the `DataReader`, accessing additional result sets in the `DataReader` is a forward-only, read-only operation.

It is important to re-iterate here that the `DataReader` will actually only hold one row of information at any given time. This means that even though ten different result sets may be available, only one row of any given result set will be available at any given time. Once a row has been passed in a `DataReader` traversal, that row is disposed of, and there is no way to retrieve it again without resetting the reader and starting over from the beginning.

For those of you who like using the `SHAPE` statement in your SQL statements to create hierarchical recordsets, you can rest assured that you can still use this with the `DataReader`. Whereas in ADO we would set a `RecordSet` object to the individual field object of a row, instead, we now set a `DataReader` object to the value of a column in the `DataReader` of the parent row.

There is plenty of information on the details of working with the `DataReader` component in Chapter 4, and information on using the `DataSet` object in Chapter 5.

Round Trips

Any time we create an application designed for data access of any kind, one of the first things we learn is to keep round trips to the data source to an absolute minimum. Actually hitting the database server for information should be considered a slow and expensive operation, to be done sparingly. The reason for this is that while operating under minimum load, you may not notice anything, but when connection resources are in use for long periods of time in a heavily burdened application, you will encounter all sorts of problems, such as resource locks, resource contention, race conditions, and the dreaded command timeout.

> Always strive to achieve the highest possible ratio of tasks to database round trips. The optimal situation is where more than one task is accomplished by a single database round trip.

Stored Procedures

Discussing stored procedures can be tricky. Many programmers will tell you that they don't buy you all that much. Others, especially database administrators, will tell you that stored procedures are the answer to all of your problems.

A programmer with an open mind and a stopwatch can probably tell you that the real answer is somewhere in between. Marathons are not won by runners with a great sprint speed, and 100-meter dashes are not won by endurance runners. The key to optimal performance when working with stored procedures is making sure that the task is given to the appropriate process.

One of the things we mentioned about reducing round trips is to keep the ratio of tasks to database requests high. One way in which you can accomplish this is to use stored procedures. For example, consider an application that has to create a new order item in response to a customer purchase request. Once an item has been ordered, a table must be updated that reduces the available stock of that item by one. If the component created the order item, and then issued a SQL statement to reduce that item's stock quantity, that would result in two full round trips. However, if a stored procedure was invoked to purchase the item, the stored procedure could then automatically decrease its stock quantity without incurring the overhead and performance hit of performing another round trip between the component's process space and the database server. This round trip becomes painfully slow when the database server is not on the same physical machine as the component issuing the requests. And, of course, the more round trips incurred, the higher the network traffic, which can also impact on the perceived speed of your application.

One of the other benefits of stored procedures is that, in general, they are less prone to failure due to simple mistakes. For example, let's take the following simple example code snippet of how we might insert a record into the database manually with a standard SQL statement:

```
string strSQL = "INSERT INTO Books(UPC, Title, Price) " +
    "VALUES('" + _UPC + "', '" + _Title + "', " + _Price + ")";
Connection.Execute(strSQL, RecordsAffected);
```

First of all, we're looking at an extremely ugly string concatenation. Not only is it extremely cumbersome to try to place the apostrophes in the right places, but because floating-point values also support the ToString method, we won't get any type mismatch errors when we try to place a floating-point value into a string field or vise versa. The other problem is that if the book's title happens to have an apostrophe in it somewhere, it will crash the statement execution. Therefore, we have to modify the above SQL statement to replace all occurrences of apostrophes with two apostrophes to make sure they don't interfere with the statement parser. If you've ever done this kind of SQL work from ADO, you know that it gets very ugly, very quickly and becomes nightmarish to debug and maintain for large queries.

Alternatively, let's take a look at what performing the same task looks like when done with a stored procedure (this can also be performed using inline SQL and parameters, but we'll just show the stored procedure here):

```
SqlCommand myCommand = new SqlCommand("sp_InsertBook", myConnection);
myCommand.CommandType = CommandType.StoredProcedure;
myCommand.Parameters.Add( new SqlParameter("@UPC", SqlDbType.VarChar, 30) );
myCommand.Parameters.Add( new SqlParameter("@Title", SqlDbType.VarChar, 45) );
myCommand.Parameters.Add( new SqlParameter("@Price", SqlDbType.Float) );
myCommand.Parameters[0].Value = _UPC;
myCommand.Parameters[1].Value = _Title;
myCommand.Parameters[2].Value = _Price;
RowsAffected = myCommand.ExecuteNonQuery();
```

This might actually take up more lines of code, but believe me, it runs faster. Even if it didn't run faster, most programmers consider code that is easy to read and maintain far more useful than fast code. Just from looking at the code without a single comment in it, we know the data types of each of our arguments, we know that we're executing a stored procedure, and we know that we've deliberately told SQL to skip the overhead of attempting to return parameters. The other major gain here is that instead of potentially corrupting data with type mismatches for the previous SQL statement, we can be assured that a type mismatch in the stored procedure will throw an exception before data is committed to the database, and, if a transaction is active, it will be rolled back.

> In general, stored procedures are faster, more reliable, less error-prone, and more scalable than building SQL statement strings manually within your components.

Compiled Query Caching

One of the features of most RDBMSs available today that many people take for granted is the ability to compile and cache stored procedures and their results based on certain parameters. As an example, let's say that our application has several different pages that all retrieve customer order history. It is possible that instead of having our component (or ASP.NET page, or Windows Forms application) issue the SQL statement to retrieve the history directly, we could simply have the component issue a request for a stored procedure and retrieve the results faster.

This performance benefit can come from the fact that SQL Server can compile the stored procedure and actually cache various results for it in memory. This means that repeated calls to the same stored procedure for the same customer could actually retrieve cached results from memory. However, we should also keep in mind that the standard query processor that processes SQL strings sent from ADO and ADO.NET components can also compile and cache queries. The ultimate test will be wiring a test harness for both modes of operation (with or without stored procedures) to see which performs in the best conditions for your application.

Configuring DataAdapter Commands

As we've seen throughout this book, the DataAdapter is the plug that can transfer information from a data store to a DataSet, as well as transfer changes from the DataSet into the data store. In most examples of a DataAdapter, we'd probably see something like this:

```
SqlDataAdapter MyDA = new SqlDataAdapter("SELECT * FROM Table", MyConn);
```

What we don't see behind the scenes is this code populating one of the properties of the DataAdapter, the SelectCommand property. Each DataAdapter has four main objects that it holds to use for the four main operations that can be performed on data:

- ❑ InsertCommand
- ❑ SelectCommand
- ❑ UpdateCommand
- ❑ DeleteCommand

When an adapter is associated with a `DataSet`, and the `DataSet` invokes the `Update` method, the adapter is then asked to propagate those changes (creations, deletions, updates, or insertions) across to the data source.

The problem is that it is all too easy to have another object do your work for you and create these commands on the fly. There are countless examples floating around in various books that recommend that we use the `CommandBuilder` objects (`SqlCommandBuilder` or `OleDbCommandBuilder`) to automatically generate the commands to perform the data update operations. While this may reduce the amount of code we have to write, chances are this won't help us in the long run, because there are many problems with using the `CommandBuilders` related to performance and reliability.

The bottom line is that, in order to make sure that changes are carried across to the data source as fast as possible, we should be building our own commands for our adapters. Not only that, but in many cases the commands that are automatically built by the `CommandBuilders` might actually cause exceptions to be thrown, because the SQL generated is faulty.

Let's take a look at some C# code that takes a `DataAdapter` and links the `CommandBuilder` object to it. The way the `CommandBuilder` object works is by just-in-time building the appropriate command object as needed. So, if we have a `DataAdapter` that has a `SelectCommand`, when the `DataSet` invokes the `Update` method, the `CommandBuilder` object will have generated commands that it deems appropriate for the intended operations. The conflict arises when the command the builder deems appropriate is either inefficient or non-functional.

Here is the source listing for our C# code that links a `CommandBuilder` to a `DataAdapter` and then prints out what the `CommandBuilder` thinks is an appropriate `UpdateCommand`.

```csharp
using System;
using System.Data;
using System.Data.SqlClient;

namespace Wrox.ProADONET.Chapter16.DACommands
{
class Class1
{
static void Main(string[] args)
{
  DataSet MyDS = new DataSet();
  SqlConnection Connection = new SqlConnection("Data Source=localhost;
    Initial Catalog=Northwind; User id=sa; Password=;");
  Connection.Open();

  SqlDataAdapter MyDA = new SqlDataAdapter("SELECT * FROM [Order Details]
    OD", Connection);
```

Here is the code that creates a new `CommandBuilder` based on the instance of our `DataAdapter`. It works by inferring what it thinks should be reasonable commands based on whatever information is available to it already.

```csharp
  SqlCommandBuilder myBuilder = new SqlCommandBuilder( MyDA );

  Console.WriteLine(myBuilder.GetUpdateCommand().CommandText);

}
}
}
```

Much to our chagrin, here is the SQL update command produced by our "automatic" CommandBuilder (found in the **DACommands** directory in the code downloads):

```
C:\527X\Chapter16\Chapter16Code\DACommands\bin\Debug>dacommands.exe
UPDATE Order Details SET OrderID = @p1 , ProductID = @p2 , UnitPrice = @p3 , Qua
ntity = @p4 , Discount = @p5 WHERE ( OrderID = @p6 AND ProductID = @p7 AND UnitP
rice = @p8 AND Quantity = @p9 AND Discount = @p10 )

C:\527X\Chapter16\Chapter16Code\DACommands\bin\Debug>
```

What's the first thing you notice about this query? Well, one of the most obvious things about the query is that its WHERE clause is needlessly large. Essentially, what is happening is that the CommandBuilder is assuming that the DataSet will be providing to the DataAdapter two *states* of data – an original state, and a new state. So, parameters 1 through 5 indicate the new state and are the arguments to the SET clause. Parameters 6 through 10 indicate the *original* state of the row and are used to locate the row in the database on which to perform the update. This is the way the CommandBuilder will always function, because it cannot make any assumptions about the underlying data source.

What kind of performance would we be looking at if none of the other fields were indexed, some of the fields were memos (SQL Text data type), and the table consisted of a few thousand rows? The situation would be grim to the say the least. We know that the OrderID column and ProductID column combine to form the unique row indicator for that table. Therefore, we could build our own UpdateCommand that only required the *original state* OrderID and ProductID and it would be far more efficient than the automatic generation.

The other problem with this automatically generated command is that it contains update columns for the OrderID and ProductID columns. These two columns together form the Primary Key for this table. I'm sure you know by now that you cannot use an UPDATE command to modify the values of Autoincrement columns. If we execute our UpdateCommand generated by the CommandBuilder we used against the Northwind database, an exception will be thrown, indicating that we cannot modify the values of a Primary Key column.

One other reason for building our own commands manually instead of using the CommandBuilder is that we can indicate to the DataAdapter that it should be using a stored procedure for an operation instead of an in-line SQL command.

To show an example of building our own command object for a DataAdapter for a stored procedure, we'll create a C# Console application called DACommands2. Then, we'll type the following into the Class1.cs file:

```csharp
using System;
using System.Data;
using System.Data.SqlClient;

namespace Wrox.ProADONET.Chapter16.DACommands2
{
class Class1
{
```

```
static void Main(string[] args)
{
  DataSet MyDS = new DataSet();
  SqlConnection Connection = new
    SqlConnection("Data Source=localhost; Initial Catalog=Northwind; User
    id=sa; Password=;");
  Connection.Open();
```

Rather than providing a simple SQL SELECT statement in the constructor to the DataAdapter object, we'll instead create a new command entirely, setting its type to CommandType.StoredProcedure. Once we have that, we can define parameters just like those we normally set. In our case, we're providing the arguments ourselves to indicate the 1996 annual sales for the "Sales by Year" stored procedure that comes with the Northwind database (ours was the copy that comes with SQL Server 2000).

```
SqlDataAdapter MyDA = new SqlDataAdapter();
MyDA.SelectCommand = new SqlCommand("Sales by Year", Connection );
MyDA.SelectCommand.CommandType = CommandType.StoredProcedure;
MyDA.SelectCommand.Parameters.Add( new SqlParameter("@Beginning_Date",
  SqlDbType.DateTime) );
MyDA.SelectCommand.Parameters["@Beginning_Date"].Value =
  DateTime.Parse("01/01/1996");

MyDA.SelectCommand.Parameters.Add( new SqlParameter("@Ending_Date",
  SqlDbType.DateTime) );
MyDA.SelectCommand.Parameters["@Ending_Date"].Value =
  DateTime.Parse("01/01/1997");
```

Here, you might be looking for some kind of "execute" method to be called on the stored procedure command we created. This is actually done behind the scenes for you when the Fill method is called on the DataAdapter.

```
MyDA.Fill( MyDS, "SalesByYear" );
```

Here we're iterating through each of the columns programmatically and displaying them to further illustrate the point that even though we used a stored procedure to obtain our records in the DataAdapter, the DataSet has been populated with a full schema.

```
foreach (DataColumn _Column in MyDS.Tables["SalesByYear"].Columns)
{
  Console.Write("{0}\t", _Column.ColumnName );
}
Console.WriteLine("\n--------------------------------------------------
  ");
foreach (DataRow _Row in MyDS.Tables["SalesByYear"].Rows)
{
  foreach (DataColumn _Column in MyDS.Tables["SalesByYear"].Columns)
  {
    Console.Write("{0}\t", _Row[_Column] );
  }
  Console.WriteLine();
}

}
}
}
```

The following is a screenshot of the console output generated by this program. The output on its own isn't entirely impressive; however, if you compile our sample and run it, and then run it again over and over again (up arrow/enter is good for this), you'll notice that, beyond the initial execution, it runs *really* fast. This is because (if configured properly) SQL has cached the compiled stored procedure, *and* the results it returns for the arguments we supplied. This allows SQL to service the request for the result set without re-querying the database for the information.

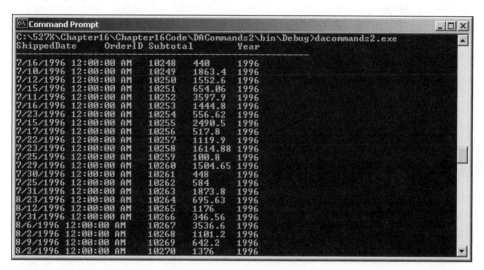

Taken on its own, this little bit of information about building your own commands might not seem all that impressive. However, when you take into account that the `DataAdapter` is used to populate `DataSet` object, which can then be visually bound to controls either on Windows Forms applications, or ASP.NET forms, the power becomes clear. By supplying our own commands, we not only get fine-grained control over how the `DataAdapter` transfers data, but we can also optimize it to transfer data in the fastest way possible using stored procedures, etc.

> The `CommandBuilder` objects are excellent at enabling us to update data when we don't know the schema of the data we're working with ahead of time. However, in most other cases, we should try to avoid using the `CommandBuilder` objects.

High-Volume Data Processing

When working with small applications, we can often ignore performance issues. However, when working with large amounts of data, large numbers of users, or both, these seemingly small issues can magnify and cause an application to grind to a halt. We've listed here a couple of things you can do to try to prepare yourself for some of the pitfalls that occur in high-volume and high-activity applications.

Latency

One of the most important things you can remember about large applications is that latency is your enemy. Latency, in our context, is the delay and locking of resources incurred while obtaining and opening a connection. We want to perform this activity as *infrequently* as possible throughout an application. If we keep this in mind, performance tuning an application may be easier than expected.

In small applications or desktop applications, when accessing local data stores such as an Access database or an Excel spreadsheet, the overhead of opening and closing connections may not be noticeable. However, when the component opening and closing the connection is on a different machine in a network (or worse, across the Internet) from the actual database server, the cost of opening a connection is very high.

For example, let's suppose a user of an application clicks a button to retrieve a list of orders. This opens a connection, obtains the orders, and closes the connection, because we've all been taught that leaving a connection open too long is also bad practice. Then, the user double-clicks on an order item and obtains a list of order details. This also opens the connection, obtains the result set, and then closes the connection again. Assuming the user continues on with this browsing behavior for ten minutes, the user could be consuming an enormous amount of time and resources needlessly opening and closing connections.

One way to prevent situations like this is to anticipate the intended use of data. We should weigh the memory cost of obtaining the information on the initial database connection against the cost of waiting until the information is needed.

`DataSets` are designed to be in-memory data caches. They are also designed to hold on to more than one table of information. They are an ideal candidate for storing large amounts of data in anticipation of disconnected browsing behavior.

> **Retrieving a large volume of data within the context of a single connection will always be faster than retrieving small portions and opening and closing the connection each time, because large-block retrieval causes less network round-trips and incurs less latency.**

Cached Data

Many applications suffering from undiagnosed performance problems are plagued by the same problem. This problem is the fact that the application is needlessly performing multiple redundant queries for the same data.

If an application is consistently hitting the database for the same data, then it can probably benefit from caching. Many performance benchmarks have been done using ASP.NET object caching and have shown remarkable speed improvements over non-cached ASP.NET applications and classic ASP.

Let's suppose that we're building an e-commerce website. All of our products are arranged in a hierarchy of categories and sub-categories. Through some usage testing, we've found that one of the most frequently performed activities on the web site is browsing items within a category.

Add to the example the fact that the site gets over 100,000 hits per day. If only 40% of customers browse products within categories, that is still 40,000 requests per day for information that probably isn't going to change except on a weekly or monthly basis.

What many companies do is retrieve the information once only at some pre-determined time. Until the next time the data needs to be changed, all of the code on the entire web site can hit the cached information instead of the actual database information. This may not seem like all that big a deal, but when we are dealing with high volumes of traffic, every single database request we can avoid is one worth avoiding. Relieving the database server of the drudgery of fetching the same item browse list information 40,000 times a day frees it up to handle more taxing things like retrieving order histories, storing new orders, and performing complex product searches.

There are several methods available for caching data. For more information on using ASP.NET's data caching features, consult the Wrox book *Professional ASP.NET*. In addition, you can use the COM+ (or MTS) package itself to cache information for you. COM+ provides a facility known as Property Groups that allows you to cache information in the package's own memory space. This way, your COM+ application that is driving your web site (you *are* using COM+ to drive your data components, aren't you?) can avoid actually hitting the database if the information has been cached.

Let's look at the Northwind database for an example. The category listing in the database (Categories table) contains binary columns that store images for the categories. If Northwind were running a high-volume web site, every single user browsing through the system would hit the database needlessly for the same nearly-static binary data, over and over again. Obviously that's not the situation we want.

Our solution is to create a COM+ component that fetches the category listing. First, it will check to see whether the category listing has been cached. If not, it will fetch it from the database, add it to the cache, and then return that result. The beauty of this solution is that any time a web site administrator adds a new category, all they need to do is right-click the COM+ application, choose **Shut Down**, and then hit the web site again and the cache will be populated with the new information. If the category is added programmatically by a component, then the component can also automatically trigger a refresh of the cache. The act of shutting down the package removes the cache. As you'll see, the cache is actually tied directly to the process in which the component is running.

Here's the source code for our COM+ component. To create this component, we went into Visual Studio.NET and created a new C# Class Library. Then, we added a reference to System.EnterpriseServices and made our component derive from the ServicedComponent class. Here is that listing:

```
using System;
using System.Data;
using System.EnterpriseServices;
using System.Data.SqlClient;

namespace PropGroupAssembly
{
public class PropGroupClass : ServicedComponent
{
public string FetchCategoryList(out bool FromCache)
{
  bool fExist;
  fExist = true;
```

We're going to use the COM+ Shared Property Group Manager to do some work for us. We'll create an instance of a group and be told if that group already exists. Then, we'll create an instance of a property and be told if that property existed. If, by the time we have the instance of our property, the fExist variable is true, then we know that we're working from a cache. Otherwise, we need to hit the database for our categories. Take special note of the ReleaseMode we've chosen. This indicates that the property will not be cleared until the process in which it is being hosted has been terminated. This is of vital importance when deciding between library activation packages (applications) and server-activation applications.

```
PropertyLockMode oLock = PropertyLockMode.SetGet;
PropertyReleaseMode oRel = PropertyReleaseMode.Process;
SharedPropertyGroupManager grpMan = new SharedPropertyGroupManager();
SharedPropertyGroup grpCache =
```

```
      grpMan.CreatePropertyGroup("CategoryCacheGroup", ref oLock, ref oRel,
        out fExist);
    SharedProperty propCache = grpCache.CreateProperty("CategoryCache",
        out fExist);
    if (fExist)
    {
      FromCache = true;
      return (string)propCache.Value;
    }
    else
    {
      FromCache = false;
```

We didn't get our information from the in-memory, process-specific cache, so now we'll get it from the database. Remembering that opening and closing the connection is a task that is our enemy, we only want to do this when the data hasn't already been cached.

```
    SqlConnection Connection = new
      SqlConnection("Data Source=localhost; Initial Catalog=Northwind;
        User id=sa; Password=;");
    SqlDataAdapter MyDA = new
      SqlDataAdapter("SELECT CategoryID, CategoryName, Description, Picture
        FROM Categories",
        Connection );
    DataSet MyDS = new DataSet();
    MyDA.Fill(MyDS, "Categories");
```

We're storing the string representation of the DataSet's internal XML data. This allows for maximum flexibility of consumers of the cache. It allows consumers of the cache that have access to the DataSet component to utilize it, but it also allows traditional COM/COM+ components invoking this component to access the data via traditional DOM or SAX components and traversals.

```
    propCache.Value = MyDS.GetXml();
    Connection.Close();
    MyDA.Dispose();
    return (string)propCache.Value;
  }

  }
  }
  }
```

The AssemblyInfo.cs file for this project (called PropGroupAssembly) contains the following custom attribute defined by the System.EnterpriseServices namespace:

```
[assembly:ApplicationName("Property Group Test")]
```

This tells the CLR that the first time this assembly has a class invoked in it, all of the classes within it will be registered in COM+, belonging to a new, library-activation application called "Property Group Test". This is where it is important to remember the difference between activation models in a COM+ application. A library-activation application will activate the components *within the context of the calling process*. A server-activation application will activate the components within its own separate process. So, if your client (or consumer) component expects the cache to persist, even though the client process has terminated, you *must* re-configure your COM+ application to activate server-side.

One more thing before we look at the code to test this caching component: always remember to place your .NET COM+ assemblies in the Global Assembly Cache, otherwise .NET components attempting to use them will be unable to locate them, even if they are in the same directory.

Here's the source to our testing harness, `PropGroupTester`, a C# Console Application. We created this by adding a reference to `System.EnterpriseServices`, and by browsing for a reference to our COM+ assembly.

```
using System;

namespace Wrox.ProADONET.Chapter16.PropGroupTester
{
class Class1
{
static void Main(string[] args)
{
  PropGroupAssembly.PropGroupClass oClass = new
    PropGroupAssembly.PropGroupClass();
  string strXML;
  bool fExist;
```

Our testing harness is storing the XML, but isn't actually doing anything with it. You could quite easily have a `DataSet` load the XML for use in a `databound` grid or some ASP.NET server-side control.

```
  Console.WriteLine("First Execution");
  strXML = oClass.FetchCategoryList(out fExist);
  Console.WriteLine("From Cache: {0}", fExist);

  Console.WriteLine("Second Execution");
  strXML = oClass.FetchCategoryList(out fExist);
  Console.WriteLine("From Cache: {0}", fExist);
}
}
}
```

What can we expect from the output of this example? Well, if our COM+ component is running in a server-activated application, then the first time we run this we should get a `False` and then a `True`. The first execution will have needed to query the database for the information. On the second execution, the information should be in the cache and we should see a `True`. To further prove that the cache is being maintained separately from our client process (again, server-activated COM+ application), we run the application again, and we should expect a `True` value for both the first and second execution. Let's test this out:

We can see from this screenshot of our console that the first time we run the application, the first execution shows that the information was *not* cached. We then see that every time we run the program after that, the information we retrieved was from the cache. As an experiment, right-click the application (or package for those not using COM+) and choose **Shut Down**. Then re-run the application, and you should see that the results are the same as the screenshot above. The cache is emptied when the process hosting the cache is terminated. This process is terminated when the server application is shut down.

> **Examine the data needs of the consumers of your application and consider caching any data that is accessed far more frequently than it changes. Two popular methods of caching are using ASP.NET's caching or COM+ Shared Property Groups.**

ASP.NET Object Caching

If you are lucky enough to be writing your data-driven application within ASP.NET, then you actually have a considerably larger toolbox available at your disposal. For example, all of the work we did above to allow us to cache arbitrary data within the COM+ server application process is completely unnecessary when you're working in ASP.NET.

ASP.NET provides a feature called object caching that automates the work we did earlier. It also provides methods for caching page and partial-page output, but those topics are better left for an ASP.NET book.

The caching mechanism is provided by an object named Cache, which exposes a dictionary-like interface, allowing you to store arbitrary objects indexed by a string key, much like the classic ASP Session object. The difference is that you can not only decide how long that information should stay cached, but you can also determine if that information should automatically become un-cached (dirty) if a change occurs in a file on disk or a database table, etc.

To quickly demonstrate caching, we'll cache a string that contains the date and time at the time of caching. We'll create an ASP page that displays the cached date/time and the current date/time so that you can see the cached time remain the same as you refresh the page.

To do this, let's create a page called `CacheSample.aspx`, with a code-behind class of `CacheSample.aspx.cs`. We'll drop two labels onto the design surface, one called `CacheLabel` and the other called `LiveLabel`. Here is the source listing for our ASP.NET caching example:

```
using System;
using System.Collections;
using System.ComponentModel;
using System.Data;
using System.Drawing;
using System.Web;
using System.Web.SessionState;
using System.Web.UI;
using System.Web.UI.WebControls;
using System.Web.UI.HtmlControls;

namespace CacheDemo
{
public class WebForm1 : System.Web.UI.Page
{
  protected System.Web.UI.WebControls.Label LiveLabel;
  protected System.Web.UI.WebControls.Label CacheLabel;

  public WebForm1()
  {
    Page.Init += new System.EventHandler(Page_Init);
  }

  private void Page_Load(object sender, System.EventArgs e)
  {
    // Put user code to initialize the page here
  }

  private void Page_Init(object sender, EventArgs e)
  {
    InitializeComponent();
```

In the code below, we test to see if there is anything stored in the named cache variable `CachedValue`. If there isn't, then we populate it with the current time and set the expiration date of the cached value to 1 minute from now.

```
if (Cache["CachedValue"] == null)
{
  Cache.Insert("CachedValue", "Cached At : " + DateTime.Now.ToString(),
    null, DateTime.Now.AddMinutes(1),
    System.Web.Caching.Cache.NoSlidingExpiration);
}
```

In keeping with the standard dictionary model, we simply obtain an object from the cache by name, and cast it to the appropriate type in order to use it:

```
CacheLabel.Text = (string)Cache["CachedValue"];
LiveLabel.Text = DateTime.Now.ToString();
}
```

```
  #region Web Form Designer generated code
  private void InitializeComponent()
  {
    this.Load += new System.EventHandler(this.Page_Load);
  }
  #endregion
}
}
```

The first time we run this in a browser, both of the labels have the same time displayed. After waiting a few seconds, we hit Refresh and get the following display:

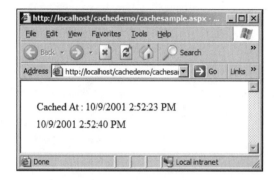

We then wait until after 2:53 and hit Refresh again to see if the cached value expired, causing our code to place a new string into the cache:

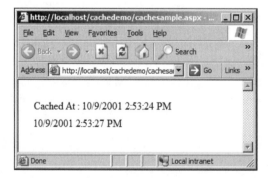

So, in conclusion, if you are writing a web application and you want to store frequently accessed information in order to increase performance, then the Cache object is your new best friend. However, if you are working on a distributed or server-side application that is using some of the performance benefits of COM+ (object pooling, etc.), you can take advantage of COM+/MTS Property Groups to utilize their in-memory data caching features. As you've seen, it is far easier to cache data within ASP.NET than it is within COM+, but at least you know that there are options regardless of your architecture.

Birds of a Feather (Functionality Grouping)

With a small application that performs very few data operations, we probably wouldn't need to be concerned with functionality grouping. However, if we're concerned about performance, we're probably not working with a small application to begin with.

Most texts on performance tuning in the Windows DNA world include rules about making sure that you never house transactional processing in the same component as you are housing non-transactional processing, as this incurs the overhead of transactional processing for read-only operations that don't need it.

The same holds true for .NET, only with slightly looser restrictions. Due to the way Assemblies are built, we can actually include a transactional and a non-transactional class in the same Assembly without worrying about the performance problems. The trouble arises when we use the same class to perform write operations and read operations.

In a slow-paced, single-user world, this wouldn't be much of a consideration. However, in high-volume applications, we want our components to start and finish their operations as quickly as possible. If a class instance is busy making a write operation when thirty other users want to use it for a simple read operation, we needlessly incur wait conditions that can be avoided.

Here we'll look at the skeleton of a data services assembly that properly separates read and write operations.

```
/*
 * The following is an illustration only and is not intended
 * to be compiled. It is intended as a guideline and starting
 * point for creating a data services component that provides
 * proper separation of functionality for optimum performance
 */

using System;
using System.EnterpriseServices;
using System.Data;
using System.Data.SqlClient;
using System.Data.SqlTypes;

using MyApplication.Common;

namespace MyApplication.DAL
{
    // Define read-only data service class for this particular
    // entity.
    [Transaction( TransactionOption.NotSupported )]
    public class MyObject: DALObject
    {
```

In most cases, the non-transactional component will have at least one method that allows for the loading of data corresponding to an individual item. Some components may have more, including loading lists or searching, but a single-item load is the most common read operation. Note that you could easily use a `DataReader` here instead of the `DataSet` for better performance if you didn't intend to modify any of the information.

```
        public DataSet Load(int ID)
        {
            // Load a single item from the database
        }
    }
```

```
namespace Transactional
{
    // define write-access service class for this particular
    // entity.
    [Transaction( TransactionOption.Supported )]
    public class MyObject: DALObject
    {
```

The transactional portion of the data access component should more than likely provide the remainder of the CRUD (Create/Retrieve/Update/Delete) functionality, providing methods for creating a new item, updating an existing item, and deleting an existing item.

```
        public int Create(...)
        {
            // use supplied arguments to create a new item in the DB.
        }

        public int Update(int ID,...)
        {
            // use supplied arguments to update an item in the DB.
        }

        public int Delete(int ID,...)
        {
            // use supplied arguments to delete an item in the DB.
        }
    }
}
}
```

> **Data service classes should provide either a read-access layer or a write-access layer surrounding the data store. They should *never* provide both within the same class.**

Marshaling Considerations

Unless an application is a single, standalone executable, or something similar, then you will more than likely encounter data marshaling at some point. Whether it is COM InterOp marshaling of data between the various wrappers, or marshaling data between two .NET processes, you will still need to be aware of how data is being marshaled in your application.

Marshaling is an expensive operation that involves moving data from one process to another without any data loss. This is a simple operation for some types such as integers, strings, and decimals. However, for complex types such as custom classes and complex structs (user-defined types in VB) the operation is considerably more expensive.

Object serialization, however, is a much faster process. The reason it is faster is that, rather than going through the extensive process of determining how to convert the complex data into a form that is suitable for transmission, the CLR can simply identify a class that supports serialization, and ask that class to serialize itself. Serialization essentially reduces the entire class to a single stream that is already in a form that is easy to transmit. This stream can then be used to re-constitute an exact duplicate of the class on the other side of the function call.

> When deciding on data formats to send between tiers or processes, try to use classes
> that support serialization to avoid costly reference-marshaling overhead.

The following is a brief list of classes that we might be using on a regular basis that already support
automatic serialization:

- ❑ `DataSet` – the `DataSet` will serialize everything including its own schema. To see this in
  action see Chapter 8.

- ❑ `DBnull` – constant representing a `null` database value.

- ❑ `Exception` – base class for all exceptions in the system.

- ❑ `Hashtable` – a collection of name-value pairs much like a Scripting Dictionary.

- ❑ `SoapFault` – contains error information wrapped in an SOAP envelope. When Web Services
  throw exceptions they are carried back to the client in a `SoapFault`.

DataSet Serialization

In Chapter 8, we discussed the serialization of the `DataSet`. The `DataSet` can actually be serialized in
several ways: into binary format, into a SOAP envelope, or into an XML document. Each of the various
serialization formats has its advantages. For example, the binary format is highly optimized for quick parsing
and deserialization. The SOAP format is used to transfer data to and from Web Services, and the XML
format is used widely throughout the CLR, including passing data between processes or application domains.

If we want to use a specific format for data serialization then instead of passing or returning the actual
object (forcing the CLR to serialize the object for us), we can pass a stream onto which we have already
serialized an object.

Let's take a look at a quick example that illustrates serializing a `DataSet` into various different formats.
To create this example, we created a new C# Console application that references `System.Data`,
`System.XML`, and `System.Runtime.Serialization.Formatters.Soap`. Then, for our main class
file we typed in the following code:

```
using System;
using System.Data;
using System.Data.SqlClient;
using System.IO;
using System.Runtime.Serialization.Formatters;
using System.Runtime.Serialization.Formatters.Soap;
using System.Runtime.Serialization.Formatters.Binary;
using System.Xml.Serialization;

namespace Wrox.ProADONET.Chapter16.SerializeDS
{
class Class1
{
static void Main(string[] args)
{
```

Our first task is going to be to populate an initial `DataSet` with some data from the `Northwind` database in our SQL Server 2000. We'll be selecting all of the customers in the system.

```
SqlConnection Connection = new SqlConnection(
  "Server=localhost; Initial Catalog=Northwind; Integrated
    Security=SSPI;");
SqlDataAdapter MyDA = new
  SqlDataAdapter("SELECT * FROM Customers", Connection);
DataSet MyDS = new DataSet();
DataSet MyDS2 = new DataSet();
MyDA.Fill(MyDS, "Customers");
```

The first serialization we're going to do is into a SOAP envelope, the format used to communicate with Web Services. To do this, all we have to do is create a new `SoapFormatter`. Then to serialize, all we do is invoke the `Serialize` function, indicating the stream onto which the object will be serialized, and the object whose graph is to be serialized.

```
Stream s = File.Open("MyDS.soap",
                      FileMode.Create,
                      FileAccess.ReadWrite);
SoapFormatter sf = new SoapFormatter();
sf.Serialize( s, MyDS );
s.Close();
```

To re-constitute a `DataSet` from the SOAP envelope we stored on disk, we basically reverse the process. We need a SOAP Formatter (a class that specializes in serializing and de-serializing object graphs using SOAP) and an input stream, and then we simply call `DeSerialize` on it.

```
Console.WriteLine("Serialization Complete.");
Console.WriteLine("De-Serializing Graph from SOAP Envelope ...");
Stream r = File.Open("MyDS.soap", FileMode.Open, FileAccess.Read);
SoapFormatter sf2 = new SoapFormatter();
MyDS2 = (DataSet)sf2.Deserialize( r );
r.Close();

Console.WriteLine("After Deserialization, MyDS2 contains {0} Customers",
  MyDS2.Tables["Customers"].Rows.Count );
Console.WriteLine("Serializing DataSet into an XML DOM...");
```

Just because we can, and to continue demonstrating the various serialization formats, we're going to serialize our recently populated `DataSet` into an XML file. Again, the procedure is very similar. We create a stream, which will be the destination of the serialization process, and then we use the appropriate formatter to perform the serialization.

```
Stream xStream = File.Open("MyDS2.xml",
                            FileMode.Create,
                            FileAccess.ReadWrite);
XmlSerializer xs = new XmlSerializer( typeof( DataSet ));
xs.Serialize( xStream, MyDS2 );
xStream.Close();
```

And finally, for the smallest of the serialization formats, we'll output our `DataSet` in serialized binary. Again, we create a stream, a Binary Formatter, and then have the formatter invoke the `Serialize` method. Much like the SOAP Formatter and an XML Formatter, the Binary Formatter is a class that specializes in serializing and de-serializing object graphs in a binary format.

```
    Console.WriteLine("Now Serializing to Binary Format...");
    Stream bs = File.Open("MyDS2.bin",
                          FileMode.Create,
                          FileAccess.ReadWrite);
    BinaryFormatter bf = new BinaryFormatter();
    bf.Serialize( bs, MyDS2 );
    bs.Close();
  }
 }
}
```

XML over HTTP

It would be difficult to discuss performance and security within ADO.NET without mentioning the use of XML over HTTP. It is also worth mentioning that XML over HTTP is *not* the same thing as SOAP. SOAP is the **S**imple **O**bject **A**ccess **P**rotocol, an industry standard that allows methods and properties to be exposed and utilized over the Internet. It is a wire protocol that, as of version 1.1, makes no requirement about the *transport* used.

The `System.Net` namespace contains two classes called `HttpWebRequest` and `HttpWebResponse`. These two classes allow code to communicate directly with any server exposing a port to the HTTP protocol. An additional benefit of these classes is that they expose streams to enable us to send large amounts of data to a web server, or receive large amounts of data from a web server. This provides a facility for all kinds of enhanced communications and back-end functionality that previously all had to be coded by hand.

We could take the code from the `DataSet` serialization example above and convert it into two portions: a client and a server. The server would be an ASP.NET page that de-serializes a `DataSet` directly off the Request stream. The client would be a console application that populates a `DataSet` and then serializes it directly onto a stream obtained by calling the `GetRequestStream` method.

Using the `DataSet` serialization code above as an example for working with streams, we should be able to take the knowledge that both the Request and Response in an HTTP conversation can be treated as streams and build this exercise fairly easily.

Connection Pooling

Opening and closing database connections is a very expensive operation. The concept of **connection pooling** involves preparing connection instances ahead of time in a pool. This has the upshot that multiple requests for the same connection can be served by a pool of available connections, thereby reducing the overhead of obtaining a new connection instance. Connection pooling is handled differently by each data provider: we'll cover how the SQL Client and OLE DB .NET Data Providers handle connection pooling.

SqlConnection

The SqlConnection object is implicitly a pooled object. It relies solely on Windows 2000 Component Services (COM+) to provide pooled connections. Each pool of available connections is based on a single, unique connection string. Each time a request for a connection is made with a distinct connection string, a new pool will be created. The pools will be filled with connections up to a maximum defined size. Requests for connections from a full pool will be queued until a connection can be re-allocated to the queued request. If the queued request times out, an exception will be thrown.

There are some arguments that can be passed to the connection string to manually configure the pooling behavior of the connection. Note that these arguments count towards the uniqueness of the string, and two otherwise identical strings with differing pool settings will create two different pools. The following is a list of SQL connection string parameters that affect pooling:

❑ **Connection Lifetime** (0) – this is a value that indicates how long (in seconds) a connection will remain live after having been created and placed in the pool. The default value of 0 indicates that the connection will never time out.

❑ **Connection Reset** (true) – this Boolean value indicates whether or not the connection will be reset when removed from the pool. A value of false avoids hitting the database again when obtaining the connection, but may cause unexpected results as the connection state will not be reset. The default value for this option is true, and is set to false only when we can be certain that not resetting connection state when obtaining the connection will not have any adverse effects on code.

❑ **Enlist** (true) – this Boolean value indicates whether or not the connection should automatically enlist the connection in the current transaction of the creation thread (if one exists). The default value for this is true.

❑ **Max Pool Size** (100) – maximum number of connections that can reside in the pool at any given time.

❑ **Min Pool Size** (0) – the minimum number of connections maintained in the pool. Setting this to at least 1 will guarantee that, after the initial start up of your application, there will always be at least one connection available in the pool.

❑ **Pooling** (true) – this is the Boolean value that indicates whether or not the connection should be pooled at all. The default is true.

The best thing about SQL connection pooling is that, besides optionally tuning pooling configuration in the connection string, we don't have to do any additional programming to support it.

> **SQL connection pooling can drastically reduce the cost of obtaining a new connection in your code, as long as the connection strings of each connection are exactly the same.**

OleDbConnection

The OLE DB .NET Data Provider provides connection pooling automatically through the use of OLE DB session pooling. Again, there is no special code that we need to write to take advantage of the OLE DB session pooling; it is simply there for us. We can configure or disable the OLE DB session pooling by using the OLE DB Services connection string argument. For example, if the connection string contains the following parameter, it will disable session pooling and automatic transaction enlistment:

```
Provider=SQLOLEDB; OLE DB Services=-4; Data Source=localhost; Integrated
Security=SSPI;
```

For more information on what values for this parameter affect the OLE DB connection, and in what way, consult the OLE DB Programmer's Reference that is available at http://msdn.microsoft.com/library.

Message Queuing

Message queuing is, quite simply, placing messages in a queue to be processed at a later time by another application or component. Users will frequently be sitting in front of either a Web or Windows application and have to wait an extended period of time for some processing to complete. In many cases this is both tolerated and expected. However, when hundreds of users are waiting for processing to complete and their tasks are all burdening the same server, the wait may be unacceptable, assuming that none of the clients experience time out failures.

Messaging is used to create the perception of increased performance by taking the user's request for a task to be performed and placing it in a queue. Some other service or process then reads the requests out of the queue and processes those tasks in an offline fashion, relieving the load on the main server.

In addition to being able to send and receive messages containing arbitrary objects from within our code, we can also make the components we write Queued Components. This allows method calls on our components to be serialized into a Queue and then serviced at a later time by another process, allowing us to not only asynchronously send messages, but also asynchronously send and respond to method calls. We'll just discuss simple MSMQ Messaging in this chapter. Microsoft has plenty of documentation on how to create Queued Components that will be fairly easy to read and understand once you have a grasp of the basics of using Microsoft Message Queues.

To Queue or Not to Queue

We might wonder why, if messaging is such a handy tool for offloading burdensome tasks, it is not used all the time for everything Just like all specialized technologies, messaging is very good at solving certain problems, but is far from ideal for solving other issues. For example, any time the user needs direct feedback as to the success or failure of their task, messaging is probably not a good idea, the reason being that the task might well not even have begun to be processed: the only feedback the user can receive is that their message has been placed in a queue.

The other reason why we might avoid using messaging concerns user feedback. Suppose a user's request is submitted to a queue, but then the service that was processing the information in the queue unexpectedly dies. If adequate precautions are not taken, thousands of messages carrying critical information could be stranded in a queue with no place to go.

Messaging is a perfectly viable tool for reducing the load on your back-end systems, as well as communicating with other loosely connected systems throughout a network or the world. Just be sure to prepare for some of the pitfalls of loosely connected messaging before you deploy your messaging solution.

Sending Messages

We're going to create an example that places into a queue a string containing the highly overused phrase "Hello World". When we create a message, we wrap an object in some header information, which includes a label for that message. The body (object) of the message can contain any object, including a `DataSet`. This can be an extremely valuable tool to take data from one data source, place it in a queue in the form of a `DataSet`, and then pick up the message to be stored in another data store.

To create our example, we create a C# Console application called `QueueSender`. Make sure that the project has a reference to the `System.Messaging` namespace. Type in the following code into the main class file to create a simple message-sending application:

```csharp
using System;
using System.Messaging;

namespace Wrox.ProADONET.Chapter16.QueueSender
{
class Class1
{
static void Main(string[] args)
{
```

It's all pretty straightforward here. We use a private queue here just to make things simpler. MSMQ has three main kinds of queues: outgoing, private, and system. The outgoing queues can participate in complex publishing policies that allow the contents of the queue to be sent to other MSMQ servers in a domain. System queues are, obviously, used by the operating system for internal asynchronous messaging.

```csharp
string Greeting = "Hello World!";
MessageQueue mQ;
if (MessageQueue.Exists(@".\Private$\HelloWorld") )
{
  mQ = new MessageQueue(@".\Private$\HelloWorld");
}
else
{
  mQ = MessageQueue.Create(@".\Private$\HelloWorld");
}

mQ.Send(Greeting, "HelloWorld");
Console.WriteLine("Greeting Message Sent to Private Queue.");
}
}
}
```

What we've done in the above code is test for the existence of a queue by using the `static` method `Exists` in the `MessageQueue` class. If it doesn't exist, then we create it. Once we know we have a valid reference to our message queue, we simply send our string to the queue. The messaging system is going to wrap up our object in a message. By default, MSMQ will use an XML serialization scheme to store objects; however, we can choose to use a binary storage system that is more efficient for transmitting things like pictures.

When we run the above example, we get the simple message that the greeting message has been sent to the queue. To see the impact of what we've just done, we'll open the **Computer Management** console on Windows 2000 (or XP) and open up the **Message Queuing** item. From there, we can open up the **Private Queues** folder and find our newly created queue. This is illustrated in a screenshot opposite:

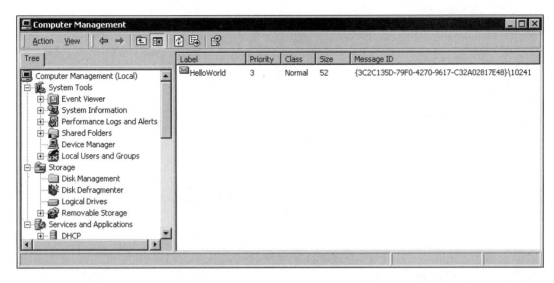

As we can see from the screenshot, we have a 52 byte message sitting in a queue called helloworld with the label of HelloWorld. We can also see that the message has been given a priority and a GUID for unique identification. Even though this screenshot was taken on Windows XP Professional, this example works just fine on Windows 2000 Professional.

Receiving Messages

Now that we've seen how we can place messages into a queue, let's take a look at pulling them out. True to their name, the queues work in FIFO order (First In, First Out). Messages are plucked out of the queue in the order in which they were placed. We created another C# Console application and called it QueueReceiver. Again, we made sure that it had a reference to the System.Messaging assembly before entering the following code into the main class:

```
using System;
using System.Messaging;
using System.IO;

namespace Wrox.ProADONET.Chapter16.QueueReceiver
{
class Class1
{
static void Main(string[] args)
{
  MessageQueue mQ;
  Message mes;
  string X;
  BinaryReader br;

  if (MessageQueue.Exists(@".\Private$\HelloWorld"))
  {
    mQ = new MessageQueue(@".\Private$\HelloWorld");
  }
  else
  {
```

```
      Console.WriteLine("Queue doesn't exist.");
      return;
   }

   try
   {
```

This is the meat of our message receiver. We create a new message by calling the `Receive` method in the message queue, also supplying a maximum three second communication timeout. We then use a `BinaryReader` to pull out the stream of data we stored and then convert it into a string.

```
      mes = mQ.Receive(new TimeSpan(0,0,3));
      br = new BinaryReader(mes.BodyStream);
      X = new String(br.ReadChars((int)mes.BodyStream.Length));
      Console.WriteLine("Received Message: {0}", X);
   }
   catch
   {
      Console.WriteLine("No Message to Receive.");
   }
   }
   }
   }
```

When we execute this code after placing a message in the private queue, our console contains the following output:

```
Received Message: <?xml version="1.0"?>
<string>Hello World!</string>
```

Now we not only know that our original text has been preserved, but it has been wrapped in the XML document created when a string is serialized.

> **Message Queues are an excellent tool for relieving the burden of critical back-end systems by providing a mechanism for offline processing and loosely coupled message-based inter-application communication.**

Security Concerns

Now that we've spent some time covering some of the ways in which we might be able to increase or maintain the performance of an application, let's talk about security. The .NET framework provides several ways in which we can not only secure data, but an application (or component) as well. The most common ways of securing an application involve either using the code access security (CAS) system or using an encryption scheme or SSL (Secure Sockets Layer) encryption for web sites.

Code Access Security

Every single .NET application interacts with the Common Language Runtime's security system. This security system is a fully configurable set of policies and permission sets that allows administrators to dictate policy at the enterprise, machine, or user level.

What it means to us, as programmers, is that it is now possible for an administrator on a machine running an application to dictate security policy. This could have the effect of preventing our application from executing. Even more interesting is that the same administrator can dictate an enterprise-wide policy that prevents *any code published by a particular company* from executing.

A very common misconception is that the code access security (CAS) system works in a similar fashion to the NTFS security permissions that can be assigned to individual files, directories and resources on windows NT/2000/XP machines. While NTFS is a system of locking down access to files and file system resources, CAS is a system of constricting the resources available to certain .NET Assemblies. The CAS administration has a very similar structure and feel to editing security policy files for locking down workstations. Windows 95/98 had *policy files* that dictated which users had access to which resources, etc. Anyone familiar with POLEDIT.EXE utility will feel comfortable navigating the .NET Framework CAS administration.

So, what does Code Access Security have to do with ADO.NET? Well, if you're using ADO.NET, then you are undoubtedly accessing resources of some kind. These resources include a SQL Server, an OLE DB Data Source, an ODBC Data Source, an Access database file, a text file, or an XML file. All of these resources are security controlled, and we should be aware of how our code functions in a secure environment.

Administration

When the final release of the .NET Framework is made available, you will have a program accessible to you from your Start menu called .NET Framework Configuration. Currently, this program is available from the Administrative Tools menu on Windows 2000, and it is unlikely that it will change before the public release.

We can administer the runtime security policy on three different scope levels: enterprise, machine, and user. When policy is evaluated, it is evaluated separately for each scope level and then intersected. The result of this is that code is granted the minimum set of permissions available from each scope.

Code Groups

The way the security policy works is that an administrator (or Microsoft, in the case of the system defaults) defines a set of **code groups**. These code groups are simply *statements of membership*. Any time an assembly is invoked, its evidence (public key, zone, version, application directory, name, etc.) is compared against the applicable code groups defined within the system. If the assembly's evidence matches a code group, that assembly is granted the applicable permission sets. We'll see a real-world example of how to apply all of this information shortly.

The code groups that ship with the framework are:

- ❑ **LocalIntranet_Zone** – identifies all Assemblies whose Zone is "Intranet".

- ❑ **Internet_Zone** – identifies all Assemblies whose Zone is "Internet".

- ❑ **Restricted_Zone** – identifies all Assemblies from the "Untrusted" Zone.

- ❑ **Trusted_Zone** – identifies all Assemblies from the "Trusted" Zone.

- ❑ **Microsoft_Strong_Name** – identifies all Assemblies built with the Microsoft public key.

- ❑ **ECMA_Strong_Name** – identifies all Assemblies built with the ECMA public key. ECMA is a standards body, the *European Computer Manufacturer's Association*.

- ❑ **My_Computer_Zone** – identifies all Assemblies residing on your computer.

Permission Sets

Permission sets are named groups of code access permissions. Each code group is assigned to a given permission set. This essentially provides the ability to grant a named set of permissions to all code matching a given criteria (or *policy*). The following is a list of the default permission sets that ship with the Framework (Beta 2):

❏ **FullTrust** – gives complete and unrestricted access to all protected resources.

❏ **SkipVerification** – grants the matching code the right to bypass security verification.

❏ **Execution** – allows the code to execute.

❏ **Nothing** – denies the code all rights, including the right to execute.

❏ **LocalIntranet** – the default set of permissions granted to code on your local intranet.

❏ **Internet** – the default set of permissions given to Internet applications.

❏ **Everything** – allows complete unrestricted access to all resources that are governed by the built-in permissions. This differs from `FullTrust` in that `FullTrust` allows unrestricted access to everything, even if those resources are not governed by built-in permissions.

Permissions

Permissions are the individual access points that protect specific system resources. Code must have been granted (either directly or indirectly through assertions, etc.) the appropriate permission before it can access the given resource. If code attempts to access a resource to which it has not been granted the appropriate permission, the CLR will throw an exception. We'll show how to grant or revoke these permissions to Assemblies in the next section.

❏ **DirectoryServicesPermission** – allows access to `System.DirectoryServices` classes.

❏ **DnsPermission** – allows the code to access the Domain Name System (DNS).

❏ **EnvironmentPermission** – governs access to reading and/or writing environment variables.

❏ **EventLogPermission** – read or write access to the event logging services.

❏ **FileDialogPermission** – allows access to files chosen by a user from an Open file dialog box.

❏ **FileIOPermission** – allows the code to read, append, or write files or directories.

❏ **IsolatedStorageFilePermission** – allows access to private virtual file systems.

❏ **IsolatedStoragePermission** – allows access to isolated storage, which is a system of storage associated with a given user and some portion of the code's identity (Web Site, Publisher, or signature). Isolated storage allows downloaded code to maintain an offline data store without encroaching on the user's otherwise protected file system/hard disk. The data will be stored in a directory structure on the system depending on the operating system and whether user profiles have been enabled. For example, on a Windows2000 machine, the files will be in <SYSTEM>\Profiles\<user>\Application Data, or <SYSTEM>\Profiles\<user>\Local Settings\Application Data for a non-roaming profile.

❏ **MessageQueuePermission** – allows access to Message Queues via MSMQ.

- ❑ **OleDbPermission** – allows access to resources exposed by the OLE DB Data Provider.

- ❑ **PerformanceCounterPermission** – allows the specified code to access performance counters.

- ❑ **PrintingPermission** – allows access to the printing system.

- ❑ **ReflectionPermission** – allows access to the Reflection system to discover type information at run time. The lack of this permission can be potentially crippling to a lot of code that the programmer or administrator might not expect. In other words, if your application depends on the use of Reflection in order to function properly, an Administrator could cripple it by revoking this permission.

- ❑ **RegistryPermission** – allows the specified code to read, write, create, or delete keys and values in the system Registry.

- ❑ **SecurityPermission** –a multi-faceted permission. Allows execute, asserting permissions, calls into unmanaged code (InterOp), verification skip, and others.

- ❑ **ServiceControllerPermission** – allows code to access system services.

- ❑ **SocketPermission** – allows the code access low-level sockets.

- ❑ **SqlClientPermission** – allows the code to access resources exposed by the SQL Data Provider.

- ❑ **StrongNameIdentityPermission** – allows one piece of code to restrict calling access to only code that matches certain identity characteristics. Often used to distribute Assemblies callable only by the publisher.

- ❑ **UIPermission** – allows access to the User Interface.

- ❑ **WebPermission** – allows access to make or accept connections on web addresses.

CAS in Action

Now that we've seen a bit of what functionality CAS provides for programmers and administrators, let's take a look at CAS in action. There are two examples we're going to go through: the first is an illustration of how to create an assembly that can be callable only by other assemblies built with the same public key – in other words, the secured assembly can only be invoked by other assemblies built with the same strong-name key file (typically a .snk file generated with the SN.EXE tool or Visual Studio .NET); the second will be an example of locking down some code and seeing the results of attempting to execute code with insufficient permission.

For our first example, we'll create a C# Class Library project called SecureLibrary. Then, we'll hit the Command Prompt and type the following in the new project directory:

```
sn -k Secure.snk
```

This generates our RSA signature file used for establishing a unique publisher ID for the component. We need the RSA signature file to guarantee us a public key that will uniquely identify us as a distinct publisher. All Assemblies built upon this RSA file will have the same public key, and hence the same publisher. RSA is an algorithm for obtaining digital signatures and public-key cryptosystems. It was named after its three inventors: R.L.**R**ivest, A.**S**hamir, and L.M.**A**delman. Now, we'll type the following into the main class file for our library (SecureClass.cs):

```
using System;
using System.Security;
using System.Security.Permissions;

namespace SecureLibrary
{
public class SecureClass
{
[StrongNameIdentityPermissionAttribute(SecurityAction.LinkDemand,
   PublicKey="00240000048000009400000006020000002400005253413100040000
     00100010095A84DEA6DF9C3"+
   "667059903619361A178C2B7506DFA176C9152540AB41E3BBA693D76F8B5F04748
     51443A93830411E"+
   "A5CE9641A4AA5234EF5C0ED2EDF874F4B22B196173D63DF9D3DE3FB1A4901C814
     82720406537E6EC"+
   "43F40737D0C9064C0D69C22CF1EFD01CEFB0F2AA9FBEB15C3D8CFF946674CC0E4
     0AF822502A69BDAF0")]

   public string GetSecureString()
   {
     return "Secret Phrase: loath it or ignore it, you can't like it
       a Week.";
   }
 }
}
```

What we're effectively doing is telling the CLR that any code attempting to access the following function must have a strong name identity that contains the public key listed. Obviously, the public key is an enormous number. In order to get the public key for this attribute, I first compiled the assembly with its strong name (the `AssemblyInfo.cs` references the `Secure.snk` file, and has a version number of 1.0.0.0) without the permission request. Then, I executed the following at the command line:

```
secutil -hex -strongname SecureLibrary.dll
```

This printed out the entire hex string (what you see above with a "0x" prefix) for the public key, as well as the version and name information required to complete a strong name for the assembly. Then, I just copied that public key onto my clipboard and pasted it, creating the above demand for the `StrongNameIdentityPermission`.

There, now we have an assembly that we're pretty sure will be completely useless to anyone who compiles an assembly against a different `.snk` file than ours. This kind of code is extremely handy in applications that have a business rule tier in that it can prevent tricky, programming-savvy customers from writing code to bypass the business rules, because they will not have access to our `.snk` file.

> **If you are ever planning on distributing assemblies outside your own company, *never* allow your `.snk` file to fall into the wrong hands. It can not only allow customers to tamper with your application, but can allow them to create new assemblies that appear to come from your organization.**

First, we'll create an assembly that was built with our `Secure.snk` file as the `AssemblyKeyFile`. In the downloadable samples, this resides in the `SecureLibrary` directory. Let's create a C# Console application called `SecureClient`. Make sure the following attribute is in the `AssemblyInfo.cs` file:

```
[assembly: AssemblyKeyFile("../../../SecureLibrary/Secure.snk")]
```

First, copy the `SecureLibrary.DLL` file from the previous example to the `obj\debug` directory of the `SecureClient` application. Then browse to that file as a project reference. Here is the source code to our main class:

```csharp
using System;

namespace Secureclient
{
class Class1
{
static void Main(string[] args)
{
  SecureLibrary.SecureClass oClass = new SecureLibrary.SecureClass();
  Console.WriteLine(oClass.GetSecureString());
}
}
}
```

It's pretty simple. It should generate the secure string as a result. When we run this application, we get the following console output:

Secret Phrase: loath it or ignore it, you can't like it.

Well, that's all well and good: everything works just fine. Now, let's actually prove that the code will fail against a client compiled without the right public key (or, for that matter, with no strong name at all). To do this, we'll create a third C# Console application called `UnsecureClient`. We won't bother setting any key file attributes. Again, copy the `SecureLibrary.DLL` file to this project's `obj\debug` directory and browse to it for a reference.

The following is the short source code for our unauthorized client application:

```csharp
using System;

namespace UnsecureClient
{
class Class1
{
static void Main(string[] args)
{
  SecureLibrary.SecureClass oClass = new SecureLibrary.SecureClass();
  Console.WriteLine(oClass.GetSecureString());
}
}
}
```

The code should look pretty familiar. In fact, it is the same. The only difference is that our second client application has no strong name, so it should fail the identity test. Well, let's run it and take a look at the console output:

It's certainly ugly, but it's also what we expected. The CLR has thrown an exception indicating that the permission request on the part of the calling assembly (our client) failed. The CLR is even nice enough to not only tell us that we failed an identity check, but what identity the CLR was looking for. Don't worry; the only way to generate this public key for your DLL is to have the accompanying private key in our .snk file (which is why it is a very good idea to keep the .snk file locked up somewhere safe if we're distributing any assemblies commercially).

Now let's see what happens when we try to revoke some permissions from existing code. To do this, we're going to go into the DACommands2 project (a sample from earlier in this chapter) and add a complete version (1.0.0.0) and a key file (DACommands2.snk in the root of the project). We'll rebuild it to create a strongly named assembly with a public key we can use.

The first thing we should do is pull up our .NET Admin Tool (should be available as a program under **Administrative Tools** by the time the public release of the SDK is available). In order to apply some security policy to our specific assembly, it needs to be a member of a specific code group. To do this, we're going to go into the machine scope and create a new custom code group beneath the **My_Computer** code group. We're presented with a wizard that allows us to supply a name (DACommands2) and description for our code group.

We then choose the membership condition. In our case, the membership condition will be a public key. Again, the wizard is nice enough to allow us to browse to a specific assembly and import that public key. The last step is to choose which permission set should be applied to group members. We'll be really extreme and set that to **Nothing** (which means that no permissions will be granted to code matching our policy).

We also need to make sure that we check the boxes that indicate that the group members will be granted only this permission set. This prevents members from inheriting other permissions from different scopes when we've explicitly denied them. When we're all done creating some tyrannical security policy for this assembly, we have an Admin Tool that looks like this:

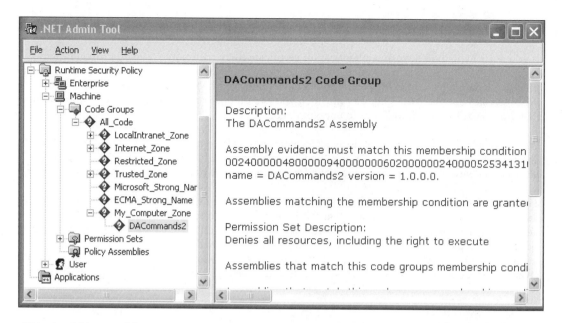

This should be suitably restrictive. Make sure you close the Admin Tool and select **Yes** to save the changes; otherwise the new rules will not take effect. Now, let's try to run the DACommands2 executable, which we know worked earlier in the chapter. Here's our console output:

Unhandled Exception: System.Security.Policy.PolicyException: Execution permission cannot be acquired.

We just modified some XML files sitting in the system somewhere with a graphic tool, and now this application cannot execute. If we were to go to the Enterprise scope and use the same public key to establish a code group, but left off the name and version, we could effectively prevent all code built against our Secure.snk from executing anywhere in our enterprise.

The bottom line is that we need to be aware of the fact that, no matter what, our code will be interacting with CAS somehow. Whether it is simply to verify that no security checks are being enforced, or to perform detailed security checks, code will still interact with CAS on some level. What this means is that any time we need access to a resource, our code should make sure that it has sufficient permission to do so, and if not, it should gracefully trap that failure and explain the issue to the user.

SSL

In addition to securing our code through permissions or identity checks, we can also secure our data. SSL (Secure Sockets Layer) is a protocol that allows encrypted, secure communications across the Internet. It works by requiring the IIS server to maintain an authentication certificate that is used in the encryption of the data. Traditionally, SSL has been used on web sites to encrypt transmissions of confidential information such as credit card numbers during e-Commerce sessions.

With the advent of Web Services, however, SSL is being used to guarantee that transmission of all kinds of data to and from Web Services is kept completely secure and private. Users can rest assured that any conversation they have with a Web Service, be it through a browser or a Windows Forms client, is completely private and no one else will be able to access that information.

Encryption

If you don't happen to have an authentication certificate (they cost money, but you can get them from companies like Verisign at www.verisign.com), or your application doesn't have a permanent Internet presence, you might want to take encryption control into your own hands and deal with your data privacy issues on your own. One way in which you can do this is to use some of the Cryptographic APIs that are available in the framework to encrypt data.

We'll take a look at an example of using a Cryptographic API to encrypt the contents of a `DataSet`, and then decrypt that into another `DataSet`. This can be a handy way of transferring private information between components across the Internet without as much of the overhead of using SSL.

The basic plan of our example is to populate a `DataSet` with some information from the `Northwind` database. Then, we're going to assume that this information needs to travel securely across an unsecure network, such as the Internet, to its final destination. We can do this by creating a cryptographic stream. To set this sample up yourself, create a C# Console application and call it `Encryption`. Then, make sure that you have references to `System.Data`, `System.Security` and `System.XML`. (Visual Studio should give you `System.Data` and `System.XML` by default). Then type in the following code for the main class:

```csharp
using System;
using System.Data;
using System.Data.SqlClient;
using System.Security;
using System.Security.Cryptography;
using System.IO;
using System.Xml;

namespace Wrox.ProADONET.Chapter16.Encryption
{
class Class1
{
static void Main(string[] args)
{
```

The first thing we're going to do is create a `FileStream` that will create a new file called `DSencrypted.dat`. This file will hold the encrypted contents of our `DataSet`. The only reason we're using a permanent storage for the encrypted data is so that, when you download the sample, you can examine this file and verify that it truly is impossible to glean any useful information from its encrypted form.

```csharp
FileStream fs = new FileStream("DSencrypted.dat", FileMode.Create,
    FileAccess.Write);
```

Next, we'll populate a `DataSet` with some source data. In our case we're going to select all of the columns from the `Customers` table in the `Northwind` database.

```csharp
DataSet MyDS = new DataSet();
DataSet MyDS2 = new DataSet();
SqlConnection Connection = new SqlConnection("Initial
    Catalog=Northwind;Integrated Security=SSPI; Server=localhost;");
Connection.Open();
SqlDataAdapter MyDA = new SqlDataAdapter("SELECT * FROM Customers",
    Connection);
MyDA.Fill(MyDS, "Customers");
```

Now we'll start doing some actual encryption work. The first thing to do in any encryption scheme is obtain a reference to the **Cryptographic Service Provider** (**CSP**) that we are looking for. In our case, we're using the **Data Encryption Standard** (**DES**). One reason for this is we don't have to seed it with any information in order for it to be able to encrypt our data.

```
DESCryptoServiceProvider DES = new DESCryptoServiceProvider();

ICryptoTransform DESencrypter = DES.CreateEncryptor();
CryptoStream cryptStream  = new CryptoStream( fs, DESencrypter,
  CryptoStreamMode.Write );
```

This next line is actually doing an incredible amount of work behind the scenes that we just don't have to worry about. We've created this object, `cryptStream`, that is a stream based on a `DESencrypter` transformation object. This means that anything placed on this stream is automatically encrypted according to the DES algorithm. Conveniently enough, the `DataSet` has an overload of the `WriteXml` method that will take a simple stream abstract as an argument. Notice here that not only are we writing the entire contents of the `DataSet` to the encryption stream, but we are also writing the schema. This means that when the `DataSet` is decrypted, all of its internal data types can be preserved.

```
MyDS.WriteXml( cryptStream, XmlWriteMode.WriteSchema );
cryptStream.Close();
```

Now we'll actually begin the task of loading our second `DataSet` with the decrypted information. To do this, we grab a read-access `FileStream`, and create a DES decryption stream based on that. Then, we create an `XmlTextReader` based on that stream and use that as the source for our `DataSet`. Once that has been done, we display some basic information about the data in the `DataSet` to prove that it loaded successfully.

```
FileStream fsRead = new FileStream("DSencrypted.dat", FileMode.Open,
  FileAccess.Read);
ICryptoTransform DESdecrypter = DES.CreateDecryptor();
CryptoStream decryptStream = new CryptoStream( fsRead, DESdecrypter,
  CryptoStreamMode.Read );
XmlTextReader plainStreamR = new XmlTextReader( decryptStream );
MyDS2.ReadXml( plainStreamR, XmlReadMode.ReadSchema);

Console.WriteLine("Customers Table Successfully Encrypted and
  Decrypted.");
Console.WriteLine("First Customer:");
foreach (DataColumn _Column in MyDS2.Tables["Customers"].Columns )
{
  Console.Write("{0}\t", MyDS2.Tables["Customers"].Rows[0][_Column]);
}
Console.WriteLine();
}

}
}
```

We can adapt the above sample so that a component in a class library returns an encrypted stream based on some data, and then the consuming application or component should decrypt the data and load it into its own `DataSet`. The resulting output should look like this:

If you really want to get fancy, you can hook up a packet sniffer and watch the encrypted data travel across your network. If you've been paying attention, you may have noticed that there is no key exchange happening, so there's no key required to decrypt the stream. This means that anyone else using the same decryption scheme could watch all of your data if they were clever and patient enough. To really secure your data you'll want to use a keyed security system.

> If keeping your data private is a concern, and SSL is unavailable, we can still manually encrypt **DataSets** for securely traveling across unsecure networks.

Summary

In this chapter, we've gained some insight on how we might be able to increase the performance of an application. In addition, we have looked at some of the ways in which we might be able to protect data from prying eyes. It is worth bearing in mind that what might be an acceptable level of performance for one programmer or one application might be considered too slow and unacceptable for another application. Also, what might be considered an adequate level of protection and security by one application might be considered an insecure situation for another application.

We have looked at the following techniques, and how they might apply to particular security and performance needs:

- ❑ Various methods to optimize data access
- ❑ Connection Pooling
- ❑ Message Queuing
- ❑ Security issues concerning Data Access.

16

Integration and Migration

While ADO.NET may be an incredibly useful and powerful tool, most people learning ADO.NET will have been programming with various technologies already. One of those technologies is ADO. Many programmers and software companies have invested considerable amounts of time, money, and resources making applications that use ADO for their data access.

In a perfect world, with any new technology, all code written in the old technology would magically transform itself to be a part of the next "Big Thing". However, this isn't usually the case. Chances are you will be forced to make the decision between reusing your existing code from your .NET managed Assemblies or re-writing your existing data access code in ADO.NET.

In this chapter, we will look at how to perform the following tasks in order to reuse as much of your existing code as possible:

- ❑ Invoking COM objects from managed (.NET) code
- ❑ Invoking functions in existing DLLs from managed code
- ❑ Upgrading your existing ADO code to ADO.NET
- ❑ Deciding when to upgrade and when to reuse
- ❑ Reusing classic code that returns ADO RecordSet objects from .NET

InterOp

The CLR provides automatic facilities for code interoperability. It allows existing COM components to make use of .NET components, and .NET components to make use of COM components. Within the .NET Framework, we can also invoke functions in standard DLLs such as those comprising the Win32 API.

COM InterOp and the RCW

COM Interoperability is implemented through an object called the **Runtime Callable Wrapper** (**RCW**). In order for code to use classic COM objects, a .NET Assembly is created that contains a wrapper for that COM object's functionality. This Assembly is referred to as an **InterOp Assembly**. When we use Visual Studio .NET to create a reference to a COM component, if the publisher has not specified an official InterOp Assemby – called the Primary InterOp Assembly – then one is created automatically.

Each method that the COM object exposes is also a method available on the RCW object created to communicate with that COM object. The method arguments and return value are then **marshaled** to and from the COM object.

In this chapter, we'll focus on using COM InterOp using ADO components from within .NET managed code.

Accessing ADO from .NET

There are a couple of things to keep in mind when accessing the ADO COM objects from within .NET. The first and foremost is that whenever you invoke a method on an ADO object, you are using the RCW, which incurs a slight per-call performance overhead. If you are making lots of function calls in a row, the performance overhead may become noticeable. The second thing to keep in mind is that data-bindable controls cannot be bound to ADODB `RecordSets`.

Whether to Access ADO from .NET

The most important decision you should make when creating your new .NET applications is whether or not you want to use ADO or ADO.NET. ADO.NET is designed to run very quickly from within managed code, and is definitely the faster alternative. We should only use ADO from ADO.NET if you absolutely have to. If there is some data source that ADO.NET will not connect to that ADO can (though with the release of the ODBC Data Provider for .NET, these occurrences should be extremely rare) then you will be forced to use ADO. Despite word from Microsoft urging people to only use ADO when technically necessary, there are typically other concerns. Companies might have a considerable amount of time and effort invested in existing code, and invoking this code from .NET and avoiding the re-write might be the only practical solution available.

Another case when ADO may be required is where your managed code needs to access files that were used to persist ADO recordsets. While an ADO.NET `DataSet` can load an ADO 2.6 XML persisted `DataSet`, the results are not pretty, and the `DataSet` cannot load the ADTG (Advanced Data Tablegram) binary `RecordSet` persistence format at all.

> **Use classic ADO only when the situation requires it, not as a preferred method of data access for managed code.**

Accessing ADO from .NET

Thankfully, Microsoft has done most of the work for us to allow .NET components to interact with existing COM components. To demonstrate this, we'll create a C# Windows Forms application in Visual Studio .NET, which we'll call `ADOInterOp`. We add a reference to the ADO 2.6 COM type library, and rename `Form1` as `frmMain`.

What we're going to do for this example is create an ADO connection. Then, we'll use that `Connection` to populate an ADO `RecordSet`. From there, we'll iterate through the `RecordSet` to populate a simple control on our form.

To build this code sample, we opened up Visual Studio .NET and created a new Windows Forms application in C#. Then, we opened up **Project Add Reference**, clicked on the "COM" tab, and selected the ActiveX Data Objects 2.7 Type Library. Keep in mind that this technique of importing COM type libraries into things called InterOp Assemblies is something that can be done to utilize *any* COM component, not just classic ADO.

Here's the source code to our `frmMain.cs` file:

```
using System;
using System.Drawing;
using System.Collections;
using System.ComponentModel;
using System.Windows.Forms;
using System.Data;

namespace ADOInterOp
{
public class frmMain : System.Windows.Forms.Form
{
private System.Windows.Forms.ListBox lbCustomers;
private System.Windows.Forms.Label label1;
/// <summary>
/// Required designer variable.
/// </summary>
private System.ComponentModel.Container components = null;

public frmMain()
{
  InitializeComponent();
```

Because we've got a reference to the ADO type library, we can create ADODB and ADOMD (ActiveX Data Objects Multi-Dimensional, used for On-Line Analytical Processing (OLAP) features) objects just as if they were standard .NET components. The RCW automatically wraps up the managed calls for us and forwards them on to the actual COM components:

```
ADODB.Connection _Connection = new ADODB.Connection();
_Connection.Open("DRIVER={SQL Server};SERVER=LOCALHOST;DATABASE=Northwind;",
"sa", "", 0);
```

This code should all look pretty familiar to ADO programmers. We simply create a new RecordSet, and then open it by supplying a SQL SELECT statement, a cursor type, and a lock type. Then we can iterate through the RecordSet using the same methods and functions we used to when invoking ADO from classic VB or C++ code:

```
  ADODB.Recordset _RS =
    new ADODB.Recordset();
  _RS.Open("SELECT * FROM Customers",
           _Connection,
           ADODB.CursorTypeEnum.adOpenDynamic,
           ADODB.LockTypeEnum.adLockReadOnly,0);
  while (!_RS.EOF)
  {
     lbCustomers.Items.Add( _RS.Fields["ContactName"].Value + " From " +
_RS.Fields["CompanyName"].Value );
     _RS.MoveNext();
  }
  _RS.Close();
  _Connection.Close();
  _RS.Dispose();
  _Connection.Dispose();
}

/// <summary>
/// Clean up any resources being used.
/// </summary>
protected override void Dispose( bool disposing )
{
  if( disposing )
  {
    if (components != null)
    {
      components.Dispose();
....}
  }
  base.Dispose( disposing );
}
}
}
```

The Windows Form designer code isn't reproduced here. To duplicate this sample on your own, just make sure the main form is called frmMain, and the ListBox on the form is called lbCustomers.

```
// Windows Forms designer code removed for brevity.

/// <summary>
/// The main entry point for the application.
/// </summary>
[STAThread]
static void Main()
{
  Application.Run(new frmMain());
}
```

When we run this program, we get the following form display:

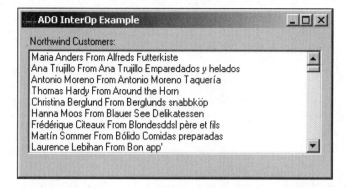

There is something else we can do in order to access our ADO data. In the above example, we had to manually add each and every customer to the ListBox because the ListBox is incapable of binding directly to an ADO RecordSet. However, we can use the OleDb Data Provider to take the contents of an ADO RecordSet and use it to fill an ADO.NET DataSet. Since the ADO.NET DataSet *can* participate in binding, we can bind the control to our DataSet. Even more useful is that once the data is in the DataSet, we can do all of the things to it that a DataSet can do to it, such as obtain its XML representation, generate an XML schema for it, or even hook up another DataAdapter to it to transfer data to another data store.

Let's take a look at an example that accomplishes the same as the above. But this time we'll use the OleDbDataAdapter to fill our DataSet using the ADO RecordSet as the source. To do this, we will create a new VB .NET Windows Application project called ADOInterOp2. Add a reference to the ADO 2.7 type library. Then enter the following code for the Module1.vb file:

```vbnet
Imports System.Data
Imports System.Data.OleDb

Public Class Form1
    Inherits System.Windows.Forms.Form

Private Sub Form1_Load
        (ByVal sender As System.Object, ByVal e
        As System.EventArgs) Handles MyBase.Load
  Dim myConnection As ADODB.Connection
  Dim myRS As ADODB.Recordset
  Dim myDA As OleDbDataAdapter
  Dim myDS As DataSet

  myConnection = New ADODB.Connection()
  myConnection.ConnectionString = _
    "Driver={SQL Server}; Database=Northwind; Server=localhost; UID=sa;PWD=;"
  myConnection.Open()
  myRS = New ADODB.Recordset()
  myRS.Open("SELECT Customers.*, ContactName + ' from ' +
      CompanyName AS FullName FROM Customers", _
    myConnection, ADODB.CursorTypeEnum.adOpenForwardOnly,
ADODB.LockTypeEnum.adLockReadOnly)
```

This is where we can really start to get the most out of code used to write to the ADO components. The `OleDbDataAdapter` has an overloaded version of the `Fill` method that allows it to `Fill` a `DataSet` from an ADODB `RecordSet` object, instead of a `SELECT` string or a `SelectCommand`:

```
    myDA = New OleDbDataAdapter()
    myDS = New DataSet()

    myDA.Fill(myDS, myRS, "Customers")
    ListBox1.DataSource = myDS.Tables("Customers")
    ListBox1.DisplayMember = "FullName"

End Sub
End Class
```

The immediate value of this might not seem all that obvious – after all, if you're selecting out of a database, why not select straight into an adapter rather than an ADODB `RecordSet`? That's an extremely good point. The only reason we used the procedure we did was to demonstrate loading an ADO `RecordSet` into a `DataSet`. The real power of this technique comes from when we have existing COM components that return ADO `RecordSets`. Using this technique, we can leverage and re-use those existing components, and still gain access to all of the advanced features found in the `DataSet` and Windows/Web Forms control binding.

> You can populate ADO.NET `DataSets` with ADO `RecordSets` returned from your existing COM objects through the COM InterOp layer without having to re-write your existing components.

Platform Invocation Services (PInvoke)

Need to access data that isn't exposed via a COM interface? Don't worry, because the .NET framework has another built-in facility supporting code interoperability that might come in handy. If you need to access a classic API exposed in the form of a standard DLL (such as the Win32 API or older database APIs like Btrieve) then you can use something called **Platform Invocation Services (PInvoke)**.

Not only can we declare an external function stored in a DLL, but we can also configure how information is marshaled to and from that external function. This is quite an obscure technology, so we will not cover it in detail here. The topic covered in-depth by *Professional .NET Framework* (ISBN 1-861005-56-3), also from Wrox Press.

We will give a brief example of how you might use Platform Invocation Services to gain access to functions in existing DLLs. To do this, create a simple C# Console Application called `PInvokeTest`. Then enter the following code into the main class file:

```
using System;
using System.Runtime.InteropServices;

namespace PinvokeTest
{
class Class1
```

```
  {
    [DllImport("winmm.dll")]
    public static extern bool sndPlaySound(string lpszSound, uint flags);

    static void Main(string[] args)
    {
      sndPlaySound("Windows XP Startup", 0);
    }
  }
}
```

This sample is pretty simple. We used the Windows API Text Viewer that comes with Visual Studio 6.0 to get the definition for the `sndPlaySound` function. We found out from this that it is defined in the `winmm.dll` library and that it takes two arguments – a string and an unsigned integer. We use the `DllImport` attribute to indicate that the following `public static extern` function is defined in the indicated DLL. Once declared, we can use the function as if it were a standard, native Framework function. When we run the application (on Windows XP) the default startup noise is played. To change this to work with any other WAV file in the `\WINNT\MEDIA` directory, just supply the filename of the WAV file without the `.WAV` extension.

The point here isn't to show how to play a sound in Windows (although that is a nice bonus). The point is to demonstrate that even though we might be planning to write new code for the .NET Framework, our old code is not lost. You don't have to re-write all your old DLLs, nor do you have to re-write all of your old COM components. Both types of functions can be accessed via code InterOp provided automatically in the .NET Framework.

Migration

Migrating is an extremely important topic when talking about moving to ADO.NET. Many people learning how to use ADO.NET, are also thinking about how their old data access code written in classic ADO can be translated. While there may be some wizards available to perform language upgrades from Visual Basic 6.0 to Visual Basic .NET, these wizards are not smart enough to interpret classic ADO access and migrate it to ADO.NET.

The biggest reason for this is that the object model and data access strategy has an entirely different focus in ADO.NET than in its predecessor. ADO's object model seems to treat offline, disconnected data access and manipulation as an afterthought, whereas this is at the core of ADO.NET's design. This next section will give you an object-by-object instruction on how to convert your existing code to work in the .NET world. In most of the previous chapters in this book, we have focused on how to do things the new way: using ADO.NET. This next section will provide a handy side-by-side comparison of both old and new.

The old-style ADO samples are written in VB6.0 for clarity, while the new-style ADO.NET samples are provided both in VB.NET and C#.

ADO Data Types

When using ADO, all of the various data types were represented by constants that began with the `'ad'` prefix. In certain languages, especially VB, it was occasionally difficult to figure out what intrinsic (language-supplied) data type to use for each of the ADO constants when supplying values for stored procedures, for instance. With ADO.NET, all of the data types are part of the CTS (Common Type System), so no matter what language you access ADO.NET from, the data types will always remain the same.

The following table should give you a handy reference for migrating your ADO data types to .NET data types. This list is not complete, and only covers some of the more commonly used data types.

ADO 2.6 Data Type	.NET Framework Data Type
AdEmpty	Null
AdBoolean	Int16
AdTinyInt	Sbyte
adSmallInt	Int16
adInteger	Int32
adBigInt	Int64
adUnsignedTinyInt	Value promoted to Int16
adUnsignedSmallInt	Value promoted to Int32
adUnsignedInt	Value promoted to Int64
asUnsignedBigInt	Value promoted to Decimal
adSingle	Single
adDouble	Double
adCurrency	Decimal
adDecimal	Decimal
adNumeric	Decimal
adDate	DateTime
adDBDate	DateTime
adDBTime	DateTime
adDBTimeStamp	DateTime
adFileTime	DateTime
adError	ExternalException

ADO 2.6 Data Type	.NET Framework Data Type
adVariant	Object
adBinary	byte[]
adChar	String
adWChar	String
adBSTR	String
adUserDefined	(not supported)

Migrating Connections

The connection is the lifeline of RDBMS-based data access. All data comes through a connection, and all changes to data return through a connection. ADO connections followed the black-box model, allowing a connection to any data source supported by OLEDB or ODBC drivers. But ADO.NET uses different connection classes to provide connections that are optimized to work as fast as possible with their particular connection type.

Syntactically, the ADO connection object and ADO.NET connection object are probably the closest in terms of duties performed and object models. The following code should look pretty familiar to ADO programmers, especially those who used VB:

```
Private Sub Command1_Click()
    Dim myConn As ADODB.Connection

    Set myConn = New ADODB.Connection
    myConn.Open "DRIVER={SQL Server};DATABASE=Northwind;" & _
                "SERVER=Localhost;UID=sa;PWD=;"
    MsgBox "Connection Object Version: " & myConn.Version
    myConn.Close
End Sub
```

The above code displays the connection version (2.7 on my test machine) in a Message Box after opening it. As usual, to snippets from a Windows Forms application, presented in both VB.NET and C#, will produce identical results.

Here is the VB.NET source code for opening and closing a SQL Connection:

```
Imports System.Data
Imports System.Data.SqlClient
```

We need to make sure that the appropriate namespaces are imported so that when we reference SqlConnection, the compiler knows that it is the System.Data.SqlClient.SqlConnection class.

```
Public Class Form1
Inherits System.Windows.Forms.Form
```

To keep things clear and easy to read, of the code generated by the Forms Designer is not included.

```
Private Sub Button1_Click(ByVal sender As System.Object, ByVal e As
System.EventArgs) Handles Button1.Click
    Dim myConnection As SqlConnection
    myConnection = New SqlConnection("Server=localhost; Integrated Security=SSPI;
Initial Catalog=Northwind;")
    myConnection.Open()
    MessageBox.Show("SQL Server Version: " + myConnection.ServerVersion)
    myConnection.Close()
End Sub
End Class
```

One thing that sticks out is the difference in connection strings. Because, when using ADO.NET, we get to choose whether we're using OleDB, ODBC, or SQL, the connection strings can be specialized rather than generic. This connection string tells SQL that we want the Northwind database on the local server, and to use NT integrated security. Also, because this connection is a SQL-specific connection, we can ask it for SQL Server's version, which is far more useful than asking it for the version of ADO used to connect to the database. In our case, this application executes and displays the SQL version 8.00.0100 (SQL 2000) in a modal dialog box:

Let's look at the C# code to do the same things:

```
using System;
using System.Drawing;
using System.Collections;
using System.ComponentModel;
using System.Windows.Forms;
using System.Data;
using System.Data.SqlClient;

namespace Wrox.ProADONET.Chapter17.CSharpConnection
{
  /// <summary>
  /// Summary description for Form1.
  /// </summary>
  public class Form1 : System.Windows.Forms.Form
  {
    private System.Windows.Forms.Button button1;
    /// <summary>
    /// Required designer variable.
    /// </summary>
    private System.ComponentModel.Container components = null;

    public Form1()
    {
      InitializeComponent();
    }
```

Like VB, VB.NET keeps many details of low-level operations hidden from the programmer. While the VB.NET form source code may not show this stuff, it is happening in the background.

```
protected override void Dispose( bool disposing )
{
  if( disposing )
  {
    if (components != null)
    {
      components.Dispose();
    }
  }
  base.Dispose( disposing );
}
```

Again, the Forms Designer code is excluded to keep things from getting too cluttered.

```
/// <summary>
/// The main entry point for the application.
/// </summary>
[STAThread]
static void Main()
{
  Application.Run(new Form1());
}

private void button1_Click(object sender, System.EventArgs e)
{
  SqlConnection myConnection = new
  SqlConnection
  ("Server=localhost;Initial Catalog=Northwind;Integrated Security=SSPI;");
  myConnection.Open();
  MessageBox.Show(this, "Server Version: " +
myConnection.ServerVersion.ToString() );
  myConnection.Close();
}
}
}
```

Aside from some syntax differences, this code should look pretty close to the VB.NET code we showed above. For more detail on using ADO.NET connections with non-SQL data sources, consult the introductory chapters in this book that detail making database connections.

Migrating the RecordSet

The connection object seemed pretty simple. Unfortunately, the same is not true for the RecordSet. As with so many other ADO components, the RecordSet encapsulates an incredible amount of functionality.

ADO.NET, on the other hand, takes an entirely different approach. For read-only result-set traversing, ADO.NET uses a `DataReader` object, while ADO still must use the `RecordSet`. For storing an in-memory cache of rows, ADO uses a disconnected `RecordSet` while ADO.NET uses a `DataSet`, which provides a wealth of functionality that simply doesn't exist anywhere in classic ADO. And for publishing data back to the database, ADO uses either a connected `RecordSet` or SQL statements or stored procedures; ADO.NET can accomplish this using `DataAdapters` hooked to a `DataSet` and a connection or stored procedures or simple SQL statements.

The following is a quick reference to help you determine which classes in ADO.NET you need to use based on the purpose for which you were using the classic ADO `RecordSet`.

ADO RecordSet Task	ADO.NET Classes Involved
Forward-only iteration for display	`DataReader`, `Connection`
Connected random (indexed) row access	`DataSet`, `DataAdapter`, `Connection`
Publishing `RecordSet` changes to DB	`DataSet`, `DataAdapter`, `Connection`
Reading/writing persisted data (XML or Binary)	`DataSet`
`GetString` or `GetRows`	`DataSet` (the purpose for `GetString` and `GetRows` is removed by the `DataSet` object's disconnected, random-access nature)

The first one we will look at is one of the most common data-related tasks: forward-only iteration. This is usually done when obtaining lists of read-only information to be displayed to users such as category lists, order history, or any other kind of "view" information. In ADO.NET, this operation is highly optimized by the `DataReader`, while ADO still uses a `RecordSet`.

Forward-Only Data Access

We'll start by looking at a VB6 example that populates a `ListBox` control with the customers list from the `Northwind` database (much like the COM InterOp sample we went through earlier).

VB6 source code for forward-only `RecordSet` iteration:

```
Private Sub Form_Load()
Dim myRS As New ADODB.Recordset
Dim myConnection As New ADODB.Connection

  myConnection.ConnectionString = _
    "Driver={SQL Server}; Server=localhost; Database=Northwind; Uid=sa;Pwd=;"
  myConnection.Open

  myRS.Open "SELECT * FROM Customers", myConnection, adOpenForwardOnly,
adLockReadOnly
  Do While Not myRS.EOF
    List1.AddItem (myRS("ContactName") & " FROM " & myRS("CompanyName"))
    myRS.MoveNext
  Loop
```

```
   myRS.Close
   myConnection.Close

   Set myConnection = Nothing
   Set myRS = Nothing

End Sub
```

It's all pretty straightforward. We use an ADO connection and an ADO `RecordSet` to iterate through the customers, adding each one individually to the `ListBox` control on our VB6 form. Let's take a look at how we accomplish this the fast way in VB .NET using a `DataReader`.

VB.NET forward-only data access example:

```
Imports System.Data
Imports System.Data.SqlClient

Public Class Form1
Inherits System.Windows.Forms.Form


Private Sub Form1_Load(ByVal sender As System.Object, ByVal e As System.EventArgs)
Handles MyBase.Load
Dim myConnection As SqlConnection
Dim myReader As SqlDataReader
Dim myCommand As SqlCommand

  myConnection =
    New SqlConnection("Server=localhost; Initial Catalog=Northwind; Integrated
Security=SSPI;")
  myConnection.Open()
  myCommand = New SqlCommand("SELECT * FROM Customers", myConnection)
  myReader = myCommand.ExecuteReader()

  While myReader.Read
    ListBox1.Items.Add(myReader.GetString(myReader.GetOrdinal("ContactName")) &_
    " from " & _
    myReader.GetString(myReader.GetOrdinal("CompanyName")))
  End While

End Sub
End Class
```

And last but not least, we have the C# sourcecode for the same example:

```
using System;
using System.Drawing;
using System.Collections;
using System.ComponentModel;
using System.Windows.Forms;
using System.Data;
using System.Data.SqlClient;
```

```
namespace Wrox.ProADONET.Chapter17.CSharp_RecordSet1
{
public class Form1 : System.Windows.Forms.Form
{
  private System.Windows.Forms.ListBox listBox1;
  private System.ComponentModel.Container components = null;

public Form1()
{
  InitializeComponent();

  SqlConnection myConnection =
    new SqlConnection ("Server=localhost;Initial Catalog=Northwind;" +
                       "Integrated Security=SSPI;");
  myConnection.Open();
  SqlCommand myCommand = new SqlCommand
                       ("SELECT * FROM Customers",  myConnection );
  SqlDataReader myReader = myCommand.ExecuteReader();

  while (myReader.Read())
  {
    listBox1.Items.Add( myReader.GetString(
      myReader.GetOrdinal("ContactName") ) + " from " +
      myReader.GetString( myReader.GetOrdinal("CompanyName") ) );
  }
}

}
}
```

All of the above examples, including the VB6 application generate output that looks similar to this:

Publishing RecordSet Changes

One of the other common things to do with a RecordSet is to leave it connected, make the appropriate changes, and then post the changes back to the database. To illustrate this example in classic ADO, we're going to use VB6 to open a connected RecordSet and insert a new customer, carrying that change across to the connected database. Then, to contrast, we'll accomplish the same goal using different techniques in VB.NET and C#.

The VB6 sourcecode to update a database using a RecordSet could look something like this:

```
Private Sub Command1_Click()
Dim myConnection As ADODB.Connection
Dim myRS As ADODB.Recordset

Set myConnection = New ADODB.Connection
myConnection.ConnectionString = "DRIVER={SQL
Server};DATABASE=Northwind;UID=sa;PWD=;SERVER=localhost;"
myConnection.Open
```

We are going to open the RecordSet in dynamic mode with an optimistic lock to give us sufficient access to allow the RecordSet to modify the underlying table directly.

```
Set myRS = New ADODB.Recordset
myRS.Open "SELECT * FROM Customers", myConnection, adOpenDynamic, adLockOptimistic

myRS.AddNew
    myRS("CustomerID").Value = "SDOO"
    myRS("CompanyName").Value = "Scooby Doo Detective Agency"
    myRS("ContactName").Value = "Scooby Doo"
    myRS("ContactTitle").Value = "Canine Detective"
    myRS("Address").Value = "1 Doo Lane"
    myRS("City").Value = "Springfield"
    myRS("PostalCode").Value = "111111"
    myRS("Country").Value = "USA"
    myRS("Phone").Value = "111-111-1111"
myRS.Update

myRS.Close
myConnection.Close
Set myConnection = Nothing
Set myRS = Nothing

MsgBox "New Customer Added"

End Sub
```

This is probably pretty familiar. ADO RecordSets use the AddNew method to create a new row and move the current row pointer to that new row. Then, they use the Update method to post those changes back to the database.

As we have seen in previous chapters, ADO.NET has no connected equivalent for enabling this kind of functionality. Not in a single class, anyway. ADO.NET uses a DataSet to store an in-memory, disconnected cache of data. A DataAdapter is then used to pump information to and from the database, in and out of the DataSet. Next we'll take a look at the sourcecode for a VB.NET application that uses a DataSet and a DataAdapter to load a DataSet with the Customers table, and then update the database with a customer added to the DataSet. This combination of classes is far more powerful than the single ADO RecordSet, in that it allows us not only to configure what information is updated in the database, but also how it is updated. The ADO.NET design of focusing the entire system around the offline data cache facilitates all kinds of features previously unavailable to classic ADO, such as the ability to work with the offline data cache from within portable devices such as PocketPCs.

Now, let's take a look at how the VB.NET comparison stands up. What we're doing is using a DataAdapter to load the DataSet, and then allowing the SqlCommandBuilder to automatically generate the necessary InsertCommand for us. Our C# example will show how to manually build the SqlCommand.

VB.NET sourcecode to insert a row using a DataSet and DataAdapter:

```
Imports System.Data
Imports System.Data.SqlClient

Public Class Form1
    Inherits System.Windows.Forms.Form

Private Sub Button1_Click(ByVal sender As System.Object, ByVal e As
System.EventArgs) Handles Button1.Click

Dim myConnection As SqlConnection
Dim myDS As DataSet
Dim myDA As SqlDataAdapter
Dim NewRow As DataRow
Dim SqlCB As SqlCommandBuilder

 myConnection =
  New SqlConnection
  ("Server=localhost; Initial Catalog=Northwind; Integrated Security=SSPI;")
 myConnection.Open()
 myDS = New DataSet()
 myDA = New SqlDataAdapter("SELECT * FROM Customers", myConnection)
```

We're here instantiating a new SqlCommandBuilder. This object will automatically create the appropriate UPDATE, INSERT, and DELETE SQL statements based on the SELECT statement that we provide to the DataAdapter. This is different from classic ADO in that the ADO RecordSet would automatically generate these commands for us without us requesting it, often incurring a performance overhead each time a classic ADO RecordSet was created. We're going to use this to automatically generate our INSERT command so that it most closely resembles the VB6 version (which is also creating an insert statement behind the scenes in the RecordSet object):

```
 SqlCB = New SqlCommandBuilder(myDA)
 myDA.Fill(myDS, "Customers")
```

The `NewRow` method creates a new row object. Unlike the `RecordSet AddNew` method, however, this new row is not automatically part of the originating table. It is simply a new, disconnected `DataRow` object that has the same columns and column data types as the originating table:

```
NewRow = myDS.Tables("Customers").NewRow()
NewRow("CustomerID") = "SDOO"
NewRow("CompanyName") = "Scooby Doo Detective Agency"
NewRow("ContactName") = "Scooby Doo"
NewRow("ContactTitle") = "Canine Detective"
NewRow("Address") = "1 Doo Lane"
NewRow("City") = "Springfield"
NewRow("PostalCode") = "11111"
NewRow("Country") = "USA"
NewRow("Phone") = "111-111-1111"
```

In order to make sure that our new row is actually placed back into the `DataSet`, we'll add the new `DataRow` to the `Rows` collection in our `DataTable` object (`Customers` table):

```
myDS.Tables("Customers").Rows.Add(NewRow)
```

Calling the `Update` method on our `Customers` table in the `DataSet` actually performs quite a bit of work in the background. First, it finds all *new* rows, and then uses the appropriate object, returned by the `InsertCommand` method, to place those new rows in the database. In addition, it finds all *modified* rows and uses the appropriate `UpdateCommand` to make those changes in the database. All *deleted* rows in the `DataSet` are then removed from the database using the adapter's `DeleteCommand`. These commands can either be standard SQL statements or they can be stored procedures in the server. As you can see, there is quite a bit of versatility and power in the `DataSet/DataAdapter` combination that simply didn't exist in previous ADO incarnations.

```
myDA.Update(myDS.Tables("Customers"))
MsgBox("New Customer Added")
End Sub
End Class
```

Now, let's take a look at the code for the C# Windows Forms application that performs this same task as well as a small amount of databinding. The difference between this application and our VB.NET sample is that this one will manually define the `InsertCommand` to perform the database insert operation in response to the new `DataRow`. As we learned in the performance chapter, this is the preferred way of accomplishing things. However, if we wanted to we could use the command builder in C#.

This example is going to have a little bit of fancy code in it. After all, you're not only interested in how to do a straight-across migration, but how to utilize as many new features of .NET as you can in the process. ADO.NET is supposed to make data access easier and better. This example demonstrates some of that power within the context of migration and upgrading. To keep things clear and simple we've removed some of the stock functions and the Forms Designer code from this listing.

Here is the C# source code for manual `InsertCommand` building:

```
using System;
using System.Drawing;
using System.Collections;
using System.ComponentModel;
using System.Windows.Forms;
```

As usual, when we're working with SQL data, we need to use the `System.Data.SqlClient` namespace.

```
using System.Data;
using System.Data.SqlClient;

namespace Wrox.ProADONET.Chapter17.CSharp_Update
{
public class Form1 : System.Windows.Forms.Form
{
 private System.Windows.Forms.Button button1;
 private System.Windows.Forms.ListBox listBox1;
```

We set the `DataSet`, `DataAdapter`, and `Connection` objects to be private member variables of the form so that both the constructor and our button-click event have access to the variables:

```
 private DataSet myDS;
 private SqlDataAdapter myDA;
 private SqlConnection myConnection;

 private System.ComponentModel.Container components = null;

public Form1()
{
  InitializeComponent();

  myConnection = new
    SqlConnection("Server=localhost; Initial Catalog=Northwind;" +
                  "Integrated Security=SSPI;");
```

The following SQL Select statement pulls all columns from the `Customers` table, as well as creating a column that concatenates two other columns. If we had used this SQL statement in our classic ADO `RecordSet` and then tried to use it to update our database, we would get an error because it would try to insert a value into the `FullName` column. Further into the listing, you'll see how we can control the way the `InsertCommand` is built to avoid this problem.

```
myDA = new SqlDataAdapter("SELECT Customers.*, ContactName + ' from ' +
    CompanyName AS FullName FROM Customers", myConnection );
myDS = new DataSet();
SqlCommand InsertCommand = new SqlCommand();

myDA.Fill(myDS, "Customers");

// Databind the listbox automatically
// to the calculated "FullName" column of our Customers table in the
// DataSet. No iteration required, still completely disconnected operation.
// Additionally, the listbox will auto-update when the DataSet changes.
listBox1.DataSource = myDS.Tables["Customers"];
listBox1.DisplayMember = "FullName";
```

Now we are going to custom-configure our `InsertCommand`. We saw earlier how to instantiate a `SqlCommandBuilder` that will automatically build the commands for us. If this is the case, then why would we want to bother entering all these lines of code to do it ourselves? Most importantly, if we did not write our own in this case, the `SqlCommandBuilder` would try and build a command that inserts the `FullName` column. Because this is a calculated column, trying to insert using that statement will raise an exception. In other cases, we might have `DataSet` columns that don't map directly to the names of the columns in the database. This can happen if we're loading data from an XML document and then using the same `DataSet` to push that data into a database. If the column names do not match, then you need to configure the `InsertCommand` manually to generate the correct column mappings.

Another case where we might want to custom-configure the `DataAdapter` commands is when we do not want certain columns to appear in certain operations. For example, if we have a `DateCreated` column that appears in a table, we probably don't want that column to appear in *any* of our commands. A good way to populate that column would be to use the column's default value property, which is used to fill the column when a row is created without that column value supplied. The `SqlCommandBuilder` will try to build complex SQL statements when building a `DeleteCommand` by deleting the row that matches *all* of the columns in the source table. This is a waste of resources, especially if there are BLOB or Memo/Text columns in the `DataSet`. A more efficient approach would be to include only the primary key in the `DeleteCommand` parameter list when removing a row.

Here we create our custom insert command:

```
InsertCommand.CommandText = "INSERT INTO Customers(CustomerID, " +
    "CompanyName, ContactName, ContactTitle, Address, City, Region, " +
    "PostalCode, Country, Phone, Fax) " +
    "VALUES(@CustomerID, @CompanyName, @ContactName, @ContactTitle, " +
    "@Address, @City, @Region, @PostalCode, @Country, @Phone, @Fax)";
```

The parameter names in this SQL statement all begin with the @ sign, much like they do in standard T-SQL stored procedures. This is no coincidence. When we create `SqlParameter` objects that use column names from the `DataSet` as mappings, we are allowing the `DataAdapter` to perform appropriate replacements and create a temporary stored procedure for us. Obviously it would be more efficient to use an actual stored procedure, which we will look at in the next section.

```
InsertCommand.CommandType = CommandType.Text;
InsertCommand.Connection = myConnection;
```

Create a parameter to map each column in the `Customers` table in the `DataSet` to a parameter in the `CommandText` property of the `InsertCommand`:

```
InsertCommand.Parameters.Add( new SqlParameter("@CustomerID", SqlDbType.NChar,
5, "CustomerID") );
InsertCommand.Parameters.Add(
new SqlParameter("@CompanyName", SqlDbType.NVarChar, 40, "CompanyName") );
InsertCommand.Parameters.Add(
new SqlParameter("@ContactName", SqlDbType.NVarChar, 30, "ContactName") );
InsertCommand.Parameters.Add(
  new SqlParameter("@ContactTitle", SqlDbType.NVarChar, 30, "ContactTitle") );
InsertCommand.Parameters.Add
( new SqlParameter("@Address", SqlDbType.NVarChar, 60, "Address") );
InsertCommand.Parameters.Add
```

```
      ( new SqlParameter("@City", SqlDbType.NVarChar, 15, "City") );
    InsertCommand.Parameters.Add
      ( new SqlParameter("@Region", SqlDbType.NVarChar, 15, "Region") );
    InsertCommand.Parameters.Add
      ( new SqlParameter("@PostalCode", SqlDbType.NVarChar, 10, "PostalCode") );
    InsertCommand.Parameters.Add
      ( new SqlParameter("@Country", SqlDbType.NVarChar, 15, "Country") );
    InsertCommand.Parameters.Add
      ( new SqlParameter("@Phone", SqlDbType.NVarChar, 24, "Phone") );
    InsertCommand.Parameters.Add
      ( new SqlParameter("@Fax", SqlDbType.NVarChar, 24, "Fax") );

    myDA.InsertCommand = InsertCommand;
}

private void button1_Click(object sender, System.EventArgs e)
{
    DataRow NewRow;
    NewRow = myDS.Tables["Customers"].NewRow();
    NewRow["CustomerID"] = "SDOO";
    NewRow["CompanyName"] = "Scooby Doo Detective Agency";
    NewRow["ContactName"] = "Scooby Doo";
    NewRow["ContactTitle"] = "Canine Detective";
    NewRow["Address"] = "1 Doo Lane";
    NewRow["City"] = "Springfield";
    NewRow["PostalCode"] = "11111";
    NewRow["Country"] = "USA";
    NewRow["Phone"] = "111-111-1111";
    NewRow["Region"] = "";
    NewRow["Fax"] ="";
    // the "FullName" column is calculated server-side. To have it show up
    // while operating disconnected, we can calculate it here. Because we
    // built our InsertCommand, we don't have to worry about this column
    // attempting to insert into the source table.

    NewRow["FullName"] = NewRow["ContactName"] + " from " + NewRow["CompanyName"];
    myDS.Tables["Customers"].Rows.Add( NewRow );
    // we'll actually see this item appear in the listbox -before-
    // it hits the database because of when we call the Update() method.
    // This allows for incredibly fast offline operation.

    listBox1.SelectedIndex = listBox1.Items.Count-1;
    // commit the changes to SQL.
    myDA.Update(myDS, "Customers");

}
}
}
```

When we run this program and then click the **New Customer** button, we see a `ListBox`, complete with the new item already selected for us:

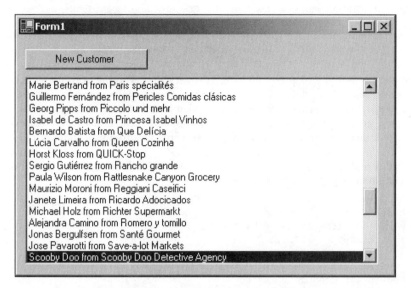

> To publish changes from a `DataSet` to a database, connect it to that database with a `DataAdapter`. The `DataAdapter` will open the connection long enough to make the changes and then close it.

Migrating Commands and Stored Procedures

So far we have seen a side-by-side comparison of ADO `RecordSets` and `Connections`, detailing what the ADO.NET code looks like to accomplish the same task as the classic ADO code. This next section will cover using stored procedures. We have seen some of the places where ADO.NET commands can be used, such as with the `DataAdapter`, but now we'll cover using a stored procedure rather than SQL strings. To do this, we'll enter the following stored procedure into our local SQL Server's `Northwind` database. All of the examples in this chapter were run against the SQL Server 2000 version of the `Northwind` database:

```
CREATE PROCEDURE sp_InsertCustomer
@CustomerID nchar(5),
@CompanyName nvarchar(40),
@ContactName nvarchar(30),
@ContactTitle nvarchar(30),
@Address nvarchar(60),
@City nvarchar(15),
@Region nvarchar(15) = null,
@PostalCode nvarchar(10),
@Country nvarchar(15),
@Phone nvarchar(24),
```

```
@Fax nvarchar(24) = null
AS
        INSERT INTO Customers(CustomerID, CompanyName, ContactName, ContactTitle,
            Address, City, Region, PostalCode, Country, Phone, Fax)
        VALUES(@CustomerID, @CompanyName, @ContactName, @ContactTitle, @Address,
            @City, @Region, @PostalCode, @Country, @Phone, @Fax)
```

The SQL statement should look pretty familiar. It is very similar to the SQL statements supplied to the InsertCommand property of the SqlDataAdapter in the previous example. The only difference between the two is that this procedure will be compiled ahead of time and saved on the server, while the procedure in the previous example will be compiled and cached only when first executed, and the caching rules will be different. In other words, the server-side stored procedure is a faster solution.

Let's take a quick look at the VB6, classic ADO sourcecode for creating a new customer in the Northwind database using this stored procedure:

```
Private Sub Command1_Click()
    Dim myConnection As ADODB.Connection
    Dim myCommand As ADODB.Command

    Set myConnection = New ADODB.Connection
    myConnection.ConnectionString = _
        "DRIVER={SQL Server};DATABASE=Northwind;SERVER=localhost;UID=sa;PWD=;"
    myConnection.Open

    Set myCommand = New ADODB.Command

    myCommand.CommandText = "sp_InsertCustomer"
    myCommand.CommandType = adCmdStoredProc
    Set myCommand.ActiveConnection = myConnection

    myCommand.Parameters.Append myCommand.CreateParameter("CustomerID", _
        adChar, adParamInput, 5, "SDOO")
    myCommand.Parameters.Append myCommand.CreateParameter("CompanyName", _
        adVarChar, adParamInput, 40, "Scooby Doo Detective Agency")
    myCommand.Parameters.Append myCommand.CreateParameter("ContactName", _
        adVarChar, adParamInput, 30, "Scooby Doo")
    myCommand.Parameters.Append myCommand.CreateParameter("ContactTitle", _
        adVarChar, adParamInput, 30, "Canine Detective")
    myCommand.Parameters.Append myCommand.CreateParameter("Address", _
        adVarChar, adParamInput, 60, "1 Doo Lane")
    myCommand.Parameters.Append myCommand.CreateParameter("City", _
        adVarChar, adParamInput, 15, "Springfield")
    myCommand.Parameters.Append myCommand.CreateParameter("Region", _
        adVarChar, adParamInput, 15)
    myCommand.Parameters.Append myCommand.CreateParameter("PostalCode", _
        adVarChar, adParamInput, 10, "11111")
    myCommand.Parameters.Append myCommand.CreateParameter("Country", _
        adVarChar, adParamInput, 15, "USA")
    myCommand.Parameters.Append myCommand.CreateParameter("Phone", _
        adVarChar, adParamInput, 24, "111-111-1111")
    myCommand.Parameters.Append myCommand.CreateParameter("Fax", _
        adVarChar, adParamInput, 24)
```

```
    myCommand.Execute
    MsgBox "New Customer Added"
    myConnection.Close
    Set myCommand = Nothing
    Set myConnection = Nothing

End Sub
```

This is the standard setup for invoking a stored procedure using ADO 2.6: we instantiate a connection, then instantiate a `Command` object. This command object then gets parameters populated with values, and finally we execute the command. It is a pretty straightforward operation.

In the last example we got a little fancy and added some features to the C# example. This time round we will spruce up the VB .NET example. We are going to bind our `ListBox` control to a `DataSet`, and we will have a button that will add a new customer to the `DataSet`. However, this time we are going to custom build an `InsertCommand` that uses our new stored procedure rather than plain SQL text. In our C# example we'll simply demonstrate the use of a stored procedure.

VB.NET sourcecode for using a stored procedure in the `InsertCommand` property:

```
Imports System.Data
Imports System.Data.SqlClient

Public Class Form1
    Inherits System.Windows.Forms.Form
    Private myConnection As SqlConnection
    Private myCommand As SqlCommand
    Private myDS As DataSet
    Private myDA As SqlDataAdapter
```

This is the event handler for the button click event on our form. In response to the button, we create a new `DataRow` object, populate the values appropriately, and then add the new row to the `Rows` collection on our Customers `DataTable`. Once we do that, we call the `Update` method which then invokes our stored procedure. If we had added two rows, our stored procedure would be invoked twice, once for each row.

```
Private Sub Button1_Click(ByVal sender As System.Object, ByVal e As
System.EventArgs) Handles Button1.Click
Dim NewRow As DataRow

 NewRow = myDS.Tables("Customers").NewRow()
 NewRow("CustomerID") = "SDOO"
 NewRow("CompanyName") = "Scooby Doo Detective Agency"
 NewRow("ContactName") = "Scooby Doo"
 NewRow("ContactTitle") = "Canine Detective"
 NewRow("Address") = "1 Doo Lane"
 NewRow("City") = "Springfield"
 NewRow("PostalCode") = "11111"
 NewRow("Country") = "USA"
```

```
  NewRow("Phone") = "111-111-1111"
  NewRow("FullName") = NewRow("ContactName") + " from " + NewRow("CompanyName")
  myDS.Tables("Customers").Rows.Add(NewRow)
  ListBox1.SelectedIndex = ListBox1.Items.Count - 1
  myDA.Update(myDS, "Customers")
End Sub

Private Sub Form1_Load(ByVal sender As System.Object, ByVal e As System.EventArgs)
Handles MyBase.Load
  myConnection = _
    New SqlConnection("Server=localhost; Initial Catalog=Northwind; Integrated
Security=SSPI;")
  myCommand = New SqlCommand()
  myDS = New DataSet()
  myDA = _
    New SqlDataAdapter("SELECT Customers.*, ContactName + ' from ' + CompanyName AS
FullName FROM Customers", myConnection)
  myDA.Fill(myDS, "Customers")
```

As usual, the databinding operation is incredibly simple and straightforward. It doesn't get much easier than this.

```
    ListBox1.DataSource = myDS.Tables("Customers")
    ListBox1.DisplayMember = "FullName"
```

Now we actually attend to the business of building our `InsertCommand`. We've initialized a private member variable called `myCommand` to be of type `SqlCommand`. We indicate that we want this command to be a stored procedure and set the `CommandText` property to be the actual name of the stored procedure. The rest of the parameter population should look nearly identical to what we did in the previous example.

```
    myCommand.CommandType = CommandType.StoredProcedure
    myCommand.Connection = myConnection
    myCommand.CommandText = "sp_InsertCustomer"
    myCommand.Parameters.Add(New SqlParameter
        ("@CustomerID", SqlDbType.NChar, 5, "CustomerID"))
    myCommand.Parameters.Add(New SqlParameter
        ("@CompanyName", SqlDbType.NVarChar, 40, "CompanyName"))
    myCommand.Parameters.Add(New SqlParameter
        ("@ContactName", SqlDbType.NVarChar, 30, "ContactName"))
    myCommand.Parameters.Add(New SqlParameter
        ("@ContactTitle", SqlDbType.NVarChar, 30, "ContactTitle"))
    myCommand.Parameters.Add(New SqlParameter
        ("@Address", SqlDbType.NVarChar, 60, "Address"))
    myCommand.Parameters.Add(New SqlParameter
        ("@City", SqlDbType.NVarChar, 15, "City"))
    myCommand.Parameters.Add(New SqlParameter
        ("@Region", SqlDbType.NVarChar, 15, "Region"))
    myCommand.Parameters.Add(New SqlParameter
        ("@PostalCode", SqlDbType.NVarChar, 10, "PostalCode"))
    myCommand.Parameters.Add(New SqlParameter
```

```
        ("@Country", SqlDbType.NVarChar, 15, "Country"))
    myCommand.Parameters.Add(New SqlParameter
        ("@Phone", SqlDbType.NVarChar, 24, "Phone"))
    myCommand.Parameters.Add(New SqlParameter
        ("@Fax", SqlDbType.NVarChar, 24, "Fax"))

    myDA.InsertCommand = myCommand
End Sub
End Class
```

The output of this VB.NET application looks almost identical to that of the C# application we wrote to do the same thing. The only difference is that this application is using a stored procedure as the InsertCommand and the C# application was using SQL Text.

Now let's take a look at a quick example of using C# to invoke the sp_InsertCustomer stored procedure:

```
using System;
using System.Drawing;
using System.Collections;
using System.ComponentModel;
using System.Windows.Forms;
using System.Data;
using System.Data.SqlClient;

namespace Wrox.ProADONET.Chapter17.CSharp_StoredProc
{
public class Form1 : System.Windows.Forms.Form
{
private System.Windows.Forms.Button button1;
private System.ComponentModel.Container components = null;

public Form1()
{
    InitializeComponent();

}

private void button1_Click(object sender, System.EventArgs e)
{
  SqlConnection myConnection = new
    SqlConnection("server=localhost;Initial Catalog=Northwind; " +
                  "Integrated Security=SSPI;");
  myConnection.Open();
  SqlCommand myCommand = new SqlCommand();

  myCommand.CommandText = "sp_InsertCustomer";
  myCommand.CommandType = CommandType.StoredProcedure;
  myCommand.Connection = myConnection;
  myCommand.Parameters.Add(new SqlParameter
                  ("@CustomerID", SqlDbType.NChar, 5));
  myCommand.Parameters.Add(new SqlParameter
                  ("@CompanyName", SqlDbType.NVarChar, 40));
  myCommand.Parameters.Add(new SqlParameter
```

```
                        ("@ContactName", SqlDbType.NVarChar, 30));
myCommand.Parameters.Add(new SqlParameter
                        ("@ContactTitle", SqlDbType.NVarChar, 30));
myCommand.Parameters.Add(new SqlParameter
                        ("@Address", SqlDbType.NVarChar, 60));
myCommand.Parameters.Add(new SqlParameter
                        ("@City", SqlDbType.NVarChar, 15));
myCommand.Parameters.Add(new SqlParameter
                        ("@Region", SqlDbType.NVarChar, 15));
myCommand.Parameters.Add(new SqlParameter
                        ("@PostalCode", SqlDbType.NVarChar, 10));
myCommand.Parameters.Add(new SqlParameter
                        ("@Country", SqlDbType.NVarChar, 15));
myCommand.Parameters.Add(new SqlParameter
                        ("@Phone", SqlDbType.NVarChar, 24));
myCommand.Parameters.Add
                        (new SqlParameter("@Fax", SqlDbType.NVarChar, 24));

myCommand.Parameters["@CustomerID"].Value = "SDOO";
myCommand.Parameters["@CompanyName"].Value =
                        "Scooby Doo Detective Agency";
myCommand.Parameters["@ContactName"].Value = "Scooby Doo";
myCommand.Parameters["@ContactTitle"].Value = "Canine Detective";
myCommand.Parameters["@Address"].Value = "1 Doo Lane";
myCommand.Parameters["@City"].Value = "Springfield";
myCommand.Parameters["@PostalCode"].Value = "111111";
myCommand.Parameters["@Country"].Value = "USA";
myCommand.Parameters["@Phone"].Value = "111-111-1111";
```

Whereas classic ADO required us to remember what flag values we would have to supply to the
Connection.Execute method in order to avoid the overhead of executing with a SQL cursor, ADO.NET
allows us to simply use the ExecuteNonQuery method, making things much easier to remember:

```
    myCommand.ExecuteNonQuery();
    myConnection.Close();
    myCommand.Dispose();
    MessageBox.Show(this, "Customer Added using Stored Procedure");
    }
    }
    }
```

> **The ADO.NET Command objects have quite a bit of power, and can be used in a
> variety of ways, such as being attached to DataAdapters to facilitate data
> communication between DataSets and databases or executing stored procedures or a
> combination of both.**

Changes in XML Persistence

As ADO progressed and advanced, so too did its support of XML as a persistence format. Attempting to load a `RecordSet` persisted to XML via ADO 2.1 into a `RecordSet` under ADO 2.6 often lead to compatibility problems. But otherwise ADO's XML persistence support was excellent.

However, there have been some changes to the way data is persisted in ADO.NET.

In ADO, the `RecordSet` was the only construct that could persist itself to XML. .NET allows virtually any class to persist itself to a vast array of different formats including binary, XML, and SOAP formats.

ADO XML persisted `RecordSets` all stored an XDR (XML Data Reduced) Schema at the start of the file or stream that indicated the structure of the `RecordSet`. ADO.NET supports either leaving off the schema entirely or storing the data with an in-line XML Schema (XSD). XSD is a newer, more refined and robust version of XDR.

First, let's take a look at a snippet of what the `Customers` table looks like when persisted via Visual Basic 6.0 and ADO 2.6:

```
<xml xmlns:s='uuid:BDC6E3F0-6DA3-11d1-A2A3-00AA00C14882'
  xmlns:dt='uuid:C2F41010-65B3-11d1-A29F-00AA00C14882'
  xmlns:rs='urn:schemas-microsoft-com:rowset'
  xmlns:z='#RowsetSchema'>
<s:Schema id='RowsetSchema'>
  <s:ElementType name='row' content='eltOnly' rs:CommandTimeout='30'>
    <s:AttributeType name='CustomerID' rs:number='1' rs:writeunknown='true'>
      <s:datatype dt:type='string' dt:maxLength='5' rs:fixedlength='true'
rs:maybenull='false'/>
    </s:AttributeType>
    <s:AttributeType name='CompanyName' rs:number='2' rs:writeunknown='true'>
      <s:datatype dt:type='string' dt:maxLength='40' rs:maybenull='false'/>
    </s:AttributeType>
```

The schema at the top of this persisted `RecordSet` is a `RowSetSchema`. According to the schema, the actual data portion of the document will consist of `row` elements. Each of those `row` elements will have attributes that indicate the columns in the `RecordSet`, such as `CustomerID` and `CompanyName`.

If we skip down through the file (it is quite large and not all that pretty) a bit to the actual data portion, we'll see that the data for each row is indeed contained within the attributes of a `row` element:

```
<z:row CustomerID='REGGC' CompanyName='Reggiani Caseifici'
   ContactName='Maurizio Moroni' ContactTitle='Sales Associate'
   Address='StradaProvinciale 124' City='Reggio Emilia' PostalCode='42100'
   Country='Italy' Phone='0522-556721' Fax='0522-556722'/>
<z:row CustomerID='RICAR' CompanyName='Ricardo Adocicados'
   ContactName='Janete Limeira' ContactTitle='Assistant Sales Agent'
   Address='Av. Copacabana, 267' City='Rio de Janeiro' Region='RJ'
   PostalCode='02389-890' Country='Brazil' Phone='(21) 555-3412'/>
```

Looking at this file, we notice some of its limitations. The main limitation is that the only type of element we'll ever get is a row element; we'll never be able to call it anything else. Additionally, even though it is XML, it is not easy to read, and we have no choice as to whether the columns are attributes or nested child elements. ADO.NET allows for all of these flexibilities and quite a bit more. However, if all we are using is purely the WriteXml method of the DataSet object, our output is going to look remarkably similar. The following is a snippet of the Customers table persisted to XML. We've decided to write the schema into the file as well so it is easier to compare side-by-side the two different implementations of XML persistence.

Here is a snippet of the schema header of the persisted XML file:

```
<?xml version="1.0" standalone="yes"?>
<xml>
  <xsd:schema id="xml" targetNamespace="" xmlns=""
xmlns:xsd="http://www.w3.org/2001/XMLSchema" xmlns:msdata="urn:schemas-microsoft-
com:xml-msdata" xmlns:app1="#RowsetSchema" xmlns:app2="urn:schemas-microsoft-
com:rowset">
 <xsd:import namespace="#RowsetSchema" schemaLocation="app1_NS.xsd" />
 <xsd:import namespace="urn:schemas-microsoft-com:rowset"
schemaLocation="app2_NS.xsd" />
 <xsd:element name="xml" msdata:IsDataSet="true">
   <xsd:complexType>
     <xsd:choice maxOccurs="unbounded">
       <xsd:element name="Customers">
        <xsd:complexType>
          <xsd:sequence>
            <xsd:element name="CustomerID" type="xsd:string" minOccurs="0" />
            <xsd:element name="CompanyName" type="xsd:string" minOccurs="0" />
            <xsd:element name="ContactName" type="xsd:string" minOccurs="0" />
```

It looks fairly similar, though it is a bit easier to read. The main difference is that the above schema is in XSD format while the previous schema was an XDR schema. ADO.NET DataSets *can* load data described by XDR schemas. And below we have some of the data generated by ADO.NET listed:

```
<rs:data xmlns:rs="urn:schemas-microsoft-com:rowset">
 <z:row CustomerID="ALFKI" CompanyName="Alfreds Futterkiste"
  ContactName="Maria Anders"
  ContactTitle="Sales Representative"
  Address="Obere Str. 57" City="Berlin"
  PostalCode="12209" Country="Germany"
  Phone="030-0074321" Fax="030-0076545" xmlns:z="#RowsetSchema" />
<z:row CustomerID="ANATR" CompanyName="Ana Trujillo Emparedados y helados"
  ContactName="Ana Trujillo"
  ContactTitle="Owner"
  Address="Avda. de la Constitución 2222" City="México D.F."
```

The difference is pretty limited. The main difference between the two XML persistence formats is which standard they conform to. The first (ADO) conforms to the XDR schema standard while the ADO.NET persistence format conforms to the XSD standard. The two standards are very similar, and in general the DataSet should be able to interpret most flat ADO 2.6 XML-persisted RecordSets. Another main difference is that ADO.NET supports multiple tables and relationships and constraints. Once these are placed into an XML file, the compatibility ends completely. By default, whenever an ADO 2.6 RecordSet is persisted, and an ADO.NET DataSet attempts to load it, it will think the main table is a table called "row".

Here is a quick C# code listing that demonstrates loading ADO 2.6 persisted `RecordSet` data into an ADO.NET `DataSet`:

```csharp
using System;
using System.Data;
using System.Data.SqlClient;

namespace Wrox.ProADONET.Chapter17.CSharp_XMLPersist
{
/// <summary>
/// Summary description for Class1.
/// </summary>
class Class1
{
static void Main(string[] args)
{
//
// TODO: Add code to start application here
//
  DataSet myDS = new DataSet();
  myDS.ReadXml(@"..\..\..\Customers_ADO.XML");

  Console.WriteLine("Customers Table, Persisted from ADO 2.6");
  foreach (DataRow _Row in myDS.Tables["row"].Rows)
  {
    Console.WriteLine("{0} from {1}", _Row["ContactName"], _Row["CompanyName"]);
  }
  myDS.Dispose();
}
}
}
```

The above sample loads a `DataSet` with the `Customers` table and then displays each row to the console. The following is a screenshot of the console output of this program:

> **XML persistence has changed between ADO and ADO.NET even though an ADO.NET `DataSet` can load an ADO 2.6 XML-persisted `RecordSet`. If you can, avoid using the old ADO format in favor of the ADO.NET persistence format. There is no guarantee that a newer version of ADO.NET will still be able to load ADO 2.6 XML `RecordSets`.**

Handling Exceptions and Errors

Catching exceptions in .NET data access applications is much more of a language and CLR function than it is a function of ADO.NET itself. ADO.NET provides its own class of exception called the `DataException`. All exceptions thrown by ADO.NET derive from the `DataException` class. In addition, certain ADO.NET objects, such as the `DataSet`, support properties that contain additional error information. The `DataSet` has a property called `HasErrors`, which indicates whether there is something wrong with the `DataSet`.

The biggest benefit in error handling by ADO.NET actually extends beyond just ADO.NET. In VB6.0, the only real way to trap errors was to use the `On Error` construct. This was moderately effective, but hardly what most people would consider robust error handling.

.NET languages support `try`/`catch`/`finally` exception trapping blocks. These are far more versatile and powerful in trapping error conditions than the `On Error` construct. First, we'll look at a classic VB6 example in which we are going to forget the trailing "s" on the `Customers` table and blindly report that something happened.

Here is the sourcecode to the VB6 error-handling example:

```
Private Sub Command1_Click()
 On Error GoTo FuncFailed
 Dim myConnection As ADODB.Connection
 Dim myRS As ADODB.Recordset

 Set myConnection = New ADODB.Connection
 myConnection.ConnectionString = "DRIVER={SQL
Server};SERVER=localhost;UID=sa;PWD=;DATABASE=Northwind;"
 myConnection.Open

 Set myRS = New ADODB.Recordset
 myRS.Open "SELECT * FROM Customer", myConnection, adOpenForwardOnly
 MsgBox "Opened Customers"
 myRS.Close
 myConnection.Close
 Set myConnection = Nothing
 Set myRS = Nothing
 Exit Sub
FuncFailed:
 MsgBox "Operation Failed: " + Err.Source & vbCrLf & vbCrLf & Err.Description,
vbCritical, "Data Operation Failure"
End Sub
```

Here's a screenshot of the VB6 application trapping an error:

Even though we're only looking specifically for when a data failure occurs, we will actually trap other kinds of runtime errors that we might not be expecting (such as COM failures, if ADO 2.6 isn't installed). The VB.NET code block below illustrates more advanced exception handling:

```
Imports System.Data
Imports System.Data.SqlClient

Namespace Wrox.ProADONET.Chapter17.VBNET_Error
 Module Module1

  Sub Main()
    Dim myConnection As SqlConnection
    Dim myDS As DataSet
    Dim myDA As SqlDataAdapter

    myConnection = New SqlConnection("Server=localhost;Initial Catalog=Northwind;
Integrated Security=SSPI;")
    myConnection.Open()
```

Here is our slightly more robust error-handling system. We have two lines of code that we're going to wrap in our handler. If either of those two lines of codes generates an exception that derives from (can be cast to) a `SqlException` then it will trigger the code in the `SqlException` `Catch` code block. If that code block does not catch it (that is, if there was an exception, but it wasn't a `SqlException`), then the fallback handler will be called.

Microsoft's documentation indicates that the `DataException` class is used whenever ADO.NET components throw exceptions. However, the `SqlException` class does *not* inherit from the `DataException` class. When using the `SqlClient` classes, `SqlExceptions` are thrown. Therefore, if our code is handling the generic `DataException` class without a fallback handler, it is quite possible that SQL errors will slip right through the cracks.

```
    Try
      myDA = New SqlDataAdapter("SELECT * FROM Customer", myConnection)
      myDA.Fill(myDS, "Customers")
    Catch E As SqlException
      Console.WriteLine("A Data Exception Occurred.")
      Console.WriteLine("Source: {0}", E.Source)
      Console.WriteLine("Message: {0}", E.Message)
      If Not E.InnerException Is Nothing Then
        Console.WriteLine("Inner: {0}", E.InnerException.Message)
      End If
      End
```

```
      Catch RE As Exception
        Console.WriteLine("An unexpected Exception has occurred.")
        Console.WriteLine(RE.Message)
        End
      End Try
      Console.WriteLine("Filled DataSet")
      myDS.Dispose()
      myDA.Dispose()
      myConnection.Close()

    End Sub

  End Module
  End Namespace
```

Let's run the application and see what results:

An unexpected Exception has occurred.
Value cannot be null.
Parameter name: dataset

It looks like we forgot to instantiate a new `DataSet`. All we did was declare it. We will fix that error by adding the instantiation line up at the top of the `Sub`. It's a good thing we had a fallback error handler. Now we can re-run the application after making the change and see what results:

A SQL Exception Occurred.
Source: SQL Server Managed Provider
Message: Invalid object name 'Customer'.

This is actually the exception we were expecting. We *cannot* trap this exception using the `DataException` class. We know that we deliberately misspelled the `Customers` table, so we knew we were going to cause a failure in the SQL Managed Provider.

One of the enormous advantages to exception handling in the .NET framework is that we can create our own classes that derive from standard exceptions. This allows us to create `Exception` classes that automatically log themselves in the Event Log, or even automatically send e-mail or pager notifications to system administrators.

Streams

The `Stream` object was introduced to ADO with the release of version 2.5. The main benefit to this was that it enabled a `RecordSet` to be persisted to a `Stream` object, rather than to a single flat file. This allowed persisted `RecordSets` to be placed in streams, converted into strings, and transferred between tiers in enterprise applications, as well as a host of other uses.

Streams are used throughout the entire framework. There are `Reader` and `Writer` objects that perform operations on `Streams`, and there are custom implementations of streams such as the `NetworkStream` and the `MemoryStream` object. Basic file input and output all takes place through the use of streams. When objects are serialized by the CLR they are serialized into `Streams`. There are in fact too many types of streams in the .NET framework to list here.

To keep the focus on migration, we'll look at the VB6 example that uses a `Stream` in a way that was common in ADO 2.5 and 2.6. Then we'll take a look at how things like that are accomplished using ADO.NET components. The key concept to remember is that streams are an integral part of nearly all I/O operations throughout the .NET Framework, and not an optional set of additional features as they were in classic ADO.

This is VB6 code to populate a textbox with the XML contents of an ADO `RecordSet`:

```
Private Sub Command1_Click()
   Dim x As ADODB.Stream
   Dim myConnection As ADODB.Connection
   Dim myRS As ADODB.Recordset
   Dim strXML As String

   Set myConnection = New ADODB.Connection
   myConnection.ConnectionString = "Driver={SQL
Server};Database=Northwind;UID=sa;PWD=;Server=localhost;"
   myConnection.Open

   Set myRS = New ADODB.Recordset
   myRS.Open "SELECT * FROM Customers", myConnection, adOpenForwardOnly,
adLockReadOnly

   Set x = New ADODB.Stream
   x.Open
```

Being able to save a `RecordSet` to an object (any object that implements `IStream`) rather than simply a filename was a welcome addition that arrived with ADO version 2.5. Here we save the `RecordSet` to the stream and then read all of the text in the stream into a simple string variable:

```
   myRS.Save x, adPersistXML
   myRS.Close
   myConnection.Close
   Set myRS = Nothing
   Set myConnection = Nothing
   x.Position = 0
   strXML = x.ReadText
   Text1.Text = strXML
End Sub
```

The `DataSet` object, on the other hand, natively gives us the ability to retrieve the XML representation of the data with the `GetXml` method. We have already seen how to use a stream to encrypt the contents of a `DataSet` in the encryption section of the previous chapter. In our next C# Console application, we see that we don't even need a `Stream` object to obtain the XML stored within a `DataSet`:

```
using System;
using System.Data;
using System.Data.SqlClient;
using System.Xml;
using System.IO;

namespace Wrox.ProADONET.Chapter17.CSharp_Stream
```

```
{
class Class1
{
static void Main(string[] args)
{
  SqlConnection myConnection = new SqlConnection
            ("Server=localhost; Initial Catalog=Northwind; " +
             "Integrated Security=SSPI;");
  myConnection.Open();
  SqlDataAdapter myDA = new SqlDataAdapter
            ("SELECT * FROM Customers", myConnection);
  DataSet myDS = new DataSet();

  myDA.Fill(myDS, "Customers");

  Console.WriteLine(myDS.GetXml());
  myConnection.Close();
  myDS.Dispose();
}
}
}
```

The XML generated above is a well-formed XML document that doesn't include any concept of rows or columns – it is simply an XML document. Here's a portion of that document:

```
<Customers>
  <CustomerID>WOLZA</CustomerID>
  <CompanyName>Wolski   Zajazd</CompanyName>
  <ContactName>Zbyszek Piestrzeniewicz</ContactName>
  <ContactTitle>Owner</ContactTitle>
  <Address>ul. Filtrowa 68</Address>
  <City>Warszawa</City>
  <PostalCode>01-012</PostalCode>
  <Country>Poland</Country>
  <Phone>(26) 642-7012</Phone>
  <Fax>(26) 642-7012</Fax>
</Customers>
```

Even though we don't use streams here, streams are used in many places throughout the Framework and are an invaluable tool.

Summary

In this chapter, we have investigated writing ADO.NET code from the perspective of the current ADO 2.6 programmer. We covered some of the procedures and decisions involved in either migrating or re-using existing ADO code. ADO.NET is an incredibly powerful tool, but there may be times when we need to keep existing ADO code. If not, then you should now have a good understanding of how to perform some of the most common ADO tasks using ADO.NET classes. At this point, you should feel comfortable with the following tasks:

❑ Invoking COM objects from managed (.NET) code

❑ Invoking functions in existing DLLs from managed code

❑ Upgrading your existing ADO code to ADO.NET

❑ Deciding when to upgrade and when to reuse classic ADO code

❑ Reusing existing code that returns ADO `RecordSets` from within .NET

17

Creating a Custom .NET Data Provider

A .NET Data Provider is an object-oriented abstraction around a particular form of data access. The providers that come with the framework, such as the SQL Data Provider and OLE DB Data Provider, expose an object hierarchy that allows access to those data sources in a standard, uniform, and often highly optimized manner. Additionally, an ODBC .NET Data Provider is available as a download from Microsoft.

Some vendors might choose to create their own .NET Data Providers to provide a more specialized or native method for accessing their particular data source. For example, you can access a Paradox table using the ODBC driver for Paradox and the ODBC .NET Data Provider. However, that form of access involves several unnecessary levels of abstraction and overhead. If someone were to provide their own Paradox-specific .NET Data Provider, it could be highly optimized for performing Paradox tasks, and not incur the overhead of COM InterOp or bridging across ODBC drivers, etc.

Another reason someone might choose to create their own Data Provider is if the data source to which they want access is either a non-traditional data source (not a relational database), or there is no available ODBC or OLE DB driver for that type of data source. This might include things like the Active Directory, complex File Systems, proprietary (vendor-specific) binary file formats or, as we'll demonstrate in this chapter, the Microsoft Message Queuing (MSMQ) sub-system.

This chapter will not only give you step-by-step directions on how to create your own .NET Data Provider, but it will also do this in tutorial fashion by creating a .NET Data Provider that is specialized for a certain task that utilizes the MSMQ technology available on Windows servers such as NT, Windows 2000, and Windows XP.

This chapter will provide you with the information you'll need to achieve the following goals:

❑ Design a .NET Data Provider Library

❑ Create a .NET Data Provider Library

❑ Use the Data Provider Interfaces as a guideline for creating your own Data Provider

❑ Create a custom `Connection`

❑ Create a custom `Command` object

❑ Create a custom `DataReader` object

❑ Create a custom `DataException` object

❑ Create a custom class that can be serialized to and from MSMQ Messages

❑ Utilize the custom Data Provider for reading, writing, displaying, and data binding

❑ Put all of the technology and information together to create a fully functioning, distributed order-entry system as a tutorial

Data Provider Library

Historically, programmers have been at the mercy of whatever data access API they were using. Typically there weren't too many alternatives. For example, to access SQL Server from Visual Basic, chances are that people used ADO.

With the .NET Framework and ADO.NET, Microsoft has changed all of that. Now, anyone who wants to can implement their own Data Provider Library, which is a single Assembly containing all of the classes, enumerations, types, constants, etc. that are required for that Data Provider to operate. Unlike the black art of creating OLE DB providers, Microsoft has made the creation of Data Provider Assemblies relatively simple – all you have to do is follow the guidelines defined by the appropriate Interfaces and you can create your own Data Provider.

Application Requirements

This chapter is going to illustrate the creation of a custom .NET Data Provider by applying a tutorial-style approach to a fictitious application need. For the purposes of our examples, a large merchant company has decided that it wants to be able to allow for an enterprise-wide, distributed order entry system. This order entry system will allow orders for stock to be taken from a traditional "brick-and-mortar" retail store, as well as from an e-commerce web site and from a telephone service linked to a phone-order catalog.

Retail Store

The retail store application must be able to take orders from customers who walk into the store and pay at a cash register. The cashier operating the application should be able to transmit the list of orders taken during a certain period of time into the MSMQ system by simply pressing a button. There's no urgency to this operation as the orders have already been fulfilled, and the need to transmit from the retail store is only for bookkeeping and central accounting purposes. The backend order processing system (fulfillment) would have a complete order history for the retail store, and be able to automatically issue re-stock requests on its behalf.

E-Commerce Site

The needs of the e-commerce site are a bit different. This site needs to be able to allow customers to browse the electronic catalog, select products and quantities, and finally check out through some form of shopping cart process. The results of this check out should then be immediately sent into the Queued back-end system for processing as quickly as possible. It should also be possible for customers to specify an alternative shipping address and name from the one that is tied to their customer record in the case of gifts or office deliveries, and so on.

Telephone Sales

The telephone sales application will function in a similar way to that of the e-commerce site. The essential difference is in the type of audience for the application. Sales people sitting at desks at our fictitious company should be able to answer a call and create an order for a given customer. As soon as the sales person has created the order, it should then be transmitted into the Queue for fulfillment as soon as possible. Fulfillment is the process by which the product ordered by the customer is actually shipped and billed to the customer.

Architecture and Design

The main problem facing the designers of our sample suite of applications is how to build the communications backend, and to standardize the format of the orders so that different programming teams can work on each application and not worry about communication failures.

The designers of this suite of applications had recently been reading up on the various technologies available with ADO.NET and remembered that ADO.NET provides a way for vendors to create their own custom data providers. This allows the folks in the corporate office to abstract and contain the entire method of accessing the disconnected, distributed order entry system. They decided that if they created a .NET Data Provider to create the message-based order communication system, they would alleviate any concerns about standardized, uniform access to distributed order information. That decision would also mean that the programmers in the corporate office could leverage the skills of the various other programmers in other teams who already knew how to use the other ADO.NET Data Providers, like the SQL provider or the OLE DB provider.

Additionally, the designers at the fictional corporate headquarters knew that they could create an OLE DB provider that could also provide access to the underlying MSMQ system. However, creating an OLE DB provider is a far more complex task than creating a .NET Data Provider. The other tremendous benefits of using the .NET Data Provider are that the Data Provider is exposed using a rich, easy to understand object model and, being a native .NET Assembly, it is far easier to upgrade, update, and maintain. The custom .NET Data Provider allows us fine-grained control over how we utilize the MSMQ system, allowing us to obtain the highest possible performance to suit our task.

Distributed Order Entry System

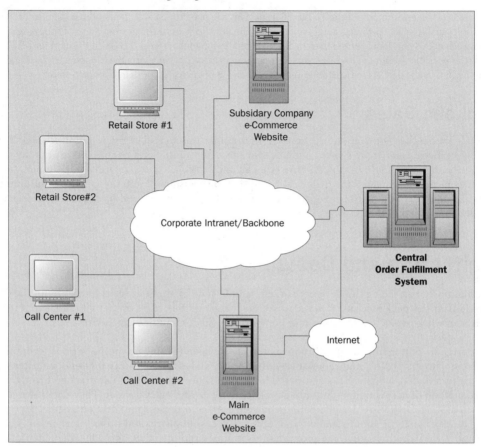

The above diagram illustrates the type of architecture that our fictitious company is trying to accomplish. There are two retail stores shown in the diagram, both of which are connected to the corporate intranet by some means. In addition, there are two call centers also attached to the corporate intranet through some means that could be anything from a local LAN, to a satellite uplink, DSL/Hi-Speed, or even line-of-sight microwave. The primary responsibility of both the stores and the call centers is for taking orders for customers and stuffing them into the amorphous "cloud" shown above indicating the Corporate Intranet/Backbone. We know at this point that the "cloud" will be some form of linked and propagated network of Microsoft Message Queues. The last two order-entry systems are two different web sites. The first could be the main corporate web site, and the second could be a web site of an owned subsidiary (maybe our fictitious company bought out its competition?). All of these input systems need to be able to place orders into a queue that will eventually be read and serviced by the Central Order Fulfillment System.

Before we discuss the mechanics of Messaging and Queues and so forth, we need to tackle a more basic issue: interchange format. We need to settle on some standard form that will represent a single "Order" entity. As all of the programmers at this fictitious company are hard-line OOP designers, they decide to come up with a class whose instances can be serialized into an XML format to allow for both portable transmission and a simple object model for accessing the data.

The Order Class and Schema

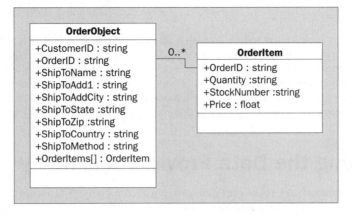

One of the things that were most worrisome about the design was how to make sure that the individual line items of an order were never separated from an order. The first round of talks simply suggested storing completely separate items – either an `Order` or an `OrderItem`. They could then be re-joined later by the fulfillment system or whatever application was pulling the items out of the Queue. This sounded like a good idea, but then what happens if something happens to the message containing an order item, but the original order message remains intact? The system will have potentially hazardous mismatches, especially in the case where something disappears between when the customer receives a receipt and when the messages arrive at the fulfillment system.

The solution was to create a class that abstracted the entire concept of an "Order", including all of the line items that belong to it. This way, when an "Order" is sent across the wire, the entire thing is sent, preventing the potential loss of dependent information.

A Sample Order

We're going to be using the `XmlSerializer` (found in the `System.Xml.Serialization` namespace) class to convert an instance of an `Order` into a portable XML format suitable for being placed into the body of an MSMQ Message. We'll go into more detail about the intricacies of MSMQ later. For now, this is a sample of what our `OrderObject` class looks like after being serialized into an XML format:

```
<?xml version="1.0"?>
<Order
   xmlns:xsi="http://www.w3.org/2001/XMLSchema-instance"
   xmlns:xsd="http://www.w3.org/2001/XMLSchema"
   OrderID="ORDER1"
   ShipToName="John Doe"
   ShipToAddr1="1 Anonymous Blvd"
   ShipToAddr2=""
   ShipToCity="Somewhere"
   ShipToState="MS"
   ShipToZip="111111"
   ShipToCountry="USA"
   ShipMethod="USPS Priority">
   <OrderItem xsi:type="OrderItem" OrderID="ORDER1" Quantity="12"
StockNumber="ITEM1" Price="14.99" />
```

```
      <OrderItem xsi:type="OrderItem" OrderID="ORDER1" Quantity="15"
StockNumber="ITEM2" Price="12.25" />
</Order>
```

Even though this may look similar to how rows in a `DataSet` might look like, it is important here *not* to confuse the two. The above format is a *Serialized XML* format, and should not be compared to the storage format used to represent the same data in a `DataSet`. While it is possible to have a `DataSet` configured to load this information, keep in mind that we'll be coding a custom class designed to serialize and deserialize itself using the above format. We'll talk more about the actual `OrderObject` class and `OrderItem` class when we get into our next section on implementing the actual Data Provider Assembly.

Implementing the Data Provider Assembly

The `System.Data` namespace is the root namespace from which all of Microsoft's Data Providers begin. For example, the SQL Data Provider exists entirely within the `System.Data.SqlClient` namespace. The OLE DB Provider for .NET is contained in the `System.Data.OleDb` namespace. Microsoft has some guidelines found in the MSDN library under the heading "*Implementing a .NET Data Provider*" to help you in creating your own Data Provider. In addition to Microsoft's guidelines, it also has a host of interfaces that define the contracts to which your components must comply in order to be considered valid portions of a Data Provider.

Microsoft's first guideline is that all of the components of your Data Provider must reside in a unique namespace. In this case, a unique namespace is one that has a reasonable guarantee that there are no other namespaces with the same name in the world. It doesn't dictate any rules or formats that your provider namespace must conform to, only that it be unique enough to never be shared by any other provider. In general, the recommendation for creating unique namespaces is to create an outer namespace for your company, then one within for the project, and so on. For our example, we're going to create an assembly that will eventually be called `OQProvider.DLL`, containing all of the entities in the namespace `Wrox.ProADONET.OQProvider`.

The OQProvider Namespace

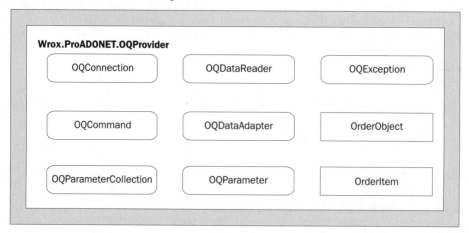

Microsoft has a detailed list of the Interfaces that a Data Provider must support by way of its classes in order to be considered valid Data Provider. Therefore, our custom provider assembly must contain classes that implement the following interfaces in order to be considered a valid Data Provider:

Interface	Description
IDbConnection	Represents a "live" connection to a data source.
IDbCommand	Represents a statement that is executed against an open, "live" data source. For traditional providers, this can be a stored procedure or a SQL statement.
IDataAdapter	Data Adapters are "plugs" that transfer information to and from DataSets.
IDataReader	Represents a means of accessing one or more forward-only, read-only streams of data obtained by a class implementing the IDbCommand interface.
IDataParameterCollection	In order to supply parameters to an IDbCommand, they must be in the form of a class that implements the IDataParameterCollection.
IDataParameter	Classes that implement the IDataParameterCollection interface maintain collections of classes implementing the IDataParameter interface.

An Assembly that contains classes that provide implementations of all of the above interfaces is considered a Data Provider. It is possible to create a limited provider that only supplies implementations of the IDataAdapter interface. By creating the limited provider, however, clients will only be able to use a very small subset of available features. This limited provider has no concept of connection, and can only transfer data to and from DataSets. Our example will, however, provide all of the required interfaces for a full implementation. Keep in mind that we don't need to implement our own DataSet, as they are completely indifferent to the source or final destination of the data they contain.

The OrderObject

Before we get into the details of implementing the various interfaces required by Microsoft to create a complete Data Provider, we're going to create our OrderObject class. This class is entirely implementation-specific and has no relation to Data Providers. It is simply the container we're going to use to house our proprietary order data. The OrderObject class is the class whose instance represents a single Order entity. This class will be designed so that it can be serialized onto a stream automatically by the CLR through the use of code attributes. Serialization is the process by which an object instance can be converted into a stream of data. This will allow the object to be serialized into the Body of an MSMQ Message. This functionality is allowed through the use of the XML serialization attributes available in the System.Xml.Serialization namespace, such as **XmlAttribute**, **XmlRoot**, **XmlElement**, and **XmlInclude** code attributes.

There's nothing overly fancy about the OrderObject class. It is really nothing more than a container for some private member variables and an ArrayList that represents the internal list of OrderItem classes. Let's take a look at the source listing for this class:

```
using System;
using System.Xml.Serialization;
using System.Collections;

namespace Wrox.ProADONET.OQprovider
{
```

The XmlRoot attribute below tells the serializer in the CLR that the class should be serialized with a root element named Order. The XmlInclude attribute tells the serialization to include a schema reference to a CLR type called OrderItem. Without that directive, we couldn't serialize an ArrayList of OrderItem instances. For more information on Code Attributes, see the Wrox book *Professional .NET Framework* (ISBN: 1-861005-56-3).

```
[XmlRoot(ElementName="Order")]
[XmlInclude(typeof(OrderItem))]
public class OrderObject
{
```

Here we declare all of the private member variables that the class instance will use to maintain all of the information it needs to store an Order. This includes an ArrayList of OrderItem instances.

```
private ArrayList _OrderItems;
private string _CustomerID;
private string _OrderID;
private string _ShipToName;
private string _ShipToAddr1;
private string _ShipToAddr2;
private string _ShipToCity;
private string _ShipToState;
private string _ShipToZip;
private string _ShipToCountry;
private string _ShipMethod;

public OrderObject()
{
    _OrderItems = new ArrayList();
}
```

In the code below, we've made an overloaded constructor so that we can build the entire class instance (except for the OrderItems) in a single constructor. Keep in mind that a class cannot be serializable unless it provides a default constructor. Also, any private variables that don't have public property accessors *will not* be able to be reconstructed properly by the serializer. Therefore, for every private member variable that our class has, we provide both set and get accessors.

```
public OrderObject(string CustomerID, string OrderID, string
        ShipToName, string ShipToAddr1, string ShipToAddr2, string
        ShipToCity, string ShipToState, string ShipToZip,
        string ShipToCountry, string ShipMethod)
{
    _OrderItems = new ArrayList();
    _CustomerID = CustomerID;
    _OrderID = OrderID;
    _ShipToName = ShipToName;
```

```
            _ShipToAddr1 = ShipToAddr1;
            _ShipToAddr2 = ShipToAddr2;
            _ShipToCity = ShipToCity;
            _ShipToState = ShipToState;
            _ShipToZip = ShipToZip;
            _ShipToCountry = ShipToCountry;
            _ShipMethod = ShipMethod;
        }
```

Below we have a method that the client application supplying the order would call in order to add `OrderItem` instances to an instance of an `OrderObject`. Note that we don't need to supply the `OrderID` parameter in the parameter list, because it is already a private member variable of the containing instance. When the method is called, we create a new instance of an `OrderItem` class and then add that reference to the private `ArrayList` we maintain.

```
        public void AddItem(string StockNumber, int Quantity, float Price)
        {
            OrderItem newItem = new OrderItem(StockNumber, Quantity, Price,
                    _OrderID);
            _OrderItems.Add( newItem );
        }

        public void ClearItems()
        {
            _OrderItems.Clear();
        }

        /*
         * Order Properties
         */
```

The `XmlAttribute` code attribute we use below tells the CLR serialization routine that the following property should be serialized (and de-serialized) as an XML attribute rather than an element. If you look back at the example we gave of a serialized order, you'll see that all of the main properties of the order are stored as XML attributes of the main `Order` XML element.

```
        [XmlAttribute]
        public string OrderID
        {
            get
            {
                return _OrderID;
            }
            set
            {
                _OrderID = value;
            }
        }

        [XmlAttribute]
        public string CustomerID
        {
            get
            {
```

```
            return _CustomerID;
        }
        set
        {
            _CustomerID = value;
        }
    }
```

In an effort to avoid boring you to tears, we've left out the rest of the property definitions. They all follow the same identical pattern and all of them sport the `XmlAttribute` code attribute. You can see all of the property definitions in the code download for this chapter.

We use the `XmlElement` code attribute here to indicate that the following property is to be serialized in the form of an element called `OrderItem`. As it is an `ArrayList`, this property will be serialized once for each item in the list, creating a sequence of `<OrderItem.../>` XML elements.

```
    [XmlElement(ElementName="OrderItem")]
    public ArrayList OrderItems
    {
        get
        {
            return _OrderItems;
        }
    }
}
```

The OrderItem

Now that we've covered our portable, XML-serializable `OrderObject` class, let's take a look at the class we're using to represent an `OrderItem`. This class is even simpler than the `OrderObject` class, only containing a few member variables and no `ArrayList` properties. Let's take a look at the source listing for the `OrderItem` class. As with all of our classes in our custom provider assembly, it is part of the `Wrox.ProADONET.OQProvider` namespace.

```
using System;
using System.Xml.Serialization;

namespace Wrox.ProADONET.OQprovider
{
```

As we did with the `OrderObject` class, we'll use a code attribute to define the name of the Root Element to be used to serialize this class. In our case we're calling this class's root element `OrderItem`. We're also using the `Serializable` attribute to re-iterate to the CLR (and to any coder examining the source) that this class can indeed be serialized.

```
    [XmlRoot(ElementName="OrderItem")]
    [Serializable]
    public class OrderItem
    {
```

There are only a handful of private member variables to keep track of for the order line item class, including the `Quantity`, `StockNumber`, `Price`, and `OrderID` to which it belongs. The `OrderID` property is there to reinforce the link between `OrderObject` and `OrderItem`, which is especially handy for creating `DataRelation` objects when placing data into a `DataSet`.

```
private int _Quantity;
private string _StockNumber;
private float _Price;
private string _OrderID;

public OrderItem()
{
    _Quantity = 0;
    _Price = 0;
    _StockNumber = "--";
    _OrderID = "";
}
```

Again, as we did with the `OrderObject` class, we've created an overloaded constructor to allow the `OrderObject` instance quick and easy instantiation of items. We've cut out a few property definitions for simplicity. All of the properties are defined with the `XmlAttribute` code attribute.

```
public OrderItem(string StockNumber, int Quantity, float Price, string OrderID)
{
    _Quantity = Quantity;
    _Price = Price;
    _StockNumber = StockNumber;
    _OrderID = OrderID;
}

[XmlAttribute]
public int Quantity
{
    get
    {
        return _Quantity;
    }
    set
    {
        _Quantity = value;
    }
}
```

So, now we've defined a class that represents an individual order, as well as a class that represents an individual line item on a given order. We've also shown how we can dictate the serialization properties of these classes using the various code attributes provided for us. Now we have a completely portable, serializable class that can be passed around through various client applications, as well as placed in the body of an MSMQ message. Before we jump right into implementing all of the various interfaces that we're required to implement, let's go through a very brief review of the MSMQ technology we're going to be using.

An MSMQ Review

Microsoft Message Queuing is a service provided by Windows servers that allows asynchronous, loosely coupled messaging between applications. We looked at it briefly in Chapter 16 as a way of deferring computationally expensive tasks until such a time that the user is unaware of the cost or delay. We can also use Message Queues to send informational messages to other applications that may or may not be connected live on a network. By placing a message in a queue, another application can receive that message whenever it gets a chance, be it an hour or a week from the time it was created.

This is the exact architecture that our application wants to take advantage of. By allowing disparate, disconnected, loosely coupled data entry systems to place orders into a queue (or system of queues) that can then be processed asynchronously by a fulfillment system, we've solved an enormous logistics problem and saved countless hours and dollars in manpower wasted on forcing disparate systems to communicate and translate in realtime.

Sending Messages

We've already covered in the previous chapter how to send a simple text message. What we'll cover here is the technology used to serialize one of our `Order` objects into a `MessageQueue` object. You'll need to understand how this works in order to understand the logistics of building an entire Data Provider Assembly around this technology.

```
// create an Order and populate it with some data.
// …

// Create a MessageQueue object and point it at an existing Queue.
MessageQueue mq = new MessageQueue(@".\Private$\OrderQueue");
mq.Formatter = new XmlMessageFormatter();
// Send an OrderObject object to the Queue. This automatically invokes the XML
serialization.
mq.Send( myOrder, myOrder.OrderID );
```

The above code will obtain a reference to an existing `MessageQueue` object. Then, it will make sure that all messages placed into that Queue are formatted via the `XmlMessageFormatter` (which uses XML serialization). When the above code is run in an actual application, you can open up one of the messages created by running the Computer Management console (Start | Programs | Administrative Tools on Windows 2000) and examine the XML-serialized `OrderObject` that resides in the Message's body. The following picture shows what the contents of a Message Queue will look like displaying orders that we will place into the Queue:

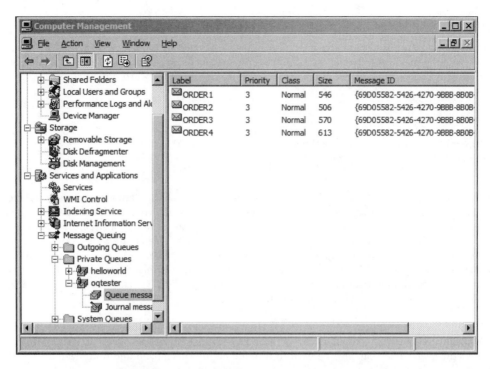

Double-clicking the **ORDER1** message in the Queue messages view then selecting the **Body** tab means that we can actually verify that our `OrderObject` has in fact been serialized and stored in XML in the body of our message:

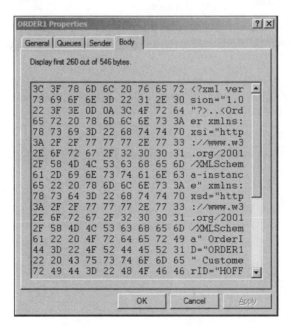

Receiving Messages

To receive an order that has already been placed in a Message Queue, we simply reverse the process we used to store the message to begin with. Some steps, such as de-serialization, are not completely automatic, so it takes a line or two more code, but it is still straightforward nonetheless.

```
MessageQueue mq = new MessageQueue(@".\Private$\OrderQueue");
Message msg = mq.Receive(new TimeSpan(0,0,3));
Streamreader sr = new Streamreader( msg.BodyStream );
XmlSerializer xs = new XmlSerializer( typeof(OrderObject) );
OrderObject myOrder = (OrderObject)xs.Deserialize(sr);
```

The above code first instantiates a new `MessageQueue` object. Then, it attempts to receive a message from that queue. If more than 3 seconds elapse before the message is received, the Messaging system will throw an exception. The body of an MSMQ message can be treated as a stream, which is especially handy for serialization of XML and large amounts of binary data. We create a `Streamreader` object to pull the raw data out of the message body. Then, we'll use the `XmlSerializer` class to de-serialize the information contained by the `Streamreader` into a new `OrderObject` instance. As the `Deserialize` method returns an `object`, and there is no implicit typecast between object and `OrderObject`, we have to explicitly supply the typecast.

Sending and receiving `Order` objects through Microsoft Message Queuing forms the core functionality of our Data Provider. Data Providers can be used to provide generalized access to data sources, such as Paradox tables, etc. They can also be used to provide highly specialized and optimized access to specific data sources, such as a Message Queue containing proprietary order objects.

The OQConnection

The `Connection` represents a connection to a data source, or some other resource. Traditionally, the `Connection` represents the physical link to a SQL Server, an Oracle database, or even an MS Access database file (`.mdb`).

> **In our particular example, the OQ (Order Queue) Connection represents a connection to a Message Queue.**

Microsoft's `IDbConnection` interface requires that the following properties and methods be implemented in order to implement a custom `Connection`. One key point to remember is that, when building your own Data Provider, you may be required to provide an implementation of certain properties or methods, but you are not required to make those implementations meaningful. This allows you to not bother with database transactions if you so choose, giving you the option of throwing a `NotSupportedException` exception when transaction-related functions are called on your provider.

Name	Type	Description
ConnectionString	Property	String used to open the resource.
ConnectionTimeout	Property	Time to wait in establishing connection before throwing an exception.
Database	Property	Name of the current database or the database to be used once the connection is opened.
State	Property	Indicates the current state of the Connection. Property is of type ConnectionState.
BeginTransaction	Method	Begins a database transaction.
ChangeDatabase	Method	Changes the current database for an open connection.
Close	Method	Closes the current connection.
CreateCommand	Method	Creates a Command object, automatically setting its connection property.
Open	Method	Opens the current connection.

Now that we've seen what is required of us in terms of implementing the required interface, let's take a look at the code we use to create our OQConnection class.

```
using System;
using System.Data;
using System.Messaging;

namespace Wrox.ProADONET.OQprovider
{
public class OQConnection: IDbConnection
{
```

We'll need to create some private member variables to maintain some of the information that the IDbConnection interface requires us to maintain, including the connection state, connection string, and timeout period. The AutoCreateQueue bool is a private member Boolean flag indicating whether or not the connection should create the queue upon opening. The queue to be created is indicated by the connection string. While the interfaces may define *which* properties we are to expose, it is still up to us to maintain the private variables that support those properties.

```
private ConnectionState _cState;
private string _ConnStr;
private int _TimeOutPeriod;
private bool _AutoCreateQueue;

private MessageQueue _Queue;

public OQConnection()
{
    _TimeOutPeriod = 3;
    _cState = ConnectionState.Closed;
    _AutoCreateQueue = true;
}
```

Other classes within our assembly, such as the `OQDataReader`, will need to be able to modify the connection state. In order to avoid allowing the end user (programmer) to have the ability to modify the connection state manually, we use the **internal** keyword. This allows us to indicate that only classes contained within this particular assembly are allowed to access this method.

```
internal void SetState(ConnectionState newState)
{
   _cState = newState;
}

public bool AutoCreateQueue
{
   get
   {
      return _AutoCreateQueue;
   }
   set
   {
      _AutoCreateQueue = value;
   }
}
```

Other classes, such as the `OQCommand`, will need to be able to access the Message Queue directly in order to send and receive data in a fashion that appears as though the information is passing through the connection. We facilitate this by allowing all classes within our Data Provider Assembly to access the `MessageQueue` object itself via the connection. No other client component or application can directly access this Queue.

```
internal MessageQueue MQ
{
   get
   {
      return _Queue;
   }
}

/*
 * IMPLEMENTATION OF IDbConnection INTERFACE
 */

/// <summary>
/// Connection string. Can only be set when the connection is closed.
/// </summary>
public string ConnectionString
{
   get
   {
      return _ConnStr;
   }
   set
   {
      if (_cState != ConnectionState.Closed)
      {
         throw new
         InvalidOperationException("Cannot set the Connection String unless
            the Connection is Closed.");
      }
```

```
            else
            {
                _ConnStr = value;
            }
        }
    }

/// <summary>
/// Timeout period of the connection in seconds.
/// </summary>
public int ConnectionTimeout
{
    get
    {
        return _TimeOutPeriod;
    }
    set
    {
        _TimeOutPeriod = value;
    }
}

/// <summary>
/// Database property. This will always return "", as this provider does not
/// actually work with Databases.
/// </summary>
public string Database
{
    get
    {
        return "";
    }
}
```

There is no ability to manually set the connection state property. The connection state property can only be set by other classes contained within the assembly or by other methods within this connection class.

```
/// <summary>
/// Indicates the current connection state.
/// </summary>
public ConnectionState State
{
    get
    {
        return _cState;
    }
}


/*
 * IDbConnection Methods
 */
```

Our Data Provider does not support Transactions. The goal of this chapter is to give you a practical example of why and how to build a Data Provider, and adding Transactions might be a useful exercise for you to do once you've got a full grasp of how Data Providers work. MSMQ has full support for transactions.

```
public IDbTransaction BeginTransaction()
{
   throw new NotSupportedException("Transactions Not
        Supported by this Provider");
}

public IDbTransaction BeginTransaction(IsolationLevel iLevel)
{
   throw new NotSupportedException("Transactions Not
        Supported by this Provider");
}

public void ChangeDatabase(string databaseName)
{
   throw new NotSupportedException("Changing Databases Not
        Supported by this Provider");
}
```

The CreateCommand method provides a shortcut for not only instantiating a new OQCommand object, but it also associates the newly created command object with the current instance of the connection class, saving the programmer a few lines of code and a few potential mistakes. By always using the CreateCommand method, rather than creating commands on their own, client programs can be written to be completely provider-independent.

```
public IDbCommand CreateCommand()
{
   OQCommand nCommand = new OQCommand();
   nCommand.Connection = this;
   return nCommand;
}
```

Typically, when a connection is opened, resources are allocated to make way for the physical connection to the data source. When the connection is closed, those resources are then disposed of. Our case is no different. When we open the connection, depending on whether the connection is configured to auto-create the Queue, it will either obtain a reference to an existing Queue, or it will create a new Queue as indicated by the connection string supplied.

```
public void Open()
{
   if (!MessageQueue.Exists( _ConnStr ))
   {
      if (!_AutoCreateQueue)
      {
         throw new InvalidOperationException("Cannot Open Queue:
             Queue Does not Exist");
      }
      else
      {
         _Queue = MessageQueue.Create( _ConnStr );
      }
   }
   else
   {
      _Queue = new MessageQueue( _ConnStr);
```

```
    }
    _Queue.Formatter = new XmlMessageFormatter();
    _cState = ConnectionState.Open;
  }

  public void Close()
  {
    _Queue.Dispose();
    _cState = ConnectionState.Closed;
  }


  }
}
```

The following few lines of code might be seen in a client application that utilizes the above
OQConnection class to open and close a connection to a Queue.

```
OQConnection Connection = new OQConnection();
Connection.ConnectionString = @".\Private$\OQTester";
Connection.Open();
Connection.Close();
```

The OQCommand

Classes that implement the IDbCommand interface are responsible for generating requests and passing them
on to the data source. In a typical relational database situation, there are four types of commands: Select,
Update, Delete, and Insert. These relate directly one-to-one with the four different kinds of SQL statements
available. In our case, there are only two things we can do to Messages in a Queue – Send and Receive
(although you can "Peek", which is something you can add to this provider as an exercise). The following is
the list of items required for us to implement the IDbCommand interface:

Name	Type	Description
CommandText	Property	String representing the text command to run against the command's associated connection.
CommandTimeout	Property	Timeout period for a command to complete before an exception will be thrown.
CommandType	Property	Indicates how the CommandText property will be interpreted.
Connection	Property	Object reference indicating the associated Connection for this Command instance.
Parameters	Property	Retrieves the IDbParameterCollection implementing class.
Transaction	Property	Gets or sets the Transaction context in which the IDbCommand instance is to execute.

Table continued on following page

Name	Type	Description
UpdatedRowSource	Property	Gets or sets how the results of command execution are to be applied to the DataRow when used by the Update method of a DataAdapter.
Cancel	Method	Cancels the execution of an IDbCommand instance.
CreateParameter	Method	Creates a new instance of an IDataParameter object.
ExecuteNonQuery	Method	Executes the CommandText with the parameters, returning only the number of rows affected.
ExecuteReader	Method	Executes the command, returning the results in an appropriately initialized IDataReader object.
ExecuteScalar	Method	Executes the command, returning the first column in the result set. All additional columns are ignored.
Prepare	Method	Creates a prepared (pre-processed or compiled) version of the command on the data source (if applicable).

Let's take a look at the code we wrote to implement the above methods for our specific need of allowing Commands to execute against a Connection that houses an active Message Queue:

```
using System;
using System.Data;

namespace Wrox.ProADONET.OQprovider
{
public class OQCommand: IDbCommand
{
```

Again we're maintaining some private member information. This time we're holding information for the TimeOutPeriod property, the Connection property, the CommandText property, and others, including the Parameters property.

```
private int _TimeOutPeriod;
private OQConnection _Connection;
private string _CmdText;
private UpdateRowSource _UpdatedRowSource = UpdateRowSource.None;
private OQParameterCollection _Parameters = new OQParameterCollection();


public OQCommand()
{
}
```

We add a little bit of specialization code here. As there's nothing all that complex about the operation we're performing against the OQConnection, we only support two different words in the CommandText property. Where the SQL Data Provider supports fully featured SQL queries and even temporary stored procedures, our Commands can only be "Send" or "Receive" operations. The reason for this is that you can only Send and Receive /from a Message Queue, and we are only going to be sending or receiving OrderObject instances. If any client code attempts to configure the command to do anything else, an exception is thrown.

```
public string CommandText
{
   get
   {
      return _CmdText;
   }
   set
   {
      if ( (value != "Send") &&  (value != "Receive"))
         throw new NotSupportedException("CommandText Must be
               either Send or Receive");
      else
         _CmdText = value;
   }
}

public int CommandTimeout
{
   get
   {
      return _TimeOutPeriod;
   }
   set
   {
      _TimeOutPeriod = value;
   }
}
```

There's some more specialization code here. We have to implement the CommandType property. However, we don't have to allow all possible values of that property. Instead, we throw an exception if any client code attempts to supply any value other than CommandType.Text. We don't support any other complex command types beyond simple words. The reason we don't simply force CommandType to be read-only and initialized to CommandType.Text is because the IDbCommand interface requires a set accessor for the CommandType property.

```
public CommandType CommandType
{
   get
   {
      return CommandType.Text;
   }
   set
   {
      if (value != CommandType.Text)
         throw new NotSupportedException("Only supported
               CommandType is Text");
   }
}

public IDbConnection Connection
{
   get
   {
      return _Connection;
   }
   set
   {
```

```
        _Connection = (OQConnection)value;
     }
  }

  public OQParameterCollection Parameters
  {
     get
     {
        return _Parameters;
     }
  }

  IDataParameterCollection IDbCommand.Parameters
  {
     get
     {
        return _Parameters;
     }
  }

  public IDbTransaction Transaction
  {
     get
     {
        return null;
     }
     set
     {
        throw new NotSupportedException();
     }
  }

  public UpdateRowSource UpdatedRowSource
  {
     get
     {
        return _UpdatedRowSource;
     }
     set
     {
        _UpdatedRowSource = value;
     }
  }

  /*
   * IDbCommand Methods (Required)
   */
  public void Cancel()
  {
    throw new NotSupportedException();
  }

  public IDataParameter CreateParameter()
  {
    return new OQParameter();
  }
```

This is the first section of code that we reach that does anything beyond meet the requirements of the interface specification. Here, we are supplying code for the ExecuteNonQuery method. The method assumes that it is performing a "Send" operation in this case. As we'll see shortly, as a business rule in our provider, the OQCommand only accepts a single parameter called Order in the case of a "Send" command, and accepts no parameters in the case of a "Receive" command. The reason for this is that we are only going to send a single OrderObject at a time, and when we Receive OrderObjects, we don't need to pass any additional information that the Connection doesn't already have. The code pulls the OrderObject reference out of the Order argument and then uses code similar to that we saw in our MSMQ review in order to transmit the Order into the Queue.

```
public int ExecuteNonQuery()
{
    _Connection.SetState(ConnectionState.Executing);
    if (_Parameters.Contains("Order"))
    {
        OQParameter tmpParam = (OQParameter)_Parameters["Order"];
        OrderObject tmpOrder = (OrderObject)tmpParam.Value;
        _Connection.MQ.Send( tmpOrder, tmpOrder.OrderID);
        _Connection.SetState(ConnectionState.Open);
        return 1;
    }
    else
    {
        throw new IndexOutOfRangeException("Order Parameter does not exist.");
    }
}
```

The ExecuteReader method simply returns a new copy of the DataReader object. You can't see it from here – you'll see it when we get to the code for the DataReader class – but the constructor we're invoking is internal. This means that the only way to obtain an OQDataReader is to invoke the ExecuteReader method on the OQCommand object. This is the way things work in the other Data Providers as well. Due to the nature of the DataReader in our implementation, no work is actually done, nor is any reading accomplished, until the reader retrieved has the Read method invoked upon it.

```
public IDataReader ExecuteReader()
{
    return new OQDataReader(_Connection);
}
```

We don't support any difference in functionality based on different values supplied for a CommandBehavior parameter to keep things simplified. However, because the IDbCommand interface dictates that we have a method that supports that argument, we simply ignore it and create a new OQDataReader, just as we did in the previous method.

```
public IDataReader ExecuteReader(CommandBehavior behavior)
{
    return new OQDataReader(_Connection);
}
```

As you saw, `ExecuteScalar` is supposed to return the first column in a resultset. We didn't feel this method would get much use when dealing with messaged `Order` objects, so we didn't provide an implementation. It could be used to simply return the `OrderObject` itself to provide a fuller implementation.

```
public object ExecuteScalar()
{
    return null;
}

public void Prepare()
{
    // do nothing.
}

}
}
```

The OQParameterCollection and OQParameter

The `OQParameterCollection` class that we're going to create is a class that implements the `IDataParameterCollection` interface. Even though we really have no need for the ability to store multiple parameters for our particular implementation, the `IDbCommand` interface dictates that the `Parameters` property be an object reference to a class that implements the `IDataParameterCollection` interface. This interface has the following requirements:

Name	Type	Description
Item	Property	Parameter at the specified index. In C#, this is the indexer property for the `IDataParameterCollection`.
Contains	Method	Indicates whether or not the `ParameterCollection` contains a given parameter name.
IndexOf	Method	Returns the index of a given parameter name.
RemoveAt	Method	Removes the parameter from the collection.

We get around the fact that the `IDataParameterCollection` interface also requires that the basic `Collection` interface also be implemented by simply inheriting our class from the `CollectionBase` class as well as implementing the `IDataParameterCollection` interface. This provides our class with all the base functionality of a collection without us having to code all of that detail work by hand. Here is the source listing for the `OQParameterCollection` class:

```
using System;
using System.Data;
using System.Collections;

namespace Wrox.ProADONET.OQprovider
{
public class OQParameterCollection:
System.Collections.CollectionBase, IDataParameterCollection
{
    private OQParameter _Param;
```

```
    public OQParameterCollection()
    {
    }
```

Our particular implementation only supports the notion of a single parameter called `Order`. Therefore, rather than maintaining an internal collection on our own, we're actually only maintaining a single `Parameter`. Any attempt to obtain *any* parameter will always give you the `Order` parameter.

```
    public object this[string parameterName]
    {
        get
        {
            return _Param;
        }
        set
        {
            _Param = (OQParameter)value;
        }
    }
```

The basic interface requirements dictate that we provide a `Contains` method. Ours is a pretty simple string check. If the `parameterName` supplied is `Order`, and we've already had the `Order` parameter created, then we return `true`. Otherwise we return a `false` indicator.

```
    public bool Contains(string parameterName)
    {
        if ( (parameterName == "Order") && (_Param != null) )
            return true;
        else
            return false;
    }

    public int IndexOf(string parameterName)
    {
        return 0;
    }

    public void RemoveAt(string parameterName)
    {
        _Param = null;
    }

    }
}
```

The `OQParameter` class has a smaller footprint than the `OQParameterCollection` as it only has to implement details concerning itself and doesn't have to conform to any interface requiring the maintenance of list information. The following is the list of requirements for the `IDataParameter` interface:

Name	Type	Description
DbType	Property	Property indicating the DbType of the Parameter
Direction	Property	Indicates the direction (In, Out, Return Value, etc.) of the Parameter
IsNullable	Property	Indicates whether or not this parameter accepts null values
ParameterName	Property	String/Textual name of the Parameter
SourceColumn	Property	Name of the source column that is mapped to the DataSet and is used for reading/writing the value
SourceVersion	Property	Indicates the DataRowVersion when loading a value
Value	Property	Gets/sets the value of the parameter itself

Let's take a look at the source code for the OQParameter class:

```
using System;
using System.Data;

namespace Wrox.ProADONET.OQprovider
{
/// <summary>
/// Summary description for OQParameter.
/// </summary>
public class OQParameter : IDataParameter
{
private OrderObject _Order;

    public OQParameter()
    {
       // do nothing
    }
```

Our own overload of the constructor takes a single object, an OrderObject, as an argument. This allows for a quick access to the private member variable storing the Parameter's internal OrderObject reference.

```
    public OQParameter(OrderObject Order)
    {
       _Order = Order;
    }

    public DbType DbType
    {
       get
       {
          return DbType.Object;
       }
       set
       {
          // do nothing
       }
    }
```

```
public ParameterDirection Direction
{
   get
   {
      return ParameterDirection.Input;
   }
   set
   {
      // do nothing
   }
}

public bool IsNullable
{
   get
   {
      return false;
   }
   set
   {
      // do nothing
   }
}

public string ParameterName
{
   get
   {
      return "Order";
   }
   set
   {
      // do nothing
   }
}
```

An `OrderObject` parameter actually contains information for multiple columns and multiple rows within a `DataSet`, so using the `SourceColumn` property in our case is quite useless.

```
public string SourceColumn
{
   get
   {
      return "";
   }
   set
   {
      // do nothing
   }
}

public DataRowVersion SourceVersion
{
   get
   {
      return DataRowVersion.Original;
   }
```

```
      set
      {
          // do nothing
      }
   }
```

Rather than retrieving and storing the information in a completely generic manner, we are instead storing an actual OrderObject reference as the Parameter's value.

```
public object Value
{
   get
   {
       return _Order;
   }
   set
   {
       _Order = (OrderObject)value;
   }
}

}
}
```

The OQDataReader

The DataReader is an object that provides forward-only, read-only access to the result set returned by a Command of some kind. In our case, the OQDataReader will provide forward-only, read-only access to the list of Messages obtained from within the Queue indicated by the OQConnection and returned by executing an ExecuteReader method against that Connection.

The following is the list of Interface requirements specified by the IDataReader interface:

Name	Type	Description
Depth	Property	Indicates the Depth of the current nesting for the current row. It is possible for nesting to be quite high when hierarchical result sets are returned from some data sources.
IsClosed	Property	Indicates whether or not the reader is closed.
RecordsAffected	Property	Indicates the number of rows changed, inserted, or deleted by the execution of the associated command.
Close	Method	Closes the current reader.
GetSchemaTable	Method	Returns a DataTable that describes the column definitions of the IDataReader.

Name	Type	Description
NextResult	Method	Advances to the next result set in the list of result sets obtained by the reader.
Read	Method	The core function of the DataReader. It advances the IDataReader to the next record.

There are some other functions (such as GetInt16, GetInt32, etc.) that must be present in order to complete the definition of an IDataReader class, and those are specified by the interface IDataRecord. We won't go into the list of requirements here, as we'll see them in our code, listed below.

```
using System;
using System.Data;
using System.Messaging;
using System.Xml;
using System.Xml.Serialization;
using System.IO;

namespace Wrox.ProADONET.OQprovider
{
/// <summary>
/// Summary description for OQDataReader.
/// </summary>
public class OQDataReader: IDataReader
{
private OQConnection _Connection;
private Message _Message;
private OrderObject _Order;
private int _ReadCount;
```

Take note of the internal keyword here. This means that a DataReader cannot be instantiated by standard client code, it can only be instantiated by classes contained within our assembly.

```
internal OQDataReader()
{
    _Order = new OrderObject();
    _ReadCount = 0;
}
```

This is another internal constructor, this one taking the associated connection as an argument. A DataReader cannot function without a connection, and it can't read from a Connection that isn't open.

```
internal OQDataReader(OQConnection Connection)
{
    _Connection = Connection;
    _Order = new OrderObject();
    _ReadCount = 0;
}
```

In place of all of the many *Getxxx* functions, such as `GetInt32`, `GetInt64`, `GetString`, etc., we supply our own method. This method retrieves an `OrderObject` class instance from the current message. We use a private counter so that we can detect if an attempt to obtain an `OrderObject` reference occurs before the first call to the `Read` method.

```
public OrderObject GetOrder()
{
    if (_ReadCount == 0)
        throw new IndexOutOfRangeException("Must first call Read method to
                load current data.");
    return _Order;
}
```

We don't support any kind of nesting, so our `Depth` is always going to be 0 (top-level).

```
public int Depth
{
    get
    {
        return 0;
    }
    set
    {
    }
}
```

We also don't support opening and closing a `DataReader`. The `DataReader` is only instantiated to pull live information from a live connection to an MSMQ Queue. There is no reason to close/re-open a `DataReader` while the connection remains live for the purposes of our sample Data Provider. Other Data Providers written for other purposes may contain logic to support the opening and closing of the `DataReader` class.

```
public bool IsClosed
{
    get
    {
        return false;
    }
    set
    {
    }
}

public int RecordsAffected
{
    get
    {
        return 0;
    }
    set
    {
    }
}
```

```
public int FieldCount
{
   get
   {
      return 1;
   }
}

public object this [string name]
{
   get
   {
      if (_ReadCount == 0)
         throw new IndexOutOfRangeException("Must first call Read method
                 to load current data.");
      if (name != "Order")
         throw new IndexOutOfRangeException("No Such Column");

      return _Order;
   }
}
```

The interface allows for named and numeric indexing into the Reader itself for access to individual columns. Due to the fact that we only have a single column (one called Order), at least in terms of the DataReader, we simply return the OrderObject reference so long as the column index is 0.

```
public object this [int i]
{
   get
   {
      if (_ReadCount == 0)
         throw new IndexOutOfRangeException("Must first call Read method
                 to load current data.");
      if (i>0)
         throw new IndexOutOfRangeException("No Such Column");
      return _Order;
   }
}
```

The IDataRecord interface specifies a *Getxxx* method for every single data type supported by the CLR. In order to spare your eyes the strain and avoid putting you to sleep rapidly, I've snipped out those definitions from the code supplied in the book (though they exist in the downloads). The essential idea is that I threw a NotSupportedException for each of the inappropriate data types.

```
// Retrieval of the unsupported types
// removed for clarity

public Type GetFieldType(int i)
{
   if (_ReadCount == 0)
      throw new IndexOutOfRangeException("Must first call Read method to
```

```
            load current data.");
    if (i>0)
        throw new ArgumentOutOfRangeException("Only Possible Column Index
            is 0");

    return typeof(OrderObject);
}

public Object GetValue(int i)
{
    if (_ReadCount == 0)
        throw new IndexOutOfRangeException("Must first call Read method to
            load current data.");
    if (i>0)
        throw new ArgumentOutOfRangeException("Only Possible Column Index
            is 0");

    return _Order;
}

public int GetValues(object[] values)
{
    if (_ReadCount == 0)
        throw new IndexOutOfRangeException("Must first call Read method to
            load current data.");

    values[0] = _Order;
    return 0;
}

public int GetOrdinal(string name)
{
    if (_ReadCount == 0)
        throw new IndexOutOfRangeException("Must first call Read method to
            load current data.");
    if (name != "Order")
    {
        throw new IndexOutOfRangeException("No such Column");
    }
    return 0;
}

public void Close()
{
}

public DataTable GetSchemaTable()
{
    throw new NotSupportedException();
}

public bool NextResult()
{
    return false;
}
```

The code below is the core of our `IDataReader` implementation. The `Read` method utilizes the associated connection to "advance a record" by pulling another Message out of the Queue. This Message is then converted into an `OrderObject` reference, which is then used internally by other *Getxx* functions.

```
public bool Read()
{
    if (_Connection == null)
        throw new OQException("Invalid Connection Object");
    if (_Connection.State != ConnectionState.Open)
        throw new OQException("Connection must be open before Reading");
    if (_Connection.MQ == null)
        throw new OQException("Connection's Internal Queue is invalid.");

    try
    {
```

Some of this code should look familiar. It is very similar to the simple Message-receiving code snippet we went through earlier in this chapter. The Message is obtained by reading from the Message Queue with a `Timespan` class indicating the timeout period as defined by the `Connection` object. Then, the `XmlSerializer` is used to de-serialize the object directly into memory in the form of an `OrderObject`.

```
        _Connection.SetState(ConnectionState.Fetching);
        _Message = _Connection.MQ.Receive(new TimeSpan(0,0,
                        _Connection.ConnectionTimeout));
        StreamReader reader = new StreamReader( _Message.BodyStream );
        XmlSerializer xs = new XmlSerializer( typeof( OrderObject) );
        _Order = (OrderObject)xs.Deserialize(reader);
        xs = null;
        reader = null;
        _ReadCount++;
        return true;
    }
    catch (MessageQueueException )
    {
        return false;
    }
    catch (InvalidOperationException)
    {
        return false;
    }
    finally
    {
        _Connection.SetState(ConnectionState.Open);
    }
  }

  }
  }
```

The OQDataAdapter

As we said before, the Data Adapter is essentially a "plug" that plugs one end into the data source via the connection (in our case, a connection to a Queue), and the other end into the `DataSet`. It is responsible for carrying changes from a `DataSet` across to the connection, and for carrying information from the connection into the `DataSet`. The following is the list of requirements for a class implementing the `IDataAdapter` interface:

Name	Type	Description
MissingMappingAction	Property	Action to take when DataSet mappings for the affected columns are not found
MissingSchemaAction	Property	Indicates whether missing source tables, columns and relationships are added to the DataSet schema, ignored, or used to generate an exception
TableMappings	Property	Indicates how a source table is to be mapped to a DataSet table
Fill	Method	Adds or refreshes rows in the DataSet to match those in the data source using the "DataSet Name"
FillSchema	Method	Adds schema definition information for a table called "Table"
Update	Method	Takes all appropriately affected rows and uses appropriate (Insert ,Update, and Delete) commands to populate

Now let's look at the code for our custom OQDataAdapter class:

```
using System;
using System.Data;

namespace Wrox.ProADONET.OQprovider
{
/// <summary>
/// Summary description for OQDataAdapter.
/// </summary>
public class OQDataAdapter: IDataAdapter
{
private OQCommand _SendCommand;
private OQCommand _ReceiveCommand;

public OQDataAdapter()
{
    //
    // TODO: Add constructor logic here
    //
}
```

We always do the same thing whether or not mappings are supplied, so here all we are doing is supplying a simple property to satisfy the requirements of the interface. We never actually use the information contained in this property internally.

```
public MissingMappingAction MissingMappingAction
{
    get
    {
```

```
        return MissingMappingAction.Passthrough;
    }
}
```

Here we are again supplying a property for the sake of satisfying the requirements of the interface. This time we are indicating that the `MissingSchemaAction` will *always* be `MissingSchemaAction.Add`.

```
public MissingSchemaAction MissingSchemaAction
{
    get
    {
        return MissingSchemaAction.Add;
    }
}
```

This property isn't supported, so we simply return a `null`.

```
public ITableMappingCollection TableMappings
{
    get
    {
        return null;
    }
}
```

The `Fill`, `FillSchema`, and `Update` methods of the `IDataAdapter` interface are essentially the core functionality of the `DataAdapter`. In our case, when `Fill` is called, we validate whether or not our `ReceiveCommand` is functioning properly. Once we have cleared the first validation code, we notice that the supplied `DataSet`'s `Orders` table will be removed. Then, we call our `FillSchema` method to define a `DataSet` schema. From there, an `OQDataReader` is used to populate the `Orders` items in the table.

```
public int Fill(DataSet dataSet)
{
    if (_ReceiveCommand == null)
        throw new OQException("Cannot Fill without a valid ReceiveCommand.");

    if (dataSet.Tables.Contains("Orders"))
        dataSet.Tables.Remove("Orders");
```

In the line of code below, we supply the parameter `SchemaType.Mapped` only because the interface requires us to supply something, even though the `FillSchema` method ignores that parameter.

```
        FillSchema(dataSet, SchemaType.Mapped);
        DataTable Orders = dataSet.Tables["Orders"];
        DataTable OrderItems = dataSet.Tables["OrderItems"];

        OQDataReader myReader = (OQDataReader)_ReceiveCommand.ExecuteReader();
        OrderObject myOrder;

        while (myReader.Read())
        {
```

```
            myOrder = myReader.GetOrder();
            DataRow newOrder = Orders.NewRow();
            newOrder["CustomerID"] = myOrder.CustomerID;
            newOrder["OrderID"] = myOrder.OrderID;
            newOrder["ShipToName"] = myOrder.ShipToName;
            newOrder["ShipToAddr1"] = myOrder.ShipToAddr1;
            newOrder["ShipToAddr2"] = myOrder.ShipToAddr2;
            newOrder["ShipToCity"] = myOrder.ShipToCity;
            newOrder["ShipToState"] = myOrder.ShipToState;
            newOrder["ShipToCountry"] = myOrder.ShipToCountry;
            newOrder["ShipMethod"] = myOrder.ShipMethod;
            newOrder["ShipToZip"] = myOrder.ShipToZip;
            Orders.Rows.Add( newOrder );
            foreach (OrderItem itm in myOrder.OrderItems)
            {
                DataRow newItem = OrderItems.NewRow();
                newItem["Quantity"] = itm.Quantity;
                newItem["StockNumber"] = itm.StockNumber;
                newItem["Price"] = itm.Price;
                newItem["OrderID"] = myOrder.OrderID;
                OrderItems.Rows.Add( newItem );
            }
        }
        // this will make everything we just put into the DataSet
        // appear as unchanged. This allows us to distinguish
        // between items that came from the Queue and items that
        // came from the DS.
        dataSet.AcceptChanges();
        return 0;
    }
```

This method creates all of the appropriate metadata in the `DataSet` by defining the appropriate tables (`Orders` and `OrderItems`), their columns, and the `DataRelations` between the two tables. It is called each time the `Fill` method is called to make sure that the `DataSet` is never corrupted and that it *always* has the metadata/schema structure appropriate for the `OrderObject` and `OrderItem` classes.

```
public DataTable[] FillSchema(DataSet dataSet, SchemaType schemaType)
{
    DataTable[] x = new DataTable[2];
    DataColumn OID_Parent;
    DataColumn OID_Child;
    DataColumn[] ParentKeys = new DataColumn[1];
    DataColumn[] ChildKeys = new DataColumn[2];

    x[0] = new DataTable("Orders");
    x[1] = new DataTable("OrderItems");

    x[0].Columns.Add( "CustomerID", typeof(string) );
    x[0].Columns.Add( "OrderID", typeof(string) );
    x[0].Columns.Add( "ShipToName", typeof(string) );
    x[0].Columns.Add( "ShipToAddr1", typeof(string) );
    x[0].Columns.Add( "ShipToAddr2", typeof(string) );
    x[0].Columns.Add( "ShipToCity", typeof(string) );
    x[0].Columns.Add( "ShipToState", typeof(string) );
    x[0].Columns.Add( "ShipToZip", typeof(string) );
    x[0].Columns.Add( "ShipToCountry", typeof(string) );
    x[0].Columns.Add( "ShipMethod", typeof(string) );
```

```
      OID_Parent = x[0].Columns["OrderID"];
      ParentKeys[0] = OID_Parent;
      x[0].PrimaryKey = ParentKeys;

      x[1].Columns.Add( "Quantity", typeof(int) );
      x[1].Columns.Add( "StockNumber", typeof(string) );
      x[1].Columns.Add( "Price", typeof(float) );
      x[1].Columns.Add( "OrderID", typeof(string) );
      OID_Child = x[1].Columns["OrderID"];
      ChildKeys[0] = OID_Child;
      ChildKeys[1] = x[1].Columns["StockNumber"];

      if (dataSet.Tables.Contains("Orders"))
         dataSet.Tables.Remove("Orders");
      if (dataSet.Tables.Contains("OrderItems"))
         dataSet.Tables.Remove("OrderItems");

      dataSet.Tables.Add( x[0] );
      dataSet.Tables.Add( x[1] );
      dataSet.Relations.Add( "OrderItems", OID_Parent, OID_Child, true );
      return x;
   }

   public IDataParameter[] GetFillParameters()
   {
      return null;
   }
```

Aside from `Fill`, `Update` is the most important method on the `DataAdapter`. This method (defined below) will use the `DataTableCollection`'s `Select` method to obtain all of the "Added" rows in the `DataSet`. We are ignoring everything other than the "Added" rows because we're maintaining the Queue model in that data can only be sent in or pulled out, and never modified while already there. Then, for each of those added rows, a `SendCommand` is executed, which as we know converts the row into an `OrderObject` (complete with line items) and then serializes that object onto the MSMQ Message's Body.

```
   public int Update(DataSet dataSet)
   {
      int rowCount = 0;
      if (_SendCommand == null)
         throw new OQException("Cannot Update Queued DataSet without
               a valid SendCommand");

      DataRow[] UpdatedOrders = dataSet.Tables["Orders"].Select("", "",
            DataViewRowState.Added);

      foreach (DataRow _Order in UpdatedOrders)
      {
         DataRow[] Items = _Order.GetChildRows("OrderItems");
         OrderObject myOrder = new OrderObject();
         myOrder.CustomerID = _Order["CustomerID"].ToString();
         myOrder.OrderID = _Order["OrderID"].ToString();
         myOrder.ShipToName = _Order["ShipToName"].ToString();
         myOrder.ShipToAddr1 = _Order["ShipToAddr1"].ToString();
         myOrder.ShipToAddr2 = _Order["ShipToAddr2"].ToString();
         myOrder.ShipToCity = _Order["ShipToCity"].ToString();
         myOrder.ShipToState = _Order["ShipToState"].ToString();
```

```
        myOrder.ShipToZip = _Order["ShipToZip"].ToString();
        myOrder.ShipToCountry = _Order["ShipToCountry"].ToString();
        myOrder.ShipMethod = _Order["ShipMethod"].ToString();
        foreach (DataRow _Item in Items)
        {
            myOrder.AddItem(_Item["StockNumber"].ToString(),
                    (int)_Item["Quantity"], (float)_Item["Price"]);
        }

    _SendCommand.Parameters["Order"] = new OQParameter( myOrder );
    _SendCommand.ExecuteNonQuery();
    rowCount++;
    }
    dataSet.Tables["OrderItems"].Clear();
    dataSet.Tables["Orders"].Clear();
    return rowCount;
}
```

The SendCommand and ReceiveCommand are both stored completely independently of each other. This allows each of the respective commands to maintain their own connections. This then allows information to be read from one Queue, displayed through a DataSet, and then pumped into another Queue to allow for some extremely sophisticated distributed processing of this order-entry system.

```
public OQCommand SendCommand
{
    get
    {
        return _SendCommand;
    }
    set
    {
    _SendCommand =  value;
    }
}

public OQCommand ReceiveCommand
{
    get
    {
        return _ReceiveCommand;
    }
    set
    {
        _ReceiveCommand = value;
    }
}

}
}
```

The OQException

The last class that we're going to implement in our custom .NET Data Provider for our distributed, Queued order-entry system is a derivation of the `DataException` class. The reason for this is that there might be some times when the client application is trapping specifically for one of the exceptions that we throw deliberately. In such a case, we throw an `OQException` rather than a standard one. It also provides us with the ability to upgrade the `Exception` class at a later date to allow it to use the Event Logging system and other complex features (for more information, see *Professional .NET Framework*, by Wrox Press, ISBN 1-861005-56-3).

Here is the brief source code to our derived `OQException` class:

```
using System;
using System.Data;

namespace Wrox.ProADONET.OQprovider
{
    /// <summary>
    /// Summary description for OQException.
    /// </summary>
    public class OQException : System.Data.DataException
    {
        public OQException()
        {

        }

        public OQException(string message) : base(message)
        {
        }

        public OQException(string message, Exception inner) :
                base(message,inner)
        {
        }
    }
}
```

As you can see, all we are doing is creating a new `Exception` class type that can be thrown and caught via the `try/catch` facilities. At some later date, we could then go back into this class and add event logging features, or more robust error tracking features if we chose.

Utilizing the Custom Data Provider

Utilizing the custom Data Provider that we've just built should actually appear quite familiar. By complying with all of the appropriate interfaces set out by the `System.Data` namespace, we provide a standard and uniform method for accessing our data source. Even though we don't support all of the methods, they are all there and the data access paradigm is similar enough so that we will be reusing our knowledge of the SQL and OLE DB Data Providers to utilize our custom provider.

At the very beginning of the chapter, we discussed that our fictitious company that was planning on providing this Queued backend infrastructure was planning on three main consumer types for this Data Provider: a Retail Store, an e-commerce web site, and a Telephone Sales call center. Next we'll go through each of these and create a very small sample application that demonstrates how each of these three main consumer types might be created for our custom Data Provider.

A Retail Store Interface

According to the design that our fictitious tutorial company came up with, the Retail Store interface simply needs to be able to provide the ability for a clerk behind the cash register to enter in orders. To do this, we'll use a `DataGrid` bound to a `DataSet`. This way, they can simply free-form enter in the information they need and then hit a button to post the orders to the Queue. Obviously, in the real world, this application would be much more robust, with a full suite of business rules to enforce, lookups, and error checking.

To create this example, we used Visual Studio.NET and created a new C# Windows Application. The first step after that was to add a reference to the DLL we generated by compiling our Data Provider Assembly (`OQProvider.dll`), which is in the `OQprovider\obj\debug` directory in the downloadable samples. Before compiling our Retail Store interface, we need to make sure that our `OQProvider` assembly is in the Global Assembly Cache (either by using the `gacutil` utility or by opening the \Winnt\Assembly folder and using the GAC shell extension). If we don't, the system will throw a `FileNotFound` exception when our application attempts to start.

We save ourselves some time by using the `OQDataAdapter`'s `FillSchema` method to pre-structure our `DataSet` before we even have any data in it. This way, we don't have to re-write code that populates the schema over and over again, and we don't have to worry about accidentally getting the schema wrong. Let's take a look at the code for the **Post Orders** button, listed below:

```
private void button1_Click(object sender, System.EventArgs e)
{
    OQConnection myConnection = new OQConnection();
    myConnection.ConnectionString = @".\Private$\OQTester";
    myConnection.Open();
    OQDataAdapter oqDA = new OQDataAdapter();
    OQCommand SendCmd = new OQCommand();
    SendCmd.CommandText = "Send";
    SendCmd.Connection = myConnection;
    oqDA.SendCommand = SendCmd;
```

The `myDS` variable in the line of code below is a private member of type `DataSet` that is initialized when the Form starts up.

```
    oqDA.Update( myDS);
    myConnection.Close();
    MessageBox.Show(this, "Orders Transmitted.");
}
```

Just like normal ADO.NET data access, everything starts with the Connection. Once we've created and opened our connection, we then create our `DataAdapter`. Then we create a new `SendCommand` object, which is just an `OQCommand` instance with the `CommandText` set to "Send". Then all we have to do is call the `Update` method on the `DataAdapter`, passing our `DataSet` as an argument, and the changes are all automatically transferred to the Queue for us. If you'll recall the `Update` code from the previous code listings, we iterate through each of the newly added rows in the `DataSet`, and create an `OrderObject` instance for each row (including its child items rows). Then, the `OrderObject` is transferred to the Queue via a `Send()` call on the Message Queue (stored in the `Connection` object).

Our Retail Store example is lacking in a couple of areas. Obviously it's not as fully featured as it can be and it doesn't contain as much error handling is it could. As an exercise, you can download the code samples and expand on them. Another lacking area is that when entering data into the `DataGrid`: if you have not moved the cursor off the current line, the `DataSet` doesn't know about it, and this can cause problems when hitting the "**Post Orders**" button. One of the application requirements mentioned at the beginning of this chapter is that some distinction be made between Fulfilled orders and Unfulfilled orders. To accomplish this, you could add a *Status* field to the `OrderObject` class and allow it to be a value of an enumerated type that would include such values as *Open, Fulfilled, Pending*, etc. That way, the distributed Order Entry system could then even incorporate a workflow or pipeline-like process where the `Order` travels from place to place, affecting various company operations until it is finally closed weeks later after the customer receives their product.

The sample code for this application is in the `RetailStore` Visual Studio .NET solution. The following is a screenshot of the Retail Store Interface in action:

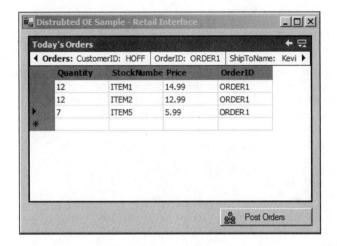

An E-Commerce Web Site Interface

Our e-commerce web site example is going to be fairly small. Rather than go through the effort of simulating the process of going through a product catalog, logging a valid customer into the system, and all the other details that make a large web site function, we'll simulate the checkout page of an e-commerce site. The checkout button is going to place the customer's order into the Queue by way of our custom Data Provider and inform the customer that their order is on its way to the warehouse.

Let's take a look at a sample of the User Interface for this simulation checkout page and then we'll look at the ASP.NET code that drives it:

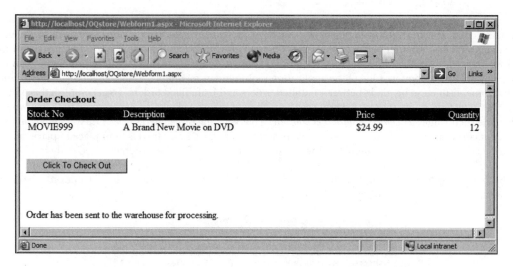

What we're looking at is a very bare-bones mock-up of a website's check-out page. The user is first greeted by the Click to Check Out button; after they click it, they are informed that the Order has been sent to the warehouse for processing. Let's take a look at the C# code in the code-behind class for the Page_Load event (we could have just as easily wired the event to the button click itself):

```csharp
private void Page_Load(object sender, System.EventArgs e)
{
    // Put user code to initialize the page here
    if (Page.IsPostBack)
    {
        // They hit the checkout button.
        OQConnection myConnection = new OQConnection();
        myConnection.ConnectionString = @".\Private$\OQTester";
        myConnection.Open();
        OQCommand SendCmd = new OQCommand();
        SendCmd.Connection = myConnection;
        SendCmd.CommandText = "Send";

        OrderObject myOrder = new OrderObject(
            "HOFF",
            "ORDER99",
            "Kevin",
            "101 Nowhere",
            "",
            "Somewhere",
            "OR",
            "97201",
            "USA",
            "FedEx");

        myOrder.AddItem("MOVIE999", 12, 24.99f);
        OQParameter myParam = new OQParameter( myOrder );
        SendCmd.Parameters["Order"] = myParam;
        SendCmd.ExecuteNonQuery();

        lblInfo.Text = "Order has been sent to the warehouse for processing.";
    }
}
```

As you can see, the process of actually getting an order into the Queue isn't all that complex. Well, it isn't complex for the consumer of the Data Provider, as they don't see all of the work that goes into facilitating that action. This application could be improved to hone your ASP.NET skills to hook the application to an XML or SQL-based product catalog, provide some forms-based authentication, and have the shopping cart actually maintain a true shopping list.

The Telephone Sales Interface

The Telephone Sales interface works very much like the web site interface. However, the difference is that it will be Windows-based and work on only one order at a time, as the people working on Telephone Sales are going to be working a single call at a time, and when they're done, they should be finished. The order should already have transmitted to the Queue with the salesperson being none the wiser.

Here's a screenshot of our Telephone Sales interface in action:

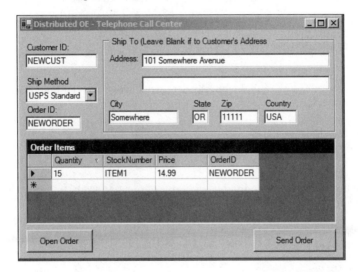

So, the Telephone Sales person gets a phone call and hits the **Open Order** button, which wipes the old data from the previous `Order` and gives them an empty slate to work with. Again, this is a sample only, and you'll find out quickly that it has a few holes (such as not typing the proper `OrderID` in the **Order Items** `DataGrid`, but that can be corrected with a little effort).

Let's take a look at the code that is executed in response to the **Send Order** button:

```
myDA.Update( myDS );
ClearOrder();
button1.Enabled = false;
MessageBox.Show(this, "Order Transmitted.");
```

In our form's initialization code, we've done the preparation work of instantiating and configuring a new `OQConnection` as well as an `OQDataAdapter` (the `myDA` variable). All we have to do is simply call the `Update` method in the `DataAdapter` and everything is handled for us. Let's take a look at the form's initialization code that goes through the motions of binding the `DataGrid` to the `OrderItems` table in our `DataSet`, as well as binding the standard controls to various columns in our `Orders` table:

```
public Form1()
{
    //
    // Required for Windows Form Designer support
    //
    InitializeComponent();

    //
    // TODO: Add any constructor code after InitializeComponent call
    //
```

Here we're going through the motions of creating and configuring the core connection supplied by our custom Data Provider. Then we create a SendCommand object that the DataAdapter will use to publish DataSet changes.

```
myConnection.ConnectionString = @".\Private$\OQTester";
myConnection.Open();
SendCmd.Connection = myConnection;
SendCmd.CommandText = "Send";
myDA.SendCommand = SendCmd;
```

We pre-configure the DataSet with the appropriate structure so we can bind to controls, even when there's no data in the DataSet.

```
myDA.FillSchema( myDS, SchemaType.Mapped );
dgItems.DataSource = myDS.Tables["OrderItems"];
```

We can bind the text boxes to the individual columns of our DataTable Orders by creating a new Binding object and adding it to that control's Bindings collection.

```
txtCustomerID.DataBindings.Add( new Binding("Text",
    myDS.Tables["Orders"], "CustomerID"));
txtOrderID.DataBindings.Add( new Binding("Text", myDS.Tables["Orders"],
    "OrderID"));
txtShipToAddr1.DataBindings.Add( new Binding("Text",
    myDS.Tables["Orders"], "ShipToAddr1"));
txtShipToAddr2.DataBindings.Add( new Binding("Text",
    myDS.Tables["Orders"], "ShipToAddr2"));
txtShipToCity.DataBindings.Add( new Binding("Text",
    myDS.Tables["Orders"], "ShipToCity"));
txtShipToState.DataBindings.Add( new Binding("Text",
    myDS.Tables["Orders"], "ShipToState"));
txtShipToCountry.DataBindings.Add(new Binding("Text",
    myDS.Tables["Orders"], "ShipToCountry"));
cboShipMethod.DataBindings.Add( new Binding("Text",
    myDS.Tables["Orders"], "ShipMethod"));

    button1.Enabled = false;
}
```

And finally, let's take a look at the ClearOrder method, which wipes the current order and sets the application user up with a fresh new order. Note that we don't have to do anything to the controls as they will automatically update whenever the DataSet changes, etc.

```
private void ClearOrder()
{
   DataRow Order = myDS.Tables["Orders"].NewRow();

   Order["CustomerID"] = "NEWCUST";
   Order["OrderID"] = "NEWORDER";
   Order["ShipToAddr1"] = "";
   Order["ShipToAddr2"] = "";
   Order["ShipToCity"] = "";
   Order["ShipToState"] = "";
   Order["ShipToZip"] = "";
   Order["ShipToCountry"] = "";
   Order["ShipMethod"] = "";
   myDS.Tables["Orders"].Rows.Clear();
   myDS.Tables["Orders"].Rows.Add( Order );
   myDS.Tables["OrderItems"].Rows.Clear();

   button1.Enabled = true;
}
```

As you can see, we're obtaining a new row, populating it with empty strings (since our schema does not allow
nulls), and then adding this new row to the Orders table. The visual controls bound to the columns of the
Orders table will automatically update and clear to reflect that the original data is no longer there.

As another exercise to polish your skills at working with the custom Data Provider, you could write a fourth
application that represents the backend administration system that continuously pulls orders out of the Queue
and simulates some processing on them, or even places them in a database using the SQL Data Provider or
OLE DB Data Provider. The possibilities are limitless, not only for this particular Data Provider, but for any
custom provider you choose to write to suit your own application and infrastructure needs.

Summary

This chapter has given you a thorough, in-depth coverage of the tasks involved in creating your own .NET
Data Provider. We've covered the reasons why you might do this, as well as the tasks involved in doing it.
In addition, throughout our coverage of .NET Data Providers we've developed a fairly complex tutorial
Data Provider that provides an infrastructure backbone for a distributed Order Entry system. After
finishing this chapter, you should feel comfortable with the following Data Provider-related tasks:

- ❑ Design a .NET Data Provider Assembly
- ❑ Create a .NET Data Provider Assembly
- ❑ Use the Data Provider Interfaces as a guideline for creating your own Data Provider
- ❑ Create a custom Connection
- ❑ Create a custom Command object
- ❑ Create a custom DataReader object
- ❑ Create a custom DataException object
- ❑ Create a custom class that can be serialized to and from MSMQ Messages
- ❑ Utilize the custom Data Provider for reading, writing, displaying, and data binding
- ❑ Put all of the technology and information together to create a fully functioning, distributed
  order-entry system

18

Case Study – Cycle Couriers

This chapter will use ADO.NET in the middle layer of a multi-tier system tracking packages for an inner city bicycle courier company. The main classes we will be working with will include:

- ❏ SqlConnection
- ❏ SqlCommand
- ❏ SqlDataAdapter
- ❏ Parameters
- ❏ DataSet, typed and untyped
- ❏ DataRelation
- ❏ DataTable
- ❏ DataGrid
- ❏ DataColumn
- ❏ DataGridTextBoxColumn
- ❏ DataGridTableStyle
- ❏ DataGridBoolColumn
- ❏ WebService

There are many ways to use ADO.NET and in this chapter we will cover the design process and the reasons behind the decisions we will make.

We will use a fictional Cycle Courier Company as an example. Let's start by taking a look at the company.

The Wxyz Consultancy Company has been contracted to develop a package tracking system for a new company called Cycle Couriers. Cycle Couriers is planning an official launch in three weeks and needs the system running before the launch. The company already has a Director, a part time Accountant and IT/Call taker person who is familiar with SQL and Windows 2000. As the company grows it intends to hire more cyclists and Call Center Operators to match demand. For the moment the Director and IT person are frantically taking calls, delivering packages, and marketing their service.

The directors expect the company to grow to handle 1000 packages a day. To handle this workload the company plans to employ:

> 1 Director
>
> 1 Accountant
>
> 1 IT/Call Center Operator
>
> 3 Call Center Operators
>
> 25 Cyclists

The IT person is expected to manage the system and has the skill to perform daily backups, archiving, and configuring the system. Each Call Center Operator will have basic IT skills.

Due to the short development time, the client has requested a staged delivery of the system. We will provide the minimum functionality to start, and then provide more features as time and money becomes available.

For this reason we will use an evolutionary development cycle, which is similar to the standard waterfall approach but enables the development to move toward several smaller staged releases. The approach also encourages the developer to design for expansion, rather than hacking a usable system that is almost impossible to modify.

Another feature of this methodology is the ability to improve the design to suit the client's requirements between evolutions, thus tailoring the system. Although evolutionary development allows for staged delivery it is important to identify all requirements before design begins. The process is shown in the following diagram:

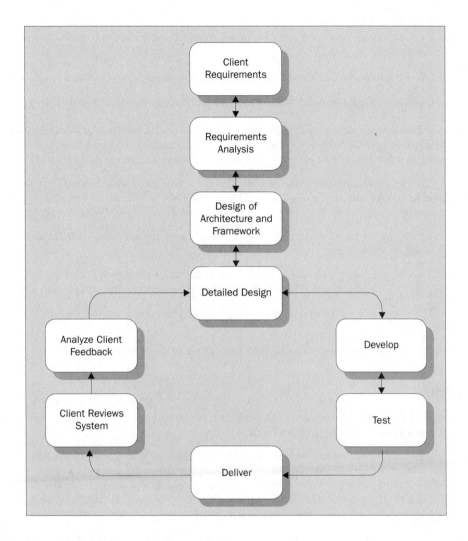

Requirements

The usual process flow is as follows:

1. The Customer places an order to the Call Center, requesting that a package or packages be collected.

2. The Call Center notifies the cyclist that there is a package to collect.

3. The Cyclist collects the package. The cyclist may choose to deliver other packages first, or may choose to pick up nearby packages before delivering those already being carried.

4. The Cyclist notifies Call Center Operator when the package has been collected.

5. The Cyclist delivers the Package. As we mentioned in Point 3, the Cyclist may decide it's easier to do other things first.

6. The Cyclist notifies the Call Center Operator when the package has been delivered.

7. The Call Center Operator notifies the Customer that the package has been delivered.

The system will have a web interface where the customer add and tracks packages. It will also have a Call Center interface where the Call Center Operator will monitor the packages and cyclists, assigning one to the other. The system will maintain a list of cyclists and their status along with lists of packages and their status.

Initially, cyclists will communicate with the Call Center via two-way radio. In the future the system could expand to a WAP interface using PDAs. This would allow the cyclist to see all the packages stacked against them and notify the Call Center Operator of deliveries and meal breaks.

The system will allow the Call Center Operator to select from a list of cyclists that are available to make collections based on their status.

The sender and addressee should be able to monitor the status of the package. Possible values are Ready for Collection, Collected, and Delivered. This information should be available through the web interface.

All data will be stored in a backend database, which will be protected from the internet and backed up on a regular basis.

Each user of the system has specific needs. Let's take a look at them now.

Customer

The customer is able to request collection of packages and monitor their movement. They will also receive an email when the package is delivered.

Customers are encouraged to make orders via the Web. However, if they wish to use a phone they can. In the initial release the Call Center Operator will simply log the order using the company web site. Future releases should add a proper telephone ordering system. If a problem arises the customer can phone the Call Center Operator. Currently the Call Operator will need to handle errors independently of the computer system, but order modification and deletion should follow in a future release.

The customer will log into the web portal using existing credentials or create a new account. If the customer has forgotten their password they may request a new one to be emailed to them.

Recipient (Addressee)

In a future release the recipient will be able to track the status of packages addressed to them using the web site but initially they can track a package by telephoning the Call Center.

Cyclist

Although the cyclist does all the work, they don't directly use the system. They use hand-held radio to receive instructions and tell the Call Center Operator of their whereabouts. This occurs when the cyclist collects a package, delivers a package, decides to go home or take a meal break. In a future release the two-way radio will be replaced with a PDA that will receive collection requests and send back delivery times.

Call Center Operator

The Call Center Operator conducts this package symphony. The Call Center Operator monitors a list containing packages that are ready for collection. When a new package appears in this list they assign it to an available cyclist and call the cyclist to add this package to their job list.

When a cyclist collects or delivers a package the Call Center Operator updates the package status, so the reported package status is always up to date. This also allows the customer to know the package's approximate whereabouts. Some tasks are automated for the Call Center Operator such as:

❑ Once a cyclist is assigned to a package the cyclist is automatically placed into the Dispatched (busy) state.

❑ When a package is marked as delivered, the system generates an email message to notify the customer of delivery.

❑ Once a cyclist has delivered all packages assigned to them their state is automatically returned to Available. A cyclist does not need to be Available in order to assign an additional package to them.

If a customer or recipient calls up the Call Center Operator the Operator must be able to have information at hand to answer questions such as "Where is my package?"

One of the Call Center Operators will double as the IT support engineer performing backups and archiving data when necessary. They will also need to know how to fix simple configuration issues. The remainder must be comfortable using a simple graphical user interface.

Design

We shall begin by determining what data is needed. This will allow us to determine the storage and transmission requirements of the data.

❑ We need information about the package. Where it is has come from, where it is, and where it is going. This information will need to be entered by the customer and passed to the Call Center Operator, and then the cyclist.

❑ Cyclist information, such as what packages they are carrying and whether they are available for work, will be required by the Call Center Operator to select to whom to assign to the package.

❑ Information about customers will be necessary so that cyclists know where to collect the packages. A customer password and email address will be useful to prevent unauthorized persons requesting pickups and viewing deliveries of our customers.

We will work with this to begin with. Later the data format will be formalized and possibly normalized.

The customer will need to place orders from a variety of locations, so the obvious interface is through the Internet. A web interface is the simplest solution to the customer data requirements – it is quite easy to build. The Call Center Operator will need access to a larger variety of information and will probably be at the same physical location as the data source. Because the Call Center Operator will be on the same LAN as the data provider this interface is not limited to web pages. The wider array of controls available to Windows applications could be used to produce a powerful user interface for the Call Center Operator.

As there are two different user interfaces accessing the same data it would be possible to lump the whole data store, process logic, application, and web interface into a single monstrous program. However, this application might be difficult to maintain and would not scale well.

This system will divide well into a client-server, n-tier architecture. In this model, processing is distributed between the client and the server, and business logic is captured in a middle tier. This model suits our purpose well as it abstracts the user interfaces from the underlying data. It enables the middle or business layer to process requests and email customers when the package is delivered. The layers are show in the following diagram:

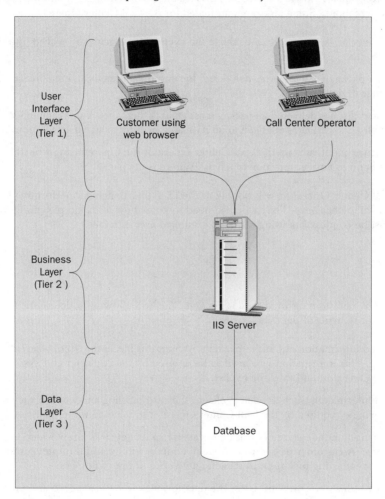

User Interface Layer

The customers, cyclists, and call operators interact with the system in different ways. We need to plan the interfaces that they will use. Let's look at the interface design for each of these groups.

The Customer View

A customer should either log into the web interface using existing credentials or create a new account. There needs to be a way a customer can request a new password if they have forgotten theirs. Emailing it to them is easy enough. To request a pickup the customer will first need to state where the package is going and possibly some delivery notes. The following form should allow this:

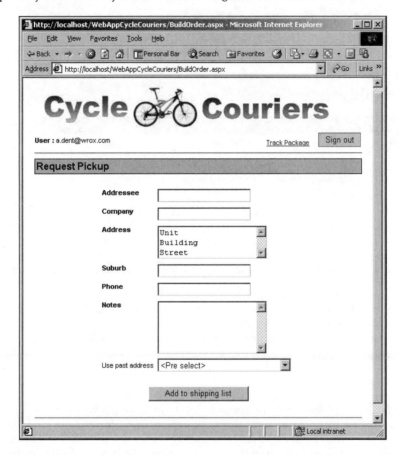

We need to allow for the customer to have more than one package for collection. As they add packages the system will add them to a list, which they may view after each new package is added. The following form should enable this:

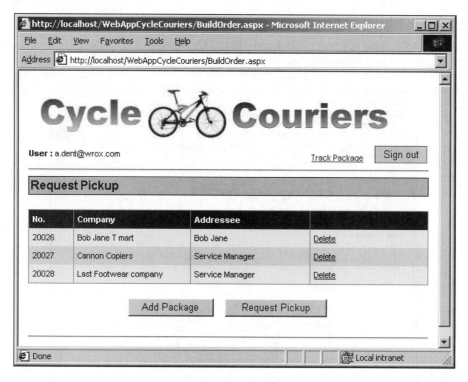

Once the customer has entered all the packages they have for collection at present, then they will need a way to notify the Call Center Operator to dispatch a cyclist. Clicking the Request Pickup button shown will put the package in a ready for collection state. The Call Center Operator will need to have access to a list of packages ready for collection and be notified of new packages in the list.

To save the customer printing out shipping dockets the request pickup command should also print the shipping dockets.

The customers also need to be able to monitor the status of all packages. To do this we should build a web form that lists the packages that they have ordered for pick-up, and provides detailed information on the selected one. As the list of packages may become very long over time the list should be in pages, and also limited in its range by dates. The form will look like this:

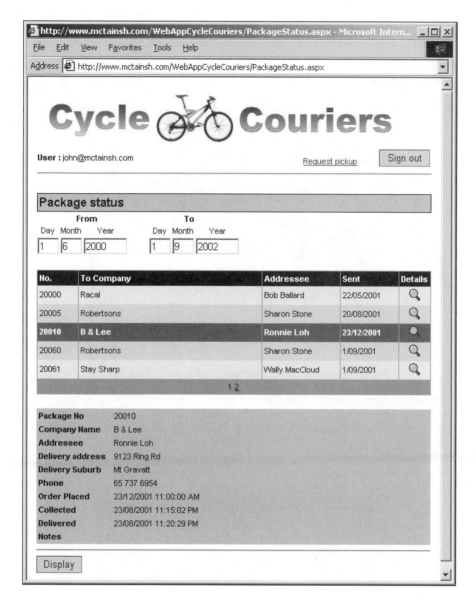

The Cyclist View

In the initial product evolution the cyclist receives all instructions from the Call Center Operator so does not directly interact with the system. However, the system may switch to a WAP interface, which should be taken into account now to enable easier implementation later.

The Call Center Operator View

The Call Center Operators' interface needs three main views:

❑   A Customer view allowing the operator to review the registered customers. There is initially no need to modify this data, it is just handy to have at hand.

❑   A table showing cyclists and their status. It should allow inactive cyclists to be filtered out since they are no longer required.

❑   A list of the currently active packages.

The Call Center Operator should also be able to change the cyclist state if need be as follows:

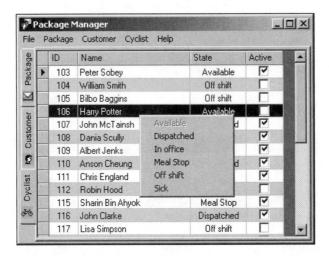

The most important information the Call Center Operator needs is the list of packages. As this is how they are notified of new packages that are ready for collection, it should be filterable on various package states. Also, to enable quick location of customer packages, the list should be filterable by customer.

Finally, the table should be sortable by column. This will allow the operator to click on cyclist column to quickly see all package assigned to that cyclist. The form should look something like this:

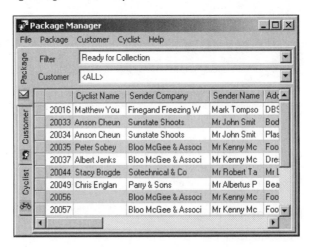

The system should prevent operators viewing all customers and all packages, as this may overload the system.

The Call Center Operator needs to be able to assign a package or group of packages to a cyclist by clicking on the packages and using a menu item to assign them to a cyclist. In the next evolution of the system when a cyclist is assigned a package, a WAP message should be sent to the cyclist's PDA and a timer set to ensure the request is acknowledged.

Business Layer

Here the business logic, which captures the rules that govern application processing, connects the user at one end with the data source at the other. The functions that the rules govern closely follow the Cycle Courier Company's everyday business tasks.

We will need business objects represent to main entities managed by the system. They include:

❑   Customer

❑   Package

❑   Cyclist

Customer

The processes that need to occur with customers are:

❑   Notify them when a package is delivered

❑   Verify the password

❑   Issue a new password

❑   Add a new customer

❑   Edit a customer's details (in future release)

Package

The processes that need to occur with packages are:

❑   Get all packages matching a filter criteria

❑   Add a new package

❑   Delete a package

❑   Get package history for a given customer

❑   Change the package state

❑   Update the package time stamps

Cyclist

The processes that need to occur with packages are:

❑   Get all cyclist data

❑   Set the cyclist state

681

❑   Dispatch a cyclist

❑   Release a cyclist from a package

❑   Change the package state

Web Services are a good choice for the business layer because they allow simple connection by both web applications and windows applications. Their tight integration to the Visual Studio .NET IDE also allows for seamless debugging and implementation.

Although it is necessary to design all business logic at this time, we will only present designs for user authentication and package status.

User Authentication

To ensure user privacy we will implement a login for the user when they want to use the system. Finally we should not be able to see the user's password at any time. To prevent anyone reading a user's password, the system will hash the password when the user enters it and the hash will be stored. To verify the password the system will hash the attempted password and compare the hashed values. This prevents the password ever being decoded. When the user forgets their password a new password will be randomly generated, sent to the user via email and hashed before storing.

Package Status Change

A package can be in one of four states:

❑   Being prepared for shipping

❑   Ready for collection

❑   In transit in the cyclist's bag

❑   Delivered to the client

The time the package enters the last three states will be useful to determine the courier's delivery performance. By creating three timestamps on the package record, Time Order Placed, Time Collected, and Time Delivered, we are able to monitor delivery statistics and determine which state the package is in. For example, if the Time Collected time stamp is set and the Time Delivered stamp is not set then we know that the package is in the "In transit in the cyclist's bag" state.

Data layer

ADO.NET provides a method of accessing most database sources so a choice of where the data comes from is basically limited by suitability and client preference. The IT person who will be maintaining the system is trained to use Microsoft SQL 2000, which is quite suitable for this purpose. Because the user interface layer never deals directly with the data layer, only the business layer would need to be modified if the data source was significantly changed.

Using OleDb data providers would allow the client to connect to a variety of data sources. However, using SqlClient will give significant performance benefits with SQL 2000 and because it is extremely unlikely the client will change from SQL 2000 we will use SqlClient.

Implementation

Implementation starts or design ends with finalizing the database detail in tables and fields. From the previous section we saw a need for data representing Packages, Customers, and Cyclists.

Database Detail

In some cases the data tables will require normalization, which will add additional tables. Where possible we will normalize the design to reduce data duplication.

Customers

The Customers table needs to hold details of each customer. The data will be entered via the Internet, detailing the customer and the package collection address. The field definitions will be as follows:

Column Name	Type	Length	Description
CustomerID	int	4	This is the primary key. The auto-incrementing column uniquely identifies the customer. It serves as foreign key to the Packages table.
CompanyName	nvarchar	40	Name of the company from which the package is being sent.
ContactName	nvarchar	30	Name of the sender.
ContactTitle	nvarchar	30	Job title of the sender.
Address	nvarchar	60	Address that the package is to be collected from.
Suburb	nvarchar	15	The suburb that the package is to be collected from. Useful for planning which cyclist to assign to a package.
Phone	nvarchar	24	The contact number to call if there are any queries regarding the package.
Email	nvarchar	50	The email address of the sender. This serves as the user name when logging into the internet portal and the address delivery confirmation is sent to.
Password	char	50	This is the user's internet login password. A cryptographic hash function stores the password, which is never decrypted. In such a case where passwords are stored, only the hash is stored and the hash is compared every time. This makes it impossible to get to know the password even if someone manages to hack into the database. This provides maximum security.
Notes	text		Notes about the customer.

Cyclists Table

The Cyclists table list the cyclists employed by the courier company to transport the packages. The list will remain fairly small, slowly growing as employees come and go. Because each cyclist can be in a limited number of states, we will normalize the state field, separating the states out into another table. The CyclistStateID will be updated regularly. The field definitions are as follows:

Column Name	Type	Length	Description
CyclistID	int	4	This is the primary key. The auto-incrementing column uniquely identifies the customer. It serves as foreign key to the Packages table.
Name	nvarchar	50	Name of the cyclist.
CyclistStateID	char	2	This is a foreign key linking to the CyclistStates table holding the current state of the cyclist. Values could be AV for available or DS for Dispatched.
Active	bit	1	Set to 1 if the cyclist is still actively working for the courier company. Cyclists who have retired or left the company are set to 0.

CyclistStates Table

The CyclistStates table contains a short list of possible states the cyclist may be in. The cyclist can only be in one state, which determines if they will be assigned to jobs or not. The state list is expected to remain static configured. It can also be used to build a pick list when the Call Center Operator is selecting what state to set the cyclist to. The field definitions are as follows:

Column Name	Type	Length	Description
CyclistStateID	char	2	This is the primary key. The unique value is a two letter short form code abbreviating the state the cyclist is in. Two states are hard coded into the system AV the status the cyclist is placed in once all packages have been delivered. DS the state the cyclist is placed in once they are assigned to a package.
Title	nchar	20	A descriptive name for the state.
Assignable	bit	1	True (1) if the cyclist can be assigned to packages in this state.

Packages Table

The Packages table links the three major elements of the system together. Each row in the Packages table represents a shipment item that is in one of the following states:

- ❑ Being prepared for shipping
- ❑ Ready for collection
- ❑ In transit in the cyclist's bag
- ❑ Delivered to the client.

Each package has only one Customer who owns it. Each package may have zero or one cyclist who is assigned to it.

The field definitions are as follows:

Column Name	Type	Length	Description
PackageID	int	4	This is the primary key. The auto incrementing column uniquely identifies the package.
CustomerID	int	4	This is the foreign key to the `Customer` who owns this package. It cannot be `null`.
CyclistID	int	4	This is the foreign key to the `Cyclist` who is currently assigned to this package. It may be `null` until the call center operator assigns a cyclist to the package.
CompanyName	nvarchar	40	Destination company name.
ContactName	nvarchar	30	Destination person or addressee.
Address	nvarchar	60	Address that the package is to be delivered to.
Suburb	nvarchar	15	The suburb that the package is to be delivered to. This can help when planning which cyclist to assign to other packages.
Phone	nvarchar	24	Phone contact of the destination addressee.
TimeOrderPlaced	datetime	8	The time that the customer finalizes the order.
TimeCollected	datetime	8	The time that the cyclist has collected the package.
TimeDelivered	datetime	8	The time that the package has been delivered to the addressee's company.
Notes	text		Free form text area where the customer may type any notes they wish to appear on the shipping docket.

Relationships

Finally we can put it all together in the following diagram:

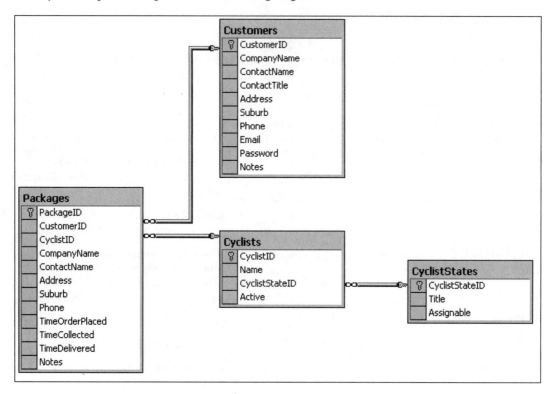

Class Description

Using a multi-tier environment allows the interface to operate without a detailed knowledge of the underlying data structure. For this reason three Web Services are developed as interfaces to represent the Customer, Package, and Cyclist. As the Web Services reside on the same machine and namespace, they also cooperate with each other. For example, when a package is delivered, the Package service calls the Customer service to send an email to the customer notifying them that the package has been delivered.

Access to the underlying database could be done using either typed or untyped datasets. In a real-life situation, we'd normally use typed datasets throughout. Typed datasets produce cleaner code, and provide greater safety because they can check for errors at compile time. In Visual Studio .NET, we can even use typed datasets to provide syntax highlighting as we type. Occasionally it is easier to simply declare a `DataSet` object, without the added hassle of subclassing it. For this reason untyped datasets are useful, and we will use them here.

We are using the `SqlClient` Data Provider for data access to obtain maximum performance from SQL Server 2000. However, if this were to be deployed on many different environments we would have used `OleDb` Data Provider as that would allow connections to a greater variety of data sources, at the cost of performance.

ServiceCustomer

The `ServiceCustomer` class represents the customer, and the actions and attributes associated with them.

The following diagram shows the service's main attributes and methods:

```
ServiceCustomer

-m_eventLog : EventLog

-m_sqlConn : SqlConnection

...

-GetCustomerID( in sEmailAddress : string ) : int

-GetCustomerEmail( in nCustomerID : int ) : string

+NotifyPackageDelivered(in nCustomerID int, nPackageID : int )

+FindEmail( in sEmailAddress : string, in bErrorState : bool ) : bool

+SetPassword( in sEmailAddress : string, in sPassword : string ) :
   bool

+VerifyPassword( in sEmailAddress : string,
   in sPassword : string ) : bool

+GetTableSchema() : DataSet

+UpdateTable( in ds : DataSet ) : bool

+GetCustomer( in nCustomerID : int ) : DataSet

+GetAllCustomers() : DataSet
```

We use `SqlCommand` Parameters to populate the datasets, as shown in the `GetCustomerID` method. `GetCustomerID` uses an email address to obtain the ID of the customer. We need to do this because the web interface uses the email address to identify the customer but packages associated with the customer are identified by `CustomerID`. Here's the code that we use:

```
public const string FIELD_CUSTOMER_ID   = "CustomerID";
public const string FIELD_EMAIL   = "Email";
public const string TABLE_CUSTOMERS   = "Customers";
public const string PARAM_EMAIL   = "@LookForEmail";
private System.Data.SqlClient.SqlConnection m_sqlConn;
...
SqlCommand sqlCmdSelEmail = new SqlCommand(
    "SELECT " + FIELD_CUSTOMER_ID +
    ", " + FIELD_EMAIL + " FROM " + TABLE_CUSTOMERS +
    " WHERE " +   FIELD_EMAIL + " = " + PARAM_EMAIL );
sqlCmdSelEmail.Parameters.Add(PARAM_EMAIL, sEmailAddress );
sqlCmdSelEmail.Connection = m_sqlConn;
SqlDataAdapter da = new SqlDataAdapter( sqlCmdSelEmail );
DataTable dt = new DataTable();
da.Fill( dt );
if( dt.Rows.Count > 0 )
    return (int)dt.Rows[0][FIELD_CUSTOMER_ID];
// Return no match found
```

In this code the following SQL select statement would be created when looking for `a.dent@wrox.com.au`:

```
SELECT CustomerID, Email FROM Customers WHERE Email =
    'a.dent@wrox.com.au'
```

The above code highlights how it is useful to define the table and field names as constants. Doing this makes changing the column names easier. The compiler can also detect mistyped constant names, while it could not detect mistyped string values. This code also shows how the `@LookForEmail` parameter is used with a `SqlCommand`.

Using `Parameter` objects avoids any SQL notation such as single quote (') and double quote (") from affecting the processing of the `SELECT` command. Sometimes users can bring down a system by including a ' in an input box on a web site, but not if we use parameters. Each SQL notation within the `sEmailAddress` string is converted into the appropriate escape sequence for its parameter type.

The `GetTableSchema` and `UpdateTable` methods highlight one of the limitations of untyped datasets. To use the `SqlDataAdapter Update` method to insert a new row into the table, it is first necessary to build the destination table schema in the `DataSet`. In this code we achieve this by calling `FillSchema` to set up the dataset. Rows are then inserted into the returned `DataSet`, which is then sent using `UpdateTable` to write to the database. This involves two round trips, one to get the schema and one to write the data. If a typed `DataSet` was used only the `UpdateTable` trip would be necessary. In this case a typed dataset would have been much more efficient, however this may not be an option in a scripting language that does not allow us to create new classes. Here is the `GetTableSchema` method:

```
public const string TABLE_NAME    = "Customers";
...
public DataSet GetTableSchema()
{
    try
    {
        DataSet ds = new DataSet();
        m_sqlDACustomer.FillSchema( ds, SchemaType.Source, TABLE_NAME );
        return ds;
    }
    catch( Exception ex )
    {
        m_eventLog.WriteEntry(
            "GetTableSchema() Failed\n" + ex.Message,
            EventLogEntryType.Error );
    }
    return null;
}
```

And here is the `UpdateTable` method:

```
public bool UpdateTable( DataSet ds )
{
    try
    {
        m_sqlDACustomer.Update( ds );
        return true;
    }
```

```
    catch( Exception ex )
    {
       m_eventLog.WriteEntry(
           "UpdateTable() Failed\n" + ex.Message,
           EventLogEntryType.Error );
    }
    return false;
}
```

When a package has been delivered an email is sent to the customer using SMTP with the following code. The code creates a mail message with a plain text body and sends it. No error is returned if the send fails:

```
MailMessage msgMail = new MailMessage();
msgMail.To = GetCustomerEmail( nCustomerID );
msgMail.From = "support@cyclecouriers.com";
msgMail.Subject = "Package " + nPackageID + " delivered.";
msgMail.BodyFormat = MailFormat.Text;
msgMail.Body = "Your package has just been delivered.";
SmtpMail.Send(msgMail);
```

Ideally this message would also contain information about the package. The `SmtpMail.Send` method will only work on Windows NT Server or Window 2000 Server that a 2000 server with an SMTP service running. The default installation of Window 2000 Server should not require configuration of SMTP but it will need access to a DNS to function.

ServicePackage

`ServicePackage` represents actions that can be performed on single or multiple packages. The `Package` is the central object in the system; it calls both the customer and cyclist objects in several instances where collaboration is necessary. The major methods and attributes are shown below:

ServicePackage

-m_eventLog : EventLog

-m_sqlConn : SqlConnection

. . .

-GetPackageCustomerID(in nPackageID : int) : int

+GetPackageCyclistID(in nPackageID : int) : int

-DbDate(in dt : DateTime) : string

+GetHistory(in dtFrom:DateTime, in dtTo:DateTime, in sEmail:string):DataSet

+GetOpenOrders(in sEmail : string) : DataSet

+GetPackets(in state : PacketStates, in nCustomerID : int,
    in nCyclistID : int) : DataSet

-GetDataSet(in sSelectCmd : string) : DataSet

+AddPackage(in ds : PackagesDataSet, in sEmail : string) : bool

---

Table continued on following page

```
ServicePackage

+DeletePackage( in nPackageID : int ) : bool

+GetPastAddresses( in sEmail : string ) : DataSet

+SetPackageState( in state : PacketStates,
    in nPackageIDs : int [] ) : bool

+TagForCollection( in nPackageIDs : int [] ) : DataSet

+AssignCyclist( in nCyclistID : int,
    in nPackageIDs : int [] ) : string
```

Adding a new record using an untyped `DataSet` meant calling the Web service twice – once to get the schema, once to write the new record. The following code uses a typed `DataSet` so only one call is necessary. Also, before the data is written to the database each record has the `CustomerID` field populated by looking up the user's email address. This is necessary because the Web Forms Application only identifies the customer by email address, but relationships to other tables are based on `CustomerID`:

```
public bool AddPackage ( PackagesDataSet ds, string sEmail )
{
    try
    {
        // Skip if no data
        if( ds.Packages.Rows.Count < 1 )
            return false;

        // Determine the Customer ID from the Email
        ServiceCustomer serCusr = new ServiceCustomer();
        int nCustomerID = serCusr.GetCustomerID( sEmail );

        // Assign Customer ID
        foreach( PackagesDataSet.PackagesRow row in ds.Packages.Rows )
            row.CustomerID = nCustomerID;

        // Add the new rows to the database
        int nRowsAdded = m_sqlDAPackages.Update( ds );
        return( nRowsAdded == ds.Packages.Rows.Count );
    }
    catch( Exception ex )
    {
        m_eventLog.WriteEntry(
            "ServicePackage.AddPackage() Failed\n" + ex.Message,
            EventLogEntryType.Error );
    }
    return false;
}
```

The state of each package is stored in the `Packages` table. Although this state is not held in any one field, it is determined by the existence of time stamps in the `TimeOrderPlaced`, `TimeCollected`, and `TimeDelivered` fields. The `PacketStates` enumeration is used to indicate the package state to read or set.

The following code sets the package state by placing a time stamp in the appropriate field. Initially an `SqlCommand` is constructed and `SqlDbType.DateTime` and `SqlDbType.Int` fields are defined. The `UPDATE` command is issued for each package passed in. Further processing occurs when a package is delivered. In this case the Customer service and Cyclist service are called to notify the customer and check if the cyclist has delivered all their packages:

```
const string TAG_TIME        = "@CurrentDateTime";
const string TAG_PACKAGE_ID  = "@CurrentPackageID";
const string TAG_TIME_FIELD  = "@TimeFieldName";
...
// Build UPDATE command string
string sUpdate ="UPDATE Packages " +
        " SET " + TAG_TIME_FIELD + " = " + TAG_TIME +
        " WHERE PackageID = " + TAG_PACKAGE_ID;
switch( state )
{
   case PacketStates.PickupRequested :
      sUpdate = sUpdate.Replace( TAG_TIME_FIELD, "TimeOrderPlaced" );
      break;
   case PacketStates.Collected :
      sUpdate = sUpdate.Replace( TAG_TIME_FIELD, "TimeCollected" );
      break;
   case PacketStates.Delivered :
      sUpdate = sUpdate.Replace( TAG_TIME_FIELD, "TimeDelivered" );
      break;
   default:
      return false;
}
SqlCommand sqlCmdUpdate = new SqlCommand( sUpdate, m_sqlConn );
sqlCmdUpdate.Parameters.Add( TAG_TIME, SqlDbType.DateTime );
sqlCmdUpdate.Parameters.Add( TAG_PACKAGE_ID, SqlDbType.Int );
m_sqlConn.Open();

// Set the TimeOrderPlaced value
foreach( int nPackageID in nPackageIDs )
{
   // Tag the record as ready to collect
   sqlCmdUpdate.Parameters[TAG_PACKAGE_ID].Value = nPackageID;
   sqlCmdUpdate.Parameters[TAG_TIME].Value = DateTime.Now;
   sqlCmdUpdate.ExecuteNonQuery();

   // If delivered the Email Customer that package has been delivered
   if( state == PacketStates.Delivered )
   {
      int nCustomerID = GetPackageCustomerID( nPackageID );
      ServiceCustomer serCusr = new ServiceCustomer();
      serCusr.NotifyPackageDelivered( nCustomerID, nPackageID );

      // Also check of cyclist is free from all current jobs
      int nCyclistID = GetPackageCyclistID( nPackageID );
      ServiceCyclist serCyclist = new ServiceCyclist();
      serCyclist.AttemptCyclistRelease( nCyclistID );
   }
}
return true;
...
finally
{
   m_sqlConn.Close();
}
```

The Packages database table could have been normalized further, by adding a table of destination addresses and referencing them through a foreign key. We won't normalize this, so that purging packages over a certain age does not require further referential integrity checks. The normalized design would require the administrator to verify an old delivery address was not linked to any packages before it could be purged.

When making an order, the customer can choose from the last ten addresses that they used. This makes it easy for the customer to reuse a earlier address by repopulating the addressee details if a selection is made from the recent addresses list. To extract this information the following SQL statement was used:

```
SELECT TOP 10 Max(PackageID) , Packages.CompanyName ,
      Packages.ContactName , Packages.Address ,
      Packages.Suburb , Packages.Phone
   FROM Packages
   INNER JOIN Customers ON
      Packages.CustomerID = Customers.CustomerID
   WHERE Customers.Email = 'a.dent@wrox.com'
   GROUP BY Packages.CompanyName , Packages.ContactName ,
      Packages.Address , Packages.Suburb , Packages.Phone
   ORDER BY 1 DESC
```

ServiceCyclist

The `ServiceCyclist` class basically encapsulates the `Cyclists` and `CyclistStates` tables, representing a `Cyclist` object. It uses typed datasets to handle and return data. Its purpose is to return the cyclist and state datasets and manage the cyclist state. The following diagram shows the structure of the class:

```
ServiceCyclist

-m_eventLog : EventLog

-m_sqlConn : SqlConnection

. . .

+GetAllCyclists() : CyclistsDataSet

+ SetState( in CyclistID : int, in sStateOld : string,
   in sStateNew : string ) : bool

+Dispatch( in nCyclistID : int ) : bool

+AttemptCyclistRelease( in nCyclistID : int ) : bool
```

`SetState` is a key method in the `Cyclist` class, which manages the change of state for the cyclist. It modifies the wizard-generated `m_sqlDACyclists DataAdapter` to return only the cyclist to be modified by appending a `WHERE` clause to it. Once the data row is read, states are verified to ensure the cyclist was actually in the state the caller believed it to be before it is modified and written back to the database.

```
// Modify the data adapter to work on a single line using where clause
string sOldSelect = m_sqlSelectCyclists.CommandText;
string sWhere = " WHERE CyclistID = " + nCyclistID;
try
{
   CyclistsDataSet ds = new CyclistsDataSet();
   m_sqlSelectCyclists.CommandText += sWhere;
   m_sqlDACyclists.Fill( ds );
   if( ds.Cyclists.Rows.Count == 1 )
   {
      CyclistsDataSet.CyclistsRow dr = (CyclistsDataSet.CyclistsRow)
         ds.Cyclists.Rows[0];
      if( sStateOld == "" || sStateOld == dr.CyclistStateID )
```

```
        {
            dr.CyclistStateID = sStateNew;
            if( m_sqlDACyclists.Update( ds ) == 1 )
                return true;
        }
    }
}
catch( Exception ex )
{
    ...
}
finally
{
    m_sqlSelectCyclists.CommandText = sOldSelect;
}
return false;
```

Web Interface classes

The Web interface consists of one HTML page in the IIS root directory and three web forms in the secure area under the directory of WebAppCycleCouriers. It allows anyone to view the opening page, then requires authentication to review or place orders.

Security is based on Forms authentication, which is sometimes called cookie-based security. To enable this, the following lines are placed in the web.config file of the WebAppCycleCouriers directory where authentication is required:

```
<configuration>
    <system.web>
        <authentication mode="Forms">
            <forms name=".cyclecouriers" loginUrl="login.aspx"
                protection="All" timeout="60">
            </forms>
        </authentication>
        <authorization>
            <deny users="?" />
        </authorization>
...
```

These settings simply direct any user to the login.aspx page unless they have been authenticated.

Opening page

The opening page could be called default.html and would contain information about the company, directing the customer to the BuildOrder.aspx or PackageStatus.aspx pages that are described later.

Login

Customers are automatically redirected to login.aspx if they do not have the appropriate cookie. Here they are given the opportunity to login, sign up, or request a new password. To login the given password is hashed and searched for in the database. If a row is returned then the credentials must be correct. The following code is called on the Web Service:

```
// Hash the password
string sHashPassword =
    FormsAuthentication.HashPasswordForStoringInConfigFile (
```

```
            sPassword, "md5" );

    // Setup the select command
    SqlCommand sqlCmdCheck = new SqlCommand(
         "SELECT Email FROM Customers WHERE Email = @CustomerEmail " +
         " AND Password = @Password" );
    sqlCmdCheck.Parameters.Add( "@CustomerEmail", sEmailAddress );
    sqlCmdCheck.Parameters.Add( "@Password", sHashPassword );
    sqlCmdCheck.Connection = m_sqlConn;
    SqlDataAdapter da = new SqlDataAdapter( sqlCmdCheck );

    // Read a datatabe if a match found
    DataTable dt = new DataTable();
    da.Fill( dt );
    if( dt.Rows.Count > 0 )
       return true;
```

We encrypt the password with `HashPasswordForStoringInConfigFile`, and use a SQL SELECT statement with a WHERE clause that only returns rows that match the email address and hashed password. Therefore only if the email address and password match, will the row count be non zero indicating a valid login. Note that the password is not decrypted at any stage. If the login is successful or a new customer is created they are redirected to the page they initially requested with the following code:

```
FormsAuthentication.RedirectFromLoginPage(
     m_tbEmailAddress.Text, m_cbRememberMe.Checked );
```

Build Order

Building an order consists of adding package pickup addresses. As each item is added it is placed in the packages table. The packages that have been entered are displayed in a grid on the Build Orders page. The user can delete them before collection is requested by clicking on the delete hyperlink on the grid. The following code deletes an item using the sender's `DataGridCommandEventArgs` to identify the row:

```
private void m_dataGrid_DeleteCommand(object source,
       System.Web.UI.WebControls.DataGridCommandEventArgs e)
{
    localhost.ServicePackage serPack = new localhost.ServicePackage();
    int nPackageID = Int32.Parse( e.Item.Cells[0].Text );
    serPack.DeletePackage( nPackageID );
    DisplayPackageList();
}
```

When a customer who has order history, places an order, the **Use past addresses** list is populated as shown opposite. The SQL command discussed in *ServicePackage* earlier produces this list. The `DataSet` of the list is held in `Session[SESSION_ADDRESS_HISTORY]` to be retrieved and used to pre-fill the address fields if the customer makes a selection from the list. Note: Unless each string in the list is unique, you will need to fill the list with `ListItem` to ensure `SelectedIndex` returns the actual selection.

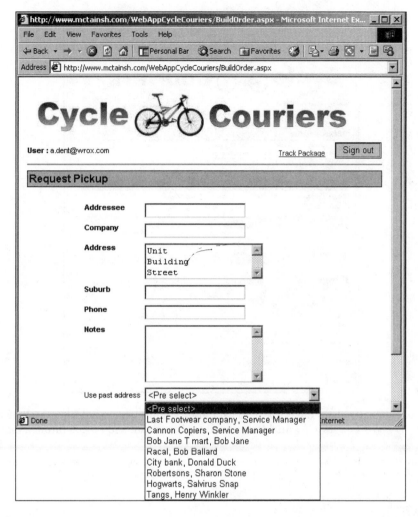

Package Status

`PackageStatus.aspx` allows the customer to review the status of all their packages. As this may be quite a long list, it is limited by date range and incorporates paging in the data display grid. The following picture shows the package in the range 1-June-2000 to 1-Sept-2002. As there are more than five packages in this range the grid enables the customer to display different pages of the listing. The details button has been pressed for package 20010:

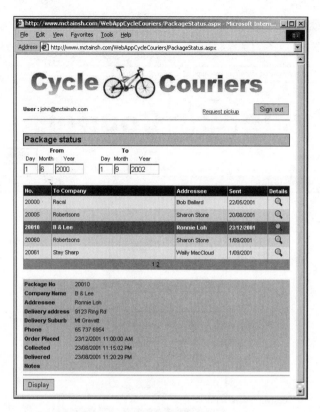

The following code populates the `DataGrid` with history information read from the Web Service. The `DataTable` is saved as a session variable and used to show detail and paging through the `DataGrid`.:

```
localhost.ServicePackage serPack = new localhost.ServicePackage();
DataSet ds = serPack.GetHistory( dtFrom, dtTo, User.Identity.Name );
DataTable dt = ds.Tables[0];
Session["dtPackages"] = dt;
m_dataGrid.DataSource = dt;
m_dataGrid.DataBind();
```

Note that storing complex objects in session variables for a large number of users can become very inefficient, and alternative methods should be sought where possible.

Call Center Operator Application

Because the Call Center Operator controls the cyclists, who in turn control the packages, the Call Center Operator must have the most up-to-date information. This is achieved by polling for the latest data. As the load on the system increases and more Call Center Operator stations are deployed the polling method would no longer be practical. With more data moving around, the Web Service should notify the client of changes as they occur. Unfortunately, the current version of the SOAP protocol does not allow for unsolicited messages with Web Services and so another communications method would be required. Microsoft .NET Remoting technology provides a framework for distributing objects across process boundaries and machine boundaries, which would suit this requirement.

The `CallCenter` application has three main views. The Customer view allows the operator to review the list of customers in a `DataGrid`. It is a read-only view and mainly used to feed data for the Package view. The Cyclist view shows a list of cyclists the company has and is using. Adding a filter to the list controls the view of active and inactive cyclists, as shown here:

```
m_dsCyclists.Cyclists.DefaultView.RowFilter = "Active = 1";
```

The display of cyclist information is made up of the information in the `Cyclists` table and state descriptions from the `CyclistStates` table. These two tables are joined in the `m_dsCyclists` `DataSet` with a `DataRelation` as follows:

```
DataRelation relCyclistState = new DataRelation( "RelCyclistState",
    ds.CyclistStates.CyclistStateIDColumn,
    ds.Cyclists.CyclistStateIDColumn );
m_dsCyclists.Relations.Add( relCyclistState );
```

The following screen shotshows the `Cyclists` table:

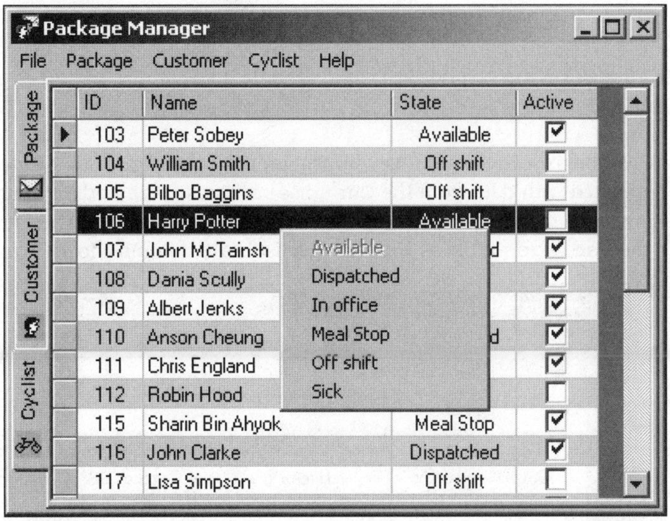

In the initial product release the cyclist state is set when the cyclist calls. If PDA's are implemented at a later date, this will be automatic when the cyclist enters data into the PDA. The cyclist state is displayed on the Cyclist view. Doing this requires another column in the `DataRelation`, which takes its data from the parent table as follows:

```
DataColumn colNew = new DataColumn();
colNew.DataType    = System.Type.GetType( "System.String" );
colNew.ColumnName = "State";
colNew.Expression = "Parent.Title";
relCyclistState.ChildTable.Columns.Add( colNew );
m_dgCyclists.DataSource = relCyclistState.ChildTable;
```

The `DataRelations` is used to display the data.

To change the cyclist state the right mouse click is captured and a context menu displayed with the possible states displayed with the following code:

```
// Determine the hit location
Point pntControl = m_dgCyclists.PointToClient( Control.MousePosition );
Control ctrl = m_dgCyclists.GetChildAtPoint( pntControl );
DataGrid.HitTestInfo ht = m_dgCyclists.HitTest( pntControl );

// Select the item and display the menu
if( ht.Row >= 0 )
{
   m_dgCyclists.Select( ht.Row );
   ContextMenu contextMenuStates = new ContextMenu();
   foreach( CyclistsDataSet.CyclistStatesRow dr in
     m_dsCyclists.CyclistStates.Rows )
   {
     MenuItem mi = new MenuItem( dr.Title,
        new EventHandler( contextMenuStates_Click ) );
     mi.Enabled = ( m_dgCyclists[ht.Row,2].ToString() != dr.Title );
     contextMenuStates.MenuItems.Add( mi );
   }
   // Get Cyclist ID
   m_nCyclistIDForConMenu = (int)m_dgCyclists[ht.Row,0];
   contextMenuStates.Show( m_dgCyclists, pntControl );
}
```

The Package view shown below provides the key information for the Call Center Operator to track packages. The DataGrid is populated with data from the Customers, Cyclists and Packages table. The **Sender Company** column is a simple data relation based on the primary CustomerID key in the Customers table and a foreign key in the Packages table as with the Cyclist **State** column shown previously:

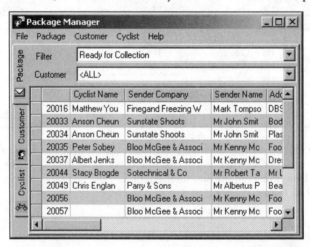

Not all packages have an assigned cyclist so this information is added using a lookup into the Customer table that is part of the typed dataset as follows:

```
public const string FIELD_CYCLIST_NAME      = "CyclistName";
public const string FIELD_CYCLIST_ID      = "CyclistID";
...
```

```
// Add additonal information columns such as Cyclist name
ds.Tables["Packages"].Columns.Add( FIELD_CYCLIST_NAME );
foreach( DataRow dr in dtPackages.Rows )
{
    // Display the Cyclist Name
    if( !dr.IsNull(FIELD_CYCLIST_ID) )
    {
        int nCyclistID = (int)dr[FIELD_CYCLIST_ID];
        dr[FIELD_CYCLIST_NAME] =
            m_dsCyclists.Cyclists.FindByCyclistID( nCyclistID ).Name;
    }
}
```

The Call Center Operator can review any package by filtering on the customer or package state. This is achieved by refreshing the data when the Package filter or Package customer droplist changes.

When a cyclist is assigned a group of packages the list of available cyclists is displayed. The information for the list is held in two tables; the cyclist Active flag is in the Cyclists table and the Assignable flag is held in the CyclistStates table. The following code loops through the list to return only the active assignable cyclists:

```
foreach( CyclistsDataSet.CyclistsRow dr in m_dsCyclists.Cyclists.Rows )
{
    CyclistsDataSet.CyclistStatesRow status =
        (CyclistsDataSet.CyclistStatesRow)dr.GetParentRow(
            FormMain.REL_CYCLIST_STATE );
    if( dr.Active && status != null &&status.Assignable )
    {
        IdStringItem ids = new IdStringItem( dr.CyclistID, dr.Name );
        m_cbxCyclist.Items.Add( ids );
    }
}
```

Hardware Configuration

To allow for future expansion of the company a scalable architecture has been chosen where each part of the system resides on a separate machine, as shown below:

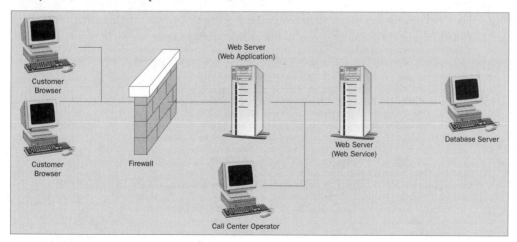

Here the customer interface is shown on the left of the diagram on the outside of the company's internet firewall. They are using web browsers with HTML and some Java Script for validation. Just inside the wall is the Web Server. The Web Server (Web application) pumps out the HTML using web forms to support customer queries and requests. The Web Server (Web Service) processes request from the Call Center Operator and Web Application to perform business processes. It is connected to the Database server. Note The Web Service server needs have access to the database server.

In the initial deployment of this system, web servers, the database server, and Call Center Operator console are actually the same machine connected directly to the Internet. However, in a single server configuration, caution must be used to ensure no security holes are left open.

How to Deploy the System

Here we will discuss how to install the files necessary to run the sample. We will not discuss how to build the projects from the source. How to build the projects will be covered in a later section. In this walk through we will assume the client windows application is on a separate machine to the web server, however they may all reside on the same machine if necessary. This is great – we can build a scalable system, but start running it with very simple hardware and you shouldn't need more than one machine to play with this example.

Installing the Web Application and Web Service

The web application and web service must run on a machine with the following software installed and operating:

❑   Microsoft Internet Information Server (IIS) 5.0 or higher

❑   Windows Component Update 1.0

❑   SQL Server 2000

In this demonstration we will call this machine AppServ01. For a scalable architecture the Web Application, Web Service, and Database could reside on separate machines. Due to the low load on this system it is not necessary.

❑   Start by copying the following files into the C:\InetPub\WwwRoot directory area on AppServ01. Note: C:\InetPub\WwwRoot is the default install location of IIS. It may be different on your machine:

```
C:\InetPub\WwwRoot\WebAppCycleCouriers\BuildOrder.aspx
C:\InetPub\WwwRoot\WebAppCycleCouriers\Global.asax
C:\InetPub\WwwRoot\WebAppCycleCouriers\login.aspx
C:\InetPub\WwwRoot\WebAppCycleCouriers\LogoLong.jpg
C:\InetPub\WwwRoot\WebAppCycleCouriers\Magnify.gif
C:\InetPub\WwwRoot\WebAppCycleCouriers\PackageStatus.aspx
C:\InetPub\WwwRoot\WebAppCycleCouriers\StyleSheet.css
C:\InetPub\WwwRoot\WebAppCycleCouriers\Web.config
C:\InetPub\WwwRoot\WebAppCycleCouriers\bin\WebAppCycleCouriers.dll
C:\InetPub\WwwRoot\WebAppCycleCouriers\Global.asax
C:\InetPub\WwwRoot\WebAppCycleCouriers\ServiceCustomer.asmx
C:\InetPub\WwwRoot\WebAppCycleCouriers\ServiceCyclist.asmx
C:\InetPub\WwwRoot\WebAppCycleCouriers\ServicePackage.asmx
C:\InetPub\WwwRoot\WebAppCycleCouriers\Web.config
C:\InetPub\WwwRoot\WebAppCycleCouriers\bin\WebSerCycleCouriers.dll
```

❏ Start Internet Services Manager and create two virtual directories one called `WebAppCycleCouriers` pointing to `C:\InetPub\WwwRoot\WebAppCycleCouriers` and the other called `WebSerCycleCouriers` pointing to `C:\InetPub\WwwRoot\WebSerCycleCouriers`.

❏ Install the sample database and data by running SQL 2000 Enterprise manager.

❏ Browse to the required server and select **Restore Database** when the **Databases** tab is selected

❏ Choose **Restore From Device** and select `CycleCouriers(SQL).Bak` as the data source. This will restore the database structure and data.

❏ Add a new user called `CycleAdmin` and give them the same privileges as `sa` with a default database of `CycleCouriers`.

❏ Modify the `WebSerCycleCouriers\web.config` file to point to the SQL 2000 database server you wish to use. It will be initially set to `localhost`. If the web server and SQL2000 are running on the same machine leave it as `localhost`:

```
<add key="connectionString" value="data source=AppSer01;initial
catalog=CycleCouriers;uid=CycleAdmin;pwd=" />
```

❏ To test the system, using the browser on the web server, navigate to the address shown below to get the login screen:

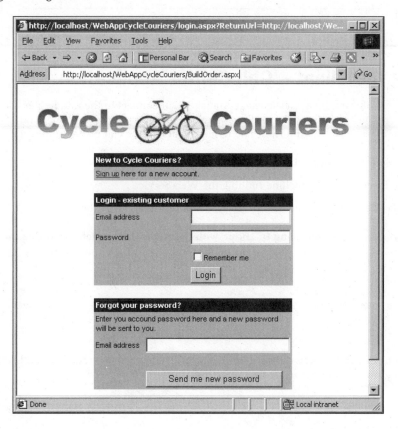

Log in using the email address of a.dent@wrox.com and a password of 1234. If the connection to the backend database is functioning correctly the Build Order screen should appear as follows:

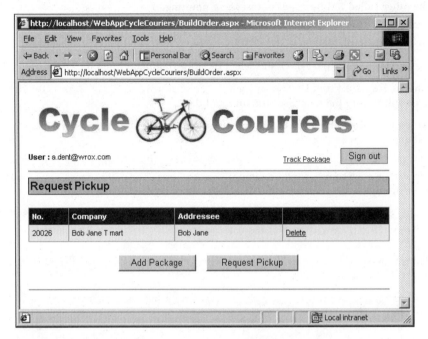

Installing the Client – Call Center Application.

The call center software, known as Package Manager will connect to the middle tier using Web Services and run on a remote machine. This machine may be the web server, a machine on the local network of the server, or even across the Internet. The requirements for the call center application are:

❑   Windows Component Update 1.0 or higher

❑   HTTP access to the machine running the Web Service

Copy the CallCenter.exe and app.config files to a directory on the client.

Edit the app.config file replacing Dilbert with the name of the machine hosting the Web Service in this case AppServ01:

```
<configuration>
  <appSettings>
    <add key="WebServerName" value="AppServ01" />
  </appSettings>
</configuration>
```

Run CallCenter.exe. A wait dialog should appear for less than 30 seconds (on a LAN) and the following window should appear.

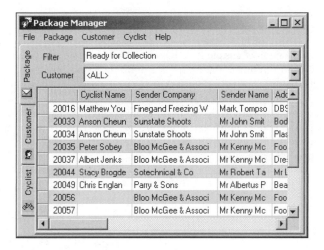

How to Build the System

Here we will discuss how to compile and run the system. To start you will need the following:

- ❑   Microsoft Internet Information Server (IIS) 5.0 or higher

- ❑   Windows Component Update 1.0

- ❑   SQL Server 2000

- ❑   Visual Studio .NET with C# installed

Start by copying the `WebAppCycleCouriers` and `WebSerCycleCouriers` development directories to the web server `wwwroot` directory and configure the web virtual directories. See *How to Deploy the System* in the previous section for details on configuring the virtual directories. Also restore the SQL Server `CycleCouriers` database as described earlier.

Build `WebSerCycleCouriers` first. Then build `WebAppCycleCouriers`. If both of these items are on the same machine there is no need to replace the web reference from `WebAppCycleCouriers`. However, if they are on separate machines then delete the `localhost` web reference and in the `WebAppCycleCouriers` project choose **Project**, **Add Web Reference** and select the machine where the Web Service is located as follows:

```
http://AppServ01/WebSerCycleCouriers/WebSerCycleCouriers.vsdisco
```

It should now be possible to rebuild and run the `WebAppCycleCouriers` project should be able to be rebuilt and run now. This also applies to the Call Center Win Forms application, which may need modification if development is not to take place on the same machine as the Web Service. However, if the deployment instructions are carried out as described earlier, it should to be possible to compile and run. the application.

Summary

In this chapter we have seen how simple it is to write a multi-tier system using ADO.NET for backend data access. We have used `DataSet` objects to pass entire tables as input and output parameters to Web Services. We have also used `DataRelation` and `Filter` objects to control how this data is displayed.

We have not covered every feature of the code presented with this chapter. Nor have we covered every possible way of using ADO.NET. However, hopefully we have covered the major points and techniques that can be used and when combined with information presented earlier in this book should enable you to build powerful multi-tier applications.

ADO.NET

Index

wrox
Programmer to Programmer™

p2p.wrox.com
The programmer's resource centre

A unique free service from Wrox Press
With the aim of helping programmers to help each other

Wrox Press aims to provide timely and practical information to today's programmer. P2P is a list server offering a host of targeted mailing lists where you can share knowledge with four fellow programmers and find solutions to your problems. Whatever the level of your programming knowledge, and whatever technology you use P2P can provide you with the information you need.

ASP Support for beginners and professionals, including a resource page with hundreds of links, and a popular ASP.NET mailing list.

DATABASES For database programmers, offering support on SQL Server, mySQL, and Oracle.

MOBILE Software development for the mobile market is growing rapidly. We provide lists for the several current standards, including WAP, Windows CE, and Symbian.

JAVA A complete set of Java lists, covering beginners, professionals, and server-side programmers (including JSP, servlets and EJBs)

.NET Microsoft's new OS platform, covering topics such as ASP.NET, C#, and general .NET discussion.

VISUAL BASIC Covers all aspects of VB programming, from programming Office macros to creating components for the .NET platform.

WEB DESIGN As web page requirements become more complex, programmer's are taking a more important role in creating web sites. For these programmers, we offer lists covering technologies such as Flash, Coldfusion, and JavaScript.

XML Covering all aspects of XML, including XSLT and schemas.

OPEN SOURCE Many Open Source topics covered including PHP, Apache, Perl, Linux, Python and more.

FOREIGN LANGUAGE Several lists dedicated to Spanish and German speaking programmers, categories include. NET, Java, XML, PHP and XML

How to subscribe
Simply visit the P2P site, at http://p2p.wrox.com/

wrox

Programmer to Programmer™

Wrox writes books for you. Any suggestions, or ideas about how you want information given in your ideal book will be studied by our team.
Your comments are always valued at Wrox.

Free phone in USA 800-USE-WROX
Fax (312) 893 8001

UK Tel.: (0121) 687 4100   Fax: (0121) 687 4101

Professional ADO.NET Programming – Registration Card

Name _____

Address _____

_____

_____

City _____ State/Region _____

Country _____ Postcode/Zip _____

E-Mail _____

Occupation _____

How did you hear about this book?

☐ Book review (name) _____

☐ Advertisement (name) _____

☐ Recommendation _____

☐ Catalog _____

☐ Other _____

Where did you buy this book?

☐ Bookstore (name) _____ City _____

☐ Computer store (name) _____

☐ Mail order _____

☐ Other _____

What influenced you in the purchase of this book?

☐ Cover Design ☐ Contents ☐ Other (please specify):

How did you rate the overall content of this book?

☐ Excellent ☐ Good ☐ Average ☐ Poor

What did you find most useful about this book? _____

_____

What did you find least useful about this book? _____

_____

_____

Please add any additional comments. _____

_____

What other subjects will you buy a computer book on soon?

_____

What is the best computer book you have used this year?

_____

Check here if you DO NOT want to receive support for this book ☐

wrox

Programmer to Programmer™

Note: If you post the bounce back card below in the UK, please send it to:

Wrox Press Limited, Arden House, 1102 Warwick Road,
Acocks Green, Birmingham B27 6HB. UK.

Computer Book Publishers